BRITISH AUTOBIOGRAPHIES

BRITISH
AUTOBIOGRAPHIES

An Annotated Bibliography of British
Autobiographies Published or
Written Before 1951

COMPILED BY

WILLIAM MATTHEWS

UNIVERSITY OF CALIFORNIA PRESS
BERKELEY, LOS ANGELES, LONDON

UNIVERSITY OF CALIFORNIA PRESS

BERKELEY AND LOS ANGELES

CALIFORNIA

UNIVERSITY OF CALIFORNIA PRESS LTD.

LONDON, ENGLAND

COPYRIGHT, 1955, BY

THE REGENTS OF THE UNIVERSITY OF CALIFORNIA

CALIFORNIA LIBRARY REPRINT EDITION 1984

ISBN 0-520-05357-5

MANUFACTURED IN THE UNITED STATES OF AMERICA

1 2 3 4 5 6 7 8 9

TO

LOIS

PREFACE

It is nearly four centuries since Benvenuto Cellini began his autobiography with the challenging assertion that "it is a duty on upright and credible men of all ranks, who have performed anything noble or praiseworthy, to record in their own writing, the events of their lives." He was apparently conscious that he was himself doing something unusual. But, as anyone knows who has scanned the back pages of literary supplements or browsed in the boxes outside secondhand bookshops, this duty, if duty it be, has since Cellini's day been taken most seriously by an overwhelming number of men, not all of them upright and some of them not entirely credible.

In English, there are few medieval autobiographies and the effective beginnings of the modern form are to be sought in the religious lives of the sixteenth and seventeenth centuries, testimonials of sin and conversion and of endeavors in behalf of the true belief by Baptists, Catholics, Presbyterians, Congregationalists Muggletonians, and, most of all, Quakers. Autobiographies of worldly experience, the accounts of military life, travel and exploration, scholarly and scientific labors, political activities, begin in the same period although they are less common than the religious. From these beginnings, the form has since been taken up by people of every sort. The call which Cellini made has been answered by statesmen, soldiers, ecclesiastics, artists, explorers, poets, all the upright and credible men he had in mind, but it has also been answered by numberless men of whom he never dreamed, peasants, drug-addicts, missionaries, housewives, fallen women, tramps, and even children. Although celebrities contribute most numerously to the examples, the genre is now a vox populi, in which anybody, even if he cannot

write, can respond to the curiosity which we all have
as to how Fortune has dealt with other people in this
bewildering and motley world.

The vox populi is not the best trained nor sweetest
of voices, and the autobiography cannot pretend to be
the most elegant of literary genres. So, despite its
popularity, it has claimed little scholarly attention
for its own sake. Scholars have regarded it, as they
have regarded other ephemera, as raw material for the
worthier scholarly concerns, useful for biographical
or historical data but not a significant form of literature, with its own history of fashions, techniques
and patterns, and even with its own minor classics. An
occasional Ph.D. student has written a thesis on this
or that aspect of its history, and later published an
odd article or two, and Mr. Bates has summarised some
of the best-known examples, but for the English autobiography there is nothing that even remotely compares
with the excellent volume which Misch wrote about the
classical autobiography.

My own interest in the form is chiefly a curiosity
as to how men operate when they write about their own
lives and personalities. The autobiography offers itself as an individual receptacle for every individual
man, and, offhand, one might expect that every autobiography would be as different from every other one
as every man is different from every other man. As a
matter of fact, however, few autobiographers put into
their books very much of that private, intimate knowledge of themselves that only they can have. Oftener
than not, they shun their own inner peculiarities and
fit themselves into patterns of behavior and character
suggested by the ideas and ideals of their period and
by the fashions in autobiography with which they asso-
ciate themselves. The laws of literature and the human
reluctance to stand individually naked combine to cheat
the expectations of readers who hope to find in autobiographies many revelations of men's true selves. On
these and kindred matters, I hope to write in fitting
detail before too long. I mention this interest here
mainly because it has sustained me during the several

years I have spent compiling this bibliography, which
in some measure is the record of my own surveys.

The bibliography, however, has been carried a long
way beyond my own requirements,so as to be of service
to scholars in a variety of studies. It should prove
of value in literary studies, of the genre itself and
also of other literary forms to which it is related,
the biography and the novel in particular. Psycholog-
ists, who have been showing a notable interest in the
form, should find it a useful guide to their further
reading. And it should be serviceable to scholars in
the humanities and social sciences who are seeking new
facts and opinions about people,events and movements;
about authors, artists, musicians, ministers, sailors
or social workers; about counties,towns and villages,
about politics, wars, religion, agriculture, working-
class life, economics, trade and industry, and so on.
The list touches on almost all human concerns in four
recent centuries and it is hoped that it will provide
scholars with untapped sources of information concerning them.

The bibliography has been in preparation since 1945
and the work for it has proceeded along two lines.The
first was to gather from a wide variety of bibliogra-
phies,from some library catalogues, from a large number of secondhand booksellers' catalogues and various
reviews the title of any book that seemed to be autobiographical, and then to examine these books in some
of the larger libraries in the United States and England. In this proceeding,my own searches and annotat-
ing were supplemented by those of assistants, notably
Mr. George Mayhew at Harvard, Miss Patricia Hann and
Mr. Kurt Ostberg in London, and Miss Audrey LaLievre
at Cambridge. The second approach was to make a shelf
search in appropriate sections of suitable libraries
for autobiographies which had not been discovered by
the first process. In 1946 and 1947,when I was enjoy-
ing the pleasantly subsidised freedom of a Guggenheim
Fellowship, I searched the shelves of the Library of
Congress,the London Library, and the Royal Empire Society Library,and the libraries of London, Cambridge,

Yale, and Harvard universities, and checked titles in the British Museum Library,   the National Library of Scotland, and elsewhere.In the years 1950 and 1951, I was again in England, in part on sabbatical leave and in part as exchange professor of English Language at the University of Manchester. During that time I visited at least two libraries in most of the counties of England,the India Office library and other government libraries, and a number of specialised and local collections in London, Ireland and Wales. In this second tour, I was greatly aided by my wife Lois, whose good humored acquiescence in unpaid labors confirms the economic doctrine that universities buy them cheaper by the pair. In between times, similar examinations have been made in the Huntington Library, New York Public Library, and the chief libraries of the University of California,and I have also tried to bring the list up to date by abstracting reviews published in the Times Literary Supplement. As it is now presented, the list includes all the autobiographies written or published before 1951 that I have been able to find in the course of the searches described above.I do not pretend that the list is a complete one: my objective when I began the work was not completeness, but comprehensiveness. I now put it out, not in the belief that it could not be extended or improved,but trusting that as a result of fairly extensive searching, it has been brought to that degree of reasonable comprehensiveness that will make it of service to other scholars.

From the outset, problems presented themselves as to what should be included. Most of them turned upon the meanings of those two deceptively innocent words, "autobiography" and "British".

The dictionary definition of "autobiography" seems clear enough. Unfortunately,however, people who write about their own lives very rarely oblige lexicographers by sticking to their no doubt proper studies;they always write about other persons and other matters as well as about themselves; not infrequently they write about themselves largely or only in relation to something or somebody else. All too often, it is not even

clear who or what is more interesting to the autobio-
grapher,himself or the other people or matters. Politicians, society ladies, soldiers, and travellers are
particularly bothersome in this respect: on occasion
they even seem to justify Seymour Hicks' dictum that
the chief appeal of the autobiography is that it en-
ables its author to write about everything except himself. In face of such dilemmas,the only recourse open
to the bibliographer is to take the arbitrary procedures forced upon anyone who has to fit individuals into categorical iron maidens.My own procedure was that
if a writer seemed to be mostly concerned with himself
he was to be included:but if his egotistical interest
was markedly subservient to his interest in other matters then he was to be excluded. Being human, too, I
claim no consistency in the application of this principle, nor do I assert that on second reading I would
always repeat the original decision; but this was the
ground of my decision, and it will explain the inclusion of some books and the exclusion of others. Sub-
sidiary to this problem was the problem of definition
of "life". Obviously, no man, not even on his death-
bed, can write about all his life: he can write only
about a part of it. How large a part, then, justified
inclusion here?My original principle was "significant
part"; but after experience of the way of autobiographers in associating themselves with some particular
event or crisis either in their own lives or in public
life, I had to modify my ideas as to what constituted
significance. Even so,I have excluded items that seem
to be restricted to only one incident or that are related very briefly. In this way, a very large number
of records of religious conversion,accidents, and the
like, and many brief, factual vitae have been excluded from the list. Fiction presented another problem,
which I have tried to solve by excluding all autobiographical novels and all works which claim to be autobiographies but struck me as being clearly fictional:
some doubtful examples I have included with a question
mark. Autobiographical poems, such as Hoccleve's <u>La
Male Regle</u> and Wordsworth's <u>Prelude</u>,to take extremes,

presented too many problems of literary convention or size to be dealt with consistently, so I decided that I would exclude them too.

As for "British", I have in general been guided by the definitions "born in the British Isles" and "naturalised British subject". As a result, a great many items are included which describe lives passed in the colonies and in foreign lands. Certain practical modifications of this principle, which have little to do with definition, must be mentioned. First, autobiographies relating wholly to life in Canada, South Africa, New Zealand, Australia, and the United States are not included, on the scores that I have already published a similar bibliography relating to Canada, that I have materials which are extensive but not yet comprehensive for New Zealand, South Africa, and Australia, and that a bibliography for the United States is now being compiled by Mr. Louis Kaplan of Wisconsin. Secondly, I have excluded autobiographies written by Hindus and other native Indians even though I have included many items relating to life in India written by British men and women; I decided to do this on the ground that so many native Indian autobiographies are written in languages I do not understand that to include only those composed in English or translated into English would misrepresent the number and variety of these interesting items. I very much regret this last decision, for it has meant excluding many excellent books. My notes on them are fairly extensive and I hope that they may be of use to some Hindu scholar who may be interested to do a more comprehensive job on the Indian autobiography. About the colonial items, there is one inconsistency which I must mention. When I published British Diaries, I excluded colonial diaries, thinking to include them in a list of autobiographies and diaries relating solely to the colonies and dominions. Having changed my plans, I had to decide what to do with the colonial diaries and I decided to include them here.

The items have been listed alphabetically according to the writers' family names, or, in the cases of the anonymous works, the first words of the titles. This

arrangement seemed best after I decided to bow to the
desire expressed by reviewers of my earlier books and
provide an index. The notes prefaced to the index explain the principles upon which it is constructed and
I hope that it will provide an adequate guide to subjects and periods.

The principle determining the style of the entries
is utility. The Christian names of authors are given
as completely as is needed for rapid identification in
library catalogues(though this fullness may be waste-
ful of time on occasion since some cataloguers appear
to prefer initials to full Christian names).Titles of
books have been shortened in many cases, but are suf-
ficiently long, I hope, to permit of immediate recognition. As in my books on diaries, I have appended to
each item a short note. This note is intended to give
a rough characterisation of the book and to indicate
the principal subjects, places and persons with which
it deals. When it seemed worth while to do so, a word
of evaluation has been added. The jottings from which
these notes were digested were mostly my own observations; several hundred of them, however, are digested
from annotations made by my assistants, and a fairly
large number are based upon reviews. It follows that
there are some variations of judgment and standard in
these notes, and they certainly vary in fullness; but
it is hoped that they will serve their turn. The form
of these notes is more telegraphic than that employed
in my other books. I wished to encompass the material
in a volume which might be sold at a price within the
reach of university scholars.With this object in mind
the notes were set down in as brief a form as was con-
sistent with clarity and utility. The same intent ex-
plains the use of photo-offset printing,short titles,
and abbreviations such as W.W.1,W.W.2, 19C (for World
War I, World War II, 19th Century), and the omission
of place of publication (or the use of "L") for books
published in London, of details of editions and page-
length, and of the biographical details about authors
which I included in my earlier bibliographies.To have
included all these additional details would certainly

have improved the book but it would also have made it
unwieldy and defeated the object I had in mind. From
my work in rechecking the titles, it would appear that
the great majority are available in one or more of the
major libraries in England and the United States; for
items which might be difficult to find, I have added a
note of where I examined them.

It is my pleasant duty to thank the assistants whom
I have previously named and also to express my thanks
to the numerous librarians and library assistants who
bore so patiently with the strange behavior of a visiting scholar who demanded mountains of books and yet
seemed satisfied to spend no more than ten or fifteen
minutes over each of them. The Englishmen among them
displayed an admirable reticence in voicing any curiosity they may have felt, but if they inclined in their
unspoken thoughts to attribute my waywardness to America, I should like to comfort them somewhat by tell-
ing them that I was no less wayward when I was English.
Once again, too, I wish to express my gratitude to the
John Simon Guggenheim Memorial Foundation and also to
the Regents of the University of California. The former did much to facilitate my work during its earlier
stages by awarding me a fellowship, and the latter, by
granting two sabbatical leaves and by making generous
research grants for assistance, have enabled me to complete it. To Mrs. Virginia Hull of the Bel-Air Secretarial Service I tender my gratitude for her patience
and skill in typing the manuscript for photo-offset,
as I also do to my good friend August Frugé who super-
vised its publication.

                              WILLIAM MATTHEWS.

Los Angeles, 1954.

ABBOTT, Maj.Gen. Augustus. Military
journal, 1838-42; service with Bengal
Artillery in the Afghan War; marches;
military details. The Afghan War, ed.
Charles R. Low (1879).   1

ABBOTT, George Washington. Events..
in the Life of an Octogenarian (1878)
Boyhood in Chelsea; impact Napoleonic
wars; theatrical life and people; society; public life.   2

ABBOTT, Richard. Narrative (Chetham
Soc. Remains, LXI, 1864). Experiences
in the Revolution, 1689-91; barbarous
experiences in prison;Lord Molyneux's
servant.   3

ABBS, Rev. John. Twenty-two Years'
Missionary Experience (1870).His work
at Travancore from 1838;difficulties;
Hindu life and customs;work of London
Missionary Society. Copy India Office
Library.   4

ABDULLAH, Morag (Murray). My Khyber
Marriage (1934). Scots woman educated
at Edinburgh University;marriage to a
Pathan; life in hills & at Delhi; and
social and racial problems.   5

A-BECKETT, Arthur William.Green-Room
Recollections (Bristol, 1896); The A-
Beckett's (1903); Recollections (1907)
Anecdotes of theatre; career as civil
servant and journalist; work on Punch
and reminiscences of its writers; humor and its fashions; social and club
life; Franco-Prussian war service; an
amusing and useful record.   6

ABERCROMBY, Sir Ralph.Naval journal
1800-1802;details of naval activities
at Aboukir. A Faithful Journal(London
1802).   7

ABERDEEN AND TEMAIR, Marquis & Marchioness of.We Twa (1925);More Cracks
(1929). Highland upbringing; Liberal
politics and reform; society in Scotland and London; Empire travels; Victoria and other celebrities; family &
domestic anecdotes.   8

ABERDEEN AND TEMAIRE, Ishbel Maria,
Marchioness of. Musings of a Scottish
Granny (1936).Highland childhood; début and romance; society and friendships in Victorian period.   9

ABINGER, Edward. Forty Years (1930)
Barrister's career and cases; famous
judges and trials; Inner Temple.   10

ABINGER, James Scarlett, 1st Baron.
Memoir, by Peter C. Scarlett (1877).
Includes fragment of autobiography of
youth, and beginning of legal career;
political and legal figures at end of
18th Century.   11

/ABLETT, William H./. Reminiscences
of an Old Draper (1876). His work in
the drapery trade; changes, fashions,
and economics; social life.   12

ABRAHAM, James Johnston. Surgeon's
Log (1911); My Balkan Log (1921). His
medical and army career; experiences
with RAMC; Salonika; WW1.   13

AN ACCURATE OBSERVER. Reminiscences
of Half a Century (1838). His travels
in England, Ireland, France and Italy
and meetings with Byron and other celebrities.   14

ACKERLEY, Joe Randolph (ed). Escap-
ers All (1932). A report of broadcast
narratives of fifteen escapees during
WW1; life in prison camps; ingenious
methods of escape; adventures.   15

ACKERLEY, Joe Randolph.Hindoo Holiday (1932). Experiences as secretary
and political agent to Indian prince;
court life.   16

ACLAND, Lady Eleanor M. Goodbye (L.
1935). Her own childhood in Westmoreland and her daughter's in Devonshire
pleasant country life.   17

/ACLAND, John E./.Through the Ranks
(1881).Peacetime army service in 70's;
Gibraltar; barrack life;attitudes and
life of rankers.   18

ACLAND, Sarah Angelina. Old lady's reminiscences of country life and Oxford where her father was a professor of medicine; early 19th Century. MS, Bodleian, Eng. Misc. d.214.   19

ACTON, Harold Mario Mitchell. Memoirs of an Aesthete (1948). Literary life; the brilliant Oxford generation after WW1; Evelyn Waugh; writers and artists.   20

ADAM, Hargrave Lee. Old Days at the Old Bailey (1932).Trials, lawyers and judges; reforms; good.   21

ADAM, Ronald.Overture and Beginners (1938). WW1 and after; London theatre productions at the Embassy.   22

ADAMS, Bill (Bertram Martin). Ships and Women (Boston, 1937).   Childhood in England; hardships at sea; farming on Cape Horn; adventures.   23

ADAMS, Henry. Some Reminiscences (L 1925). A civil engineer for 75 years; public works and docks;amusements and social life; London; science.   24

ADAMS, Capt.John Bernard P. Nothing of Importance (1917). Cambridge; service with Welsh regiment in France in WW1; fresh and sensitive.   25

ADAMS, Joseph. Fifty Years' Angling (1938). Reminiscences of sport in English, European, Canadian rivers.   26

ADAMS, William. An Old English Potter (1904). Work and life in Staffs.; travels in England and Europe; end of 18th Century.   27

ADAMS, William Alexander.Twenty-Six Years' Reminiscences (1892). Country life in Scotland; mainly devoted to a technical description of the shooting of grouse.   28

ADDISON, Lt.Col.Henry Robert. Diary of a Judge (L.1860); Recollections of an Irish Police Magistrate (L. 1862); All at Sea (1864).Work as a subaltern and police magistrate in Limerick, in the twenties; journey to West Africa, to take up official post; administration.   29

ADOLPHUS, John.Recollections of, by

Emily Henderson (1871). Mainly autobiography and diary; legal career;social life in London; artists, writers visits to Paris.   30

ANON. Adventures of a Young Lady (L 1880). A farmer's daughter who worked as governess in diplomat's family;her capture by Arabs, sale as slave; rescue, marriage; fiction?   31

ADYE, Major-Gen. Sir John. Soldiers and Others I Have Known (1925). Army career from 1876; Egypt,India & South Africa; Boer War; WW1; Staff College; celebrities.   32

ADYE, Gen. Sir John Miller. Recollections (1895). Artillery; surveyorgeneral of ordnance in Crimea, Indian Mutiny, Egyptian War; 1854-82.   33

AFLALO, Frederick George.Salt of My Life (1905). Lifetime of sea-fishing, England and abroad.   34

AGATE, James Evershed. Ego (1935). Begins as autobiography of childhood; journalism and theatre in London up to 1932; diverges into diaries.   35

AGG-GARDNER, Sir James.Some Parliamentary Recollections (1927). Harrow; Cambridge; M.P. for Cheltenham; Conservative politics and politicians in 1868-1911.   36

AGNEW, Derek. Bevin Boy (1947). Pit work in Kent under Bevin plan, WW2; a realistic picture of mining life. 37

AINGER, Arthur Campbell.Memories of Eton (1917). Schoolboy in 50's; sport traditions, masters,celebrities. 38

AINSLIE, Ainslie Douglas.Adventures Social and Literary (1922).Diplomatic career; anecdotes of public personages society and writers; travels; England and France.   39

AINSLIE, Philip Barrington ("Philo-Scotus").   Reminiscences of a Scottish Gentleman (1861). Edinburgh life and society in 1790's; early years in the navy; Napoleon; West Indian planter; business in Liverpool; travels; may be fiction.   40

AINSWORTH, Leopold.Merchant Venturer (1930); __Confessions of a Planter__ (n. d.). Trading in Malaya, and rubber planting at Kedah; adventures and experiences with natives.   41

AIRD, Andrew.Reminiscences (Glasgow 1890). Scottish journalism and printing, 1830-90.   42

AIRY, Sir George Biddell. __Autobiography__ (Cambridge, 1896). Cambridge; work at Royal Observatory; Astronomer Royal; science and scientists 1836 to 1881.   43

AITKEN, Samuel."Memories" (__Gloucester Journal__, 1925-26). Social and industrial life in Lancs, Derby, Gloucester, mid-19th Century. Cuttings in Gloucester City Library.   44

AKROYD, Charles H.__A Veteran Sportsman's Diary__ (Inverness, 1926). Eton; Yorkshire; shooting and fishing in the British Isles and Canada.   45

ALBANI, Emma. __Forty Years__ (L. 1911) Canadian childhood; concert and opera career; oratorio; Wagner; travels in the Empire; anecdotes.   46

ALBEMARLE,George Thomas Keppel, 6th Earl of.__Personal Narrative of Travels in Babylonia__(1824);__Personal Narrative of a Journey from India__(1827); __Narrative of a Journey across the Balkan__(L 1831); __Fifty Years of My Life__ (1876). Official travels and descriptions;his education;family and Court life;military career, Waterloo, India,Ireland; politics;Napoleon;society life, sport pleasures, to 1850's.   47

ALCOCK, Sir Rutherford. __The Capital of the Tycoon__ (1863). Diplomatic work as ambassador in Japan, 1858-60;travels; Japanese scene and customs.   48

ALDERTON, Haddon. __One Man's Meat__(L. 1937). Ranching in Canada; osteopath military service in Philippines & in France, WW1; adventures.   49

ALDIN, Cecil C. W. __Time I Was Dead__ (1934).Career as illustrator; country life and sport; London Bohemian life; Kipling.   50

ALDINGTON, Richard. __Life for Life's Sake__ (N.Y.1941). Reminiscences of po-litics, writing, literary life.   51

ALDIS, Janet. __A Girl Guide Captain in India__ (1924). Social work; running a troop of girl guides; Eastern life; Western ideals.   52

ALDRIDGE, Olive. __Retreat__ (1916).Her service in field hospitals in Serbia, WW1; retreat with Serbian army.   53

ALEC-TWEEDIE, Ethel Brilliana.__Behind the Footlights__ (1904); __Thirteen Years__ (1912); __My Table-Cloths__ (1917);__Me and Mine__ (1932); __Tight Corners__ (1933).The travels & adventures of a Scotswoman; theatrical ambitions;Ibsen; marriage; journalism; famous people in arts and public life;her painting; celebrities she knew; journalistic; lively.   54

ALEXANDER, Alec. __A Wayfarer's Log__ (1919); __Wayfarer's Caravan__ (1921).His life at fairs and on open road; caravanning; athletics, walking, gymnastics; sports, from 60's.   55

ALEXANDER, Alexander. __Life__ (Edin. 1830). Harsh boyhood in Scotland; at sea and in army; Ceylon; West Indies; adventurer's picaresque life; a dictated autobiography.   56

ALEXANDER, David Alfred.__Cum Notitia__ (Bristol,1949). A general practitioner's posthumously published memories and notes on medicine addressed to his son who chose another profession.   57

ALEXANDER, Ann. Quaker diary, 1849-1850; visiting Quaker schools in West Indies; Coddrington College; missionary work with husband;pleasant record MS. Friends Society Library, London, N.W.1.   58

ALEXANDER, Boyd. Travel diary,1908-1910; expedition to the Cameroons;exploration, anthropology, topography & natural history.__Boyd Alexander's Last Journey__ (1912).   59

ALEXANDER, Edward. __Memoir__ (1849). A Quaker ministry in Limerick.   60

ALEXANDER, Gilchrist Gibb. __From the Middle Temple__(1927); __Tanganyika Memories__(1936);__The Temple in the Nineties__ (1938).Career as a colonial magistrate in the Fijis to 1920 and in Tanganyika during early days of colony;justice & administration;people;amusements; and memories of his study at Temple; work in courts and at Parliamentary bar and legal celebrities of nineties.   61

ALEXANDER, Heber M. A.On Two Fronts (1917).Service with Indian male corps WW1; France and Gallipoli.   62

ALEXANDER, Sir James Edward. Passages in the Life of a Soldier (1857). Military and social life, 1848-55; in Canada; Crimean War.   63

ALEXANDER, Mary. Some Account (York 1811).Suffolk Quaker's religious life and travels in ministry in the British Isles.   64

ALEXANDER, Patrick(Patrick A.Meade) As the Sparks Fly Upwards(1938); Born to Trouble(1942).Army service and adventures in Africa,Russia, before and during WW1;farm boyhood;adventures as political officer in India,and police officer in Singapore.   65

ALEXANDER, Lt. Col. William Gordon. Recollections of a Highland Subaltern (1898). With Colin Campbell; service in Indian mutiny; relief of Lucknow; army personalities.   66

ALFORD, Frances. Reminiscences of a Clergyman's Wife (1860). Wife of Dean of Canterbury;London and country life and the poor; visiting; old friends; pleasant.   67

ALINGTON, Rev. Cyril A. Schoolmaster's Apology (1914); Things Ancient and Modern (1936).Marlborough; Oxford teaching in the great public schools; views on education; his work and life as Dean of Durham; good.   68

ALISON, Sir Archibald. Some Account (Edin. 1883). Career as lawyer, Edinburgh; sheriff of Lanarkshire; social life and public affairs, in Scotland; Crimean War; Indian Mutiny.   69

ALLAN, James MacGrigor. Last Days (1862). Bachelor's social life, love affairs, travels; fiction?   70

ALLAN, John Robertson. Farmer's Boy (1935,1948). Autobiography of farming life and work.   71

ALLAN, Maud. My Life (1908). Career and travels as a dancer; the Suffragist movement.   72

ALLEN, Bernard M. Down the Stream (1948). Schoolmaster at Harrow; Churchill; service with Technical Education Board; progress of education in England; useful.   73

ALLEN, George.Machine Breaker(1831) Working-class life; apprenticeship; a profligate career and lost job; conspiracy to destroy machines;imprisonment and repentance.   74

ALLEN, Rev. Isaac Nicholson. Diary, 1841; service as chaplain on expedition into Sind and Afghanistan; with Nott's troops; topography. Diary of a March through Sinde (1843).   75

ALLEN, J. Archibald. One of Ten (L. 1929). Amusements of child in a large family; school; sports.   76

ALLEN, John. Lives of Early Methodist Preachers, by Thomas Jackson (L., 1838) III. Autobiography of itinerant preacher, in Northumberland and North of England, 18th Century.   77

ALLEN, Mary S. Lady in Blue (1936). Militant suffragette; organizing the women police; sex crimes; drugs; war work in the service; travels.   78

ALLEN, Oswald. History of the York Dispensary (York 1845); MS, York Public Library. Medical work in York in 18th Century; York Dispensary; family and personal affairs.   79

ALLEN, Rev. Roland. Diary, 1900; a chaplain's account of siege of Pekin; Christian behavior. Siege of the Peking Legations (1901).   80

ALLEN, Rose. Autobiography, ed. by a Lady (1849).Servant's life and work in country houses; society life;families she worked for; her moral crises may be fiction.   81

ALLINGHAM, Philip. Cheapjack (1934) Oxford; life at fairs; fortune-teller cheapjack, hawker, salesman; amusing career of gentle grafter; slang.   82

ALLISON, William. My Kingdom (1919)

Memories (1922). The life & work of a
sporting journalist and Tory; horse-
racing; The Sportsman; Bohemians; and
celebrated sportsmen.   83

ALLTREE, George W. Footlight Memories (1932).Liverpool boyhood; theatrical and vaudeville agent from 1905;
anecdotes comedians and actors.   84

ALLWOOD, Montagu C.Third and Fourth
Generation (1940). Village life, Sussex;career as nurseryman; reminiscences of Wivelsfield Green.   85

ALMEDINGEN,Martha Edith von. Tomorrow (1941); Almond Tree (1947);Within
the Harbour (1950). Nostalgic account
of her life in St. Petersburg before
WW1; university career; ignores Revolution; society; Rome in 20's; struggles as writer; English scene, people
and her love for England.   86

ALMOST ANYBODY. About Nothing What-
ever (1936). Reminiscences of bewil-
dered person; sex, love, bigamy; con-
cern about war and strikes; artistic
and philosophical inclinations.   87

ALPORT, Arthur Cecil. House of Curious (1937).Experiences and anecdotes
of medical student and doctor.   88

ALSOP, Alfred. Ten Years(Manchester
1879). Work as a missionary in slums;
Manchester working people;sketches of
depravity; relief work.   89

ALSOP, Christine R. Memorials of,by
Martha Braithwaite (1881). Early life
in France;Quaker life and ministry in
England and France.   90

ALVERSTONE, Richard E. W., Viscount
Recollections (1914). Busy legal career, 1868-1900;company law and cases
and secrets of success; famous judges
and barristers; L.C.J.   91

AMATOR ETONAE. Random Recollections
(1846). His life as a student at Eton
in forties; studies, games, boys, and
masters.   92

AMERY,Rt.Hon.Leopold. Days of Fresh
Air (1939); In the Rain (1946). Travels, mountaineering, politics, public
life, WW1; Empire travels and work; &
his sporting activities.   93

AMES, Leslie. How's Zat (1938). The
career and sporting reminiscences of
Kent and England wicketkeeper & batsman; English & Australian players. 94

ANDERSON, Surgeon. Diary, 1763; his
capture and prison experiences at Patna as prisoner of Suraj-ad-daula.Wal-
ter K.Firminger, The Diaries of Three
Surgeons of Patna (Calcutta,1909) pp.
38-70.   95

ANDERSON, Alex. Windjammer Yarns(L.
1923). Boyhood in sailing ships; ways
of the sea in the 60's;clipper ships;
voyages; port life;romance.   96

ANDERSON, David.Reminiscences(Glasgow, 1937). Education in Glasgow and
German universities; tutor in Greece;
ministry & parish life, Scotland. 97

ANDERSON,David. Surveyor's Trek (L.
1940). Cambridge; work as civil servant in Nigeria;surveys;tropical life
and adventures.   98

ANDERSON, Doris G. Nigger Lover (L.
1938). Experiences of an Englishwoman
married to American negro writer; her
lecture tours in America; vindication
of Christianity.   99

ANDERSON, James R. An Actor's Life
(1902). Theatrical life and actors in
London and provinces; tours; Charles
Matthews to the Bancrofts.   100

ANDERSON,Rev. John Henry. Memorials
(1882).Work as minister among poor in
Islington; emigration to N.Z.   101

ANDERSON, Lt.Col. Joseph J. Recollections (1913). Military career and
adventures;Peninsular War; at convict
station in N.S.W.;Gwalior campaign in
India; 1805-48.   102

ANDERSON, Sir Robert. Lighter Side
of My Official Life(1910). His police
career in Ireland and at Home Office,
1867-95; Scotland Yard; robberies and
political offenses; anecdotes.   103

ANDERSON, Capt.Robert Patrick. Personal Journal of the Siege of Lucknow
(1858). Military affairs and civilian
life during the siege.   104

ANDRÉE, Rosemary(pseud.).   My Life

Story (1945). London girlhood; family opposition to stage; artist's model; her career in musical comedy and dancing; her running fights with the local watch committees; the nude.   105

ANDREW, Jane. Autobiography (1889); Recorded Mercies (1890). Her life in a Methodist home; Cornish farms; work and travel in ministry. Copy, Exeter P.L.   106

ANDREWS, Charles Freer. Inner Life (1939). Cambridge; work as missionary in India; friendship with Tagore and Gandhi; his spiritual life.   107

ANDREWS, Octavius William. Seamarks (1927). Surgeon's career in the navy, from 1889 & experiences in China & in WW1.   108

ANDREWS, William Linton. Haunting Years (1930); Yorkshire Folk (1935). Journalist in Leeds and West Riding; Territorial in France in WW1; Adventures and people; anecdotal.   109

ANGELO, Henry C. W. Reminiscences (1828-30); Angelo's Pic Nic (1834). A fencing master's recollections of high society, the theatre, clubs, court and celebrities for 80 years; Byron, Kean, Macklin, etc.   110

ANGIER, John. A Narrative, by Oliver Heywood (1683). Brief religious autobiography; visit to New England.   111

ANGLE, Bernard John. My Sporting Memories (1925). Lifetime of sport; especially boxing.   112

ANGLESEY, Arthur Annesley, 1st Earl Memoirs (1693). Religious life and moralisings; 17th Century.   113

ANGLO-AUSTRALIAN. After-Glow Memories (1905). Upbringing in Herts; literary parents; youth in Australia and visits to England.   114

[ANNESLEY, James]. Memoirs of an Unfortunate Young Nobleman (1743). Claim to be son of Earl of Anglesey; profligacy of father; shipped as a slave to Pennsylvania; love affairs & vicissitudes in England; his struggle for the title.   115

ANONYMOUS. Autobiography of woman's spiritual life & religious struggles. Said to be a relation of Cromwell. MS B. M., Add. 5858.   116

ANONYMOUS. Autobiography of a young lawyer, 1660-89; civil law studies at Cambridge; his religious life. MS, in Cambridge U.L., Add. 6596.   117

ANON. Military journal, 1763; experiences of a prisoner of Cossim Ali at Patna. MS, B.M. Add. 29209.   118

ANON. Military journal, 1763-64; a march from Burdwan to Surseram in the East Indies. MS, India Office Library A.1, 70 pp.   119

ANON. Diary, 1779; military service in war with Hyder Aly; army movements and battle of Arcot. MS, "A Narrative of the Second War," Clement's Library Ann Arbor, Michigan.   120

ANON. Diary, 1800; details of a stay at Mocha; Arab customs; apparently by a naval surgeon. MS, India Office Library, Eur. E.2, pp. 37-76.   121

ANON. Military journal, 1805; Delhi army life; service with Lord Lake; the capture of Aligarh. MS, India Office Library, Eur. D.117, 40 pp.   122

ANON. Travel journal, 1827-29; notes of a tourist in the Mediterranean and Egypt and Palestine. Private Journal of a Visit to Egypt and Palestine (L. 1836).   123

ANON. Travel diary, 1838; notes on a voyage to Mauritius. MS, Royal Empire Soc. Library, 483 Case.   124

ANONYMOUS. Autobiography of soldier in early part of 19th Century; mainly campaigns & battles of Peninsular War Sherwood Foresters' Regimental Annual 1921-22.   125

ANSON, Gen. Sir Archibald E. H. About Others and Myself (1920). Woolwich and army career in infantry; Crimean War; Malaya; adventures; anecdotes.   126

ANSON, Lady Clodagh. Book (1931); Another Book (1937). Irish childhood; marriage and social life; ranching in Texas; welfare work among down and out in London; juvenile crime.   127

ANSON,Harold. Looking Forward(1938)
Oxford; ministry in England and N.Z.;
rural dean; Master of Temple; religious movements; clerical life.   128

ANSON,Peter Frederick. Harbour Head
(1944); Roving Recluse (Cork, 1946).
Life in Caldey and other monasteries;
travels in Europe and Canada; life at
sea; religion; adventure.   129

ANSTED,David Thomas. Scenery (1854)
Travels and work of mining engineer &
geology professor; Europe, Africa and
America; slavery; geology.   130

ANSTRUTHER-THOMSON,Col. John. Eighty Years' Reminiscences (1904). Life
and service in Fifeshire regiments at
home and in South Africa; sports, and
foxhunting with Pytchley,Scottish and
Welsh packs; Conservatism.   131

ANTHONY, Francis. A Man's a Man (L.
1932). Orphanage upbringing; bandboy
in Hussars; with Black Watch in WW1;
odd jobs; poetry; journalism; affec-
tion for the well-to-do.   132

ANTON, James. Retrospect of a Mili-
tary Life (Edin. 1841). Army career;
QMS in a Scottish regiment during the
Peninsular War.   133

ANTROBUS, George Pollock.King's Mes-
senger(1941). Travels of foreign service messenger, 1918-40; politics and
foreign affairs.   134

APEX. Uneasy Triangle (1931). Four
years' service with army of the Rhine
politics and relations of British and
French and Germans.   135

APPERLEY, Charles James. Life of a
Sportsman (1842, 1948); Hunting Reminiscences (1843, 1927); My Life and
Times (1927)."Nimrod's" reminiscences
of life among the aristocracy & country gentry during the Regency; chase,
hunting, racing; celebrities; lively
picture and anecdotes of the sporting
journalist.   136

APPLIN, Col. Reginald V. K. Across
the Seven Seas (1937). Adventures and
military career; Malaya; Africa; WW1;
from late 19th Century.   137

AQUILA. With the Cavalry(1922). Experiences of subaltern with cavalry;
WW1 in France.   138

ARBENINA,Stella (Stella Z. Wishwaw,
Baroness Meyendorff). Through Terror
(1929). Englishwoman's adventures in
Russia before and during the Bolshevik
revolution;wife of an aristocrat; her
exciting escape.   139

ARBUTHNOT, Sir Alexander John. Memories (1910). Rugby, Arnold, Hughes;
55 years in public service, in India;
director of public instruction Madras
Madras University; Council of India;
society and friends; good.   140

ARBUTHNOTT, Sir Alexander Dundas Y.
Memoir(Brighton, 1884). Naval service
as boy; Peninsular war; diary.   141

ARCH, Joseph. Story of His Life (L.
1898).Agricultural laborer, Warwickshire;labor leader; struggles to form
Agricultural Labourers Union; member
of Parliament; important.   142

ARCHER,Frank. Actor's Notebooks (L.
(1912). Reminiscences of literary and
theatrical celebrities, 1845-99.   143

ARCHER,Dr. George. Plantation diary
1828-41; plantation work in Jamaica;
Spring Mount and Greenfield; slaves &
their behaviour. MS. B.M. Add. 33294,
147 fos.   144

ARDITI, Luigi. My Reminiscences (L.
1896). Italian upbringing; experiences as conductor and composer in London; court; musical circles.   145

ARGALL, Phyllis. Prisoner in Japan
(1945).Twenty years in Japan; work as
missionary, teacher, journalist, editor;imprisonment during WW2; life and
character of Japanese.   146

ARGYLL, George D.Campbell, 8th Duke
Autobiography (1906); Passages (1907)
Social, literary,and political life;
Palmerston and Derby administrations;
Postmaster-General;Scottish life and
church; celebrated figures.   147

ARIA, Eliza (Davis). My Sentimental
Self (1922). Childhood; designing and
journalism in London; theatrical and
literary celebrities.   148

ARKELL-HARDWICK, Alfred. An Ivory-Trader in North Kenia (1903). Hunting and trade in Kenya;adventures; native tribes.   149

ARKWRIGHT, Maj. Albert S. B. Return Journey (1948). WW2 prisoner in Germany; plans for escape; adventures in crossing Germany to Holland and Spain his benefactors.   150

ARLINGTON, Lewis Charles. Through the Dragon's Eyes (1931). Fifty years with Chinese navy,customs service and post office;Sun Yat Sen; politics and revolution.   151

ARLISS, George. Up the Years (1927) On the Stage (1928); George Arliss,by himself (1940). Struggles and success as actor on stage and screen; London; Hollywood; actors and producers. 152

ARMISTEAD, J.J. Piloted (1906); Ten Years (1913). Business in Leeds; fish culture in Scotland; Quaker life; his missionary work in Arctic lands North of Norway; travel and adventures. 153

ARMITAGE, Capt. Albert B. Cadet to Commodore (1925). Boyhood on sailing ships;work on P. and O. liners; Polar expeditions;troopships WW1; adventure for boys.   154

ARMSTRONG, Anthony (A. A. Willis). We Like the Country(1940). An account of his life in Sussex; country ways & people; novelist and humorist.   155

ARMSTRONG,Chester. Pilgrimage(1938) Pursuit of self-reliance; religious & political revolt; work for the Labour Party; Durham.   156

ARMSTRONG, George Gilbert. Memories (1944). Religious life and journalism in Yorks and London; liberal politics and educational work;Children's Newspaper; Unitarianism; peace work. 157

ARMSTRONG, James M. Legion of Hell (1936). Scotsman's service in French Foreign Legion in Morocco and Syria; his crimes and prison life.   158

ARMSTRONG,Martin D. Victorian Peepshow (1938).Recollections of boyhood; family, schools, holidays, houses and places; a boy's world.   159

ARMSTRONG, Thomas. My Life in Connaught (1906). Presbyterian clergyman and superintendent of schools and orphanage; his work; Irish life & great famine;religious rivalry; interesting record of 1840-60's.   160

ARMSTRONG, Warren. Saltwater Tramp (1944).Ship's engineer and unemployed travels in many lands; journalism and adventures, 1919-39.   161

ARMYTAGE,Percy. By the Clock (1927) Usher to the King; state occasions; & London life and society from 1870;celebrities.   162

ARNOLD, Frederick. Reminiscences of a Literary and Clerical Life (1889). Cambridge and Oxford;life and work as minister; scholarship and writing in London; magazines; preachers.   163

ARNOLD,Julian B. Giants in Dressing Gowns (Chicago, 1942). Childhood reminiscences of son of Sir Edwin Arnold; Garibaldi,Darwin, Swinburne, Crookes; Conan Doyle, etc.   164

ARNOLD, Thomas. Passages(1900). His boyhood in literary society; Oxford; Tasmania and N.Z.; Newman and Anglo-Catholicism;teaching at Oxford; religion, politics, literature.   165

ARNOT,Frederick Stanley. Garenganze (1889). Missionary work from 1881; in Northern Rhodesia; simple heroism and good details of native life.   166

ARNOT,William. Autobiography (1877) Life and work of minister in Glasgow and Edinburgh; Free Church.   167

ARNOTT,Peter. This Impertinence (L. 1941). Army career in India; engineer with Public Works Dept.;railways; and descriptions of Indian life,medicine, sport; adventures; anecdotes.   168

⟨ARTHUR, Sir Allan⟩.Hotch-Potch and Kedgeree (Calcutta, 1916). Shipowner; businessman; British India Steam Navigation Company; Indian life, society and celebrities.   169

ARTHUR, Sir George C. A. Septuagenarian's Scrap-Book(1933); From Phelps to Gielgud (1936); Not Worth Reading (1938). Eton, Oxford; career as soldier and writer; public and social events; reminiscences of stage and actors; friendships with royalty, statesmen and famous soldiers.   170

ANON. Artillery and Trench Mortar Memories(1933). Reminiscences of service on Western Front in WW1 by three rankers (J.E. Prince, V.H. Larr, and T. Slane); personal; 32 Division. 171

ASCHE, Oscar. Oscar Asche (1929). A theatrical autobiography; with Benson and Tree; travels & tours; his roles; sport; anecdotes.   172

ASH, George. Adventures(1923). Life as cowboy and Texas Ranger; adventure in Far East and Palestine; chronicles of a rolling stone.   173

ASHBEE, Charles Robert. Diary,1918-1923; work as adviser to the city of Jerusalem; reconstruction; Zionism; & celebrities. A Palestine Notebook (L. 1923).   174

ASHBRIDGE, Elizabeth. Some Account (Dublin, 1820).Quaker's sufferings at hands of drunken soldier husband; family and religious life, 1713-55. 175

ASHBURNHAM,John. A Narrative (1830) Army and political activities;attendant on Charles I from Oxford to Scottish army, 1646-47.   176

ASHBY,Lillian Luker. My India (Boston, 1937). Childhood in Bengal; domestic life in Orissa from 1874;Anglo-Indian life; Sakchi Steel Mills; good familiar knowledge.   177

ASHE, Thomas. Memoirs (1815). Seduces French maid; imprisonment; travel and adventures in N.and S. America; diamond mines; picaresque; it may be fiction.   178

ASHFORD, John. Life's Leaves (1869) Spiritual autobiography in verse; nature; loneliness;religion; source and solace of his poetry.   179

⎾ASHFORD, Mary Ann⏌. Life of a Licensed Victualler's Daughter (1844). Orphan & servant; adventures with employers and sons; marriage and family life in London; Chelsea College;difficulties in her life.   180

ASHLEY, Frederick William. My Sixty Years (1936). Clerk to Justice Avory; law, lawyers, judges; Avory.   181

ASHMAN, William. Lives of Early Methodist Preachers, ed. Thomas Jackson (1838)III. Life and work of itinerant preacher in Somerset and South of England; 18th Century.   182

ASHMOLE, Elias. Memoirs (1717). His career as astrologer and goldsmith; a rambling,amusing record; domestic and personal; health; remedies; difficulties; religion.   183

ASHTON, Arthur. Fifty Years' Work (Lowestoft, 1936). Attractive, simple picture of life and work of a Suffolk country parson.   184

ASHTON, Arthur Jacob. As I Went on My Way (1924). Lancs schooling; Balliol; legal career and cases; painting in France and Germany.   185

ASHTON,Julian Rossi. Now Came Still Evening On (1941). Boyhood in Devon; art studies in London;successful career as portrait-painter in Australia; friend of R. L. Stevenson; his travel and adventures.   186

ASHTON-WOLFE, Harry. The Underworld (1926);Thrill of Evil (1928). Work as interpreter at civil & criminal courts abroad; work with Sureté Nationale in Paris; international crooks.   187

ASHURST, Frederick. Memoirs (1898). Professional reminiscences of a young country surgeon.   188

ASHWELL,Lena. Myself a Player(1936) Canadian childhood;theatrical career; Irving and Lyceum;management Kingsway Theatre; concerts in France in WW1; & private life; good.   189

ASHWORTH,John. Life and Labours, by A.L.Calman (Manchester, 1875). Methodist upbringing; house-painter; work for Rochdale Chapel for destitute and travel and preaching in England and in America; good details of life of poor in Lancs; diary.   190

ASPINALL, Henry Kelsall. Birkenhead (Liverpool, 1903). Business career in Birkenhead and reminiscences of town and people from 30's.   191

ASQUITH, Lady Cynthia. Haply I May Remember (1950). Family life from the late 19th Century; society and public figures; George Wyndham; her literary interests.   192

ASQUITH, Hon. Herbert. Moments of Memory (1937). Boyhood and his father at Hampstead; Winchester and Oxford; service in WW1; public and political personalities.   193

ASSHER, Ben. Nomad (1931). A lively and amused account of an artilleryman in France during WW1.   194

ASTLEY,Sir John Dugdale.Fifty Years of My Life (1894). Eton and Oxford; a career in the army; Crimean War; M.P. for N.Lincs; social life and sport at home and abroad; racing; hunting. 195

ASTON, Anthony. The Fool's Opera(L. 1730?) Autobiography in preface; the breezy and brief chronicle of actor's many jobs in many countries; possibly fictional.   196

ASTON, Sir George Grey. Memories of a Marine (1919);Secret Service (1930) Woolwich and Greenwich; Boer War; intelligence work for Navy; WW1; Staff College;Camberley; educational, staff work; anecdotes.   197

ASTON, Walter H. Nor Iron Bars (L. 1946). Adventures of three prisoners of war in WW2; Dunkirk; captivity and escape; war conditions in France. 198

ANON. At the Front (Paisley, 1914). Personal narrative of a soldier in the Crimean War and Indian Mutiny.   199

/ATALL, John/. The Adventures of an Author(1767). Legal training & career in London; love, politics, debts; his life in Jamaica; his partnership with a Polish Jew;odd jobs; his success as a religious writer.   200

ATHERLEY-JONES, Llewellyn Archer. Looking Back(1925). Manchester School Chartism; legal career; Liberal politics and reform; Home Rule; Member of Parliament; judge of City of London; varied career; reminiscences of Lloyd George, Parnell, etc.   201

ATHILL,William Lombe. Recollections (1911). Irish boyhood; Dublin in 40's medical study and practice in Dublin; Rotunda Hospital; antiquarianism and sport; public events.   202

ATKIN, Frederic. Reminiscences of a Temperance Advocate (1899). Travels & lectures through England;anecdotes of drunkards, publicans, converts, temperance personalities from 1845.   203

ATKINS,John Black. Incidents (1947) Marlborough;Cambridge; literary journalism;war correspondent for Manchester Guardian; wars of late 19th Century; judicious.   204

ATKINSON, Charles. Life and Adventures (York, 1818). Military surgeon; travels in England; satirical account of native foibles.   205

ATKINSON,Charles J.F. Recollections (1934). Doctor's life in a village in Wharfdale; people and customs.   206

ATKINSON, John Christopher. Forty Years (1891). Clergyman's life & work in Yorkshire moorland parish of Danby natural history; antiquities and folk lore; good.   207

ATKINSON, Robert Le Lacheur. Island Going (1949). Attractive record of 15 years of travel, exploration, and adventures in remote and uninhabited islands of the Hebrides;natural history observations.   208

ATKINSON, William. Memoirs (Rotherham, 1817). Sinful childhood; life as tradesman in Rotherham; overwhelming sense of sin and damnation;redemption in Church of England.   209

ATTWOOD, William. The Man Who Could Grow Hair (1949). A journalist's travels and adventures in Europe, Africa etc. after WW2; amusing tales.   210

AUBREY, John. Miscellanies (1696). Preface has autobiographical details; of 17th Century antiquary; alarms and excursions.   211

AUSTIN,Alfred. Autobiography (1911) Childhood;schools; law studies; work as journalist, writer, and poet; Poet Laureate; European travels.   212

AUSTIN, E. Anecdotage (1872). Journalist's recollections of excitements
and public affairs in Bristol; crimes
and Chartism.   213

AUSTIN, Guy K. Pilgrim Father(1934)
Covered Wagon (1936). Travels and ups
and downs of English family in America
during the depression.   214

AUSTIN, Brig. General Herbert Henry
Gun Running in the Gulf (1926); Some
Rambles of a Sapper (1928). Military
career of an Engineer in India, 1894-
1920; adventures with gun-runners on
the frontier; social life.   215

/AUSTIN, John/. Return via Dunkirk,
by Gun Buster(1940). Experiences during 1940 campaign in Belgium; Dunkirk
rear guard and evacuation.   216

AUSTIN,Lorimer John. My Experiences
(1915). Red Cross doctor in France in
WW1; arrest; treatment in German prison camps.   217

AUSTIN, Maj. Thomas. Old Stick-Leg,
ed. H. H. Austin (1926). His military
experiences during the Peninsular War
from reminiscences and diary.   218

ANON. Autobiography of a Journalist
ed. Michael Joseph (1929). Experience
in free lance and staff journalism in
Fleet Street.   219

ANON.Autobiography of a Navvy (Macmillan's Mag., V, 1861-62). Laborer's
various jobs and travels for work;his
drunkenness; marriage; reform.   220

ANON.The Autobiography of a Poacher
ed.Caractacus (1901). Activities of a
deer-poacher on Exmoor;later a keeper
and water-bailiff;Exmoor dialect. The
editor is Frederick John Snell;may be
fiction.   221

ANON.The Autobiography of a Private
Soldier (Sunderland, 1838). Army life
in Ireland in early 19th Century; his
earlier work as chemist's apprentice;
brutality of service; nostalgia.   222

ANON. Autobiography of a Scotch Lad
(Glasgow, 1887). Ayrshire childhood &
religious upbringing from 1815; printer's apprentice; his missionary work
in Glasgow; pastorates.   223

ANON. Autobiography of a Shipowner
(Plymouth, 1909). Life of an apprentice fitter and ship mechanic; repair
of boats; experience as a "shipowner"
told flippantly; it may be fiction. A
copy in Bodleian.   224

ANON. Autobiography of a Thief(Macmillan's Mag., 1879). Criminal activity; relations with police; narrated
in thieves' cant.   225

ANON.Autobiography of an Irish Traveller (1835). Travels with a pauper
in USA; claiming inheritance, Ireland
and travels there; naval commissary;&
his adventures in India, Siberia, and
China.   226

ANON. Autobiography of an Ordinary
Man (1903?). Boyhood as a cowherd in
Banffshire from 1834; early poverty;
Calvinism; drapery business, Ireland;
reform school in Glasgow.   227

AVON. How I Became a Sportsman (L.
1882).Veteran sportsman's memories of
country sports from boyhood;mostly of
foxhunting.   228

AWDRY, Frances. In the Isles of the
Sea (1902). Her fifty years of travel
and adventure in Melanesia.   229

B., G. Narrative of a Private Sol-
dier(Glasgow 1819). Glasgow education
and enlistment; service in Peninsular
war and Ireland; discharge; sins; religious life.   1

BABBAGE, Charles. Passages from the
Life(1864). School; Cambridge; invention of calculating machine;engineer-
ing; science and famous scientists of
19th Century; social life and social
scene; good.   2

/BABINGTON, T. M./. Soldiering Yarns
by B. A. B. (Madras, 1905). Army and
civilian life in India; social life;
celebrities; the supernatural, India
Office Library.   3

BACK, Philip. From Terrier Boy(Plymouth,n.d.). Hunt servant for Trelaw-
ney on Dartmoor; a huntsman and field
master; country life and sport. Copy

in Barnstable Athenaeum.   4

BACKHOUSE, Hugo. Among the Gauchos (1950). Experiences in South America, from time he left home as a boy;ranch work, cattle, sport in Argentina,etc. and gaucho life and ways; good.   5

BACON, Capt. Alban F. L. Wanderings (1922). With Territorials in WW1;service in France,Egypt, Palestine; good unglamorized picture of war.   6

BACON, Gertrude. Memories (1928). A lively record of pioneer flying; WW1; adventures as journalist;travels as a lecturer.   7

BACON,John Francis. Six Years (1838) Experiences at sieges of Bilbao and in Carlist war, 1830-37.   8

BACON, John Mackenzie. Record of an Aeronaut (1907). First part autobiography of boyhood in Berkshire village reminiscences of Tom Hughes.   9

BACON, Adm. Sir Reginald. From 1900 (1940); A Naval Scrapbook (1925). His early life in navy, from 1877; review of navy in his time; WW1;critical reminiscences.   10

BADCOCK, Lt.Col. George H. Tell Him (1945). Autobiography of a dog trainer; army reminiscences.   11

BADCOCK,Lt.Col.Lovell. Rough Leaves (1835). Military observer in Portugal and Spain during civil war 1832-34;an account of war and travel book.   12

BADDELEY, John Frederick. Russia in the Eighties (1921). Special correspondent for "Standard" 1879-93; sport and politics.   13

BADEN-POWELL, Sir Robert Stephenson Smyth, Baron. The Downfall of Prempeh (1896); Memories of India (1914); My Adventures as a Spy(1915); Lessons of a Lifetime(1933);Adventures and Accidents (1934). Scouting during Ashanti expedition; early army life and sport in India; espionage work in the Boer War; education at Charterhouse;military career,travels,sport; work in the Boy Scout Movement.   14

BADGER, Rev. W. Collins. God Pursu-

ing Me (Brinkley, 1909). Boyhood and clerical work in Cambridge & Birmingham. Tract, Wilts Archaeological Soc., Devizes.   15

BADLEY, John Haden. Schoolmaster's Testament (Oxford, 1937). Founding of Bedales School and his 40 years there curriculum & educational experiments; practical and wise career.   16

BAGOT, Mrs. Charles (Sophy Louisa). Links with the Past (1902). Childhood with father in navy; marriage; Staffs society and London; 1842-70; Wellington, etc.   17

BAILEY, John. Poor Pilgrim (1810). Baptist's spiritual life; sins; conversion; ministry at Alie Street. 18

BAILEY, Philip James. Autobiographical fragment; poet's life. MS, Nottingham Public Library.   19

BAILLIE, Matthew. Autobiography of 18th Century physician. MS,Royal College of Surgeons. See, Practitioner, LVII (1896).   20

BAILLIE, Mrs. W. W. Days and Nights of Shikar (1921). Big-game hunting in India during many years of residence; from early 20th Century.   21

BAILY, Francis Evans. Twenty-Nine Years' Hard Labour (1934).Work as literary journalist; WW1 service in Tanganyika; literary views.   22

BAIN,Alexander. Autobiography(1904) Poor student in Scotland; studies and mental growth; philosophy; Aberdeen & London universities; his writings and teaching at Aberdeen; Carlyle.   23

BAINBRIDGE,Henry Charles. Twice Seven(1933). Life and adventures Russia before WW1; St. Petersburg; Corvo and Farbergé.   24

BAINES, Frederick Ebenezer. Forty Years (1894); On the Track (1895). A personal narrative of surveyor-general for telegraph and inspector of mails; mostly the work.   25

BAIRNSFATHER,Bruce. Wide Canvas (L. 1939); Career of cartoonist; creation of Old Bill;Churchill and other celebrities; travels Europe and USA.   26

BAKER, Daniel. Autobiography, 1690-
1705; God's providences; escapes; often violent or amusing. MS, Bucks Museum, Aylesbury.   27

BAKER,George. Soul of a Skunk(1930)
Somewhat smug apologia of conscientious objector in WW1; Wormwood Scrubs;
public attitude.   28

BAKER,Sir Herbert. Architecture and
Personalities(1944). Kentish boyhood;
architectural work from 1885;churches
public buildings & monuments; London;
S. Africa, India, USA.   29

BAKER, John. Diary, 1751-58; family
and social life in Sussex and London;
work as Solicitor-General of Leeward
Isles; personal and social life; detailed and lively.   The Diary of John
Baker, ed. Philip C. Yorke (1931). 30

BAKER, John. Autobiographical notes
1772-1803; medical work; childbirths;
folk beliefs. MS, Reading Public Library.   31

BAKER, Richard St. Barbe. I Planted
Trees (1944). Career and travels of a
silviculturist.   32

BAKER,Sir Samuel White. Eight Years
Wanderings in Ceylon (1855). The work
and problems of a planter, from 1845;
native life and labour; social life &
hunting.   33

BAKER, Silvia. Alone and Loitering
(1946); Journey to Yesterday (1950).
Painter's travels from 1938; Mediterranean, West Indies, India, Sth Seas;
childhood, stage training, Zoo painter; life in Chelsea; her search for
pre-industrial scenes.   34

BAKER, Sir Thomas. Autobiographical
jottings of Lord Mayor of Manchester.
19th Century. MS, Manchester Central
Library.   35

BAKER, Thomas. Battling Life (1885)
Civil service career; Health Department; Royal Sanitary Commission; inspection and public health work; travels and work in India.   36

BAKER, William. A Brief Memoir, by

John Bowen (Taunton, 1854). Autobiography;boyhood in Bridgewater, Somerset; theatre, Kean; hobbies; natural
history; militia; pleasant.   37

BAKER-CARR,Christopher d'Arcy. From
Chauffeur to Brigadier(1930). Machine
guns and tanks in France, WW1.   38

BALDRY, George. The Rabbit Skin Cap
(1939). Autobiography of country laborer in Norfolk 1869 to 1922; Norfolk
dialect.   39

BALDWIN,Monica.I Leap Over the Wall
(1949). Experiences, impressions, and
emotions in the outside world after 28
years in a nunnery;service in WW2 and
Stanley Baldwin; very sensitive writing; good.   40

BALDWIN, Oliver. Six Prisons (1925)
Questing Beast (1932). Eton; criticism of schools; socialist; Armenian &
Bolshevik revolutions; and his adventures in Anatolia, etc.; labor politics.   41

BALDWIN, William Charles. African
Hunting (1863). Travels in unexplored
Africa from Natal to the Zambesi from
1852; hunting and adventures; natives
and their ways.   42

BALFOUR, Arthur James, 1st Earl of.
Chapters of Autobiography(1930).Eton;
Cambridge; philosophical studies; en-
try into politics; Parliamentary car-
eer; Disraeli, Gladstone, Reform Bill;
WW1; Society; important.   43

BALFOUR, Lady Frances. Ne Oblivisc-
aris(1930). Public and political life
and society, 1880-1900.   44

BALFOUR, Harold Harrington. Airman
Marches (1933). Flying in WW1; journalism for "Daily Mail,"; M.P.;Conser-
vative politics; 1914-32.   45

BALFOUR, Jabez Spencer. My Prison
Life (1907). Parkhurst and Portland;
routine; the physical & psychological
effects; suggestions for reform.   46

BALL,Derrick. Bungalow by the Beach
(1950).Experiences of himself and his
wife while living on the Caribbean island of Grenada; domestic life in the
tropics.   47

BALL, Sir Robert S. Reminiscences (1915). Irish childhood; Trinity; Irish social life;mathematics & astronomy; professor at Royal College Science and at Cambridge.   48

BALL, Valentine. Jungle Life in India (1880). Irregular journal kept by a geologist, 1864-78; Indian life and natural history; hunting; scientific observations; detailed.   49

BALLANTINE, William. Some Experiences (1882); The Old World and the New (1884). Law studies; legal career and cases; Sergeant-at-Law; lawyers, writers, and clubs; Garrick Club; London social life; good.   50

BALLANTYNE,Robert Michael. Personal Reminiscences (1893). Experiences in lighthouse,fire brigade, mines; travels and adventures; moral reflection; gathering materials for his books for boys.   51

BALLARD, Philip Boswood. Things I Cannot Forget (1937). Education; work as school inspector,Wales and London; career, travels, writings;reminiscences of schools, teachers, etc.   52

BAMBERGER,Sir Louis. Memories(1929) Bow Bell Memories (1931). His career; timber and pianoforte trades, London; memories of London social life, business men, etc.; interesting.   53

BAMFIELD, Col. Joseph. Apology (The Hague? 1685). Royalist commander during reign of Charles I; experience in Civil Wars.   54

BAMFORD,Samuel.Passages in the Life (1844); Early Days (1859). Education; middle-class life in Lancashire;weaving;Corn Law riots; work as agitator, poet & journalist; imprisonment; life of a radical; good.   55

BAMPTON, C.F.L. Memorials of a Life of Adventure (1883).Travels in various parts of world,including Australia and New Zealand.   56

BANCROFT,George Pleydell. Stage and Bar (1939). Legal studies and career; clerk of assize; anecdotes of lawyers and judges; and intimate reminiscences of Victorian theatre and players; son

of Squire Bancroft.   57

BANCROFT, Sir Squire and Mrs. Marie Effie. Mr. and Mrs.Bancroft (L. 1888) The Bancrofts (L. 1909); Empty Chairs (1925).Their careers and roles on the stage; plays, playwrights, actors and the theatrical scene; social life and friendship with Dickens and others of the Eminent Victorians; good.   58

BANDERAS. Sporting Reminiscences of South America(1929). Naval service in South America, 1919-1921; social life, sport, hunting.   59

BANGS, Benjamin. Memoirs (1757). A Quaker life and ministry at Stockport and through England, later 17th & earlier 18th Century.   60

BANKES, James. Memoranda Book (Inverness, 1935). Estate work on Lancashire manor near Wigan,1586-1617; family life;dialect. Copy at Manchester Public Library.   61

BANKES, Viola. Why Not? (1934). An author's life in country;literary society in London.   62

BANKS,Mrs.Emily. White Woman on the Congo(1943). Missionary work and domestic life at Wangata & Bolenge.   63

BANKS, John. Journal of the Life(L. 1712).Quaker's education; conversion, ministry, travels through England and Ireland; sufferings; Sunderland.   64

BANKS, Sir Joseph. Journal, ed.Sir J. D. Hooker (1896). Scientific work& travel experiences during Cook's first voyage in the Endeavour,1768-71;South Seas, Australasia, East Indies.   65

BARBER, Maj. Charles H. Besieged in Kut (1917). Military experiences WW1; siege of Kut; capture; prison life in Bagdad; exchange.   66

BARBER,Donald Herbert. Twenty Years (1947). Bank clerk; free lance writer and editor; journalist's life.   67

BARBER, James Henry. A Family Memorial, ed. H. M. Doncaster (Sheffield, 1905). Boyhood and education in Yorkshire; Quaker life; USA, West Indies; work in banking; 1820-47.   68

BARBER, Mrs. M. Five Score and Ten (Crewkerne,1840). Dictated; long life of poverty and sufferings; a servant; life of poor in Ireland; family. Copy Bristol Central Library.   69

BARBICAN, James. Confessions (1927) English airman turned rum-runner; the USA during prohibition; adventures in trade.   70

BARCLAY, Sir Thomas. Thirty Years (1914). Times correspondent in France 1876-1906; politics; diplomacy; society.   71

BARCLAY,Thomas Patrick. Memoirs and Medleys(Leicester, 1934). Bottlewasher;working-class life; socialism; his reading; friendship with Shaw.   72

BARCROFT,John.Brief Narrative (Dublin, 1730). Quaker autobiography; Irish travels and social conditions;his ministry in Ireland.   73

BARD, Samuel A. (pseud). Adventures on the Mosquito Shore (1856). Travels and adventures in British Honduras; & details of native life; by Ephraim G. Squier.   74

BARHAM,Francis. Alist(1840). Author's life; religion and morals; cult of Alism; writings; interesting record of a crank in 18th Century.   75

BARING,Sir Francis Thornhill. Journals and Correspondence (Winchester, 1905). Winchester;Oxford; liberal politics;Parliamentary and governmental career, 1808-1852; literature; Reform Bill; penny postage.   76

BARING, Maurice. Puppet Show (1922) Childhood; Eton; writing and journalism; travels in Russia and Balkans; a pleasant record of 30 years.   77

BARING-GOULD, Sabine. Early Reminiscences (1923); Further Reminiscences (1925). Devonshire parson; religious, social, country life, antiquarianism, folklore, teaching, writings; rise of new ideas; travel abroad; good.   78

BARKE, James. Green Hills (L.1940). Childhood in Scotland;school, country and sport; WW1 service; life in Glasgow; far-off days.   79

BARKER, Albert. Memories(1921). WW1 experiences of a sapper in Macedonia; naive and simple.   80

BARKER, Sir Ernest. Father of the Man (1949). Cheshire upbringing; village life and schooling; Manchester Grammar School; Balliol;his education and his debt to teachers.   81

BARKER,Fred Drummond. Angler's Paradise (1929). Reminiscences of twenty years' fishing in West Ireland.   82

BARKER,George M. Tea Planter's Life in Assam (Calcutta, 1884). The everyday life and work of a planter; labor conditions;domestic life;natural history; government policies.   83

BARKER, Sir Herbert A. Leaves from My Life (1927). Struggles and success as manipulative surgeon in Manchester and London;fight with General Medical Council for recognition.   84

BARKER, J. Ellis. My Testament of Healing (1939). Career as homeopathic practitioner; cases; a defence of his beliefs.   85

BARKER,James P. Log of a Limejuicer (1933). Dictated; boyhood; apprentice to sea; life in sailing vessels; voyages around Cape Horn; yarns.   86

BARKER, Joseph. History and Confessions (1846); Life (1880). Yorkshireman's self-education;teetotalism and ministry; Barkerite movement in England and USA: free thought; joins the secularists.   87

BARKER, Matthew Henry. Floating Remembrances (1854). Service in British navy; people and incidents; his share in capturing a deserter.   88

BARKER, Robert. Genuine Life (1809) Lancs childhood; in shipbuilding; his voyages as carpenter to Africa and Antigua on slavers; loss of sight; his dreams; religion; writings.   89

BARLOW,Richard Gorton.Forty Seasons (Manchester, 1908). Career and games of Lancashire cricketer;work as coach and umpire; Australian tours.   90

BARNARD,Lieut. Frederick Lamport. A

Three Years' Cruize (1848). His naval service off Mozambique in 40's; slave traffic; chasing slavers; native life shipwreck and adventures. 91

BARNES, Alpheus G. Master Showman (1938). Life in the circus; anecdotes of people and beasts; good. 92

BARNES, Derek G. Cloud Cover (1943) Intelligence officer in WW2; service with RAF; night-flying. 93

BARNES,George Nicoll. From Workshop (1923). Early poverty;trade unionism; career in Parliament; Pensions minister in war cabinet;Labour Party chairman. 94

BARNES, James Thomas Strachey. Half a Life (1933);Half a Life Left (1937) Eton,Cambridge, and Sandhurst; flying with RFC during WW1; journalist & war correspondent; sympathy with Fascism; Mussolini and his virtues. 95

BARNES, John H. Forty Years (1914). Stage career from 1874 in England and USA; plays, actors, anecdotes. 96

BARNETT, Lt.Col. George Henry. With the 48th Division (1923). Service in WW1;Italian Front and Austrian offensive; supply and administration. 97

BARNETT,John Francis. Musical Reminiscences (1906). Musical studies in Germany; career in England; teaching at Guildhall School; his compositions English musicians; pianist. 98

BARONTÉ,Gervée.Life and Adventures. (1935).Travels and adventures of writer and prodigal daughter;Mrs.Charles Breckenridge. 99

BARR, Amelia Edith. All the Days of My Life (1913). Lancashire days; USA; spiritual memories and sorrows; lyric and verse-writing; Christian journalism; sentimental. 100

BARR,David. Climbing (1910). Struggle and success of a village lad as a salesman and estate agent; Methodist church and class work; prosperity and religion in Birmingham. 101

BARR, James. Lang Syne (Glasgow, 1949). Life and work of a Scots minister, social reformer, and M.P.; temperance, betting, & other social problems; Parliamentary affairs. 102

BARR, Robert. I Travel (1945). From motor mechanic to bus owner;travel by road; motor tourism. 103

BARR, Lieut. William. Journal of a March from Delhi (1844). Artilleryman with Wade on his march to Peshawur and Kabul in 1839; military affairs; Himalayan scenery. 104

BARRAUD, E. M. Set My Hand (Worcester,1946). Five years as land girl in WW2;work and workers; changing values simple; interesting. 105

BARRETT, Daniel William. Life and Work (1880). Clergyman's mission work amongst men building Midland Railway; their ways and slang. 106

BARRETT,Edward John Boyd. Ex-Jesuit (1931). Boyhood Ireland; novice; study at Louvain; teaching at Clongowes; bitter experience teaching Irish boys and withdrawal;professor of education in USA; politics. 107

BARRIE, James M. A Window in Thrums (1889).Humor and pathos in a Scottish village; a fictitious setting typical of playwright's early life. 108

BARRINGTON, Charles George. Seventy Years' Fishing (1906). Salmon & trout fishing, England and Scotland. 109

BARRINGTON, Charlotte, Viscountess. Through Eighty Years (1936).Childhood London and Hampton Court;marriage and country house and London Society; politics; travel; WW1 effects. 110

BARRINGTON, George. Memoirs (1790). Irish boyhood; career as a pickpocket trials and prison experiences; acting in Glasgow; deportation. 111

BARRINGTON,Sir Jonah. Personal Sketches(1827-32). Politics and Parliament in Ireland; admiralty judge; Irish political and social life; rebellion; theatres; women; sport; drinking and wild comedy. 112

BARRINGTON,Jonah.And Master of None (1948).Varied career; music-master at

Uppingham;chorus-master for BBC; ENSA and eight years journalism.   113

BARRINGTON,Rutland.Rutland Barrington(L.1908); More Rutland Barrington (1911). Career as singer and actor in Gilbert and Sullivan;tours;sport and social life; anecdotes.   114

BARRON, David. Book of Remembrance (1927). Scottish clergyman's ministry in Eastbourne; poems; prayers.   115

BARROW, Gen. Sir George de Symons. Fire of Life (1942). Military career, from 1884; Boxer Rebellion; India; at Staff College, Quetta; with Allenby & in Eastern Command to 1928.   116

BARROW, Sir John. Travels in China (1804); Voyage to Cochin China (1806) An Auto-biographical Memoir (L. 1847) Business in Liverpool; at sea;service in embassy of Macartney into China in 90's; South Africa; pioneer travels & 40 years with Admiralty.   117

BARROW, Katherine Mary. Three Years in Tristan da Cunha (1910). The life of a missionary's wife from 1905; religious work, education,medicine; and social and domestic life;natural history; life of islanders.   118

BARRY, Alice F. Armchair Reflections (Brighton, 1946). An old lady's notes on her social, domestic, family life in Victorian days; the familiar, everyday scene. Worthing P.L.   119

BARRY, Charles. Unsought Adventure (1939). Soldier in Russian Army; the revolution; spy in Russia for British; editorial work for ILO;writing detective and adventure stories; real name was Charles Bryson.   120

BARRY, William. Memories (1926). At Oscott College; priest's parish work, Dorchester & Leamington; writing for Dublin Review;advocacy of social justice; travels.   121

BARRY, Tom B. Guerilla Days in Ireland (Dublin, 1949). Political memories of a still bitter Irish rebel and his activities while leading guerrilla company in West Cork 1919-21.   122

BARRY, William Jackson. Up and Down (1879).Fifty years of travel, pioneer life and adventures from 1828; India, China, Pacific, Australia, California; gold-rushes,gambling,speculations and lecturing; lively.   123

BARSLEY, Michael Henry. Wolf at the Door (1946). Liverpool;Oxford; advertising;radio work with BBC in wartime and odd jobs; flippant.   124

BARTLETT, Ellis Ashmead. Some of My Experiences (1918). Experiences of a journalist during WW1; at sea, France and Gallipoli; disjointed.   125

BARTLETT, Vernon. This is My Life (1937). His career as journalist and radio commentator; News-Chronicle and BBC; international affairs.   126

BARTON, Edwin Alfred. Doctor Remembers(1941); Running Water (1944). His career as doctor in London; hospitals and Harley Street from 70's;anecdotes and reminiscences of fishing; interesting for medical fashions.   127

BARTON, Francis Alexander. Jack of All Trades (1938).Dover; Harrow; Cambridge; medical study and practice in Norwich, etc.; flying; non-alcoholic wine; sport; Victorian social scene; varied and interesting.   128

BARTON, "Freddie" (Frederick Page). We'll Go No More A-Roving (1937). His social life, travels, sport; at Monte Carlo; career as bridge expert & writer;introduced contract; anecdotes of celebrities.   129

BARTON, Tilney. Life of a Country Lawyer(Oxford, 1937). Training as solicitor; work at Truro; official receiver; work with prisoners in Egypt and Jerusalem.   130

BARTRAM, Lady Alfred. Recollections of Seven Years' Residence, by a Lady (1830). With her husband in Mauritius in early century; government work and French and English society; Creoles; missionaries;domestic and social life and anecdotes; good.   131

/BARTRUM,Katherine Mary7. A Widow's Reminiscences (1858).Experiences of a doctor's wife at siege of Lucknow;her hardships and dangers;the loss of her husband in the siege.   132

BARTTELOT, Captain Edmund Musgrave. Military journal, 1887-88; commander of the rear column with the Emin Pasha relief expedition.Life,by W. L. Barttelot (1890).   133

BARWICK, T. To India; Under Arms; Through the Jungle;Last of the Seven; Memories. Pamphlets by a Barnstaple man on his army experiences, 1883-90; Ireland,India; in the ranks. Bound in one volume in library of North Devon Athenaeum, Barnstaple.   134

BASHFORD,Sir Henry Howarth.Lodgings (1935); Fisherman's Progress (1946). Social and personal life of himself & his family and friends;angling, Devon Wiltshire, Norway.   135

BASSETT, George. This Also Happened (1947).Methodist chaplain to hospital in India; Indian life & India in wartime; WW2.   136

BATEMAN, Henry Mayo. H. M. Bateman (1937). His training as an artist at Westminster; work for Tatler & Punch, etc.; London Sketch Club.   137

BATEMAN, Josiah. Clerical Reminiscences, by Senex (1880). Life and parish work of a parson in Staffs, India, Wilts, Yorks, Kent, etc.   138

BATES,Frank. Reminiscences (Norwich 1930).Career as organist and musician mainly at Norwich Cathedral; festival and church music in England.   139

BATHGATE,Janet. Aunt Janet's Legacy (1894). Pious upbringing; child servant in various families;marriage to a saddler & widowhood; life in Selkirkshire in early 19th Century.   140

/BATTEN, Harry Mortimer/. Mountains of the Morning, by Stravaiger (Edin. 1938). Boyhood in Scotland; his life in India; Nilgiri Hills; Rudyard Kipling; emigration to Canada; backwoods life there.   141

BATTEN, John. Dirty Little Collier (1947). Work as radio officer; coasting colliers, in WW2; comradeship of the sea; unglamorized picture of naval life in wartime.   142

BATTERSEA, Lady Constance (de Rothschild) Flower. Reminiscences (1922). Her family and social life from 50's; politics; social work; Reform; celebrities.   143

BAX, Sir Arnold E. T.   Farewell My Youth (1943). Studies and career as a musician and composer;musical personalities and movements.   144

BAX, Clifford. Ideas & People (1936) Evenings in Albany (1942);Here's Rosemary(1948); Rosemary for Remembrance. (1948).Autobiography and reminiscences of artist and writer;Holst, Bennett & Playfair and the famous figures of the artistic and literary world;lament on vulgarity of the times.   145

BAX, Emily. Miss Bax (Boston, 1939) English girl stenographer at the American Embassy in London 1902-14;celebrities; social events.   146

BAX, Ernest Belfort.   Reminiscences (1918). Socialist politics and journalism; Victorian literature, art and philosophy; legal life, political and journalistic work; rise of the Labour Party;clubs; personalities; important for socialist movement.   147

BAXTER,Archibald. We Will Not Cease (1939). New Zealand farmer; conscientious objector WW1; deported, drafted sent to France; release and return to NZ; spiritual resistance.   148

BAXTER, Arthur Beverley.   Strange Street (1935). Life in Canada; salesman; journalism after WW1; editor of "Daily Express"; Beaverbrook; Blumenfeld; the Empire.   149

BAXTER,John. Intimate Thoughts, ed. A. Muir(1942). Mellow experiences and reflections of antiquarian bookseller in Edinburgh; books; authors.   150

BAXTER, Richard. Reliquiae Baxterianae (1696). God's providences; Civil War; nonconformity and anti-Papism; a spiritual and religious life; Plague; Great Fire; a classic of the spiritual autobiographies.   151

/BAYLEY, Frederick William Naylor/. Four Years' Residence (1830). Work of a sugar planter in Barbados, St.Lucia

St. Vincent, Trinidad from 1826; the social and military scene; slaves and slavery.   152

/BAYLEY, Capt. John Arthur/. Reminiscences of School and Army Life (1875) Eton in 40's; ensign with army in India and Ireland; the Mutiny; civilian life in England.   153

BAYLEY, Victor. Nine-fifteen from Victoria (1937); Indian Artifex (1939) His work and adventures as railway engineer;the Khyber Railway; India during WW1 and after; good.   154

BAYLISS, Sir Wyke. Olives (L.1906). Art studies; drawings of churches and cathedrals; the Gothic; clubs, societies, Royal Society British Artists; Watt, Hunt, and other Victorians; artistic creeds.   155

BAYLY, Capt. George. Sea Life Sixty Years Ago (1885). Exploring & trading in South Seas and New Zealand; transporting convicts to NSW; adventures; pioneer life; natives.   156

BAYLY, Hugh Wansey. Triple Challenge (1935). Career of Harley St. specialist;navy and army service WW1; politics and scandals after war.   157

BAYLY, Adm. Sir Lewis. Pull Together (1939). His naval career, 1872-1921; anti-submarine campaign; torpedoes; & convoying US troops.   158

BAYLY, Colonel Richard. Diary (1896) Narrative of his military service in India, 1796-1830; Tippoo Sahib; later military experiences in Mauritius and Ireland.   159

BAYZAND, William. "Coaching in and out of Oxford from 1820 to 1840," Oxford Hist. Soc. Collectanea IV, 1905. Anecdotes and reminiscences of an old Oxford janitor.   160

BEALE, Thomas Willert. The Light of Other Days (1890). His career as theatrical and operatic company manager; His Majesty's;London social life; the theatrical and musical scene.   161

BEALES, Hugh L. and LAMBERT, Richard (eds.), Memoirs of the Unemployed (L. 1934). A vivid collection of autobiographies by anonymous unemployed men and women of many trades; sociology & humanity.   162

BEAMAN, Ardern A. H. The Squadroon (1920). Experiences with the cavalry in France,WW1; Cambrai; the great advance.   163

BEAMAN, Ardern George Hulme. Twenty Years (1898). Work as lawyer in Levant consular service in 70's and 80's;the Egyptian rebellion; journalism in the Balkans.   164

BEARD, John. My Shropshire Days on Common Ways (Birmingham,1948). Schooldays; farm and building laborer; random notes on Shropshire life and people.   165

BEARD, Thomas. Holy Seed, by Joseph Porter (1711). Contains autobiography of Beard; sins and conversion; spiritual life of nonconformist at the end of 17th Century.   166

BEARDSALL, Francis. Autobiography, 1799-1842;religious experiences after his conversion to Methodism;Sheffield affairs. MS, Sheffield City Libraries Sheffield Collection.   167

BEASLEY, Benjamin. Stammering (1902) School; work in steel business; cures himself of stammering; success of his school for stammerers.   168

BEATON, Cecil W. H. Ashcombe (1949) The artist's memories of social life, conversation and famous guests in the arts and society during long tenancy of a house in Wiltshire.   169

BEATON, Revd. Patrick. Creoles and Coolies (1859). Five years' work as a missionary in Mauritius;native life & morals; slavery; labour problems; and economics.   170

BEATTIE, Malcolm Hamilton. On the Hoogly (1935). His work as a pilot on the Hoogly,1878-1913; life in Calcutta; adventures; famous ships and sailors; anecdotes.   171

BEATTY-KINGSTON, William. Men,Cities and Events (1895); Music and Manners (1887). Career as journalist and foreign correspondent;Telegraph; society court; musicians; writers.　　　　172

BEAUFORT, Douglas. Nothing up My
Sleeve (1938). Experiences of society
entertainer and magician; performances before royalty and schools.　　173

BEAUMAN, Katharine Bentley. Wings
(1943). Airwoman WW2; balloon centre;
Air Ministry; Bomber Command Headquarters; growth of WAAF.　　　　174

BEAUMONT, Agnes. Narrative of the
Persecution, ed. G. B. Harrison (1929)
Nonconformist's spiritual life & persecution; picture of Bunyan; a lively
narrative and good dialogue.　　175

BEAUMONT, Sir Barrington. Reminiscences (1902). Society and court life
in 18th Century; Walpole; Versailles;
politics; pseudonymous and is possibly
spurious.　　　　　　　　176

BEAUMONT, Cyril William. Flashback
(1931). His boyhood at turn of century
home, hobbies, games, etc.　　177

BEAUMONT, John C. H. Ships and People (1926). Scotland; medical officer
on liners; White Star Line; in merchant navy WW1; meetings with celebrated
passengers.　　　　　　　178

BEAUMONT, William Comyns. A Rebel in
Fleet Street (1944). His forty years
as journalist; The World; anecdotes &
criticism of newspapers and journalists.　　　　　　　　　179

BEAVAN, Arthur Henry. Fishes (1905)
Reminiscences of fishing, mainly deep
-ea; England; Australia.　　180

BEAVEN, Thomas P. A Sportsman (Trowbridge, 1939); A Sportsman's Fireside
Memories (1940). Country sports, Wiltshire from boyhood; shooting, fishing
and country life; local characters and
humors; fond memories.　　　181

BEAVER, Philip. African Memoranda
(1805). Experiences in the attempt to
establish a British settlement at Bu-
lama, Sierra Leone, in 1792; natives,
slavery, trade.　　　　　182

BEAVER, Wilfred N. Unexplored New
Guinea (1920). Travels and adventures
of a resident magistrate in interior;

life and customs of the natives of New
Guinea.　　　　　　　　183

BECHER, Augusta Emily. Personal Reminiscences (1930). A lively picture
of Indian society and social life from
1830 to 1888; the Mutiny.　　184

BECHERVAISE, John. Thirty-six Years
(1839). Sea adventures; schooner captain, Newfoundland, Brazil; bankrupt;
in Winchester Gaol; naval service in
West Indies and Far East.　　185

BECKETT, Arthur. Adventures (1933).
Sussex village life, sports, customs,
character; with diary extracts.　186

BECKWITH, Lady Muriel Beatrice (Gordon Lennox). When I Remember (1936).
Country house life; London society and
pleasures; Goodwood; sport; Edwardian
social scene and customs.　　187

BEDDINGTON, Mrs. Claude (Frances E.)
All that I Have Met (1929). Reminiscences and anecdotes; politics, society
theatre, music, literature, sport; celebrities.　　　　　　　188

BEDDOE, John. Memories (Bristol, 1910)
Childhood Wales; medical studies London and Edinburgh; Crimean War; Bristol
practice; anthropological study; medical officer, Edinburgh.　　　189

BEDFORD, Hastings W.S. Russell, Duke
of. The Years of Transition (L. 1949)
Eton and Balliol; work with YMCA during WW1; social service and religious
work; pets and animals; violent political views; unhappy record.　190

BEDFORD, Paul John. Recollections
(1864). Early days; theatre at Bath;
career of comedian; Adelphi theatre;
anecdotes; amusing.　　　191

[BEE, Allan Gordon]. Rolling Home,
by The Idler, (1936). His education in
Edinburgh; medical studies; career as
naval surgeon; WW1; practice in South
Africa; travels.　　　　192

BEECHAM, Sir Thomas. A Mingled Chime
(1943). Lancs childhood; Oxford; music
in Bayreuth; life in opera and music
from 1900; Russian Ballet; orchestras
controversies; anecdotes of musicians
and society.　　　　　　193

BEEDEL, F. Autobiography (Sydney, 1905). Early life in Reading; boyhood factory work;emigration to Queensland and his business and ministry at the Baptist Church in Sydney.Copy Reading P.L.   194

BEERBOHM, Julius. Wanderings in Patagonia (1879). His travels in Patagonia in 70's; ostrich-hunters; trade and adventures.   195

BEESTON,Sir William. Journal, 1655-1680; largely deals with Jamaican affairs and naval activities in the West Indies and Jamaica; log notes mostly. MS, B.M. Add. 12424, 12430.   196

BEHAGUE, John C. I Found Shangri-La (Birmingham, 1945). Adventures of RAF radio operator in the Himalayas 1945; Eastern life. Cambridge U.L.   197

BEITH, Rev. Alexander. Memories of Disruption Times (1877). Work in the Church of Scotland & Free Church; the disruption of 1843.   198

BELCHER, Joseph. Pastoral Recollections (1837). Everyday life and work of clergyman; instances of piety and conversion; moral tales.   199

BELFRAGE, Cedric. Away from It All (1937); They All Hold Swords (1941). Escapist's travels in Far East; emotional career of gentleman and journalist; sex in large doses;Daily Express Labour Party; egotistical.   200

BELL, Adrian. Corduroy (1930); Silver Ley (1931); The Balcony (L.1934); Apple Acre (1942). Literary primitivism; boyhood, nursery schools, evocation of small things; return to country,work as farmer in Suffolk; yeoman and squire; revival of agriculture in war years; social; economics.   201

BELL, Charles Dent. Reminiscences (1889). Ulster boyhood;poet's reminiscences of boyhood in Ireland; folklore; Scottish school; friends.   202

BELL,Edward Albert.These Meddlesome Attorneys(1939). Solicitor's life and memories; courts, judges & lawyers; a lively collection of stories.   203

BELL,Evelyn. So Kind to Youth (1938

Memory Be Good(1939). Essex boyhood, musical training and career;Victorian and Edwardian musical scene; his life in India;attempts to reconcile East & West; social reforms.   204

/BELL, Sir George/. Rough Notes by an Old Soldier (1867). Lively account of military career; Peninsular & Crimean wars; India; Canadian rebellion; West Indies; Ireland; personal, social, sport, adventures.   205

BELL, Sir Henry Hesketh J. Glimpses of a Governor's Life (1946); Witches and Fishes(1948). Work as administrator in Leeward Isles, Uganda, Nigeria and Mauritius from 1899; social life; economics; studies of natural history and folklore.   206

BELL, Isaac. Huntsman's Log Book(L. 1947).Rivalry of hunting and schooling; master of hunts in Ireland,Wiltshire; hounds, runs, breeding.   207

BELL, John Joy. I Remember (Edin.; 1932); Do You Remember (Edin.,1934). Middle-class life in Glasgow; Glasgow scene and Victorian ways; literature and journalism in London;70's to 90's pleasant and amusing.   208

BELL, Robert. Reminiscences (1924). Fifty-five years of medical life;Durham and Glasgow; research into cancer small-pox,women's diseases; travel in Europe and America; WW1; social life & sport.   209

BELL, Thomas. Pioneering Days(1941) Working class life,Glasgow; ironmoulder;trade unions; socialist movement; pacifist work;work in Communist Party and internationals;General Strike and imprisonment; political career.   210

BELL,Vicars W. The Dodo (1950). His own schooldays and his work as village schoolmaster; his creed as a teacher; hostility to modern education; & love of the country; interesting.   211

BELL, Capt. William. Journal, 1830; army administration and slavery; Barbados.MS, Clements Library, Ann Arbor Michigan.   212

BELLAMY,George Anne.An Apology for the Life(1785). Theatrical career and amours of Covent-Garden actress; high society;sufferings from deluding men; splendors and miseries.   213

BELLETT, Rev. George. Memoir (1889) Irish boyhood; training for ministry; work at Bridgenorth and Whitborne;religious,family, social life. Hereford City Library.   214

BELLEW, Capt. Francis John. Memoirs of a Griffin (1843). Life of a cadet; Indian social life and travel; partly fiction.   215

BELLINGHAM,William. Diary, 1884-87; laborer with the University Mission at Lake Nyassa; transporting stores; his work and personal life;unusual detail of mission work; very good. The Diary of a Working Man (1890).   216

BELLMAN,Sir Harold. Cornish Cockney (1947). Cornish boyhood; Methodism; a business career from 1900; at Railway Clearing House; the Ministry of Munitions; Abbey Road Building Society; & Liberal politics.   217

ANON. The Bells Go Down (1942). The experience of member of National Fire service in WW2; London Blitz; private affairs; diary.   217A

BELOE, William. Sexagenarian (1817) Literary and scholarly reminiscences and anecdotes;social and personal affairs; later 18th Century.   218

BELSON, S. H. Son of the Sea (Whitstable, 1939). Life on sailing ships and steamers; service in Far East; at Singapore; retirement to Kent.   219

BELT, Thomas. The Naturalist in Nicaragua (1874). Four years as commissioner for a gold-mining company; the geology and natural history of Nicaragua; native life; travels.   220

BELTON, Fred. Random Recollections (1880). Actor's experiences in London and provincial theatres, 1815-71; reminiscences and anecdotes of the great actors.   221

BENEDETTA,Mary. Girl in Print(1937) Work in journalism and publicity;features for Daily Express;script writing for radio; interviews with stage and film actors.   222

[BENGAL OFFICER]. Recollections of the First Campaign (1845). A critical account of the operations of Nott in Afghanistan; personal and detailed. A copy in Harvard U.L.   223

BENGOUGH,Sir Harcourt Mortimer. Memories (1913). His army life; Crimean War;Indian service; Zulu campaign and later administration in Jamaica;regimental life and sport; chatty.   224

BENN, Sir Ernest J. P. Confessions of a Capitalist (1925); Happier Days (1949). Schooling; advertising salesman;trade journalism; success as publisher;combative defense of materialism and nostalgic memories of pre-WW1 scene; Wells and other writers.   225

BENN, William Wedgwood. In the Side Shows (1920). Personal narrative; experiences WW1;Egypt, Gallipoli; with RFC in Mesopotamia; the Italian front interesting.   226

BENNETT, Charles Frederick. Memoirs (1817). London childhood;study at the Temple; mental and literary development;career as actor in the provinces and his poems; bantering.   227

BENNETT,Francis William.Leaves from My Log (1869). Twenty years as naval officer; his adventures in many parts of the world.   228

BENNETT, Frank. Forty Years in Brazil (1914). Business, economics, travels and general conditions.   229

BENNETT, Frank Debell. Narrative of a Whaling Voyage (1840). Experiences of a naturalist in California, Indian Ocean and Central Pacific; scientific observations.   230

BENNETT, Joseph. Forty Years (1908) Work and reminiscences of musical critic of "Telegraph"; opera; musicians; festivals; societies.   231

BENNETT, Lieut. Mark H.J. Under the Periscope(1919). Experiences in British submarines during WW1.   232

BENNETT, Sgt. Thomas. Following the Drum, ed.Sir John W. Fortescue (Edin.

1931). Soldier's personal experiences in Peninsular War; Waterloo.   233

BENNEY,Mark (H. E. Degras). Low Company(1936). Excellent account of slum childhood and criminal career; industrial school, Borstal & prison; clear record of activities and mental reactions.   234

BENNISON,B. Giants on Parade (1936) Reminiscences of sporting journalist ; and of celebrities in every field of sport.   235

BENSON,Arthur Christopher. Memories and Friends(1924). Literary and scholarly life; sketches and impressions of interesting people he knew; essays form. His Gate of Death (1906); House of Quiet(1904), though autobiographical in form, seem to be fiction. 236

BENSON,Lady Constance. Mainly Players (1926). Theatrical experiences in Benson Company from 80's; Shakespeare and poetical drama; Lyceum; plays and players; tours.   237

BENSON, Edward Frederic. Our Family Affairs (1920); Final Edition (1940). Clerical family in Lincoln and Truro, from 1867; prep school and Cambridge; career and interests as a writer; his friendships; travels; informal.   238

BENSON, Sir Francis Robert. My Memoirs (1930). Winchester, Oxford; his theatrical career from 1880; Irving & Ellen Terry; formation of Benson Company; anecdotes of stage.   239

BENTINCK, Lady Norah I. E. My Wanderings (1924). Reminiscences of society and political life from 1900;reflections and comments.   240

BENTLEY,Edmund Clerihew. Those Days (1940).St. Paul's; Oxford; legal studies; literary career; journalism and novels; Chesterton and other literary friends; Liberalism and public scene; good.   241

BENTLEY, William Holman. Pioneering on the Congo (1900). Travel and work of a Baptist missionary; native life; Biblical translation; exploration and meeting with Stanley; life in Central Africa.   242

BENTWICH,Norman de Mattos. Wanderer in the Promised Land (1933); Wanderer between Two Worlds (1941). Liberalism and politics from 1908; his work for Zionist cause; Jews in Europe and Palestine; travels.   243

BENWELL,John. Extracts from a Diary (Bristol, 1825). Autobiography; Quaker religious life at Sidcot; written in old age.   244

BENYON-TINKER, W. E. Dust Upon the Sea (1947). Service with the Levant Schooner Flotilla in WW2; adventures in armed caiques in Aegean.   245

BERESFORD, Adm. Charles William De La Poer, Baron. Memoirs (1914). Irish upbringing; naval career 1859 to 1907 Egyptian and Soudan campaigns; Khartoum; Disraeli; Admiralty; naval affairs in Parliament;Irish social life and sport; lively.   246

BERESFORD, George Charles. Schooldays (1936). School-days at Westward Ho, 1878-82;with Kipling; reminiscences of M'Turk.   247

BERESFORD, Sir Marcus. Diary,1836-1841 and 1854-59; work as military secretary in India;Indian rulers; political affairs; travel, social life & sport; written for his daughter. MS, India Office Library, Eur. C. 70-72, three vols.   248

BERGER, Francesco. Reminiscences(L. 1913); "97" (1931). His musical career from 1848;singer,composer; Philharmonic Society; London musical life; Dickens and other celebrities.   249

BERGH, Francis. Story of a Sailor's Life (Gosport, 1852). Adventures during fifty years at sea;religious life and God's mercies. Harvard U.L.   250

BERINGER, Oscar. Fifty Years (1907) Pianist's reminiscences of composers and performers in Germany and England; teaching; Philharmonic Society.   251

BERKELEY,George Charles G. F. Reminiscences of a Huntsman (L.1854); My Life (1865-66); Anecdotes (1867). The life of a country gentleman and politician; West Country social life and sport; M.P. for Gloucester; anecdotes of high society.   252

BERKELEY OF STRATTON, John Berkeley
1st Baron. Memoirs of Sir John Berke-
ley(1699). Diplomatic activities; negotiations with Cromwell for restoring
Charles I.   253

BERKELEY-HILL, Owen Alfred Rowland.
All Too Human (1939). Education; sex
life; his psychiatrical studies; work
in Indian medical service;mental hospital at Ranchi; studies; family life
and sport in India.   254

BERNARD,John. Retrospections of the
Stage (1830);Retrospections of America (N.Y., 1887). Work as comedian and
theatrical manager in provinces;Beef-
steak Club; plays & tours; later with
American companies.   255

BERNARD, Oliver Percy. Cock Sparrow
(1936).Poor boyhood, London; odd jobs
in theatre;sailor; billiards;bookmak-
ing; scene designer; WW1 at sea; USA;
the theatre; hard life and his griev-
ances.   256

BERNARD, Sir Thomas.   Pleasure and
Pain, ed. J.B. Baker (1930). Reminiscences and diary of philanthropist in
late 18th Century;   lawyer; workhouse
reform, work for chimney sweeps & for
artists; Foundling Hospital; & social
life; interesting.   257

BERNARD, Thomas Dehany. Autobiographical Notes (1909?).Somerset farming
life;Shrewsbury and Oxford; religious
training and ordination; Newman & the
Oxford Movement. Bath P.L.   258

BERNARDI,Maj. John. A Short History
(1729). Joins army as a boy; in Dutch
service; with James II in Ireland; 33
years in Newgate as prisoner of state;
picaresque adventures.   259

BERNAU, Rev. John Henry. Missionary
Labours in British Guiana (1847). His
work for CMS; religion; native life &
customs; natural history & adventures
with animals.   260

BERNERS,Gerald Hugh Tyrwhitt-Wilson
Baron.First Childhood(1934); Distant
Prospect (1945). Eton; relationships
of schoolboys; at Elmley; country social life and sport; family; discove-

ry of music and dance; Wagner;the development of musical interests;compo-
sitions;sensitive account of emotional and artistic development.   261

BERRETT, James. When I Was at Scotland Yard (1932). Career as policeman
and detective inspector;famous crimes
the CID, its members and methods. 262

BERRINGTON, Benjamin Shepherd. Exciting Leaves (1891). Ordination and
curacies in Essex, Herts, Sark; parishioners and friends.   263

BERRY, Erick (pseud.). Mad Dogs and
Englishmen (1941). The experiences of
Mrs. Herbert Best, wife of a resident
magistrate in Nigeria; amused picture
of native life.   264

BERRY, James. My Experiences (1892)
Policeman from 1874; executioner for
Edinburgh from 1884;criminals; execution methods; the book was suppressed
by the government.   265

BERRY, William Henry.   Forty Years
(1939). Career of a comedian; musical
comedy;Daly's, Gaiety, Adelphi, anecdotes of the theatre.   266

BERTHON, Edward Lyon. A Retrospect
(1899). Boyhood; studies; scientific
interests; life in Dublin; Irish character; work as clergyman.   267

BERTRAM,Charles. Isn't It Wonderful?
(1896); A Magician (1911). Career and
world-travels as entertainer and conjurer; theatrical anecdotes.   268

BERTRAM, James Glass ("Peter Paterson"). Glimpses of Real Life (Edin.
1858); Behind the Scenes (Edin. 1859)
Some Memories(Westminster, 1893). The
life of an entertainer in Scotland and
North of England;booth-theatres; circus; ballet; pantomime; Hamlet in the
booths; Edinburgh book trade; writers
and periodicals.   269

BESANT, Annie. Annie Besant (1893).
Her mental and spiritual development;
marriage & family; Bradlaugh's influence; atheism, socialism & theosophy;
her spiritual pilgrimage.   270

BESANT, Sir Walter.   Autobiography
(1902).London and Cambridge universi-

ties;scholarship; antiquarianism; his
novels; Society of Authors; literary
friends; social work.   271

BESSEMER, Sir Henry. Autobiography
(1905). Career of the great engineer
to crash in 1875;inventions, improvements in manufacture of materials;the
Bessemer process; saloon steamships;
travels.   272

BESTE, Henry Digby. Four Years in
France (1826); Italy as It Is (1828);
Personal and Literary Memorials(1829)
Oxford education; conversion to Catholicism; travels with family, France
and Italy; memories and anecdotes, of
churchmen and scholars,from Warburton
and Johnson to Shelley; antiquarian &
linguistic studies.   273

BETAGH, Capt. William. Voyage round
the World (1728). Experiences and descriptions; captain of marines, with
Clapperton and Shelvocke.   274

BETHAM,Ernest Burton. House of Letters (1905). Suffolk life, including
diaries connected with Rev. William
Burton, antiquary of Stoneham.   275

BETHAM-EDWARDS,Matilda Barbara. Re-
miniscences(1898); Anglo-French Reminiscences (1900); Mid-Victorian Memo-
ries(1919). Suffolk village life; her
trips in Germany and France; Kensington & London Society; Karl Marx meetings; social life & literary friends;
Patmore,Harrison, Henry James, George
Eliot, Mark Rutherford, etc.; a very
pleasant series.   276

BETHUNE,Col. John Drinkwater. Autobiography; military, naval, political
life and events in 18th Century. MS,
National Library of Scotland.   277

BETTESWORTH, Frederick. Bettesworth
Book,ed. George Bourne (1911); Memoir
of a Surrey Labourer(1907). Conversations with an old farm labourer;inci-
dents in his life and work;a delighted evocation of country scene and the
pleasure of country life, traditions,
and practices; a classic.   278

BEVAN, Major Henry, Thirty Years in
India (1839). Surveying and military
police work in the Presidencies from
1808; robber bands in Central India;

Indian life; sport.   279

BEVAN, Llewelyn David. Life and Reminiscences (1921). Dictated; career
of leading Congregational minister in
London, America & Australia; religion
and social history.   280

BEVAN, Theodore Francis. Toil, Travel and Discovery (1890). His travels
and exploration in British New Guinea
in the eighties.   281

BEVANS, John.The Sedgefield Country
by Richard Ord (Darlington,1904). Has
Bevans' autobiography of early life on
a Lincs farm; work as groom and whip-
per-in with foxhunts in Hungary and in
South Durham.   282

BEWICK, Thomas. Memoir (1862). Life
and work of Northumberland engraver;
country life, society; moralisings; &
relations with Scott, Haydon, Hazlitt
etc.; good.   283

BEWLEY, George. Narrative (Dublin,
1750). Autobiography of a ministering
Quaker; Cork, Dublin; travels in England and Ireland.   284

BEWSHER, Paul. "Green Balls" (1919)
Personal narrative of London clerk in
WW1; flying; night bombings; terrors;
personal adventures.   285

BIARD, Captain Henri Charles. Wings
(1934). Experiences as test pilot in
Supermarine aircraft; Schneider Cup &
races.   286

BICKERSTAFF-DREW, Francis Browning
Drew, Count.Pages from the Past(1922)
Boyhood in Wales; social life; public
events; London society; his career in
writing. (Pseud. John Ayscough). 287

BICKFORD,Rev. James. An Autobiography (1890). Devon boyhood in the 20's
and career as missionary in Demarara,
West Indies, Australia, 1838 to 1888;
travels, preaching, reading.   288

BIDDLECOMBE,Sir George. Autobiogra-
phy(1878). His naval career from boyhood; convict ship; cruises; capture
of St.Jean d'Acre;part in Baltic campaign 1854; sights, curiosities. 289

BIGG-WITHER,Thomas P. Pioneering in

South Brazil(1878). Mining engineer's travels in Paraná in 70's; colonists; natural history; hunting. 290

BIGLAND, Eileen. Awakening (1946). Scottish girlhood;Calvinism;advertising salesman;novelist; travels; politics; her own development. 291

BIGLAND, John. Memoir (Doncaster, 1830).Amusing record of a self-taught Yorkshireman; antiquarian and historian of Yorkshire. 292

BILAINKIN,George. Hail, Penang! (L. 1932). Work as journalist and editor in Malaya; racial attitudes and problems; influence of films & plays; the Straits Echo. 293

BINGFIELD, William (pseud). Travels and Adventures (1753). Voyages, shipwreck, miraculous preservation; with account of the bird-dog. 294

BINNS, John. Recollections (Philadelphia, 1854). Political career of a United Irishman;the rebellion of 1791-1798; anecdotes; history. 295

BIRCHENALL, John. Life, by Alfred J. French (1881). Autobiography; surgeon turned Methodist minister;travels and work in ministry; introspection. 296

BIRD, Henry Llewellyn Johnson. Episode (1911). Work and observations of a tutor in a noble Russian household, in the seventies. 297

BIRDWOOD, William Riddell Birdwood, Baron. Khaki and Gown (L.1941); In My Time (1945). Clifton; Sandhurst; long army career; Boer War; India; commander of Anzacs WW1; Gallipoli; France Home Guard; history; anecdotes. 298

BIRKIN, Sir Henry R. S. Full Throttle (1932). Career as racing motorist after WW1; motor industry; sponsors; lure of speed; races. 299

"BIRMINGHAM, George A." (Rev. James Owen Hannay). Padre in France (1918); Pleasant Places(1934). Experiences in WW1 as chaplain behind lines;his early years;parish work in Ireland; carreer as novelist; Irish politics and religion at Mells; memories of Irish life. 300

BIRON, Sir Henry Chartres. Without Prejudice (1936). Eton and Cambridge; law studies and practice; magistrate, at Old Street and Bow Street; crimes, criminals, Bottomley; Liberal Party & politics. 301

BIRRELL, Augustine. Things Past Redress (1937). Eighty years' recollections of life,people, politics, books Liverpool; Cambridge; legal study and literary criticism. 302

BISHOP, Cecil. From Information Received(1932). Boy before mast; career as policeman and detective; criminals Crippen case;guard to celebrities; an amusing record. 303

BISHOP, George Adderley. Memoir of a Cambridge Undergraduate (1876). Uppingham and Cambridge in 70's; religious life and ordination. 304

BISHOP, Harry Coghill Watson. Kut Prisoner (1920). Subaltern in Indian army; WW1 service; Mesopotamia; siege of Kut; capture and escape. 305

BISHOP, Priv. Matthew. Life and Adventures (1744). His naval & military experiences under Marlborough,Shovell etc.; Oudinard; New England; lively, but may be fiction. 306

BISHOP, Reginald W. S. My Moorland Patients (1922).Life and work of doctor in North Riding; moorland people; anecdotes; WW1; from 1894. 307

BISHOP, Sydney Oliver. A Touch of Liver (Allahabad, 1909). Experiences as a medical officer in Assam, India, Panama, Peru in 70's; London in 60's; amusing anecdotes. Copy in India Office Library. 308

BISSET, James. Brief Memoirs (Leamington Spa,1818). Art training, Perth Academy; work in Birmingham area; art gallery in Leamington Spa. Birmingham P.L. 309

BLACK, Adam. Memoirs (Edin. 1885). Autobiography of the Edinburgh bookseller and publisher to 1872;some diaries; books, authors, politics, social life in Edinburgh. 310

BLACK,Sister Catherine.King's Nurse

by Blackie (1939). Donegal; career as nurse; London Hospital; France in WW1; nurse to George V;his death; appealing record.   311

BLACK, William. Lives of the Early Methodist Preachers,by Thomas Jackson (1837-38) III. Huddersfield; his sinful youth and conversion; life & work of itinerant preacher in Nova Scotia; America; to 1788.   312

BLACKADER,John. Memoirs (Edinburgh 1823). Life and troubles of covenanting minister in Scotland; prisoner at Bass Rock;ejected from Trocqueer; his theology, politics, adventures; 17th Century.   313

BLACKBURNE,Harry William. This Also Happened(1932). Personal narrative of chaplain with infantry in France,WW1; breezy account of work and of providing comfort for troops.   314

BLACKER, Capt. Latham V. S. On Secret Patrol (1922). Lively adventures in WW1; guerilla work with Pathans in Persia, Turkestan, Afghanistan.   315

BLACKETT, Herbert Field. Two Years in an Indian Mission (1884). Work as a missionary; education; problems;and Hindu religion; anecdotes.   316

BLACKHAM,Col. Robert James. Scalpel Sword and Stretcher (L.1931). Medical training in Ireland; Victorian medicine; army surgeon in India and Afghan border; service in WW1; social.   317

BLACKIE,John Stuart. Altavona(Edin. 1882);Day-Book (Lond. 1901); Notes of a Life (Edin.1910). Scottish boyhood; Scottish life and travel and folklore; education in Germany;literary friendships; professor of classics in Edinburgh and Aberdeen; Liberal politics; religion; social; good.   318

BLACKLEDGE, William J. Hell's Broth Militia (1936). Remarkable adventures with Kurram Militia on N.W. Frontier; exciting.   319

BLACKSTOCK,Edward. Mercy Manifested (1853). Conversion; life and ministry of nonconformist; thirty years ministry at Wolverhampton, Potton & London and in Manchester; to 1842.   320

BLACK TAB. On the Road to Kut(1917) Personal experiences WW1;Mesopotamian campaign; siege of Kut.   321

BLACKWELL, Elizabeth. Pioneer Work (1895). Bristol childhood; early life in America; student at Barts; medical practice; work for women's rights and opening of medicine to women;practice in America.   322

BLACKWELL,Lt. Thomas Eden. Military journal, 1822-29; young officer's experiences in India; Burmese War; his observations on Indian culture & art. MS, B.M. Add. 39811-12.   323

BLACKWOOD,Algernon. Episodes before Thirty (1923). Boyhood; brought up in Moravian brotherhood; sent to Canada; misfortunes; adventures in New York's slums; New York reporter, 19 C.   324

BLACKWOOD,Lady Alicia. Narrative of Personal Experiences (1881). With her surgeon husband at Scutari during the Crimean War; Florence Nightingale;her work and hardships;soldiers and their wives.   325

BLACKWOOD,John. Reminiscences(Edin. 1908). Boyhood and medical studies in Edinburgh;reminiscences, Scott, John Brown & Hugh Miller; medical practice near London;social work and religion; working class life.   326

BLAIKIE,James Brunton. I Go A-Fishing(1928). Experiences with trout and salmon in England and Norway.   327

BLAIKIE, William Garden. Autobiography (1901). Scottish life; religious and social questions; his writing Church of Scotland.   328

BLAIR,Dorian. Russian Hazard (1937) Adventures of secret service agent in Russia during W.W.1 and the Bolshevik revolution.   329

BLAIR, Hugh. General Account (Edin. 1908). Life and work of 18th Century minister in Fife and Edinburgh; Scottish church affairs;from 1762 professor of rhetoric in Edinburgh.   330

BLAIR, Robert. Memoirs (Edin. 1754) Life, ed. T. M'Crie (Edin. 1898). The life and work of minister of St. Andrews,1593-1636; a record of religious troubles,protest and sufferings; valuable for covenanting period.   331

BLAKE, Rev. Henry J. C. The Cantab (Chichester, 1845). His undergraduate studies and social life at Cambridge, early 19th Century; some later adventures and misadventures.   332

BLAKE, Major Wallace. Quod (1927). Work as prison governor from 1902; at Pentonville, Borstal, Wandsworth, reform work, religion, training of officers; anecdotes; reflections.   333

BLAKE, Wilfrid T. Ports of Call (L. 1933). Guide to pleasure cruises and a few personal reminiscences.   334

BLAKELEY, John Rix. Brief Memoirs (Norwich,1838). Brief; early military life, conversion, Baptist ministry in Norfolk. Ipswich P.L.   335

BLAKEMORE,Anne. Rich in My Heritage (1942); Out of Old Fields (1944). The experiences of a novice farmer in the Cotswolds between wars;farming during WW2; government agencies.   336

BLAKENEY,Capt. Robert. A Boy in the Peninsular War (1899). Service during war; Danish campaign; Spain; Waterloo and Grand Review; subaltern's personal experiences.   337

BLAKER,Nathaniel Paine. Reminiscences (1906). Village life in Sussex in 1840-1906; medical work in Brighton; bygone days and ways.   338

BLAKEY, Robert. Memoirs (1879). His boyhood in N. England;studies; philosophy; scholar friends; professorship in Belfast;teaching and writing; Cobbett, Godwin, Bewick, etc.   339

BLAKHALL,Gilbert.Brieffe Narration (Aberdeen, 1844). Work of priest with Scots mission in France and in Netherlands and Scotland, 1631-1649; travel and adventures; lively.   340

BLAKISTON, Maj. John. Twelve Years' Military Adventures (L.1829); Twenty Years of Retirement (1836). Military service in India; and with Wellington in Peninsular War; farming and sport in Midlands; country life, social and political affairs, etc.   341

/BLAMPIED, Capt. H.J./. With a Highland Regiment (Bombay,1918). Fighting in France and Iraq during WW1;details of daily life. India Office.   342

BLAND, Robert Henderson, Actor-Soldier-Poet(1939). Reminiscences of his theatrical work and tours; theatrical celebrities; his poems; army service in France during WW1.   343

BLAND,Sarah Nash. The Field and the Garner (1854). Religious life; Sunday School and mission work in Reading in 1840's.   344

BLAND-SUTTON, Sir John. Story of a Surgeon (1930). Medical education and career, 1855 to 1910; Royal College of Surgeons; travels.   345

BLASER, Bernard. Kilts (1926). Battalion scout and mapper in Palestine, WW1; life and interests of non-coms ; fighting against Turks.   346

BLATCHFORD, Robert. My Life in the Army (1910); My Eighty Years (1931). Early experiences in ranks; political work and journalism; labour and socialist movements; The Clarion & Sunday Chronicle; labour leaders.   347

BLATHWAYT,Raymond. Through Life (L. 1917); Tapestry of Life (1923); Looking Down the Years (1935). Education for church; curate in East London;his career and travels as journalist,England, the East, Hollywood; invalidism and forces which moulded him;celebrities in the arts.   348

BLAUGDONE, Barbara. An Account of (1691). Quaker's testimony; ministry, persecutions, travels in South-West of England and Ireland.   349

BLENKINSOP, Adam. Memoirs of (1852) Gloucestershire; London society; medical practice; with Wellington's army in Spain and in America; inheritance and financial ventures; return to medicine; graphology.   350

BLIGH, Eric Walter. Tooting Corner (1946).Affectionate, humorous account of boyhood in London suburb; rich detail of bygone family life.   351

BLISS, William. Pilgrimage of Grace (1937). Solicitor and Roman Catholic; work in Lincoln's Inn Fields; travels meetings with Wilde, Shaw, Morris, &c; vigorous and Shandean.   352

BLOMEFIELD, Leonard. Chapters in My Life (Bath, 1889). London; Cambridge; ordination; ministry; work in natural history; publications; scientific societies in Bath. Bath P.L.   353

BLOMEFIELD, Mrs.Mathena. Nuts in the Rookery(1946); Bulleymung Pit (1946); Bow-Net and Water-Lilies (1948). Life of child on West Norfolk farm in 80's; education, games, animals, old customs family; deliberately charming.   354

BLOMFIELD, Capt. Charles James. Once an Artist (1921). Experiences in the Artists' Rifles from 1882; service in WW1, France; anecdotes; people.   355

BLOMFIELD, Sir Reginald Theodore. Memoirs (1932). Haileybury & Oxford; career as an architect; art movements and personalities; social life.   356

BLOOD, Sir Bindon. Four Score Years and Ten (1933). Military career; Aldershot; India from 1871; Boer War; & social and sport.   357

BLOOM, Ursula. Mistress of None (L. 1933); Without Make-Up (1938); Log of No Lady (1940); Time, Tide & I (1942) No Lady Buys a Cat (1943); No Lady in Bed (1944); Me, After the War (1945); The Changed Village (L.1945); No Lady Meets No Gentleman(1947);No Lady with a Pen (1947); No Lady in the Cart (L. 1949) etc. Noisy, flippant, chattering reminiscences of childhood, many jobs, journalism, popular writing, experiences during war; marriages, motoring; anything to make a new book; a notable representative of the fashion for perpetual gossip-column instalment autobiography.   358

BLOOMFIELD, Georgiana, Baroness. Reminiscences (1883); Gleanings (1902). Reminiscences of society and politics during whole of Victoria's reign; her life at court and at embassies, Berlin Russia, Vienna; diplomats, celebrities public affairs.   359

BLOOMFIELD, Paul. Half the Battle.

(1936); B.B.C. (1941). Autobiography of his youth, including his diaries at Harrow; art, current ideas, WW1, sex and insecurity; work at the B.B.C. in Birmingham; Talks Department; critical and personal.   360

BLOUNT, Sir Edward Charles. Memoirs (1902). Career as attaché in Rome and Paris; banker and railway promoter in France; Franco-Prussian War; sport and social life in Staffs.   361

BLOW, Sydney. The Ghost Walks (1935) Theatrical career; playwriting; anecdotes of London theatre and music hall and of actors and plays.   362

BLUECHER VON WAHLSTATT, Evelyn Mary, Fuerstin von. An English Wife in Berlin (1920). Personal record of public events, politics, daily life in Germany during WW1 and revolution.   363

BLUNDELL, Peter (Frank Nestle Butterworth). Confessions of a Seaman(L. 1924). A pleasant autobiography of an engineer on tramp steamers; deck life, and ports; amusing.   364

BLUNDEN, Edmund Charles. Undertones (1928).Personal experiences and reactions while serving in France in WW1; trench life; sensitive.   365

BLUNT, Fanny Janet Sandison, Lady. My Reminiscences (1918). Childhood in Turkey; with consul-husband in Constantinople to 1901; social life; diplomacy, etc.   366

BLUNT, Reginald. Those Were the Days Reminiscences of engineer; chiefly local affairs and daily life in Chelsea. MS, Chelsea Public Library.   367

BLUNT, Wilfred Scawen. Travel diary, 1883-84; in India during Ripon's viceroyalty; travels; political and social conditions; good. India Under Ripon (1909).   368

BLYTON, William Joseph. Landfalls (1940). Newspaper editor; farmer; and traveller; politics, literature, and country life; mental development; his meetings with famous men.   369

BOARDMAN, William H. Vaudeville Days (1935). Orphan; Lancs; boy in circus;

musician; manager of music-hall; reminiscences of the great days of variety and the great performers.   370

BOASE,Mabel M. Happy Potterer(1928) I Stir the Poppy Dust (Cupar, 1936). Childhood on east coast of Scotland in 70's and 80's; country life in Fife; pleasant and mild.   371

BODDY, Alexander Alfred.   From the Egyptian Ramleh(1900). His travel and social life in the Delta, Lower Egypt and Alexandria in the 90's.   372

BODKIN, Matthias M'Donnell. Recollections (1914). Life and work of an Irish lawyer, judge, journalist; Parliamentary and public affairs.   373

BODKIN,Thomas. My Uncle Frank(1941) Boyhood at uncle's farm in Ireland; a boy's life and amusements.   374

BODLEY, Col. Ronald Victor Courtenay Indiscretions (1931); Wind in the Sahara(1944); The Quest(1947). Eton and Sandhurst;WW1 service;Lawrence; Paris embassy and Peace Conferences;service with Algerians; life as nomad,shepherd in Sahara;mysticism and his quest for peace of mind in Java and East.   375

BODLEY, Sir Thomas. The Life(Oxford 1647, 1913). Family exiled by catholicism; return under Elizabeth; ambassador; rivalry of Burleigh and Essex; retirement and setting up library for Oxford students; brief and dry.   376

BOGER, Alnod John. Road I Travelled (Bristol, 1936). Winchester, Oxford; legal studies; climbing and big-game hunting in India, Far East, Uganda, & Norway, etc.   377

BOGGIS, Robert James Edmund. I Remember (1947). Clerical work and social life in Exeter.   378

BOGLE, J. Linton. More Meanderings (1938). Doctor's trips in England and on continent.   379

BOLITHO, Henry Hector. Thistledown & Thunder(1928); Older People (1935). A New Zealand author's travel notes,1915 to 1927,Empire,America, Europe; youth in N.Z.;career as writer; writing,the arts; Shaw, Ellen Terry,Lawrence, and

other celebrities.   380

BOLTON,Glorney and Sybil. Two Lives Converge (1938). Dual autobiography; his work at Bodleian;Oxford life; and journalism in Yorkshire;her education at convent in Holland;childhood in W. Riding;anglo-catholicism; journalism; public affairs.   381

BOLTON, John.   Personal Narrative (Ulverston, 1871).Residence in Barnsley 1818-42;industrial & labour troubles; Chartism; Jacquard loom.   382

BOLWELL, F. A. With a Reservist in France(1917). Simple narrative of his service with Lancs Regiment in France WW1; Mons to Loos.   383

BOND,Jessie. Life and Reminiscences (1930). Cockney childhood; choir work in Liverpool; musical training; singing; her career in Gilbert and Sullivan operas.   384

BOND, Reginald C. Prisoners (1934). Experiences in France WW1; Mons; capture; three years in German prisons; escape; Holland internment.   385

BONDFIELD, Margaret. A Life's Work (1949). Somerset; London shop girl; a career in trade union and labour movement; WW1; Russian diary; Parliamentary career; the cabinet; retirement & retrospect of 30's.   386

BONE, Sir David W.The Brassbounder (1910, 1949); Merchantman Rearmed (L. 1949). His experiences as a merchantseaman in sailing and steam ships and his services in WW2 transporting children to USA and troops to Mediterranean, French and Far Eastern theatres of war; good.   387

BONHAM, Colonel John. Oude in 1857 (1928). Reminiscences of his service in Indian Mutiny; military affairs in outstations of Oude.   388

BONNEY,Thomas George. Memories(Cambridge,1921). School; Cambridge; travels, climbing, geology; Victorian social life; Kingsley; daily life. 389

BONWICK,James. An Octogenarian's Reminiscences(1902). London boyhood and education;training and work as teacher and later career in Australia.   390

BOOKER,Beryl Lee. Yesterday's Child
(1937).Derbyshire childhood and family life, 1890-1909; boarding schools;
middle-class family piece.   391

BOON,John. Victorians (1928). Journalist's work and reminiscences,1883-
1926;Times and Mail; Parliament; war;
special correspondent; public affairs
and public men.   392

BOOSÉ,James R. Memory Serving(1928)
Clerk, librarian, travelling commissioner;50 years in Royal Colonial Institute; imperial affairs.   393

BOOSEY, William. Fifty Years (1931)
Music publishing with Boosey and Chap-
pell, 1880-1939;   London musical life
and anecdotes.   394

BOOTH,Doris Regina. Mountains, Gold
and Cannibals (1929). Goldmining with
her husband in New Guinea in the 20's
at Bolulo River; humanitarianism; her
hospital work; travels.   395

BOOTH,John Bennion. Master and Men
(1926); Pink Parade (1933); Sporting
Times (1938);Life, Laughter and Brass
Hats (1939); Days We Knew (1943). His
life and work as a sporting journalist
with "The Pink 'Un";racing and sport;
music halls and theatre;Bohemian life
and celebrities; anecdotes.   396

BOOTH, Mary Warburton. My Testimony
(1947). Spiritual autobiography; religious life;social work in the London
slums; mission work in India.   397

BOOTH,W. Bramwell. Echoes & Memories
(1925); These Fifty Years (1929). His
parents and religious upbringing;life
work and travels for Salvation Army;
struggles and triumph; Rhodes, Stead,
and famous churchmen.   398

BOOTHBY, Capt. Charles. A Prisoner
of France(1898); Under England's Flag
(1900). Service in Peninsular War; at
Talavera;capture; experiences in prison in France.   399·

BOOTHBY,Com. Hubert Basil. Spunyarn
(1935). His life at sea 1878-1928; in
merchant navy; R.N.R.; naval anecdotes
and experiences in many parts of the

world; suggestions for reform.   400

BOOTHBY, Laetitia. Memoirs (1872).
theatrical life; Covent Garden; Garrick;companion; intrigue; amours; it
may be fiction. Derby P.L.   401

BORDEN, Mary. Journey Down a Blind
Alley (1946). Novelist's experiences
in France in early days of WW2;with a
hospital unit in N. Africa.   402

BORODIN, George. One Horizon (1948)
A doctor's world-wide travels, adventures and medical experiences,especi-
ally in the South Pacific.   403

BORROW,George. Bible in Spain(1843)
Experiences as agent of Bible Society;
adventures with gypsies and Basques and
troubles; prison reflections.   404

/BOSANQUET, Augustus Henry/. India
Seventy Years Ago (1881). His boyhood
in India;family life and sport; early
service with East India Co.   405

BOSTOCK, Edward Henry.   Menageries
(1927). Bucks; life in circuses, menageries and theatres;tours throughout
British Isles; anecdotes.   406

BOSTON,Thomas. Memoirs (Edin. 1776)
Life and ministry at Ettrick; controversies in Church of Scotland.   407

BOSWELL, John. Pig's Head (n.d.). A
partial autobiography of his fight vs.
drink and work at the Birmingham Gospel
Temperance Mission. Copy in Birmingham
P.L.   408

BOSWELL-STONE,Lucia Catherine. Memories (1895). Dorchester; childhood &
family life; townspeople; dreams and
spiritualism; Dorchester people, customs and antiquities. Copy, Dorchester C.L.   409

BOTELER,Captain John Harvey. Recollections (1883; Navy Records Society,
1942). Pleasant record of his ships,
his men,his naval career; and general
account of sea life &c. 18 Cent.   410

/BOTT, Alan John/. An Airman's Out-
ings, by Contact (1917). Experiences
and adventures of a flyer during WW1;
with RFC in France; early military air
craft.   411

BOTTLE, Dorothy M. Reminiscences of a Queen's Army Schoolmistress (1936). Work teaching soldiers' children;Ireland, Kent, Jamaica, Near East.   412

BOTTOME, Phyllis. Search for a Soul (1947). Psychologically frank account of childhood and family relations and their effect on her character.   413

BOTTOMLEY, Horatio William. Bottomley's Book (1909). His work in a lawyer's office; career in politics and M.P.for Hac.ney; activities among the London poor.   414

BOUGHTON, Capt. George Piper. Seafaring (1926). Boy in sailing ships; the old sea life;pirates; South Seas; steamships; marvels & adventure.   415

BOULESTIN,Xavier Marcel. Myself (L. 1936); Ease and Endurance (1948). His early life in Perigord and Paris;nostalgic memories of artistic society & his discovery of London; London scene and society before WW1;work as interpreter in WW1; gastronomy and restaurants; writing; gossip.   416

BOULLIER, John A. Jottings by a Gunner(1917). Methodist chaplain; gunner with RFA in France; chaplain with the infantry; WW1.   417

BOULNOIS,Henry Percy. Reminiscences (1920). London childhood; King's College; engineering in Exeter and other towns; sanitary work.   418

BOULTON, Alexander C. F. Adventures (1939). Canadian boyhood; legal work, journalism, politics in England; M.P. colonial interests; arbitration in N. England.   419

BOURNE, Gilbert Charles. Memories (1933). School life at Eton in 70's; mostly deals with rowing.   420

BOURNE,Pamela. Out of the World (L. 1935).Her travels and adventures; New Zealand, Fiji, Tonga, Raratonga.   421

BOUTFLOWER,Andrew. Personal Reminiscences (Salford, 1916). Chorister at Manchester Cathedral; church life and religion; Tractarians.   422

BOWATER,Sir William. Birmingham and

I (1931). Business and public life in Birmingham; city life; politics; career of self-made man;Lord Mayor. Published in "Evening Despatch";cuttings in Birmingham Public Library.   423

BOWDICH,Thomas Edward. Mission from Cape Coast Castle (1819). His embassy to Ashanti in 1817;court life; native customs on Gold Coast; diary.   424

BOWEN, Catherine S. D. Friends and Fiddlers (1936). Pleasant memories of family life and amateur music.   425

BOWEN, Elizabeth. Seven Winters (Dublin, 1942). Childhood in Dublin & County Cork, early century; education and family life; early impressions; a graceful record.   426

BOWEN, Marjorie. See under, LONG, Gabrielle Margaret Vere.   427

BOWEN,Stella. Drawn from Life(1941) Australian childhood;London art studies;painting in Sussex and France;expatriate artists and writers; life in London to 1940.   428

BOWEN,Zacchery, ed. Up and Down the World,by a Passionate Pilgrim (1916). Woman's early life in Scotland;school and church; travel in Philippines and China.   429

BOWER, Fred. Rolling Stonemason (L. 1936). Liverpool boyhood; training as mason; work in Canada and USA; tradeunionism; Upton Sinclair; Jim Larkin; WW1; gold-digging in Australia.   430

BOWER, Frederick Orpen. Sixty Years (1938). Repton; Cambridge; professor of botany; London, Glasgow; botanical scholars and studies, from 1875.   431

BOWER, Capt. Hamilton. Exploration journal, 1891-92; exploring in Tibet; return via China; Tibetan life & customs; hardships. Diary of a Journey Across Thibet (1894).   432

BOWERS,Lt. William. Naval Adventures (1833). Boy at sea; travel and adventures and hardships of seaman's life; a cheerful record.   433

BOWES, John. Autobiography (Glasgow 1872). Conversion to Methodism; indefatigable travels and preaching;diary and articles. 434

BOWES,William ("Bill"). Express Deliveries (1949). Cricketing memories and anecdotes of the Yorkshire & England fast bowler; games, players, and tours. 435

BOWKER, Archibald Edgar. Behind the Bar (1947). Legal reminiscences; famous trials and lawyers;Marshall Hall; Birkett, etc. 436

BOWLER, Louis P. Gold Coast Palaver (1911). Mining for diamonds and gold; railway construction; natives & settlers; from 1901. 437

BOWLES, Thomas Gibson. Flotsam and Jetsam (1882). Personal life, reading and anecdotes, but mainly experiences as yachtsman. 438

BOWMAN,Humphrey Ernest. Middle-East Window (1942). His work in schools in Egypt,Sudan, Iraq, Palestine, 1903 to 1936; educational affairs. 439

BOWNAS, Samuel. Account of the Life (1756). Autobiography of Westmoreland Quaker; ministry and travels in British Isles, West Indies, America. 440

BOWRING, Sir John. Autobiographical Recollections (1877). Boyhood and early business life; Westminster Review & its contributors; politics, Parliament, public affairs;reminiscences of celebrities in public life. 441

BOWYER, George W. Lively Ahoy(n.d.) Work as pilot and ship-builder for 58 years at Southampton.Copy Southampton Public Library. 442

BOWYER,William. Brought Out in Evidence (1941). Summing-up at 50; reactions to public affairs & intellectual, spiritual, and political ideas of his time, with brief notes on everything in general. 443

BOX, Edward Gaspar. Commoners in My Time (Winchester, 1936). Memories of Winchester College in 50's; Fearon's House; school life; customs. 444

BOYD,Andrew Kennedy Hutchison.Twenty-Five Years(1892); Last Years(1896)

St. Andrews and Elsewhere (1894). His work as minister; parish work; social life in St. Andrews; the Church; education; literature; people. 445

BOYD, Donald. Salute of Guns (1930) Good personal narrative of artillery officer in France, WW1; Somme, Ypres, 1918 offensive. 446

BOYD, Frank M. Pelican's Tale(1919) St.Andrews; 50 years as journalist in London,etc.; sporting journalism; The Pelican;Bohemian London; clubs; theatres. 447

BOYD,Joyce. My Farm in Lion Country (1933). Her farming experiences after WW1 in Tanganyika; family and domestic affairs;social life; gardening; lions and adventures. 448

BOYD, Mark. Reminiscences of Fifty Years(1871). Politics and politicians from Pitt onwards; largely Scottish; Campbell the poet; celebrities. 449

BOYD, Martin. Single Flame (1939). Boyhood hopes contrasted with experience; ideals, religion & disillusionment in war; politics; writing. 450

BOYDEN, James. The Man of Two Lives (1828). Two existences; German, English; accumulating evidence of metempsychosis during Westminster schooldays;retracing former life in Germany Fuseli; Mesmer. 451

BOYES,John. John Boyes, King of Wakikuyu(1911). Runaway to sea; service in South African police;life as trader in Uganda; personal rule of Kikuyu tribe until ousted by government. 452

BOYLE, Daniel. Keeping in Trouble (1937). Scotsman's emigration; hobo & bootlegger in Canada and USA: adventures in Pacific and in Franco's Spain picaresque story. 453

BOYLE, Frederick. Adventures Among the Dyaks (1865). His life and adventures in Sarawak; Rajah Brooke's rule native life; European residents; and explorations. 454

BOYLE, George David. Recollections, (1895).Edinburgh;Scott; Charterhouse & Oxford; ministry in Midlands; Dean

of Salisbury; church, politics, literature.   455

BOYLE, Mary Louisa. Mary Boyle - Her
Book (1901). Court and country house
society; literature and arts; Hampton
Court; Dickens, Tennyson, Browning, &
Lowell, etc.   456

BOYNE, Don (pseud.). I Remember Maynooth (1937). College life, classwork
exams, games; theological disputes; a
gravely humorous record.   457

BOYS, Capt. Edward. Narrative of a
Captivity (1827). Naval service in the
Napoleonic wars; capture; prisoner in
France; escape; 1803-9.   458

BRABROOK, Sir Edward. Some Notes(L.
1932). London; career as actuary; insurance work; antiquarianism and anthropology; public work; Methodism; a
busy and varied life. Copy in Croydon
P.L.   459

BRACKENBURY, Sir Henry. Some Memor-
ies(Edin. 1909). Military career from
1853; Indian Mutiny; Franco-Prussian
war; Ashanti War; military attaché in
Paris; professor of military history;
journalism.   460

BRADDOCK, Joseph E. Bright Ghost(L.
1936). Boyhood in Lancashire & London
before WW1; simple & graphic account;
slightly fictional.   461

BRADDON, Sir Edward Nicholas Coventry. Thirty Years of Shikar (Edinburgh
1895). Hunting boars & tigers in Bengal; social and station life in Oudh;
the Santhal Mutiny.   462

BRADFORD, Samuel. Shell-Backs (1933)
Sailor's parson in Marseilles, Belfast
Liverpool, etc.; practical Christian-
ity; life of sailors.   463

BRADLEY, Arthur Granville. Other Days
(1913); Exmoor Memories (1926); When
Squires and Farmers Thrived (1927). At
Marlborough; Twyford school; Cambridge;
farming in Scotland, Wilts, Canada and
Virginia; Devonshire sporting life and
sportsmen; country life from 1869. 464

BRADLEY, Cuthbert. Good Sport (1910)
Fox-Hunting (1912). Sporting journalist's reminiscences of Quorn, Belvoir

and other hunts; runs, packs, masters
"The Field".   465

BRADLEY, Eliza. An Authentic Narrative (Boston, 1821). Liverpool woman;
shipwrecked, captured by Arabs, 1818;
her sufferings.   466

BRADLEY, Josephine. Dancing through
Life(1947). Work as teacher of ball-
room dancing; friends and celebrities
she met and taught.   467

BRADLEY, Kenneth Granville. Diary of
a District Officer(1943). Administrative work as district officer; tribes
of Northern Rhodesia; law and justice;
native life.   468

BRADLEY, Patrick. While I Remember
(Clonakeagh, 1938). Boyhood in Ireland
and Irish country life; Irish sport &
politics; writing; his impressions of
America.   469

BRADLEY, Shelland. The Adventures of
an A.D.C.(1910). Work and social life
in Monaling hill station; amusements
of Anglo-Indian and Indian life; light
and lively.   470

BRADSHAW, Percy Venner. Drawn from
Memory (1943). Childhood; commercial
artist; running an art school; famous
pupils; his experience in WW1 and WW2;
trips to USA, Switzerland, etc.   471

BRADSTREET, Capt. Dudley. Life and
Uncommon Adventures (Dublin, 1755). An
Irish adventurer's picaresque life as
buck, magician, pimp, etc.   472

BRAITHWAITE, Cecil. Fishing Vignettes
(1929); Fishing Here and There (1932)
Sporting life; mostly his reminiscences of trout fishing, Scotland.   473

BRAKE, Charles. Recollections of My
Life(Brighton, 1836). Bath schooling;
early struggles in London; spiritual
troubles and conversion; ministries in
Cambridgeshire, London, Brighton. 474

BRAKE, Hezekiah. On Two Continents
(Topeka, 1896). Early years at Sherborne; Methodist religious work; jil-
ted; work as groom; marriage; emigration to USA: frontier life.   475

BRAMPTON, Sir Henry Hawkins, Baron.

Reminiscences, ed. R. Harris (1904).
Life in the Law (1907). Conversations
and interviews; Bedford school; legal
career; barrister and judge; judges &
lawyers; sporting interests.   476

BRAMSTON, Sir John.   Autobiography
(1845). Legal study, Middle Temple, &
legal career;politics and public life
during the Restoration; retirement at
Skreens under Commonwealth.   477

BRAND, Lt. Charles. Travel journal,
1827-28;journey afoot across Andes to
Peru and across Pampas;scenery. Journal of a Voyage (1828).   478

BRAND, John. Memoirs. Early days in
College of Edinburgh; tutor; clerical
work and life at Bo'ness; personal &
family affairs; public events to 1727
MS, National Library of Scotland, No.
1668, 190 fos.   479

BRAND, Patrick.   Garret in Chelsea
(1935). Bohemian life in London 1926-
1934; writing; theatre and travelling
shows, poverty and struggles.   480

BRANFORD,John R.I Sailed with Kings
(1941). Early days at sea; officer on
royal yachts; later on staff of Sergeant-at-Arms in House of Commons; his
meetings with celebrities.   481

BRANGWYN, Sir Frank. Brangwyn Talks
by William de Belleroche(1944). Autobiography reminiscences in interviews;
career as artist in Belgium and Engl-
and; Bruges, Ditchling; views, anecdotes, gossip.   482

BRANSBY, Leslie. I Went A-Roving(L.
1948).Travels of one trying to escape
from civilisation; escapism & travels
to islands and deserts;service in WW2
and in Finnish war.   483

BRASBRIDGE, Joseph. Fruits of Expe-
rience(1824). Merchant in London; reminiscences of London life, merchants
actors, writers,quacks, writers; Mrs.
Piozzi.   484

BRAUN,Hugh. The Centuries Look Down
(1947). War experiences of an architect; his visits to ancient buildings
in France, Malta, Middle East.   485

BRAY,Charles. Phases of Opinion and

Experience(1884). Studies in religion
philosophy,phrenology; publishing the
Coventry Herald; free trade; philosophy of necessity;science; manufacturing at Coventry;Victorian fashions in
science and psychology.   486

BRAY,John Francis. Autobiography of
American-born social, political, and
religious reformer, 1822-42. MS, London School of Economics.   487

BRAY, Norman N. E.   Shifting Sands
(1934).WW1 experiences in Arabia; the
Arab revolt; Lawrence.   488

BRAYE, Alfred Thomas Townshend Verney, Baron. Fewness of My Days (1927)
Eton and Oxford; classical study; his
travels; the Victorian scene; career
in army;South Africa; WW1; Parliament
and House of Lords; defence of Roman
Catholicism.   489

BREADALBANE,Alma I. C. L. Campbell,
Marchioness of. The High Tops (1907).
Scottish society; country life in the
Highlands; sport; staghunting.   490

BREARLEY, Harry. Knotted String (L.
1941).Work as steel-maker; Sheffield
University; metallurgical research;in
Riga; Russian steel; socialism; minor
official of ILP.   491

BREEDEN, Henry.   Striking Incidents
(1878).Work of United Methodist preacher; Flintham, Nottingham; personal
religious life. Methodist Book Room,
City Road, London.   492

BREEN,Dan. My Fight for Irish Free-
dom(Dublin, 1924). Life and adventure
of an Irish politician, 1914-22; IRA;
Tipperary.   493

BREMER, Mounsteven. Memoirs (1930).
Education in England; coffee-planting
in Ceylon 1875-96; & later travels in
the Empire; London Life; WW1.   494

BRENNAN, Robert. Allegiance (Dublin
1950).An Irish rebel's account of the
politics and revolt of 1914-22 and of
his part in helping to throw off British rule; Irish leaders.   495

/BRENT,John Frederick7. Memories of
a Mistaken Life (1897). Early career
on stage; rivalry with actress wife;

he gives up but she continues; family
life and disappointments.   496

BRENTON, Sir Jahleel. Memoir of the
Life (1846). His naval career, 1790-
1818; Peninsular War; at Cape of Good
Hope; exploring in S.Africa.   497

BRERETON,Robert Maitland. Reminisc-
cences of an Old English Civil Engineer
(Portland, Oregon, 1908).Copy in Library of Congress.   498

BRETT-JAMES,Anthony. Report My Signals (1948). Personal account of war
service; the Burmese campaign of WW2;
work of the Fifth Indian Division of
Royal Signal Corps.   499

BREWER,Sir Alfred Herbert. Memories
(1931). Organist and composer; Oxford
Coventry,Gloucester, Manchester; festivals; choral music; English composers and music.   500

BREWER, Charles.   Spice of Variety
(1948). Experiences and anecdotes of
a man of many occupations;his medical
studies;work as airman, lecturer, entertainer, civil servant, journalist,
composer, producer; strange tales.501

BREWSTER, Adolph Brewster. King of
the Cannibal Isles (1937). Work as a
commandant and commissioner of native
constabulary in Fijis in 70's; social
life and politics.   502

BRIANT,Keith Rutherford. Oxford Limited (1937). His experiences at the
university;education, sport, politics
dons, sex, etc.   503

BRIDGE,Sir Cyprian A.G. Some Recollections (1918). Boyhood;naval career
from 1853;stations in Australia; life
and work in South Seas.   504

BRIDGE, Sir John Frederick. A Westminster Pilgrim (1919). His career as
organist and musician;Westminster Abbey music and celebrations;music and
musicians in England; hunting, sport,
society.   506

BRIDGES, Sir George Tom M. Alarms &
Excursions(1938). Lively narrative of
army career; mainly WW1; Washington,
Balkans, S. Russia after War; diplomacy and soldiering.   507

BRIDGES, John Affleck. Sportsman of
Limited Income (1910); Reminiscences
(1906);Victorian Recollections (1919)
Country life and farming in Shropshire
Worcestershire and Essex; elections;
labour; local politics.   508

BRIDGES, Thomas Charles. Florida to
Fleet Street (1926). Sport and social
life in Florida; freelance journalism
and his Dartmoor home;natural history
and Fleet Street journalism.   509

BRIDGETT,Robert Currie. By Loch and
Stream (1922); Tight Lines(1926). His
fishing reminiscences;mostly of trout
fishing in Scotland.   510

BRIDIE, James (Osborne Henry Mavor)
Some Talk of Alexander(1926); One Way
of Living (1939). Childhood;education
medical studies; WW1 service as army
doctor; general practitioner; work as
playwright; London theatre; players &
writers; whimsical.   511

BRIERLEY, Benjamin.   Home Memories
(Manchester, 1886). Workingman's life
in Lancashire; cotton mills; religion
and social life; literary interests &
activities.   512

BRIERLEY, Henry. Rochdale Reminiscences (Rochdale, 1923). A solicitor's
account of family life in Rochdale and
the local scene.   513

BRIGGS, Isaac George. Surgeon Goes
to Sea (L.1939);They Gave Me a Crown
(1944).Lively career of medical life
on sea and land; navy; Singapore;Ran-
goon; Australia; army doctor and registrar; odd cases and patients.   514

BRIGGS,Sir John Henry. Naval Administrations (1897). Career as reader &
clerk at Admiralty; reminiscences of
Lords of Admiralty, naval affairs and
politics, 1827-92.   515

BRIGHTON, Hilda. No Bridge to Yesterday (1949). Family life in theatrical circles; Edgar Cohen,   Charlot,
the Venturers, actors, contemporary
society and first-nighters in early
20th Century.   516

BRIMBLE, E. Lilian. In the Eyrie of
the Hohenzollern Eagle(1916). Governess at German Imperial court; house-

hold; her charges; gossip.   517

BRINSLEY-RICHARDS,James.Seven Years at Eton (1883). Lively account of his schooldays, 1857-1864; institutions & famous Etonians; Churchill, Rosebery, and others.   518

BRISBANE,Gen. Sir Thomas Makdougall Reminiscences (Edin. 1860). Military career 1789-1852; Peninsular War; his later relations with Wellington; governor of New South Wales; it includes diaries.   519

BRISTED, Charles Astor. Five Years (1852). A New Yorker's experiences at Trinity, Cambridge; the English university system.   520

BRISTOW, James. A Narrative of Sufferings (1793). Service with the East India Co. 1771-91; captured by Hyder Ali; sufferings in prison, Mysore and Seringapatam.   521

BRITISH SEAMAN.Life on Board a Man-of-War(Glasgow, 1829). Short but good account of seaman's life; his ships; battle of Navarino. Bodleian.   522

BRITTAIN,Sir Harry Ernest. Pilgrims (1946); Happy Pilgrimage (1949). Boyhood;Oxford;long association with the dominions;Imperial Press Union; politics, travel, sport.   523

BRITTAIN, Vera Mary.   Testament of Youth (1933);Thrice a Stranger (1938) Life in Newcastle; Oxford; nursing in WW1; impact of war and public events; journalism and writing;experiences in America as wife of professor in state university; lecturing.   524

BRITTEN, Sir Edgar Theophilus. Million Ocean Miles(1936). Sailing ships and with Cunard Line; WW1 transport & hospital ships; commander, White Star liners; famous passengers.   525

BRITTON,John. A Brief Memoir (1825) Autobiography (1850).Misery as London apprentice; education; antiquarianism and scholarly writing;Wiltshire; literary life in London; eminent scholar friends.   526

BROADHEAD, Augustus G. The Navy as It Is (Portsea, 1854). A midshipman's

ten years; exposé of conditions, cruelty of officers; reform and counterblast to novelistic sentiment.   527

BROADHURST,Henry. Story of His Life (1901).Workingclass life and his early hardships; stonemason; trade union work;career in Parliament; early days of Labour Party;Treasury bench; political issues of time.   528

BROADHURST, Joseph F. From Vine St. (1936). With Metropolitan Police from 1900; detective, Scotland Yard & Vine Street;WW1 service as provost-marshal in Egypt; inspector of CID for Palestine government to 1932.   529

BROCKWAY, Archibald Fenner. Inside the Left (1942). Socialist political work and journalism, 1906-40; I.L.P.; editor "New Leader"; pacifist in WW1; prison;with Clydeside group after the war; M.P. for East Leyton; useful record of left-wing politics.   530

BRODHURST-HILL,Evelyn. The Youngest Lion, by Eve Bache (1934); So This Is Kenya! (1936). Life on a Kenya farm, after WW1; natives and settlers; education and social life; experience of ex-soldiers.   531

BRODIE,Sir Benjamin C.Autobiography (1865). Winterslow Rectory; medical study and apprenticeship; his work at St. George's;anatomy research;Sergeant Surgeon;reminiscences of teachers and doctors and medical life.   532

BRODIE,Robert. Reminiscences (Bristol,1942). Training as railway engineer, Scotland; work on Scottish railways; construction & maintenance work Lancs, Wales, Bristol.   533

BRODRICK, George Charles. Memories (1900). Norfolk;Eton; Oxford; academic and legal career; Times journalism Liberal politics;Huxley, Arnold, etc. warden of Merton College.   534

BROMET,Mary Pownall. Response(1935) Childhood and schooling; art study in Paris and Rome;career as sculptor and views on English art; social and domestic life; pleasant.   535

BROMILOW, William Edward.   Twenty Years Among Primitive Papuans (1929).

Work of Methodist missionary; native
life and customs in New Guinea and the
Fijis; the Dobus.   536

BROMLEY,Albert Nelson. Work & Sport
(Nottingham,1934). Architectural study in Italy in 1870's; work as architect in Nottingham; fishing and golf;
rural preservation.   537

BROOK, James. Jim of the Seven Seas
(1940).Career as an engineer in navy;
bush life in Australia; work, travels
and adventures as trader in Gilberts,
Solomons, etc.; cannibalism.   538

BROOKE, Charles A. J. Ten Years in
Saráwak (1866). Naval career, 1852 to
1862; suppression of pirates;policing
and administration in Sarawak;life of
Dyaks; Empire building; life as white
chief; good; mainly diary.   539

BROOKE,Gen. Geoffrey F. H. Brotherhood of Arms (1941). Military career;
experiences in WW1; the life, and its
heroisms and humours; social.   540

BROOKE, Sir James. Narrative of Events in Borneo and Celebes   (1848).
Diaries,1839-46, at Singapore & Sarawak; occupation and rule of Sarawak &
expeditions against pirates; natives;
local customs; exploration; journals
of Rodney Mundy included.   541

BROOKE, Jocelyn.The Military Orchid
(1948).Kent childhood; Bedales school
and early interest in botany; his war
service in Africa and Sicily in a V.D.
unit; botany and war; amusing.   542

BROOKE, Richard Sinclair. Recollec-
tions(1877). Clergyman's college days
in Dublin in 20's;curacies in Ireland
and reminiscences of Irish churchmen
and church happenings.   543

BROOKFIELD, Arthur Montagu. Annals
(1930). Rugby; Sandhurst; Cambridge;
with Hussars in India; marriage; Conservative M.P. for Rye; politics and
country life; Germany before WW1. 544

BROOKFIELD,Charles H. E. Random Reminiscences (1902). Cambridge; literary society; career as actor; London
Bohemian life; visit to USA; theatrical anecdotes; theatrical personages &
social scene.   545

BROOKS,Collin. Devil's Decade(1948)
Editor of Truth; the 1930's; notable
personalities; Shaw; Churchill; Beaverbrook; somewhat impersonal.   546

BROOME,Henry Arthur. Log of a Rolling Stone (1913). Norfolk man-of-all-
trades;policeman, magistrate, sailor,
labourer,whaler, sculptor; travels in
many countries.   547

BROOME, Lady Mary Ann Barker. Life
in South Africa(1877);A Year's House-
keeping in South Africa(1879); Colonial Memories(1904). Social & domestic
life in governmental circles in second
half of century;New Zealand,Australia
Trinidad, Mauritius, S.Africa.   548

BROOMFIELD, Sidney Spencer. Kacha-
lola (1930). Medical studies in Edinburgh; exciting experiences in remote
areas; Borneo; Africa; Tibet; Venezuela; trading, hunting, prospecting in
60's and 70's; lively.   549

BROTHERS, Richard. A Revealed Knowledge of the Prophecies (L. 1794);The
Writings (1798). Autobiography of the
religious fanatic and latter-day prophet; revelations; the new cosmology;
18th Century.   550

BROUGHAM AND VAUX,Henry P. Brougham
Baron.   Life and Times (Edin. 1871).
His education, travels, and political
career from 1834 to the Melbourne Cabinet; the Reform Bill.   551

BROUGHTON,Elizabeth. Six Years Residence in Algiers (1839). Reminiscences and diary of her life in Algiers,
1806-12; consul's wife; domestic life
social life, politics & Algerian life
and manners.   552

BROWN, Albert Curtis. Contacts (L.
1935). His work and experiences as a
literary agent; early work as a journalist; Kenneth Grahame; anecdotes of
literary men.   553

BROWN,Alfred G. Ground Staff (1943)
RAF squadron leader;Vienna during the
Anschluss;with ground staff of Bomber
Command during the Blitz.   554

BROWN, Alfred J.   I Bought a Hotel
(1949). Experiences of an ex-soldier
and his wife as novice proprietors of

a small country hotel; work, guests, personal life; literary views.   555

BROWN, Beatrice Curtis. Southwards (1948). Childhood in St.John's Wood; life in Chelsea; office work; social life, walks, theatre, London scene; a simple everyday record.   556

BROWN,Charles Barrington & LIDSTONE William.Fifteen Thousand Miles on the Amazon (1878). Travels and adventures of a geologist and an engineer 1873-4 preparing mining report.   557

BROWN,Sir Edward. Memories (Burnley 1934). Business career in eggs, poultry from 1880; editor of "Live Stock Journal"; National Poultry Society;& the national and political scene. 558

BROWN, Edwin A. Indiscreet Memories (1934). His business and social life in Singapore and Malaya,1901-4; anecdotes and trivia.   559

BROWN, Frederick. "Boxer" and Other China Memories (L.1936). Chaplain and interpreter with British forces;siege of Pekin; missionary in North China; a pleasant, modest account.   560

BROWN, Dr. George. An Autobiography (1908). Fifty years' work as Wesleyan missionary in Samoa, New Britain, New Ireland, New Guinea, Solomons; native life; explorations.   561

BROWN, George E. R. Grant. Burma as I Saw It (1926). Work as magistrate & revenue officer in Burma, 1889-1917; social and domestic life; Burmese art and customs.   562

BROWN, Hercules Langford. By the Water's Side (1936). Experiences as a fisherman, mainly in South-West of England; the Teign and Taw.   563

BROWN,Hildegarde Gordon.Conclusions (1908).Experiences and views on every day problems connected with emancipation; marriage, education; literature and the arts.   564

BROWN,Hugh Stowell. His Autobiography (1887). Career and parish work of a Baptist minister in Isle of Man and Liverpool; social and domestic life & local affairs.   565

BROWN, James. Turkish Days (Sydney, 1940). Experiences in WW1; Sinai 1916 and capture by Turks;prison experiences; medical work.   566

BROWN, Jane (pseud). I Had a Pitch (1946).Twenty years in the Caledonian Market; London market life and work & characters; amused.   567

BROWN,Jean Curtis.To Tell My Daughter (1948). Artless picture of childhood in North of England parsonage at end of Victoria's reign; sympathetic and humorous.   568

BROWN, John. Sixty Years' Gleanings (Cambridge, 1858). Boyhood poverty; & varied jobs;soldier, actor, shoemaker & wanderer; Cambridge; the University Billiard Rooms; amusing.   569

BROWN, John. Autobiography (1867). Country boyhood; factory work; Chartist riots;Methodism; Christianity and industrialism;plea for reconciliation of classes and for philanthropy and no socialism; propaganda?   570

BROWN, Mrs. John (Mary Solomon). An Account of Her Social Work, edited by Angela James and Nina Hills (1937). Dictated reminiscences of early life in Edinburgh; work in slums; labour, co-operative & temperance movements; Keir Hardie; later association with Olive Schreiner in South Africa; an excellent record.   571

BROWN, John. I Was a Tramp (1934); Road to Power(1937).Workingclass life in South Shields;odd jobs; rigger; at sea; tramp; Ruskin College and career in Labour Party; views of a socialist and imperialist;travels in Europe and USA.   572

BROWN, Capt. Lewis. Private Journal (Bombay, 1841). Experiences occupying a British outpost at Kahun with Bombay Infantry. War Office Library.   573

BROWN, Lindsay W. Suivez Raison and I.T.(1933). Many jobs and travels all over the world; undertaker to colporteur; poor writing.   574

BROWN,Percy. Round the Corner(1934) Shrewsbury boyhood; work as carpenter and teacher of cleating; service WW1;

experiences at Ruhleben.   575

BROWN,Percy. Almost in Camera(1944)
Work and assignments of a newspaper-
photographer; Graphic and Mail; notes
on celebrated subjects; 1919-40.   576

BROWN, Robert. Passages in the Life
by Helen Colvin(1867). Includes diary
of his life in India and Ceylon; work
as merchant; conversion and religious
activities in Bombay.   577

BROWN,Sir Robert Charles.Sixty-Four
Years(Preston, 1922). Lancashire medical practice; study London and Dublin
and work at Preston Hospital; general
medical topics; social; hobbies.   578

BROWN, Thomas. Reminiscences (Edin.
1835).Long travel experiences in many
parts of Europe; travel material. 579

BROWN, William. A Narrative (York,
1829). Devon childhood; naval service
in Napoleonic wars; hard times after
Waterloo; work as schoolmaster at Mid-
dleham, Yorks; poems.   580

BROWN, William. Autobiography (Kilmarnock, 1829). Working-class life in
Scotland; enlistment; service in Peninsular War and in Ireland; good narrative; life of troops. Copy in New
York P.L.   581

BROWN, Capt. William. Home is the
Sailor(1940). Career as merchant captain in the East Indies and as a pilot
at Penang from 1890;adventures; anecdotes; good.   582

BROWN, William John. Land of Look-
Behind (1949). Voyage to Jamaica and
stay there; life and politics.   583

BROWN, William John. So Far (1943).
London childhood and poverty; career
in Civil Service;organization of Civil Service trade union;M.P. Coventry;
Labour politics;critical, independent
and combative views.   584

BROWNE, Eddie. Road Pirate (1934)
Life and adventures of an English criminal; England, Canada, USA; national
differences in crooked ways.   585

BROWNE, Edward. Travels and Adventures (1739). Merchant's experiences

and observations in France,Italy, Levant, Malta, Egypt.   586

BROWNE,Rt.Rev. George Forrest. Recollections (1915). Career and anecdotes; church and public life; Bishop of Bristol; church history and antiquities.   587

BROWNE,Henzie. Pilgrim Story (1945)
Work with the Pilgrim Players, 1939-
1943; performances for the services;
"better" plays; theatrical idealism;
organizing.   588

BROWNE, Gen. Horace Albert. Reminiscences of the Court of Mandalay(Wok-
ing, 1907). Administration and public
work in Mandalay; Chinese and Burmese
life and ideas; includes his diary of
years 1859-79.   589

BROWNE,John H.B. Forty Years (1916)
Recollections (1917). His career as a
barrister; Parliamentary bar work and
private legislation;corporations;some
lawyers;political speeches; elections
his writing and reading.   590

BROWNING,Elizabeth Barrett. Hither-
to Unpublished Poems (Boston, 1914).
Includes "Glimpses of my own life and
literary character"; a short account
of herself and her literary interests
to age of fifteen.   591

BROWNING, Oscar. Memories of Sixty
Years (1910); Memories of Later Years
(1923). Society, scholarship, writing
and education; Browning, Tennyson and
others; political and church affairs;
work at Eton and Cambridge;travels in
Germany,Italy, Russia, India; crowded
& somewhat superficial account of his
role in Victorian scene.   592

BROWNLOW,Capt. Cecil A. L. Breaking
of the Storm (1918). A good personal
narrative WW1; gunner in France; Mons
to Ypres.   593

BROWNLOW,Emma Sophia Cust, Countess
of. Slight Reminiscences (1867); Eve
of Victorianism (1940). Reminiscences
of court, court life, politics, society in early 19th Century;interesting
anecdotes.   594

BROWNRIGG,Admiral Sir Douglas E. R.
Indiscretions (1920). Career in navy;

work as naval censor; Admiralty; WW1
activities.   595

BROWNRIGG, Gen. Sir Wellesley D. S.
Unexpected (1942).Military life 1905-
1939; India; WW1; Mesopotamia; Gallipoli; Sandhurst, War Office; defence
of Shanghai and Hong Kong; home guard
in WW2; sport, anecdotes; light.   596

BRUCE, Sir Charles. Broad Stone of
Empire (L. 1910); Milestones (Glasgow
1917). His experiences as administrator in Crown Colonies;problems of Empire defence;professor of Sanskrit at
King's College and rector of the Royal
College,Mauritius; director of public
instruction in Ceylon;a varied, valuable career, from 1868.   597

BRUCE, Charles (pseud. of Arthur B.
C. Francis).   Twenty Years in Borneo
(1924). Work as policeman and magistrate in Borneo;medicine; social life
and sport; travels; humours.   598

BRUCE,Hon.Charles Granville. Twenty
Years in the Himalaya (1910); Himalayan Wanderer (1934). Military career,
in India; WW1 service; sport in India
and his Alpine and Indian climbs; the
Everest expedition.   599

BRUCE, Henry James. Twenty Years(L.
1939).Life in navy as a diver and his
work and adventures; WW1; Gallipoli;
his ships; anecdotes.   600

BRUCE,Henry James. Silken Dalliance
(1946);Thirty Dozen Moons (1949). His
diplomatic career before WW2; St. Petersburg, Vienna, Berlin; society and
ballet; marriage with Karsavina; travels; Diaghilev; nostalgic.   601

BRUCE, Sir Michael W. S. Sails and
Saddles(1929). Many jobs; soldier and
sailor, cowboy, journalist, teacher,
engineer, film actor; policeman in S.
Africa; Rupert Brooke & Lloyd George;
reflections on color bar.   602

BRUCE, Peter Henry. Memoirs (1782).
Soldier of fortune;military adventure
in Prussia, Russia, Turkey & West Indies, 1706-45; lively.   603

BRUCE, Lieut.Talbot Baines. Missing
(Edin.1930). WW1 adventures of airman
in Belgium in disguise as peasant; is

hunted by Germans.   604

BRUCE, W.J. Reminiscences (Aberdeen
1929).His ministry in Church of Scotland; theology; church affairs; celebrities; gossip; kindly.   605

BRUNEL, Adrian. Nice Work (L. 1949)
His thirty years in British films as
actor, writer, producer and director;
Film Society; lively.   606

BRUNTON, John. John Brunton's Book
(Cambridge, 1939). Boyhood in a Welsh
mining valley; work with Stephenson &
Brunel; railway engineering, building
bridges, tramways; archaeology study;
seventy years life and work; pleasant
record of great engineer.   607

BRUST,Harold. I Guarded Kings(1935)
In Plain Clothes(1937). Scotland Yard
detective;guard to political missions
ministers and kings; adventures among
political criminals, etc.   608

BRYAN, Hugh. Autobiography (1866).
Killarney boyhood; school and family;
Irish sentiment and youthful activit-
ies as rebel, early 19th Century. 609

BRYANT, James. Happy Jim, ed. E. W.
Jealous (1937). Kentish boyhood; early experiences of dipsomania; attempt
at reform;conversion; work as farrier
and mission work in South London;tem-
perance lecturer to troops in WW1 and
at race courses.   610

BRYANT,John Frederick. Verses(1787)
Includes autobiography;London; school
in Bristol;seeking work; tobacco pipe
maker and poet.   611

BRYDGES, Sir Samuel Egerton. Recollections of Foreign Travel(1825); and
The Autobiography (1834). Reflections
on writers, writing, Parliament, manners; development of his literary and
antiquarian tastes; country life; his
friendships and quarrels;estimates of
friends and enemies; publishing; can-
tankerous.   612

BRYSSON, George. Memoirs of William
Veitch and George Brysson (Edin. 1825)
Life of Edinburgh merchant; life of
covenanters; travels and hardship on
the continent; public events from the
Restoration to the Revolution.   613

BUCHAN,Anna (O. Douglas, pseudonym) Unforgettable (1945). Scottish childhood; Glasgow family and social life; reading; marriage to John Buchan; and domestic, literary, and society life in Scotland, England, Canada.   614

BUCHANAN, Capt. Angus. Three Years of War (1919). WW1 military service; adventures in campaigns in German East Africa.   615

BUCHANAN,Dugald. Diary (Edin. 1836) Sinful youth in Stirling; conversion; spiritual life;religious and missionary labours in Perthshire.   616

BUCHANAN, Francis. Journal (Patna, 1925). Diary of a survey and tour in Patna and Gaya, 1811-12; archaeological and scientific observations; and natural history.   617

BUCHANAN,George. Opera Omnia (Edin. 1715). Contains a brief "vita ab ipso scripta" 1580; a dry statement of the facts of his studies, writings, religious activities.   618

BUCHANAN,Sir George William.My Mission (1923). Diplomatic career, 1876-1918;Vienna, Bulgaria, St. Petersburg public events and personalities & his travels.   619

BUCHANAN, Meriel. Diplomacy (1928). With her diplomat father in many capitals; Berlin, Sofia, Constantinople, St.-Petersburg; social life; society, and daily life.   620

BUCHANAN-TAYLOR,W. Shake the Bottle (1942);Shake It Again (1943);One More Shake (1944). Journalism, advertising and entertaining; ventriloquism; London theatrical and Bohemian life;travels in Europe and America;an amusing picture.   621

BUCKINGHAM, James Silk. Autobiography (1855). His adventurous life from age of nine;merchant marine and navy; speculations; scheme for opening Red Sea route; adventures in Egypt, Near East, India, to 1825.   622

BUCKINGHAM, John Sheffield, Duke of Works (1723) II. Contains memoirs of early career in navy; the Dutch wars; quarrel with Rochester; the Monmouth

plot; political contrivances.   623

BUCKLAND,Francis Trevelyan.Log-Book (1875).Quizzical reminiscences, anecdotes; fisherman and zoologist.   624

BUCKLER,John. A very brief autobiographical sketch of a minor artist of 18th Century. MS,William Salt Library Stafford.   625

BUCKLEY, John. A Village Politician (1897).Childhood poverty in Chilterns and agitation against Corn Laws; the education,propaganda, and troubles of a young reformer to 50's; a valuable picture of working-class life in country; Claywick.   626

BUCKMASTER, Herbert. Buck's Book(L. 1933). Service in Boer War and WW1 ; adventures and misadventures as a man about town; country life, society and sport.   627

BUDD, Henry. Memoir (1855). Boyhood life; ordination; parish work & chaplain at Bridewell.   628

BULLEN, Frank Thomas. Log of a Sea Waif(1899); With Christ at Sea (1900) Confessions of a Tradesman(1908); Recollections(1915). His boyhood at sea and religious experiences on ship;his brief career and failure as shopkeeper his career and travel as lecturer and author; attractive.   629

BULLOCK, Shan F. After Sixty Years (1931). His early life in Ulster; family, social, religious life at Lough Erne; politics; problems.   630

BULMAN, Brian. Four Years (1939). A diary of his last years suffering from tuberculosis; Italy; Tyrol; his pleasures and amusements.   631

BUNBURY,Sir Charles James Fox. Life ed. Frances J. Bunbury (1894). Begins with autobiography of boyhood and early manhood; geologist.   632

/BUNBURY, Col. Thomas/. Reminiscences of a Veteran (1861). His military career to 1846; Peninsular War; garrisons in Ireland; taking convicts to Australia;Maori Wars; India; his campaigns; social; travels; personal and military adventures.   633

BUNN, Alfred. The Stage (1840). His work as lessee of Drury Lane and Covent Garden; theatrical fashions; audiences, actors, plays, critics, playwrights.   634

BUNYAN, John. Grace Abounding (1666) Relation of the Imprisonment (L.1765). His spiritual anguish and conversion; his preaching; arrest, trial, imprisonment in Bedford; release.   635

BURALL, Paul.   Cornwall to America (1932). Life and work of Cornish Methodist; mostly experiences in Philadelphia 1783-84; language and spelling is very interesting.   636

BURCH, William. Life, Sermons, and Letters, ed. T. Russell (1866). Kentish minister; weaver's son; apprentice to bootmaker; sins; conversion; business troubles; ministry.   637

BURDETT, Frederick David. Odyssey of an Orchid Hunter (1930); Odyssey of a Pearl Hunter (1931); Odyssey of a Digger (1936). Dictated reminiscences of his adventures in W.Australia, Borneo and Philippines in search of fortune; early 20th Century.   638

BURDETT, Osbert H. Memory & Imagination (1935). Childhood; school; Cambridge; choice of profession & career as writer.   639

BURDSALL, Richard. Memoirs (Thetford 1823). Sins and conversion; Wesleyan Methodist ministry; religious life and work in Yorkshire to 1822.   640

BURGE, Charles Ormsby.   Adventures (1909). Fifty years as railway engineer in England, Ireland, India, South Africa, Utah & Australia; social life and sport; literary and political celebrities he met.   641

BURGIN, George Brown. Memoirs of a Clubman (1921); More Memoirs (1922); Many Memories (1922); Some More Memories (1925). Social and literary life in London; theatres & clubs; friends, authors & journalists; his own books; pleasures and anecdotes.   642

BURKE, "Billie" (Mary W. Ziegfeld). With a Feather on My Nose (1949). Her career as comedienne with Hawtrey and

Ziegfeld Follies; marriage with Ziegfeld; career in Hollywood.   643

BURKE, Thomas. Living in Bloomsbury (1939); Son of London (1946). Childhood in London; career as journalist and short-story writer; Cockney scene and ways; anecdotes of writers and artists; a devoted Londoner.   644

BURKE, William P. Señor Burky (1936) Experiences of a trader and sanitary engineer in Peru & Santa Domingo; odd jobs; tropical life on river beats; & breezy story of adventures.   645

BURN, Gen. Andrew. Memoirs (1815). Scottish religious upbringing; at sea and poverty in Jamaica; service in the Marines; six years in France; debauchery and penury; spiritual state; later journals of military service and religion, America, East Indies, etc. 646

/BURN, James Dawson/. Autobiography of a Beggar Boy (1855). Childhood with stepfather; drunkenness, beggary, charity, peddling, gaols; picaresque; his own progress in Nth.Country hat trade and lecturing for Oddfellows; vicissitudes of chequered life; excellent for life of working classes.   647

BURNAND, Sir Francis Cowley. My Time (1874); The A.D.C. (1880); Records and Reminiscences (1904). Persiflage; his social life since a boy; anecdotes of Cambridge dramatic club; literary and social life; Punch and its contributors; the theatre; good.   648

BURNE, Gen. Sir Owen Tudor. Memories (1907). His military career and politics; Crimean War; India; Afghanistan, and work at India Office.   649

BURNELL, John. Bombay in the Days of Queen Anne (1933). Includes an account of adventures in Bombay in 1712. 650

BURNET, Gilbert. History of My Own Time (1724, 1734). General history of England and Europe from Restoration to Treaty of Utrecht, and intermixed personal affairs; professorship at Glasgow; his part in politics; service to William of Orange; appointment to see of Salisbury; standard.   651

BURNET, William. Gleanings (1905).

His curacies in various parts of England; churchmen and church work; congregations;missionary work among Jews
of Paris.   652

BURNS, Sir Alan Cuthbert. Colonial
Civil Servant (1949). His boyhood in
Leeward Isles; administration in Nigeria and Bahamas;governor of Honduras
business,economics, politics; reports
and reflections.   653

BURNS,Jabez. Retrospect (1875). His
early life and business in Yorkshire;
independent minister in London for 40
years;London poor and religious scene
temperance & social work; social conditions; travel in England, USA.   654

BURNS, James. Historical Fragments,
ed. James Maidment (Edin. 1833). Contains Burns' memoirs of the civil war
in Scotland 1644-61; bailie of city of
Glasgow.   655

BURNYEAT, John. Journal of the Life
(1661). Quaker converted by Fox; ministry and sufferings;England, America
and West Indies;one of the models for
Quaker autobiographies.   656

BURR, Malcolm. A Fossicker (1933)
Slouch Hat (1935). Life in Angola;ad-
ventures, exploring, slave trade;life
of Portuguese and natives;medical service in Balkans during WW1;Serbian and
Salonika campaigns.   657

BURROUGH,Edward. A True Description
(1663). Religious adventure, hardship
and spiritual life of a Presbyterian,
turned Quaker; a life despised though
glorious.   658

BURROUGHS, Capt. Frederick William.
Journal of his army service in India;
experiences in the Mutiny. MS,Nation-
al Library of Scotland.   659

BURROW,Francis Russell.Centre Court
(1937). Tennis referee; organization;
Wimbledon and other tournaments; famous players and games.   660

BURROWS, Capt. Montagu. Autobiography (1908). Early life in Navy; South
Africa;Oxford studies of history; his
career as Chichele professor of modern
history;church work; Oxford life; his
writings.   661

BURSTALL,Sara Annie. Retrospect and
Prospect(1933). Aberdeen; London; the
Buss school;Girton; career as teacher
in girls' schools in Manchester;views
on education.   662

BURSTOW, Henry. Reminiscences (Horsham, 1911). Childhood in Horsham and
apprentice to shoemaker; bellringer;
memories of Sussex life, people, customs, at Horsham.   663

BURT,T. Seymour. Memoranda (Dorking
1886).Schooling in Addiscombe; military career in India;society; disjointed; early 19th Century.   664

BURT, Thomas. Autobiography (1924).
Durham; a pit boy and miner; life in
colliery villages; trade unions; labour conditions and strikes; M.P. for
Morpeth from 1874; Liberal politics;
Parliament; Labour Party; valuable as
record of early labour movement. 665

BURTON, Major Gen. Edmund Francis.
Reminiscences of Sport (1885); Indian
Olio (1888). Big-game hunting in In-
dia; military affairs; social life; &
Indian life and customs.   666

BURTON,Henry. Narration of the Life
(1643). Ardent anti-Catholic;court of
Charles I; his books against Rome and
Star Chamber trial; imprisonment; release; pious and dull.   667

BURTON,Lady Isabel. The Romance of,
ed. W. H. Wilkins (1897). Unfinished
autobiography; childhood, youth, society; marriage to Sir Richard Burton;
devoted love and romantic travels and
adventure in many parts of the world;
woven in with Wilkins' text.   668

BURTON, John. A Genuine and True
Journal (1749; Edin. 1884). Escape of
the Young Chevalier; from Culloden to
landing in France;from mouths and diaries of those who assisted.   669

BURTON, Percy. Adventures among Im-
mortals (N.Y. 1937). Dictated to Lowell Thomas; Press agent; Barnum; manager for Irving, Tree, Bernhardt etc.
anecdotes of clients.   670

BURTON, Brig. Gen. Reginald George.
Sport and Wild Life (1928). His forty
years of big-game hunting in the Dec-

ran; perils from wild beasts.   671

BURY, Right Rev. Herbert. A Bishop amongst Bananas (1911);Here and There (1916). Church work as Bishop of Honduras;negroes and banana trade; chaplain and Bishop of North & Central Europe during WW1.   672

BUSS,Henry. Eighty Years Experience (1893). Education at London Mechanics Institute; influence of Birkbeck; his medical training at Royal College Surgeons; practice; experiments with new therapies;travels; marriage; valuable for working-class education.   673

BUSSEY,Harry Findlater. Sixty Years (1906). Journalist and Parliamentary reporter;Manchester; Manchester politicians, Disraeli, Gladstone; debates in Parliament;Tichborne and other famous trials; from 1844.   674

BUTLER, Alfred J. Court Life (1887) Short career as tutor to the Khedive of Egypt's sons; Cairo; social life & court.   675

BUTLER, Andrew S. G. Recording Ruin (1942). Architect's work; experiences in WW1 and firefighting during London Blitz; social life between wars. 676

BUTLER,Charles.Reminiscences (1822) Catholic upbringing; writings on history, politics, religion; reminiscences of education,law, politics; mostly impersonal.   677

BUTLER, Elizabeth Southerden, Lady. From Sketch-Book (1909);Autobiography (1923). Artist's travels in S. Africa Ireland, Egypt & Italy; her art study in Italy; young Amazon turned painter marriage to soldier; social life; military paintings;Franco-Prussian war; popularity of her work.   678

BUTLER, Frank Hedges. Fifty Years of Travel (1920). Adventures of professional traveller and hunter; land,sea and air; the long bow.   679

BUTLER, Sir Harold. Confident Morning (1950). Boyhood; Oxford and continental universities; his career as civil servant; Local Government Board and Home Office; the creation of the ILO and his work with it; management-

labour problems; politics;social life rambling.   680

BUTLER, Major John. Travels and Adventures (1855). Military career in Assam 1841-54; administration; exploration; life of hill tribes.   681

BUTLER,Josephine Elizabeth.Personal Reminiscences (1896);Autobiographical Memoir (1909). Religious upbringing; life devoted to social work; outcast women in Liverpool;crusade for purity and against licensed prostitution;for women's education;crusade of violence and sweetness; excellent.   682

BUTLER, Lt. Col. Patrick Richard. A Galloper at Ypres (1920). A cheerful narrative of experiences in France in WW1.   683

/BUTLER, Robert/. Narrative of the Life and Travels of Serjeant B.(Edin. 1823). Peebles; poverty; enlistment; service in Ireland and India 1807-14; religion, war, native life.   684

BUTLER, Sir William Francis. Autobiography (1911). Ireland;the famine; military career in India, Canada, Egypt, Sth Africa; Boer War; War Office empire building, sport,social; a good military record.   685

BUTTERFIELD, Sir Frederick W. L. My West Riding Experiences (1928). Study in Germany and America;music and law; work on family estate in Yorks;social political and public work; activities as Mayor of Keighley.   686

BUTTERWORTH,Alan. The Southlands of Siva (1923). Civil servant and judge in Southern India from end of the 19th Century; travels and social life; Indian religion and customs.   687

BUTTERWORTH, William (Henry Schroeder). Three Years' Adventures (Leeds, 1823). A boy running away to sea and his adventures on a slaver and later in Africa, West Indies, USA; a lively record.   688

BUTTS, Mary. Crystal Cabinet (1937) Childhood in Dorset; family; schools; Westfield College; psychological and sentimental development;intimacy with nature; animism; a novelist's subtle and beautiful self-portrait.   689

BUXTON, Maj. Anthony. Fisherman Na-
turalist(1946); Travelling Naturalist
(1948). Reminiscences of his lifetime
experiences in field sports and natural history study; fishing, shooting,
hawking; Norfolk and East Anglia; and
travels in Europe; pleasant.   690

BUXTON, Mary Aline. Kenya Days (L.
1927). Experiences of farming at Nairobi; social life; natives.   691

BUXTON, Noel Edward (Noel-Buxton).
Travels and Reflections(1929). Labour
M.P.'s travels in Balkans,Persia, Armenia, Japan, before WW1; his work as
relief agent in 1912 Balkan war. 692

BUYERS, William.   Recollections of
Northern India (1848).Missionary work
at Benares; Indian religious beliefs;
Indian customs.   693

BYRNE,J. C. Twelve Years' Wanderings
(1848). Travel experiences in British
colonies, including Australia.   694

/BYRNE,Mrs. Julia Clara/. Gossip of
the Century (1892); Social Hours with
Celebrities (1898). Gossip, anecdotes
and reminiscences; court,society, law
music, stage, art, etc.   695

BYRNE, Miles. Memoirs (Paris 1863);
Some Notes of an Irish Exile (Dublin,
1910). Life and political activity of
a United Irishman; his part in rebellion of 1798; history of the struggle
his comrades; account of his life in
exile.   696

BYRNE, Muriel St. Clare. Common or
Garden Child (1942). Edwardian childhood; family, domestic, social life &
customs; personal; emotional.   697

BYRON, John. The Narrative (1768).
Shipwreck on coast of Patagonia & his
sufferings, 1740-46; Indian customs;
the poet's grandfather.   698

C. S.(Retired). Leaves from a Diary
in Lower Bengal (1896). Civil servant
in Chittagong and Calcutta; his early
years of administration; Indian life;

covers the period 1862-70.   1

CADDICK, Helen. White Woman in Central Africa (1900). Missionary work;
visiting missions and native villages
in Central Africa from Zambesi to the
Lakes; solitary travels.   2

CAFFYN, William. Seventy-One (Edin.
1899). Surrey and England cricketer's
reminiscences of his matches from fifties; famous games and players; tours
in America and Australia.   3

CAILLARD, Mabel. Lifetime in Egypt
(1935). With her father in Egypt from
1876; political and government work;
social and everyday life;familiar and
pleasant.   4

CAINE, Sir Thomas Henry Hall. My
Story (1908). His early days in Isle
of Man and Liverpool; his career as a
novelist; literary life & friendships
including Rossetti;social life in the
Isle of Man.   5

CAIRNS, David S. David Cairns(1950)
Puritanical religious life in Scottish
family from 1860's;life in the manse;
his revolt from puritanism; theological writing; friendships.   6

CAIRNS, Elizabeth. Memoirs (Glasgow
1762). Spiritual autobiography; work
as preacher for Reformed Church,Stir-
ling.   7

CALAMY, Edmund. Historical Account,
ed. J. Rutt (1829). A history of his
own times and the dissenters; church,
state, nonconformity, and himself; it
is modelled on Burnet but is somewhat
more personal.   8

CALDWELL,Rt. Rev. Robert. Reminiscences (Madras, 1894).Glasgow boyhood;
work as missionary in Madras and Tinnevelly;Bishop of Tinnevelly; studies
of language and religion.   9

CALLADINE,Sgt. George. Diary (1922)
Mostly autobiography,1793-1837; military life and adventures in England,
Ireland, Ceylon; ordinary life of the
soldier; simple and good.   10

CALLOW,William. Autobiography(1908)
Boyhood; art study in Paris; teaching
and drawing in London; water colorist

& illustrator; his life in Great Missenden; tours.   11

CALLWELL, Gen. Sir Charles Edward. Service Yarns (1912); Experiences of a Dug-Out (1920); Stray Recollections (1923). Haileybury and Woolwich; military career from 1878 in India; Boer War; Staff College; Intelligence Dept and War Office; WW1 service; Dardanelles;munitions problems; cabinet and councils;his opinions, criticisms and anecdotes.   12

CALTHROP,Dion Clayton. My Own Trumpet (1935). Family; Bohemian life in Paris and London; theatrical life and playwriting; WW1 service.   13

CALVERT,Adelaide Helen. Sixty-Eight Years (1911). Reminiscences of career as an actress;actors, plays, tours in England and USA.   14

CAMBRIDGE,T. R. In the Land of Turkana (1921). Military service in WW1; Central Africa.   15

CAMDEN, Charles. When I Was Young (1872). Childhood in a Welsh village; family,playmates, adventures, village life and folk.   16

CAMDEN, William."Memorabilia de se ipso" in Thomas Smith's Vita (1691). Brief notes on his life to 1622; his journeys, studies, publications, and illnesses.   17

CAMERON,Sir Charles Alexander.Autobiography (Dublin, 1920). Reminiscences of Dublin life, theatres, music & celebrities; and his work as doctor & chemist in public health.   18

CAMERON, Mrs. Charlotte. Two Years in Southern Seas (1923). Her travels and adventures; New Guinea; Fijis and Melanesia.   19

CAMERON,Sir Donald Charles. My Tanganyika Service (1939). His work as Governor in Tanganyika and Nigeria; & problems of colonial life; education, law, administration.   20

CAMERON, Capt. Evan Percival. Goodbye Russia (1934). Last days of Tsarist Russia; evacuating White refugees from Odessa and Batoum; horrors & his adventures.   21

CAMERON,Lieut. Col. George Poulett. The Romance of Military Life (1853). Partly describes his early service in the army in India.   22

CAMERON, Capt. John. John Cameron's Odyssey (1928). Adventures of sailor in sailing ships in the South Seas in 1850-1925; hearty; dictated.   23

CAMERON,Lucy Lyttelton. The Life of (1862).Includes autobiography and diary extracts; Worcestershire childhood daughter of Chaplain to George III;in London;Hannah More;minister's wife in Salop and Lincs; family life.   24

CAMERON, Ludovick C. R. Rod, Pole, and Perch (1928). Reminiscences fishing and otter hunting.   25

CAMERON, Lady Mary. Merrily I Go to Hell (1931). Rebellious daughter of a bishop; in VAD during WW1; munitions work;goes on stage; great gusto; little too good; pseudonymous.   26

CAMERON,Verney Lovett.Across Africa (1877). Extensive travels in Central Africa in 70's;opening up of tropical Africa; native life; slavery; commercial prospects.   27

CAMM, Dom Bede. Anglican Memories (1935). His conversion to Catholicism and his work and spiritual life in his Anglo-Catholic days.   28

CAMPBELL, Archibald Bruce. With the Corners Off (1937); Bring Yourself to Anchor (1941); Come Alongside (1946); Into the Straight (1950). Adventures of a rolling stone; schooldays; hunter and trapper in Canada; in merchant navy;with minesweepers and armed merchantmen in WW1; lecturer, entertainer and radio personality; the Brains Trust; yarns.   29

CAMPBELL, Charles. Memoirs (Glasgow 1828).Seaman in war of 1812; overseer in Jamaica; slave plantations; cotton spinner in Glasgow;working-class life and adventures; written in gaol while charged with murder; sordid realism; interesting.   30

CAMPBELL,Donald. A Narrative of the

Extraordinary Adventures (1796). His adventures on an overland journey to India,1781-85; shipwreck; experiences as prisoner of Hyder Ali; adventures in Bengal; humours.   31

CAMPBELL, Dugald. In the Heart of Bantuland (1922); Wanderings in Central Africa (1929). Exploration and pioneering in Central Africa & Bantuland from 1890;native life and ethnology; slavers;sport and adventures; a lively record.   32

CAMPBELL, Duncan. Secret Memoirs of (1732). A famous deaf mute; astrology and fortune-telling; advice to lovers and stories about his clients. Sequel to the "Life of Duncan Campbell"possibly by Defoe.   33

CAMPBELL, Duncan. Reminiscences and Reflections (Inverness,1910). Farming background in Highlands;church, landlords, eccentrics; antiquarianism and folk-lore; journalism; editor of Northern Chronicle; valuable.   34

CAMPBELL, Ethyle. Can I Help You , Madam(1938). Selling women's clothes; experiences with customers, sellers & designers; part fiction.   35

CAMPBELL, Sir George. Memoirs of My Indian Career (1893). Haileybury; his administrative work in Orissa, Bengal and Oude; Sepoy Mutiny; personal life and history of India in his time. 36

CAMPBELL,Capt. George F. Soldier of the Sky (Chicago, 1918). Training and flying experiences with RFC in France; WW1.   37

CAMPBELL, Sir Gerald. Of True Experience (1948). Repton, Cambridge; his career as consul and diplomat; Brazil Congo, Italy & Abyssinia; USA during WW2; High Commissioner at Ottawa; political events,people, public opinion and personalities; good.   38

CAMPBELL,Admiral Gordon. My Mystery Ships (1928); Number Thirteen (1932). Experiences and adventures in the navy; training of cadets; West Indies, South Africa, Pacific; anti-submarine work during WW1; awarded VC.   39

CAMPBELL, Helen. An Eastern Diary

(Tenby, 1922). The experiences of a soldier's wife in India and Burma, in 1909-12;and later at Bushire and Bagdad; simple.   40

CAMPBELL, Col. Ian Maxwell. Wayward Tendrils (L. 1947); Reminiscences of a Vintner (1950). Recollections of an expert wine-lover;sport; playing with Grace; WW1 army service; rambling. 41

CAMPBELL, Lt.Col. James. Excursions Adventures and Field Sports (1843). A soldier's career in Ceylon; administrative and military affairs; law and business; social life.   42

CAMPBELL of Ardkinglass, Sir James. Memoirs(1832). Scotland; military career; Seven Years War; battle of Minden;social life and amusements; meets Voltaire; London society, clubs, theatres; Pandemonium Club; good.   43

CAMPBELL,John, 1st Baron. Life, ed. Mrs. Hardcastle (1881). Autobiography to 1847;Scottish childhood; education St.Andrews; journalism & law; London and on circuit; M.P.for Stafford; Reform Bill; Parliament; Solicitor-General; society; Brooks Club.   44

CAMPBELL, Sir John. Personal Narrative (1864). Military operations in the hills of Orissa; efforts to suppress human sacrifice in Khondistan; Hindu life; 1837-50.   45

CAMPBELL, John. Thirty Years' Experience(1884). Surgeon on convict ship and in English prisons; the treatment of prisoners; sociological.   46

CAMPBELL,John McLeod. Reminiscences (1873).His early ministry in Scotland at Row; ideas and ideals; progress of his thought and teaching.   47

CAMPBELL,Sir Malcolm. Autobiography (1934); My Thirty Years of Speed (L. 1935); Speed on Wheels (1949). Adventures of a sporting career; yachting, flying, motoring; attempts at world's records.   48

CAMPBELL,Neil. Shadow and Sun (1947) Dublin boyhood; Presbyterian family;a period in banking;runs away to sea and adventures under sail and steam;later life in South Africa.

CAMPBELL, Mrs. Patrick (Beatrice S. Cornwallis-West). My Life & Some Letters(1922). Her career in the theatre 1888-1918; plays, roles, & theatrical scene; her friends; Barrie, Shaw, and Fauré.   50

CAMPBELL, Dr. Peter. Journal, 1763; surgeon's experiences as a prisoner of Suraj ad Daula at Seringapatam; massacres. Walter K. Firminger, Diaries of Three Surgeons of Patna (Calcutta, 1909).   51

CAMPBELL,Phyllis. Back of the Front (1915). Work as nurse in Belgium and France; behind the lines, WW1.   52

CAMPBELL, Reginald. Teak-Wallah (L. 1935). Work and adventures of forest assistant in the teak forests and jungles of Northern Siam   53

CAMPBELL, Reginald John. Spiritual Pilgrimage(1916). Ulster; Oxford; his nonconformist ministry in Brighton and London;City Temple; withdrawal to the high church movement; his work in the Labour movement.   54

CAMPBELL, Robert. Reminiscences of a Long Life (Dunedin, 1894). Early life in Scotland; later in New Zealand. 55

CAMPBELL,T.J. Fifty Years of Ulster (Belfast,1941). A barrister's reminiscences of press, politics, law, public events and troubles.   56

CAMPBELL, Colonel Walter. My Indian Journal(Edin. 1864). Highland boyhood and his military career in India; but mostly big-game hunting.   57

CAMPION,John S. On the Frontier (L. 1878). Englishman's adventures in the Wild West; Colorado; prairie life and Indian skirmishes.   58

CAMPION, Sidney R. Sunlight on the Foothills(1941);Towards the Mountains (1944); Reaching High Heaven (1945); Only the Stars Remain (1946). Leicester; poor boyhood; struggles; Ramsay Macdonald; self-education and experiences as schoolmaster, barrister, and author; politics; travels; WW1 & WW2; meetings with many celebrities;rather egotistical and flimsy; in the fashion of the instalment autobiography.   59

CANCELLOR,Henry L. Life of a London Beak (1930). Work as magistrate; police courts; delinquents; social work; good sense.   60

CANDLER, Edmund. Youth and the East (Edin.1924). Experiences of young man in India in early 20th Century;literature and art; his spiritual life; an interesting record.   61

CANNELL, Bertram G. A. From Monk to Busman(1935). A boy at Llanthony monastery;Father Ignatius; novice's life his marriage; work as bus conductor; daily life, beliefs; candid.   62

CANNELL,John Clucas. When Fleet St. Calls (1932). Travels and excitements of London journalist; interviews; the romance of journalism.   63

CANZIANI,Estella. Round About Three Palace Green (1939). Painting in London; late Victorian life; reminiscences of artists; travels; social. 64

CAPADOSE, Col. Henry. Sixteen Years (1845). Military and social life and travels in 1839-55;Trinidad, Barbados and Guianas.   65

CAPPE, Catharine. Memoirs (1822). A record of her religious life; at York and in North of England.   66

CAPPER, Alfred Octavius. Rambler's Recollections (1915). Career and travel as a professional mind-reader and entertainer; actors and spiritualists; anecdotes of show business.   67

CAPPER, Com. Henry D. Aft from the Hawsehole (1927). Long career in navy his ships and cruises; changes in the service and conditions of sailors and their work; adventures.   68

CAPPON,Thomas Martin. Then, Now and Whither (Edin. 1935). Training as an architect; military service in volunteers;Black Watch; Scottish life; his work with conscription in WW1.   69

CARBERY,Mary (Toulmin), Lady. Happy World(1941). A Victorian childhood at Childwick; country life and ways; her family and friends; Herts.   70

CARDEN, Adm. John Surman. Curtail'd

Memoir(1912). Naval career, 1780-1850 fighting pirates in East Indies; surrender to Americans in war of 1812 and his disgrace; vivid account of adventure and naval life.   71

CARDIGAN, Chandos S. C. Brudenell-Bruce, Earl of. I Walked Alone (1950) Capture by Germans before Dunkirk and his wanderings and adventures in his escape from Belgium to Gibraltar; good narrative.   72

CARDIGAN AND LANCASTER, Adeline L.M. Countess of. My Recollections (1909). Girlhood in 1830's; court life, society, country houses; her two marriages politics; sport; yachting; memories of celebrities.   73

CARDINALL, Allan Wolsey. In Ashanti and Beyond (1927). Work as a resident magistrate on Gold Coast; native life and ethnology; culture and cults. 74

CARDUS, Neville. Autobiography (L. 1947); Second Innings (1950). Boyhood in Manchester slums; odd jobs; gifts for music and writing; exploration of mind and spirit; work as a cricket and music reporter for Manchester Guardian and as coach at Shrewsbury; celebrated artists and sportsmen; good.   75

CAREW, Bampfylde-Moore. An Apology (1749). Devonshire youth; living with gypsies; in America; king of beggars; West Country adventures; slang.   76

CAREW, Dudley C.H. The House is Gone (1949). His boyhood and youth in Edwardian times; Lancing; classical education; literary journalism; London Mercury and Sir John Squire; cricket; films.   77

CAREW, Dr. Francis Wylde, (ed.). No. 747 (Bristol, 1891). Autobiography of gypsy and poacher in Devon and South-West; service with L'Estranges; marriage, sport, adventures.   78

CAREW, Paul. Dust, Dope and Sawdust (1937). Early days of flying; service with RNAS in WW1, Gallipoli, Africa; hunting in India; journalist in Buenos Aires; cocaine racket; revolution in Argentina; circus-owner.   79

CAREY, Eustace. Diary, 1815-1835; a missionary's life in India; teaching Hindus and soldiers; his disputes with Brahmins. Eustace Carey, by Mrs. Eustace Carey (1857).   80

CAREY, Lewis. My Gun and I (1933). Fowling and rabbiting; hunting in Sth Africa; fond recollections of sporting life since boyhood.   81

CARLETON, Capt. George. Military Memoirs(1728; 1929). Soldier of fortune 1672-1713; service in Spain; prisoner at Denia; volunteer in Low Countries; partisan leader; adventures; a stirring life; sometimes held to be fiction and propaganda by Defoe.   82

CARLETON, William. Life of, by David O'Donoghue(1896). Contains autobiography of early life in County Tyrone and Dublin; poverty; candidate for priesthood; reading, tutoring, writing; difficulties with landladies; his literary work before he became established; entertaining.   83

CARLILE, John C. My Life's Little Day(1935). Religion and social reform for 50 years; Bradlaugh, Besant, Spurgeon; educational work; editor of the Baptist Times; movements for unity of free churches.   84

CARLIN, Francis. Reminiscences(1927) Scotland Yard detective; Etham Common murder and other noted crimes and his part in tracking down criminals.   85

CARLTON(Arthur Philps).Twenty Years of Spoof (1919). Poor boyhood; rise as entertainer and conjuror; in markets, fairs, music halls; tours; lively anecdotes of show business.   86

CARLYLE, Alexander. Autobiography (1860; 1910). Life and work of minister of Inveresk; leader of the moderate party in Church of Scotland; his friendships with Hume, Smollett, Adam Smith, etc.; excellent for Scotch life and society in 18th Century.   87

CARLYLE, Thomas. Reminiscences, ed. J.A. Froude (1881). Parents, wife and friends; Edward Irving, Southey, Wordsworth, Lord Jeffrey; their influences on him; his life in Scotland.   88

CARLYON, Clement. Early Years (1836)

Fellow of Pembroke;studies in Germany literature and philosophy; meditation on history, theology, medicine;literary acquaintances, Coleridge, Scott & Wordsworth; medical work.   89

CARNEGIE, Mrs. V. M. A Kenyan Farm Diary (1930). Her daily work building up a farm in Kenya,1919-28; sheep and cattle; native labour.   90

CARNIE, William. Reporting Reminiscences (Aberdeen, 1902-6). Journalism Aberdeen, 1850-1900; Aberdeen affairs and people.   91

CARON, Francis. Majorca (1939). The painter's salad days;romance; amours; illustrated.   92

CARPENTER, Edward. My Days & Dreams (1916).Cambridge University extension and adult education work;lecturing in North and London; farm at Millthorpe; socialist work and journalism; labour movement and friends.   93

CARPENTER, Minnie L. Angel Adjutant (1921). Life and work of a Salvation Army officer and social worker.   94

CARPENTER,Richard. Experience(1642) Cambridge student;becomes a Catholic; Douai monastery; ordination; mission to England;rejoins Church of England; ministry in Sussex; acrid propaganda vs. Rome.   95

CARPENTER, Right Rev. William Boyd. Some Pages of My Life (1911); Further Pages (1916). Early years, Cambridge; career in Church of England; bishop; London, Ripon, Leeds; public life and figures; Browning; Tennyson.   96

CARR, William Guy. Hell's Angels of the Deep (1932); Brass Hats (1939). A boy's experiences at sea;service with Harwich naval force under Tyrwhitt in WW1; submarine work; lively.   97

CARRUTHERS,Anthony Douglas Mitchell Beyond the Caspian (Edin. 1949). The extensive travels and adventures of a geographer and naturalist in Russian Asia during three years; hunting for museums; natives; sports.   98

CARSLAKE, Bernard. Jockey's Memoirs (1938). Early days in Australia; rac-

ing there;career as jockey and trainer in Hungary,South Africa, India and England; sportsmen; scandals.   99

CARSTAIRS, John Paddy. Honest Injun (1942); Hadn't We the Gaiety (1945). Schooldays; author and film director in Hollywood;film stars; broadcasting and films; life in RNVR & experiences in London Blitz.   100

CARSTAIRS, Robert. The Little World of an Indian District Officer (1912). His work and life in Bengal,1872-1903 medical,legal, police affairs; social life; Hindu traits.   101

CARSWELL, Catherine R. Lying Awake. (1950).Mostly describes her upbringing in a Glasgow bourgeois family in late Victorian period; religion; puritanism;little about her literary life or about D. H. Lawrence.   102

CARTER, Albert C. R. Let Me Tell You (1940).Art critic's experiences in art & literature;auctions and behind the scenes anecdotes.   103

CARTER, Barbara Barclay. Old Nurse (1936).Welsh nanna and her charges in Brecon; Welsh country life & children and their ways; good.   104

CARTER, George. Hound and Horn, by I. H. Gale (1885). Reported reminiscences of West Country life and people and hunting.   105

CARTER,George G. Able Seaman (1948) His career in the merchant navy;experiences in Pacific and West Indies; & farming in England; lively.   106

⟦CARTER,Capt. Harry⟧. Autobiography of a Cornish Smuggler,ed. J.B.Cornish (Truro,1894). Lively account of activities as smuggler to 1809 and of his religious life;authentic; interesting language.   107

CARTLAND,Barbara. The Isthmus Years (1943); Years of Opportunity (1948). Her work, as journalist and novelist; public events,society, the war years; covers 1918-43.   108

CARTON,Ronald. The Gentle Adventure (1933). A child's life in suburbia in reign of Victoria;domestic and middle

class life; patriotism; robust, heal-
thy childhood.   109

CARTON DE WIART, General Sir Adrian
Happy Odyssey (1950). War experiences
of a Belgian-born British general; in
Boer War as private;WW1 in France; in
Poland after war; in Lybia, Italy and
China in WW2;adventures in remarkable
career of a committed soldier; milit-
ary and political celebrities.   110

CARVER, Mrs. John. Recollections of
My Old Homes(Liverpool, 1908). Domestic life in Liverpool in reign of Victoria. Copy Liverpool Athenaeum.   111

CARVOSSO, William. Memoir (1847). A
Cornish Methodist minister; religious
life in Redruth. Methodist Library,
City Road, London.   112

CARY,Catherine E. Memoirs(1825). In
service of Queen Caroline; court life
and anecdotes of society and royalty;
sentimental and disguised.   113

CASE, Mrs. Adelaide. Day by Day at
Lucknow (1858). Diary of a soldier's
wife at the siege; sufferings of civ-
ilians and soldiers.   114

CASE, Thomas Henry. Memories (Cambridge, 1899). Chorister at King's in
30's and 40's; routine; and anecdotes
of church musicians.   115

CASSE,George Richard.Authentic Nar-
rative(1841). Kentish sailor captured
by French;imprisonment 1809-14; hardships, atrocities. Maidstone Museum
Library.   116

CASSELLS,Joe. With the Black Watch.
(1919).With original BEF in France in
WW1; Mons; hospital life; good.   117

CASSERLEY, Julian Victor Langmead.
No Faith of My Own (1950). Spiritual
autobiography; his atheistic upbringing and his gradual conversion; life
as Church of England rector.   118

CASSERLY, Major Gordon. Life in an
Indian Outpost (1914). Military life,
sport and social affairs in Himalayas
in late 19th Century.   119

CASSIDY,Thomas. Autobiography of an
Augustinian priest, in Irish;life and

adventures. MS, Royal Irish Academy,
SR.E.iv.1;another copy in B.M., Egerton 9.   120

CASSON, Stanley. Steady Drummer (L.
1935). Experiences in WW1; mostly the
Balkan campaign, Salonika & Caucasia;
personal.   121

CASTLEHAVEN,James Touchet, 3rd Earl
Memoirs of James Lord Audley (L.1680)
Autobiography of his activities in the
Irish wars, 1642-51; military affairs
and politics.   122

CASTLETOWN, Bernard E. B. FitzPat-
rick, 2nd Baron. Ego (1923). Military
career;Franco-Prussian War; Egypt and
Boer War; WW1; travel, hunting, Irish
country life, anecdotes.   123

CATHCART-JONES, Lt. Owen. Aviation
Memoirs (1934). Naval flying 1925-29;
& civil flying thereafter; his record
flights to Australia; dangers, adventures, triumphs; social life.   124

CATLING, Thomas. My Life's Pilgrimage (1911). Early life from 1838; his
career in journalism; editor, Lloyd's
Weekly; national events and politics;
social changes.   125

CATON, William. Journal of the Life
(1689). A foundation Quaker autobiography, 1652-64; his ministry and sufferings in England, Holland, Germany;
Lancashire.   126

CATTLEY, Stephen. Autobiography of
Camberwell business man (1751-1821).
trading in Russia;family affairs and
business. MS, owned by Rev. J. Adams,
Landulph Rectory, Saltash.   127

CAUDWELL,Francis. The Cross in Dark
Places(1903). Parish work of a Church
of England vicar;North & East London;
slums; workingclass life.   128

CAUGHEY,James. Earnest Christianity
(1857). Spiritual record of Methodist
minister in Yorkshire; revivalism in
Huddersfield in 40's and 50's.   129

CAVALIER,Anthony Ramsden. In Northern India (1899). Missionary work in
zenanas; medical work; travels; religious life; observations on a tour of
the missions.   130

CAVALRY OFFICER. Military Service & Adventures in the Far East(1847). His army service in India;Afghan and Sikh campaigns; Sir Harry Smith.   131

CAVANAUGH, Timothy.   Scotland Yard (1893).His career in the police force from 1855; The Borough; chief inspector at Scotland Yard;the social scene in London;music halls,theatres, shows and Drury Lane and Covent Garden. 132

CAVE, Sir Genille Cave-Browne. From Cowboy to Pulpit(1926). Early days as sailor and in circus;mining, ranching and evangelism in America; ordination and Church of England ministry; tales from an extraordinary career.   133

CAVE OF RICHMOND, Ann Estella Sarah Penfold, Countess. Odds and Ends (L. 1929). Domestic life; society; public figures; fashions; servants; collecting.   134

CAVENAGH, Sir Orfeur. Reminiscences of an Indian Official(1884). Military career;   cadet in Straits Settlement; administration and diplomacy in India Burma and Malaya;social life; 1837 to 1880.   135

CAVENDISH, Francis W. H.   Society, Politics and Diplomacy (1913). Precis writer to Russell and Clarendon; Whig political and international affairs; society gossip; anecdotes.   136

CAYLEY, Cornelius. Life and Conversion(Manchester, 1819). Early days in London;spiritual autobiography of lay preacher in London and Wales.   137

CECIL,Edward Herbert Gascoyne, Lord Leisure of an Egyptian Official(1921) His eighteen years as British official in Egypt;diplomacy; official & social life; the lighter side.   138

CECIL OF CHELWOOD, Edgar Algernon Robert Gascoyne-Cecil, 1st Viscount. Great Experiment (1941); All the Way (1949). Statesman's career;public affairs and society in Edwardian and recent times; the League of Nations and his part in it.   139

CENNICK, John. Life (1789). Reading man's sins & conversion to Methodism; the Wesleys and Whitfield;his work at

Hitchin and teaching at Kingswood;   a brief account. Reading P.L.   140

CHADWICK,William S. Man-Killers and Marauders(1929). Twenty-five years as guide and professional hunter in Central Africa; kills; escapes.   141

CHAILLÉ-LONG,Col. Charles. My Life (1912). Military career and travel in four continents; Gordon; the Egyptian campaigns; chief of staff; criticisms of the campaign.   142

CHALKLEY,Thomas.Journal of the Life (1749).Spiritual autobiography; travels of Quaker in England and America; Friends' meetings; 18th Century. 143

/CHALLENGER,Charles/. Five Years of Colliery Life,by Jonathan Presto(Manchester, 1884). Bristol man's experiences as collier boy in Somerset mine; work and dangers, conditions, pay and other interesting details.   144

CHALMERS, James. Work and Adventure in New Guinea (L.1885); Pioneering in New Guinea (L.1887); Pioneer Life and Work in New Guinea (L.1895); Autobiography and Letters (1902).His boyhood and early religious work in Scotland; pioneer missionary work in Rarotonga, and New Guinea from 1877; adventures; explorations; native life, religion & customs.   145

CHAMBERLAIN,John. Journal extracts, 1798-1817; life in Bristol; religious activities; missionary work & travels in India; his own spiritual life and introspection. Memoirs, by William Yates.   146

CHAMBERLAIN,Sir J. Austen. Down the Years (1935); Seen in Passing (1937). Study in Paris and Berlin; political career, public events and issues, and political figures; chief statesmen of the 20's; some domestic items; travel in Europe and art impressions.   147

CHAMBERS,Adm.Bertram Mordaunt. Salt Junk (1927).Naval career and reminiscences, 1881-1906; Egyptian war; social,sport, notes on the places he had been to and things he had seen. 148

CHAMBERS, George F. East Bourne Memories (Eastbourne, 1910). A lawyer's

account of people and things in Eastbourne from 1845; and his part in the
affairs of the town; author, astronomer, churchman, local official.   149

CHAMBERS, William. Story of a Long
and Busy Life (Edin. 1882). Scottish
education; literary journalism; Chambers' Journal; his publisher and writer friends in Edinburgh and London;
interesting.   150

CHAMBRE, Major Alan. Recollections
(1858). London;Eton; army service and
travels; India, Brazil, Jamaica, USA,
Ireland;social life in London and Paris;theatres; personalities and West-
End life; Beau Brummell.   151

CHAMIER, Frederick. Life of a Sailor
(1832). Naval career from 1809;war of
1812; South American revolution; rise
from midshipman to captain;adventures
and naval life.   152

CHAMPION DE CRESPIGNY, Rose (Key).
This World and Beyond (1934). Psychic
experiences; Principal of the College
of Psychic Science; séances, mediums
and sceptics; experiments.   153

CHAMPNESS,Thomas. Diary, 1857-1905;
work of a Wesleyan missionary; Sierra
Leone; later parish work in Yorkshire
and Lancashire; temperance work. Life
Story, by Eliza Champness (1907). 154

CHANNING, Francis Allston. Memories
(1918). Liberal politics, 1885-1910;
M.P. for East Northants; free trade;
labour movement; farming interests; &
anecdotes, Gladstone, Asquith.   155

CHANNING,Mark. Indian Mosaic (1936)
Subaltern in India; his growing sympathy toward Indian life and beliefs;
Yoga; philosophy; his spiritual life;
the heart of India; interesting. 156

CHANTER, John Mill. Wanderings (Ilfracombe, 1887). Dictated reminiscences of the Vicar of Ilfracombe; country life, work, journeys in North Devonshire; gentle.   157

CHAPMAN, Abel. Retrospect (L. 1928)
Memories of Fourscore Years (1930). A
zoologist's reminiscences;hunting and
nature study in three continents; the
Border moors; Spain; sport and philo-

sophy of nature study.   158

CHAPMAN, Captain Charles. First Ten
Years (1876). Fulham orphanage; cabin
boy; boyhood at sea, studies & promotion to officer;adventures and am ours
with native girls.   159

CHAPMAN,Col. Frederick Spencer. The
Jungle is Neutral (1949). His service
in the jungles of Malaya in WW2; good
account of activities with the Chinese
guerrillas against Japanese.   160

CHAPMAN,George H.Leaves from a Life
(Northampton, 1931). His work and experiences in boot and shoemaking factories in Northants.   161

CHAPMAN,Guy. Passionate Prodigality
(1933). Fragments of autobiography; a
record of personal experience,impres-
sions, and reactions on Western Front
in WW1.   162

CHAPMAN,Herbert Turlay. Reminiscences (Maidstone,1932). County surveyor
of Kent; highway work; colleagues and
Boards in various counties.   163

CHAPMAN-HUSTON,Desmond. The Lamp of
Memory (1949). His varied life as an
actor,politician, soldier and writer;
Edwardian society, politics, and public figures.   164

CHARKE, Charlotte. A Narrative of
the Life (1755).Theatrical career and
amours of Colley Cibber's daughter; a
record of splendeurs et misères; high
society.   165

CHARLEMONT,James Caulfeild,1st Earl
Autobiography of his political career
and work as commander of Irish Volun-
teers,written for his sons. MS, Royal
Irish Academy, SR.12.R.7; H.M.C. 12th
Report, App. Pt. X.   166

[CHARLES, Mrs.]. Life as I Saw It
(1924). Religious life and philosophy
in London; conversion to Roman Catholicism; visit to Lourdes.   167

CHARLES,Elizabeth (Rundle). Our Seven Homes (1896). Author's child hood
in Tavistock; pleasant environment and
governesses; marriage and widow hood;
life in London and Hampstead; religion & Oxford Movement; her poetry and

writing; inner life; fond, sentimental record.   168

CHARLES, Thomas. Brief History, ed. Edward Morgan(1828); Life and Letters (1881). Autobiography of minister of Bala; Welsh religious life and work; inner life and moralisings.   169

CHARLTON, Barbara. Recollections of a Northumbrian Lady (1949). Her life at Hesleyside in 1815-66, written up from diaries; convent education; family life; parental troubles; marriage and domestic life; social scene; difficulties of everyday life; railroad; Patrick Bronte,Swinburne, Mrs. Wordsworth; very interesting.   170

CHARLTON, Lionel E. O. Charlton (L. 1931); More Charlton(1940). Victorian childhood; Sandhurst life; service in Boer War and Montserat; training as a flyer and flying service in WW1; Air Commodore;retirement; socialism, writing, BBC; crises of 30's.   171

CHARTERIS,Brig.Gen. John. At G.H.Q. (1931). Experiences at Western Front Headquarters 1914-18; letters amplified by recollections; higher command; mostly impersonal.   172

CHARTERS, James. This Must Be the Place(1934). Childhood in Chatham and nine years as barman in Montparnasse; with anecdotes of customers.   173

CHATFIELD, Alfred Ernle Montacute, Lord. The Navy and Defence (1942); It Might Happen Again (1947). His naval career from 1893; Controller of Navy; 1st Sea Lord, Minister for Co-ordination of Defence; wide experiences of a devoted public servant; some personal and family, but mostly didactic; an important record.   174

CHATFIELD-TAYLOR, Hobart Chatfield. Cities of Many Men (1925). Experience as a boy in London, Paris, New York & Chicago;impressions of souls of towns former customs; social history; family life; tolerant.   175

CHATTERTON, Right Rev. Eyre. India Through a Bishop's Diary (1935). Work in Nagpur diocese,1903-26; missionary activities; education; celebrities; & service with Indian Corps,WW1, France

and Mesopotamia.   176

/CHATTO,William Andrew/. Scenes and Recollections of Fly Fishing, by Stephen Oliver (1834). Reminiscences of sport in Lake District & the northern counties; in dialogue form, modelled on Compleat Angler.   177

CHEESMAN, Lucy Evelyn. Hunting Insects (1932). Her adventures and observations during entomological expeditions to the South Seas.   178

CHEKE,Marcus. The Licking (Winchester, 1931).Army officer's son; recollections up to WW1; school; holidays; country sports; sensitive account of a fortunate childhood.   179

CHELSEA PENSIONER. Jottings from My Sabretasche(1847). Shropshire boyhood and enlistment in Dragoons;Peninsular War; Waterloo; soldier's life; pleasant simple record; low language.   180

CHESHIRE, Leonard. Bomber Pilot (L. 1943). Personal narrative of service in WW2; training as flyer, squadron-leader; missions over Germany; danger and escapes.   181

CHESSYRE, Henry T. N. Recollections (1861). Inheritance; five years' life and sport in Norway; customs and folk lore.   182

CHESTER, Francis. Shot Full (1938). Morphine and cocaine addict;cardsharper, clown, poacher, cook, shoplifter and informer; unpleasant.   183

CHESTERTON,George Laval. Peace, War and Adventure (1853). Military career 1812-20; Peninsular War and 1812 War; New Orleans; captain in Colombian army and service in S.America; Bolívar; later service in British prisons and houses of correction.   184

CHESTERTON, Gilbert Keith. Autobiography (1936). Quizzical, argumentative account of life, tastes, beliefs; literature, religion, politics; cult of Notting Hill;romance of bourgoisie and his political and literary friendships.   185

CHETTUR, Govinda K. Last Enchantment (1934). Experiences of a Hindu at New

College, Oxford, 1918-21; friends and spirit of Oxford;Yeats, Symons, Masefield.   186

CHETWYND,Sir George. Racing Reminiscences(1891). Life on Turf, 1869-90; horses,races, owners; his work at the Jockey Club; training, handicapping & breeding.   187

CHEVALIER, Albert. Record (L.1895); Before I Forget (1901). Reminiscences of great musichall comedian;his Cockney studies;tours; ups and downs; the social life of the theatres.   188

CHEYNE, George. Account of Himself (1743). Brief account of the career, studies, and writings of a mystic and physician.   189

CHICHESTER, Francis Charles. Ride on the Wind(1936). Travels and adventure of tramp and airman;England, Pacific, China, Northern Canada.   190

CHIGNELL,Arthur Kent. An Outpost in Papua (1911). His missionary labours in New Guinea; native life.   191

CHILD,Harold. Poor Player(Cambridge 1939). Account of his not very brilliant theatrical career,1894 to 1914; London plays; anecdotes.   192

CHILDS, Sir Borlase Elward Wyndham. Episodes and Reflections (1930). The general's military career; Boer War; Ceylon; South Africa; WWl; India; and social life and sport; reflections of a reactionary on contemporary events and customs.   193

CHIROL,Sir Ignatius Valentine.Fifty Years (1927). Observations of public events from Paris Commune 1871 to Versailles; a journalist's record of politics and war; impersonal.   194

CHOLMLEY, Sir Hugh. Memoirs (1787). His family; childhood & married life and business, and his adventures as a royalist during the Civil Wars; siege of Scarborough and affairs in Yorks.; interesting.   195

CHOLMONDELEY, Mary. Under One Roof (1918). Her childhood in a Shropshire rectory; the family; clerical and domestic life in Victorian era.   196

CHORLEY,Henry Fothergill. Music and Manners in France and Germany (1841); Thirty Years' Musical Recollections (1862); Autobiography (1873). Career and reminiscences of critic of "Athenaeum"; early life in Lancashire; literary and musical life in London and friendship with chief Victorian writers and artists; opera, art, travels; his own verses and writing.   197

CHOYCE,James. The Log of a Jack Tar (1891). Life of master mariner, 1793-1820; whaling; capture and slavery in S. American mines; whaling and adventures in Spanish and British ships sea actions during Napoleonic wars; a lively life.   198

CHRISTIE,A. V. Brass Tacks(Kilmarnock, 1943); More Brass Tacks(Kilmarnock, 1944). Childhood in Kilmarnock; his hardware shop;music and theatres; people, local events, pastimes.   199

CHRISTIE, Dugald. Ten Years in Manchuria (1895);Thirty Years in Moukden (1914). Work and travels of a medical missionary;medical education; plague; Chino-Japanese war; Boxer Rebellion; Red Cross work.   200

CHRISTIE, Ella Robertson & STEWART, Lady Alice Margaret King. A Long Look at Life.(1940). The life of two sisters from the 60's;their girlhood and social life in Scotland; music interests; travel in the East; Stevenson; Andrew Lang, etc.   201

CHRISTIE, Octavius Francis. Clifton School Days (1930). His experience at Clifton when it was a new school; the education, masters, boys, and sports, in 1879-85.   202

CHRISTISON, Sir Robert. Autobiography (1885). Edinburgh university; medical studies; practice and teaching in Edinburgh and London; reminiscences of doctors, medical practice, and experiments;hydrophobia; body-snatching; social life; medical fashions; & climbing and sport.   203

CHRISTY, Cuthbert. Big Game (1924). Hunter and naturalist in Congo; guest of Okapi; adventures; native life.204

CHRISTY, Theodore. Random Recollections (Colchester, 1939). Essex farmer & sportsman; his steeplechasing; hunting, staghunting; musichalls; and celebrities; Florence Nightingale; & reactions to Quaker upbringing.   205

CHUBB, Thomas. The Posthumous Works (1748). Preface contains brief autobiography of the theologian's earlier work as stove-maker and chandler; the circumstances leading to his début as an author.   206

CHURCH, Alfred John. Memories (1908) School & Oxford; country curacies and teaching; fishing and cricket; farming and reminiscences of literary life and books.   207

CHURCH, Sir Arthur Herbert. Records and Recollections (Gloucester, 1899). Study of chemistry; research at Oxford and London; professor at Cirencester and Kew; publications; hobbies.   208

CHURCHER, Emery James. Some Reminiscences, by a Mutiny Veteran (1909). Seventy years of a barrister's life; the old days in India; administration politics and sport; the Mutiny.   209

CHURCHILL, Jenny Spencer (Lady Randolph Spencer Churchill). Reminiscences (1908). Memories of politics and diplomacy from 1869; society & social life; Boer War; her travels.   210

CHURCHILL, Rt. Hon. Winston Leonard Spencer. My Early Life (L. 1930); Amid These Storms (1932); Thoughts and Adventures (1932); The Gathering Storm (1948); Their Finest Hour (1949); The Grand Alliance (1949); Hinge of Fate (1950). The political and military career of a happy warrior; adventures in journalism, war, politics; painting & hobbies; celebrities, scenes & events; Boer War to WW2; his political offices events leading to WW2; Battle of Britain; victory and peace; personal and historical.   211

CHURCHWARD, William B. My Consulate in Samoa (1887); "Blackbirding" in the South Pacific (1888). Experiences as acting consul in 80's; labour recruiting; King Laupepa & other celebrities adventures.   212

CIBBER, Colley. Apology for the Life (1740). Education & choice of profession; historical review of stage since the Restoration and his own theatrical career; classic.   213

/CIERPLIKOWSKI, Antoine7. "Antoine" (1946). Gossip and anecdotes of a society hairdresser; work and clients; egregious but amusing.   214

CITY MAN. Greystones (Edin.1932). A Scotsman's reminiscences of Scottish politics and society, and of Scottish celebrities; Bonar Law, Campbell-Bannerman, Haldane, etc.   215

CLANRICARDE, Ulick de Burgh, Marquis of. Memoirs (1722). Public affairs and politics in Ireland 1650-52; patriotism and family pride.   216

CLAP, Roger. Memoirs (Boston, 1731) A brief account of his Devonshire background; experiences in New England from 1630; life of pilgrims.   217

CLAPHAM, Henry Sheffield. Mud and Khaki (1930). Personal experience in WW1; trench warfare in Flanders; the early months of the war.   218

CLAPPERTON, Captain Hugh. Journal of an Expedition (L. 1826); Journal of a Second Expedition (1829). Records of two explorations into the interior of Central and North Africa; native life, travel conditions.   219

CLARE, John. Sketches in the Life (1931). The poet's early days; country labourer; village life 1793-1821; family and personal life; education and beginnings as poet.   220

CLARENCE, Oliver Burchett. No Complaints (1943). His theatrical career from 1891; musicals, plays and films; Benson Company; tours in England, and in America; theatrical scene; players and performances.   221

CLARENDON, Edward Hyde, 1st Earl of The Life (Oxford, 1759). Autobiography of the Lord High Chancellor, from birth to Restoration and banishment in 1667, written for children; closely related to his history of the rebellion; political, civil, military history and his part in it; related in 3rd person and quasi-historical.   222

CLARK, Alexander. Reminiscences of (Aberdeen,1873). Experiences of a police officer in Aberdeen.   223

CLARK, Cumberland. Life and Works (Shrewsbury,1940). London boyhood and life in New Zealand and other dominions;pioneer life; writing and lecturing on the Empire; anecdotes.   224

CLARK,H.Atwood. Those Were the Days (1933). Wiltshire farming,sport, natural history, country life, beginning of the century.   225

CLARK, John. Memoirs (Bath, 1810). Religious life and work of dissenting minister of Trowbridge, Wilts.   226

CLARK,Norman. All in the Game(1935) Blundell's School; with RAF in WW1; a boxing career;National Sporting Club; famous fighters, patrons, etc.   227

CLARK, Rev. Robert. A Brief Account (Lahore,1883). Work of Methodist missionary in Sind and Punjab, 1852-82; organization of missions.   228

CLARKE,Capt. Arthur O. T. Transport and Sport(1938). Experiences with divisional train ASC; horse transport & RASC; WW1 in France; sport.   229

CLARKE, Basil. My Round of the War (1917). Experiences of Daily Mail war correspondent in France and the Balkans, WW1.   230

CLARKE,Gen. Dudley W. Seven Assignments(1948). Experiences in WW2 of an unorthodox soldier;his assignments in Norway, Near East, etc.   231

CLARKE, Sir Edward George. Story of My Life (1918). Career as lawyer and solicitor-general; school; study and cases;M.P. for Plymouth; Conservative politics; 1867-1906.   232

CLARKE,Dr. George. Autobiography of experiences in war and politics up to 1727. H.M.C., F. W. Leyborne-Popham's MSS (1899) 259-289.   233

CLARKE,James Fernandez. Autobiographical Recollections(1874). Career in medicine from 1823;schools, hospitals personalities, societies, fashions in medicine, Westminster Hospital; University of London;establishment of The Lancet; Mesmerism; quacks.   234

CLARKE, Mary E. B. Sketches of My Childhood (Edin. 1874). Family life & life as orphan; may be fiction.   235

CLARKE, Mary Victoria Cowden. My Long Life(1896). Her upbringing, marriage,literary work; friendships with eminent writers; theatres and music; travels in Europe.   236

CLARKE, Moma. Light and Shade(1939) Forty years in France as art student; later as journalist and critic for The Times; interviews with celebrities in art, literature, theatre.   237

CLARKE,Samuel. Lives of Sundry Eminent Persons (1683). Contains a brief autobiography of the puritan minister to 1681;at Emmanuel under Hooker; his Puritan leanings; persecution.   238

CLARKE, Samuel R. Among the Tribes in South-West China (1911).Missionary work; 33 years with the China Inland Mission at Kweichow; Chinese life and customs.   239

CLARKE,Thomas J. Glimpses of an Irish Felon's Prison Life (Dublin,1922) Irish rebel & political prisoner; his life in Hurst Castle prison from 1883 to 1898.   240

CLARKSON,Henry. Memories (Wakefield 1887). Work as surveyor at Wakefield; social life and people there.   241

CLARKSON, Lieut. John. Diary, 1792; his work as governor of Sierra Leone; natives, slavers, and slaves; plantation life. Sierra Leone Studies Vol. VIII (1927).   242

CLAVELL, John. A Recantation of an Ill-Led Life (1628). Poetical account of the sins of a young highwayman and his operations at Gads-Hill.   243

CLAY, Arthur Lloyd. Leaves from a Diary in Lower Bengal (1896).Life and work of a civil servant in 60's; travels, social life, sport.   244

CLEEVE,Marion. Fire Kindleth Fire (1930). Experiences of a schoolteacher and headmistress, in an industrial slum; struggles with parents, pupils, staff; educational means and ends; an interesting record.   245

CLEGHORN, Hugh. Travel diary, 1795-1796; from London to Ceylon; work as government agent;annexation of Ceylon travels and return;lively & personal. Cleghorn Papers, ed. William Neil (L. 1927).   246

CLEMENS, Louisa P. C. Narrative of a Pilgrim (Edin. 1870). Religious education; governess in Scotland, Ireland; insanity and visions; meetings with Edward Irving;settlement USA and anti-slavery work;marriage; return to Scotland.   247

CLEMO, Jack. Confessions(1949). His Cornish boyhood; schools; mysticism & spiritual struggles;neo-Calvinist and follower of Karl Barth; his writing; novels; critical views.   248

CLERK, Sir John. Memoirs, ed. J. M. Gray (1895). Scotsman's autobiography 1676-1755; Scottish education; M.P.; justice and commissioner on the Treaty of Union; court of Queen Anne; Scottish rebellion;South Sea Bubble; family and domestic life;very interesting and historically valuable.   249

CLIFFE,John Henry. Notes and Recollections (1860). Rambling, climbing, and fishing in Wales.   250

C(LIFFORD), A. M. On the March (Madras, 1904). Recollections of wife of a soldier; army life and marches; India; Delhi; amusing details. Copy in India Office Library.   251

CLIFFORD, George Reid. My Experiences (Boston, 1928). Flying service in WWl; captain in RFC; his missions and adventures.   252

CLIFFORD, Sir Hugh Charles. Bush-Whacking(1929). Career in the Malayan Civil Service from 1890; administrative work; troubles with natives; his travels and visitors.   253

CLIFT, C. Winifred Lechmere. Very Far East (1909); Seng Chang Sees Red (1928).Domestic and religious work in Southern China; wife of medical missionary;Chinese ways; Chinese-British relations; anti-foreign agitation in the twenties.   254

CLIFT, William. Reminiscences (Basingstoke, n.d.). Farm childhood; life in Bramley; old customs; tenant farming for 45 years; old songs. Copy in Winchester P.L.   255

CLINKER KNOCKER.Aye, Aye, Sir(1938) Life in merchant marine and navy from 1908; cabin boy and able seaman; work on destroyers and minesweepers in WW1; conditions on the lower deck; farming in Canada after the war.   256

CLINTON, Henry Fynes. Literary Remains(1854). Scholar's autobiography largely about classical studies. 257

CLODD, Edward. Memories (1916). The banker's reminiscences; free thought; agnosticism; famous friends; Spencer, Huxley, Meredith, Gissing.   258

CLONCURRY, Valentine Browne Lawless 2nd Baron. Personal Recollections of (Dublin, 1849). Education and social life in Ireland in 1780's;law studies at Middle Temple; Irish law, politics and rebellion; his work with the United Irishmen; imprisonment; his part in the political and social history of Ireland to 1846; religion.   259

CLONEY, Thomas. Personal Narrative (Dublin, 1832). United Irishmen; personal experiences in County Wexford in 1798 rebellion; his trial.   260

CLOUGH, Margaret Morley. Missionary diary,1823-26; Yorkshire woman's journey to Ceylon;missionary work there & her own religion and health. Extracts from the Journal (1829).   261

CLOUSTON, Harry. Happy Hobo (1937). Five years of travel on a round the world tour.   262

CLOWES, William. Journals (1844). A Primitive Methodist's life, from 1810 to 1838;conversion; call to ministry; progress of Primitive Methodism. 263

CLYDE, Colin Campbell, Lord. Life, by Lawrence Shadwell (1881). Contains copious extracts from his diaries; of his early experiences in the Peninsular War, siege of Antwerp, and military career in England, India, China & Crimean War.   264

CLYNES,John Robert. <u>Memoirs</u> (1937). Boyhood poverty and hardships;work in cotton mills;trade unionism; activities in Labour Party;Parliamentary career;Home Secretary; national affairs and WW1; temperate account and useful for history of Labour Party, but somewhat dull.   265

COAD, John. <u>Memorandum of the Wonderful Providences</u> (1849). A Somerset puritan's experience 1685-90; the Monmouth rebellion & the Revolution; his sufferings, banishment; life at Port Royal.   266

COATS, Joseph. Travel diary, 1879-80 Glasgow professor's observations; New Zealand, Australia, Ceylon, and Egypt <u>Notes on Sea and Land</u> (1898).   267

COBBE,Frances Power. <u>The Life</u>(1894) Early life in Bristol; conditions of the poor; life in Italy; London life in 70's and 80's; journalism with The Echo; social reforms; interviews with celebrities; useful.   268

COBBETT, William. <u>Life & Adventures of Peter Porcupine</u>(Philadelphia 1796) <u>Life</u> (London 1835). Brief autobiographical sketch of farmer, journalist & politician. See also, <u>The Progress of a Ploughboy to a Seat in Parliament,</u> ed.W. Reitzel (1933) made up from the autobiographical elements in Cobbett's writings.   269

COBORN, Charles. <u>The Man Who Broke the Bank</u> (1928). Entertainer's career busking, tours, concerts, musichalls, pantomimes; anecdotes of vaudeville & comedians.   270

COCHRAN, Charles Blake. <u>Secrets of a Showman</u> (1925);<u>I Had Almost Forgotten</u> (1932); <u>Cock-a-Doodle-Doo</u> (1941); <u>Showman Looks On</u> (1945).His career in show business and the theatre: circus prize-fights, ballet, musical comedy; poverty and early struggles;promotion and publicity; Noel Coward; rambling and anecdotal.   271

COCHRANE, Captain Charles Stuart. <u>Journal of a Residence</u> (1825). Travel and residence in Colombia, 1823-24; a

somewhat impersonal account of Spanish society, industry, politics.   272

COCHRANE, Thomas.   <u>Fifty-One Years</u> (Edin.1898). Childhood in Peebles and apprentice in Edinburgh;Sunday School work; ministry and missions in Fife & among workingclass in Edinburgh; social conditions.   273

COCK, Mrs. Alfred. <u>A Country Diary</u> (1905). Removal from London; new home in village;country life and amusement and her health.   274

COCKS, Richard. Journal, 1615-22; a factor's work and business at English factory in Japan. <u>The Diary</u> (Hakluyt Society, 1883).   275

COCO THE CLOWN.   <u>Behind My Greasepaint</u> (1950). Life, work, anecdotes; travels; fairs and circuses.   276

COFFIN, Charles Hayden. <u>Hayden Coffin's Book</u> (1930). Theatrical career, 1884-1930;musical comedies; anecdotes of actors and shows.   277

COGHLAN, Margaret. <u>Memoirs</u> (1794). With her soldier-father and husband in USA; military and social life; Revolution; her admirers and keepers; the splendors and miseries of a courtesan in America.   278

COHEN, Chapman. <u>Almost an Autobiography</u> (1940). Intellectual development; intellectual movements of time; struggle for freedom of speech and of press; editor of The Freethinker from 1915.   279

COHEN, Israel. <u>Ruhleben Prison Camp</u> (1917). Capture in WW1; 19 months in German prison; social life; treatment of prisoners.   280

COHEN, Max. <u>I Was One of the Unemployed</u> (1945). Cabinet-maker; hunger, dole, problems of ways and means; unemployment as a life; difficulties of readjustment; interesting.   281

COIGLY,James. <u>Life</u> (1798). An Irish clergyman's life in politics; United Irishmen; the rebellion of 1791. 282

COKE, Desmond F. T. <u>Confessions of an Incurable Collector</u> (1928). Child-

hood at Aldershot; visits to Dublin;
his collecting of curios, prints, en-
gravings, silhouettes.   283

COKE, Henry John. Tracks of a Rolling Stone (1905). School; Cambridge;
reading; wanderlust and travels thro
Europe, North and South America; literary interests and sport.   284

COLAM,Lance.One Jump Ahead of Death
(1940); Death Over My Shoulder (1947)
Edinburgh student; adventures in many
lands; gunrunning in Korea; elephant
hunting in Uganda;macabre experiences
in Africa, Philippines, Brazil. 285

COLCHESTER, Charles Abbot, 2d Baron
Memoranda (1869). His life & politics
1798-1859; chiefly activities in Parliament and notes on political affairs
and the political scene; with details
of his life at sea; admiral.   286

COLE,Sir Henry. Fifty Years of Public Works (1884). Career in the civil
service 1823-51;in Public Records Office, Post Office, docks; work on international exhibitions, museums. 287

COLE, Margaret Isabel.   Growing Up
Into Revolution (1949).   Roedean and
Girton; her parents; her work in the
Labour Movement, teaching, and Fabian
research; WW1 and WW2; marriage; life
in London and Oxford; politics; Webbs
and Macdonald; Shaw, Wells, Pound and
Eliot; varied but disjointed.   288

COLE, Philip Tennyson. Vanity Var-
nished (1931). Early days painting in
South Africa,India, Australia; Rhodes
and Boer War;work as a portrait painter; court and society; reminiscences
of celebrities.   289

COLE,William. Life in the Niger (L.
1862). Liverpool man's experiences as
a trader; slavery; native life; business; journey up the Niger with Laird
in 1859-60.   290

COLEMAN, Charles George. On Sea and
Prairie (1901). Norwich; boy at sea;
in U.S.naval service; romance in West
Indies; desertion; ranching in California and Texas; jobless in England;
success in America; marriage and settlement near Norwich.   291

COLEMAN, Frederic. With Cavalry in
1915 (1916);From Mons to Ypres (1916)
Chauffeuring cavalry officers on Western Front; with French; WW1.   292

COLEMAN, John. Fifty Years (1904).
Actor and manager's career; reminiscences of Scottish and provincial theatres and of famous players.   293

COLERIDGE, Arthur Duke. Eton in the
Forties, by an Old Colleger (L. 1896)
Reminiscences (1921).Pleasant account
of days at Eton; Hodgson, Hawtrey etc.
games, customs,institutions; his life
at Ottery St. Mary;music and law; social life of Victorian period. 294

COLERIDGE,Bernard John Seymour, Baron. This for Remembrance (1925). His
studies at Eton and Oxford; his legal
career and trials;Lord Chief Justice;
politics and his work in the House of
Commons; memories of music and of the
stage.   295

COLERIDGE,Gilbert J. D. Eton in the
Seventies (1912); Some & Sundry(1931)
Fond memories of teachers and the life
at Eton;Oxford; Jowett; OUDS; his law
career; famous judges; drama; Arnold,
Ellen Terry, Irving, Wilde; the Lyric
Club; anecdotes.   296

COLERIDGE,Samuel Taylor. Biographia
Literaria(1817). Mainly criticism but
some personal material about his stay
in Germany and the Quantocks.   297

COLERIDGE, Sara. Memoir and Letters
(1873). Contains autobiography of her
childhood in the Lake District in letter to her daughter.   298

COLES,Charles Edward. Recollections
and Reflections (1918). His work as a
police administrator in Egypt,1873 to
1913; prison work and prison reforms;
social life and sport.   299

COLEY,Rev. James. Journal, 1845-47;
chaplain to Hardinge's forces; religious work; description of Sutlej campaign. Journal of the Sutlej Campaign
(1856).   300

COLLES,Ramsay. In Castle and Court-
house (1911).Thirty years of journal-

ism in Ireland;The Irish Figaro; Parnell,politics, theatre, writers, social life.   301

COLLEY, William. News Hunter (1936) Forty years as reporter for Mail etc. special correspondent Paris and N.Y.; Versailles and other peace conferences; personalities.   302

COLLIER, Mrs. A Bible-Woman's Story (1885).Methodist class-worker in Birmingham; drunkenness and sin; working class life;family troubles; an interesting record.   303

COLLIER, Constance. Harlequinade(L. 1929). Her childhood and her career in the theatre; the Trees.   304

COLLINGWOOD, Robin George. Autobiography (1939). Story of his study and mental life; home, Rugby, Oxford; the philosophies and philosophers of his time; applications to practical life; professor at Oxford.   305

COLLINS, Dale. Bright Vista (1946). Australian boyhood; travels in Papua, Fijis, Japan, Bali, Ireland; work as press censor WW1; his novels; Aldous Huxley.   306

COLLINS, George E. Farming and Fox Hunting (1935). Farming in Lincolnshire from 80's; round of work; sport and hunting.   307

COLLINS, Horace. My Best Riches (L. 1941).Travels around world; London in 90's;Drury Lane, the theatre, musical comedy,radio; work as publicity agent for Drury Lane.   308

COLLINS, John Churton. The Life and Memoirs (1912). Literary journalism & reviewing;teaching in Birmingham; interviews and friendship with Browning, Carlyle, Swinburne, etc.   309

COLLINS,Jose. Maid of the Mountains (1932).Career of musical comedy singer;vaudeville, revues, Ziegfield Follies; Daly's musical comedies; later Lady Robert Innes-Ker.   310

COLLINS, Michael. Michael Collins's Own Story (1923). Dictated; his part in the Irish rebellion; civil war and negotiation from 1916.   311

COLLINS,Sarah Mabel.The Alien Years (1949). Life with Viennese husband in Berlin and Vienna from 1938;Nazis and war-time Germany; effect of air-raids on German outlook.   312

COLLINS,Tom. School & Sport (1905) Bury; Cambridge; teaching,Birmingham and Newport;shooting, hunting, athletics; public and grammar school; reflections on pedagogy and games.   313

COLLINS, William E. W. Episodes of Rural Life (Edin. 1902); Leaves from an Old Country Cricketer's Diary (Ed. 1908). Village life in Scotland; people, dogs,events, characters; village cricket, players, umpires.   314

COLLINS,William John Townsend. Rugby Recollections (1948). Sports writer, South Wales Argus; work in Rugby football and work for the same; some great matches, from 70's.   315

COLLINSON, Clifford Whiteley. Life and Laughter (1926). His experiences as a trader in the Solomons;officials missionaries and natives.   316

COLLIS, Joyce. The Sparrow (Dublin, 1943). Conversion to Catholicism; her work as VAD in England in WW1; Christian Science; Maud Royden; patient in Swiss tuberculosis sanitorium; religious experiences.   317

COLLIS, Maurice S. Trials in Burma (1938). Work as a district magistrate in Burma in 30's;administration; political unrest; prison mutiny.   318

COLLIS, Robert. Silver Fleece (N.Y. 1937).Rugby; Cambridge; Yale; medical student and footballer; house physician at Johns Hopkins; return England; medical study and sports.   319

COLLISON, William. Apostle of Free Labour(1913). Work with National Free Labour Association vs. trade unions; labour movement and its leaders & his war with them; strikes, police; political propaganda.   320

COLLODON,Augustus C. Congo Jake (L. 1933); Congo Jake Returns (1934). His life at sea and in the army; pirates; slave-traders;adventures in the South Seas and South America;big-game hunting in India and Rockies.   321

COLLYER,Margaret. Life of an Artist (1935). Woman artist's career; study in Germany and Royal Academy School; country interests; uncanny experiences; life in East Africa.   322

COLMAN, George. Some Particulars of the Life (1795). Brief autobiography of the elder Colman; his theatrical & playwriting career; misfortunes with patrons; Covent Garden.   323

COLMAN,George. Random Records(1830) Life of Colman the younger;Oxford social life; London; his beginnings in the theatre; literary life and entertainments; his plays; tours, Scotland and English watering-places.   324

COLOMB, Capt. Philip Howard. Slave-Catching in the Indian Ocean (1873). Adventures of a naval officer;chasing slavers in Indian Ocean;Zanzibar; and native customs.   325

COLQUHOUN , Archibald Ross. Dan to Bersheba (1908). Life in India, Burma and Siam from 60's; administration in South Africa; Rhodes; work in Central America.   326

COLQUHOUN ,Maj. James A. S. Journal, 1878-1879; service in the Afghanistan expedition;military details. With the Kurram Field Force (1881).   327

COLSON,Percy. I Hope They Won't Mind (1930); What If They Do Mind (1936); Close of an Era (1945); Those Uneasy Years (1947). A journalist's reminiscences of events and people;music and musicians, writers, actors, the social scene in London; life in W.W.1 and the interwar years; a somewhat malicious record.   328

COLUM, Mary Gunning (Maguire) (Mrs. Padraic Colum). Life and the Dream(L. 1947). Childhood;convent school; college in Dublin; Irish literary revival;Abbey Theatre; Yeats, Joyce, Singe and other writers;politics; the Irish rebellion;American literary scene and writers; humorous; critical.   329

COMBE, Lieut. C. Journal, 1857-59; service with QVO Light Cavalry in the Indian Mutiny. G. M. Molloy,The Poona

Horse (1933).   330

COMPTON, Denis Charles Scott. Playing for England (1948). His career as a cricketer; from ground-boy at Lords to playing for Middlesex and England; games, tours, players.   331

COMPTON,Fay (Virginia C. Mackenzie) Rosemary (1926). Education; career in the theatre; musical comedies; Shakespeare;theatrical scene; anecdotes of plays and players.   332

COMPTON-RICKETT,Arthur. I Look Back (1933). Cambridge; career as journalist, novelist, lecturer; Fleet Street and politics;theatre; literature; and his psychic experiences.   333

COMYN, David Charles Edward ffrench Service and Sport in the Sudan (1911) With the Camel Corps; administration; policing; pioneer life; racial difficulties; hunting.   334

COMYNS-CARR,Mrs. Joseph (Alice Vansittart).Reminiscences (1926). Childhood in Italy;stage designing;costuming; theatre; eminent actors and writers; social, theatrical and literary life in London under Victoria.   335

COMYNS-CARR, Joseph William. Some Eminent Victorians(1908). His work in literary journalism and at bar;criticism of art; reminiscences of Victorian painters, poets, actors.   336

ANON. Confessions of a Convert from Baptism in Water (1845). Early doubts and argument about complete immersion and adoption of paedo-baptism.   337

ANON. Confessions of a Dancing Girl (1913). London life; poverty; apprentice to acrobat;continental tours and change to dancing;travels, misfortune and recovery.   338

ANON. Confessions of a Medium(1882) Experiences in spiritualism; development as medium; fellow-practitioners; exposé of frauds.   339

ANON. Confessions of a Too Generous Young Lady(1859). Disingenuous girl's marriage to spendthrift; ruin, family estrangement; later bereavement & her remorse in old age;"Esther Lawne"; it may be fiction.   340

ANON. Confessions of a West End Us-urer (1875). Birth; Jewish life; talent for money-making; details of his dealings;vindication of usury; Israel Macgregor; burlesque?   341

ANON. Confessions of a Woman (1893) "Mrs. Ashton Harcourt"; passion, art and love; marriage and misery; escape to Paris and devotion to painting;her emotional upsets; fiction?   342

ANON.Confessions of an English Doctor(1904). His medical career; condition of profession; criticisms; needed reforms.   343

ANON.Confessions of an English Hachish-Eater (1884). Experiences of drug addict; growth of habit;reactions and fantasies.   344

ANON. Confessions of an Unbeliever (1932). Protestant background; drifts away from religion; philosophy; need for Humanitarian Duty.   345

ANON. Confessions of an Unexecuted Femicide (Preston, 1828). Early life in Stirling; moral depravity; murder of fiancée;trial and acquittal; posthumous confession.   346

CONNELL,J. Confessions of a Poacher (1901). Sporting life,poaching, country life in late 19th Century; fragmentary; disguised names.   347

CONNER,Rearden. Plain Tale from the Bogs(1937). Dublin childhood; nationalism in Ireland; IRA, Collins and De Valera; rioting; life in England as a landscape and jobbing gardener.   348

CONNOLLY, Jane.   Old Days and Ways (1912). Life and politics in Ireland; West Meath;rebellion of 1898;with her father, a naval chaplain, in Woolwich; Irish folk-lore.   349

CONOLLY, Arthur.   Diary, 1841-42; a soldier's experiences in Afghanistan; imprisonment at Bokhara; later executed. MS(copy), Chelsea P.L., and B.M. Add. 37232, 38725.   350

CONQUEST, Joan. Strange Beds (1937) Childhood; novelist's travels and ad-

ventures in Europe, Asia, Africa & No. and S. America; thrills.   351

CONRAD, Joseph.   Mirror of the Sea (1906);Some Reminiscences (1912). The novelist's reminiscences of his life in Poland; how he joined English merchant service and experiences at sea; his artistic compulsions,his universe and his writing; odd people and good stories, but reticent.   352

CONRAN, Major Henry Mascall. Autobiography (1870).Early religious life and military career in India, 1832 to 1855; missionary work in India; Hindu religion and customs.   353

CONRAN, John.   Journal of the Life (Philadelphia,1877). A Quaker's religious life, ministry, travels; mainly in County Down; 18th Century.   354

CONSTANDUROS,Mabel. Shreds and Patches (1947). Monologuist's career and success in musichalls and radio; domestic comedy;her experiences with the BBC at Savoy Hill, etc.   355

CONSTANTINE, Learie N.   Cricket & I (1933); Cricket in the Sun (L. 1946); Cricketer's Carnival (1948); Cricket Crackers (1949). Career of the great West Indian all-rounder;Trinidad,West Indies,Lancashire League, Test games; games, players, anecdotes.   356

ANON. Consule Planco (1909). Pleasant reminiscences of schooldays; Eton in mid-19th Century.   357

CONWAY, James (J.C. Walter). Recollections of Sport(1902).Fishing, deer and otter hunting & shooting in North of England, Scotland, Ceylon.   358

CONWAY OF ALLINGTON, William Martin Conway, Baron.   Episodes in a Varied Life (1932); A Pilgrim's Quest (1936) Education, Repton and Cambridge; his sporting life; mountaineering, winter sports,Alpine exploration; collecting and art history;philosophy; spiritual life;man and nature; and his questing for God.   359

CONYBEARE, Crawford J.M. Naval Reminiscences (1930). His naval career; 1868-91; voyages; Soudan campaign; on Arctic expeditions; admiral.   360

CONYBEARE, William Daniel. Letters
and Exercises (1905). Contains autobiographical fragment;Westminster and
Oxford;reading; literary and antiquarian interests;pleasant nostalgia for
his youth.   361

CONYERS, Dorothea. Sporting Reminiscences (1920). Childhood and family
life in County Clare; Irish peasants;
foxhunting in Ireland.   362

CONYERS-KEYNES, Stephen. White Man
in Thailand(1951). Uninspired reminiscences of the life and work of businessman in Siam.   363

COOK, Sir Albert Ruskin. Uganda Memories (Kampala, 1945). His 45 years
in Uganda;work as medical missionary;
tropical diseases; hospitals; native
life; Sudanese War and WW1; sport and
social life.   364

COOK, Ann. Ann Cook and Friend, ed.
R. Burnet (1936); reprinted from latter part of her "Professed Cookery."
Narrative of her experiences as a cook
and housekeeper on country estate; an
amusing record of 18th Century.   365

COOK, Sir Theodore Andrea. Sunlit
Hours (1925); Sweet Hours (1925). His
schooldays; country life, sport, nat-
ural history; work in journalism; St.
James Gazette, Telegraph; ed. of The
Field; travels in England & USA.   366

COOKE, Bella. Rifted Clouds (1886).
Autobiography and diary of a Yorkshire
Methodist; marriage and family; mis-
fortunes in business; emigration, New
York in 1847; hard times and afflic-
tions; religious work.   367

COOKE, Charles W. R. Four Years in
Parliament (1890). Work and observation of a conservative member; a back
bencher's criticisms; essays.   368

COOKE, Edward Douglas Montague Hunter. With the Guns, by Arnewood (Plymouth, 1923); Clouds that Flee (1935)
His experiences with the artillery in
France and Palestine, WW1; education,
Eton; London social life in the 90's;
army career in artillery;Egypt, India
and WW1; Germany after the war; sport
and social life; WW1 service in France
and Palestine; capture Jerusalem. 369

COOKE,Capt. Sir John Henry. Memoirs
of the Late War(1831); A Narrative of
Events(1835). Service with Wellington
in Peninsular War; mostly historical;
and in war of 1812; battle of New Orleans.   370

COOKE,Sophia Sutton. Memoirs (1829)
Moral wanderings; Jamaican married in
London to young officer;ups and downs
à la Becky Sharp; picaresque and entertaining. Copy in William Salt Library, Stafford.   371

COOMBES,Bert Lewis.These Poor Hands
(L.1939); Those Clouded Hills (1944);
Miner's Day (1945). Life and observations while coalminer in South Wales;
effects of WW1 and the depression;un-
employment, strikes and 1926 stoppage;
condition of mines and miners and the
improvements in mining methods.   372

COOMBS, J. Recollections (Bedford,
1889). Medical studies in 30's, practice in Bedford; county social life &
sport; local politics; work as alderman of Bedford. Copy, Bedford County
Library, Bedford.   373

COOPE,Col. William Jesser. Prisoner
of War (1878). His service as mercen-
ary in Imperial Ottoman Gendarmerie;
imprisonment in Russia.   374

COOPER,Adolphe R. The Man Who Liked
Hell (1933). Twelve years as sergeant
in French Foreign Legion;service WW1;
hard living and fighting in Africa and
Dardanelles.   374A

COOPER,Arthur Nevile.Round the Home
of a Yorkshire Parson (1904).His pastorates;anecdotes; rambles; Yorkshire
life.   375

COOPER, Charles Alfred. An Editor's
Retrospect (1896). His fifty years as
a journalist;Scottish affairs; editor
of The Scotsman;politics, Reform, and
Home Rule; publishing; celebrities; &
Thackeray.   376

COOPER, Charles W. Town and Country
(1937). Footman's forty years service
with aristocracy; Kensington Palace,
royal yacht, German Embassy; Princess
Louise and other royalty.   377

COOPER, Ernest Read. "Nineteen Hundred and War Time,". Town clerk, harbour manager; Southwold; major in the Suffolk Volunteers; home defence WW1. MS, Imperial War Museum.   378

COOPER, George Henry. Fifty Years' Journalistic Experiences (Cleckheaton 1938). Homely reminiscences of reporter in industrial and factory circles; West Riding; social; political.   379

COOPER,Gladys. Gladys Cooper (1931) Her career as an actress;roles, writers, actors; society life & fashions; anecdotes.   380

COOPER, Herbert Noel. Fifteen Years a Store Detective (1940). His work as detective in big department stores and experiences with shoplifters, staff & managers; visit to USA.   381

COOPER, Sergt. John Spencer. Rough Notes of Seven Campaigns (1869; Carlisle 1914). Service with Royal Fusiliers in Peninsular War and the War of 1812.   382

COOPER, Margaret. Myself and My Piano (1909). Life and work of popular musician and singer; concerts in London; Palace Theatre, etc.   383

COOPER, Thomas. Life (1872). Shoemaker, schoolmaster, Methodist, lecturer, journalist & Chartist; working-class life;his activities in Chartist movement; journalism in Leicester; an important record.   384

COOPER,Thomas Sidney. My Life(1890) Early days in Canterbury; his work as coachbuilder;theatrical scene painter at Canterbury; study at Royal Academy and in Brussels.;career as a painter; exhibitions;clubs; literary, social & artistic life; anecdotes.   385

COOPLAND,R. M. A Lady's Escape from Gwalior (1859). Life of the widow of an army chaplain in India, 1856-58; & her experiences at Agra during Mutiny; escape.   386

COOTE, Howard. While I Remember (L. 1937). Family life in Cambridgeshire and South coast resorts;nonconformity and middle class life; Rugby; farming in Fen country; business at St. Ives; Lord Lieut. Hunts; Liberalism.   387

COPE, Charles West. Reminiscences, by C. H. Cope (1891). Autobiography, 1811-82; art study in Italy; painting sitters, society life in London; Victorian painters; art in USA.   388

COPE, Joan Penelope. Bramshill (L. 1938).Twelve year old's life in village in N.Hants.;mummers' play; and her views on adult world; pleasant.   389

COPE,Richard. Autobiography (1857). Religious life and work as minister in Cornish parishes; travel USA.   390

COPE,William. A Faithful and Particular Account (Birmingham, 1830). The conversion and religious life of Methodist. Birmingham P. L.   391

COPEMAN, Fred. Reason in Revolt (L. 1948). Childhood poverty; orphanage; left-wing political activities;Invergordon Mutiny; unemployment in London in 30's; Spanish Civil War; renunciation of Communist Party and conversion to Catholicism; interesting.   392

CORAGGIOSO,Cagliardo.Wandering Minstrel (1938). Italian boyhood;begging musician in England; adopted by Yorkshire fishmongers; success as restaurant keeper;bankruptcy; business success in Edinburgh.   393

CORBALLIS, James Henry. Forty-Five Years (1891). Sporting life and anecdotes; riding, shooting, deerstalking falconry, fishing, etc.   394

CORBETT, Clare. Happy Hunting Days (1931). Childhood and youth pre-WW1; farming and social in Wilts; fox and stag hunting.   395

CORBETT, Sir Vincent Edwin. Reminiscences(1927). Diplomatic career from 1884; Berlin, Hague, Rome, Turkey and Greece; public affairs and diplomatic commentary; courts; social.   396

CORCORAN, Capt. Austin P. The Daredevil of the Army (N.Y. 1919). Experiences WW1;"buzzer", motor cycle despatch rider, wireless operator.   397

COREY, Winifred (Graham). That Reminds Me (1945); Observations (1947); I Introduce (1948). Discursive reminiscences of a grande raconteuse; her

social life; literary career; friends
travels; anti-Mormon campaign; notes
on celebrities; anecdotes.　　　398

CORFIELD,Mary Hay. Some Memories of
a Scotswoman (1934). Old shipping family in Glasgow;shipping and yachting
before WW1; social life.　　　399

CORK, Richard Boyle, first Earl of.
The Lismore Papers, ed. A. B. Grosart
(1886-88).Chronicle of public affairs
family matters,business of estates in
Ireland, social matters; partly diary
and correspondence.　　　400

CORK AND ORRERY, William Henry Dudley Boyle, Earl of. My Naval Life (L.
1942). Naval career of admiral, from
the 80's;naval history; activities in
WW1.　　　401

CORKRAN, Henriette. Celebrities and
I (1902); Oddities (1904). Literary,
artistic, political life in England &
France,1850-1900; Thackeray, Disraeli
Samuel Butler,Millais, Whiteing etc.;
gossip, anecdotes.　　　402

CORNFORD, Philip Henry. Missionary
Reminiscences (1856).A Baptist's mission work in Jamaica in 40's; slavery
and emancipation.　　　403

CORNISH, George W.　Cornish of the
Yard (1935). Police work from 1895; a
superintendent at Scotland Yard; famous crimes in London.　　　404

CORNISH,James George. Reminiscences
of Country Life (1939).Vicarage youth;
tutor; his own parishes in Berks and
retirement to Devon; pleasant memories
of village life.　　　405

CORNWALLIS,Kinahan. My Life and Adventures (1860). Picaresque adventure
of Irish lawyer's son in some remoter
parts of world; medicine, lions, love
affairs; fiction?　　　406

CORNWALLIS-WEST,George F. M. Edwardian Hey-Days (1930);Edwardians　Go
Fishing (1932). Military service Boer
War and WW1; social life, sports, especially trout and salmon fishing;so-
ciety.　　　407

CORRI,Eugene. Thirty Years a Boxing
Referee (1915);Refereeing 1000 Fights

(1919); Fifty Years (1933). His life
as boxing referee; reminiscences boxing and fights in London.　　　408

CORRIE,Right Rev. Daniel. Religious
diary,1804-36; missionary work in India; Cawnpore, Calcutta, Madras; diocesan work and administration as Bishop of Madras. Memoirs (1847).　　409

CORRIGAN,Andrew J. A Printer (1944)
His life and craft in Dublin;printing
and its development;work at the Cuala
Press; Irish literary world.　　410

COSBY,Lt. Col. Henry A. M. Military
journal, 1767-78; military service in
East India Company's forces;campaigns
in the Carnatic;Pondicherry; a rather
impersonal record. MS.British Museum,
Add. 29898.　　　411

COSBY,Pole. Autobiography, 1703-37,
of Irish country life,family affairs,
visits to England.Journal Co. Kildare
Archaeol. Soc. V (1906-8).　　412

COSTELLO, Edward. Adventures (1841)
With Rifle Brigade in Peninsular War;
civil Wars in Spain; humorous account
of Irish soldier's life to 1836.　413

COSTER,George Thomas.Points from My
Journal (1908). Ministry and travels
of a congregationalist clergyman from
1859.　　　414

COSTIGAN, Arthur William.　Sketches
of Society and Manners (1787). Series
of letters relating to military service for Spain, 1778-87; observations
on Portuguese scene and society.　415

COTES, Peter.　No Star Nonsense (L.
1949). His experiences as actor, manager,producer; the group principle in
acting; detailed account of his productions and survey of the modern theatre.　　　416

COTTON,Rt. Rev. George Edward Lynch
Religious diaries,1858-66; educational, administrative and religious work
as Bishop of Calcutta; social life; &
his earlier years in education;teach-
ing at Rugby and Marlborough; Arnold.
Memoir (1871)　　　417

COTTON, Sir Henry.　Indian and Home
Memories(1911). His thirty-five years

in the Indian Civil Service; politics and administration;   some social life and sport.   418

COTTON, Sir Sydney John. Nine Years on the North-West Frontier (L. 1868). Military service, administration, and sport; the Mutiny.   419

COTTON, William. Certain Reminiscences. Anecdotes of artists and writers, national events, theatre, social happenings, first half 19th Century. MS, owned by G. Hamilton-Edwards, 3 Nelson Gardens, Stoke, Plymouth.   420

COULTON, George Gordon. Fourscore Years (Cambridge, 1943). Boyhood Lynn; Felstead school; Cambridge; schoolteaching; professor of history Cambridge; scholarship and study; colleagues and students; his historical writings; the mellow record of one of the last Eminent Victorians.   421

COUNSEL, Dr. Herbert E. 37 The Broad (1943). London; Guy's Hospital; practice in Oxford from 1897; Jowett and other celebrities; student life; the OUDS: European travels.   422

A COUNTRY VICAR.   Cricket Memories (1930); Second Innings (1933). Boyhood and village cricket; Lord's; county, varsity, and Test cricket; reprinted from The Cricketer; by Randolph Hodgson & J. N. S. Sewell.   423

COURNOS, John. Autobiography (1935) Novelist's childhood in Russia; emigration to USA; career as novelist and writer in London from 1912.   424

COURTENAY, Arthur. Autobiography and Letters (1834). Diplomatic and social life in India; sentimental affairs; it may be fiction.   425

COURTENAY, William.   Airman Friday (1937). Bellhop on liners; WW1 service as a flyer in Egypt and near East; civilian pilot; developments in civil aviation; lecturing; journalism. 426

COURTHOPE, Sir George. Memoirs 1616-1685; travels in Italy, France, Turkey and public work; anti-catholic; financial officer during Commonwealth; Parliament; Restoration. Camden Soc.Misc. XI (1907) 103-157.   427

COURTLAND, Arthur C. Stray Notes of a Wayfarer (1904). Items from his social life, friendships, social work & domestic life.   428

COURTNEIDGE, Robert. I Was an Actor Once (1930). Career as actor and manager; London theatre, actors, theatrical life; anecdotes.   429

COURTNEY, Janet Elizabeth. Recollected in Tranquillity (1926). Childhood in country; clerical life in Lincoln and Oxford from 70's; work as clerk, teacher, journalist; WW1.   430

COURTNEY, Roger. The Claws of Africa (1934). His varied jobs in Central Africa; store-clerk, ranger on a timber concession, professional hunter, and guide; anecdotes.   431

COURTNEY, William Leonard. Passing Hour (1925). Bath; Oxford; work as a London journalist; literature and the theatre in London.   432

COUSINS, Dennis Lewis. Extracts from the Diary (1847). Workhouse chaplain in 40's; case histories; religious and social conditions; repentances. 433

COUSTOS, John. The Sufferings (1746) Freemason's experiences with Inquisition at Lisbon; imprisonment; torture and four years in galleys; release by intercession of George II.   434

COWAN, Charles. Reminiscences (Edin. 1878). Social life, politics, travel; Reform Bill, Corn laws; Switzerland; USA.   435

COWAN, Gibson. Loud Report (L. 1938) Working-class life & poverty, London; his odd jobs and work as a showman and in the theatre.   436

COWAN, John James. From 1846 to 1932 (Edin. 1933). Edinburgh; St. Andrew's; Scottish residence and world-wide travels; books, art, theatre, pastimes, Oxford Group; WW1.   437

COWAN, Samuel. Humorous Episodes in the Life (Birmingham, 1913). His work in Inland Revenue and newspaper office newspaper editor in Scotland; Liberal agent in Perth; printing, journalism, politics, Scottish affairs.   438

COWARD, Sir Henry. Reminiscences(L. 1919). Self-help;apprentice and workman in cutlery factory; amateur music and teaching in Sheffield; career as choral conductor;editor. MS Sheffield City Libraries. 439

COWARD,Noel. Present Indicative (L. 1937). Childhood in theatre and difficulties with education; poverty and fortunes as actor and playwright; reminiscences of theatrical world and of famous players; frank. 440

COWELL, Elizabeth B. Leaves of Memory (1892). Girlhood in Ossington;her travels in France, Italy, India; meditations; love of nature; partly done in verse. 441

COWELL, George. Memorials of a Gracious Life, by Ruth Cowell (1895). It includes diaries of religious life of lay preacher and writer, mid 19 C.442

COWELL, Henry J. These Forty Years (1940); Seventy Years' Pilgrimage (L. 1941). Religious life and work; Baptist Free Church; sub-editor, Baptist Times;Free Church activities; WW1 and politics; historical value. 443

COWELL, Joseph. Thirty Years (1844) Comedian's career in English and American theatre;London, provinces, Philadelphia; anecdotes of actors. 444

COWEN, Sir Frederic Hyman. My Art and My Friends (1913). Musical career from 1856; studies, England and Germany;composer and opera conductor; the London Philharmonic; anecdotes. 445

COWLES, E. Sand-Hills and Mountains (1932).Work as a school inspector and customs official in the Bahamas and in Zanzibar. 446

COWPER,William. Memoirs of the Early Life (1816). The poet's schooldays in Bedfordshire; religious experiences;influence of Herbert's poems; and early fear of madness. 447

COWTAN,Robert.Memories of the British Museum (1872). Employment in Museum library from 1835; happenings and changes there; Ellis, Panizzi & other librarians. 448

/COWTAN,Robert/. Autobiography of a "Man of Kent" (1866). His social life in Canterbury in the twenties;Kentish life and people;religion; his work in London. 449

COX, Alfred. Among the Doctors (L. 1950). Boyhood in the North Country; education; medical training; successful career; work as secretary of the BMA: medical celebrities. 450

COX, Sir Edmund Charles. My Thirty Years in India (1909). His work as a tea-planter and in the educational and police service; adventures; sport and social life. 451

COX,George Valentine. Recollections of Oxford (1868). Don's record of Oxford life and personalities from 1789 to 1860; dons, preachers, Tractarians and movements. 452

COX,Maj. Harding Edward de Fonblanque.Chasing and Racing(1922); Sportsman at Large (1922); Dogs and I(1923) His unacademic boyhood;sporting life, fox-hunting, steeple-chasing, riding; jockeys, characters, dogs. 453

COX, Henry Boys. Memoir (1851). Religious life and ministry of Wesleyan Methodist; diary extracts 1849. 454

COX, Capt. Hiram, Military journal, 1796-97; service with the East India Company's forces at Amarapoorah; Burmese court life; Burmese customs; and life at Rangoon. Journal of a Residence in the Burmahn Empire (1821).455

/COX, John Edmund/. Musical Recollections of the Last Half Century (L. 1872). Critical reminiscences of London musical life; composers & orchestras; mainly opera, concerts and virtuosi; rather impersonal. 456

COX,Sir Richard. Autobiography, ed. R.Caulfield (1860). Family life Cork; law study, Gray's Inn; government and legal work in Ireland; ascent to Lord Chancellorship of Ireland;a brief and bald record; 17-18 C. 457

COXERE, Edward. Adventures by Sea (Oxford,1945). Delightful autobiography of life and adventure of a seaman and Quaker in 17th Century; conversion and troubles; good language.   458

COXON, Stanley Williams. And That Reminds Me (1915); Dover during the Dark Days (1919). Commander's memories of a life at sea; with marines and police in Andamans, India, Burma, Australia; and with destroyers and Dover Patrol during WW1.   459

COXWELL, Henry Tracey. My Life and Balloon Experiences (1887-89). Trials experiments and adventures; work for government; shows; ascents in 60's and 70's.   460

COZENS, Charles. Adventures (1848). Black sheep; school; Cambridge; joins Horse Guards; transportation; convict life in New South Wales; work there as policeman and tax collector; return to Wales in 1846.   461

CRADOCK, Joseph. Literary and Miscellaneous Memoirs (1828). Memories of antiquarian and eccentric; theatres & literature; antiquities; his eminent friends; travel; country life.   462

CRAIG, C. W. Thurlow. A Rebel for a Horse (1934). Life at São Paolo; his experiences as a rebel horseman during the Chaco War; 1932 revolution.   463

CRAIG, Edith. Edy, edited by Eleanor Adlard (1949). Her career in theatre; work and productions of Pioneer Players 1911-21; intellectual drama; anecdotes character sketches; family life.   464

CRAIG, George Alexander. From Parish School to University (Birmingham 1899) Scottish life, education, culture and social life in 50's; physician; rather impersonal.   465

CRAIGMYLE, Thomas Shaw, Baron. The Other Bundle (1937). Education in the 50's; influences on him; legal study; his career as a lawyer in Scotland; & politics and social life.   466

CRAIK, Henry. Passages from the Diary (1866). Student at St. Andrew's, Edinburgh; tutor in Exeter; reading; spiritual life; Baptist pastor; his Hebrew studies and writing.   467

CRAN, Marion. Story of My Ruin (1924)

Her homes and gardens in Kent and Surrey; people; horticulture.   468

CRANE, Charles Paston. Memories of a Resident Magistrate (Edin. 1938). A Yorkshire boyhood; Irish magistrate, 1880-1920; Killarney, Sligo and Kerry; Irish life and politics; service Boer War.   469

CRANE, Walter. An Artist's Reminiscences (1907). Apprenticeship; painting and stage designing; pre-Raphaelites; social work and socialism; travels in Italy and Europe.   470

CRANWORTH, Bertram Francis Gurdon, 2nd Baron. Kenya Chronicles (1939). His life in Kenya and East Africa from 1910 to 1939; politics, war, sport and social life.   471

CRAUFORD, Russell. Ramblings of an Old Mummer (1909). Actor's experience in stock companies and in supporting roles; tours in Europe, USA, Empire; anecdotes of old days.   472

CRAVEN, Lady Elizabeth (Margravine of Anspach). Autobiographical Memoirs (1826). Lively reminiscences and anecdotes of family, court, social, political life in England, Europe and Turkey.   473

CRAWFORD, Capt. Abraham. Reminiscences of a Naval Officer (1851). Irish childhood; naval career as boy and officer during Peninsular War, 1800-15; anecdotes of officers, etc.   474

CRAWFORD, Allan B. I Went to Tristan (1941). His adventures during a scientific expedition; life and ways of the islanders.   475

CRAWFORD, Archibald. Guilty as Libelled! (1938). Career as criminal lawyer; work in Scottish courts; criminal psychology.   476

/CRAWFORD, Arthur Travers/. Reminiscences of an Indian Police Official, by T.C. Arthur (1894). Police work in India from 1850; Bombay; crime, thugs dacoits; Mutiny; famines; social life and anecdotes.   477

CRAWFORD, Daniel. Thinking Black (L. 1912). His life and missionary work in

Africa,1889-1911; long grass country; native life and the religious challenge.His diary for the same period is printed in G. E. Tilsley's Dan Crawford (1929).   478

CRAWFORD, E. May. By the Equator's Snowy Peak (1913). Medical missionary work with her husband in Uganda, from 1904; native life; travels.   479

CRAWFORD, James H. Autobiography of a Tramp (1900). Experiences with his parents; tramp from boyhood; people & places; travel; adventures.   480

CRAWFORD, John Dawson. Reflections and Recollections(1936). Ireland; the career and cases of lawyer and judge; Liverpool; Northern circuit in 80's; county court work;Workmen's Compensation; Rent Restriction Acts.   481

CRAWFORD, Robert John. I Was an 8th Army Soldier(1944). Dictated autobiography of driver's experiences in WW2; with Montgomery in Africa; a grim and humorous narrative.   482

CRAWFURD, John. Brief Narrative of an Embassy (1828); Journal of an Embassy(1829). Resident at the Javanese court;services on embassy from Governor of India to Siam and Cochin-China and later to Court of Ava.   483

CRAWSHAY-WILLIAMS,Eliot.Leaves from an Officer's Notebook (1918); Simple Story (1935). Experiences WW1; France and Sinai campaign;M.P. Leicester and political life; marriage; his novels; writing for theatre and films.   484

CREAGH, Sir Garrett O'Moore. Autobiography (1924). Army career, mostly in India; 1866-1916; Afghan war; India Office; commander-in-chief in India.   485

CREEVEY, Thomas. The Creevey Papers ed. Sir H. Maxwell (1904); Creevey's Life and Times, ed. John Gore (1934). Reminiscences of political life, high society and court;Prince Regent, Wellington; spicy gossip; the early 19th century.   486

CREICHTON,Capt.John. Memoirs (1731) Military service and adventures; the Old Pretender; Jacobites and Scottish

affairs; "digested" by Swift.   487

CREIGHTON, Oswin. With the Twenty-Ninth Division (1916). Chaplain's experiences at Gallipoli, WW1.   488

CREMER, John. Ramblin' Jack (1936). Amusing account of life in navy and in merchant ships 1708-30;excellent detail of ordinary sailor's life;humor and pathos; interesting language. 489

/CRESSWELL, Mrs. Gerard/. Eighteen Years on a Sandringham Estate, by The Lady Farmer(1888). Farming in Norfolk with husband and alone;Royal landlord and society; work; difficulties with huntsmen; independent and vigorous account of work and views. Copy,Norwich P.L.   490

CRESSWELL,Walter D'Arcy. The Poet's Progress (1930). New Zealand; service in WW1; difficulties in England; door to door selling of poetry; critical & literary views; unusual.   491

CRESTON, Dormer (Dorothy J. Baynes) Enter a Child(1939). Childhood London and Wiltshire; delighted account of a golden childhood;country house life in distinguished company.   492

CRESWICK, William. An Autobiography (1886). Theatrical career 1835-85; in London and provinces; Australian tour anecdotes of famous actors.   493

CRICHTON, Kate. Six Years in Italy (1861). Social life and travel in the 50's; music, politics, religion, social; the scene and people.   494

/CRICHTON, Miss Makgill/. Recollections of My Early Scottish Home(Edin. 1876). Early life and hardships, village friends; a trip to St. Andrew's; early 19th Century. Cambridge University Library.   495

CRICHTON-BROWNE, Sir James. Victorian Jottings(1926); The Doctor's Second Thoughts (L. 1931); The Doctor's After Thoughts (1932); The Doctor Remembers (1938). A famous physician's career and reminiscences; student in Edinburgh; work in Yorkshire, London; memories of doctors and medicine, and celebrities in science and the arts; Hardy, Lytton, Bret Harte, Gladstone,

Huxley, Browning, etc.　　　　496

CRICK,Throne. Sketches from the Diary (1847); Reminiscences of the Road (1848).Travels and events in the life of a commercial traveller; hotels and travel conditions; people.　　　497

CRISP, Dorothy. A Life for England (1946). Incidents in life of a publicist and publisher; her struggles to revive Conservative Party.　　　498

CRISP,Margaret. Utility Nurse(1947) Volunteer Red Cross Nurse 1942-45;her work, comrades, friends; the hospital system; air raids.　　　499

CRISP, Stephen. A Memorable Account (1694);Short History of a Long Travel (1765). Spiritual autobiography of an early Quaker;ministry, sufferings and controversy; inner light.　　　500

CRISPE,Thomas Edward. Reminiscences (1910). Childhood; legal training and career; King's Counsel; judges, lawyers and trials; theatre and Bohemian life in London.　　　501

CRISTY, Theodore. Horse and Hounds (1937); My Ups and Downs (1931). The sporting life of an amateur jockey and master of staghounds.　　　502

CRITTALL,Francis Henry. Fifty Years (1934). Nonconformist; schooling; his work as plumber and window-maker;success story; social experiments in his business;munitions work WW1; a simple account of business life.　　　503

CROAL, David. Early Recollections (Edin.1898). Journalist's experiences in Edinburgh and Glasgow 1832-59; his work as reporter;editors and journalists; local life; Crimean War.　　　504

CROFT, Gen. Henry Page Croft, Baron Twenty-Two Months (1917); My Life of Strife(1948). Member of Parliament in Territorials WW1; Western Front; the Somme; political career in Commons; & Under-Secretary of State for War,WW2; public affairs.　　　505

CROFT-COOKE, Rupert. World is Young (1937); The Circus Has No Home (1941) Youth in Buenos Aires; teaching English; Argentinian life; experiences in

small Rosaire circus touring in British Isles.　　　506

CROFTS,Charley. Memoirs (Cork 1829) Autobiography of a Paddy;army life in Ireland; rake, humorist, good fellow; his troubles; amusing tales.　　　507

/CROKE, Charles/. Fortune's Uncertainty, by Rodolphus(1667). Wild oats of a young Oxford scholar; picaresque adventures, England, Virginia, Portugal; escapades and loves.　　　508

CROKER, John. "Brief Memoir," The Friends' Library, XIV (Philadelphia, 1850). Short account of life and ministry of a Plymouth Quaker; religious life & travel, England, America. 509

CROLL,James.Autobiographical Sketch (1896).Stonemason's son; Scottish education;village life; odd jobs; reading and study; geological work; civil service in Edinburgh; science.　　510

CROMAR, John. Jock of the Islands (1935). Voyages and adventures of a trader and labour recruiter in Solomons.　　　511

CROMER, Ruby F. M. Baring, Countess of. Such Were These Years (1939). Her life and travels with her husband; in Palestine, India, Canada; society and politics in England while her husband was Lord Chamberlain.　　　512

CROMPTON, Col. Rookes E. B. Reminiscences (1928). Army career in India, Boer War, WW1; transport; work as electrical engineer, Italy, Balkans and Sweden; celebrities.　　　513

CROOK, David Moore. Spitfire Pilot (1942).Training as flyer; experiences in Battle of Britain.　　　514

CROOK, John. A Short History of the Life (1706). A Hertford man's life as a Quaker in 17th Century; religion; & his sufferings in ministry.　　　515

CROPTON,John. Road to Nowhere(1936) Boyhood romance and dreams;soldiering in WW1; Gallipoli; post-war failures and disillusionment.　　　516

CROSLAND, Mrs. Newton　(Camilla). Landmarks of a Literary Life (L.1893)

Social and literary affairs from 1820; public events; spiritualist and writer figures in literature and arts of Victorian period;Brownings, Hawthorne etc.   517

CROSLAND,. Newton. Rambles Round My Life (1898). America, Montreal; youth on Wilts farm;clerk in London; literature, philosophy, spiritualism; marriage and social life;views on Darwin art, astrology, spiritualism; travels in France; celebrities.   518

CROSS, George. Suffolk Punch (1939) Suffolk family; his successful career in business, commencing as a butcher; real estate; his creed.   519

CROSS, John Keir. Aspect of Life(L. 1937). Lanarkshire; a clerk in Perth; actor, atheist,ventriloquist; attempted suicide; travels and adventures; Eastern religion and the evolution of his creed.   520

CROSS, Thomas. Autobiography of a Stage Coachman (1861, 1904). His work as coachman, London and South; social scene, customs, travel conditions and his passengers.   521

CROSS, William. Diary, 1832-1839; Wesleyan Methodist's missionary work; Friendly Islands and Fijis;conversion and backslidings of natives. Rev.John Hunt, Memoir of..(1846).   522

CROTCH, William. Memoirs of a Norfolk musician,early 19th Century. MS, Norwich Public Library.   523

CROUCH, Archer Philip. Diary, 1886; experiences with laying a cable; West coast of Africa; traders and natives. On a Surfbound Coast (1887).   524

/CROUCH, Emma Elizabeth7.   Memoirs of Cora Pearl (1886). Plymouth girl's adventures and profligacy in France; courtesan's scandals; translated from French.   525

CROUCH,William. Posthuma Christiana (1712):Friends' Library,XI (Philadelphia, 1847).Experiences in early days of Quaker movement during Restoration; Quakers and their sufferings.   526

CROW, Capt. Hugh. Memoirs (1830). A slave-trader's voyages and adventures; imprisonment in France;slave trade in Africa and West Indies;an interesting apologia.   527

CROWE, Sir Joseph Archer. Reminiscences (1895).Journalist's experiences 1830-65; Daily News; Times; war correspondent; Crimea, Indian Mutiny and Germany.   528

CROWLEY,Aleister (Edward Alexander) The Spirit of Solitude (1930). Childhood among Plymouth Brethren; schools and Cambridge;sport; climbing; marriage; his writing; experience in magic and spiritualism.   529

CROWLEY, Ann.   Some Account of the Religious Experience (Lindfield 1842) Friends' Library, VII (1843). Quaker spiritual life and ministry, Southern counties, from 1791; Gurneys.   530

CROWTHER, Samuel; and TAYLOR, John Christopher. Diary, 1857-59; 1862-63; missionary travels; Niger expedition of Church Missionary Society; native life and customs. Gospel on the Banks of the Niger (1859-63).   531

CROXTON, Arthur. Crowded Nights (L. 1934). Lancashire; journalism in Manchester and London; weeklies; advertising; publicist for Stoll's theatres and musichalls.   532

CROZIER,Frank Percy. A Brass Hat (1930);Impressions (1930); Five Years Hard(1932); Angels on Horseback(1932) Men I Killed (1937). Military career and experiences;Boer War; WW1; Lithuania, Ireland; warfare, organization, politics, later pacifism.   533

CROZIER,John Beattie. My Inner Life (1898). Personal autobiography of his spiritual evolution;reading of Darwin Spencer, etc.; Canadian.   534

CRUDEN, Alexander. The Adventures of (1754).Experiences of an 18th Century religious fanatic & Biblical student; sufferings in lunatic asylum.   535

CRUICKSHANK, Brodie. Eighteen Years (1853).His administrative work on the Gold Coast; culture of Ashanti tribes and government relations; Legislative Council.   536

CRUTCHLEY,Com. W. Caius. My Life at Sea (L.1912). Transition from sail to steam; service in mercantile marine; Secretary of Navy League.   537

CRUTCHLOW, William. Tale of an Old Soldier (1937). Cabin boy; soldiering in WW1,India, France, Middle East; in merchant navy and army after war; odd jobs.   538

CUDDEFORD, D.W.J. And All for What? (1933).Rough and ready account of his service in Scots regiments; France in WW1; with native troops in Africa.539

CULLING, Eve H. V. S. Arms and the Woman (1932). Canteen worker in WW1, with French army; director of canteen at Revigny; French troops.   540

CUMBERLAND, Gerald (Charles F. Kenyon). Set Down in Malice(1918); Written in Friendship (1923). Manchester journalist; music, theatre; reminiscences of writers, artists, performers Bennett, Barry Pain, etc.   541

CUMBERLAND, Richard. Memoirs (1806) His career in the theatre; playwriting;literary society; actors and writers; Johnson; travel and adventures, health, patrons.   542

/CUMBERLAND,Robert Bakewell/. Stray Leaves from the Diary of an Indian Officer (1865). Military career; social life in India; theatricals; sport and Hindu religion; varied; good. Copy in India Office Library.   543

CUMBERLEGE,Adm. Claude. Master Mariner (1936). Apprentice in last days of sail; commander of brig; yarns of South Seas and strange places.   544

CUMING,Sir Alexander. Autobiographical notes written 1764; misadventure of a picturesque soldier, debtor, and astrologer;affairs with Cherokees. MS B.M. Add. 39855.   545

CUMMING, Gen. Hanway R. A Brigadier (1922). With infantry in France, WW1; German offensives and retreats; good descriptions of campaigns.   546

CUMMING, Lt. James Slator. Journal, 1837-42; military activities in Punjab; Afghan campaign; morality & cul-

ture in India; social life. Six Years Diary (1847).   547

CUNYNGHAME, Gen. Arthur Augustus T. An Aide-de-Camp's Recollections(1884) With Saltoun at Hong-Kong, 1841-1843; military affairs;travels; economy and customs of China.   548

CURLING,Henry. Recollections (1855) Scattered and discursive anecdotes of plays, actors, theatre; and of military service Peninsular War.   549

CURRAN, John Adye. Reminiscences(L. 1915). Barrister, county court judge and chairman of Quarter Sessions; legal and political affairs in Ireland; Phoenix Park murders.   550

CURTIS, Mrs. George James. Memories of a Long Life (1912). Religious life and social work in Derby;Chartism and French threats;travels; life of poor; religious revivalism;daily life; long and interesting life. A copy in Derby P.L.   551

CURTIS, Julia. Mists and Monsoons (1935). Early life in Scottish Highlands; domestic life on coffee estate in India in 80's; social life.   552

CURTIS-WILLSON,Rosemary. C/o G.P.O. London(1949). Her experiences serving with Women's Royal Navy services overseas.   553

CURZON OF KEDLESTON, George Nathaniel Curzon, 1st Marquis. Leaves from a Viceroy's Note-Book (1926). Reminiscences of his administration; India, 1899-1905; history; travels; people & places.   554

CUSACK, Mary F. C. Nun of Kenmare (1888).Autobiography of Irish nun and her work among poor in Kenmare.   555

CUST,Robert Needham.Memoirs of Past Years (Hertford,1899). Education; his 25 years in Indian Civil Service; later travel, politics, religion & work for international congresses.   556

CUSTANCE,Henry.Riding Recollections (1894).Career and experiences of jockey; famous horses, jockeys & owners; ways of turf; 1863-86; a useful record of sporting life.   557

CUTHBERTSON, David. Revelations (L. 1923); Thirty-Three Years (1910). His work as librarian 1876-1923;Edinburgh University; teachers, students, celebrities, Stevenson; anecdotes.   558

"D. 83222." I Did Penal Servitude (Dublin, 1945). Imprisonment in various Irish jails; emotional reactions; difficulties of rehabilitation.   1

D., E. Recollections of a Nurse (L. 1889). Medical work with Universities Mission at Zanzibar; service in Boer War; private cases.   2

DAFT, Richard. Kings of Cricket (L. 1893); Cricketer's Yarns (1926). The sporting career and reminiscences of the Notts. and England batsman, 1858-1891;famous players and games; social life at Trent Bridge.   3

DAGGERWOOD, Sylvester (pseud.). Memoirs (1806). Purports to be autobiography of comedian; generally vague & seems more like fiction.   4

DAILY,Starr (pseud.). Release(1942) Experiences as criminal;redemption by Christianity; inner light and religious experiences.   5

DALE,Harrison. Vanishing Trails (L. 1926). Sailor's ten years' experiences; radio man; adventures ashore and in many ports.   6

DALGLISH,Doris N. We Have Been Glad (1938).Clapham; Oxford; reading, literary interests,religion, intellectual life; mainly spiritual autobiography of one of lost generation.   7

DALL, Ian. Sun Before Seven (1936). Memories of his childhood in Argentina in late 19th Century; Buenos Ayres; a record of boyhood daydreams, raptures spirit and senses.   8

DALLAS,Alexander R. C. Incidents in the Life,by his widow(1871). Autobiography 1791-1820; service in commisariat in Peninsular war; Waterloo; marriage; going up to Oxford.   9

DALLISON,Buck. Lookin' Back (1939);

Still Lookin' Back(1941). Reminiscences of colliery work in North England; family life; in humorous and dialectal style.   10

DALRYMPLE, Gen. Sir Hew Whiteford. Memoir(1830). Military service; Spain 1806-8; campaigns of Peninsular.   11

DALRYMPLE,Sir James, Viscount Stair Apology for Himself, 1690 (Bannatyne Club, Edin.1825). Affairs of the 17th Century Scottish historian.   12

DALRYMPLE-HAY,Adm. Sir John Charles Lines from My Log-Book (1897). Career in navy from the thirties.   13

DALTON, Charles. With the Dublin Brigade(1929). Political life; experiences with IRA, during the Irish rebellion 1917-21.   14

DALTON, Clive (Frederick S. Clark). A Child in the Sun(1937). Memories of five years in Malaya as a boy;pull of East and West; early 20th Century. 15

DALY,Mrs. De Burgh (Emily Lucy). An Irishwoman in China (1915). Her work in hospitals in Ningpo,1888-1912; and social life, Chinese customs; war and travels.   16

DALY,Sir Henry Dermot. Diary, 1848-1857;military service in Oudh Cavalry and at Delhi during the Mutiny; agent for Governor-General in Central India. Memoirs (1895).   17

DAMPIER, Sir William C. Cambridge and Elsewhere (1950). His education & later scientific work at the university; studies of heredity, dairy farming, history of science.   18

DANCE,Charles Daniel. Recollections of Four Years in Venezuela (L. 1876). and Chapters from a Guianese Log-Book (Georgetown, 1881). Religious work, travels, and adventures of a mission priest in Guiana & Venezuela.   19

DANDO, Ellen D. Out of Romanism (L. 1938). County Durham; conversion from Catholicism to Methodism and religious experiences;missionary work in London slums.   20

DANE,Ebba. A House of My Own (1950)

Return from war service;settlement in France and life with her family in the French countryside; local affairs. 21

DANIELL, John Edgecombe. Journal of an Officer(1820). In commissariat dept. in Peninsular War in Portugal, Spain, France, Netherlands; with army of occupation, 1816-18.   22

DARBYSHIRE, Charles. My Life in the Argentine Republic (1917). Business & social life in Buenos Ayres, 1852-74; lively details of politics, dictators gauchos and outlaws.   23

D'ARCY, Rt. Rev. Charles Frederick. Adventures of a Bishop (1934). Family life in Dublin; Trinity; ministry in Church of Ireland; Belfast, Ossory, & Down;Bishop of Armagh; administration and dioceses, etc.   24

DARE, Phyllis. From School to Stage (1907). Her education;her career as a child actress; her troubles with gossip.   25

DAREWSKI, Herman. Musical Memories (1937).Experiences and reminiscences; musichalls, theatres; travels; Bohemian life; composer.   26

DAREWSKI,Mme.Max (Ruby Miller). Believe Me or Not (1933). Actress's reminiscences of theatres, musichalls, early films, actors, society; tours; married life with Max Darewski.   27

DARK, Sidney.   Mainly About Other People(1925); Not Such a Bad Life (L. 1941). Boyhood and family;journalism in London; Daily Express; John O'London's;literature, theatre, criticism; public affairs;religious work; Savage Club and Bohemian life;his friends in the arts and public life.   28

DARLEY,Maj. Henry. Slaves and Ivory (1926); Slaves and Ivory in Abyssinia (1935). Travel, exploration, hunting for ivory in Sudan and Abyssinia from 1907; frontier-agent in Abyssinia after WW1; native life.   29

DARLING, Frank Fraser. Island Years (1940). Three years on Isle of Rona; studies of natural history off Scottish coast.   30

DARLING, Sam. Reminiscences (1914). Life and work as trainer, rider, owner; Beckhampton stables; outstanding events and personalities during forty years of racing.   31

/DARLING, William Young/.   Private Papers of a Bankrupt Bookseller(1931) Bankrupt Bookseller Speaks Again (L. 1938). His experiences in bookselling and his failure in business; service in WW1; France; Gallipoli.   32

/DARLING, William Young/. Old Mill by Penelope Potter (Edin. 1934). Her experiences turning an old mill into a tea-room; catering work, Scotland; marriage; fiction?   33

DARLINGTON,William Aubrey.I Do What I Like (1947). Schooling;teacher; WW1 service and humors of army life;drama critic for Telegraph; his huge enjoyment of theatre.   34

DARWIN,Bernard R. M. Green Memories (1928); Life is Sweet, Brother(1940); Pack Clouds Away(1941). Eton and Cambridge; journalism; Salonika in WW1; sports journalism for Times; golf and other sports; reading, social, literary friends.   35

DARWIN, Charles R. Life and Letters (1887) I,26-107; Autobiography (1929) Lively account of grammar-school days and study at Edinburgh University;his mental and personal development; geology and natural history; travels and scientific studies; success of Origin of Species; his other writings; Carlyle, Macaulay, S.Smith and his other friends.   36

DASENT, Sir George Webbe. Annals of an Eventful Life (1870). Warwickshire and West Indies; Oxford; love affairs and life in Warwickshire; travels in Greece; legacies; autobiography mixed with fiction.   37

DATAS. Datas: The Memory Man (1932) Career of musichall entertainer; celebrities in music hall and crime from Barnum to Crippen.   38

DAVENPORT, Major E. M. Life and Recollections (1869).Military experiences 1835-50;Canada, British Isles and

West Indies; station life, sport, and social.   39

DAVENPORT,Henry S. Memories at Random(1926). Foxhunting from 1859; Melton and Harborough hunts;sporting and social life; personalities.   40

DAVEY, William J. Recollections (L. 1936). Work with London engineers on public projects;Methodist church work in London;social and temperance activities. Methodist Book Room.   41

DAVIDGE, John. Conversion of a Metropolitan Policeman (1878). Work as a policeman; his sense of sin; conversion and spiritual life.   42

DAVIDGE, William. Footlight Flashes (N.Y.1866). Comedian's work in London and provincial theatres, and later in USA; Dickens, Kemble, Kean.   43

DAVIDSON,D. Remembrances of a Religio-Maniac (Stratford-upon-Avon 1912) Long and curious autobiography of religious enthusiast who was twice committed to an asylum.   44

DAVIDSON,Lt.Col. David. Memories of a Long Life (Edin. 1890). Early life in Scotland; military career, mostly in India; Christian activities.   45

DAVIDSON, Lillias Campbell. Confessions (1902). Widow's life in country town; her daughters and their schemes for marrying them; her own remarriage fiction?   46

DAVIDSON, Samuel. Autobiography and Diary (Edin. 1899). Presbyterian religion and theology; study in Belfast and Germany; professor at Lancashire Independent College; studies; English and German scholars.   47

DAVIDSON-HOUSTON, Col. James Vivian Armed Pilgrimage (1949). His military activities with Chinese Defence Force and Chinese-American forces in Burma; liaison work with Chinese; travels in Asia; lively.   48

DAVIES, Catherine. Eleven Years Residence (1841). Governess in France & with Murat family in Naples; Napoleon at Fontainebleau;Murat's elevation to throne of Naples;affairs of the Murat

family & her adventures with them;ill health and return to England.   49

D(AVIES), C(harles) H.Recollections of a Bolton Grammar-School Boy (1907) Minister's son in Lancashire; boyhood life; experiences at Bolton School in 1856-65; Lancs life.   50

DAVIES,Christian(Mother Ross). Life and Adventures(1740). Adventures of a woman who served as foot-soldier under Marlborough; dictated; has been attributed to Defoe.   51

DAVIES, Ellen Chivers. A Farmer in Serbia(1916). Nursing in WW1; in Serbia with British Farmers military hospital unit; Serbian life.   52

DAVIES, George Middlecott. Chaplain in India (1935). Boyhood & education in Norfolk; 21 years as army chaplain in India;Archdeacon of Nagpur; return to parish work in Norfolk.   53

DAVIES,John. Lower Deck (1945); The Stone Frigate(1947). Experiences WW2; gunner on destroyer; lieutenant RNVR; training ship work near Falmouth; experiences in convoy and anti-submarine work; interesting.   54

DAVIES,Jonathan Ceredig. Life, Travels and Reminiscences(Llanddewi Brefe, 1927). Not seen.   55

DAVIES,Lady Lucy Clementina. Recollections of Society (1872). Her life in high society;social, political and court life and celebrities;Talleyrand etc.; anecdotes.   56

DAVIES,Richard. Account of the Convincement (1710). Welshpool Quaker's conversion,ministry in Wales, sufferings, imprisonment.   57

DAVIES, William. Diary, 1814-1818; missionary work in Sierra Leone;tribulations of missionary life; & native life and culture. Extracts from the Journals (Llanidloes, 1835). Copy in Bodleian: Methodist Book Room.   58

DAVIES,William Henry. Autobiography of a Super-Tramp (L.1908);Later Days (1925). Boyhood; begging and tramping in America and England; low life both sides of Atlantic;his writing; literary development and friendships; WW1; politics.   59

DAVIS, Edward G. Some Passages from My Life (Birmingham, 1898). Working-class life in Aston; drunkard father; marriage; religious life; a brief and pleasant account.   Copy in Birmingham P.L.   60

DAVIS, Mrs. Elizabeth (Cadwaladyr). Autobiography (1857). A Welshwoman's picaresque adventures;difficulties of childhood; runs away; travels in England, West Indies, Brazil, Australia, South Africa,working as nurse and domestic servant; service as nurse during Crimean War; Balaclava; unusual & very interesting.   61

DAVIS,James Percival.Rolling Stones (1940). Cathedral organist; mountaineering;European travels; evolution of a system of religion.   62

DAVIS,John.Some Account of the Wonderful Operations (Manchester, 1844). His early sins;conversion by Friends; Quaker life and ministry.   63

DAVIS, Sydney C. H. Racing Motorist (1949). Experiences and adventures in thirty years as a racing driver; work as sports editor of Autocar.   64

DAVISON, Dorothy G. M. Three Children at Home (Oxford, 1933).Simple and naive evocation of childhood in country; household associations; imagination of children;visits to London and seaside.   65

DAVY, Colin. Ups and Downs (1939). Army life after WW1; Egypt and India; riding experiences; his horse "Desert Chief"; pleasant.   66

DAVYS, Owen. A Long Life's Journey (1913). Chester, Peterborough; clerical home; religious study and ordination; parish work at Stilton, Peterborough, Ambold; rector of Wheathampstead; church work.   67

DAWSON,Adam. Rambling Recollections (Falkirk, 1867). Forfarshire life in early 19th Century; social, fashions, customs, people.   68

DAWSON,Sir Douglas F. R. A Soldier-Diplomat (1927). Military attaché in Vienna, Paris & The Hague, 1874-1900; society, sport, etc.   69

/DAWSON, G. A. R./.Nilgiri Sporting Reminiscences,by an Old Shikarri (Madras, 1880). Adventures as a big-game hunter in India, 1856-80. Copy, India Office Library.   70

DAWSON, H. Autobiography of a Company Promoter (1892). Attractions and riches of land. Bodleian.   71

DAWSON, James. Autobiography (Truro 1865). Actor and manager's recollections of playing Shakespearean parts; egotistical but undetailed.   72

DAWSON, John. Excise officer's life and personal affairs in Leeds and London. MS, Dewsbury Public Library. 73

DAWSON, Adm. Lionel. Flotillas (L. 1933); Mediterranean Medley (L. 1935) Gone for a Sailor (L. 1936); Sound of the Guns (L. 1949). His war experiences and naval career from 90's; Nile; Boer War; with destroyers and torpedo boats in Mediterranean in WW1 & with commandos in Africa and Italy in WW2; adventures of war and naval life. 74

DAWSON,William James. Autobiography of a Mind (1925). St. Albans; Methodist family life; his spiritual vagaries and awakening; preaching in small towns; poet, author & lecturer; later days in USA:the influence of country town, art, religion.   75

DAY, Charles William. Five Years' Residence in the West Indies (1852). Residence and social life, 1846-1851; descriptions of the islands.   76

DAY,Henry C.Cavalry Chaplain(1922). Macedonian Memories (1930);Army Chaplain's War Memoirs (1937). A chaplain in WW1; Gallipoli and Macedonia; his work; soldiers' life; popular & lively; Catholic padre.   77

DAY,Samuel Phillips. Life in a Convent (1848);Down South (1862). Former monk's breach with Catholicism;monastery life and system; indictment; his later experiences as correspondent of London newspaper in the American Civil War; general events of war; refutation of pro-Confederate bias.   78

DAY, W.C. Behind the Footlights (L. 1885). Reminiscences of amateur theatricals and his part in them; Scenic Club and its productions.   79

DAY, William. Reminiscences (1886). Life of horse-trainer; famous owners and trainers; impersonal.   80

DEACON, Abraham. Memoir (1912). His childhood; working-class life; boy in stocking-factory; religion; ministry at Leicester. Leicester P.L.   81

DEADFALL.Experiences of a Game Preserver (1868). Chronicle of a country squire in North of England; everyday life and work;trapping and preserving, keepers, poachers.   82

DE AINSLIE, Charles Philip. Life as I Have Found It (Edin. 1883). School; military service in Canada, India and Ireland;West Indies command; Tory politics; social life.   83

DEAN, Edward J. Lucky Dean (1944). Press photographer's assignments; the chief public events of 20's and 30's; his triumphs.   84

DEANE, Anthony Charles. Time Remembered (1945). London boyhood; schools and Cambridge; his parishes; canon of Windsor; writing, broadcasting, reading, literary and social life.   85

DEARDEN, Harold. Medicine and Duty (1928); Wind of Circumstance (1938); Time and Chance(1940). Family, school and medical study, Cambridge & London; service in RAMC in France during WW1; medical practice and experiences West End of London; patients.   86

DEARDEN, Com. Richard Lionel. Watch On Deck (1934); A Seafarer's Harvest (1935). Adopted child; life in merchant marine; WW1 service in navy; life and adventures of a sailor.   87

ANON. Death in the Air (1933). Good account of adventures in WW1; officer in fighter-squadron of RFC.   88

DEAZLE, Mr. Autobiographical notes of teacher at King Edward Grammar Sch. in Stafford, 1731-42; family life and domestic troubles; brief. MS, William Salt Library, Stafford.   89

DE BEAR,Archie. Reminiscences(1938) Entertainer's career and reminiscences musichalls, variety, reviews; shows; performers.   90

DE BLOWITZ, Henri Stephan. My Memoirs(1903). Bohemian youth; career as journalist; Times; public affairs in Europe; foreign correspondent.   91

DE CASTRO, Jacob. Memoirs (1824). A comedian's career;Astley's Royal Circus;eminent London actors;playwrights and theatrical scene.   92

DECIES,Lady Elizabeth W. Beresford, Baroness.Turn of the World (1937). An American wife in English and European high society; WW1 events.   93

DE COSSON,Maj. Emilius Albert. Days and Nights (1886). Army service with Graham in Egypt during Suakin campaign of 1885; campaign details.   94

DE COURVILLE, Albert P. I Tell You (1928). Life as journalist; work as a producer; musichalls, revues & opera; reminiscences of actors, celebrities, gaming, and sport.   95

DE CRESPIGNY, Sir Claude Champion. Memoirs (1896); Forty Years (1910). A lifetime in sport; big-game hunting, riding, steeplechasing; military service; Boer War; travels.   96

DE FRECE, Lady Matilda A. Recollections of Vesta Tilley (1934). Musichall career in London and provinces; anecdotes of her stage experiences; & marriage and life in society; work in WW1.   97

DE GUELPH, Prince John. The Memoirs (N.Y.1910). Experiences of a claimant to royal birth;alleged birth at Windsor Castle in 1861; adventures, India Burma, USA.   98

D'EGVILLE, Alan Hervey. Adventures in Safety (1937). London; his varied life as actor in Berlin, skier, guide to American tourists in Near East,intelligence officer WW1;extensive travels;memoirs of celebrities; humorous skit.   99

DE HALSALLE, Henry. Who Goes There (1927). His experiences & adventures while doing espionage work in Germany during WW1.   100

DE HEGEDUS,Adam.Don't Keep the Van- man Waiting (1944). London correspon- dent of Hungarian newspaper;experien- ces and army service WW2.   101

DEICHMANN,Hilda Elizabeth, Baroness Impressions and Memories (1926). Life of private family in London and Germ- any; diplomatic, court, society life; sport; personalities.   102

DE KUSEL, Samuel Selig, Baron. An Englishman's Recollections(1915). His career as customs official with Egyp- tian government; controller-general; politics; social life.   103

DE LA BECHE,Sir Henry Thomas. Diary 1823-24;visit to his sugar plantation in Jamaica;work for suppressing slave trade. MS, National Museum of Wales, Cardiff.   104

DE LACY,Gertrude.Some Recollections (1910). Experiences with musical com- edy company in India and Java,1905-7; theatres; hotels;soldiers. Copy India Office Library.   105

DELAND, Margaret Wade. If This Be I (1935). Attractive evocation of child life in Manchester in 60's; daily rou- tine, schools, etc.   106

DELANY, Mary (Pendarves). Autobio- graphy(1861-2). In letters to Duchess of Portland; her marriage to Mr. Pen- darves; interests of a bluestocking; court life and society to 1740.   107

DE LENOIR, Cecil. The Hundredth Man (1933). Joys and horrors of addiction to drugs; underworld traffic; cure; & moralisings.   108

DE LISLE,Adele. Leaves (1922). Her work in V.A.D. during WW1; lively and genial account of her experiences and of soldiers of various nations.   109

DE LISLE,Gen. Sir Beauvoir. Reminis- cences (1939). Cavalryman's career in Egypt and India; Boer War; WW1; sport polo, hunting, racing from 1883.   110

DELISLE, Francoise. Friendship's Odyssey (1946). Childhood in France; young woman in London;intimate record of friendship with Havelock Ellis.111

DE MONTMORENCY, Hervey. Sword and Stirrup (1936). Childhood France; his military career and travels;Gibraltar Boer War, WW1 & Sinn Fein rebellion ; riding and steeplechasing; musichalls and theatres;treasure-hunting; multi- farious adventures.   112

DE MORGAN, Sophia Elizabeth. Three Score Years and Ten (1895). Literary and political life in London; fashion social reform; celebrities; Coleridge Lamb, Carlyle, etc.   113

DEMPSEY,John J. Storms over the Da- nube (1938).Irish journalist's adven- tures in Balkans during WW1;Bela Kun; communist rebellion; film-making with Korda; politics and rebellion in Ire- land; smuggling in Dublin.   114

DEMPSTER,Charlotte L. H. Manners of My Time (1920).Scottish childhood and poverty; her life in country houses & in Italy and Southern France;books on France, romance, etc.   115

DE NAVARRO,Mary Anderson.A Few More Memories (1936). A theatrical idol's reminiscences of her interests during retirement; country life; her brilli- ant friends; Henry James, Barrie, El- gar, Coquelin, Tennyson, etc.   116

DENHAM, Capt. Prison journal, 1842; experiences of a sailor imprisoned by the Chinese.Journals Kept by Mr.Gully and Captain Denham (1844).   117

DENHAM, Sir James. Memoirs (1922). Social, court, diplomatic life; Vict- orian and Edwardian political & legal celebrities; sport.   118

DENISON,George Anthony. Notes of My Life (1878); Supplement (1893). Educ- ation and clerical career as vicar of East Brent and archdeacon of Taunton; religion and politics; Gladstone and the church.   119

DENISON, Henry Phipps. Seventy-Two Years (1925). Childhood in Tasmania; Winchester and Oxford; Catholic revival; ministry in Somerset, Kensington and Wells; social work; theology and ritual; his catholicism.   120

DENISON, Sir William Thomas. Varieties of Viceregal Life (1870). Career as Governor-General of Australia and as Governor of Madras;administration and society; politics; native life.   121

DENMAN,Thomas. Autobiography; Derby education;medical training; surgeon's mate in navy; success in London; surgeon and midwife;written 1779; interesting. MS, Derby Public Library. 122

DENNETT, R.E. Seven Years Among the Fjort (1887). Work and travels of a trader in the Congo area; negroes and traders.   123

DENNIS, Owen. The Rest Go On (1942) Anti-aircraft gunner with transports; WW2; Dunkirk; with a troopship around Africa; convoy work in Atlantic.   124

DENT,Hastings Charles. Diary, 1883-1884;work of railway surveyor in Brazil; explorations; scientific observations; Rio and Bahia. A Year in Brazil (1886).   125

DENT,Joseph Mallaby. Memoirs (1928) His education and reading; success as publisher in London;books and writers Everyman library.   126

DENT, Olive. A V.A.D. in France (L. 1917). Naive and emotional account of work in French hospitals in WW1; life and work as nurse.   127

DENT,Thomas(pseud.). Then a Soldier (1934). School; sex and youth; psychological experiences in WW1; written in third person;said by publishers to be well-known writer.   128

DENVER, John. Life Story (Dublin, 1910).Irish politics in England; Home Rule, Fenians,Parnell; journalism and politics; literature, theatre.   129

DE QUINCEY, Thomas. Autobiographic Sketches (1853, 1854); Confessions of an English Opium Eater (1822). School in Manchester;Oxford; travels; literary work and friendships; Wordsworth, Coleridge, Southey and Lakeland society; books and intellectual life; his

addiction to opium and its effects on his mind and dreams; self-analysis; & triumph over the habit.   130

DE POLNAY,Peter. Death and Tomorrow (1942). Writer's experiences in fall of France and German occupation 1940; in Vichy prison; escape to Spain; internment and release.   131

DERBY, James Stanley, 7th Earl of. Account of main events of life to 1650 with theological and religious reflections and notes from reading. MS copy at Chetham's Library, Manchester. 132

DE REYA,Capt. Guy. Nomad of the Sea (1936).Cabin boy to captain and smuggler; gunrunning in North Africa; imprisonment by Moors; adventures, WW1; arms smuggling to Ireland,Finland and Spain; adventures.   133

DERING,Sir Edward. Autobiographical notes, 1598-1640, mainly relative to estate work. MS in Bodleian Library, Gough Kent 20, 170 pp.   134

DERING, Heneage. Autobiographical notes by Dean of Ripon; mainly family affairs, 1665-1735. Yorkshire Diaries (Surtees Soc. LXV, 1875).   135

DESART, Hamilton John A. Cuffe, 5th Earl of. A Page from the Past (1936). His daughter's (Lady Sybil Lubbock) & his own reminiscences; school; travel to South America as a boy; Cambridge university;social life and society in London; sport; to 70's.   136

DE STACPOOLE,George Stacpoole, Duke Irish and Other Memories (1922).Irish country life, society, sport, personalities;travel in Europe, Turkey, USA and Burma; 1857-1920.   137

DE STEIGER,Isabelle. Memorabilia(L. 1927). Woman writer and artist; music art, literature; memories of Eminent Victorians; Ruskin, Sharpe, Wilde and singers.   138

DE STOEKL, Baroness Agnes (Barron). Not All Vanity(1950). Irish birth and social life in later 19th Century;her marriage to a Russian diplomat & life as a grande dame; the Revolution; and subsequent poverty and work as dressmaker; a personal example of the age of revolution; interesting record. 139

DES VOEUX, Sir George William. My
Colonial Service(1903). His career as
magistrate and governor in Guiana, W.
Indies,Fijis, Australia, Newfoundland
and Hong Kong,1863-93; administration
law, politics; social life.   140

DEVANT, David. Woes of a Wizard (L.
1903); My Magic Life (1931); Secrets
(1936). Career as entertainer; tricks
and devices of conjurer and magician;
Maskelyne and Devant; colleagues and
rivals; tours; social life in London;
theatrical world.   141

DEVAS,Fr. Dominic. From Cloister to
Camp(1919). Franciscan's service with
Irish regiment in France,1915-18; the
life of the troops.   142

DEVENISH, Dorothy. A Wiltshire Home
(1949). Charming evocation of child's
life at Little Durnford; family, garden, Wilts scene.   143

DE VERE,Aubrey Thomas.Recollections
(1897). Boyhood in Ireland;literature
politics and social life; his poetry;
literary life; the Wordsworth circle;
Catholicism; Manning, Newman.   144

DEVEREUX, Ernest Cecil. Life's Memories (1936). His life as shopkeeper
in Eton; seven headmasters, Goodford
to Elliott; sports; colours.   145

DE VERTEUIL,Frederick Joseph. Fifty
Wasted Years (1938). Career as lawyer
in India; legal life and people; politics; sport; social life.   146

DE VILLIERS, Sir John A. J. My Mem-
ories(1931). Early life in tea-trade;
linguistic studies; on staff of British Museum; Hackluyt Society; work as
civil servant at Hague in WW1;geogra-
phical research.   147

DEVOY,John. Recollections (New York
1929). Activities of an Irish rebel,
1860-1920; Irish politics; the Fenian
movement.   148

DEW,Walter. I Caught Crippen (1938)
Northampton;London; his career in the
London police;Scotland Yard inspector
and his cases; Crippen; Jack the Ripper, etc.   149

DEWAR, George A. B.   A Younger Son
(1920). Boyhood,country life, Oxford;
work in journalism and politics; WW1
service; travel in Italy.   150

DEWAR, Adm. Kenneth G. B. Navy from
Within(1939). His naval life and naval history 1893-1928; naval gunnery;
service on warships; W.W.1 service in
Dardanelles and at Jutland; Royal Oak
court-martial 1929.   151

D'EWES, J.   Sporting in Both Hemi-
spheres(1858). Hunting, fishing, travel and adventure; Europe, Australia,
India, China.   152

D'EWES, Sir Symonds. Autobiography,
ed. J.O. Halliwell (L. 1845); College
Life (1851). Diary, written up; study
of law and antiquities; domestic; religious; contemporary history; James
I and courtiers; prior experiences as
fellow-commoner at St. John's 1618 to
1620.   153

DE WINDT, Harry. My Restless Life
(1909);My Notebook (1923). Cambridge;
London society in 70's; fiction writing and journalism;adventures of buck
and Bohemian; travels and adventures
in Japan,Siberia, America, Arctic and
Europe.   154

DE WOLFE, Elsie (Lady Mendl). After
All (1935). Early life in New York;
work as interior decorator; marriage
and experiences as society hostess; a
volunteer nurse in WW1;theatrical activities in USA: beauty advice.   155

DEXTER, Capt. Walter E. Rope-Yarns
(1938). Lifely account of experiences
as apprentice and before mast in sailing ships; nostalgic.   156

DEY, Thomas Henry.   Leaves from a
Bookmaker's Book(1931). Reminiscences
of horse-racing and gambling; stories
about celebrities.   157

DEYNCOURT, Sir Eustice H. W. A Ship
Builder's Yarn(1948). Career and work
of Admiralty director of naval construction.   158

DIAPEA, William. Cannibal Jack (L.
1928).Record of fifty lively years in
the South Seas;trader and beachcomber
his wives and children; violence; an

amusing, garrulous record.   159

DIAPER, Capt. Tom. Tom Diaper's Log
(1950). His career as a yacht skipper
and anecdotes of famous owners;Thomas
Lipton; Wilhelm Il.   160

ANON.Diary of a Staff Officer(1941)
Experiences of intelligence officer at
advanced headquarters in France during
Blitzkrieg of 1940; air forces.   161

DIBDIN, Charles. Professional Life
(1803).Life of actor, dramatist, composer, novelist; tours; reception of
his works; Covent Garden, Garrick and
London stage; business transactions &
abortive voyage to India.   162

DIBDIN,Thomas Frognall. Reminiscences (1836). Playwright's anecdotes of
literary and theatrical life; tours;
actors; London theatre management and
his operas.   163

DIBDIN, Thomas John. Reminiscences
(1827). His life in music and theatre
at Covent Garden, Drury Lane, Haymarket; comic operas; theatrical scene,
from end 18th Century.   164

DICEY, Albert Venn. Memorials, ed.
R. S. Rait (1925). Includes autobiographical fragment and diaries; legal
academic, political work; Oxford and
famous Oxonians;the great writers and
thinkers of the time; Rhodes scholar-
ships; Whig politics; valuable material for later 19th Century.   165

DICK, Alan. Walking Miracle (1942);
Inside Story (1943). Life and work of
newspaperman; fight against tuberculosis; his new spiritual life; events
leading to WW2 at home and abroad;the
Blitz.   166

DICKENS, Sir Henry Fielding. Recollections (1934).His father and family
life; education; legal career; trials
and cases at Cambridge; Common Sergeant; social life, theatre & politics,
to 1917.   167

DICKENS, Monica. One Pair of Hands
(1939); One Pair of Feet (1942). Her
adventures in brief career as a cook
and domestic servant in London; experiences as probationer nurse in WW2,
near London; sociological.   168

DICKEY, Herbert Spencer. The Misadventures of a Tropical Medico (1929).
His travels and medical work in Brazil and Ecuador; Amazon Indians.   169

DICKIE, J. L. Forty Years of Trout
and Salmon Fishing (1921); Comedy and
Drama(1939). Fishing in Scotland; his
schooldays and medical studies; Aberdeen University; practice in asylum,
Assam, Scotland; WW1 service in RAMC;
sport, social life, anecdotes.   170

DICKINSON,James.Journal of the Life
(1745).Quaker's conversion, spiritual
life and ministry; Cumberland; travel
in British Isles, Holland, and American colonies.   171

DICKINSON, Jonathan. Journal of the
Travels (1759). Quaker's sufferings &
God's mercies; a shipwreck in Gulf of
Florida; adventures with Indians dur-
ing journey to Pennsylvania.   172

DICKINSON, Joseph H. C. A Trader in
the Savage Solomons (1927). Eighteen
years as a trader and planter in the
Eastern Solomons; missionaries;native
life; violence and romance.   173

DICKINSON,Peard. Memoirs (1803). A
Methodist minister's conversion; work
in London and Topsham;friendship with
Wesley.   174

/DICKSON, Samuel/. Memorable Events
in the Life of a London Physician (L.
1863). Reminiscences of medical practice in London in earlier 19th Century, doctors, controversies, theories,
and his part.   175

DIEHL, Alice Mangold. Musical Memories (1897); True Story (1908). Early
life of novelist,writer and musician;
student years in Germany; playing and
teaching; family and social life; reminiscences of great players and singers of 50's and 60's.   176

DIGBY,George. Goose Feathers (1938)
Down Wind (1939); Red Horizons (1939)
Light and amusing narratives of trav-
els and adventures in Asia, America,
Australia, China; curious people and
scenes.   177

DIGBY, Sir Kenelm. Private Memoirs
(1827-8). Memoirs a clef; amorous and

romantic adventures of sailor, courtier, diplomat, to 1620; courtship of
Venetia Stanley; entertaining.　178

DIGHTON, Allen Adair.　My Sporting
Life (1934). Cheltenham school; medical study, Edinburgh; life as sporting journalist; dogs, horses, sportsmen; anecdotes.　179

DILNOT, Frank. Adventures (1913). A
newspaperman's adventures; Parliament
crime, public events and excitements;
Central News.　180

DIMMOCK,Frederick H. Bare Knee Days
(1937). Scouting in Scotland; service
WW1;　editor of The Scout; jamborees,
travels, writings for scout movement;
lifelong pranks.　181

/DINGLE,Aylward Edward/. Rough Hewn
(1933). Modern Sinbad; runs away as a
boy to sea;travel, love, business adventures in many parts of world;jour-
nalism; South Seas.　182

DISBROWE, Charlotte A. A.　Old Days
in Diplomacy (1903). Reminiscences of
octogenarian daughter of diplomat;her
memoirs of society,courts, statesmen;
Germany, Sweden, Holland.　183

DISNEY,Gervase.Some Remarkable Passages (1692). Religious life of puritan at Nottingham and Ollercar; sins,
temptations, God's mercies; poems and
letters.　184

DISNEY,W. H. Incidents During Thirty Years (1898).Parish work in Tralee
and other Irish churches; controversy
with Catholics;medical work; clerical
life and work in Leicestershire and in
Peterborough; workhouses.　185

DIVALL, Tom. Scoundrels and Scally-
wags (1929). Thirty years with Metropolitan Police; CID; Jockey Club; the
criminal world and its ways; gangs on
racecourses.　186

DIXON, Alec. Singapore Patrol (1935)
Tinned Soldier (1941). Police work in
Singapore in 20's; Oriental crime and
vice; service in ranks during WW1;the
Tank Corps; Lawrence; good.　187

DIXON,Ella Hepworth. As I knew Them
(1930). Reminiscences of Eminent Vic-

torians and Edwardians in literature,
theatre; journalistic.　188

DIXON, Henry. Reminiscences, Essex
Review, XXIII-XXV (1914-16). Medical
education;practice for fifty years in
and around Witham,Essex; politics and
social life and changes.　189

/DIXON, Henry Hall/.　The Post and
the Paddock, by Druid(1856). Reminiscences of racing,jockeys, owners, and
celebrities;　Sam Chigney, George IV,
etc.; impersonal.　190

DIXON, H. Sydenham. From Gladiateur
to Persimmon (1901).Sporting journalist, 1865-96; horses, jockeys, owners
and races; visits to Sandringham as a
racehorse expert.　191

DIXON, William Scarth.　Men, Horses
and Hunting(1931). Schooling; farming
in Cleveland;　work as sporting journalist; hunting, horse-shows; country
life in Yorks.　192

DOBBIE, Sybill.　Grace under Malta
(1922).　Secretary to General Dobbie;
WW2 experiences during siege of Malta
record of high courage.　193

/DOBBS, Bettie/. Autobiography of a
Charwoman (1900). Squalid adventures
and heroic labours of a poor Londoner
dictated to Annie Wakeman and recorded in phonetic style.　194

DOBBS, Major Gen.　Richard Stewart.
Reminiscences of Life in Mysore (Dublin, 1882); Reminiscences of Christian
Life (n.d.).　Career of Irish soldier
in Mysore, Burma, and South Africa; &
work in religion; Hindu education and
religion. Cambridge U.L.　195

DOBBS,Rosalind. Incomplete autobiography; late 19th Century. MS, London
School of Economics.　196

DOBIE, William G. M. Winter & Rough
Weather (1938).　Life of a sportsman;
staghunting, fishing,shooting; nature
study in Scotland; sketches.　197

DOBSON,Richard Partway. China Cycle
(1946). Business and travels of a ci-
garette salesman in China in thirties
Japanese invasion;　lively details of
Chinese life.　198

DODD, Catherine. Vagrant Englishwoman (1905). European travels; German
university town; Hungary, Serbia; woman's emancipation;pursuit of romance
and depressions;everyday life in England.   199

DODD, William. Narrative of the Experiences (1841). Sufferings of cripple; factory life; a pamphlet against
industrialism; 18th Century.   200

DODDS, James. Personal Reminiscen-
ces(Edin. 1887). Boyhood in Annan and
study in Edinburgh;Free Church minister of Dunbar;Scottish personalities;
Chalmers, Edward Irving, Thomas Campbell, Sir Walter Scott.   201

DOGGETT, H. W. Tuppence, Please (L.
1943). Reminiscences and anecdotes of
chair-ticket collector in the London
Royal Parks.   202

DOHERTY, William J. In the Days of
the Giants (1931). Career as pugilist
in bareknuckle days; his championship
fights and Empire travels;Jem Mace to
Sullivan.   203

DOLBEY,Robert Valentine. Regimental
Surgeon(1917). Service in WW1; Marne,
Ypres,La Bassée; capture; experiences
in four German prison camps; hospital
work.   204

DOLIN,Anton. Ballet Go Round (1938)
Events in career of the Irish dancer,
1915-37; his companies, partners, and
ballets; tours; troubles.   205

DOLLING, Robert W. R. Ten Years in
a Portsmouth Slum (1897). Winchester
College; ministry & theological troubles;mission work in Portsmouth; life
of the poor; useful.   206

DOLMAN, Arthur. In the Footsteps of
Livingstone (1924). Travel and explo-
ration in Central Africa in mid-19th
Century; brief notes.   207

DOMVILLE, Admiral Sir Barry. By and
Large (L.1936); From Admiral to Cabin
Boy (1947). Critical and chatty reminiscences of naval life; his career &
his political opinions; reactionary;
interned under Regulation 18B during
WW2; efforts to escape.   208

DONALDSON,Sgt.Joseph. Recollections
of the Eventful Life (Glasgow, 1824).
Early life in navy; military service
in Peninsular War;French barbarities;
adventures, military life.   209

DONALDSON, Walter Alexander. Recollections (1865); reprinted as, Fifty
Years of Green Room Gossip(1881). His
experiences in theatre from 1809;Dub-
lin, Scotland, provinces; reminiscences of eminent actors,playwrights and
theatres.   210

DONEGALL,Marquess of. I've Taken My
Fun (1940).Social columnist of Sunday
Dispatch;society, gossip, journalist-
ic work and travels.   211

DONELLAN, John. The Genuine Case of
(1781). Poisoner's declaration of his
innocence.   212

DONNELLY,Peter. The Yellow Rock (L.
1950). Irish upbringing and study for
priesthood;factory work in Barrow-in-
Furness;industrial life; unemployment
interesting.   213

DONOGHUE, Stephen. Just My Story(L.
1923); Donoghue Up (1938). Autobiography of famous jockey; apprenticeship and career;his mounts and races;
Derby winners; famous sportsmen. 214

DONOHOE,Maj. Martin Henry. With the
Persian Expedition (1919). A personal
narrative of service in WW1; Persia &
Iraq; intelligence work.   215

DONOVAN,Michael. March or Die(1932)
Experiences in French Foreign Legion;
Algeria, Morocco; brutalities of the
officers; bitter complaint.   216

DOORLY, A. R. C.   Music in My Life
(Surbiton,1945). Naive account of his
singing in Gilbert and Sullivan and at
concerts; effect of various composers
and performers on him.   217

DOORLY, Capt. James Gerald Stokely.
In the Wake(1937). Trinidad; a boy at
sea;on relief ship to Scott in Antarctic;West Indies banana trade; on N.Z.
coastal service; in transport in WW1;
Houdini, Conan Doyle.   218

DORAN, Alban. Memories of a doctor

and antiquarian in 19th Century. MS, Royal College of Surgeons.   219

DORAN, George Henry. Chronicles of Barrabas (1935). Toronto; his career as publisher in America and England; reminiscences of English writers,publishers and editors.   220

DORMER, Hugh. Hugh Dormer's Diaries (1947). Catholic serving in WW2 with Irish Guards; romantic, mystical, and idealistic crusading; with the Maquis in France; violence and quietism.   221

/DOUGLAS, A.C./. Niger Memories, by Nemo (Exeter, 1927). Work as district commissioner in Nigeria in 90's; native life; breezy record. Copy, Royal Empire Society.   222

DOUGLAS, Lord Alfred Bruce. Oscar Wilde and Myself(1914); Autobiography (1929); Without Apology (1938). Early days at Winchester and Oxford;his relations with Wilde and Wilde's friends and self-defence in Wilde affair; his writings, literary journalism, literary friendships; country houses, social life, Bohemia.   223

DOUGLAS, Sir George Brisbane Scott. Diversions of a Country Gentleman (L. 1902). Roxburgh life and society; his sports;fishing, shooting, hunting and hawking.   224

DOUGLAS, Rt. Rev. John. Short autobiography; Dunbar, Oxford; army chaplain in Lowlands;country curacies and clerical career to 1776; MS, British Museum, Egerton 2181, 59 fos.   225

DOUGLAS,Norman. Looking Back (1933) Memories suggested by visiting cards; boyhood,work on English Review and at Foreign Office;travels in Mediterranean; reminiscences of Sir E. Arnold, Doyle, Doughty, etc.   226

DOUGLAS,Robert. Adventures of a Medical Student (1848) 2 v. Apprenticeship; study at Guy's; romantic adventures as ship's surgeon; fiction? 227

DOUGLAS, Robin. Sixteen to Twenty-One (1925). Difficulties of youth in London; down and out; tramp; looking for work;Salvation Army; with a dance band; journalism.   228

DOUGLAS,William. Soldiering in Sunshine and Storm (Edin. 1865). Private in the Hussars; service in India; the Crimean War; life in the ranks. 229

DOUGLASS, Albert. Memories of Mummers (1924); and Footlight Reflections (1934).Childhood in theatrical family and sixty years in theatre as manager etc.; reminiscences and anecdotes of plays and performers;the Old Standard Theatre.   230

DOUIE, Lt. Charles. The Weary Road (1929);Beyond the Sunset (1935). Personal experiences WW1, with infantry in France; study at Oxford; at Board of Education; book-reviewing; social work and prison teaching;literary and theatrical friendships.   231

DOVETON, Capt. F. B. Reminiscences of the Burmese War (Taunton, 1852). A personal narrative of service with the Madras Fusiliers, 1824-26.   232

DOWER, Kenneth Gandar. The Spotted Lion (1937). Big-game hunting in Central Africa; rare lions.   233

DOWNES, Capt. Walter Douglas. With the Nigerians (1919). Personal record of WW1 service with Royal Sussex and Nigerian regiments in East Africa;his campaigns.   234

DOWNEY, Edmund. Twenty-Years Ago(L. 1905).Anecdotes of literary life and writers in 70's and 80's.   235

DOWNIE, W. I. Reminiscences (1912). Cheerful account of life as midshipman in 60's; life on frigate of Black Wall Line; passengers.   236

DOWNING, Rupert. If I Laugh (1941). Adventures in exodus from Paris, WW2; German advance; escape.   237

DOYLE, Sir Arthur Conan. Memories and Adventures (1924). Medical study and practice;whaling; service in Boer War; politics, sport, WW1; experiences in spiritualism;his novels; literary success of Sherlock Holmes. 238

DOYLE,Sir Francis Hastings Charles. Reminiscences and Opinions(1886). His education at Eton and Oxford; career in law;poetry; Professor of Poetry at

Oxford; literary reminiscences; notes on politics, society, etc.   239

DOYLE, Lynn (Leslie A. Montgomery). Ulster Childhood (Dublin, 1921). His boyhood & family life in County Down; peasant life and sport.   240

DOYLE, Richard. A Journal (1885). A fifteen year old artist's daily life; London in 1840; early Victorian scene and family life; illustrated.   241

D'OYLY, Sir John, Diary, 1810-1815; activities as British Commissioner in Ceylon; trade; government life; social affairs; court of Kandy. The Diary of ed. H. W. Coddrington (Colombo, 1917) Royal Empire Soc. Library   242

D'OYLY, Sir Warren Hastings. Tales Retailed (1920). His thirty years in the Indian Civil Service from sixties, administration and law; social life, sport, celebrities; later life, Sussex and Scotland.   243

DRACOTT, Alice Elizabeth. The Voice of Mystic India (1930). Her childhood in India; occult studies; lamas, and yogis and fakirs; her visions. India Office Library.   244

/DRAGE, Lt.Col. Gilbert/. Gazpacho, by Marsouin (Leominster, 1949). Life in the marines; travel, sport, places where he was stationed; West Indies, Canada, Spain, Italy. Copy, Hereford City Library.   245

DRAKE, Capt. Peter. Memoirs (Dublin 1754). Military adventures of an Irish soldier of fortune, 1690-1720; service with Jacobites, with French in War of Spanish Succession and in West Indies and with Marlborough; lively.   246

DRAKE, Richard. Autobiography of his life at Pembroke College, Cambridge, to 1640; antiquarian interest; copied by Hearne. MS, Bodleian Library, Rawlinson K (Hearne) 173.   247

DRAKE, Vivian. Above the Battle (L. 1918). Personal experiences with Royal Flying Corps in WW1.   248

DRAPER, Mrs. Muriel Gurdon (Sanders) Music at Midnight (1929). Musical life in London before WW1; composers, play-

ers and her brilliant circle; Sargent and Henry James.   249

DRAWBELL, James Wedgwood. Drifts My Boat (1947). Work and travels of journalist; his many friends from various walks of life.   250

DRAYSON, Maj.Gen. Alfred Wilks. Experiences of a Woolwich Professor (L. 1886). Military education and service and his work as teacher at Royal Military Academy; anecdotes; curriculum; scientific interests.   251

DRESSEL, Dettmar. Up and Down the Scale (1937). London boyhood; career as violinist; music, musicians and social life, England and Germany.   252

DREW, Mrs. John (Louisa). Autobiographical Sketch (N.Y. 1899). Lambeth childhood in theatrical family; career as child actor; emigration to USA and her theatrical career there; reminiscences of Kembles, etc.   253

DREW, Nicholas (Robert Harling). Amateur Sailor (1944). Service in WW2; Dunkirk evacuation; RNVR: convoying in Atlantic.   254

DRINKWATER, John. Inheritance (1931) Discovery (1932). Boyhood and family; Oxford and Warwickshire; office work; acting with Birmingham Rep; his poetry and verse-plays; literary friendships; social life and sport.   255

DROBUTT, Richard. I Spy for the Empire (1939). Intelligence and espionage work during WW1; India, Persia and Afghanistan.   256

DROUGHT, Captain J. B. Green Memory (1937); A Sportsman Looks at Eire (L. 1949). His lifetime of sport in Ireland; fishing; shooting; Irish scene; personalities.   257

DRUMMOND, John. Through Hell (1944) Official naval reporter's experiences in WW2; convoying, submarine-hunting; adventures at Murmansk, Iceland, and in Atlantic.   258

DRUMMOND, John. Inheritance of Dreams (1945). Farming and estate work in the Carse of Gowrie; twenty-year plan for an inherited estate; delightful story of his life and his neighbors in rural Scotland.   259

DRUMMOND-HAY, Sir John. Journal of an Expedition (Cambridge,1848);Memoir (1896). At the Moroccan court in 1846; Scottish boyhood;Sir Walter Scott;his career as diplomat;Egypt, Turkey, and Morocco;local customs, personalities, events.   260

DRURY,Col. Herber. Reminiscences of Life and Sport (1890). Military life in India; acting resident at Travancore; administration; travel, hunting and social life.   261

DRURY, Robert. Madagascar (1722). A report on experiences and observation during 15 years' captivity on island; language, customs, resources.   262

DRURY,Lt.Col.William Price. In Many Parts(1926). Sandhurst; his career in the marines and in naval intelligence; anecdotes of royalty and celebrities; his painting and writing.   263

DUBERLY,Mrs. Henry (Frances Isabella). Journal Kept during the Russian War (1855);   Campaigning Experiences (1859). Experiences of soldier's wife in the Crimean War and the Mutiny;her travels;army movements; Central India and Rajpootan.   264

DUBOIS-PHILLIPS, Dare.   Wanderlust (1934). Adventures in Europe, America Africa, China, as hobo, rancher, hunter, gambler, etc.; white-slavers and the underworld.   265

/DUBUS, Raoul/. Reminiscences of 20 Years' Pigsticking (Calcutta, 1893), Hunting in Bengal.   266

DUCKERS, James Scott.   Handed-Over (1917). Solicitor's experiences as a conscientious objector in WW1;life in Maidstone Prison.   267

DUCKETT,Sir George Floyd. Anecdotal Reminiscences (Kendal, 1895). Herts & Oxford; military service in Ireland; historical and antiquarian writings; country life, mountaineering, public events, social life; rambling.   268

DUCKWORTH, L. B.   Cricket My Love (Birmingham, 1946). The career of the

England wicketkeeper; Yorkshire; the Bradford League; great players; great games.   269

DUDLEY, Joshua. Memoirs (1772). The autobiography and self-revelations of a wastrel;written in Newgate.   270

DUFF,Charles. No Angel's Wing(1947) Irish boyhood; work on boats; interpreter in WW1; in Foreign Office News Department; service with republicans in Spanish Civil War; activities of a leftist and anti-Catholic.   271

DUFF,Douglas Valder. Sword for Hire (1934);Galilee Galloper (1935); Rough with the Smooth (1940); May the Winds Blow (1948). Adventures of a soldier of fortune;police work in Ireland and Palestine; shipwrecked as a boy; commanding schooner-fleet at Tobruk;service in WW1 and WW2; largely composed for boys.   272

DUFF, Sir Hector Livingston. African Small Chop(1932); This Small World(L. 1936).Experiences in British West Africa;life in Castle Grim; himself and his house; Scottish country life, society, sport, reading, etc.   273

DUFF,   Sir Mountstuart Elphinstone Grant. Notes of an Indian Journey (L. 1876); Notes from a Diary (1897-1905) Military life and administration, India, 1851-1901; public affairs; travels; government; social life.   274

DUFF-GORDON,Sir Alexander Cornewall Recollections of Thirty-Nine Years in the Army (1898). Army career from the forties; service in India; the Mutiny Gold Coast; China expedition; observer at siege of Paris; campaigns. 275

DUFF-GORDON, Lady Lucy Christiana. Discretions and Indiscretions (1932). Her social career, work and travels; London, Paris, New York; career as a dress designer.   276

DUFFERIN AND AVA, Hariot Georgina, Marchioness of. Our Viceregal Life in India (1890); My Canadian Journal (L. 1891).Lively diaristic accounts; life in governmental circles in Canada 70's and India in 80's; society,sport, and travel; official life.   277

DUFFIELD,Alexander J. Recollections of Travels Abroad (1889). Travels and adventures;work as miner; Chile, Canada, New Zealand, etc.　　　　278

DUFFIELD,Kenneth Launcelot. Savages and Kings (1945). Johannes Factotum's adventures in news-reel style; ships, sheep, theatre, savages; droving and broncho-busting;his musical plays;the Savage Club; famous cartoonists.　279

DUFFY, Sir Charles Gavan. My Life (1898). Early life in Dublin; Belfast journalism; nationalist politics and agitation, editor of The Nation;Young Ireland Party; in Newgate; emigration to Australia; politics and government there.　　　　　　　　　　　280

DUGDALE, Blanche E. C. Family Homespun (1940). Schooling; Scottish life in Inverary and Edinburgh, to 1900 ; literary life and society;and Saintsbury, etc.　　　　　　　　　281

DUGDALE, Capt. Geoffrey. Langemarck and Cambrai (Shrewsbury, 1932). Personal experiences in WW1;the two battles.　　　　　　　　　　　282

DUGDALE, Sir William. Brief Account in his Heraldic Miscellanies (n.d.). Staffs upbringing; work as antiquarian, surveyor of monuments, librarian, herald; events of Civil War; his publications.　　　　　　　　　283

DUGMORE,Capt.Arthur Radclyffe. When the Somme Ran Red (1918); Autobiography (1930). Education; experiences as naturalist, photographer, writer upon nature subjects; Mark Twain; service, WW1, Yorks regiment; Somme.　284

DUGUID,Julian. I am Persuaded(1941) Spiritual autobiography;progress into agnosticism and back to religion;what determined his development.　285

DUKE, Joshua. Recollections of the Kabul Campaign(1883). Personal record of work in Bengal medical service during Afghan War, 1879-80; military details; diary.　　　　　　　286

DUKES, Sir Paul. Red Dusk (L. 1922) The Story of St. 25 (1938); Unending Quest (1950). Teaching at Riga; work in British intelligence service in the

USSR:Revolution; in service of Whites and Reds; Russian conditions; attack on communism; study of yogi.　287

DUNALLEY, Henry Cornelius O'Callaghan Prittie, Lord. Khaki and Rifle Green (1940). His military & sporting career; Boer War, Egypt, England,WW1; hunting and shooting.　288

DUNBAR, Sir George Duff-Sutherland. Frontiers(1932). His military service in Assam and on North-West Frontier in 1901-14; Abor expedition.　289

/DUNCAN, Alfred H./. Private Life of a Ceylon Coffee Planter(Colombo n.d.) Familiar and personal record of everyday life and work of planter in Ceylon domestic life and sport. Royal Empire Soc. Library.　　　　　　290

DUNCAN, Eric. From Shetland to Vancouver Island(Edin.1937). His boyhood in the Shetlands in mid-19th Century & later life in Canada.　291

DUNCKLEY, Fan. C. Eight Years in Abyssinia (1935). Experiences of wife of a journalist at Addis Ababa in the twenties; Abyssinian life and customs and her adventures.　292

DUNDAS,Anne Louise. Beneath African Glaciers (1924). Wife of a Tanganyika official; change from German to British rule;official society; people and places.　　　　　　　　293

DUNDAS,Admiral Sir Charles Hope. An Admiral's Yarns(1922). Fifty years in navy; training on Britannia; service in China and Japan; anecdotes.　294

DUNDONALD,Douglas M.B. H. Cochrane, 12th Earl of. My Army Life(1926). His military career,1884-1918; service in Egypt, South Africa, Canada, WW1. 295

DUNDONALD,Thomas Cochrane,10th Earl of. Autobiography of a Seaman (1860). His naval career 1793-1814;conditions of sea life;service against French in Napoleonic wars; work in Parliament; Stock Exchange trial.　296

DUNLOP, Andrew. Fifty Years (Dublin 1911). Irish politics and journalism; Dublin Daily News; Home Rule, Parnell Land War; from 1857.　297

DUNLOP, Robert Henry Wallace. Service and Adventure (1858). His work as
a civil servant in Bengal; service in
Meerut Volunteer Horse at Meerut during the Mutiny.   298

DUNN, James. From Coal Mine Upward
(1910). Work as coalminer; with Works
Corps in Crimea; spiritual awakening;
work for London City Mission.   299

DUNN, James. Paperchase (1938). Adventure and work of journalist; Wolverhampton and London;Daily Mail correspondent abroad; crime, notorieties
and celebrities; pungent Tory.   300

/DUNNE,John Joseph/. Here and There
Memories,by H.R.N. (1896). Legal, political and social life in Ireland; &
anecdotes of friends and Irish politicians.   301

DUNRAVEN,Windham Thomas Wyndham-Quin
Earl of. Past Times(1922). Boyhood in
Ireland;travel, sport, society, celebrities & public events; politics and
land troubles in Ireland.   302

DUNSANY, Edward J. M. D. Plunkett,
Baron. My Ireland (1937); Patches of
Sunlight (L.1938); While Sirens Slept
(1944); Sirens Wake (1945). Childhood
London and Dunstall; Eton & Sandhurst
and army career;Boer War and WW1 service;sport, travel, social, politics;
his novels, plays, poetry and lecturing; oncoming of war; experiences in
Blitz and WW2.   303

DUNSTERVILLE,Maj.Gen.Lionel Charles
Stalky's Reminiscences (1928); Stalky
Settles Down (1932); Stalky's Adven-
tures(1933). Kipling's friend; childhood; at school with Kipling; Woolwich;
army career in India; China War 1900;
service in France in WW1;Indian frontier and Indian problems; adventures
into journalism; social.   304

DUNTON,John. Life and Errors (1705)
Apprentice bookseller; characters of
booksellers;marital and religious affairs; merchants and preachers in London.   305

DUNVILLE, T. E. Autobiography of an
Eccentric Comedian (1917). Schooling;
life as entertainer on tour;musichall
comedian; anecdotes.   306

/DUPPA,Richard/. Memoirs of a Celebrated Literary & Political Character
(1813). Experiences in journalism and
politics, mid-18th Century; political
society; Fox, Pitt, Newcastle.   307

DUPUIS, Joseph. Journal of a Residence in Ashantee (1824). Travels and
negotiations on Gold Coast; consul in
Ashantee; politics; court life. 308

DURAND, Col. Algernon G. O. Making
of a Frontier(1899). His military and
administrative activities while British Agent at Gilgit and in the eastern
Hindu-Kush.   309

DURAND, Sir Edward Law. Rifle, Rod,
and Spear (1911).Lively adventures of
big-game hunter; India; Persia.   310

DUTTON, Maj. Charles. Life in India
(1882). Military service in Bengal;
social life; hunting; Indian society;
hints for travellers.   311

DUTTON, Joseph E.   An Evangelist's
Travels (Kilmarnock, 1927). A Gospel
preacher's ministry, adventures, and
sufferings in Europe, Near East, and
America.   312

DUVEEN,James Henry. Collections and
Recollections (1935);   Secrets of an
Art Dealer (1937). His experiences as
an art dealer;searching out treasures
and buying and selling; great collections;his coups and deals; crimes and
secrets of trade.   313

DYCE, Charles M. Personal Reminiscences (1906). Thirty years experience
of a businessman in Shanghai; Chinese
and English society; sport.   314

DYER, Robert. Nine Years of an Act-
or's Life (1833). Experiences acting &
managing; Theatre Royal, Plymouth;his
experiences, mostly in theatres of the
West Country.   315

DYKE, Lady Zoë Hart. So Spins the
Silkworm (1949). Lively record of her
enthusiasm for silkworms from girlhood
and of her silk farm in Kent; the use
of silk for parachutes & royal robes;
pleasant.   316

DYNEVOR,Walter FitzUryan Rhys, Lord
My Reminiscences (Carmarthen,1937). A

boyhood in Wales;Eton and Oxford; his political career as Conservative M.P. and in House of Lords;Lord Lieutenant for Carmarthen;his friends, amusement and recreation.   317

E., B. History of a Man, ed. George Gilfillan (1856). Scottish education; theological and church affairs;literary life and views,first half of 19th Century.   1

EADE,Sir Peter. Autobiography(1916) Boyhood and youth to 1847; schools in Norfolk; medical studies, London.   2

EADIE, Hazel Ballance. Lagooned in the Virgin Islands (1931). Residence in Tortola; experience among negroes; native customs and ideas.   3

EAGAR,M. Six Years (1906). A simple account of six years as nurse to royal children in Russia;nursery affairs in the palaces.   4

EAMES,Emma. Some Memories (New York 1927). Harsh childhood;experiences as opera singer; censorious views on the musical profession.   5

EARDLEY-WILMOT, Sir Sainthill. Forest Life (1910); Leaves from Indian Forests (1930). Experiences during 25 years as inspector of forests in India mainly forestry and sport.   6

EARDLEY-WILMOT, Adm. Sir Sidney. An Admiral's Memories (1927). Sixty-five years in the navy and Naval Intelligence; his voyages; reflections on the old and new navies,on war and prevention; celebrities.   7

EARLE, Mrs. Charles William (Maria Theresa). Memoirs and Memories (1911) Her parents and mid-Victorian childhood;marriage and life in Canada; her garden and nature study; memories of Ruskin.   8

EARLE,Sir Lionel.Turn Over the Page (1935). Career of civil servant,1900-1933;Colonial Office; Office of Works and London Parks; society, politics & celebrities.   9

EASTON, Dorothy. You Asked Me Why (1936). Addressed to her son; country life; writing in London; flower-growing in Kent; marriage; her son.   10

EASTON, Fred H. Barak (1928). Experiences of a missionary in China told through mouth of his donkey;it may be entirely fictional.   11

EASTON,John. Three Personal Records (1929). Personal experiences of officer in France in WW1; joint work with R. H. Mottram & E. Partridge.   12

EASTWICK, Capt. Robert W.E. Master Mariner (L.1891). Lively account of adventures at sea;service on East Indiamen; wrecks and escapes; captured by the French during Napoleonic wars; excitements; dictated; good.   13

EBERS,John. Seven Years (1828). Experiences of the manager of the King's Theatre, Haymarket, 1821-27; Italian singers;French opera; difficulties of manager's life.   14

ECHLIN, Elizabeth Gladys. Keep Off Death (Glasgow, 1939); Live Unafraid (1944); Vertigo (1946). Her clerical and minor literary activities;life in Britain during WW2; air raids; shelters;her fight and victory over tuberculosis; poems; translations.   15

ANON. Echoes of the Eighties,ed. W. Partington (1921). Gossip, scandals, anecdotes of high society and literary interests; from the diary of a Victorian lady.   16

EDGE, Selwyn F. My Motoring Reminiscences (1934). Experiences in racing automobiles and motorboats from 1895; Brooklands; engineering.   17

EDGE-PARTINGTON, James. Random Rot (Altrincham, 1883). An ethnologist's three years'of world travel,including New Zealand and Australia.   18

EDGER,Samuel.Autobiographical Notes (1886). London childhood; nonconformity; education; ministry at Kimbolton and Abingdon; later in N.Z.   19

EDGEWORTH, Richard Lovell. Memoirs (1820). Childhood in Ireland; Oxford,

the Temple; London life; his two marriages; his technical inventions and
friendships with Mr.Day, Erasmus Darwin; visit to Rousseau; goes to 1780;
completed by Maria Edgeworth.   20

EDMONDS, Charles (C.E. Carrington).
Subaltern's War (1929).   A realistic
account of experiences in France WW1;
Somme, 3rd Ypres; 1914-18.   21

EDMUNDSON,William. A Journal of the
Life (1715). Spiritual autobiography
and adventures of an Irish Quaker; in
Cromwell's army; ministry in Ireland,
America, West Indies.   22

EDRICH, William J. Cricket Heritage
(1948); Cricketing Days(1950). Career
of the Middlesex and England all-rounder; Test cricket; games, players and
tours; commentary.   23

EDWARD,Eliza. Diary of a Quiet Life
(1887). Afflictions; retirement from
social life;spiritual meditations and
literary studies.   24

EDWARDS,Charles. An Afflicted Man's
Testimony (1691). Spiritual life and
sufferings of an Oswestry nonconformist clergyman.   25

EDWARDS, Charles Edward. Round the
World (Ludlow, 1949). Lively account
of adventures of an old Shropshireman
on cattle-selling trip;his adventures
in Spain and Lisbon, Australia, South
Africa. Shrewsbury P.L.   26

EDWARDS, F. W. Paper, Sir? (1912).
Autobiography and reminiscences of an
old newspaper seller.   27

EDWARDS, George. From Crow-Scaring
to Westminster (1922). Farm labourer
in Norfolk; organization of labourers
and work in Trade Union movement; MP;
country life and working-classes; an
important record.   28

EDWARDS, Henry Sutherland. Personal
Recollections(1900). Life as journalist; sixty years recollections of the
theatre, music & literature; travels;
anecdotes of his friends.   29

EDWARDES, Maj. Herbert B. A Year on
the Punjab Frontier (1851). Life and
work of a political officer; military

administration, 1848-49; conquest of
Bunnoo.   30

EDWARDS, Ifan. No Gold on My Shovel
(1947). Welsh working man;odd jobs in
South Wales and Midlands; labourer's
experiences of work and unemployment;
athletics; political activities.   31

EDWARDS, Jane. Recollections of Old
Sevenoaks; Kentish social life, topography, etc. MS, Sevenoaks Public Library, L. 548.   32

EDWARDS, John Passmore. A Few Footprints (1905). Working-class life in
Manchester; journalism for The Echo;
philanthropic and social work; hospitals, mechanics' institutes; working-
class education. Cambridge U.L.   33

EDWARDS, Lionel D. H. Reminiscences
of a Sporting Artist (1948). Work as
an artist; horses and hunts; England,
Ireland, Wales.   34

EDWARDS,Norman.Through a Young Man's
Eyes(1928).Sailor and theatrical journalist in 20's;impressions and opinions about education,people, the times
and religion.   35

EDWARDS,William.Personal Adventures
(1858); Reminiscences of a Bengal Civilian (1866); Reminiscences of Forty
Three Years in India (1874). His long
career as a judge in Bengal; administration and law; travels; Indian Mutiny; a vivid record.   36

EGERTON,Capt. Francis. Diary, 1850-
1851;sailor's travels in India; lively account of scenes and society, Nepal mainly.Journal of a Winter's Tour
(1852).   37

ANON.1871-1935(1936). Old-fashioned
but lively reminiscences of literature
and the theatre by an old lady;poetry
recitations; and her views on people,
books, plays, etc.   38

ELDRIDGE, Captain T. J. Knots in a
Sailor's Life (1937). His service in
the Indian and Chinese maritime services;mostly adventures while policing
Chinese waters; lively.   39

ELERS, Capt. George. Memoirs (1903)
Family and school; military career as

young man in India;   country life and
sport in Suffolk; up to his marriage;
excellent.   40

ELGIN,James Bruce, 8th Earl. Diary,
1857-62; account of two missions into
China;activities as Viceroy of India;
military and official matters; social
life;his troubles among lesser breeds
Letters and Journals, edited Theodore
Walrond (1872).   41

ELIBANK,Gideon Murray, 2nd Viscount
A Man's Life(1934). Scottish boyhood;
business in London; colonial administration in New Guinea, South Africa,
and West Indies;Food Commissioner and
Air Ministry in WW1; reflections and
reminiscences; interesting.   42

ELIOT, E. C. Broken Atoms (L. 1938)
His career in the colonial service in
Argentina, Gilberts, Ellice Islands,
Gold Coast, Uganda, West Indies; and
experiences of officialdom,1888-1931,
travels; social life.   43

ELLAN, B. J. Spitfire (1942). Experiences of fighter-pilot in RAF in
WW2; Dunkirk; Battle of Britain.   44

ELLENOR, Thomas Bell. Rambling Recollections of Chelsea (1901). An old
inhabitant's recollections of life in
Chelsea in early Victorian period;in-
stitutions; events. Chelsea P.L.   45

/ELLERSLIE, Alma7. Diary of an Actress, ed.Henry C. Shuttleworth (1885)
Three years in provincial theatres and
her difficulties and anxieties; daily
life and work told with religious and
moral bias. Bodleian.   46

ELLIOT, Sir Henry George. Some Revolutions (1922). His career as a diplomat, 1841-77; travels, politics and
public affairs in Italy, Greece, Turkey, Australia.   47

ELLIOT, John. Narrative of the Life
and Death (1787). Includes his apologia for his attempted murder of Miss
Mary Boydell.   48

ELLIOT, John. Darlington man's memoirs of his life at sea to 1782; midshipman on the Resolution; Cook's 2nd
voyage round the world. MS in British
Museum, Add. 42714.   49

ELLIOT,Robert Harry. Experiences of
a Planter in the Jungles of Mysore(L.
1871); Gold, Sport, and Coffee-Plant-
ing(1894). Work of a planter, 1855 to
1893;native labour; technical detail,
government; native customs;scenery; &
social life; interesting.   50

ELLIOT, William Gerald. In My Anec-
dotage(1925). Eton and Cambridge; his
career on the stage; social and political life in Roxburghshire; the Bancrofts and Forbes Robertson.   51

ELLIOTT, Ebenezer. Life, Poetry and
Letters, by John Watkins (1850). Contains short autobiography of his boyhood and youth; schooling; work in a
foundry; beginning of his poetry. See
also, Athenaeum, Jan. 12, 1850 and MS
Sheffield City Libraries, B. E158 SF,
which is a short autobiographical essay of the Corn-Law poet.   52

ELLIOTT, Grace (Dalrymple). Journal
of My Life (1859). A vivid account of
her experiences in France during the
Revolution; imprisonment after execu-
tionof her friend the Duke of Orleans
and her adventures.   53

ELLIOTT, Sir James Sands. Scalpel &
Sword (Sydney, 1936). Boyhood in New
Zealand; medical studies in Edinburgh
and career as army surgeon; Boer War
and WW1 work;medical life, travel and
army life.   54

ELLIOTT, John Malsbury Kirby. Fifty
Years(1900). Reminiscences of hunting
with Grafton,Belvoir and other packs;
characters and celebrities.   55

ELLIS,Capt. Fred W. Round Cape Horn
in Sail (Croydon, 1949). Memories of
his first voyage as a boy;on a barque
from London to Chile and Peru, around
the Horn.   56

ELLIS, Havelock. My Life (1939). An
autobiography of 80 years;his life in
Australia and England;family affairs;
work in sexual problems and his writings; his friends, Olive Schreiner and
John Symonds, etc.; important.   57

ELLIS, Henry. Journal, 1816-1817; a
commissioner's account of diplomacy &
ceremonies during an embassy to China;
interview with Napoleon on St. Helena;

Journal of the Proceedings (1817). 58

ELLIS, Gen. Sir Samuel B. Memoirs & Services (1866).His career in Marines from 1804; Trafalgar and the Peninsular War;War of 1812; Cape Town, China includes diaries.   59

ELLIS, William. A Brief Account of the Life (1710). Airton man's spiritual life and sufferings in the Quaker ministry.   60

ELLIS, Reverend William. Polynesian Researches (1829). His six years as a missionary in New Zealand and islands of South Seas; ethnology and customs of natives.   61

/ELLIS, William/. Reminiscences and Reflections of an Old Operative(1852) Working-class life;apprenticeship and work as engineer; labour conditions & unions, co-operative societies, economics; advice on education.   62

ELLISON, Grace. An Englishwoman in a Turkish Harem (1915). Her work at the Ottoman court; Turkish life, customs; feminist; lively.   63

ELLISON, Seacome. Prison Scenes (L. 1838).An English sea-captain captured by French in 1804; four years experience of French prisons; escape.   64

ELLISON,Thomas. Gleanings and Reminiscences (Liverpool, 1905).   Thirty years of journalism;Liverpool D a i l y Post; chief events and figures of the cotton trade.   65

ELLISON,Wallace. Escaped (Edinburgh 1918); Escapes and Adventures (Edin. 1928).His four years in German prison camps in WWl; various attempts to escape; at large in Germany.   66

ELLISS,Albert F. Adventuring in Coral Seas (1936).His youth; travels in South Seas;investigation of phosphate deposits on Ocean Island and Naurk; & adventures.   67

ELLMAN, Edward Boys. Recollections (Hove, 1912;1925). Oxford; his career as parson; Sussex parishes; rector of Berwick;Sussex life and people; religious and educational work.   68

ELLWOOD,Thomas. History of the Life (1714). Quaker conversion and ministry; low life in England; experiences in Newgate;troubles and adventures; a lively record.   69

ELPHINSTONE,Gen.Sir Howard Crauford Journal of the Operations (1859). An impersonal account of the invasion of the Crimea and the winter campaign of 1854-55.   70

ELSMIE, George Robert. Thirty-Five Years in the Punjab(1908). Haileybury education; career as commissioner and judge at Peshawur; administration and law; largely diary.   71

ELSTOB, Peter. Spanish Prisoner (L. 1939).Adventure in Spanish Civil War; flying for Republicans;arrest as spy; prison experiences.   72

ELTON, Godfrey Elton, Baron. Among Others (1938);The Two Villages (1949) Education, WWl service, socialism and politics, radio work; reflections and impressions in a Midland village during one day.   73

ELTON,James Frederick. Diary, 1873-1877; his work as consul, Mozambique; tour of inspection with view to suppressing the slave-trade. Travels and Researches (1879).   74

ELWES,Henry John. Memoirs of Travel (1930). Eton; Scots Guards; travels & sport in many lands, and his studies in ornithology, botany, zoology, and horticulture; collecting specimens in Asia, Europe, South America.   75

ELWIN,Verrier. Leaves from the Jungle (1936). Mostly diary of his life in a Gond village,1932-35; educational work; village life.   76

EMANUEL, Louis. Jottings and Recollections of a Bengal "Qui Hye!"(n.d.) His social life in Calcutta; servants and sahibs. Copy in Royal Empire Soc. Library.   77

ENGLISH OFFICER. Society Recollections (1907); More Society Recollections (1908). Anecdotes and gossip of high society, sport, spas, operas and theatres, 1879-1904; mostly impersonal; attaché in Europe.   78

AN ENGLISHMAN. Five Years Residence in Buenos Ayres (1827). Life there in 1820-25; Uruguay; police; shipping on the Plate; Argentinian life.   79

ANON. Episodes in the Life of a Retired Chaplain(1882). Work in Norfolk parish; army chaplain, India & Burma; Rangoon; Travancore villages; educational and missionary work; his later life in a Hereford parish.   80

ANONYMOUS. Episodes in the Life of an Indian Chaplain (1882). Military & religious life in India. India Office Library.   81

EPSTEIN, Jacob. Let There be Sculpture(1940). New York childhood; study in Paris and thirty years of sculpture and artistic struggle and controversy in England;artistic movements and his place in them.   82

ERNLE,Rowland Edmund Prothero, Lord Whippingham to Westminster(1938). His upbringing and education; Oxford; his writing; literary criticism; politics and public service;M.P.; President of Board of Agriculture; political journalism.   83

ERSKINE,Angela St. Clair, Lady. Memories (L. 1923); Fore and Aft (1932) London social life and society;sport; travels around the Empire.   84

ERSKINE, John Elphinstone. Journal, 1853; travels of a naval officer; the Fijis and Western Pacific;customs and institutions. Journal of a Cruise (L. 1853).   85

ERSKINE OF CARDROSS,Sir David. Memoirs(1926). Early years and marriage; forty years as sergeant-at-arms in the House of Commons;reminiscences of Parliament,court, Victoria's jubilee and WW1.   86

E7. I Am a Spy (1938). Experiences of a professional spy for many countries; lone hand excitements.   87

ESCOTT, Thomas Hay Sweet. Platform, Press, Politics and Play(1895). Early life in Somerset; Balliol; politics & literature in 60's and 70's;Gladstone

Disraeli, George Eliot, etc.   88

ESMONDE, Sir Thomas Henry Grattan. Hunting Memories (1925). Travels and shooting in Canada, USA, Ireland.   89

ESPINASSE, Francis. Recollections (1893).Edinburgh boyhood; the British Museum library;Manchester about 80's; his literary journalism; Scott, Campbell,the Carlyles, Leigh Hunt, Hannay and other writers.   90

ESPINOSA,Edouard Henry. And Then He Danced (1948). A lifetime's work as a dancer and teacher of dancing;British Ballet.   91

ESTE, Charles. My Own Life (1787). Chaplain at Chapel Royal, Whitehall; theatre; journalism.   92

ETHERTON, Col. Percy Thomas. Adventures (1928);All Over the World(1947) A Soldier in India; consul in Chinese Turkestan; with Kitchener's Scouts; a gold prospector in Australia; travels and hardships in Canada, USA,Asia and Australia.   93

AN ETONIAN. Recollections of Eton (1870). "Charles Norton's" life at the school as a boy; studies, sports, and masters and boys.   94

EURALYUS. Tales of the Sea (1860). Irish boyhood;experiences as midshipman in 20's; adventures in China War; life in many seas.   95

EUSTON, Arabella. Lover's Looking Glass(1800?). Devonshire milkmaid and her affair with a tradesman's son;family difficulties and her troubles to eventual happiness and wealth.Probably fiction.   96

EVANS, Alfred John. Escaping Club (1922).Experiences of a flyer in WW1; imprisonment in Germany and attempts to escape.   97

EVANS, Capt. Anwyl Rees. Sailor's Way (1934). His life in sailing ships around the Horn; life, work, and romance of the sea.   98

EVANS, Herbert M. M. Why I Left St. Michael's(1903). Clergyman's apologia for resigning from Shoreditch benefice and for catholic practices.　　　99

EVANS, Hugh. Gorse Glen (Liverpool, 1948).Liverpool journalist's memories of bygone Wales; translated.　　　100

EVANS, Margiad. Autobiography (Oxford, 1943). Country life before WW2; passing emotions of a woman; detailed minutiae of sensation.　　　101

EVANS, Thomas. A Welshman in India (1908).Work and travels of sailor and evangelist in ports; missionary work in India; destroying Hindu gods; temperance work; fascinating record of a hell-fire Baptist.　　　102

EVANS, Thomas Wiltberger. Memoirs (1905).Court dentist to Napoleon III; political, military, and society matters at court.　　　103

EVELYN,John. Memoires for My Grand-Son, ed.Geoffrey Keynes (Oxford 1926) Reminiscences and reflections in old age; life and ways of a country gentleman in 17th Century; estate, house, books, family duty; modelled on Varro and largely a conduct book.　　　104

ANON.The Eventful Life of a Soldier (Edin.1827). The experiences of Scottish infantry sergeant in the Peninsular war; campaigns in Spain, Portugal and France.　　　105

EVERARD, Edward Cape. Memoirs of an Unfortunate Son of Thespis (Edinburgh 1818). Theatrical training; pupil of Garrick; work in provincial theatres and 23 years at Drury Lane; interesting account of theatrical life in the 18th Century.　　　106

EVEREST, Elsie. Finding a Soul(1922) Spiritual life; childhood in agnostic family; influence of Beethoven; education in convent; conversion to Catholicism.　　　107

EVERETT,Katherine. Bricks & Flowers (1949). Childhood near Killarney in the 70's; drabness of Irish domestic life;country house life in Leicestershire;study at Slade; career as house and garden designer;society anecdotes pleasant.　　　108

EVERY, Right Rev. Edward F. Twenty-

Five Years in South America (L.1929). Travels and missionary work of Anglican bishop in Argentina; social life, politics in Argentina.　　　109

EVILL, William. Rambling Records(L. 1904). Bath boyhood; his training as railway engineer and work in railroad construction;in business in Battersea and London social life,amusements and travels. Bath P.L.　　　110

EWART, Sir John Alexander. Story of a Soldier's Life (1881). Military career in Mauritius, Turkish and Crimea campaigns,Indian Mutiny; aide-de-camp to Queen Victoria.　　　111

EWART,Lt. Wilfrid H. G. Scots Guard (1934). Service in France in WW1; later social life and sport in England; and trips to Mexico and USA; his novels and writing.　　　112

EWENS, William Thomas. Thirty Years (1924). Life and work of newspaperman working at Bow Street Police Court; criminals, trials, police.　　　113

EX-CIVILIAN. Life in the Mofussil (1878). Education; civil service work as magistrate and collector in Lower Bengal; Mozufferpore, Dacca; hunting; social life; by G. Gordon?　　　114

ANON. Experiences (1926). Spiritual autobiography of woman; telepathy and mental tribulations;conversion to Catholicism; visions.　　　115

ANON. Experiences of a War Baby (L. 1920). Naval service in WW1; cadet at Dartmouth; Jutland; Scapa Flow; naval routine and diversions.　　　116

ANON.Experiences of a Workhouse Visitor (1857). Charity and social work in and around Frome in 50's;condition of workhouses; mission work.　　　117

ANON. Experiences of an Officer's Wife in Ireland (Edin. 1921). Adventures and perils of Scotswoman during IRA troubles; anti-Irish.　　　118

ANON. Experiences of Mack (1906). A readable account of the work, travels sport and social pleasures of Glasgow businessman; European travel, fishing etc.　　　119

EX-PRIVATE X. War is War (1930). A class-conscious ranker's narrative of experiences in WW1, insisting on horror and brutality of war.   120

ANONYMOUS. Extracts from the Diary of a Field Officer in the Bengal Army (1853). Journey to India; his military service; Indian life & scene; geology; reflections on Indian service.   121

ANON. Extracts from the Diary of a Living Physician, ed. L. F. C. (1851) Death-bed and court scenes; narratives of psychological and ethical interest concerning his patients.   122

ANON. Extracts from the Journal of a Young Traveller (Newcastle, 1825). Orphan's extensive travels and adventures; Russia, Asia, China, Indonesia India, Arabia, Africa; customs, sights written up for her children.   123

ANON. Extraordinary Confessions of a Detective Policeman (1852). Sensational experiences in London police in 30's and 40's; feats of detection and capture of criminals.   124

EYRE, Giles E. M. Somme Harvest (L. (1938). Life in the ranks in WW1; experience in and about Loos and in the battle of the Somme.   125

EYRE, Lt. Sir Vincent. The Military Operations at Cabul (1843). Experiences during the Afghan rebellion 1841, and the attempts to suppress it; sufferings in prison.   126

EYRE-TODD, George. Leaves from the Life(Glasgow, 1934). Autobiographical essays of Scottish man of letters; reminiscences of older Scottish life and customs.   127

EYRE-WALKER, Basil. Rolling On (1936) Adventures of a rolling stone; cowboy in western USA: farming and odd jobs in New Zealand.   128

EYSTON, George E. T. Flat Out (1933) Adventures in speed; racing with cars and motorboats from 1921.   129

F., A.M. Foreign Courts and Foreign Homes(1898). Domestic and social life in Germany, England, France; diplomatic and court life.   1

FABER, Mary Anne. Recollections of Indian Life (1910). Domestic life in Calcutta with her soldier-husband from 50's; simple and pleasant. Copy, India Office Library.   2

FABIAN, Robert. Fabian of the Yard (1950). Career and experiences as constable and detective from 1921; exciting cases; modern police methods.   3

FAGAN, Elisabeth (editor). From the Wings, by The Stage Cat (1922). Theatrical career, plays, tours; the Benson Company; Daly comedies; anecdotes and opinions.   4

FAGAN, James Octavius. Autobiography (N.Y.1912). Scottish boyhood and education; travels and railway work in S. America, Africa, and mostly USA: free enterprise and individualism.   5

FAGG, Michael (pseud.). Life and Adventures of a Limb of the Law (1836). Irish upbringing; experiences as lawyer's clerk; adventures and wild oats; legal study at Temple; eventual marriage to an old Irish flame.   6

FAIRBAIRN, Lt. Com. Douglas. Narrative of a Naval Nobody (1929). Naval career and social life, 1907-24; but mostly experiences in WW1; Gallipoli and Dardanelles.   7

FAIRBROTHER, Sydney. Through an Old Stage Door(1939). Childhood; her early acting in stock companies; touring USA with Kendals; experiences in music halls, musical comedies, plays; anecdotes of theatrical life.   8

FAIRFAX, Thomas Fairfax, 3rd Baron. Short Memorials (1699). His military service in the Civil War; sieges and battles in Yorkshire, 1642-3.   9

FAIRFAX-BLAKEBOROUGH, John Freeman. Sporting Days (1925); Paddock Personalities (1935). Journalism and sport; hunting, horse-racing, steeplechasing; owners, trainers, jockeys, celebrities and anecdotes of 30 years.   10

FAITHFULL, Lilian Mary. In the House

of My Pilgrimage(1924);Evening Crowns the Day (1940). Her childhood and family;study at Somerville; teaching at Royal Holloway and King's Colleges and her career as principal of Cheltenham Ladies College;friendships, pleasures social and religious work.   11

FALCONER, John Downie. On Horseback (1911). Travels and explorations of a geographer in Nigeria and the Central Sudan.   12

FALCONER, Capt. Richard. The Voyage Dangerous Adventures and Imminent Escapes (1720). Picaresque adventure on sea and land;West Indies; shipwrecked marooned & married to Indian; engagements with Spanish.   13

FALK, Bernard. He Laughed in Fleet Street (1933); Five Years Dead (1937) Journalist's humorous account of life in Manchester and Fleet Street; Daily Mail; celebrities of arts, crime, politics, etc.   14

FALKLAND, Amelia Cary, Viscountess. Chow-Chow(1930). Her journal in India Egypt, Syria; social and domestic life of Governor of Bombay,1848-53; travel and observations of Hindu life; witty and observant.   15

FANE, Lady Augusta Fanny. Chit-Chat (1926). Childhood in 60's; court, society,country house life; hunting and memories of huntsmen;travel in Canada and WW1 work and experiences.   16

FANE, Col. Henry Edward. Five Years in India (1842). Diary of an aide-de-camp, 1836-41, in Bengal, Afghanistan and on the frontier; descriptions and military details; overland journey to England.   17

FANSHAWE, Lady Anne. Memoirs (1829) Wife of the ambassador to Portugal and Spain;service to Charles I and II and hardships and adventures during Civil War and in exile; career of a devoted wife and royalist.   18

FANSHAWE,George A. F. C. Memoirs of a Person of Quality, ed. Ashton Hilliers(1907). Picaresque adventures in late 18th Century;highwayman, murderer, etc.; fiction?   19

FARJEON, Eleanor. A Nursery in the Nineties (1935). Whimsical and pleasing account of the artistic and literary Farjeons,including herself in the nursery.   20

FARLEIGH, John. Graven Image (1940) Artist's reminiscences, 1914-35; work and experiments as wood engraver and book illustrator; teaching at Rugby; techniques.   21

FARMER,Biddy. History (Dublin 1760) Adventures and amours of a servant in fine London society; seems a by-blow of Pamela; fiction?   22

FARMER, H.F. The Log of a Shellback (1925).Pleasant reminiscences of life in sailing ships at end of 19th Century;experiences of a rough and brutal life.   23

FARNELL, Lewis Richard. An Oxonian Looks Back (1934). London childhood; City of London School; Oxford; travel and research in archaeology; work and administration at Exeter College.   24

FARNES,Kenneth. Tours and Tests (L. 1940). Reminiscences of the Cambridge University, Essex, and England bowler with reports on tours to Australia,S. Africa, and West Indies.   25

FARNINGHAM,Marianne (pseud.). Working Woman's Life (1907). Childhood in Kent; schools and religion; her work and travel in religious education and journalism; editing the Sunday School Times.   26

FARQUHARSON, Robert. In and Out of Parliament(1911). Edinburgh; Scottish social life and politics; service in Guards;career in Parliament as a Conservative; Aberdeen; theatre, music, travel, society.   27

FARR, Thomas. Traveller's Rambling Reminiscences (1838). Clergyman's eye witness account of Carlist wars;British Auxiliary Legion in Spain;investigations; defence of Palmerston's foreign policy.   28

FARRAN,Roy Alexander. Winged Dagger (1948).Adventures in WW2; escape from Greece;partisan in Italy; in Wavell's

Libyan campaign; Palestine; trial for murder.   29

FARRAR, David. No Royal Road (Eastbourne, 1947). Autobiography of British film actor.   30

FARRELL,William. Carlow in '98, ed. Roger McHugh (Dublin, 1949). Boyhood in 1770's; idealised picture of Irish scene; unwilling participation in the 1798 rebellion;eye-witness account of activities of United Irishmen;reading of Swift and Goldsmith.   31

FARRER, Thomas Henry Farrer, Lord. Some Farrer Memorials(1923). Disjointed but interesting record of boyhood and youth to 1840; Hampstead schools; evangelism, social life, family; life in Bedford Place.   32

FAUGHNAN, Sgt. Thomas. Stirring Incidents (Toronto, 1879). Irish youth; military service of a loyal soldier in the ranks;Crimean War; Egypt; Spain; West Indies; Canada.   33

FAULDS, Henry. Nine Years in Nipon (1885). Missionary work in Japan and work as surgeon in a Tokyo hospital in the 70's; travels; Japanese life and horticulture.   34

FAUSSET, Hugh I'Anson. Modern Prelude(1933). Orphan's spiritual life and sufferings;school and father; his artistic and emotional leanings; his search for reality and faith; literature, sin, religion; struggles with a modern neurosis.   35

FAWCETT, Millicent. What I Remember (1925). Childhood;schools; Cambridge; Victorian literary figures; her work as militant suffragette; women's work in WW1; work for Labour Party.   36

FAWCETT, William. Turf, Chase, and Paddock (1932). Yorkshire sportsman's reminiscences of horses,hounds, hunts races and sportsmen.   37

FAY, Sir Sam. The War Office at War (1937). His work at War Office, from 1886; Boer War; mostly WW1; director of movements and in charge of railway transport.   38

FAY,William George. The Fays of the

Abbey Theatre(1935). Excellent narrative of his early theatrical life; on tour in Ireland and England;repertory work in Dublin;later acting in London anecdotes and personal.   39

FAYERS,Thomas.Labour among the Navvies(1862). His missionary work among railway workmen in Westmoreland;their living and labour conditions.   40

FAYRER, Sir Joseph.   Recollections (1900). Lakeland and Liverpool; medical study in London;army medical service in India and Burma; the Mutiny; professor at Calcutta;his posts, honours, travels, social life & research work.   41

FEA, Allan. Recollections of Sixty Years (1927). His work as a painter; the India Office; his art and writing and contemporary artists; the social scene.   42

FEATHERSTONE, Peter. Reminiscences (1905). Grocer's apprentice at Whitby his conversion and ministry and travels as Wesleyan minister.   Methodist Book Room.   43

FEDDEN, Romilly. Golden Days (1919) Reminiscences of a painter and fisherman in Brittany.   44

FELIX. Recollections of a Bison and Tiger Hunter (1906). A subaltern's 26 years of big-game hunting;large-scale slaughter of Indian game.   45

FELLOWES, Edmund Horace. Memoirs of an Amateur Musician (1946). Winchester and Oxford; career as clergyman; his researches in heraldry and genealogy; work on the Tudor polyphonists and his part in the revival of Tudor music; a modest, pleasant record.   46

FELSTEAD,Sidney Theodore. In Search of Sensation (1945). Thirty years as journalist and freelance; crime,sport politics, theatre, law, etc.   47

FENNAH, Alfred. Retaliation (1935). British sergeant's experiences, WW1; trench warfare in France; Zeppelins ; appraisal of war.   48

FENNELL,James. Apology for the Life (Philadelphia, 1814). Adoption of the stage; life as actor; his misfortunes and moral perils; a warning for parents; latter part Philadelphia.   49

FENTON, Mrs. Journal (1901). Travel of a woman in Tasmania, India, Mauritius; pioneer life; her hardships; a simple autobiography.   50

/FENTON, Capt. Albert/. Memoirs of a Cadet, by A Bengalee (1839). Military service with the East India Co.in Bengal; military affairs; Indian life and wonders of the East.   51

FENTON, Lt. Col. Layard Livingstone The Rifle in India(Berlin, 1923). His long years of big-game hunting in India. India Office Library.   52

FENTON,Seamus. It All Happened(Dublin,1949). Kerry childhood; work as a pupil teacher,teacher, school inspector; professional travels; studies of Gaelic culture and folk-lore; and his Gaelicising activities.   53

FERGUSON, James. Select Mechanical Exercises (1773); A Short Account of the Life (1826). Short autobiography of the 18th Century Scottish physicist, astronomer & inventor; patrons; high thought and low living.   54

FERGUSON, Margaret. Bid Time Return (1941). Her unusual childhood, youth, in Persia; imprisonment during W.W.1; adventures.   55

FERGUSSON, Robert Menzies (ed). My College Days (1887). Scottish student at Edinburgh and St. Andrew's; theological studies; professors, students, landladies,social life, rags; trivial fond records.   56

FERGUSSON, W. N. Adventures (1911). Adventures and hazards during expeditions from Shanghai to Tibet, with J. W. Brooke, 1906-8.   57

FERGUSSON,William. Notes and Recollections (1846). Career as army surgeon during Napoleonic wars and in West Indies; military life, medicine, general observations.   58

FERNYHOUGH, Capt. Thomas. Military Memoirs of Four Brothers (1829). The military career of four Staffordshire

men in the Peninsular War, and war of 1812; Waterloo; USA; largely extracts from diaries.   59

FERRIER, J. Kenneth. Crooks & Crime (1928).Career as policeman and detective;Scotland Yard; police methods in England and USA.   60

FFOULKES,Charles John. Arms and the Tower (1939). Shrewsbury and Oxford; studies in armour; naval service WW1; work as Master of Armouries at Tower of London, and as curator of Imperial War Museum; scholarship, antiquarianism; busy and happy life.   61

FFOULKES, Maude M. C.   My Own Past (1915);All This Happened to Me (1937) Childhood in 80's; Brussels finishing school; flight from her environment & work as clairvoyant,ghost writer, secretary, journalist; travels, adventures, society.   62

FIELD,Cecil. I Always Was Lucky (L. 1948). Journalist's reminiscences of voyages to many parts in merchantmen; reflections on people & places.   63

FIELD,Sir John, Journal, 1841-1892; military and social life in India;1st Afghan War and Abyssinian expedition. Jottings from a Journal (1911).   64

FIELD,Josephine. Wife Ashore (1941) Daily life of naval officer's wife in port towns before and during WW2; family and domestic life; her devotion to the navy; pleasant.   65

/FIELD, Julian Osgood/. Uncensored Recollections (1924);Things I Shouldn't Tell (1925); More Uncensored Recollections (1926). Social gossip and anecdotes of high society and of cosmopolitan high-jinks and politics, in late 19th Century.   66

FIFE, Lt.Col. Ronald d'Arcy. Mosaic of Memories(1943). Military career in India, Africa, WW1; country life and sport.   67

ANON. Fifteen Years in India (1822) Experiences of an officer's wife 1805 to 1819; military travels; campaigns of Mahratta war. Copy in India Office Library.   68

ANON. Fifty Years of London Society (1920). Anecdotes and glamour of high society and the newly rich; appeal to snobs; satire.   69

FIGGIS, Darrell. Chronicle of Jails (1917); Second Chronicle (1919); Recollections of the Irish War (L.1927) Reminiscences of Irish nationalist and writer;the Irish troubles 1913-21 and his part in them; his life in English and Irish prisons; lively.   70

ANON.Fighter Pilot (1942). A simple but good account of his work with RAF in the battle of France.   71

FIGHTER PILOT. Tattered Battlements (1943). Personal narrative of service in RAF in WW2; battle of Malta.   72

FINCH, George Ingle. The Making of a Mountaineer (1924). His training as a climber from boyhood; climbs in the Alps & Himalayas; Everest expedition; techniques; adventures.   73

FINCK,Herman. My Melodious Memories (1937); In the Chair (1938). Amusing reminiscences of composer and conductor; Palace, Drury Lane; musical comedy,musichalls, pantomime, ballet and theatre;reminiscences of Great Edwardians; Bohemian life.   74

FINDLAY, Col. J. M. With the Eighth Scottish Rifles (1926).Experiences of Battalion commander in WW1; Gallipoli Egypt, Palestine, France.   75

FINDLAY,James L. O. B. Fighting Padre (1941).Scottish bank clerk turned army chaplain;plain account of travel and work; Boer War; WW1.   76

FINGALL, Elizabeth M. M. Plunkett, Countess of.Seventy Years Young(1937) Youth in West Ireland;gaiety of young married life in Dublin and Meath; Irish social, literary, political life; the Great Edwardians; lively.   77

FINLAY, David White. Reminiscences of Yacht Racing (Glasgow, 1910). His boats, races and regattas, 1862-1904. Cambridge U.L.   78

FINLAY, George. A History of Greece (1877)Vol. I. Contains brief autobiography; outline of his career as student;travel, farming; historical study and writing.   79

FINLAYSON, George. Mission to Siam and Hué (1826). Journal of observations kept during Crawford's mission, 1821-2; Cochin-China.   80

FINN, Elizabeth Anne. Reminiscences (1929). With her husband, the Polish consul at Jerusalem,from 1846; Jewish life; politics; Hebrew studies; dictated in her old age; good.   81

FINNEMORE, Hilda. Mountain-Sides of Dreams (1914). Childhood in Wales;the romance and fantasy of childhood, and the Welsh countryside.   82

FINZI, Kate John. Eighteen Months (1916). Her work as nurse at Boulogne hospital in early part of WW1.   83

FIRBANK,Thomas. I Bought a Mountain (1940). Experience of sheep-raising & estate work in the Welsh mountains in the twenties.   84

FIREBRACE, Sir Aylmer. Fire Service Memories (1949). His career in London Fire Brigade;fire-fighting in WW2 and the London Blitz; anecdotes.   85

FIRTH, S. Reminiscences of an Old Commercial (Leicester, 1889). Amusing and interesting experiences of travelling salesman; travel; hotels; railways; colleagues. Leicester P.L.   86

FISH, William F. Autobiography of a Counter Jumper (1929). His experiences as assistant and draper in the East End of London in 80's; later business career and work as councillor and mayor in Cape Town.   87

FISHER, Arthur O. Exmoor and Other Days (1930). Staghunting and fowling in Devonshire and abroad.   88

FISHER, Maj. Charles Hawkins. Reminiscences of a Falconer (1901). Experiences and incidents in falconry and in training of falcons; country life and sportsmen in Gloucs.   89

FISHER,Douglas. Little World (1948) Childhood and village life in Eastern Cotswolds between wars; farming,sport manor-houses, local affairs.   90

FISHER, Adm. Sir Frederic William.
Naval Reminiscences (1938). His naval
career 1865-1914; chatty notes on his
social life and adventures, especially
on India and China stations.   91

FISHER, Herbert A. L. An Unfinished
Autobiography (1940). Sussex and New
Forest; education at Oxford and Paris;
reminiscences of famous scholars, writers and painters; Pater, Jowett, Carroll, Taine, Renan; his work at Board
of Education; historical studies; travels in Canada, USA, etc.   92

FISHER, James. Life and Travels (Toronto, 1890). Scottish sergeant-major;
service in Crimea, India, China; later
settles in Canada.   93

FISHER, John Arbuthnot Fisher, Baron
Memories(1919); Records (1919); Memories and Records (N.Y. 1920). His naval career 1854-1919; life and work at
sea and in naval administration; bold
styled story of strong-minded, strong-
handed admiral; controversial.   94

FISHER, Lieut. Col. R. E. Personal
Narrative (1863). Military service at
Canton, 1857-60; Chinese customs; for-
tifications; disciplinary measures on
seizure of British factories.   95

FISHER, Robert Howie. Outside of the
Inside(1919). Spiritual and religious
life and work of minister of St.Cuth-
bert's, Edinburgh; his parishes, editorial work, anecdotes.   96

FITCH, C. G. Queer Horses and Queer
People (1948). A happy-go-lucky life
in the Yeomanry; country life, hunting
and racing; Ireland, New Zealand. 97

FITCH, Henry. My Mis-Spent Youth(L.
1937). Naval career as assistant clerk
and admiral's secretary; India; adventures in WW1; Dardanelles; naval mission to Serbia and defence of Belgrade
Salonika and Serbian offensive; a high
spirited narrative.   98

FITCH, Herbert T. Traitors Within
(1933); Memoirs of a Royal Detective
(1935). His work in Special Department
of Scotland Yard; shadowing political
suspects and counterspy in WW1; Lenin
and Trotsky; work from 1911, as guard
to Royal Family and reminiscences and

anecdotes of royalty; interesting. 99

FITZBALL, Edward (Ball). Thirty-Five
Years of a Dramatic Author's Life (L.
1859). Boyhood on Cambridge farm; Norwich printer; marriage; early literary
efforts and success; writing for London theatre; ventures as manager; theatrical life.   100

FITZCLARENCE, Lt.Col. George. Diary,
1817-18; journey from England to India
and military operations against Pin-
darries and Mahrattas. Journal of a
Route Across India (1819).   101

FITZGERALD, Adm. Charles Cooper Penrose. Memories of the Sea(1913); From
Sail to Steam(1916). His naval career
from 1854 to 1905; cruises and service
and adventures; changes in the navy;
naval architecture; social life, sport
and anecdotes.   101A

FITZGERALD, Percy Hetherington. Pictures of School Life (1873); Recreations of a Literary Man(1882); Memoirs
of an Author (1895); Stonyhurst Memories (1895); see also, Schooldays at
Saxonhurst (1867); Autobiography of a
Small Boy (1869). Public school life,
1843-49; boys, masters, games, plays;
notes on his life as a writer; reminiscences of the chief Victorian novelists, dramatists, journalists, actors;
social life.   102

FITZMAURICE, Mrs. F.M. Recollections
of a Rifleman's Wife (1851). Travels
with husband in early 19th Century; at
stations in Ireland, Devon and Malta;
army life and travel notes.   103

FITZROY, Sir Almeric. Memoirs(1925)
His work as Clerk of the Privy Council
1898-1923; official ceremonies, public
events, society, celebrities; diaries;
rather impersonal.   104

FITZROY, Yvonne A. G. With the Scottish Nurses in Roumania(1918). Simple
notes on her nursing service in Rumania in WW1.   105

FITZSIMONS, Frederick William. Opening the Psychic Door(1933). His thirty years as an investigator of psychic
work and phenomena; poltergeists, mediums, obsessions; principally in Sth.
Africa.   106

ANON. Five Years for Fraud (1936). Experiences in New Zealand and English prisons;Shrewsbury, Maidstone, Walton gaols; inmates and prison personnel;a balanced account of prison life & its problems.   107

ANON.   Five Years in a Protestant Sisterhood(1869). Anglican upbringing and education; Puseyanism and religious influences; life in sisterhood at Helston and her difficulties; conversion and ten years in a catholic convent; convent life and work.   108

ANON.   Five Years' Penal Servitude (1877). Account of his experiences in Newgate,Millbank, Dartmoor; prisoners and prison life and problems; suggestions for reform.   109

FLAD, Johann Martin. Notes from the Journal (1860). Work of pioneer missionary in Abyssinia in 50's; unrest and native opposition;his negotiation with the king.   110

FLAMSTEED, John. An Account of the Rev. John Flamsteed, by Francis Baily (1835). Contains an autobiography assembled from his writings and touched up; his education, health, researches in astronomy, relations with the Royal Society, quarrels with Newton; covers 1646-1716.   111

FLANAGAN,James. Scenes from My Life (1907). Slum life in London; life of an evangelist; revivalism and its methods; criticism of preachers.   112

FLEET, Adm.Sir Henry Louis. My Life (1922).His naval career 1864-1903 and later service in coastguard;his ships and cruises; anecdotes of naval life and personalities.   113

FLEMING, Sir John Ambrose. Memories of a Scientific Life (1934). Studies in electricity and engineering;London University; teaching at Rossall; professor of engineering at Nottingham & London;his research, lecturing, writing; progress of science; scientific friends. MS of the book is in Lancaster Public Library.   114

FLEMMING, Sir Oliver. Narrative (L. 1660). How he came to execute office of Master of Ceremonies; comportment

therein and his sufferings for nearly 18 years; a tract.   115

FLETCHER, Eliza (Dawson). Autobiography (Carlisle 1874). Social life & literary interests;Scotland and Yorkshire; Wordsworth interest.   116

FLETCHER, Frank. After Many Days(L. 1937). His life in education; schooldays at Rossall; Balliol; teaching at Rugby, Marlborough, Charterhouse, and headmaster of Rossall; personal life and his experiences in and thoughts on education; good.   117

FLETCHER, James Phillips. Autobiography (1853). Boyhood and religious leanings;study and training as a missionary and his work in Nineveh; clerical life and scenes.   118

FLETCHER, Joseph Smith. Memories of a Spectator (1912). Farming in Yorkshire; pleasant account of Yorkshire life and people; literary interests & Tory politics; writing and lecturing; workingmen's clubs.   119

FLETCHER, Margaret.   O, Call Back Yesterday (Oxford, 1939). Conversion to Catholicism 1896; editing Catholic Women's Magazine; leader in Catholic Action; work as painter and as Christian feminist; interesting.   120

FLETCHER, Marie Jane. Diary, 1853; details of her life in India;extracts in biography. Francis Espinasse, Lancashire Worthies (1877).   121

FLOCKHART, Robert. Street Preacher (Edin. 1858). Scottish soldier's life in India; conversion & his religious labours and missionary work in Edinburgh; dictated.   122

FLORA, Calpensis. Reminiscences of Gibraltar (1880). A slight account of her family and social life in Gibraltar from 1845. Colonial Office.   123

FLOWER, Sir Newman. Just As It Happened (1950).His career as journalist and publisher;Cassell's; literary and social life in London; character studies,Stevenson, Wilde, Gosse, Bennett Hardy; life in Dorset.   124

FLYNN,John Stephen. Cornwall, Forty

Years After (1917). Reminiscences of Cornish life and people in late 19th Century.　　　　　　　　　　　125

FOLEY,Lt.Col. Cyril P. Autumn Foliage (1935). Military career and service in Boer War and WW1; mostly sport and social life; cricket, shooting, & golf.　　　　　　　　　　　126

FOLEY,Thomas. I Was an Altmark Prisoner (1940).Sailor on the Doric Star sunk by Graf Spee; experiences aboard the Altmark; rescue; WW2.　　　127

FOLLOWS, Ruth. Memoirs, ed. Samuel Stansfield(Liverpool, 1829). Quaker's ministry in England and Ireland; spiritual life, Quaker meetings & family life; Leicestershire.　　　　　128

FOOT, Stephen. Three Lives (1934); Three Lives and Now(1937); Life Began Yesterday (1935). Childhood; official of Standard Oil in Singapore, Mexico, C.America; WW1 service in France with Tanks; schoolteaching in Eastbourne; international affairs,religion, problems of individual in society; relations with Oxford Group.　　　129

FOOTE,Alexander. Handbook for Spies (1949). His work and adventures as a Russian spy 1938-47 in Switzerland and Germany; training in Moscow; recruitment of spies.　　　　　　　　130

FORAN, Maj. William Robert. Kill or Be Killed (1933);A Cuckoo in Kenya(L. 1936).Adventures of big-game hunter in India and Africa;Roosevelt; work as a police officer in Kenya in early days of colony; lighter side.　　　131

FORBES, Lady Angela S. B. Memories (1921).Country house life and society and her work in canteens in WW1. 132

FORBES,Anna. Insulinde (Edin. 1887) Adventures of a naturalist's wife in Dutch East Indies; descriptions;based on her diary.　　　　　　　133

FORBES,Archibald. My Experiences of the War (1871); Souvenirs (1885). Adventures and observations of special correspondent; Russo-Turkish & Franco Prussian wars; travel and society in Australia, N.Z. and USA.　　　134

FORBES,Frederick Edward. Five Years in China (1848); Dahomey and the Dahomans(1851). Army man in China, 1842 to 1847 and later in Central Africa; coin-collecting; occupation of Lubuan and Borneo; Chinese life; experiences at court of Dahomey.　　　135

FORBES, James. Oriental Memoirs (L. 1813; 1834). Somewhat impersonal description of Indian scene and affairs, during his residence there, 1765-84. See also his "Memoirs of the Campaign 1775," describing military activities in Bombay area. MS, India Office Library, Eur. B.3, 233 pp.　　　136

FORBES, Maj. Jonathan. Eleven Years in Ceylon (1840). Somewhat impersonal account of Ceylon; scenery & natural history;history and antiquities; life of people; sport.　　　　　137

FORBES, Reginald G. Red Horizon (L. 1932).Lurid and brutal experiences in French Foreign Legion; North African campaigns; desertion.　　　138

FORBES,Rosita. Gypsy in the Sun (L. 1944);Appointment with Destiny (1946) Travel and adventure in many parts of the world 1920-43; lecturing; society and celebrities.　　　　　139

FORBES, Sir William. Memoirs of a Banking-House (1860). His career with Coutts' Bank in Edinburgh and London, to 1803; his work, his partners & the banking business; good.　　　140

FORBES-MITCHELL, Sergeant William. Reminiscences of the Great Mutiny (L. 1893). Service in Sutherland Highlanders during Mutiny; siege of Lucknow; Oude and Rohilcund campaigns.　　141

FORBES-ROBERTSON, Sir Johnston. A Player under Three Reigns (1925). His career as actor and manager; the London theatre; tours in Europe and USA; reminiscences of plays, players, and authors.　　　　　　　142

FORD,Ford Madox (Hueffer). Memories and Impressions (1911); Return to Yesterday (1932); It Was the Nightingale (1933). Reminiscences of Pre-Raphaelite poets and artists; country life, politics, social life, visits to USA;

his writing and his literary friends; Joyce, Pound,Proust, Belloc, Galsworthy, etc.   143

FORD, Reginald W. Record of a Pilgrimage (1936). A spiritual autobiography; ill-health, work, love, religion, psychic phenomena.   144

FORD, Thomas Murray (Thomas Le Breton). Memoirs of a Poor Devil (1926). His early life and sport; his work as journalist and novelist; reminiscences of actors, publishers, artists and writers.   145

FORDER,Archibald. With the Arabs in Tent and Town (1902). Missionary work and travels in Moab, Edom and Arabia, late 19th Century.   146

FORMAN, Simon. Autobiography & Personal Diary, edited J.O. Halliwell(L. 1849). Events in the career of a 16th Century schoolmaster, physician, and astrologer; his patrons; the Court; & his legal troubles.   147

FORMBY, Catherine. Formby Reminiscences(1897). Her childhood and family life at Formby;trips to France; written in letter form. Copy in Cambridge U.L.   148

FORMER CHORISTER. Old Magdalen Days (1914). Choral and church work, 1847-1877; Magdalen in the days of Routh; parish life as rector of rural parish in Oxon.   149

FORSHAW, Harry. Stillage Makes His Way (Altrincham, 1948). His success & failure in clothing business,Manchester;Home Defence service in WW1; emigration to Canada and hard times; his later ups and downs in Manchester and Cheshire, and his rising fortunes; he writes as "Rupert Stillage".   150

FORSYTH,Sir Thomas D. Autobiography and Reminiscences (1887).Liverpool & Haileybury; work in ICS and memories of the Mutiny; trade missions to Turkestan;political mission to Mandalay; government service and archaeological interests.   151

FORT, George Seymour. Chance or Design?(1942).Pioneer and administrator in New Zealand,Australia,New Guinea ,

and South Africa in latter part of 19th Century.   152

FORTESCUE, Sir John William. Author and Curator (1933). Cambridge education;government service, Windward Is. and N.Z.;librarian at Windsor Castle; scholarship, writing, social.   153

FORTESCUE,Sir Seymour John. Looking Back (1920). Naval career from 1870; South Africa, Egypt; social life; and on royal yacht.   154

FORTESCUE, Lady Winifred. There's Rosemary (1940); Trampled Lilies (L. 1941); Mountain Madness(1943); Beauty for Ashes(1948); Laughter in Provence (1950). Suffolk childhood; wife of an historian; dress designer; convalescence in Dauphiné;life in Provence and Sussex;work for Free French and evacuees; return to Provence; social life and gossip; Oppenheim; trivial.   155

FORTIE, Maruis. Black and Beautiful (1938).Trading and safaris in Central Africa; village life in Tanganyika; & negro labour and negro sorrows.   156

FORTUNE, Robert. Three Years' Wanderings (1847); A Residence among the Chinese (1857). Work in the Chinese tea and silk trades in 40's and 50's; travels; Chinese customs & politics; pirates.   157

FORWOOD,Sir William B.Recollections (Liverpool,1911). Liverpool schooling and business life; church and public work;local politics, schools, justice music, sport; a seventy years' reflex of Liverpool; good.   158

FOSTER,Ernest. Editor's Chair(1909) Editor,Cassell's Saturday Journal for 20 years; his work, famous authors and the methods and contents of a popular weekly.   159

FOSTER,Francis. Separate Star(1938) Journalism in London before and after WW1; WW1 service in France, Egypt and India; philosophical & religious speculation; conversion to Catholicism & ordination to priesthood.   160

FOSTER, Frank. Clowning Through (L. 1937);Pink Coat (1948). Autobiography and reminiscences of circus ring-master; clowns, strange experiences with men and beasts; Bertram Mills.   161

FOSTER,George. Spice of Life (1939) Comedian's long life in London music-halls; The Gaiety; nightclubs; Bohemian life and anecdotes of comedians, managers, etc.   162

FOSTER, Henry Clapham. At Antwerp & the Dardanelles(1918). Experiences of WW1 chaplain, with 2nd Naval Brigade; training and trial at Gallipoli; Rupert Brooke; simple and good.   163

FOSTER, John. Life and Experiences (Gainsborough, 1824). Religious life and ministry of a Yorkshire Methodist travels and preaching   164

FOTHERGILL, Claud Francis. A Doctor in Many Countries (1945). Medical and religious work;travels with Camps and Tours Union; climbing and sport; his spiritual life.   165

FOTHERGILL, Edward. Five Years in the Sudan (1910). Work as an engineer on government steamers plying water-ways of Southern Sudan, 1900-5; life in out-stations.   166

FOTHERGILL, George A. Riding Retrospect (Edin.1895); Notes from the Diary (Lon. 1901). Boyhood in Kent and Westmoreland; Uppingham School; medical student at Edinburgh; practice in Staffs and N.Wales; later work as artist;horses, hunting, racing, life in a sporting family; pleasant.   167

FOTHERGILL, John. An Account of the Life (1753).Quaker spiritual life and travels in ministry; England,W.Indies and America; religious life in Wensleydale, Yorks.   168

FOTHERGILL, John. Confessions of an Innkeeper (1938);My Three Inns (1949) Hotel work and literary reminiscences of proprietor of poet's pubs at Thame Ascot & Market Harborough; unromantic details and his eclectic clientele;an aesthetic antiquarian.   169

FOULKS,Theodore. Eighteen Months in Jamaica (1833). Planters and negroes in Jamaica; rebellion of 1832; atrocities; attack on anti-slavers.   170

ANON. Four to Fourteen (1939). Grim Victorian childhood in 80's; ruthless mother and weak father; school discipline & childhood submission; character sketches; vivid.   171

FOWLER, George. Three Years in Persia (1841). His travels in Persia and Kurdistan; native life.   172

FOWLER, John Kersley. Echoes of Old Country Life (1892); Recollections of Old Country Life (1894). Middle-class social life and farming in Buckinghamshire, 1830-70; agriculture, town and country,Volunteers, racing, shows and social scene; good.   173

FOX,Eliza. Memoir, ed. Franklin Fox (1869). Her girlhood, family, friends in Chichester to 1820.   174

FOX, Ernest. Contracts and Contacts (1943). Work of a Bournemouth estate agent; apprenticeship, business success, auctions, practice, travels and hotels; nonconformity.   175

FOX, Sir Francis. Sixty-Three Years (1924). Family and education; work as civil engineer on railways, bridges & tunnels; restoring ancient buildings; social and war work.   176

FOX, Franklin. Glimpses of the Life (1862).British sailor aboard American whaler;the slave-trade in China; part fiction.   177

FOX, George. A Journal of the Life (1694); many editions, the best edited by Norman Penney (Cambridge, 1911) for additions to which, see, Journal Friends' Hist. Soc. IX-XXI (1912-24); Penney also edited the Short Journal (Cambridge, 1925). Prototype of the Quaker spiritual autobiography; inner light and Christian witness; endless travels in ministry; imprisonment and sufferings; excellent picture of Quakerism in the days of its trial and the 17th Century religious scene.   178

FOX, George Washington. Some Memories (1931). Literary and legal notes and memories; reprinted from the Surrey Comet.   179

FOX, Richard Michael. Smoky Crusade

(1937). Engineering work in Ireland & Clydeside; work in unions and socialist movement; strikes; conscientious objection and imprisonment in WW1; at Ruskin College; the Russian famine of 1921;with IRA; adventures of a militant left-winger.   180

FOX, Uffa. Crest of the Wave (1939) Life and work of a yacht designer and builder; international races; social life at Cowes.   181

FRANCILLON, Robert Edward. Mid-Victorian Memories(1914). Gloucester and Cheltenham; Cambridge university; legal studies and practice; famous writers and literary life in seventies & eighties; social life; anecdotes; interesting.   182

FRANCIS, Frederick S. Fred Francis (1940). Wellington College; childhood and marriage; life and work on Stock Exchange; hunting and sport; life in Kent; travels.   183

FRANCIS, Gen. Henry. Autobiographical notes, 1842-72; military service with East India Company; the Sutlej & Punjab campaigns; siege of Lucknow; & social and family life. Percy Adams, A History of the Douglas Family (Bedford, 1921).   184

FRANCIS, J. G. Notes from a Journal (1847). Travels in Italy and Sicily, 1844-46; antiquarian and literary interests.   185

FRANCIS, M. E. (Mary E. Blundell). Things of a Child (1918).Evocation of childhood in Ireland; a child's mind and activities; her early reading and writing.   186

FRANCIS,Sir Philip. Diary, 1777-81, his public life and administration in India; the Council, Coote, Hastings; private opinions;official society and social life.Memoirs, by Joseph Parkes (1867). The MS is in India Office Library, Eur. E.23, 344 pp.   187

FRANCK, Richard. Northern Memoirs (1694, 1821). Cambridge; Cromwellian trooper in Scotland;residence in Nottingham;mostly natural history, fishing, reflections in Scotland, done in dialogue form and modelled on Walton's

Compleat Angler.   188

FRANK, Arnee. Quaker autobiography, 1766-1856; youth in Bristol and life as shopkeeper there; conversion, Quaker religious life and observance. MS Friends' Soc. Library, London, N.W.1, Box A.   189

FRANKAU, Gilbert. Self-Portrait (L. 1939). Novelist's life; childhood and family;career of an egocentric; journalism, novels, etc.   190

FRANKAU, Pamela. I Find Four People (1935). Life in boarding-school, as a journalist and writer, with advertising firm;social life, Windsor and the Riviera; friendship with Rebecca West Bennett, G. B. Stern, etc.   191

FRANKLAND,Sir Edward. Sketches from the Life (1902). Boyhood; apprentice to apothecary; work as research chemist; professor at Owen's College,Manchester; X Club; travels.   192

FRASER, Alexander Campbell. Biographica Philosophica (Edin. 1902). Boyhood and schools;Edinburgh University and philosophical studies;work on the North Britain Review;teacher of philosophy at Edinburgh & the university and its work;cultural development and influences on him.   193

FRASER, Sir Andrew Henderson Leith. Among Indian Rajahs and Ryots (1911). Service in Indian Civil Service 1871-1908; administration, education, and police in Bengal and Central Provinces; social life and sport.   194

/FRASER, C?/. Diary, 1831-33; kept by a revenue officer at Saugor; travels in India; Indian life. MS, India Office Library, Eur. E.97.   195

FRASER,Donald. Autobiography (1892) His education and religious training in Scotland; Presbyterian ministry in Canada, and in Inverness and Marylebone; sermons.   196

FRASER, George. Memoirs in the Life (Glasgow, 1808). Early years in Scotland;failure as grocer and enlistment his fortunes and hardships as soldier in Scotland and Ireland; Irish rebellion; capture & escape; return to his business in Glasgow.　　　197

FRASER, James. Memoirs of the Life
Edin. 1738); MS, National Library of
Scotland. Trials and tribulations of
the minister of Brea; imprisonment in
Bass, Tolbooth, and London; religious
life in Scotland in later Seventeenth
Century.　　　198

FRASER, James Baillie. Diary, 1815;
travels of a political agent;military
affairs and descriptions of Himalayan
areas;sources of Jumna and the Ganges
Journal of a Tour (1820).　　　199

FRASER,John. Sixty Years in Uniform
(1939). His army life in India; Kipling;thirty-five years as a beefeater
at the Tower; Tower ceremonies.　200

FRASER,Mary C. A Diplomatist's Wife
in Japan (1899); A Diplomatist's Wife
in Many Lands (1911); Further Remini-
scences(1912). Society and court life
abroad from 50's; Rome, Pekin, Vienna
South America; diplomacy; celebrities
Browning, Sargent, etc.　　　201

FRASER, Gen. Sir Thomas. Recollections (Edin.1914). Service with Royal
Engineers 1862-78; military attaché &
observer; Franco-Prussian and Russo-
Turkish wars.　　　202

FRASER, W.M. Recollections of a Tea
Planter (1937). Work on Assam estates
from 1894;planters & plantation work;
social life in Calcutta.　　　203

FRASER,Sir William Augustus. Hic et
Ubique(1893). Vignettes and reminiscences since early days; social life,
reading, thought.　　　204

FRASER, Sir William J. Ian. Whereas
I Was Blind(1942). Blinded during WW1
training at St. Dunstan's; work there
for education of blind; journalism; &
his work on BBC and as a Conservative
M.P.　　　205

FREDERICK, E. Journal, 1810; military service with Malcolm in Persia; &
escort work. MS, India Office Library
Eur. D. 110-111.　　　206

FREE,Richard William. Dearly Beloved Brethren(1933). A pleasant account
of life and work of an Anglican priest

in East End and suburbs of London;the
human side.　　　207

FREEBODY, Capt. James H. Heat, Hell
and Humour (1935). Adventures of merchant captain in Central Africa;ports
and natives.　　　208

FREEMAN,Ann. Memoir of the Life and
Ministry (1826). Religious life of a
Methodist, Bryanite, and Quaker; her
ministry and travels in Ireland, Devonshire, etc.　　　209

FREEMAN, Rev. Thomas Birch. Journal
of Various Visits (1844). Travels and
missionary work of Wesleyan Methodist
in Ashanti, Aku, and Dahomey.　210

FREEMAN, Win Frank. Age Challenges
Youth (1949).Old man's memories; his
work in Methodist education; training
at Westhill College;lecturing for the
Wesleyan Sunday School Department and
travels in Empire and USA.　　　211

FREESTON, Joseph. Memoirs (Derby,
1823). Autobiography of Baptist religious life and work; minister of the
Baptist church at Hinckley.　　　212

FREMANTLE, Sir Edmund Robert. The
Navy as I Have Known It (1904). Naval
career and service 1849-99; N.Z. war;
Ashanti war;East India and China com-
mands; at Plymouth; naval life, chief
events, reminiscences.　　　213

FREMANTLE, Maj. John Morton. Diary,
1900 and 1904-13;army service in Boer
War;work as political officer in Northern Nigeria; administration; sport;
lively. Two African Journals (1938).
Colonial Office Library.　　　214

FREMANTLE,Sir Sydney Robert. My Naval Career(1949). Buckinghamshire; at
Greenwich; training and rise from the
ranks to admiral; administration; the
Admiralty;Aegean command in WW1; Commander-in-Chief at Portsmouth; naval
personalities.　　　215

FREMANTLE, William Henry. Recollections (1921). Eton and Oxford; parish
work;Dean of Ripon; evangelical revival and Tractarian movement;theologi-
cal controversies; social reform; the
Broad Church opposition to Newmanism;
modernist.　　　216

FRENCH, Evangeline; CABLE, Mildred; FRENCH, Francesca. A Desert Journal (1934). Experiences of three missionaries in China during 30 years; hardships and travels.   217

FRENCH,Rt. Rev. Thomas Valpy. Diary 1867-91; missionary work in India and educational work as Principal of Lahore College; travels; Indian life and culture. The Life, by Herbert Birks (1895).   218

FRENCH, William. Some Recollections of a Western Ranchman (1928). English man's experiences in Wild West; ranch life on the New Mexico frontier 1883-1899; Geronimo, rustlers, etc.   219

/FRERE, Benjamin7. Adventures of a Dramatist (1813). Experiences in London while trying to sell a play; the London scene, theatre, bookshops, and politics; fiction?   220

FREWEN, Moreton. Melton Mowbray and Other Memories (1924).Boyhood, Sussex and Ireland; Cambridge; horse-racing and hunting; cattle ranching in USA; later social and politics in England, and visit to Balkans.   221

FREY, Joseph S. C. F. Narrative of (1809). Franconian Jew converted; his work for London Missionary Society in East End of London.   222

FRITH, William Powell. My Autobiography (1887); Further Reminiscences (1888). Career of a Victorian painter and reminiscences of artists, writers social life, and fashions.   223

FROHMAN, Daniel. Memories of a Manager (N.Y. 1911). Experiences at the Lyceum from 1885;new trends in drama; Pinero & Arthur Jones; famous actors; incidents of stage life.   224

ANON. From Dartmouth to the Dardanelles (1916). A midshipman's experiences in the early days of WW1; naval service in Dardanelles.   225

FROST, George "Jack". Flying Squad (1948). His career in police force; mostly as a driver with Flying Squad; excitements.   226

FROST,John. Horrors of Convict Life

(1856). Newport man's trial for treason, imprisonment, and transportation in 40's.   227

FROST, Thomas. Forty Years' Recollections (1880); Reminiscences (1886) Boyhood in London suburbs; journalism in Birmingham,Lancs, Yorks.; Chartism and Owen's socialism;the reform movement and social work in London; popular literature,entertainment and the plebeian scene; excellent.   228

FRY, Caroline (Wilson). An Autobiography (1848). Kentish childhood and her upbringing;social life in London; her conversion and religious life and travels with husband;intellectual interests;views on education; her writings.   229

FRY, Charles Burgess. Life Worth Living (1939). Public school; Oxford; his career in cricket; great days and players of the game;hunting and other sports; journalism; work on League of Nations as India representative; administration.   230

FRY, Sir Edward. A Memoir, by his daughter(1921). Largely autobiography of the L.C.J.; Bristol youth; his law practice, work as judge, arbitration work; University College, London; his friends; Crabb Robinson.   231

FRY, J. H. Boulogne and Berlin (L. 1916). Genial reminiscences of anAnglican chaplain at English churches on the continent.   232

FRYER, E. R. M. Reminiscences of a Grenadier (1921). Adventures in WW1 & short account of battles fought by the Grenadiers.   233

FULLARTON, William. Prison journal, 1763; experiences of a surgeon; captive of Suraj ad daula at Patna.Walter K. Firminger,Diaries of Three Surgeons (Calcutta, 1909).   234

FULLER, James Franklin. Omniana (L. 1916). Irish octogenarian's reminiscences of his schooling and Irish politics; literary affairs; & his social life in Cork and Dublin.   235

FULLER, Maj.Gen. John F. C. Memoirs of an Unconventional Soldier (L.1936)

Controversial military career;work as chief of General Staff of Tank Corps, in WW1; his fight for adoption of the tank and his work with it;problems of military tactics.   236

FULLER, Sir Joseph Bampfylde. Some Personal Experiences (1930). Administrative work in Bengal, Assam, Egypt; travels in North and South America; & colonial problems.   237

FULLER, Loie. Fifteen Years (1913). The career and art of a modern dancer; literary and artistic friends, especially in France.   238

FULLER, Robert A. Recollections (L. 1912). A retired detective-inspector; experiences in crime and detection; & famous cases.   239

FULLER, William. The Whole Life of (1702). Lively account of the adventures and misadventures of government agent in England and France, to 1691; written in Newgate.   240

FULLER-MAITLAND, John Alexander. A Doorkeeper of Music (1929). Reminiscences of Times music critic; musical life in London; anecdotes of performers.   241

FULLERTON, Lady Georgiana Charlotte The Inner Life of (1899). Contains an autobiography of her Staff's childhood and her early Catholic sympathies;and diary notes entirely devoted to religious meditations.   242

FULLERTON, W. Y.   At the Sixtieth Milestone (1917).Baptist evangelist's nearly forty years of travel and meetings through Great Britain.   243

FURBER, Edward Price. London Doctor (1940). Charterhouse; St. Barts; his medical career as medical officer in N.W. London and in fashionable practice in West-End; masonic affairs and social life;celebrated patients; Surrey sport.   244

FURLEY, Sir John. Struggles and Experiences (1872); In Peace and War(L. 1905).Volunteer medical and Red Cross work from 1854; Franco-Prussian War & siege of Paris;Boer War; hospital work and relief of suffering.   245

FURNISS, Harry. Confessions (1901); My Bohemian Days(1919). His career as cartoonist and illustrator; Punch and its contributors;Savage Club and London social and artistic life;reminiscences of writers,painters, actors of late 19th Century.   246

FURSE, Katharine. Hearts and Pomegranates (1940). Education; Victorian conflicts; life in Switzerland and Italy with J. A. Symonds; literary life and reminiscences;her work with V.A.D. in WW1.   247

FURZ,John. Lives of Early Methodist Preachers, ed. Thomas Jackson (1837). II. Autobiography of an 18th Century itinerant Methodist preacher mainly in South of England.   248

ANON. Fusilier Bluff(1934). Service with Welch Fusiliers in Near East WW1; Macedonia and Transcaucasia;political views on war.   249

FYFE,Henry Hamilton.My Seven Selves (1935). Whimsical account of various aspects of his career and personality; reporter,war correspondent, editor of Daily Herald; Labour Party and reform; his artistic and literary tastes;travels; friends; pleasant.   250

FYTCHE, Lt. Gen. Albert. Burma Past and Present (1878). Experiences of a soldier and administration in India & Burma, 1839-71; Chief Commissioner of British Burma; economics; native culture; sport and social life.   251

G.,Major-General.An Apology for the Life of(1792). The apologia of a rake and native Casanova.   1

G., J. The Prisoner Set Free (Preston,1846). Poor youth near Ribchester atheism and ignorance; marriage; profligacy and theft; imprisonment; conversion in prison; with notes by John Clay, chaplain.   2

G., R.   Diary, 1828-29; journey to Demarara and residence there; life in West Indies and North America. MS, in Liverpool Athenaeum, 84 pp.   3

GAHAGAN,Major. Historical reminisc-
cences of military service in Peninsular War and garrison life in India.
New Monthly Mag., 1838-39.   4

GALBRAITH,Winifred.The Dragon Sheds
His Skin(1928). Experiences as teacher in a Chinese family at Hunan; the
tragedy of China in revolution; young
intellectuals in 20's.   5

GALLACHER, William. Revolt on the
Clyde(1936); Rolling of Thunder(1948)
Lively, combative account of career &
opinions of Communist M.P.;industrial-
ism & working class life in Scotland;
his struggles;Clyde in wartime;Russia
after revolution; General Strike;and
Spanish Civil War; his work in Parliament and unions.   6

GALLAGHER,Frank. Days of Fear (1928)
Irish nationalist leader; experiences
in Mountjoy Prison and his sufferings
during hunger strike, 1920.   7

/GALLAGHER, Patrick/. My Story, by
Paddy the Cope (1939). His boyhood in
Donegal; founding of the Templecrone
Co-operative; campaign vs. merchants;
social work among Donegal peasants; &
life and beliefs in Ireland.   8

GALLIE, W. B. An English School (L.
1949). Reminiscences of his school in
Yorkshire; liberalism and religion in
education; curriculum, masters, games
and friends; reflections.   9

GALSWORTHY, Ada. Over the Hills and
Far Away (1937). Travels with husband
in Europe,N. Africa and America; places and people; reminiscences of John
Galsworthy.   10

GALT, John. Autobiography (L.1833);
Literary Life (1834).Scottish boyhood
and reading; business career; travels
in Balkans; business travels in Canada and founding of Guelph; difficulties in Canada; political affairs; his
literary works;Byron; comments, books
and plagiarism; good.   11

GALTON, Sir Francis. Memories of My
Life (1908). Medical studies; travels
& hunting, Africa; studies in meteor-
ology, geography, anthropology, heredity;ideas about race improvement and
his writings.   12

GALTREY,Sidney. Memoirs of a Racing
Journalist (1934). Horse-racing, England and India;famous stables, trainers, jockeys, owners, races; journalism,Daily Telegraph; anecdotes of the
sport.   13

GAMBIER, Com. James William. Links
in My Life (1906). Naval career from
1854;Baltic, Crimea, China, Far East;
cruises and adventures.   14

GANDER,Leonard Marsland.After These
Many Quests (1949). His work, travels
and adventures during his career as a
journalist and war correspondent; the
Times of India; WW2 in Italy, France,
and Germany.   15

GANDY, Ida. A Wiltshire Childhood
(1929). Fond memories of country and
village life by clergyman's daughter;
early 20th Century.   16

GANT,Frederick James. Autobiography
(1905). Medical career in London; the
Royal Free Hospital; reflections upon
medicine, nursing, science, & women's
work; religious life.   17

GANT, Roland. How Like a Wilderness
(1946).Experiences of medical orderly
in Airborne Division in WW2; capture;
experiences in Muhlberg.   18

GANTHONY, Robert. Random Recollections (1899). Anecdotes from his career as writer, ventriloquist, conjur-
or, cartoonist; musichalls; tours in
America and S. Africa.   19

GAPE, W. A. Half a Million Tramps
(1936). Entertaining account of experiences during 22 years as a tramp in
England and America;Hoboes Union; the
humors of the life.   20

GARDINER,William. Music and Friends
(1838-53).Lively but rather impersonal reminiscences of a commercial traveller; travels, anecdotes on celebrities and friends;preponderating notes
on music.   21

GARDINER, Wrey. Colonies of Heaven
(Billericay, 1941);The Once Loved God
(1943); Dark Thorn (1946). The poet's
autobiography and mind; country life
in England and France; wanderings and
depression;reflections on poetry, art

sex, war; ashes of romanticism.   22

GARDNER, Maj. FitzRoy.Days and Ways
(1921); More Reminiscences(1926). His
military career; Franco-Prussian War;
assistant provost-marshal in WW1; the
Rhine occupation; society, club life,
hunting, journalism, theatre manager;
Bohemian life in London.   23

GARDNER, Com. James Anthony. Recol-
lections(1906). Attractive account of
sailor's life, 1775-1814; his ships &
cruises; social life and duties; hum-
ane interest.   24

GARDNER, James Peter. Reminiscences
(Boston, 1940). A boyhood on Scottish
border in 80's;   school and sports at
Melrose; religion; social life.   25

GARDNER, Percy. Autobiographica (Oxford,1933). London boyhood; Cambridge
and appointment to British Museum;his
classical and archaeological studies;
teaching at Oxford; theology; Modern-
ism; religious life.   26

GARLAND,Thomas Charles. Leaves from
My Log(1882); East End Pictures(1885)
Work of Wesleyan missionary around the
Port of London for 25 years; seamen &
slum dwellers; his social & religious
work; interesting.   27

GARRATT, Samuel. Life and Personal
Recollections (1908). Parish work of
Vicar of Ipswich;recollections of the
religious movements and church events
of period 1830-80.   28

GARRATT, Vero W. Man in the Street
(1939). Warwickshire boyhood; work in
factory; self-education; work as commercial traveller; Suffragette movement and work in Temperance; journalist on John Bull and English Review;
contemporary events.   29

GARRETT, Eileen Jeannette. My Life
(N.Y. 1939).Irish childhood; religion
and visions; social work and in Labor
movement in London; Edward Carpenter;
development of psychic gifts and work
as medium;studies at Duke University;
serious and well-written account of a
spiritualist.   30

GARRY,Thomas Gerald. African Doctor
(1939). Education in Ireland; medical

studies; work as surgeon on W.African
steamers and as army surgeon in Egypt;
Egyptian customs and morals; the drug
traffic; good.   31

GARVIE, Alfred Ernest. Memories and
Meanings (1938). Poland; education in
English universities; pastor in Scotland; professor and principal of New
College, London; religious education
and theology;his religious and social
work.   32

GARWOOD, Alfred Edward. Forty Years
(Newport, 1903). Engineering work in
Russia, Egypt, and Newport; administration, business, politics; work on
railways.   33

GATES, Caleb Frank. Not to Me Only
(Princeton, 1940). Life and work as a
missionary in Turkey and Mesopotamia,
1881-1932.   34

GATHORNE-HARDY, Alfred Erskine. My
Happy Hunting Grounds(1914). Leisurely reminiscences of sport and natural
history in Channel Islands, Scotland,
etc.   35

GATHORNE-HARDY, Robert. Three Acres
and a Mill (1939). A horticulturist's
travels in search of rare plants; his
home and garden in village near Reading.   36

GATLIFF,James. Stations, Gentlemen!
(1938).His military career and adventures in India and China 1782 to 1814;
joins church,imprisoned for debt; later minister at Gorton.   37

GATTY, Alfred. A Life at One Living
(1885). Rather impersonal account of
church and parish work and affairs at
Ecclesfield, Yorks.   38

GAULD, H. Drummond. The Truth from
the Trenches (1922).Experiences of an
infantryman in W.W.1; first battle of
the Somme and later.   39

GAUNT, F. The Immortal First (1917)
Army career before WW1;with B.E.F. in
France;1st battle of Yser; written up
from diary in hospital.   40

GAUNT, Admiral Sir Guy.Yield of the
Years (1940). Career at sea; sailing
ships and navy; Samoa and S. Pacific;

naval attaché in Washington and chief of British Intelligence in USA, during WW1; anecdotes of celebrities.   41

GAUTREY,Thomas. Lux Mihi Laus(1937) His career as a teacher and work with London School Board,1871-1904, as secretary and member;schools and educational movements.   42

GAY,J. Drew. The Prince of Wales in India (Toronto, 1877). Travels with Prince Edward in India in 1875; festivities; ceremonies; hunting.   43

GAY, Maisie. Laughing through Life (1931). Theatrical career from childhood; her work in musichalls, revues, musical comedies; anecdotes of actors and theatrical life.   44

GED, William. Biographical Memoirs (1781). Edinburgh printing; work as a type-founder;with a London stationer; invention of stereotyping process and his activities in printing;first half 18th Century.   45

GEEN,Philip. What I Have Seen(1905) Days Stolen for Sport (1907).His long years of fishing, sports, and country life; trout and salmon fishing.   46

GEIKIE, Sir Archibald. Scottish Reminiscences (1904);A Long Life's Work (1924). Scottish life, religion, and character; his education and work in geological surveys and as a professor; presidency of Royal Society.   47

GELL, Mrs. Edith Mary. Under Three Reigns (1927). Social life; society; London, Oxford, country houses; religious interests.   48

GENT, Thomas. The Life (1832). Work as printer in London and then in York; printing rivalries; social and family life; vigorous and interesting record written in 1746.   49

ANON. Genuine and Authentic Memoirs of a Well-Known Woman of Intrigue (L. 1787). Yorkshire girl in business as a courtesan with her mother; London & York; anecdotes of members of society interesting. Bodleian.   50

GERARD, Fr. John. During the Persecution(1886). Experiences of a Jesuit priest in England in 17th Century;imprisonment and torture in Marshalsea; persecution of Catholics; the Gunpowder Plot; trans. from Latin.   51

GERARD, Lt.Gen. Sir Montagu Gilbert Leaves from the Diaries (1903). Army life and campaigns in India and Egypt, 1865-85; Afghan Wars; hunting; life of ruling caste.   52

GERHARDI,William Alexander. Memoirs of a Polyglot (1931). Boyhood,Russia; military service; Oxford; journalism; travels; political and literary reminiscences; Wells, Shaw, D.H.Lawrence, Lloyd George, Beaverbrook.   53

GERMON, Mrs. R. C. Diary, 1857; her experiences in siege of Lucknow;hardships. A Diary (1870).   54

GERVIS, Captain Henry. Arms and the Doctor (1920). Experiences of an army surgeon before and during WW1;work at hospitals in Brighton, etc. A copy in Worthing P.L.   55

GIBB, John Philip. Edinburgh Man's Recollections (Edin. 1934). Schools; work in druggist's and as a commercial traveller in Shetlands; life on road; sports.   56

GIBB, Robert Shirra. Farmer's Fifty Years (Edin.1927). Training as doctor and work as farmer in Lauderdale; the Scottish agricultural scene.   57

GIBBON,Edward. Autobiographies, ed. John Murray (1896); various editions. Account of his dedication to history, his scholarly training for his task, what shaped his work,and the work itself.   58

GIBBON,Monk. Mount Ida (1948). Emotional experiences in his life,in the George Moore manner; three women, his sensibilities and philosophizing. 59

GIBBON, Skeffington. Recollections (Dublin,1829). Reminiscences of country life,sport, the nobility and gentry in Ireland, 1796-1829.   60

GIBBONS, John. I Gathered No Moss (1939).Londoner's cheerful account of village life and of travels, mainly in Portugal.   61

GIBBONS, John Skipworth. Eton, Oxford and Afterwards (Worcester, 1941) Life of a Gloucestershire squire; his passion for sports; anecdotes of the open air. Gloucester City Library. 62

GIBBS, Major Arthur Hamilton. Grey Wave (1920). Experiences in the ranks and as officer in WW1; Serbia and the Western Front.   63

GIBBS, Henry S. Autobiography of a Manchester Cotton Manufacturer (1887) Family life at Bath;work as inspector & manager in Manchester cotton-mills; intellectual life there; vicissitudes of trade; emigration.   64

GIBBS, John. Life and Experience of (Lewes,1827). Boyhood hardships; work as servant and unemployment;solace in religion and his preaching;activities at Lewes Chapel & troubles with rival preachers.   65

GIBBS, Leonard Angas. Notes from a Diary(1930). Family, personal, travel notes of a long-lived dilettante; his wealthy and cultured life. London L.66

GIBBS, Sir Philip Hamilton. Adventures in Journalism (L.1923); Pageant of the Years (1946); Crowded Company (1949).Travels and experiences of the famous journalist and war correspondent and novelist; his many papers and critical views of a Liberal on newspaper business; memories of statesmen artists, writers, celebrities.   67

GIBBS, R. P. M. Not Peace(1943). An airman with RAF before and during WW2; Coastal Command; commander of torpedo squadron in WW2; expansion of RAF and his personal adventures.   68

GIBNEY, William. Eighty Years Ago (1896). Medical training at Edinburgh and Dublin; experiences as army surgeon in Peninsular War; Waterloo; the occupation of Paris.   69

GIBSON,Ashley. Postscript to Adventure (1930). Experiences in literary journalism and publishing; travels in India and Africa; service in WW1; his literary friendships.   70

GIBSON, Charles Bernard. Life Among Convicts (1863). Work as prison chap-

lain in English and Irish prisons in 40's and 50's;opinions on prisons and penal methods.   71

GIBSON,Sir Christopher H. Enchanted Trails (1948). His life and explorations in Central South America; Bolivia,Paraguay, Brazil; Indian life and ways; dangers and adventures.   72

GIBSON, John. Life, ed. Lady Eastlake (1870). Mostly an autobiography of his childhood; art studies, Italy; long career as a sculptor in Rome and notes on Roman life.   73

GIBSON, John Frederick. Dark Seas Above (1947); Memory Bay (1950). His service in submarines during WW2; his adventures as a child in Cornwall and at sea; in Lapland; around the world, by sailboat;literary hackwork; films; retirement to Cornwall.   74

GIELGUD, John. Early Stages (1939). Childhood;training in the theatre and the Bensons; Oxford; his plays, roles and development of his talent.   75

GIELGUD,Val Henry. Years of the Locust (1947). Nostalgic account of his years before WW1; his career in radio and films; work with BBC; development of radio drama.   76

GIFFARD, Adm. Sir George. Reminiscences of a Naval Officer(Exeter 1892) Naval career to 1858; West Indies and China stations; Crimean War; siege of Sebastopol.   77

GIFFORD,William. Memoir (1827). His early life; Devonshire; work on coaster and as shoemaker's apprentice; at Exeter College; tutor; beginnings of his writing;his translations; patrons short but vigorous.   78

GILBERT, Ann(Taylor). Autobiography (1874). The writer's childhood & early life,1782 to 1813, at Lavenham and Colchester.   79

GILBERT, George. Recollections and Reminiscences (Canterbury, 1938). The cathedral, services, clergy, townsmen at Canterbury in 60's. Dean & Chapter Library, Canterbury.   80

GILBERT,William. Memoirs of a Cynic

(1880). Orphan; midshipman with East India Co.; life in London as a music critic and newspaper editor; investigation of lunatic asylums;insight into social conditions.   81

GILL, Eric. Autobiography (L.1940). Childhood and schools; work as artist architect and monumental mason;career as letter-cutter and designer;religious and spiritual life; good.   82

GILL, Maud. See the Players (1938). Career of character actress;stock and repertory;stage manager at Birmingham Repertory; melodrama, Shakespeare; an unimportant actress but lively story of love of theatre.   83

GILL, William. Life in the Southern Isles (L. 1876); Selections from the Autobiography (1880). Missionary work of a Devon man in Samoa and the Herveys to 1880;London Missionary Society partly diaries.   84

GILLARD, Frank. Reminiscences, by Cuthbert Bradley (1898). A huntsman's career 1860-96, with Belvoir Hounds; events and people in foxhunting.   85

GILLIES, Robert Pearse. Memoirs of a Literary Veteran (1851). A writer's work and social life; anecdotes about politicians and writers,especially in Scotland; Scott, Campbell, Wordsworth Maturin, etc.   86

GILLILAND,Capt.Horace Gray. My German Prisons(1918). Officer of N.Lancs regiment; three years as prisoner of war, WW1.   87

GILLMORE, Parker. Adventures (1873) Gun, Rod and Saddle(1896); Encounters with Wild Beasts (1881); Leaves from a Sportsman's Diary (1896). Experiences of sports in many parts of world; fishing, big-game hunting, etc.   88

GILMOUR, James. Journal, 1870-1887; a Scotsman's missionary work in Pekin and Mongolia; preaching, medical work and education. James Gilmour, ed. Richard Lovett (1908).   89

GILMOUR,Oswald W.Singapore to Freedom (1943); With Freedom to Singapore (1950). Life in Singapore;an exciting account of escape from Japanese invaders;planning for the reoccupation of Singapore.   90

GILPIN, Mary Ann. Memoir (1841). A Bristol girl's religious preoccupation and illness, mainly diary.   91

GILSON,Charles J. L. Chances & Mischances(1932); Men and Chances (1932) Adventures as a soldier in Boer War and WW1; travels & excitements in various parts of world;his books for boys and his audience; journalistic.   92

GIRALDUS CAMBRENSIS. Autobiography, ed. H. E. Butler (1937). Lively, vain record of his activities in church and state affairs; England, Paris & Rome; later 12th Century.   93

GLADSTONE, William Ewart. A Chapter of Autobiography (1868). A justification of his activities in connection with the Church of Ireland.   94

GLASFURD, Col. Arthur I. R. Leaves from an Indian Journal (Bombay, 1903) Rifle and Romance (1905); Musings of an Old Shikari (1928). His boyhood in India; military career; social life & travels;mostly big-game hunting. Copy of first, India Office.   95

GLASGOW, David Boyle, 7th Earl of. Memoirs (Edin.1918). His childhood in Scotland;cruises as a naval cadet and captain.   96

GLASS, Frederick C. Adventures with the Bible (1923). Missionary work of an evangelist in Brazil;Bible-selling & preaching; Catholic opposition.   97

GLASS, James. Chats over a Pipe (L. 1922). Youth in Dunfermline; business as stationer and importer in Edinburgh and extensive travels; & his rolling-stone brother; genial.   98

GLAVE, E. J. Six Years of Adventure (1893). Pioneer officer for Stanley; travels, exploration & hunting in the Congo area.   99

GLEDHILL, Samuel. Memoirs (Kendal, 1910). Yorkshireman and soldier's reminiscences & moralisings on his life written for his children.   100

GLEED,Ian Richard. Arise to Conquer

(1942). Vivid account of life of WW2 pilot and wing-commander; battles of France and Britain.　　　101

GLEICHEN,Gen. Lord Edward. With the Camel Corps (1888); With the Mission (1897); Guardsman's Memories (1932). Military career 1863-1918;Sudan, Gordon at Khartoum, Boer War; Ireland; & WW1; life in Guards.　　　102

GLEICHEN, Lady Helena. Contacts and Contrasts(1940). Society life; mostly her hospital work in Italy during the 1st World War.　　　103

GLEIG, George Robert. The Subaltern (Edin. 1825). Chaplain's service during Peninsular War, 1813-14; military affairs in Southern France.　　　104

GLENBERVIE,Douglas Sylvester, Baron Diaries, ed. F.Bickley (1928). Begins with his early life, mid 18 C.　　105

GLINDONI, H. G. Short autobiography of popular painter and exhibitor R.A. mostly 19th Century. MS,Dagenham Public Library.　　　106

GLOVER,Archibald Edward. A Thousand Miles of Miracle in China (1904). His perils and miraculous escapes from the Chinese during the Boxer rebellion; a missionary.　　　107

GLOVER,Lady Elizabeth Rosetta. Memories of Four Continents(1923). Society and diplomatic life and travel before WW1;Ireland, Newfoundland, Paris India, Egypt.　　　108

GLOVER, James Mackey. Jimmy Glover (1911); Jimmy Glover and His Friends (1913); Hims (1926). Youth in Ireland work as translator and musician;music halls and Drury Lane;reminiscences of theatrical life and shows,clubs, performers, etc.　　　109

GLOVER, John. Some Memoirs (1774). Norwich man's religious work and spiritual life after his reformation in 1736.　　　110

GLOVER,Sir John Hawley. Naval diary 1857-58; exploration up the R. Niger; with the Baikie Expedition.The Voyage of the Dayspring,by A. C. G. Hastings (1926).　　　111

GLOVER, Richard. Memoirs of a Celebrated Literary and Political Character (1813). Critical reminiscences of public affairs, 1742-57; politics and intrigue;associate of Chatham and the Grenvilles.　　　112

GLOVER, Terrot Reaveley. Cambridge Retrospect (1943). Cambridge university life and famous scholars during half a century;St. John's; university reform; anecdotes; pleasant.　　　113

GLOVER, William. Reminiscences of a Cambridge Chorister (1885); Reminiscences of Half a Century (1889). Trinity College in 20's and 30's; musical life,the theatre, literature, society and its changes & sport; an excellent picture of the Victorian scene and of its celebrities especially in music & at Cambridge.　　　114

GLYN, Elinor. Romantic Adventure(L. 1936). Childhood in Jersey; marriage and society in 90's; her travels; her career as a novelist; her experiences in Hollywood.　　　115

GLYNN, John. More Stories (Chatham, 1937). His work in Liverpool shipping business and as lay reader; religious life and experiences.　　　116

GODFREY, Sir Daniel Eyers. Memories and Music (1924). Musical education & 35 years as conductor; military bands music at Bournemouth;anecdotes, British music, musical outlook.　　　117

GODFREY, Derek. We Went to Blazes (1941).Journalist's experiences as an auxiliary fireman in WW2; before and during the Blitz.　　　118

GODFREY, George. History of George Godfrey (1828). Pseudonymous; his life of crime;sentenced; reprieved; transported to Australia; life there.　　119

GODFREY, Thomas. Autobiography of a Kentish man; family and domestic life and his military service in early 17 C MS, B.M., Lansdowne 235.　　　120

GODLEY, Sir Alexander John. Life of an Irish Soldier (1939). The general's boyhood in Ireland and education; his army career and service;Boer War; WW1 and occupation in Germany.　　　121

GOGARTY, Oliver St. John. As I Was Going Down Sackville Street (L. 1937) Tumbling in the Hay (L.1939); Rolling Down the Lea (1950). Study at Trinity and Dublin hospitals; grim humours of medicine;taverns, social & night life of Dublin; nationalist politics, literary life, theatre, folklore; Joyce, Yeats; Irish character & countryside; romantic, fantastic, lively. 122

GOLDIN,Horace.It's Fun to be Fooled (1937). Career and travels of a stage magician for 48 years;his secrets and his triumphs. 123

GOLDING, Louis. World I Knew (1940) Manchester childhood; Oxford; travels and work as a journalist and novelist; inter-war politics; and the growth of Nazism. 124

GOLDMAN, Willy. East End My Cradle (1940).Jewish life and poverty Whitechapel; sweatshops, unemployment, sex and anti-Semitism; his work as author; and sociology. 125

GOLDRING,Arthur. Some Reminiscences (1926). Exuberant memories of iconoclastic clergyman; church reform movements and life in general. 126

GOLDRING,Douglas. Odd Man Out(1935) South Lodge (1943); Life Interests(L. 1948). School and family; Oxford; his experiences in literary journalism and novel-writing;the political events of the 20's; publishing and writing and literary affairs of Edwardians;London haunts;Flecker, Lawrence, Ford, Violet Hunt and English Review. 127

GOLDSWORTHY, Edward Francis. Recollections of Taunton (Taunton, 1883). Reminiscences of the town and people, and his life there, in the early part of the century. Bodleian. 128

GOMES,Edwin Herbert.Seventeen Years among the Sea Dyaks (1911). Work and adventures of a missionary among Dyaks of Borneo. 129

GOOCH, Sir Daniel. Diaries (1892). Begins with autobiography of his happy childhood, his work in an ironfoundry and his work as engineer for the Great Western Railway. 130

GOOCH, Elizabeth Sarah Villa-Real. Entredas; The Life of(1792). Marriage and divorce and the road to sin; 18th Century Becky Sharp;written from prison. 131

GOOCH, William. Travel diary, 1791-1792;experiences at sea and in Rio de Janeiro; Brazilian life and ways; the observations of an astronomer. MS, in Cambridge U.L. Mm.6.48. 132

GOOD,Meyrick G. B. Good Days (1941) His work in sporting journalism; "Man on the Spot" of Sporting Life; rider and owner;turf celebrities; musichall people; anecdotes. 133

GOODALL, Frederick. Reminiscences (1902). His early life; work as painter; patrons; Royal Academy; reminiscences of Turner and other Victorian painters; social life, travels, theatre; social changes. 134

GOODENOUGH, Adm. Sir William Edmund Rough Record (1943). His naval career 1882-1926; South Africa; Jutland and WW1 experiences; the Nore; his work & reflections on navy. 135

GOODMAN,Margaret. Experiences of an English Sister of Mercy (1862).Social work in slums & service with Nightingale in Crimean War; hospital work at Scutari and Balaclava. 136

GOODRIDGE, Charles Medyett. Narrative of a Voyage (1832). A boyhood at sea;shipwreck and two years on deserted island in South Seas; rescue and eight years in Tasmania. 137

GOODSALL,Lieut. Robert H. Palestine Memories (1926).Personal narrative of an airman in WW1; Allenby's campaign; later visit to Palestine. 138

GOODWIN, Jack. Myself and My Boxers (1924).Work as boxing trainer; famous fighters; his life in East End. 139

GORDON, Major Archibald Alexander. Culled from a Diary (Edin.1941). Army career to 1939; mostly liaison work & on Western Front in WW1. 140

GORDON,Charles Alexander. Experiences of an Army Surgeon in India(1872)

Life on the Gold Coast(1874). Medical work in India from 40's;expedition to Gold Coast in 1847-8;army life; travel; medical work; anecdotes.   141

GORDON, Gen. Charles George. Diary, 1884;detailed account of the siege of Khartoum; explanation of his activity and self-justification. Journals, ed. A. E. Hake (1885).   142

GORDON, Douglas George Hamilton . Fifty Years of Failure (1905). Humorous account of his life of odd jobs and travels; literary, Bohemian life in London; work for church publishers British Museum, art societies.   143

GORDON, Lady Edith Susan. Winds of Time (1934). Ireland in 90's; society in London; travels; WWl; nationalist politics in Kerry to 1930.   144

GORDON,Lord Granville Armyne.Sporting Reminiscences (1902). Reminiscences of many sports; fishing, hunting, cricket, golf, billiards, etc.   145

GORDON, Sir Home Seton C. M. Background of Cricket (1939). His clubs & cricketing friends; progress of game; great players.   146

GORDON,Jane (Peggy L. Graves). Married to Charles (1950). The married life of two journalists; domestic and social life;travels; work as hospital nurse in WW2.   147

GORDON, John. Memoirs of the Life (1733).Account of Scotsman's thirteen years at Scottish College in Paris;an anti-catholic record.   148

GORDON, John. My Six Years with the Black Watch (Boston, 1929). Aberdeen man's service in Egypt, 1881-87; Nile expedition; army life; good.   149

GORDON,John Digby.Work and Play in India and Kashmir (1893). Legal life and cases of a lawyer;social life and sport in India and Kashmir.   150

GORDON,Gen. Joseph M. Chronicles of a Gay Gordon(1921). Military life and sport in Ireland; Boer War; experiences in journalism and police;business life in New Zealand and Australia.151

GORDON,Pryse Lockhart. Personal Memoirs(1830). Entertaining life on the continent in time of Napoleon;reminiscences of Lady Hamilton,Burney, Rodney; antiquarian interests.   152

GORDON, General Sir Thomas Edward.A Varied Life (1906).Career in army and civil service;Afghanistan,India, Persia and Central Asia,1849-1902; sport and travel; language studies.   153

GORDON, Winifred. Echoes and Realities (1934). Education, social life & music in Vienna and Paris; court life in London;Bath during WWl; travels in Africa and Asia;salon celebrities and politics.   154

GORDON-ALEXANDER, Lt. Col. William Gordon. Recollections of a Highland Subaltern (1898). Military service in India, 1857-9;with Campbell in Indian Mutiny.   155

GORDON-CUMMING, Constance Frederica At Home in Fiji (Edin. 1881); In the Himalayas (Edin. 1884); Two Happy Years (Edin. 1892); Memories (Edin. 1904).A lifetime of travels; South Seas,India Ceylon, Japan, USA; social life,planters,missionaries, officials, natives and her Highland childhood,social life in England; interest in spiritualism; Crimean War; Indian Mutiny.   156

GORDON-STABLES,William. Leaves from the Log (1906). His life in the navy; retirement to English village; everyday life of a bachelor in the country; marriage; yarns.   157

GORE, Frederick St. John. Lights & Shades of Hill Life(1895). His travel with a surveyor in Himalayas; Afghanistan and Punjab; administration, social life in Kuram.   158

GORHAM, Maurice. Sound and Fury (L. 1948). Oxford; journalism; editor of Radio Times; work in broadcasting for BBC and for armed forces in WW2;television work; BBC anecdotes.   159

GORST, Harold Edward. Much of Life is Laughter (1936). Education in German education and music;journalism in London; lecturer at girls' school;experiences in WWl.   160

GOSLIN, Harry. Up & Down Stream (L. 1927). Early days as Thames waterman; trade union work; member of LCC; work organizing dockers; M.P. and Minister of Transport; Labour Party.   161

GOSS, Fred. Memories of a Stag Harbourer (1931). Work as harbourer and keeper with the Devon & Somerset Stag Hounds;Devonshire sport, customs, social life, celebrities.   162

GOSSE, Sir Edmund William. Father & Son (1907). Family life; struggle between temperaments of father and son; development of moral and intellectual concepts; good.   163

GOSSE, Philip. Memoirs of a Camp-Follower (1934); Go to the Country(L. 1935); Naturalist Goes to War (1942) Apple a Day (1948). Lively account of work and impressions of a medical officer in France and India,WW1; return to Sussex between wars, with memories of Haileybury and boyhood;further experiences as medical officer; medical practice in Colchester hospital and in private practice in Essex;antiquarian interests; reflections; good.   164

GOSSE, Philip Henry. A Naturalist's Sojourn in Jamaica (1851). Expedition and natural history.   165

GOUGER,Henry. Personal Narrative of Two Years' Imprisonment (1860). Travels and business of merchant in Burma siege of Rangoon; imprisonment 1824-6 hardships.   166

GOUGH, Sir Hugh Henry. Old Memories (1897). Military service in India in the 50's; the Mutiny; siege of Delhi; Lucknow; gets the VC.   167

GOUGH, James. Memoirs of the Life (Dublin, 1781). Education in North of England; conversion; Quaker ministry and travels in England, Wales,Ireland etc.   168

GOUGH,John Bartholomew. Autobiography (1886). Kentish childhood; alone at 12 to USA; hard times in New York; success as temperance lecturer; tours in America and England.   169

GOUGH,William Charles. From Kew Observatory (1927). Twenty-eight years

as detective at Scotland Yard;famous crimes.   170

GOULD, Frederick James. Life Story of a Humanist (1923). Poverty in London; reading; work as journalist; activities in agnosticism and with Ethical Society to 1905.   171

GOULD,Nathaniel. The Magic of Sport (1909). Early days in Australia; his literary career in London and novels; Bohemian life; horseracing in England and Australia.   172

GOULDSBURY,Charles Elphinstone.Life in the Indian Police (1912); Tigerland (L.1913); Reminiscences of a Stowaway (1920).A lifetime of adventures mainly in India; crime and police work in India; social life; big-game hunting in Bengal.   173

GOWER, Pauline. Women with Wings(L. 1938). Career of a woman pilot; business enterprise in commercial aviation and her adventures.   174

GOWING,Sgt.Maj. T. Soldier's Experience(Nottingham, 1885). Ranker's experiences in Crimean War, Indian Mutiny and Afghan campaign, 1854-63; the hardships and horrors of war.   175

GOWLAND, John Stafford. War is Like That (1934). A youth's experiences in the infantry in WW1; discomforts and hardships.   176

GOYDER, David George. My Battle for Life (1857). Autobiography of a phrenologist; reading, religious opinions Swedenborg's influence; a minister of new church;work as painter; phrenological studies and lectures;sociological interests.   177

GRACE, William Gilbert. Cricketing Reminiscences (1899). His career as a cricketer;mostly reminiscences of the game and famous players; Gloucester & England; Australian tours.   178

GRAFTON,Augustus Henry Fitzroy, 3rd Duke of. Autobiography (1898). Childhood; court, political, state affairs to 1783; Whig ministries; & political events and his part in them;important but largely impersonal political history.   179

GRAHAM, Eleanor. Head o'Mey (1947)
Her grandmother's childhood and her
own; life in far North of Scotland;
19th and 20th Centuries.   180

GRAHAM, Lt.Gen. Sir Gerald. Diaries
1854-85; service with Gordon in China
and Egypt; military activities; reading and work. Life, Letters & Diaries
ed. R. H. Vetch (Edin. 1901).   181

GRAHAM, Joe F. An Old Stock-Actor's
Memories (1930). His work in theatre,
from 70's; theatrical life; reminiscences of actors and acting.   182

GRAHAM, John Parkhurst. Forty Years
of Uppingham (1932). His experiences
as boy and teacher, from 1888; school
life and personalities.   183

GRAHAM, Maria. Journal of a Residence in India (Edin.1812); Journal of
a Residence in Chile (1824). Trave ls,
India 1809-11;Indian scene; experiences in Chilean war of liberation; and
notes on Cochrane, San Martin, O'Hig-
gins, etc.; interesting.   184

GRAHAM,Sir Reginald. Foxhunting Recollections (1907). Brief. notes on
military life;mostly hunting with the
most famous hunts from 1863.   185

GRAHAM, Gen. Samuel. Memoir, edited
James J. Graham(1862). Includes autobiography of his service with British
forces during American revolution.186

GRAHAM, Stephen.   A Private in the
Guards (1919). Personal essays about
his service in France, WW1.   187

GRAHAME-WHITE,Com.Montague. At the
Wheel (1935). Forty years of motoring
yachting, motorboating; racing trials
and sporting life.   188

GRAIN, Corney. Corney Grain (1888).
Career as entertainer and performer of
sketches.   189

GRAND, George Francis. Narrative of
the Life of a Gentleman (Cape of Good
Hope, 1814;Calcutta, 1910). Experiences of an ensign and soldier-of-fortune; in India for 30 years from 1766;
Cornwallis; intrigues; his troubles;
partly in indigo trade; interesting.
India Office Library.   190

GRANT, Dr. Alexander. Physician and
Friend (1902). Scottish education and
medical training; career in India and
China from 1837;improvement of Indian
Medical Service as Apothecary-General;
Dalhousie and other personalities;the
Mutiny; partly diaries.   191

GRANT, Ann. Memoirs and Correspondence (1844). Brief autobiography of
childhood in Glasgow, family life and
widowhood at Laggan; literary interests and writing; religion; covering
1755-1805.   192

GRANT, Bernard. To the Four Corners
(1933).Travels and adventures of news
photographer;crimes, disasters, sport
in Balkans, WW1; South Pacific.   193

GRANT, Brewin. The Dissenting World
(1869). Studies for ministry at Glasgow;congregational minister, Birmingham and Sheffield; & his dissent from
congregationalism.   194

GRANT, (Charles) Graham. Diary of a
Police Surgeon (1920). Crime and medical work in East End.   195

GRANT, Elisabeth(Smith). Memoirs of
a Highland Lady (1911). Childhood and
youth in early 19th Century; gay society in Scotland; Edinburgh celebrities; estate life at Rothiemurchus; a
lively record.   196

GRANT, George Hook.   The Half Deck
(Boston, 1933). A boy's experience of
rough life on cargo ships.   197

GRANT, J.Glenelg. Heart beneath the
Uniform (1917). Experiences as entertainer to troops during WW1.   198

GRANT, Sir James Hope. Military diaries, 1857-8 and 1860; army service;
personal experiences in Sepoy War and
China War. H. Knollys, Incidents in
the Sepoy War (Edin. 1873); Incidents
in the China War (Edin. 1875).   199

GRANT, Marjorie. Verdun Days in Paris (1918) Her experiences in canteen
work in Paris, 1916.   200

GRANT, Robert.   Reminiscences of a
Clergyman (1873). Forty years in Dorset parish; mission work among railway navvies; views on poor law, tem-

perance, liturgy, morals, etc.   201

GRANT-WATSON,Eliot Lovegood. But to
What Purpose (1947); Departures(1948)
Biologist's life, travels, and mental
development;Darwin and Huxley; inter-
action of scientific, religious, and
social ideas; country life in England
Australia, Fijis, etc.   202

GRANVILLE, Augustus Bozzi. Autobiography (1874). His long life and work
as physician in foreign countries and
work for Royal Society; Italy, Greece
Portugal, Russia & West Indies, etc.;
foreign society and customs.   203

GRANVILLE, Mary (Delany). Autobiography and Correspondence (1861), 6v.
Mostly correspondence, but Vol.I contains autobiographical chapters on her
childhood and early life at court, to
1724.   204

GRATTAN,Thomas Colley. Beaten Paths
(1862). Anecdotes of himself and his
literary friends;Moore, Campbell, Coleridge, Wordsworth; and of diplomats
actors, etc.   205

GRATTAN, Lt. William. Adventures of
the Connaught Rangers (1847). Activities of the regiment in the Peninsular
war,1808-14; lively but rather impersonal.   206

GRATTON, John. Journal of the Life
(1720). Cheshire Quaker's conversion,
ministry, imprisonment, sufferings in
England, Ireland, Scotland.   207

GRAVES, Alfred Perceval. To Return
to All That (1930). Irish boyhood in
50's;Trinity College; London life and
the PreRaphaelites; work as inspector
of schools; London education in 90's;
his family; WW1 experiences; comments
on Robert Graves.   208

GRAVES, Charles. Gone Abroad (1932)
Off the Record(1942); Londoner's Life
(1943); Great Days (1944); Pride of
the Morning (1945). The frothy life &
reminiscences of Bohemian and columnist; high life, journalism, sport and
society in England and abroad, with a
slight background of WW2.   209

GRAVES, George. Gaieties and Gravi-
ties (1931). His career as a comedian

in musical comedies and pantomime and
musichalls;Daly's; Drury Lane; social
and theatrical life.   210

GRAVES, J. G. Some Memories (Sheffield,1944). Apprentice to watchmaker
in Sheffield; the printing business;
member of Sheffield City Council, and
alderman; religion and social work in
Sheffield. Sheffield P.L.   211

GRAVES, Robert. Goodbye to All That
(1929). His childhood,schools and family; service in France in WW1, with
commentary on war;university teaching
in Egypt; his novels.   212

GRAY, Alexander Hill.   Sixty Years
Ago (1925). Boyhood in India; adventures at sea; diamond seeking; travel
in Asia and Africa.   213

GRAY, Bernard. War Reporter (1942).
Experiences with British troops in WW2
up to Dunkirk; racy, critical narrative of war correspondent.   214

GRAY, Cecil. Musical Chairs (1948).
Career of a composer,music critic and
scholar; travels;music and musicians;
writers, painters; Delius.   215

GRAY, Edward Ker.   Thirty Years of
the Lights and Shades(1902). Work and
sermons of London clergyman; domestic
and family; St. George's Chapel. 216

GRAY,Frances Ralph.And Gladly Wolde
He Lerne (1931).   Her experiences in
women's education;her own schools and
Newnham;classics teacher at Westfield
and her career as high mistress of St.
Paul's Girls School;views on curriculum, educational problems, etc.   217

GRAY, Frank. Confessions of a Private (1920);Confessions of a Candidate
(1925). Experiences in France, WW1;&
Liberal M.P. after war; House of Commons and politics; work of whip. 218

GRAY,George. Vagaries of a Vagabond
(1930). Varied experiences;tramp, doing odd jobs,actor, parson; reminiscences of theatre and music halls;cha-
rities; celebrities.   219

GRAY, John. Gin and Bitters (1938).
Childhood in pubs; factory work; typing for famous novelists; his own no-

vels; religious life and work for the Church Army.   220

GRAY, Dr. John Alfred. My Residence at the Court of the Ameer (1895). His experiences as physician at court of Amir of Afghanistan from 1889; epidemics; court customs.   221

GRAY, John Hamilton. Autobiography (Edin. 1868). Boyhood in Scotland at beginning of century; ill health and education by tutors;Oxford; curate at Bolsover; travels in Europe; delicate and precise.   222

GRAY,Robert. Reminiscences of India and North Queensland (1913). Military experiences of a subaltern in India; the Mutiny; later pioneer and station life in North Queensland.   223

GRAY, William Dorchard. Travels in Western Africa (1825). The travels of a surgeon,1818-21, from the Gambia to the Niger.   224

GRAY, Lieut. William John. Military journal, 1857; service in the Mutiny; march from Ferozepore to Delhi. Journal of Society of Army Hist. Research X (1931) 1-16.   225

GREAVES, General Sir George Richard Memoirs (1924). Military career 1849-1893; Sandhurst; service in India and the Mutiny; New Zealand and Maori War Ashanti War;Adjutant-General in India social life and adventures.   226

GREEN, Arthur. Story of a Prisoner of War (1916). With Somerset Infantry in WW1;capture; German prison experiences; interesting language.   227

GREEN, Gen. Arthur Frank Umfreville Evening Tattoo (1941). Woolwich; army career; mostly service in France and on Italian Front in WW1;later service at Malta.   228

GREEN, Charles H. S. In Deaths Oft (1901).Experiences of a missionary in the Boxer rebellion; imprisonment and maltreatment.   229

GREEN, G.Garrow. In the Royal Irish Constabulary (1905). Police work and crime; social life, Ireland.   230

GREEN,George Clark. Collections and Recollections(1886). Eton; Cambridge; life as Devonshire vicar;fishing, otter hunting,yachting; observations of a naturalist.   231

GREEN, Henry. Pack My Bag (L. 1940) Days at school and at Oxford; country life and sport; a good life told in a poetical style.   232

GREEN, John. Vicissitudes of a Soldier's Life (Louth, 1827). A runaway apprentice's experience in Peninsular war, 1806-15.   233

GREEN, William. The Sufferings of (1774). Brief account of his work and experiences during seven years transportation to Maryland.   234

GREEN,William. Brief Outline of the Travels and Adventures(Coventry 1857) Experience and adventures of a bugler in the Rifle Brigade during the Peninsular War, 1802-12.   235

GREEN, William Charles. Memories of Eton and King's (Eton, 1905). Recollections of school and university by an old boy; historical.   236

GREENE, Harry Plunket. Where the Bright Waters Meet (1925); From Blue Danube to Shannon (1934). His career and travels as a singer; fishing and social life in Hants.   237

GREENE, Herbert. Secret Agent in Spain (1938). Adventures of official British agent during the Spanish Revolution of 1937.   238

GREENFIELD, M. Rose. Five Years in Ludhiana(1886). Experiences of a missionary in the Punjab in 70's; zenana work;conversions; medical work; Hindu women.   239

GREENHAM, G.H. Scotland Yard Experiences (1904). Detective work, crime, criminals, work of CID; his duties as guard during journeys of Queen Victoria.   240

GREENLY,Edward. A Hand through Time (1938).Intimate account of love story of himself & his wife; his geological studies and work as director of Geological Survey;religious views; reminiscences of eminent men.　241

GREENWALL, Harry James. Scoops (L. 1923); Round the World (1935); I Hate Tomorrow (1939); Three Years of Hell (1943); Farewell France (1949). Travels and adventures of a star reporter and war correspondent ; Daily Express WW1 and WW2; nostalgia over France in pre-WW1 days; international celebrities and events; interviews.　242

GREENWOOD,James. In Strange Company (1873).Daily Telegraph correspondent; investigations;slums, pubs, missions, hopping in Kent, prisons, industrialism, costermongers.　243

/GREENWOOD, Mary/. Passing Strange (1899). Orphan in Rochester; mission work among sailors, soldiers, dockers Quaker life and work; & working-class conditions.　244

GREER,Sarah. Quakerism;or the Story of My Life (Dublin, 1851). Account of her Quaker upbringing; worship; education; satirical account of religious life in Ireland.　245

GREGORY, Alfred Thomas. Recollections of a Country Editor (Tiverton, 1932).Proprietor and editor of Tiverton Gazette; journalism,public events and education in Devonshire;interesting.　246

GREGORY, Benjamin. Autobiographical Recollections (L. 1903).Conversion to Methodism; his education; ministry in Norfolk.　247

GREGORY, H. Never Again (1934). His military service in WW1; personal experiences; anti-war sentiments.　248

GREGORY,Isabella Augusta, Lady. Our Irish Theatre (1914). The Irish theatrical renaissance and her part in it; Abbey Theatre;Gaelic League; National Theatre Society; Yeats, Johnson, Robinson, etc.　249

GREGORY,John Duncan. On the Edge of Diplomacy (1929). A humdrum member of the Foreign Office's comments on diplomatic life and diplomats.　250

GREGORY,Robert. Autobiography(1912)

Work in Liverpool shippers;ordination and parish work in country and town; Dean of St. Paul's 1868-1912; religious controversies and problems; Tractarian movement and his part.　251

GREGORY, Sir William Henry. Autobiography (1894).Public & social life in Ireland; M.P. for Galway; work as Governor of Ceylon 1872-75.　252

GRENFELL, Francis Wallace Grenfell, Baron. Memoirs of a Field-Marshal (L. 1925). Milton Abbas; military training and service in Kaffir Wars, Sudan Boer War; Governor of Malta; service with Red Cross in WW1; army administration; reticent style.　253

GRETTON, Frederick Edward. Memory's Harkback (1889). Hereford childhood & cathedral social life; Shrewsbury and Cambridge; country life in Leicester, Rutland, Wales; judges he knew.　254

GREVILLE,Lady Beatrice Violet. Vignettes of Memory (1927).Her childhood and Victorian social life, literature amateur theatricals, philanthropy and sport.　255

GREW,Joseph Clark. Sport and Travel in the Far East (1910). Travels from 1902 in Malaya, India, Kashmir, China and big-game hunting.　256

GREY,Edwin. Cottage Life in a Hertfordshire Village (St. Albans, 1935). Boyhood in Harpenden in 60's; village life and work; his work at Rothamsted Experimental Station, with anecdotes of staff to 1920's.　257

GREY, Harry. Autobiography (L.1861) Life and work of Church of England minister.　258

GREY,Capt. J. R. World's End (1946) Adventures on sea and land in Pacific; Tahiti and Fiji; coconut plantations; colonial administration;vigorous view of officials and missionaries.　259

GREY OF FALLODON, Edward Grey, Viscount. Twenty-Five Years (1925). His career in public affairs and at Foreign Office;crises and policy; events leading to WW1; Allied Diplomacy. 260

GRIBBLE,Francis Henry.Seen in Passing(1929). Oxford in 80's; journalism for Observer and Graphic;Authors Club and literary groups of 90's;work as a biographer;travels in Europe; internment in Germany during WW1.　　　261

GRIERSON,Henry. Ramblings of a Rabbit (1924). Sporting experiences and reminiscences; mostly Rugby Football; Leicester and Cambridge; club cricket and his law studies.　　　262

GRIERSON, John. Air Whaler (1949). Experiences of pilot attached to Norwegian whaling factory-ship;technical aspects& adventures of reconnaissance work in the Antarctic.　　　263

GRIFFIN, Frank. I Joined the Army (1937). Unemployed man who joined Tank Corps;transfer to Departmental Corps; jaundiced account of six years as an army misfit.　　　264

GRIFFIN,Gerald. The Dead March Past (1937). Journalist in Dublin and London; his part in Irish rebellion; celebrities, eccentrics, turbulence in Ireland; fact and fantasy.　　　265

GRIFFIN, Maj. Henry Lysaght. An Official in British New Guinea (L.1925) Harrow and Woolwich; service in Royal Artillery;Boer War; administration in New Guinea;traders, planters, natives and missionaries.　　　266

GRIFFIN,James. Memories of the Past (1883). Congregational minister's recollections of his work among Manchester poor and in Hastings; memories of Chalmers, Edward Irving, etc.　　　267

GRIFFITH, George. Going to Markets (1870); Reminiscences (Bewdley, 1880) His education; & Staffordshire public affairs, politics & social life, from 1830 to 1880.　　　268

GRIFFITH, John. Journal of the Life (York, 1830). Quaker religious autobiography; conversion; emigration to America and ministry there; return to England and ministry in Yorkshire and Essex, etc.; mid 18 C.　　　269

GRIFFITH, Llewellyn Wyn. Up to Mametz (1931); Spring of Youth (L.1935); Wooden Spoon(1938). Sensitive account of service in France in WW1; poetical

account of his childhood and youth in Cardigan;farm life, schools, religion and his courtship; poet.　　　270

GRIFFITH, William. Diary, 1835-40; observations of a scientist in Assam, Burma, Afghanistan; natural history; tea-planting. Posthumous Papers (Calcutta, 1847-8) Vol. 1.　　　271

GRIFFITH,William Peter. Memoirs and Life, comp. by H.J.Piggott (typewritten copy at Methodist Book Room, London). Difficult childhood in Ireland; work as printer in London; success in business; Methodist observance.　　　272

GRIFFITH,Mrs. William Peter. Reminiscences (1908).Early life as wife of Methodist preacher; travels to Canada and New Zealand; family life. Copy in Methodist Book Room.　　　273

GRIFFITH-BOSCAWEN, Sir Arthur S. T. Fourteen Years in Parliament (L.1907) Memories (1925). Career as Conservative M.P. and minister of Pensions and of Agriculture; public affairs, politics; Boer War; WW1.　　　274

GRIFFITHS, Major Arthur. In Tight Places (1900). Retired officer's adventures as detective;exploits in Algiers, Egypt, Spain; crooks in society; his love affairs; fiction?　　　275

GRIFFITHS, Arthur G. F. Fifty Years of Public Service (1904).His military service in Crimean War, Canada & Gibraltar;inspector in charge of convict prisons in Chatham and London; prison life, organization, etc.　　　276

GRIFFITHS, Capt.Charles John. Diary 1857-8; a lively and detailed account of siege of Delhi. Narrative of the Siege of Delhi (1910).　　　277

GRIGG, Sir Percy James. Prejudice & Judgment (1948). Career of an important civil servant; private secretary to five Chancellors of Exchequer; and War Secretary in WW2; public affairs; financial problems and ideas; public figures; his education, liberalism and nonconformity.　　　278

GRIMBLE,Augustus.Leaves from a Game Book(1898); More Leaves (1917). Fishing, shooting, country house life and country sports from 70's.   279

GRIMSHAW, Beatrice Ethel. Isles of
Adventure (1930). Her thirty years in
New Guinea and South Seas;travels and
native life; journalism.   280

GRIMWOOD, Ethel St. Clair. My Three
Years in Manipur (1892). Experiences
of wife of political agent in Manipur
court, domestic and social life; the
Mutiny; adventures and escape.   281

GRINNELL-MILNE, Duncan William. An
Escaper's Log(1926);Wind in the Wires
(1933). Prison experiences in Germany
in WW1 and escape to Holland;training
as airman and service with RFC in WW1
capture and escape.   282

GRONOW,Capt. Rees Howell. Reminiscences (L. 1862); Recollections (1863)
Celebrities of London and Paris(1865)
Last Recollections (1866). Collected
form: Recollections and Reminiscences
(1889).Social life in Grenadiers; his
clubs and life as a buck;society life
sport, gallantry, gossip about society, literary, political personages in
first half of the century.   283

GROSSEK,Mark. First Movement (1937)
Polish-Jewish boy in London elementary
schools; family background; his early
literary interests.   284

GROSER, Fr. St.John B. Politics and
Persons (1949).Catholic priest's life
and work in Stepney from 1930's;soci-
al work;poverty, unemployment, Labour
Party, Communist Party; a sympathetic
record.   285

GROSSMITH, George. A Society Clown
(Bristol, 1888); Piano and I (1910);
"G.G." (1933). Long career as entertainer; tours in England and America;
work in musical comedy and in Gilbert
and Sullivan operas; social life and
theatrical scene.   286

GROSSMITH, Weedon. From Studio to
Stage (1913). Schools; study as painter;amateur theatricals and career in
theatre from 1885; Savage Club; social life in London.   287

GROUNDSELL,Frank. Lunatic Spy(1935)
His tours and travels as an entertainer; in Germany during WW1 and work as

British Agent; escape.   288

GROVES,Anthony Norris. Diary, 1829-
1852;work and travels of a missionary
in India and Bagdad; educational work
missionary rivalries; native life and
poverty; medical affairs. Memoir, by
Mrs. Groves (1856); Journal of a Residence at Bagdad (1832).   289

GRUBB, Wilfrid Barbrooke. Among the
Indians of the Paraguayan Chaco(1904)
Missionary work in Paraguay in 90's at
the Chaco mission; ethnography;Indian
ways.   290

GRUNDY, Anthony George. My Fifty
Years in Transport (1944). His career
as a pioneer in passenger transport on
railways and trams.   291

GRUNDY, Francis H. Pictures of the
Past (1879). Lancs boyhood; work as a
civil engineer on railways in Lancs &
Yorks;friend of Patrick Bronte; later
experiences in Australian goldfields;
Brisbane, Sydney.   292

GRUNDY, George Beardoe. Fifty-Five
Years at Oxford (1945). School; student at Oxford; tutor in ancient history; Brasenose and Corpus; scholars &
celebrities; books; good.   293

GUBSKY, Nikolai. Angry Dust (1937);
My Double and I (1939). Youth in Russia; misfortunes in Revolution; exile
in England and struggles;unemployment
and odd jobs; writing in London. 294

GUERIN, Eddie. Crime (1928); I Was
a Bandit (1929). Life of a criminal;
slums and poverty; prison life in USA
France and England; has some sociological value.   295

GUGGISBERG,Sir Frederick Gordon. We
Two in West Africa(1909). Travel with
his wife on Gold Coast and in Central
West Africa.   296

GUILLEMARD, Francis H. H. The Years
that the Locusts Have Eaten (MS, Bodleian Library, Eng. Misc. d. 189-192,
196, 236). Childhood at Eltham; youth
at Cambridge; medical study at Barts;
residence in S.Africa and Madeira and
travels; discursive reminiscences.297

GUILLEMARD, Sir Laurence N. Trivial

Fond Records(1937). Work and problems of the Governor of Straits Settlements from 1919; the lighter side.   298

GUISE, Anselm Vener Lee. Six Years in Bolivia (1922). Adventures of manager of a tin mine in Bolivia; travel and native life; engineer.   299

GULLY, Robert. Prison journal, 1842 his experiences and hardships as captive of the Chinese. Journals Kept by Mr. Gully (1844).   300

GUMMER,George. Reminiscences of Rotherham (Rotherham, 1927). Alderman's recollections of his work and of public life over sixty years.   301

GUNN,Clement Bryce. Leaves from the Life of a Country Doctor (Edin. 1935) Medical study in Edinburgh & practice in Fife; his work and social life on the border; his visits to London; an entertaining local record.   302

GUNNING,Henry. Reminiscences of the University (1854). His career at Cambridge; Christ's; education, dons and town and gown; development of university; social life and public affairs, 1784-1830.   303

GURNER, Stanley Ronald Kershaw. I Chose Teaching (1937). Career of representative teacher; Clifton, Haileybury, Marlborough, Strand, Whitgift; sensible reflections & proposals from his experience.   304

GURNEY,Emelia Russell. Diary, 1865-1866; travel and social life, Jamaica Letters, ed. E.M. Gurney (1902).   305

GURNEY, Priscilla Hannah. Memoir of the Life (Bristol, 1834). Quaker family life and religious observances in Norwich, etc.; reading; inner light; Quaker leaders.   306

GUTHRIE,Duncan. Jungle Diary (1946) Personal narrative, WW2; experiences as a commando on the Burma-Siam frontier; the Burmese.   307

GUTHRIE, Ellen Emma. Retrospection (Edin. 1876). Memories in verse form; her happy childhood on Skye; shepherd life and folk-lore; her sadness as an exile; nature and the open air.   308

GUTHRIE, Kate. My Year in an Indian Fort (1877); Life in Western India(L. 1881). Residence and extensive travel in India; mainly impersonal descriptions of Indian life and scene.   309

GUTHRIE, Thomas. Autobiography and Memoir (1874-5). Scottish education and student life in Edinburgh; foundation of Free Church and ministry at Arbirlot and Edinburgh to 1843; work in temperance and ragged school movements; good.   310

GUTHRIE, Thomas Anstey ("F.Anstey") Long Retrospect (1936). Wry, humorous account of education,legal studies & writings as humorist; work for Punch; Henry James, Meredith, Irving, literary friends.   311

GUTHRY, Henry. Memoires (1702). The Scottish theologian's account of Scottish affairs from royalist and episcopalian point of view;rebellion against Charles I; historical account of public affairs 1637-49.   312

GUY, William. Mostly Memories(Edin. 1949). His life and work as dentist, from later 19th Century; interests in acting, poetry, photography.   313

GWATKIN-WILLIAMS, Capt.Rupert Stanley. Under the Black Ensign (L. 1922) Naval service in WW1 in trawlers,destroyers,minesweepers; raiding; lively and personal.   314

GWIN, Thomas. Quaker autobiography and journal, 1656-1717; attendance at Falmouth meetings and visits to Devon and Cornwall meetings; ministry; personal life. MS, Friends' Society Library, London, MS.77.   315

GWYNN,Mary M. X. From Hunting Field to Cloister (1947). Conversion; life as nun; biography with some extracts from diary.   316

GWYNN, Stephen Lucius. Experiences of a Literary Man (1926); Memories of Enjoyment (Tralee, 1946). Irish boyhood; Oxford; Dublin in 80's; schoolteaching; London social and literary life and his writings;M.P. for Galway and Irish politics; his recreations , reading, pleasures, friends; a pleasant record.   317

GWYNNE,Capt. John. Military Memoirs (Edin. 1822). A Welshman's account of his most laudable activities in service of Charles I; military exploits & bravery; interesting.   318

GWYNNE-VAUGHAN, Helen C. I. Service with the Army (1942). Her work as the organizer of women's auxiliary services in WW1 and WW2;service on Western Front;professor at London and work as botanist; conservative politics; Parliamentary candidate; good.   319

H. Reminiscences of a Red Coat(London, 1895).Service in Lancers in England, South Africa, India.   1

H., A. L. Escape: A Confession(1940) Her spiritual life; studies of spiritualism and philosophy;faith lost and regained.   2

H., J.C. Reminiscences of a Professional Politician (1899). Liberal's account of political activities, 1886 to 1896; campaigning in the Orkneys & Shetlands; manoeuvres.   3

HACKETT, B. Memorials of a Ministry (1901). Religious zeal; study at Nottingham; first pastorate at Ashbourne and his vocation.   4

HADDON, C.G. Gordon. My Uncle, King George V (N.Y. 1929). Alleged life in high society; claims to be illegitimate son of Duke of Clarence; bandboy, soldier in India and China;service in WW1.   5

HADFIELD,George. Personal Narrative Covers 1787-1878;family and religious life; founding of Lancashire Independent College and work for Rusholme Rd Chapel; M.P. for Sheffield; political affairs; repeal of Test laws. MS copies in Sheffield City Libraries, Manchester Central Library.   6

HAGGARD, Lt. Col. Andrew Charles P. Under Crescent and Star (Edin. 1895). His military service in Egypt 1882-5; the Nile expedition.   7

HAGGARD,Henry Rider. The Days of My Life (1926). Education; life and travels in South Africa; his career as a novelist; public work; politics.   8

HAGGARD,Lilias Rider (ed.).I Walked by Night (1935).Dictated by the "King of the Norfolk Poachers"; 75 years of country life and sport & his troubles with the law;ballads, songs, old ways and people.   9

HAIG-THOMAS, David. I Leap before I Look (1936). Eton & Cambridge; career as an oarsman;climbing and travels in Canada, Iceland, Pyrenees etc.   10

HAIME, John. Short Account of God's Dealings (1792). Military service in the Dragoons;conversion; preaching of Methodism in Army;later work as itinerant minister, largely in Devonshire and Southwest.   11

HAKE, Dr. Thomas Gordon. Memoirs of Eighty Years (1892). Classical study; medical studies and practice in Scotland and England; literary and theatrical interests;friendship with pre-Raphaelites.   12

HALCOMBE, Charles J. H. The Mystic Flowery Land (1896). Experiences in China in 80's; Hongkong; Canton; Chinese life and literature; his poems & his marriage to a Chinese girl.   13

HALDANE, Archibald Richard Burdon. By Many Waters (1940). Reminiscences of walking and fishing, Scotland.   14

HALDANE, Charlotte. Music, My Love! (1936); Truth Will Out (1949). London childhood;work as journalist & novelist; marriage to J.B.S. Haldane; divorce;conversion to communism; Spanish war;Russia in WW2; disenchantment and rejection of communism; her devotion to music;record of experiences in her grand passion.   15

HALDANE, Elizabeth Sanderson. From One Century to Another (1937).Experience in transition from Victorianism; social,economic, political life; Liberalism,women's rights, trade unions; literature and society;an interesting sociological record.   16

HALDANE, Sir James Aylmer Lowthrop. Soldier's Saga (Edin. 1948). Military career; seven campaigns; India, Boer War, Japan, Manchuria, Iraq; travels; celebrities he knew.   17

HALDANE,John W.C. Life as an Engineer (1904). Apprentice; work on ships and railways at Birkenhead and Crewe; consulting engineer;advance of engineering.   18

HALDANE,Mary Elizabeth. A Record of 100 Years (1925). Autobiography deals with childhood in 20's and 30's; the early Victorian scene, education, family life, etc.   19

HALDANE,Richard Burdon Haldane,Viscount. An Autobiography(1929). Career as a barrister to 1905;work in Liberal Party and public affairs; Minister for War in WW1; Lord Chancellor; part in Labour government; record of great public servant.   20

HALDEN, Margaret. First Year Out(L. 1943). Her experience as teacher in a special school.   21

HALE, Sgt.James. Journal (Cirencester, 1826).Gloucestershire man's service in 9th Foot Regiment during the Peninsular War 1803-14; a general account of movements and campaigns;Portugal,Spain, France. Copy, Gloucester City Library.   22

HALES,Alfred Greenwood. Broken Trails(1931). Travels and varied jobs of novelist;pearling and range-riding in Australia; professional soldier, Turkey;war correspondent; adventures and celebrities he met.   23

HALES, Harold K.   Autobiography of "The Card" (1936). Lively account of days at school with Arnold Bennett and of his work and deals as a commercial traveller; life in Burslem; M.P. for Hanley.   24

HALFAR, Raichal Das. English Diary (Dacca, 1903). Life of Hindu student at Oxford and London universities, in the 60's; Max Mueller; tours.   25

HALFORD, Frederic Michael. Angler's Autobiography (1903). Experiences of trout, salmon, and sea fishing, mostly in South of England;journalism for The Field.   26

HALHEAD, Myles. Book of Some of the Sufferings(1690). Autobiography of an early Quaker; conversion, ministry, & sufferings in prison and at hands of crowd; God's visitations.   27

HALKETT, Lady Anne (Murray). Autobiography(Edin. 1701; Camden Society 1875). Fragmentary; education, family life,courtship; her loyal devotion to her husband during the Civil War; the sufferings of a royalist;an excellent story of a devoted wife.   28

HALKETT, G. R. Dear Monster (1939). Rambling autobiography of life in Germany; court life at Weimar; the days of the Nazis;excellent account of intellectual life and arts.   29

HALKETT, J.G. Hay. Magistrate's Fun (1940). Career as a lawyer; his work as a London magistrate; cases; incidents grave and gay.   30

HALL,Sir Alfred Daniel. Digressions of a Man of Science (1932). A professional autobiography of Kentish farmer botanist and soil specialist.   31

HALL, Captain Basil. The Midshipman (1862); Voyages and Travels(1895). An account of his early naval career and life on shipboard;selections from his many books of travel in America,Spain Africa, etc.; lively but loose. 32

HALL, David. Some Brief Memoirs (L. 1758). Yorkshire schoolmaster; teaching at Skipton;religious life and observances of Quakers at Skipton; travels in the ministry.   33

HALL, George. Gypsy's Parson (1915) His friendship with gypsies and religious work among them;rector of Ruckland, Lancs.   34

HALL, Herbert Byng. Adventures of a Bric-a-Brac Hunter (1868). Experience collecting china and antiques through Europe; mostly impersonal.   35

HALL, Herbert C.   Barrack and Bush (1923). Soldiering, police work, and sport in Northern Nigeria;WW1 service in Africa.   36

HALL, J. H. W.Scenes in a Soldier's Life (Montreal, 1848). Military serv-

ice in India and Afghanistan, 1839-43
life in the ranks; simple. 37

HALL, James Norman. Kitchener's Mob
(N.Y. 1916). American serving as private with British Army in France, WW1
humors and everyday life. 38

HALL, John. Memoirs of the Right
Villainous John Hall (1708). Apologia
of a criminal dictated in Newgate before his death. 39

HALL, John Ames.Retrospect of Eight
Decades (1930). Lay preacher and amateur horologist; his hobbies and interests. Typed MS, Portsmouth Public
Libraries. L.C. 921. 40

HALL, John B. Random Records (Dublin, 1928). Experiences of journalist
in Dublin;rather impersonal recollections of politics, law, theatre, social life, personalities. 41

HALL, John Vine. Autobiography of
(1865). His sins and redemption; temperance work & lecturing; his philanthropic work;work among prisoners and
in gaols; important. 42

HALL, Rt.Rev. Joseph. Works, edited
Josiah Pratt (1808) I, Pref. Contains
autobiography of studies & religious
career; political and religious controversies of the early 17th Century;
bishop; written in Tower. 43

HALL, Martin J. In Full & Glad Sur-
render (1905). Work and travels of a
CMS missionary in Uganda and Victoria
Nyanza district. 44

HALL, Col. Melvin A. Journey to the
End of an Era (1948). A lively record
of his military career and travels in
Asia and Europe;excitement and horror
of running a secret telephone line in
WW1. 45

HALL, Newman. Conflict and Victory
(1874);Autobiography (1898). Work and
travels as an evangelist & temperance
reformer; pastorates in Hull and Surrey Chapel, London; meetings with celebrities in politics and religion; a
good Victorian record. 46

HALL, Samuel Carter. Book of Memories (1871);Retrospect of a Long Life

(1883). Journalism and politics 1800-
1883;with reminiscences and anecdotes
of chief politicians,writers, artists
and public figures. 47

HALLAM, Jo. Seventy Years' Hard (L.
(1934). Adventures and anecdotes of a
long life at sea; experiences of merchant skipper. 48

HALLAM, Thomas. Manchester scholar;
studies and researches in phonetics &
English dialects to 1887.MS, Bodleian
Library, Eng. Lang. d.32. 49

HALLE, C. E. Notes from a Painter's
Life (1909). Work in Chelsea; reminiscences of painters,exhibitions, gal-
leries & fashions in painting at home
and abroad; anecdotes. 50

HALLÉ,Sir Charles. Life and Letters
(1896). Early life in Germany; musical career, Manchester and London; his
piano recitals; the Hallé Orchestra;
music and musicians. 51

HALLÉ,Gustave. Mayfair to Maritzburg
(1933). His early life in Manchester &
London;some social life in England and
notes on celebrities (Tennyson,Brown-
ing, etc.); mostly his career in South
Africa. 52

HALSHAM, John. Idlehurst (1898). A
year in a cottage on the Sussex Weald
village life and activities. 53

HALWARD, Leslie. Let Me Tell You(L.
1938). Poverty and elementary education in Birmingham; factory work, odd
jobs,boxing; his struggles and career
as fiction writer. 54

HALYBURTON, Thomas. Memoirs of the
Life (Edin. 1715, 1847). Professor of
Divinity at St.Andrews; his religious
development; introspection & sense of
sin; God's mercies; from 1674. 55

HAM, Elizabeth. Elizabeth Ham, ed.
Eric Gillett(1945). Life and struggle
of governess in Ireland, Channel Islands, Dorset; family, farm life, religion, teaching, seeking husband and
gossip; entertaining; 1783-1820. 56

HAMAND, Dr. Louis Arthur. An Organist Remembers (St. Albans, 1949). His
career as organist and choirmaster at

Malvern Priory Church from 1910;music
and antiquities.   57

HAMBLOCH,Ernest. British Consul (L.
1938).Thirty years as consul and commercial diplomatic officer in Belgrade
and Rio de Janeiro.   58

HAMBOURG, Mark. From Piano to Forte
(1931). His musical career from 1889;
recitals, tours, travel; musical life
and musicians in London, etc.   59

HAMBROOK, Walter.   Hambrook of the
Yard (1937). Constable at Vine Street
and Paddington; detective work, Scotland Yard; famous cases and crimes; &
the Dartmoor mutiny.   60

HAMERTON, Philip Gilbert. Intellectual Life(1873); Autobiography (1897)
Lancashire child; miseries at school;
development of interest in literature
and art;journalism and art criticism;
notes on Ruskin, Thackeray, writers &
painters; from 1834.   61

HAMILTON, Arthur. Confessions of a
Scribbler(Merthyr Tydfil, 1880?). His
experiences in writing and publishing
a "modern" book.   62

HAMILTON, Cicely Mary. Life Errant
(1935). Schools; work as suffragette;
war work in France; travels in Europe
after war; her novels and writing and
literary society.   63

HAMILTON, Cosmo. Unwritten History
(1924). Work as playwright; theatrical life; visit to theatres in America
and Hollywood.   64

HAMILTON,Ernest William, Lord. Forty Years On (1922); Old Days and New
(1923). Childhood in Ireland; Baron's
Court and country life; Harrow; experience as soldier; social and country
house life; sport; travel to America;
anecdotes of places and people.   65

HAMILTON, Francis (Buchanan). Diary
1795;travels and observations of surgeon on a journey from Bengal to Ava.
Antiquities. MS, India Office Library
Eur. C. 12, 13.   66

HAMILTON, Frederic Spencer, Lord.
Here, There and Everywhere(1921); The
Vanished Pomps(1919); The Days before

Yesterday(1920); gathered together as
My Yesterdays (1930). Diplomatic life
and society in Berlin, Vienna, Lisbon
Russia, Brazil; viceregal life in India, Canada; amusements, social life,
fashions, personalities and politics,
from 1870.   67

HAMILTON,George Francis, Lord. Parliamentary Reminiscences (1916, 1922)
2v.Parliamentary career of a Manchester economist and a Tory free-trader;
politics and politicians in his time;
Parliamentary affairs.   68

HAMILTON,Gerald. As Young as Sopho-
cles(1937). Novelist's travels, China
Japan, Russia;interest in Catholicism
and Buddhism; work for Sinn Fein, and
for Save the Children Fund; Germany &
rise of Nazis.   69

HAMILTON,Gen. Sir Ian Standish Mon-
teith.When I Was a Boy(1939); Listen-
ing for the Drums (1944).Childhood in
Scotland; Cheam and Wellington; Sandhurst; military service and army social life in Ireland,India, Egypt; memories of Kipling, Churchill; adventures and escapades.   70

HAMILTON, John. Sixty Years Experience (1894). Farming, social, religious life in Ireland; his troubles as
a landlord in Donegal; the famine of
1846.   71

HAMILTON,John Potter. Reminiscences
of an Old Sportsman (1860). Shooting,
fishing, hunting, in England, Europe,
South America, for 40 years.   72

HAMILTON, Lady Margaret. A Pairt of
the Life (Edin. 1827). Marriage 1598;
pregnancies;deserted; family life and
troubles; difficulties with husband;
destitution; second marriage.   73

HAMILTON, Maria. A Narrative of the
Life (Bristol, 1833). Upbringing and
posts as governess; domestic misfortunes; elopement; chronicle of troubles from fire, shipwreck, robbers; an
inane, prim pamphlet.   74

HAMILTON, Mary. Green & Gold (1948)
Fictionalised autobiography of growing up in County Meath in the 80's and
90's; Irish country life; and visits
to Dublin.   75

HAMILTON, Mary Agnes. Remembering My
Good Friends (1944). Upbringing, Manchester, Glasgow, Aberdeen; education
at Cambridge; political work for Labour Party; her writings.   76

HAMILTON, Vereker Monteith. Things
that Happened(1925). Work and social
life of planter in India and Ceylon in
60's; evocative, mystical events & co-
incidences in chain of life;painting;
sports.   77

HAMMERTON, Sir John Alexander. With
Northcliffe (1932); As the Days Go By
(1941); Other Things Than War (1943);
Books and Myself (1944). Childhood in
Scotland; career in provincial & London journalism; Daily Mail and Northcliffe;editorial work, publication of
encyclopoedias and volumes of popular
education; experiences in WW2 Blitz;
literary friendships;reminiscences of
writers and journalists.   78

HAMMOND, Walter R. Cricket My Destiny
(1946); Cricket My World(1948). The
sporting career of the Gloucester and
England batsman;players, games, anecdotes.   79

HAMNETT, Nina. Laughing Torso (1932)
Schooling; Bohemian life in Paris and
South of France with expatriates; re-
miniscences of writers and painters;
Joyce, etc.   80

HAMON, Count Louis ("Cheiro"). Confessions (1932). Experiences of hand-
writing expert and palmist; reminiscences of royalty & the celebrities of
the stage and professions.   81

HANBIDGE, William. The Memories (St.
Albans, 1939). Boyhood in Wicklow at
beginning 19th Century; farming; his
teaching in London ragged schools and
missionary work, Whitechapel.   82

HANBURY, Charlotte. Autobiography
(1901).Childhood and family life; her
work for ragged school at Bonchurch &
family and country life at Blackdown,
Somerset.   83

HANBURY-SPARROW, Col. Arthur Alan.
Land-Locked Lake (1932). Forceful account of experiences in WW1; with the
unlucky 1st Division in France.   84

HANBY, Thomas. Lives of Early Methodist Preachers, edited Thomas Jackson
(1837) I. Autobiography of itinerant
Methodist preacher in 18th Century in
Carlisle and North.   85

HANCOCK, Norman. An Innocent Grows
Up(1947). Draper's sober, industrious
career from childhood;family life and
the trade; Kipps in real life.   86

HANCOCK, Thomas. Narratives of the
Reformation (Camden Society, 1859). A
protestant clergyman's troubles during
reign of Queen Mary; interesting dialogue and spellings.   87

HANDLEY, Maj. Leonard Mourant H. Hunter's Moon(1933); Time's Delinquency
(1935). Twenty-two years' big-game in
India and Siam; adventures and impressions of soldier and traveler, mostly
in Asia.   88

HANDLEY, Mrs. M. A. Roughing It in
Southern India (1911). Experiences of
wife of a forestry officer; elephants
and hunting; natural history; life in
country with Hindus.   89

HANDLEY, Tommy. Handley's Pages (L.
1938). His career in musichalls, revues, musical comedy, but largely his
work as radio comedian; anecdotes of
B.B.C. and theatre.   90

HANDLEY-TAYLOR, Geoffrey. Magenta
Moments (1946). Odd jobs as secretary
editor & actor; London clubs and personalities; army life in WW2.   91

HANGER, Col. George. Life, Adventures
and Opinions (1801).Picaresque adventures of soldier-of-fortune, buck and
gallant, ending in gaol.   92

HANLEY, James. Broken Water (1937).
A vigorous account of early life; his
passion for sea and voyages;beginning
of his career as novelist.   93

HANNAN-CLARK, Thomas. Some Experiences of a Court-Martial Officer (1932)
Army trials in Belgium and France after WW1; vindication of system.   94

HANNAY, James. "Reminiscences of a
Provincial Editor," Temple Bar, XXIII
(1868). Humorous account of Scottish

journalism;work on the Edinburgh Courant. 95

HANSON,James. Rolling Stone (Liverpool, 1939). Lancashire boyhood; work in dairy business in Liverpool,London Peterborough,Australia; ups and downs in business. 96

HANSON, Lawrence. Shining Morning Face (1948). Memories of his boyhood; parents and governess; social life in middle-class home;his study of Coleridge. 97

HANSON, Thomas. Lives of Early Methodist Preachers,edited Thomas Jackson (1838)III. Autobiography of itinerant Methodist preacher in Yorkshire and N. England. 98

HAPGOOD,Edris Anthony. Football Ambassador (1944).Career of Arsenal and England soccer captain; games, tours; soccer during WW2. 99

HARBORD, Maurice Asshton. Froth and Bubble (1915). Cheerful reminiscences of soldier, rider, sportsman, hunter; experiences in Boer War, Rhodesia and East Africa. 100

HARDING, Col. Colin. Far Bugles (L. 1933). Boyhood and youth in Somerset; later life in S. Africa as prospector and commander of police in Mashonaland and administrator in Barotseland; and service in WW1. 101

HARDING, Geoffrey. Escape Fever (L. 1932). Airman's adventures WW1; capture and imprisonment at Strohen, and escape; humorous. 102

HARDING, Rowe. Rugby (1929). Sporting reminiscences of Cambridge Rugby footballer; international matches for Wales in 20's. 103

HARDINGE, Sir Arthur Henry. Diplomatist in Europe(1927); Diplomatist in the East(1928). His career in Foreign Office and abroad from 1884; in Spain Egypt, Russia, Persia. 104

HARDINGE OF PENSHURST, Charles Hardinge, Baron. On Hill and Plain (1933); Old Diplomacy(1947); My Indian Years (1948).Hunting and sport in India;his long career in diplomacy; politics and

statesmen;quest for power; WW1; Viceroyalty of India;partition of Bengal; imperial relations; important. 105

HARDMAN, Samuel. In the Days of My Youth (Radcliffe, Lancs., 1921). Boyhood in Lancs; work in mills and cotton trade; social history; effects of American civil war. Copy in Manchester P.L. 106

HARDWICKE,Sir Cedric. Let's Pretend (1932).His career on stage and films; London theatre; Birmingham Repertory; reminiscences of actors and theatrical life and audiences. 107

HARDY, Capt. Jocelyn Lee. I Escape (1927). Capture in WW1; imprisonment in Germany; escape to Holland. 108

HARDY, Thomas. Memoir (1832). Scottish youth from 1752; shoemaker; his friends and political interests, London; founding London Corresponding Society; sympathies with French Revolution and arrest for treason; parliamentary reforms. 109

HARDY, Thomas. Early Life, by Florence Hardy (L.1928); Later Years, by Florence Hardy (1930). Biography incorporating Hardy's recollections of early days, with extensive quotations from his notebooks during novel period that constitute something like a diary of people, scenes, social life and his career. 110

HARE, Augustus John Cuthbert. Memorials of a Quiet Life(1872); Story of My Life (1896-1900) 6v. Very leisurely account of boyhood, literary life in England and abroad;writing; social life and literary and society friends and domestic; much of it quoted from diary of 1855-1900. 111

HARE, Kenneth. No Quarrel with Fate (1946).Poet and adventurer; imaginative childhood; Oxford;London literary circles before WW1; army service WW1; exuberant. 112

HARGRAVE, John. At Suvla Bay (1916) Scoutmaster's service in Army Medical Corps, Gallipoli campaign. 113

HARGROVE,Charles. From Authority to Freedom (1920).Religious life and de-

developments;Plymouth Brother; Catholic priest and monk; 35 years Unitarian minister at Leeds.   114

HARINGTON, General Sir Charles. Tim Harington Looks Back (1940). Military career; Sandhurst; Boer War; work at Staff College; service in WW1, India, Gibraltar.   115

HARRIOTT, John.   Struggles through Life (1807). Lively and varied career Northampton childhood; boy at sea; a farmer in S. Africa and America; magistrate in Thames Police;domestic affairs; perils.   116

HARKER, Joseph. Studio and Stage(L. 1924). A childhood in theatre; career as theatrical scene painter; Gilbert and Sullivan, Irving & Tree; fashions in scenery and design.   117

HARLAND, Elizabeth M. Farmer's Girl (1942). Businesslike account of farming work in Norfolk in WW2.   118

HARLAND-EDGECUMBE, Francis W. Lord High Executioner (1934). A criminal's experiences in English & in American prisons; sociology.   119

HARLEY, Captain John.   The Veteran (1838). A boyhood in Ireland; 40 years in army; service in Egypt, Peninsular War; adventures, army life.   120

HARLEY, Percy. My Life in Shipping (1938). Career in shipbroker's; tankers, refrigerated ships & development of shipping;1889 Dock Strike; WW1 experience; Highbury life.   121

HARMAN, Neal. Loose End (1937). His youth in Bucks; work in London silver shop; travels America, Burma, Africa; adventures of footloose man.   122

HARPER, Allanah.   All Trivial Fond Records (1950). A pouting account of her childhood and youth from 1908 and travels as a child in Far East, Egypt and France; her debut; critical.   123

HARPER, Harry. Twenty-Five Years of Flying (1929). Learning to fly; early experiences with balloons and planes; development of aviation.   124

HARPOLE, James.   Leaves from a Sur-

geon's Case Book (L.1937); Behind the Surgeon's Mask (1940). Work and cases of a surgeon;thoughts and feelings in his work; pseudonymous.   125

HARRAP, George Godfrey. Some Memories (1935). Publisher's career; publishing, literary fashions; history & anecdotes of books, writers.   126

HARRIS, Frank.   My Life and Loves (Paris and Nice, 1922-27);   Life and Adventures (1947). Career and adventures of author, editor, and lover; & his exploits and vanities;Oscar Wilde and writers he knew.   127

/HARRIS, Mrs. G./.   A Lady's Diary (1858). With her soldier-husband; the siege of Lucknow; details of civilian experiences.   128

HARRIS,George. Autobiography (1888) Childhood and education; legal study; career as lawyer and judge; his writing, scholarship, lecturing; literary friendships.   129

HARRIS, George Harold. Prisoner of War and Fugitive (Aldershot, 1947). A personal narrative of WW2; capture in N.Africa, 1942; in Italy; escape and recapture; adventures.   130

/HARRIS, James/.   Confessions of a Scribbler (Merthyr Tydfil, 1882). His meagre schooling; work as boy in Cardiff; experiences as writer with critics and publishers; inflated.   Copy in Bodleian.   131

HARRIS, Major-General James Thomas. China Jim (1912). Cadet in India 1849 army life and service;the Mutiny; and march to China and life and adventures there; sport.   132

HARRIS,John. My Autobiography (Falmouth, 1882). Boyhood on Cornish farm and country life;early reading, writing of poetry; work as miner; family life; later books; good. Copy, Exeter P.L.   133

HARRIS, John. Recollections, ed. H. Curling (1929). Good personal account of experiences of a rifleman in Peninsular War.   134

HARRIS,Joseph. Random Notes and Re-

flections (Liverpool, 1912); Further
Random Notes (1914). The experiences
of a Russian-Jew; settlement in England;business success; reflections on
Judaism.   135

HARRIS,Odee (Oscar Drew). Unsettled
in Places (1937). Fifty years' travel
throughout world; many jobs; journalism,stage managing, soldiering, hotel
and pub managing.   136

HARRIS, Sir Percy. Forty Years in &
out of Parliament (1947). Public work
of a persistent Liberal; M.P. Bethnal
Green; work in L.C.C.; chief whip of
Liberal Party; frank and instructive
account of politics and public affairs
and Liberal fortunes.   137

HARRIS, Richard W.   Not So Humdrum
(1939).Career of a civil servant from
1890; Tax Department; National Health
Insurance.   138

HARRIS, Sir Robert Hastings.   From
Cadet to Admiral (1913). Naval career
1853-1908;chatty reminiscences of his
service and sport in many parts of the
world; Boer War; S.Africa.   139

HARRIS, Samuel. History and Conversion (Bradford, 1833). A Polish Jew's
religious upbringing; emigration; his
hardships in England; his conversion
to Methodism; fortunes as a footman &
ship's steward.   140

HARRIS, Stanley. Old Coaching Days
(1882).Historical and antiquarian reminiscences of coaching and coachmen;
earlier 19th Century.   141

HARRIS, Tindall. Here and There (L.
1924). Reminiscences and anecdotes of
fishing; England and abroad.   142

HARRISON, Alexander James. Eventful
Life (1901). Irish background; educa-
tion; scepticism and conversion; work
as Methodist preacher and transfer to
Church of England; religious work in
Lancs and Newcastle; discussions with
Bradlaugh.   143

HARRISON,Benjamin. Harrison of Igh-
tham (Oxford, 1928). His 83 years in
Kentish village;local shopkeeper;loc-
al scene; geological interests; remi-
nescences of Tennyson, Wendell Holmes

etc.; pleasant.   144

HARRISON, Clifford. Stray Records
(1892). Professional life of a poetry
reciter; theatrical and literary reminiscences;Tennyson, Taylor, Stanley
etc.   145

HARRISON, David. Melancholy Narrative (1766). Sea captain's adventures
on journey from West Indies;gale, famine, cannibalism; rescue.   146

HARRISON, Frederic. Autobiographic
Memoirs (1911).Oxford; social life in
London; his writing and lectures; reminiscences of celebrities in politics
and literature; social problems. 147

HARRISON, Jane Ellen. Reminiscences
(1925). Childhood; her career as teacher and classical scholar.   148

HARRISON, M. C. C., and CARTWRIGHT,
H. A. Within Four Walls (1930). Joint
account of experiences in German prison camp in WW1; endeavors to escape:
humours.   149

HARRISON, Maude. Spinner's Lake (L.
1941). Account of her cure in mental
hospital; hospital life.   150

HARRISON, Gen. Sir Richard. Recollections (1908). His army career 1857
to 1900; Mutiny; China; Zulu War and
Sekukuni war; Canada, Egypt, and home
service.   151

HARRISON, Robert.   Notes of a Nine
Years' Residence (1855). His life and
observations in Russia in 40's. 152

HART, Heber Leonidas. Reminiscences
and Reflections (1939). Scattered recollections of his work as lawyer and
judge; London University; writers and
politicians;public events and women's
suffrage, 1880-1930.   153

HART,Solomon Alexander. Reminiscences (1882). Brief dictated notes; his
career as a painter;Royal Academy and
its presidents; Victorian artists and
theatre.   154

HARTE, Frederick E. The Road I Have
Travelled (Belfast, 1947). Work of an
Irish Methodist minister; Irish reli-
gious life; travels.   155

HARTFORD, George Bibby. Commander, R. N. (1927). Naval career from 1898; service on destroyers & in convoys in WW1; adventures; amusements.   156

/HARTL, Rollin Lynde/. Confessions of a Clergyman (1916).A satirical account of training and work as country clergyman; conventions, fashions, and bothers of the life.   157

HARTLEY,Harold Thomas. Eighty-Eight Not Out (1939). Early life in London; work as publisher; hobby of illustrated books and his exhibitions;collections and hobbies; theatre; art.   158

HARTMAN,Capt. Howard. The Seas Were Mine (1935). Wild life on sea & land; perils from animals and men; wrecks, war, mutiny, travels; notes on Conrad and Stevenson.   159

HARTRICK, Archibald Standish. Painter's Pilgrimage (1939). Study in Paris with Van Gogh and Gauguin;drawing for The Graphic; New Art Club and International Society of Painters;   art movements and artists.   160

HARTSHORNE, Lt.Arthur George. Diary 1863-64; service with the Pioneers in the Sattara campaign;simple. Diary of the Sattara Campaign (1864).   161

HARVEY, Basil. Growing Pains (1937) Harrow; Cambridge; work as stockbroker, shopwalker, cashier, actor, playwright; his love-affairs and complexes; a bitter-sweet record.   162

HARVEY, F. W. Comrades in Captivity (1919).Military service, WW1; capture and experiences in seven German prison camps; lively and cheerful.   163

HARVEY,John Henry. With the Foreign Legion in Syria (1928); With the Secret Service in Morocco, by Ex-Legionaire 1384 (1933);   The Black Arab, by Operator 1384(1937). Service with the French Foreign Legion in North Africa and Syria; desert warfare; flamboyant story of miseries and brutalities and code of the Legion.   164

HARVEY,Richmond. Prison from Within (1937).   His experiences in Wormwood Scrubs; official and unofficial life; the routine, prisoners, hospital; his

emotions and daydreams; good.   165

HARVEY, Thomas Newenham.   Autobiography (Waterford, 1904). Education; work as stationer in Waterford; Quaker religious life and ministry; sport and social life.   166

HARVEY,William Fryer. We Were Seven (1936). Amusing account of his childhood; nursery life and schooling with his brothers and sisters; in a Quaker household.   167

HASLAM, A. D. Cannon Fodder (1930). Army service in France, WW1; prisoner in Germany;perverse opposition to almost everything.   168

HASLAM,William.From Death into Life (1880); Not Yet I (1883); Leaves from My Notebook (1889).Minister of Curzon Chapel, Mayfair; his Christian tribulations and triumphs; evangelism and open-air missions; work in temperance movement.   169

HASLETON, Richard. Strange and Wonderful Things (1595). His experiences as a slave among the Moors, 1583-1593 Moorish life and ways.   170

HASSALL, Arthur Hill. Narrative of a Busy Life (1893). Teddington; medical study in Dublin; practice in London and at Royal Free Hospital; scientific researches; later work, Ventnor and on continent.   171

HASTINGS, Archibald G. C. Nigerian Days (1925). Life of a political and judicial officer in Nigeria from 1906; administration,tours, hunting, native life.   172

HASTINGS, Francis Rawdon Hastings, 1st Marquess. Private Journal (Allahabad, 1907). His work and experience as Governor-General of India, 1813-18; official and social life; travels and hunting; Indian customs and religion; for his children.   173

HASTINGS, Frederick.   Pages from a Joyous Life (1923). Clergyman's life; travels on bicycle; experiences in No. and So. America and Europe.   174

HASTINGS, Major Lewis. Dragons are Extra (1947). Military life; & random reminiscences and reflections; on his travels and adventures.   175

HASTINGS, Nicholas. Round the Next Corner (1949). Autobiographical jottings of a London shopkeeper, 1939 to 1948; experiences as a naval officer; life in Kenya; slight.   176

HASTINGS,Sir Patrick. Autobiography (1948). Career as a barrister and Attorney-General;famous lawyers, trials and judges; his work in Labour Party; Labour Government.   177

HASTINGS,Warren. Journals, 1773 and 1784; details of journey to Benares & visits to Benares and Lucknow; treaty negotiations. MS, B.M. Add. 29212 and 39879.   178

HASWELL, John. Pages from My Past (1924). Engineering studies and shipbuilding in Sunderland;secretary Wear Shipbuilding Association; social life in North; literary friendships. Copy Cambridge U.L.   179

HATHAWAY, Katharine Butler. Little Locksmith (1943). Social and psychological experience of a facially disfigured woman from childhood.   180

HATHERLEY, William Page Wood, Baron A Memoir, by W. R. W. Stephens (1883) Vol. I contains autobiography written 1863;Winchester, Cambridge, Lincoln's Inn; law career, judge, in Parliament and Vice-Chancellor; factual.   181

HATTON, Sidney Frank. The Yarn of a Yeoman (1930). WWl service with Middlesex Regiment; Gallipoli, Salonika, Allenby campaign; extrovert's account of daily life in army.   182

HAVARD, R. A. Portland Spy (1939). Secret service work in WWl;with Portland garrison; convoys; later in Ireland; arms smuggling.   183

HAVERGAL, Frances Ridley. Memorials by Maria Havergal (1880). Autobiography of first 25 years; religious life and aspirations; and her life in Germany; poet.   184

HAWEIS, Hugh R. My Musical Life (L. 1884); Travel and Talk (1896). Music studies and performances;music critic

and violinist; life in Bethnal Green; missionary activities and wide travel in USA and the dominions.   185

/HAWEIS, Thomas/. An Authentic Narrative (1764). Orphan's troubles as a boy; life at sea; temptations; amours and conversion;religious life and his ministry at Aldwinkle to 1763.   186

HAWKE, Maj. James. From Private to Major (1938). Factory work; career in army; India and WWl service; in Royal Signals.   187

HAWKE, Martin Bladen Hawke, Baron. Recollections and Reminiscences(1924) Eton and Cambridge;devotion to cricket; Yorkshire, M.C.C., and tours; his minor sports; hunting;big game; anecdotes of sportsmen.   188

HAWKER, Henry Edward. Notes on My Life (Gloucester, 1919). Life in Somerset from childhood; social life of Taunton and neighborhood; service as station master with G.W.R. A copy in Gloucester City Library.   189

HAWKES, Charles Pascoe. Heydays (L. 1933). Cambridge University; life in Tangier; in militia; work as lawyer; sport, Old Stagers; memories of Kipling and other writers.   190

HAWKES, Clarence. Hitting the Dark Trail (1915). Thirty years blindness; work in nature study.   191

HAWKINS, Sir Anthony Hope. Memories and Notes (1927). Marlborough; Oxford legal studies and law work; literary and theatre work; his novels; visits to America; social scene.   192

HAWKINS,Laetitia Matilda. Anecdotes (1822); Memoirs(1824). Bluestocking's reminiscences of society, social life and literature;the Johnson circle and 18th Century celebrities.   193

HAWKSHAW, Sir John. Reminiscences (1838). Travels of an engineer in So. America, 1832-34; description of Venezuela.   194

HAWTREY,Sir Charles Henry. Truth at Last (1924). Eton;teaching; career in the theatre; his plays and tours; and his varying fortunes.   195

HAWTREY,Stephen T. Reminiscences of a French Eton (1867). Work at a lycée in Toulouse; comparison of French and English education.   196

/HAY, Malcolm Vivian/. Wounded and Prisoner of War, by an Exchanged Officer (Edin. 1916). WW1 service, Mons and Cambrai;in hospital and prison at Wurzburg; exchange.   197

HAY, William. Deformity (1754). An account of his life as a cripple; the reactions of others and his emotional life.   198

HAY, Captain William. Reminiscences under Wellington (1901). Boy-officer in Peninsular War & Waterloo; service in Canada and at home to 1828; dictated in a lively, colorful style.   199

HAY,Capt. William Rupert. Two Years in Kurdistan (1921). Work and social life of a political officer, 1918-20; his troubles.   200

HAYDON, Benjamin Robert. Life, by Tom Taylor (1853); Autobiography and Memoirs, ed. A.Penrose (1927). Begins with autobiography, 1786-1820; career as painter and teacher; ups and downs and his literary and artistic friendships; excellent.   201

HAYES, Alice. A Legacy (1723). Quaker autobiography; spiritual life and the Lord's dealings with her from her youth; ministry in Herts, etc.   202

HAYES,Sir Bertram. Hull Down (1925) Forty-five years in merchant ships and liners;transporting of troops in Boer War and WW1; his passengers.   203

HAYES, Capt. Matthew Horace. Indian Racing Reminiscences(1883); Among Men and Horses (1894). Military life in India; sport; horse-breeding and racing; Indian sportsmen. Copy of first in Cambridge U.L.   204

HAYES, Thomas. Recollections (1902) London boyhood in 20's; office clerk; Methodist missionary work at Mission House in Hoxton; literature and antiquities of Methodism.   205

HAYLEY,William. Memoirs of the Life (1823). Sussex;Eton; Cambridge; early

poems;Garrick and literary circles in London; settled in Sussex;family life his biographical writing; friendships with Blake, Cowper, Gibbon.   206

HAYNES, Edmund Sidney Pollock. The Lawyer (1951). A selection from jottings 1877-1949;life in London and at Primrose Hill; comments and observations on society, food and wine, conversation,public affairs, and Eminent Victorians; sturdy and lively.   207

HAYNES,Gen. Robert. Diary, 1805-35; plantation work and social life; Newcastle, Barbados; family and domestic affairs; slaves and slavery.Barbadian Diary (Medstead, 1934). Royal Empire Soc. Library.   208

HAYTER, Frank E. African Adventure (1938). Work of prospector and hunter for London Zoo in Gambia, Abyssinia; police work in Palestine; gold prospecting in Abyssinia.   209

HAYWARD, Capt. H. B. Military diary 1868;service on Abyssinian expedition and at battle of Magdala.Sherwood Foresters' Regimental Annual (1927) pp. 269-311.   210

HAYWOOD, Lt.Col. Austin H. W. Sport and Service in Africa (1926).Military service in Nigeria, Cameroons, Togoland from 1903; hunting.   211

HAZLITT, William. Liber Amoris (L. 1823). Account of his infatuation for Sarah Walker; conversations; letters; rupture of affair;interesting psychological record.   212

HAZLITT, William Carew. Confessions of a Collector (1897). Development of interests of bibliophile and antiquary auctions,books, scholars, booksellers literary friends; his writings.   213

HEAD, Alice M. It Could Never Have Happened (1939); work as a journalist on women's magazines;The Academy; her work for Hearst; England; USA.   214

HEAD, Colonel Charles Octavius. No Great Shakes (1943). Irish upbringing Woolwich;army service in India, South Africa and WW1; residence in Ireland; anti-nationalist sentiments.   215

HEAD, Sir Francis Bond. Rough Notes

(1826). Work as inspector of mines in South America;Rio de la Plata & Chile gold and silver mines; finance; travels; gaucho life.　　　216

HEAD, Hugh Stanley. Diary, 1883-84; travels and social life in Australia, Java, Malaya, India. Journals & Letters(1892). Copy in Royal Empire Soc. Library.　　　217

HEADLAM, Maurice. Rod, Horn and Gun (1942); Irish Reminiscences (L. 1947) Fishing and hunting;his career as the Treasury Remembrancer in Ireland; the Irish rebellion and its aftermath;Irish politics and society; opinions of a conservative.　　　218

HEALEY, George. Life and Remarkable Career (n.d.). Odd jobs and hardships of a bootblack,factory worker, salesman, grocer; travels through England; his ultimate salvation. Copy in Birmingham P.L.　　　219

HEALY,Christopher. Confessions of a Journalist (1904). Work & adventures; politics; seamy side of London life; Dreyfus, Kropotkin, Morris; anecdotes of celebrities.　　　220

HEALY, Maurice. Old Munster Circuit (1939). His legal career in Ireland, from 1893; social life in Cork; anecdotes of judges, lawyers, cases. 221

HEALY, Timothy Michael. Letters and Leaders (1929). His work in the law, journalism and politics;Parliamentary career; Governor-General of Ireland; the troubles;anecdotes of the leading figures in Irish life.　　　222

HEARN, Sir Walter Risley. Some Recollections (1928). Thirty-five years in the consular service from 1883; in USA, Norway, France, Brazil, Germany; politics; business; anecdotes.　　223

HEARSEY, Sir John. Autobiography of military service in India in 1st half of 19th Century;the Mutiny. H. Pearse The Hearseys (1905).　　　224

HEATH, Vernon. Recollections (1892) Work as a photographer from 1841; his friends and acquaintances;social life and country life.　　　225

HEATHCOTE, Wyndham Selfe. My Salvation Army Experience(1891). Religious life from his conversion at Oxford; a career in Salvation Army in London and provinces;resignation; critical views on the organization.　　　226

HEBDEN,Roger. Plain Account of Certain Christian Experiences(1700). The religious life and sufferings of 17th Century Quaker;imprisonment; ministry and spiritual life.　　　227

HEBER, A. Reeve and Kathleen M. In Himalayan Tibet (1926). Their twelve years in Lesser Tibet; anthropological and historical details.　　　228

HEBER, Right Rev. Reginald. Diary, 1823-26; Bishop of Calcutta; journey through India and Ceylon; scenery and religious work;India and Ceylon. Narrative of a Journey (1828); A Selection, ed. P. R. Krishnaswami (1923).　　229

HEDDERWICK, James. Backward Glances (Glasgow, 1891). Work as a journalist on Glasgow Citizen; reminiscences of Glasgow social life, public affairs & politics during 50 years.　　　230

HEDGES, Sir William. Diary, 1681-7; travel to Bengal and his work as agent there; business; Indian life. Diary (Hakluyt Soc. 1887-9).　　　231

HEITLAND, W. E. After Many Years (Cambridge,1926). Academic and social life at Cambridge; teaching; scholarship; pleasant reminiscences.　　232

HELE, John. Reminiscences (Exeter, 1870). Postmaster of Alphington; his education; apprentice-tailor; work as constable and postmaster;village life and Devonshire customs;an interesting local record. Exeter P. L.　　233

HELM,William Henry. Memories (1937) Journalist's career and anecdotes;the literary editor of Morning Post; literary figures; anecdotes.　　　234

HELME,Eleanor Edith. After the Ball (1931).Reminiscences of Surrey golfer her games; great women golfers.　　235

HELPS, Mary Alice. Memories (1924). Village life in the Chilterns; sentiment and romance;local characters and customs; Ruskin.   236

HEMINGFORD, Dennis Henry Herbert, Baron. Back-Bencher and Chairman (L. 1946).Work and observations as Member of Parliament from 1918; work as the Deputy-Speaker & the Chairman of Committees.   237

HEMINGWAY,R.D'Oyly. Memories, Fresh and Salt (1937). Chatty reminiscences of sea and fly-fishing.   238

HEMY,Thomas M. Deep Sea Days (1926) Painter's life at sea; a boy in sailing ships in the sixties; cruises and adventures.   239

/HEMYNG,S.Bracebridge/. Eton School Days, by an Old Etonian (1864). Eton school life;study, teachers, boys and sports, etc.   240

HENDERSON, Kathleen C. T. Sporting Adventures (Madras, 1918). Memsahib's lively account of big-game hunting in Nilgiri. India Office Library.   241

HENDERSON, Sir Neville. Failure of a Mission (L. 1940); Water under the Bridges (1945). Work as a diplomat in Hitler's Germany; events leading to & failure to avert WW2;private & social life; lighter side; anecdotes.   242

HENDERSON, Captain Robert. Soldier of Three Queens (1866). Adventures of soldier-of-fortune in Portugal; service with British Legion in the Carlist Wars; with the Lancers in India; the Crimean War; sport; social life. 243

HENDERSON, Robert. Ninety Years in the Master's Service (Edin.1911). His Scottish boyhood; study in Edinburgh; ministry in Ireland;the disruption in Scottish Church; later evangelism in Australia.   244

HENDERSON, William. My Life (1879). Amusing memories of fishing experiences from childhood; trout and salmon; Scotland and Durham.   245

HENDREN,Patsy (Patrick). My Book of Cricket (1927); Big Cricket (L. 1934) Reminiscences of the great batsman; a record of his games for Middlesex and England; tours; players.   246

HENDRY,Capt. Frank Coutts. From the Log-Book of Memory, by Shalimar (Edin. 1950). Memories of his early days at sea;sailing ships; escape of his ship from eruption of Mt. Pelée.   247

HENEGAN, Sir Richard R. Seven Years Campaigning(1846). Experiences in the Field Transport Dept. in the Peninsular campaigns and the Netherlands, in 1808-15; somewhat impersonal, technical details.   248

HENLY,Peter (Peter Robertson). Life of (1799). Boyhood in a Wilts village and at sea;warfare in West Indies and Canada; army service; his settlement in New England; beginning of Revolution; in debtor's prison. Copy,Wilts. Archaeol. Soc., Devizes.   249

HENNING, Fred W. J. Some Recollections (1888). Work as a sports journalist; reminiscences of great prize fights of early 19th Century.   250

HENREY, Robert. A Century Between (1937); Farm in Normandy (1941); Return to the Farm (1947). A sensitive picture of boyhood in clerical family and experiences as journalist in 20's marriage and farming life in Normandy before and after WW2; good details of French rural life; his work for BBC; interesting.   251

HENRIQUES,Basil L. Q. Indiscretions of a Warden (1937); Indiscretions of a Magistrate (1950).Work as warden at St. George's Settlement & as chairman of East London juvenile court; educational and social problems;Jewish and slum life; his court; anecdotes. 252

HENRY, Jack. Detective-Inspector Henry's Famous Cases (L.1942). Twenty five years at Scotland Yard; memories of detection and famous crimes;broadcasting; sports anecdotes.   253

HENRY, Leonard. My Laugh Story (L. 1937). Career in musichalls; success as radio comedian;anecdotes of entertainment field.   254

HENRY, Walter. Events of a Military Life (1843). Irish boyhood; career as an army surgeon; Peninsular War, Waterloo; service in India, St. Helena & Canada.   255

HENRY,Warren. <u>Confessions of a Ten-</u>
<u>derfoot Coaster</u> (1937). Frank account
of experiences as trader on W.African
coast; social life; French colony at
Grand Lahou. 256

HENSCHEL, Sir George. <u>Musings and</u>
<u>Memories</u> (1918). Boyhood and musical
education in Germany; career as conductor and singer in England; society
life; friendship with musicians, writers, etc. 257

HENSON, Right Rev. Herbert Hensley.
<u>Retrospect</u> (1942). Clerical career of
Bishop of Durham; parish work, London
and his bishoprics;administration and
church politics; somewhat impersonal,
but forms a useful view of the church
in his time. 258

HENSON, Leslie. <u>My Laugh Story</u> (L.
1926); <u>Yours Faithfully</u>(1948). Career
of a comedian; roles; musical comedy;
WW1 entertainments;theatrical life in
London; friends; school days; good.259

HENWOOD, Loveday. <u>Extracts from the</u>
<u>Memoir</u> (1847). Spiritual life of Qua-
ker and Methodist;her ministry, Cornwall and Southwest; her dealings with
God; 19th Century. 260

HEPBURN, Capt. George. Diary, 1766.
his sufferings when shipwrecked on an
island at mouth of the Ganges. MS, in
B.M., Add. 23679. 261

HERBERT, Sir Alan Patrick. <u>Indepen-</u>
<u>dent Member</u> (1950). Unorthodox career
as M. P. for Oxford University & his
WW2 work patrolling the Thames; Parliamentary causes, divorce, betting &
renaming the stars; the Thames scene;
personal and lively. 262

HERBERT, Aubrey Nigel H. M. <u>Mons,</u>
<u>Anzac and Kut</u> (1919).Military service
in WW1; with the Irish Guards on the
Western Front;intelligence officer at
Salonika; campaigns against the Turks
a good personal account. 263

HERBERT, Dorothea. <u>Retrospections</u>
(1929-30). Very entertaining account
of her childhood in Ireland in latter
part of 18th Century and later social
life in Irish clerical circles;covers
1770-1806. 264

HERBERT, George. <u>Shoemaker's Window</u>
(Oxford, 1948). Life in Banbury; work
as shoemaker and photographer; peram-
bulation of Banbury;interesting story
or workingclass life. 265

HERBERT,Henry. <u>Autobiography</u> (Gloucester,1876). Life of Gloucestershire
cobbler told in doggerel verse; country life and work; temperance. A copy
in Gloucester City Library. 266

HERBERT,J.D. <u>Irish Varieties</u> (1836)
Fifty years' reminiscences; Ireland;
religion,law, society, theatres, people, customs. 267

HERBERT, Sir Thomas. Diary, 1627-9;
travels in Africa and Persia;topogra-
phy, antiquities and local customs. <u>A</u>
<u>Relation of Some Years' Travaile</u> (L.
1634);<u>Travels into Persia</u>, ed.William
Foster (1928). 268

HERBERT OF CHERBURY,Edward Herbert,
Baron. <u>Life</u>, ed. C.H. Herford (1928);
first published 1764. A modest-proud
account of his gallantries and prowess
as swordsman; British champion's dis-
plays of knightly and amorous superi-
ority over the French; together with
advice on education and morals; vain
but delightful account of 17th Century
eccentric. 269

HERD, Alexander (Sandy). <u>My Golfing</u>
<u>Life</u> (1923). Dictated; boyhood at St.
Andrews; career as golfer; championships,players, tours; social celebrities on the links. 270

HERD, Harold. <u>Press Days</u> (L. 1936).
Minor happenings in career as journalist in Yorkshire and North Wales;mag-
azine editor; proprietor of a correspondence school. 271

HERKOMER, Sir Hubert von. <u>My School</u>
<u>and My Gospel</u> (L.1908); <u>The Herkomers</u>
(1910-11).Career as an art teacher in
Bushey; students; art problems; lives
of his parents and himself from 50's;
art studies; career as painter & teacher;The Slade; country life; arts in
his time. 272

/HERMON-HODGE, Hon. Harry Baldwin/.
<u>Up Against It in Nigeria</u>, by Langa
Langa (1922). Work of a political of-

ficer in Nigeria, 1908-18;administra-
tion, sport, social life.   273

HERMON-HODGE, Nona C. Call of the
Land (1936). WW1 experiences in Land
Army;Oxford, Cheshire, Worcester; and
dairy farming in the twenties;village
life.   274

HERON,Barney. Such As I Have (1941)
His work as farmer in Ireland; social
life; country ways; autobiography but
partly fictionalized.   275

HERON, Sir Robert. Notes (Grantham,
1850). His career as M. P. for Grimsby; politics, political life, statesmen, 1812-50.   276

HERRIES, James William. I Came, I
Saw (Edin. 1937). Outstanding events
in the career of an Edinburgh journalist in WW1 and later.   277

HERRING,Richard. Lecture on Personal Experiences (1877). His invention
of a telegraph instrument; difficulty
with the Post Office.   278

HERRINGHAM, Gen. Sir Wilmot P. Physician in France (1919). His work as
consulting physician to overseas forces during WW1; RAMC; hospitals; org-
ganization; medical problems in time
of war.   279

HERTSLET, Sir Edward. Recollections
of the Old Foreign Office (1901). His
career as librarian in Foreign Office
and reminiscences of Palmerston, sec-
retaries of state, etc.   280

HERVEY, Capt. Albert. Ten Years in
India (1850). Young officer in Madras
Infantry, 1833-42; military life and
sport.   281

HERVEY, General Charles Robert West
Some Records of Crime (1892). Service
in the Indian Police; crime, Thugs and
Dacoits.   282

HERVEY, Mrs. Thomas Kibble (Eleanor
Louisa). Adventures of a Lady (1853).
Pioneer travels in Tartary, Kashmir,
Tibet,China; scenery; native life; in
diary form.   283

HESLOP,Derwent Gordon. Through Jungle, Bush and Forest (1934). Work of

of a railway engineer in Assam, India
China, Africa, etc.   284

HESS, Charles. Millionaire of Love
(1909). A workingman's life; religion
and conversion;evangelist; teacher in
adult schools.   285

HEWETT, George M. A. The Pedagogue
at Play (1903).Schoolmaster's holiday
activities; fishing, shooting, winter
sports, sailing; at home and on continent.   286

HEWINS,William A. S. Apologia of an
Imperialist (1929). Work as secretary
to Chamberlain's Tariff Commission and
as M.P.; Director of London School of
Economics;politics, tariffs, imperial
economic relations.   287

HEWITT, Harald. From Harrow School
to Herrison House Asylum (1923). His
seven years in an asylum; neurosis; &
the responsibility of Harrow education
for his condition.   288

HEWITT, Kathleen. Only Paradise (L.
1945). Novelist's education; acting &
odd jobs; literary career; books; and
Bohemian life and expedients.   289

HEWLETT, Sir William Meyrick. Forty
Years in China (1943). His career in
the consular service from 1898; China
and the Chinese; diplomacy, politics,
nationalism, Japanese threat.   290

HEWS,Francis. Spoils Won in the Day
of Battle (Bedford, c. 1799). Spiritual autobiography of a Dunstable man;
Baptist belief; God's mercies.   291

HEYWOOD, Oliver. Autobiography and
Diaries, ed. J. H. Turner (Brighouse,
1872-85). Life and work of a nonconformist clergyman in later 17th Century; Yorkshire and Lancashire; family
life; good.   292

HIBBERT, Henry George. Fifty Years
of a Londoner's Life (1916); A Play-
goer's Memories(1920). Journalism and
dramatic criticism;newspaper life and
theatrical world; night-clubs; musichalls; anecdotes.   293

HICHENS, Robert. Yesterday (1947).
His career as journalist and novelist
literary world;glimpses of celebrated

writers; travels; slight.   294

HICKEY, Capt. Daniel E. Rolling into
Action (1936). Service with Tanks in
WW1; Ypres, Passchendaele, Cambrai and
Amiens; personal adventures.   295

HICKEY, William. Memoirs, ed. Alfred
Spencer (1919-25) 4v. Boyhood & early
life in London; social life & customs;
his career in India as a factor in the
time of Hastings; business, military
affairs, Indian life; excellent.   296

HICKS, Ethel Kathleen. From Rock to
Tower (1948). Life of the wife of the
Bishop of Lincoln; clerical, diocesan
affairs and society; Trollopian style
in its detail; good.   297

HICKS, Frederick Coddrington. Forty
Years among the Wild Animals of India
(Allahabad, 1910). Work as a forester
in India; big-game hunting in all its
phases.   298

HICKS, Sir Seymour. Seymour Hicks,
by Himself (1910); Between Ourselves
(1930); Not Guilty (1939); Me and My
Missus (1939); Hail Fellow Well Met
(1949). Career as actor & playwright;
theatrical life and celebrities; Ellaline Terriss and his theatrical work
with her; Wyndham, Ellen Terry, Alfred
Gilbert; social life; hobby of attend-
ing the Old Bailey; an unending stream
of anecdotes.   299

HIGGINBOTHAM, Frederick James. The
Vivid Life (1934). Reporter; editor of
Pall Mall Gazette; politics and public
affairs; Home Rule; crimes; celebrities, 1881 to 1911.   300

HIGGINSON, Gen. Sir George. Seventy
One Years (1916). Career in Guards;
mostly his experiences in the Crimea;
siege of Sebastopol.   301

HIGGS, Dorothy Pickard. Guernsey
Diary (1947). Experiences in Guernsey
during WW2; German occupation; farming
morale; liberation.   302

HILEY, Richard W. Memories of Half
a Century (1899). An excellent record
of clerical life; Oxford and Newman;
parish work and teaching in Liverpool
and as vicar of Wighill; social life
in a Yorkshire village.   303

HILL, Benson Earle. Recollections
of an Artillery Officer (1836); Playing About (1840); A Pinch of Snuff(L.
1840). Irish youth; military life in
Ireland; service in Peninsular War and
at New Orleans; mostly social life in
the army; later career as actor; life
of theatre; famous actors; anecdotes
of celebrities.   304

HILL, Capt. Charles. Journal, 1829;
regimental life in a small provincial
cantonment at Cannanore, India; social
life. MS, India Office Library, Eur.
A. 29, 204 pp.   305

HILL, Charles Fitzmaurice. Journal,
1800-2; officer's journey from India
to Egypt; garrison life. MS, India Office Library, Eur. D. 108.   306

HILL, Frederick. Autobiography of
Fifty Years (1894). Social life; politics and Reform to 1853; Reform Bill
and its prologue; social life in Birmingham and Edinburgh.   307

HILL, Captain George Alexander. Go
Spy the Land (1932). Espionage work in
Russia during WW1; adventures.   308

HILL, Herbert. Retreat from Death
(1936). A good account of experiences
in WW1 in France; enlistment at 16; a
signaller in the 1918 retreat; blown
about by fate.   309

HILL, J. Arthur. From Agnosticism to
Belief(1924). Spiritual life of Bradford man; his investigation of spiritualism; conversion.   310

HILL, Matthew Davenport. Journal of
a Third Visit (Bristol, 1865). Investigation of prisons and the treatment
of prisoners in Ireland; observations
of the Recorder of Birmingham and his
daughter, Rosamund.   311

HILL, M. D. Eton and Elsewhere (L.
1928). Eton and Oxford; his career as
biology teacher in various schools and
comments on educational matters & the
educational scene.   312

HILLABY, John D. Within the Streams
(1949). Fishing experiences and anecdotes.   313

HILLARY, Richard. The Last Enemy (L.

1942). Excellent account of an Oxford student and Spitfire pilot during WW2 the Battle of Britain; experiences in hospital after being shot down.   314

HILLIAM, B.C. Flotsam's Follies (L. 1948). Career of an entertainer;anecdotes of stage and audiences.   315

HILLOCKS, James Inches. Life Story (1860); My Life and Labours (L. 1865) Life Struggles (Glasgow, 1876); Hard Battles (1884). Boyhood in Dundee and Scottish workingclass life;a weaver's apprentice; education; experiences as a Chartist, schoolmaster, businessman temperance lecturer; a congregational minister in London and Darlington;his writings; good Victorian record.   316

HILLS,John Waller. My Sporting Life (1936). Reminiscences of fifty years, of fishing and deer-stalking;   North of England; Cumberland.   317

HILLYARD, George Whiteside. Forty Years of First-Class Lawn Tennis (L. 1924). Experiences and games as tennis player and umpire; anecdotes.   318

HILLYARD, William Heard. Recollections of a Physician (1861). Medical work in Scotland and England; stories about himself and his patients;psychological interest.   319

HILTON, Harold Horsfall. My Golfing Reminiscences (1907). Experiences as a golfer; anecdotes of games, famous players, etc.   320

HILTON,Jack. Caliban Shrieks (1935) Half-timer in a mill;errand-boy; army service during WW1; life in prison; & his interest in eugenics & socialism; sociological interest.   321

HILTON, General Richard.   Military Attaché in Moscow (1949). His experiences after WW2;Russian suspicion and his difficulties;   study of Marxism; the ballet.   322

HINCHINGBROOK, Edward G.H. Montagu, Viscount (later 8th Earl of Sandwich) Diary, 1878-9; administrative work in India and Ceylon;travels; society and Indian life. Diary in Ceylon & India (1879).   323

HIND,Charles Lewis. Naphtali (1926) His career as a literary journalist & memories of writers; influences upon him; Victorian literary scene.   324

HINDERER, Mrs.Anna. Seventeen Years in the Yoruba Country (1872). Work as missionary at Ibadan,West Africa, and medical and educational work,1852-69; native customs.   325

HINDLEY, Charles (editor). Life and Adventures of a Cheap Jack (1876). 40 years in fairs and markets; tricks of the trade;characters; travels through England; manners; lively.   326

HINDS, E. M. Nothing Venture (1941) A schoolmistress abroad; France, Canada,Australia, New Zealand; Kent; her travels and teaching; poor.   327

HINE, Rt.Rev.John Edward. Days Gone By (1924). Boyhood; Oxford; training as medical missionary; work and travel in Zanzibar, Tangier, and Northern Rhodesia.   328

HINE, Reginald L. Confessions of an Uncommon Attorney (1945). Career as a solicitor in Hitchin; his antiquarian pursuits and writing; Quaker life and work; humanitarianism; reminiscences of writers,doctors, parsons; Shaw and Wells; interesting.   329

HINTON, Sir John. Memoires (L.1679, 1814). A Royal physician's account of adventures while serving Charles II; the Civil Wars;his financial troubles covers 1642-60.   330

HINTON, William T.T. Poulett, Viscount. Epitome of My Life (1897). The hard-luck story of pretender to earldom; his noble descent; pamphlet sold when organ-grinding. Bristol Central Library.   331

HIRST,Francis W. In the Golden Days (1948). Early life;political journalism and the political scene at the end of 19th Century; formerly editor, The Economist.   332

HISCOCK, Eric C. I Left the Navy(L. 1946). Service in a submarine-chaser in WW2; work in a war-factory and as a farm labourer.   333

HISLOP, John. Echoes from the Border
(1912); Langholm as It Was(1912). His
life in the Lake District;reminiscen-
ces of old scenes and people.   334

HIVES, Frank. Momo and I (L. 1934).
His experiences as an administrator in
Nigeria; adventures of a careless and
lively career.   335

HOBART-HAMPDEN, Admiral Augustus C.
Never Caught, by Captain Roberts (L.
1867); Sketches from My Life (1887).
His career in navy, 1836-86; suppres-
sion of slave trade in Brazil;Crimean
War; blockade running during the U.S.
Civil War; commander in Turkish Navy;
adventurous life.   336

/HCBBES, R. G./. Reminiscences and
Notes of Seventy Years' Life, by a Retired Officer of H.M.'s Civil Service
(1893-5).Military service in India in
40's;interest in literature & science
civil servant in dockyards;varied and
interesting.   337

HOBBES, Thomas. Life of Mr. Thomas
Hobbes (1680).Latin verse and English
translation; study at Oxford; work as
tutor; philosophical studies and publications; astronomy; physics; Royal
Society; brief but interesting.   338

HOBBS, Henry. The Digressions of a
Ditcher (Calcutta, 1925). Experiences
of a prospector and settler in Mombasa
Nairobi and Kenya in 20's; estimates
of prospects of settlers. Copy, India
Office Library.   339

HOBBS, John Berry. My Cricket Memo-
ries(1924); My Life Story (1935). His
early days as Cambridge county cricketer; career for Surrey and England;
tours,games, players; achievements of
the great batsman.   340

HOBDAY, Sir Frederick Thomas George
Reminiscences(1937). Fifty years as a
veterinary surgeon; science, research
and teaching; Principal of Royal Veterinary College; good.   341

HOBSON, Rev. Richard. What God Hath
Wrought (1903).His missionary work in
Ireland; long ministry in Liverpool;
church work and problems;workingclass
and slum life.   342

HOBSON, Samuel George. Pilgrim to
the Left (L.1938). Quaker upbringing,
work in Fabian Society and the Labour
Movement; Guild Socialism; activities
of a modern revolutionist.   343

HOBY, Sir Thomas.   A Booke of the
Travaile and Lief(Camden Soc. Miscellany, X, 1902). Ambassador; travel in
Italy and Germany; schemes for translating The Courtier; domestic life at
Bisham Abbey;briefly covers the years
1547-64.   344

HOCKING, Silas K. My Book of Memory
(1923). Novelist's early life, Lancs.
and London; preaching, travel, journalism; Boer War and political affairs
literary life; anecdotes of Meredith,
Chesterton, etc.   345

HODDER, George. Memories of My Time
(1870). Work as journalist on Morning
Post;literature, society, clubs, mid-
century; Punch writers; Dickens, Sala
Thackeray, Jerrold, Christopher North
etc.   346

HODDER WILLIAMS, John Ernest (ed.).
One Young Man (1917). Personal narra-
tive of WW1 service;YMCA; his life on
Western Front; wounded at Somme. 347

HODGE, Herbert.   It's Draughty in
Front (1938); Cab, Sir? (1939). Working class life in London; his work as
a taxi-driver; its interests, humors,
trials; London life; his development
as a writer.   348

HODGE, John.   Workman's Cottage to
Windsor Castle (1931). Working-class
life and labour; steel-workers; trade
unionism; career as Labour M.P.;later
as Minister of Pensions.   349

HODGES, Frank.   My Adventures as a
Labour Leader (1923). His boyhood in
South Wales; Ruskin College; work as
miner,teacher, mining union official;
Royal Commissions; International Conferences; career in Parliament; Lord
of Admiralty in Labour Government; an
interesting record.   350

HODGETTS, E. A. Brayley. Moss from
a Rolling Stone(1924). His boyhood in
Berlin;European travels as journalist
and correspondent; Boer War; celebri-

ties he met; public events.   351

HODGMAN, George. Sixty Years on the Turf (1901). Victorian sporting life; horses and races; jockeys; owners and gambling; social life.   352

HODGSON, Charles. Autobiography of missionary work at Benares; religious disputes; ethnology. C. B. Leupolt, Recollections of an Indian Missionary (1863), preface.   353

HODGSON, Christopher Pemberton. A Residence at Nagasaki and Hakodate(L. 1861). Experiences of first British consul in Japan; diplomatic relations and business;natural history, resources, politics, customs.   354

HODGSON, Capt. John. Autobiography, ed. J. H. Turner (Brighouse, 1882). A Yorkshireman's account of activities in the Civil Wars, 1642-63 and of his troubles during the Restoration; service on Parliamentary side.   355

HODSON,Arnold Wienholt. Seven Years in Southern Abyssinia (L.1927); Where Lion Reign (1929). Work as consul in Ethiopia;Addis Ababa and Gordula; politics, war, social life, sport. 356

HODSON,James Lansdale. Gentlemen of Dunkirk (L.1940); Towards the Morning (1941); Before Daybreak (1942); Thunder in the Heavens (1950). Experience of a Manchester journalist in WW2; at Dunkirk and in the Blitz;military and civilian activities;democracy and war the post-war scene;wide interests and observations.   357

HODY, Major E. H. With the Mad 17th (1920). His experiences in WW1; with divisional supply during the Italian campaign of 1917-18.   358

HOFFMAN, Capt. Frederick. A Sailor of King George(1901). Experiences and adventures in the navy,1793-1814; the Nore Mutiny; Trafalgar; imprisonment in France; lively.   359

HOFFMAN, Richard. Some Musical Recollections (N. Y., 1910). An English pianist's studies and performances in the forties; English musical scene; & his later career in New York. 360

HOFFMANN, William. With Stanley in Africa (1938). Experiences of servant to Stanley during his travels in Central Africa in 80's and 90's. 361

HOFFNUNG-GOLDSMID,Cyril Julian. The Diary of a Liaison Officer(1920). His personal experiences and adventures in WW1; 1918 Italian campaign. 362

HOGARTH, David George. Wandering Scholar (1896); Accidents of an Antiquary's Life (1910). Study and training as an archaeologist;work in Lycia Crete,Cyrene, Egypt, etc. in the 80's and 90's; Oxford life.   363

HOGARTH, Robert George. The Trent and I (Nottingham, 1940). A doctor's study and career; work at Nottingham General Hospital; social work, sport, people, in Nottingham. Copy, Nottingham P.L.   364

HOGARTH, William. Anecdotes, edited J. B. Nichols (1833). Consists mostly of the famous artist's views on art & artists; in the form dictated to John Ireland c.1764.   365

HOGG, Garry. The Road Before Me (L. (1948).A writer's rambles through the English countryside after WW2; random experiences and observations on country life.   366

HOHLER, Sir Thomas Beaumont. Diplomatic Petrel (1942). His career as a diplomat;commentary on public events; Turkey, Egypt, Russia, Japan, Mexico, Abyssinia.   367

HOLBROOK, Ann Catherine. The Dramatist (Birmingham, 1809). Her troubles with audiences and managers during her nine years on the stage,mainly in provincial theatres.   368

HOLCROFT, Thomas. Memoirs (L. 1816; 1852; 1926). Interesting & important account of his rise from a stableboy; workingclass life; self-education and work as writer and politician;radical activities; trial for treason; individualism and human perfectibility; an important liberal record.   369

HOLDEN, John Watkins. Wizard's Wanderings (1886). Career as a conjurer;

world-wide tours; interest in spiritualism and folk-lore.　　　　　370

HOLDEN, Joseph. Autobiography (Bolton, 1872). A builder's life and work
in Bolton; interest in phrenology and
teetotalism. Manchester P.L.　　371

HOLDEN, Margaret. Grace o'Life (L.
1935). Benevolent account of life in
the country; village customs.　　372

HOLE, (Samuel) Hugh Marshall. Looking Life Over (1934). Eton; army life
and service in Boer War and WW1;legal
studies at Inner Temple;political affairs, Derby and Notts.　　　　373

HOLE, Samuel Reynolds. Memories (L.
1892); More Memories (1894); Then and
Now (1901). Dean of Rochester; life &
work; country and social life; public
affairs; reminiscences of celebrities
in arts, sport, church.　　　　374

HOLIDAY, Henry. Reminiscences of My
Life (1914). Training and career as a
painter; Pre-Raphaelite friends; travels abroad; socialist activity; work
in stained glass.　　　　　　375

HOLLAMS, Sir John.　Jottings of an
Old Solicitor (1906). Law studies and
career in the law from 1820's; legal
personalities; land registration; and
public affairs.　　　　　　376

HOLLAND,Sir Henry. Recollections of
Past Life (1872). Medical studies and
social life in Edinburgh; Sir Walter
Scott and other celebrities; practice
of medicine;Royal Physician; literary
and political personalities.　　377

HOLLAND, Henry Fox, 1st Lord. Life
and Letters of Lady Sarah Lennox (L.
1904) contains his memoirs of political affairs in 1760's and a romantic
episode with Lady Sarah.　　　378

HOLLAND, Henry Richard, third Lord.
Foreign Reminiscences (1850); Memoirs
of the Whig Party (1852-4). Political
and Parliamentary affairs, 1820-1821;
diplomacy in France, 1791-1814; memories of Napoleon,Talleyrand, Mirabeau
etc.　　　　　　　　　379

HOLLAND, Henry Scott.　A Bundle of
Memories (1915). Clerical life & work

in London; professorship of Divinity,
at Oxford;academic and religious life
and prople;Toynbee, Green, Hugh Scott
and others.　　　　　　　380

HOLLENDER, Bertie.　Before I Forget
(1935). Memories and persiflage; his
social life,sport and amusements; before WW1.　　　　　　　　381

HOLLES, Denzil, Baron. Memoirs (L.
1699). Activities and self-justifica-
tions of a Presbyterian and Royalist;
military affairs; Civil Wars; attacks
on Cromwell; mostly history.　　382

HOLLINGSHEAD, John. My Lifetime (L.
1895); Gaiety Chronicles (1898). Work
in the theatre; manager of the Gaiety
Theatre; theatrical life and people;
social life in London; literary figures; anecdotes.　　　　　383

HOLLINS, Alfred.　A Blind Musician
Looks Back (1936). Career as organist
church music; music and musicians in
England; Empire travels; family life;
musical opinions.　　　　　384

HOLLINS, James.　Pastoral Recollec-
tions(1857). His six years of mission
work among sailors and watermen,Glou-
cester;workingclass life & conditions
and religion.　　　　　　385

HOLLIS,Thomas. Memoirs, ed. Francis
Blackburne (1780). Activities of the
18th Century philanthropist; benefac-
tions to Harvard; literary interests;
criticism of Dr.Johnson; a mélange of
quotations.　　　　　　　386

HOLLOWAY, Henry.　A Voice from the
Convict Cell (Manchester, 1877). Poverty and crime in Manchester; conversion; folly of drink.　　　387

HOLMAN, Gordon. Commando Attack (L.
1942). WW2 service under Mountbatten
and Keyes; training; the invasion at
St. Nazaire.　　　　　　388

/HOLMAN, Thomas/. Life in the Royal
Navy, by a Ranker (Portsmouth, 1891).
Life of a seaman, gunner, and warrant
officer; navy life, its demands & its
opportunities. Bodleian.　　　389

HOLMES, Benjamin. Collection of the
Epistles and Works (1753). Contains a

short autobiography of the ministry of
a Welsh Quaker and his travels in England, Ireland and America.   390

HOLMES, Sir Charles J. Self & Partners (1936). Eton and Oxford; work as
a book publisher;editor of Burlington
Magazine;Slade Professor; director of
National Gallery;art criticism; reminiscences of artists; social.   391

HOLMES, Edmond Gore Alexander. In
Quest of an Ideal (1920). Irish life;
work as school inspector; his spiritual life; philosophy; mysticism; nature and poetry.   392

/HOLMES,Edward/. A Ramble among the
Musicians of Germany, by a Music Pro-
fessor(1828). Visits to musicians and
musical scenes; Germany; Austria. 393

HOLMES, G.V. The Likes of Us (1948)
Her childhood in a Dr. Barnardo home;
village life, schooling, social & domestic life; the staff and governors;
interesting.   394

HOLMES, Miss Gordon. In Love with
Life (1944). Her success in the stock
and share business.   395

HOLMES, Jessie. The Private Nurse
(1899). Her nine years' work as nurse
college and slums.   396

HOLMES,Robert. My Father Was a Gentleman (1939). Experiences in the Irish rebellion and in France in WW1;on
the dole; later work as a second-hand
car dealer.   397

HOLMES, Sgt. Maj. Samuel. Journal,
1792-3;simple observations of soldier
with Macartney during the embassy to
China. Journal (1798).   398

HOLMES, W. L. An Englishman among
Gangsters (1933). His life as private
detective in USA; American crime and
criminals.   399

HOLT, Joseph. Memoirs (1838). Life
of an Irish politician and rebel; the
1798 rebellion; activities as general
capture; transportation to Australia;
return; simple, lively narrative of a
militant Irishman.   400

HOLT, William. I Was a Prisoner (L.

1935); I Haven't Unpacked (1939). His
early poverty in Yorks; working-class
movement; labour agitation; the Means
Test and his experiences in prison for
agitation against it.   401

HOLTHAM,Edmund Gregory. Eight Years
in Japan (1883). Work as civil engineer with Japanese government, 1873-81;
bridges,railways, surveys; a pleasant
account of Japanese life.   402

HOLTOM, Ernest Charles. Two Years'
Captivity in German East Africa,by C.
E. H.(1919). Experiences of a surgeon
captured by Germans in East Africa in
WW1; medical conditions.   403

HOLYOAKE, George Jacob. Among the
Americans (Chicago,1881); Sixty Years
of an Agitator's Life (1892); Bygones
Worth Remembering (1905). A lifetime
of radical agitation, journalism, and
politics in Birmingham and Midlands;
anti-Corn League; co-operation, atheism; travel in USA; reminiscences of
public figures; George Eliot.   404

HOMAN, F. In the Days of Long Ago
(1912). Pleasant recollections of his
childhood in a happy home.   405

HOME, Sir Anthony D. Service Memories (1912). Surgeon-general's career
in the army, 1848-64; Crimean War and
Indian Mutiny; China work; hospitals;
medical work.   406

HOME, Daniel Dunglas. Incidents in
My Life (1863-72). Edinburgh boyhood;
early life and spiritualism in America; performances as medium in England
and Europe; fight against scepticism;
comment on Browning's "Mr. Sludge"; &
his legal troubles.   407

/HOME, George/. Memoirs of an Aristocrat (1838). Scottish boyhood;naval
service in Napoleonic wars; sympathy
with Napoleon;family affairs in Scotland; lawsuits; disappointments. 408

HOME, Michael (Christopher Bush).
Autumn Fields (1944). Village boyhood
in East Anglia; local amusements and
local worthies.   409

HOMEWOOD,Isabel Georgina. Recollections of an Octogenarian (1932). Her
social and domestic life; world-wide

travels; Victorian scene; Dickens and Mrs. Dickens.   410

HONE, William. Early Life and Conversion (1841); see also, Frederick W. Hackwood's Life of William Hone(1912) and B.M.Add. MS 40121. His early life as a London apprentice; beginnings of his writing and political interests; London life; books and Methodism; an interesting record.   411

HONIGBERGER, Johann Martin. Thirty-Five Years in the East(Calcutta 1905) A doctor's experiences in Near East & India in early 19th Century; Transylvanian; work as physician at court of Lahore.   412

/HOOD/, Sydney Paxton. Stage See-Saws (1917). Life and roles of actor; provinces and London; manager of the Zancigs; theatre anecdotes.   413

HOOKER, Sir Joseph Dalton. Journal, 1848-51; explorations of the naturalist in the Himalayas; scientific details. Himalayan Journals (1854). 414

HOOKER, Rufus W. Ship's Doctor (L. 1943). Experiences of fourteen years' medical work at sea.   415

HOOLE, Elijah. Madras, Mysore, and the South of India (1844). Missionary work and travels, 1820-8; Indian missions; conflicts with Jesuits.   416

HOOLEY, Ernest Terah. Hooley's Confessions (1924). A financier's rise & fall; millionaire in 90's; operations in high society;blackmailed, bankrupted and imprisoned.   417

HOOTON, Charles. St. Louis Isle (L. 1847). English emigrant settler's experiences in Texas in 40's; hardships disillusionment and return.   418

HOPE, Elizabeth Reid Cotton, Lady, Sunny Footsteps (1879).Stories of her childhood in India; family life; adventures; told for children.   419

HOPE,James L.A. In Quest of Coolies (1872). Life as blackbirder in South Pacific;recruiting labour; adventures at sea.   420

HOPFORD, Wim. Twice Interned (1919)

Experiences of military internment in the Transvaal during Boer War and in Ruhleben during WW1.   421

HOPKINS, Edward. "Memoirs". English Hist. Rev. XXXIV (1919). Memories of polite society in the time of William Anne and the early Georges;Parliament and politics; M.P. for Coventry. 422

HOPKINS,Francis Powell. Fishing Experiences (1893). Half a century of sport in Wales, Southern England, and India; anecdotes; advice.   423

HOPKINSON,Sir Alfred. Penultima (L. 1930). Career as barrister; memories of public affairs, science, religion, literature, education, and Victorian social and domestic life, from middle of the 19th Century.   424

HOPKINSON, Arthur Wells. Pastor's Progress(1942). An attractive account of a curate's life in Dorset; boyhood in Manchester; Oxford education; his devotion to individual and social welfare.   425

HOPKINSON, Evelyn. Story of a Mid-Victorian Girl (1928). Her childhood in Dresden; school and university at Manchester; happy marriage; experiences in the world of engineering & science.   426

HOPPER, Christopher. Lives of Early Methodist Preachers, ed. Thomas Jackson(1837) I. Autobiography of itinerant Methodist minister, mainly in the North of England;religious life, Durham, in 18th Century.   427

HORAN,Malachi. Malachi Horan Remembers, by G. A. Little (Dublin, 1943). Dictated reminiscences of older Irish life; country life near Dublin, folklore, local events, etc.   428

HORE, Edward Coode. Tanganyika (L. 1892). Master mariner's work for CMS, 1877-88; shipbuilding, water travel & missionary work in Tanganyika.   429

HORLER, Sydney. Excitement (1933); Strictly Personal (1934);More Strictly Personal (1935). Youth and work as a reporter in Bristol and London; his novels;literary world; notes on ideas and things that took his fancy.   430

/HORLOCK, K.W./. Recollections of a Foxhunter, by Scrutator (1861). Wilts boyhood; hunting with various packs; Duke of Beaufort's Hounds; hunting in North Wales.   431

HORN, Alfred Aloysius(pseud.). Life and Works, ed. E.Lewis (1927); Waters of Africa (1929). Remarkable career & adventures of a trader in Cameroons & on Ivory Coast in the 70's.   432

HORNBY, Clifford. Shooting Without Stars (1940); Rural Amateur (1943). A photographer's experiences obtaining background scenes for films; village life in Essex from boyhood; interests in birds and photography.   433

HORNBY,Sir Edmund Grimani. Autobiography (1928). His career in the law and diplomacy in mid-19th Century; in consular service in near and far East, judge of Chinese Supreme Court.   434

HORNBY, Emily. Sinai and Petra (L. 1907). Travels and descriptions, 1899 to 1901; religion; social life.   435

HORNE, Eric. What the Butler Winked At (1930). Experiences in the service of nobility for 57 years;high life as seen from below stairs;his doings and doings of his employers; humility and subservience.   436

HORNE,William Ogilvie.Work and Sport (Edin. 1928). Career in ICS from 1882 and nostalgic picture of a collector's life in India before reform; hunting, racing, administration.   437

HORNER, David. Was It Yesterday (L. 1939).Childhood in France; the French and their ways; a pleasant account of eccentricities.   438

HORNER, Lady Frances.   Time Remembered (1933). Home life at Mells and social life in London;family; friendship with Eminent Victorians; writers and painters; pre-Raphaelites.   439

HORNER,Francis. Memoirs and Correspondence (1843). Boyhood in Edinburgh legal and philosophical studies; work in law and politics in London in early 19th Century; mainly journal.   440

HORNIBROCK, F. A.   Without Reserve

(1935).His life in Australia and Ireland; experiences as a physical culturist in England.   441

HORNSEY, F.Haydn. Hell on Earth (L. 1930). Personal experiences in France in WW1; everyday life of the troops; trench warfare; battle of Lys.   442

HORNUNG, Ernest W.   Notes of a Camp Follower(1919). Work with the YMCA in France during WW1;   entertainment and service work.   443

HORSLEY, John Callcott.   Recollections (1903). Career of the Victorian painter and Royal Academician; social life; the theatre; anecdotes of painters and celebrities.   444

HORSLEY,John William. Jottings from Jail (1887).First part contains autobiography of a thief written in cant; adventures and crimes.   445

HORSLEY, John William.   I Remember (1912). Oxford; career as country curate;social work in London slums; his work among criminals and prisoners and ministry in Walworth.   446

HORSLEY, Terence. Odyssey of an Out of Work (1931). Miseries of a Scot in the twenties;   unemployment; hopeless quest for work;tramp; life in lodging houses; sociological interest.   447

HORSNELL, Horace. The Album (1945). Family life in Bath in the nineteenth century; partly autobiography.   448

HORTON, A. E.   When I Became a Man (1931).   Schoolteacher's service as a machine-gunner in WW1; France, Italy; good personal record.   449

HORTON,Robert Forman. Autobiography (1917).Education and career of a congregationalist clergyman; parish life and work;social work;later nineteenth century.   450

HORWELL, John E.Horwell of the Yard (1947).Thirty-five years as policeman and detective;   Scotland Yard; famous cases he handled;happy lot of policeman; advice to the wayward.   451

HOSE, Charles. Fifty Years of Romance and Research (1927). Boyhood in

Norfolk;Cambridge; administration and scientific work in Sarawak;government posts in England in WW1 and after;his studies in natural history.   452

HOSIE,Sir Alexander. Three Years in Western China (1890).Work as a consul in Szechuan in 80's; trade; travels; Chinese life and scene;his linguistic studies.   453

HOSKENS, Jane. Life and Spiritual Sufferings (Philadelphia, 1771). Her conversion to Quaker belief; missionary trips to America, Barbados, Ireland;work as a schoolmistress; London life to 1760.   454

HOSMER, Harriet. Letters and Memories (1913). Social life in London; artistic and literary life; Brownings and other eminent Victorians.   455

HOSPITAL NURSE. Memories (L. 1910). Training; work in private and public hospitals; her cases. Bodleian.   456

HOTHAM, Admiral Sir William. Pages and Portraits(1919). His life and his naval career, 1786-1814, based on his diaries and reminiscences; S. Africa, the Nore Mutiny, Camperdown; memories of Hood, Nelson, etc.; good.   457

HOUGH, Right Rev. John. His table-talk; reminiscences of ecclesiastical and political affairs, 1703-43; work as Bishop of Worcester. Collectanea, II (Oxford Historical Soc., XVI 1890) pp. 383-416.   458

HOUGHTON,George William. Adventures of a Gadabout (1936).Work as journalist and caricaturist;cosmopolitan society; the playgrounds of Europe; the inter-war period.   459

HOUGHTON, Georgiana.   Evenings at Home (1881). Her experiences in spiritualism;development as a medium; the spiritualist movement; lively.   460

HOUSMAN, Laurence.   The Unexpected Years (1936).His boyhood; family life in London; visits to USA; career as a writer; his plays; friendships; W.W.1 experiences.   461

HOUSTON, Mrs. M. C. Twenty Years in the Wild West (1879); A Woman's Memories (1883). Her life in Connaught in 19th Century;Irish country life; literary celebrities and social life from the thirties.   462

HOUSTOUN,James. Memoirs of the Life (1747). Boyhood; medical career, 1690 to 1747; surgeon to Royal Africa Company in West Indies;Darien Settlement and South Sea Bubble; a lively record of adventures and work.   463

HOWARD, Catherine Mary. Reminiscences (Carlisle, 1836-37). Her life in Cumberland; children and family; the events of Napoleonic wars;social life in London and Cumberland; life of the country aristocracy.   464

HOWARD, Edmund. A Narrative of Some Occurrences. Life and work in London, 1709-85; gardener to Sir Hans Sloane; later, a clockmaker; Chelsea affairs. MS,Chelsea P.L.; see Friends Quarterly Examiner, 1906.   465

HOWARD,Ethel. Japanese Memories (L. 1918).Experiences as teacher in house of Japanese nobleman, 1901-8; life of Japanese nobility.   466

HOWARD, Gen. Sir Francis. Reminiscences(1924). Boyhood in Germany; army career; Sandhurst, Canada, India; the Afghan wars;his adventures, sport and social life to 1890.   467

HOWARD,Frederick Thomas Rowland. On Three Battlefronts (N. Y. 1918). The service of a private in WW1; with the Australians in Gallipoli & with the Canadians on Western Front.   468

HOWARD, J. Bannister. Fifty Years a Showman (1938). Touring with melodramas;producing and management, London; ups and downs in business; theatrical and social life; celebrities.   469

HOWARD, Keble (John Keble Bell). My Motley Life (1927). Oxford; work as a journalist;drama critic and editor of The Sketch; Savage Club; literary and theatrical life and people.   470

HOWARD,Luke. Love & Truth in Plainness Manifested (1704). Apprentice to shoemaker in Dover;religious life and ministry with Baptists and Quakers in 17th Century; sufferings.   471

HOWARD OF PENRITH,Esmé William Howard,1st Baron. Theatre of Life (1935-1936). Education; diplomatic career, 1863-1936; in France, Italy, Germany, Spain, USA, West Indies; Boer War and WW1;international conferences; interest in rubber trade.   472

/HOWARD-WILLIAMS, Ernest Leslie/ . Something New Out of Africa, by H. W. (1934).Life,work and adventures during three years service with the RAF in Sudan in the 30's.   473

HOWE, J. Burdette. A Cosmopolitan Actor (1888). Archly humorous record of theatrical experiences; his tours in many parts of world.   474

HOWE, M. S. Osborn. By Fire & Cloud (1894). Missionary work and travel in India and South Africa from 70's; revivalism with Moody.   475

HOWEL, Thomas. Diary, 1787-9; journey from Madras to Venice,via Armenia and Anatolia;adventures. A Journal of the Passage from India (1789).   476

HOWELL, Com. Edward. Escape to Live (1947). Wing-commander's experiences in WW2; German invasion of Crete; his adventures and escapes.   477

HOWELL, John. Journal of a Soldier (Edin. 1819). Military service; South America,Peninsular War, Waterloo; the battle experiences of a common soldier told interestingly.   478

HOWITT, Mary, Autobiography (1889). Girlhood in Uttoxeter; literary life; journalism in London;Quaker religious life and work; social work; the anti-slavery movement; travels.   479

HOY, Hugh Cleland. 40 O. B. (1932). Personal narrative of WW1 service; at Admiralty; naval intelligence.   480

HUDSON, William Henry. Far Away and Long Ago (1918).Boyhood in country in England and on farms in Argentina;impressions of boyhood; early interests in natural history.   481

HUEFFER, Ford Madox (Ford). Ancient Lights (1911). His life among the pre Raphaelites; literature and art; the artistic views and the social life of

the brotherhood; criticism.   482

HUGHES, Alice. My Father and I (L. 1923). Life with her painter-father; her own career as a painter and photographer; their sitters; artistic and social life in London.   483

HUGHES, Sir Edward. Naval journals, 1778-85;activities while commander of squadron in East Indies;naval engagements. MS, India Office Library, Eur. F. 27-29.   484

HUGHES, Henry. Glimpses of My Life (1902). Travel and work as commercial traveller from the sixties; memories of people and places.   485

HUGHES, John Scott. Sailing through Life (1947). Career at sea; deck-hand and yachtsman;his writings; authority on yachting.   486

HUGHES,Joseph Edward.Eighteen Years on Lake Bangweulu (1933). Experiences of a native commissioner in North-West Rhodesia, 1901-18; work as trader and hunter and guide; natural history and native life.   487

HUGHES, Katherine (Barrett). Story of My Life(1945). Girlhood and family life; her life as the wife of a Methodist minister; social work; the West London Mission.   488

HUGHES, Mary Vivian. A London Child of the Seventies (1934); London Girl (1936);London Home (1937); London Family (1940). A charming and detailed account of her family life in London, at Canonbury; schooling and teaching; Bedford College; her married life and the humours of family relationships & changing customs; travels.   489

HUGHES, Patrick Cairns ("Spike"). Opening Bars(1946). Boyhood, Ireland; musical study; musical career as conductor and composer; ballet, jazz and new movements in music.   490

HUGHES, Spencer Leigh. Press, Platform and Parliament(1918). Boyhood in Ipswich; career as foreign correspondent, political journalist, lecturer, prior to WW1; Liberal politics; M.P. for Stockport; social life, clubs and eminent public figures.   491

HUGHES, Thomas. Early Memories for the Children (1899); selections in the Cornhill Magazine,1925. Early life of the novelist in Uffington and London; legal studies; writing; socialism and work at Working Men's College.   492

HUGHES-HALLETT, Captain F. Victor. Bran Mash(1931). Education at Haileybury; work as a brewer's apprentice; cut off by his father; the gay life of a spendthrift;varied life as actor soldier, sportsman, writer.   493

HUGILL, Lt. Com. John A. C. Hazard Mesh (1946). Experiences in WW2; the invasion of Normandy; London and the Blitz; his duties.   494

HULBERT,Charles. Memoirs of Seventy Years (Providence Grove, 1852). Life at Shrewsbury; Shropshire life; antiquarianism; his friends.   495

HULL, Edward.   Reminiscences of a Strenuous Life (1910). A geologist's career from 1850; work for Geological Survey in England; professor of Geology in London; simple.   496

HULLAH,John Pyke. Life, by his wife (1886).Opens with autobiography up to 1843; musical studies; Royal Academy; work as organist; and his activities in singing.   497

HULME, Edward. Alphabet of Life (L. 1949). Enlistment in the army as boy; invalided out in WW1; his struggles; work of the Disabled Soldiers & Sailors Agencies.   498

A HUMAN WOMAN. Me, Some Men, Some Women and Affairs (Birmingham, 1930). Superficial details of Suffragette activities; conservative politics; WW1; work in munitions; love story.   499

HUMBLEY, Captain William Wellington Waterloo.Journal of a Cavalry Officer (1854). Military career in India; the Sikh campaign of 1845-6; his travels; Indian life and customs.   500

HUME, David. The Life (L. 1777) and Philosophical Works, I (Edin. 1826). Brief outline of his literary career; neglect and popularity;defence of his History; his own character.   501

HUME, George. Thirty-Five Years in Russia(1914). His training as a naval engineer at Ipswich; the Crimean War; work with agricultural machinery,Russia; Russian scene, life, politics; & his business affairs.   502

HUME, General John R. Reminiscences (1894). Military career; mostly deals with the campaigns of the Crimean War 1854-55.   503

HUME-GRIFFITH, Mrs. M.E. Behind the Veil (1909). Wife of medical missionary in Persia and Turkish Arabia;mission work; family life; status & life of Persian women.   504

HUME-WILLIAMS, Sir Ellis. The World the House and the Bar (1930). Career as barrister and M.P.;divorce courts; conservative politics; WW1 Coalition government;social life; public events and legal and political figures. 505

HUMPHREY, Frederick. Experiences of a Temporary C. F. (1916). The work of a Baptist Chaplain during WW1; in the Near East with British forces.   506

HUMPHREYS, A. L.   When I Was a Boy (1933).Simple and pleasant account of his boyhood in Somerset in the 70's; country life and pleasures.   507

HUMPHREYS, Charles. The Life (n.d.) Life of a poor boy from 1850's; work in London bookshops; his own bookshop homely business advice. Copy, Croydon P.L.   508

HUMPHREYS, Eliza Margaret ("Rita"). Recollections of a Literary Life (L. 1936). Career of a popular novelist; Victorian social life; Boer War; WW1; literary changes and fashions; women novelists; publishers; her successes; lively.   509

HUMPHREYS, Travers.   Criminal Days (1946). His career as a lawyer in the criminal courts;High Court judge; his views of crime,punishment, and reform of the law; sketches and anecdotes of legal celebrities; good.   510

HUMPHRIES, W.R. Patrolling in Papua (1923). Work and travel as patrol officer in New Guinea from 1918.   511

HUNGERFORD, Sir Anthony. His autobiography;country life in Oxon; Black
Bourton in the late 16th & early 17th
Centuries. MS, British Museum, Add.
42504.   512

HUNT, Agnes Gwendoline. Reminiscences (Shrewsbury, 1935); reprinted as,
This is My Life(1938). Family life in
1870's; adventures in Tasmanian bush;
training and work as nurse in England
and her work for cripples; foundation
of orthopaedic hospital.   513

HUNT, Cecil. Authorbiography (1934)
Ink in My Veins (1948).His experience
as freelance writer,editor of a trade
paper, fiction editor for Daily Mail,
novelist,literary agent, broadcaster;
opinions on writers.   514

HUNT, Dick. Bygones (Lewes, 1948).
Veterinarian among omnibus horses;his
memories of coaching and coachmen in
the South; Edwardian sportsmen; good
old days.   515

HUNT,Henry. Memoirs (1820). Radical
politics; trial and imprisonment for
political activities; experiences in
Ilchester Gaol.   516

HUNT,James Henry Leigh. Autobiography and Reminiscences (1860). Career
as an author and journalist; travels
in Italy;friendship with Keats, Byron
and Shelley. His recollections of his
imprisonment in Surrey Gaol are printed in his Correspondence (1862), pp.
74-82; MS in Berg Collection,New York
Public Library.   517

/HUNT, Rev. John/. Clergymen Made
Scarce,by a Presbyter (1867). Boyhood
in Scotland;ordination; curate in the
North and in London; his difficulties
with superiors;protest against Puseyanism.   518

HUNT, John. Pioneer Work in the
Great City (1895). Wilts upbringing;
work as a missionary in London slums;
pubs and workhouses.   519

HUNT,Violet. The Flurried Years (L.
1926). Her personal, literary, public
life up to beginning of WW1; writing;
family and friends;D.H. Lawrence; the
drift to WW1.   520

HUNT, William. Then and Now (Hull,
1887). His fifty years as journalist;
Devonshire; Yorkshire; country journalism; development of press; organization of Newspaper Guild.   521

HUNTER,Capt. Charles. Adventures of
a Naval Officer (1905). Adventures of
a sailor in Malaya and Sumatra in the
40's;pirates, natives, Dutch; capture
and escape; sport.   522

HUNTER,George McPherson. When I Was
a Boy(Boston, 1920). His interests as
a boy; schools, sports and customs in
Scotland in 70's; the Clyde area; and
Kelvinhaugh.   523

HUNTER,George W. His diary adapted
in the biography by Mildred Cable and
Francesca French,Apostle of Turkestan
(1948). Life and work as pioneer missionary of China Inland Mission; work
and travel in Central Asia; imprisonment by NKVD.   524

HUNTER, Isabel Fraser King. Land of
Regrets (1909). Social life & travels
of an English spinster in India; her
low opinions of Hindus. India Office
Library.   525

HUNTER, J. A. White Hunter (1939).
Experiences of a professional big-game
hunter in Kenya, etc.   526

HUNTER, Captain James Edward. Ups &
Downs (1923). Career in the navy; his
experiences in the Chinese War,Kaffir
War, etc.   527

HUNTER, General Sir Martin. Journal
(Edin. 1894).His military career from
1774 to 1800;American Revolution; India and Gibraltar;Indian affairs; social life and sport.   528

HUNTER, William. Lives of Early Me-
thodist Preachers, ed. Thomas Jackson
I (1837). Autobiography of itinerant
Methodist preacher in 18th Century in
Northumberland and North.   529

HUNTER-BLAIR, Right Rev. Sir David.
Medley of Memories (1919); New Medley
(1922); Memories and Musings (1929);
More Memories (1931); Last Medley (L.
1936); In Victorian Days (1939). His
education at Eton and Oxford; life as

a Benedictine monk; Abbot of Dunfermline; rambling account of religious,
literary and social life; travels and
pilgrimages;eminent friends in literature,public life and religion; Wilde
and others;the pleasures of books and
music; pleasant.   530

HUNTINGTON, William. God, The Poor
Man's Guardian (1784). Autobiography
of his spiritual life; an account of
God's mercies to him.   531

HUNTLEY,Sir Henry Veel. Seven Years
Service on the Slave Coast (L. 1850).
His work as governor of Gambia, 1830-
1837;investigation and suppression of
slave-trade in Sierra Leone & Gambia
and personal affairs.   532

HUNTLY, Charles Gordon,   11th Marquis. Travel, Sport and Politics (L.
1887);Milestones (1926);Auld Acquain-
tance(1929); Cock o' the North (1926)
Memories of a Scottish Grand Seigneur
his estate work; social life in Scotland;university affairs; the House of
Lords;Victoria and Eminent Victorians
and Scottish Lairds; good.   533

HURD,Sir Archibald Spicer. Who Goes
There? (1941). Journalist's reminiscences of naval affairs; navy politics
and personalities from 1885; writings
and journalism.   534

. HURD, Right Rev. Richard. Works, I
(1811). Brief notes on occurrences in
the life of the Bishop of Worcester &
on episcopal matters.   535

HURNARD,James. A Memoir (1883). His
boyhood;emigration to USA; conversion
to Quaker belief; return to Essex and
Quaker ministry there; anti-Corn Law
agitation; his poetry.   536

HURREN,Bernard John. Stand Easy (L.
1934);Eastern Med (1943). The lighter
side of navy life;naval and air operations with the Fleet Air Arm based at
Malta in WW2; good.   537

HURST,Sir Arthur Frederick. A Twentieth Century Physician (1949). Education and medical training at Oxford
and Guy's;practice of medicine & psychiatry; WW1 service; changes in medicine and medical attitudes during his
lifetime.   538

HURST, Sir Gerald Berkeley. Closed
Chapters (Manchester, 1942). Bradford
and Oxford; legal work in Manchester;
Conservative M.P.; Parliamentary and
legal career;civic and social life in
Manchester.   539

HURST, Ida. Vagabond Typist (1937);
Break Away(1939); Dare to Live (1940)
Typist in China (L. 1941); I've Been
Around (1946). Adventures of a typist
secretary and journalist; insatiable
taste for travel in dangerous places;
Africa, Prague, Danzig, Shanghai etc.
superficial zest.   540

HUSSEY, Samuel M. Reminiscences of
an Irish Land Agent (1904). Education
in Dublin; work as a farming and land
agent in Cork; the Kerry Land League,
Irish social life, politics, religion
from the thirties.   541

HUTCHEON, William. Gentlemen of the
Press (1933).His forty years of journalism in Aberdeen,Bradford, Manchester and London;journalistic scene and
his colleagues and friends.   542

HUTCHINS, Sir Philip Percival.   An
Indian Career (Preston, 1927). School
at Haileybury;career as administrator
collector and judge at Madras;work in
India Office; 1858-1908; activity for
imperial relations.   543

HUTCHINSON,Horatio Gordon.When Life
Was New (L.1911); Fifty Years of Golf
(1919).His golden boyhood in Devon in
60's and 70's;country life, sport and
amusements;amateur golf, championship
play,organization; golfers and famous
socialites.   544

HUTCHINSON,Lucy.Memoirs of the Life
of Colonel Hutchinson (1810). Preface
contains fragment of autobiography; a
fulsome estimate of the virtues of her
family and her husband; domestic life
in 17th Century.   545

HUTCHINSON,Thomas Joseph. Ten Years
Wanderings among the Ethiopians (1861)
Buenos Ayres (1865); The Paraná(1868)
Two Years in Peru (1873). Experiences
as British consul in Nigeria, Argent-
ina, Peru;commerce; local customs and
South American politics.   546

HUTCHISON,Lieut. Col. Graham Seton.

Footslogger (L. 1931); Warrior (1934)
Education; military career in the Sudan, India, WW1; business and fortune
seeking in Australia and South Africa
politics; his writing; filming of "W
Plan"; celebrities he met; heroic but
querulous.   547

HUTCHISON, Percy. Masquerade (1936)
Theatrical career and reminiscences;
Empire tours; Wyndham & other actors;
from the nineties.   548

HUTCHISSON, W. H. Florio.   Pen and
Pencil Sketches (1883). Reminiscences
of 18 years in Bengal; travels; views
on Indians and Anglo-Indians.   549

HUTTON, Surgeon-Major George A. Reminiscences in the Life (1907). Study
of medicine in Newcastle;career as an
army surgeon in South Africa, Canada,
England; ambulance work in coalfields
and on railways; the St. John's Ambulance Association; good.   550

HUTTON, Isabel Galloway   (Emslie).
With a Woman's Unit (1928). Nursing &
medical work in WW1; Serbia, Salonika
and the Crimea.   551

HUTTON, R. N.Five Years in the East
(1847). His life at sea; experiences
in India and Far East in 40's.   552

HUTTON, Leonard. Cricket is My Life
(1949). His boyhood in Pudsey; career
as Yorkshire and England batsman; and
reminiscences of games,players, tours
etc.   553

HUTTON,William. "The Life of an Old
Soldier," Derbyshire Biography (n.d.)
Hardships as boy and apprentice; wan-
derings; life in the army, 1733-1762.
Copy, Derby P.L.   554

HUTTON, William. Life (1816, 1872).
Boyhood in Derby;work in mills; business as papermaker; nonconformity and
public life in Birmingham; industrial
revolution;historian; charming record
of the English Franklin.   555

HYAMS,Edward S. From the Waste Land
(1950). Work as a market gardener in
Kent;reclaiming waste land; crops and
prices;local scene; extensive digressions on many topics of public & private interest.   556

HYATT, Ernest.   All Over the Place
(1935). Travel and adventures in many
parts; sailor; N.W. Mounty.   557

HYATT, Stanley Portal.   Diary of a
Soldier of Fortune (L. 1910); Off the
Main Track (1911). Novelist's travels
and many jobs in Australia, S. Africa
India and USA; engineer, trader, sol-
dier, tramp, blockade-runner.   558

HYNDMAN, Henry Mayers. Record of an
Adventurous Life (1911); Further Reminiscences (1912). Work for socialist
movement from 1889; journalism, politics, labour movement; Shaw and Fabi-
ans; history and personal activities;
criticisms.   559

HYNDSON,Capt. J. G. W. From Mons to
the First Battle of Ypres.(1933). Re-
gular officer's service in France in
WW1; plain and detailed.   560

HYNE, Charles John Cutcliffe Wright
My Joyful Life (1935). Seafaring and
wanderings; adventures in remote places; treasure-seeking; work as novelist; Captain Kettle.   561

ANON. I Am an Alcoholic (1948). Account of his dipsomania by a Fleet St.
journalist.   1

ANON. I Had a Row with a German; by
R.A.F.Casualty (1942). Wounded fighter pilot of Battle of Britain; experiences in hospital; plastic surgery;
convalescence.   2

ANON. I Lost My Memory (1932). Experiences of an aphasiac; struggles to
recapture lost world;new mental world
fascinating psychological story.   3

IDDON,Jean H. Fragrant Earth (1947)
Experiences of Land Girl in WW2; village life and farm work in Yorkshire;
anecdotes.   4

/ILLINGWORTH, Capt. Arthur E./. Fly
Papers: by The Whip (1919). Personal
narrative of WW1; service with Royal
Flying Corps.   5

INCE, Richard. Shadow Show (1932).

London;office clerk; ordination; curacy in Midlands; loss of faith; journalism;reading; adoption of mysticism a frank spiritual record.   6

INCHFAWN,Fay. Adventures of a Homely Woman (1926). Poet's life in country; domestic, gardening, social.   7

INFANTRY OFFICER. Memoirs of an Infantry Officer (Edin.1833). Campaigns of the Peninsular War. 1809-16. Copy, War Office Library.   8

INGE, Lieut. Col. Denison M. A Subaltern's Diary (1894). Career in the Hussars, 1854-72; England, Malta, and India; service in the Mutiny; sport & pleasure.   9

INGE, William Ralph. Vale (1934). A review of his life by the Dean of St. Paul's;Yorkshire; Eton and Cambridge; career in the church; philosophical & mystical study; his work for Eugenics Society and Modernist movement;teaching at Oxford.   10

INGLIS,James. Sport and Work on the Nepaul Frontier (1878); Tent Life (L. 1888). Indigo planter's reminiscences of work and sport on Nepaul frontier, 1863-75;big-game; social life; Indian customs.   11

INGLIS, James. Oor Ain Folk (Edin. 1894). N.S.W.statesman's recollection of his boyhood in Scottish parsonage; village and glen life and people; old ways; the 1843 Disruption.   12

INGLIS, John. In the New Hebrides (1887). Work of Presbyterian missionary mainly on Aneityum and among Maoris, 1850-77; preaching, schooling, & labour traffic; hardships.   13

INGLIS, Lady Julia Selina. Siege of Lucknow (1892). Daily account of the siege by wife of one commander of the defence; personal details.   14

INNES, Alex Taylor. Chapter of Reminiscences(1913). Scottish advocate's memories of boyhood, relations of the state and church in Scotland; Principal Rainy; Gladstone.   15

INSKIP, Right Rev. James Theodore . Man's Job (1948). Bishop of Barking's

career; the clergyman & congregations he worked with;sermons; diocesan work and journeys; his busy life.   16

IRELAND, Annie Elizabeth. Longer Flights (1898). Writer's continental travels, recollections of writers and notes on literary and general social subjects.   17

IRELAND,Denis. From the Irish Shore (1936). Life in County Down; literature, theatre, politics & social life in Ireland; service in WW1.   18

IRELAND, John B. A Journal of Five Years (N. Y. 1859). Extensive travels in the 50's;Palestine, Near East, India, Afghanistan, China etc.   19

IRELAND, William Henry. Confessions (1805). The story of his career as a literary forger; antiquarianism & his Shakespearean forgeries.   20

IREMONGER, Lucille. It's a Bigger Life(1948). Journalist's year in West Pacific islands before WW2.   21

IRON,Capt. John. Keeper of the Gate (1936). Harbour-master of Dover; life at sea;work at Dover in peace and war and adventures on Goodwin Sands.   22

ANON. Iron Times with the Guards:by an O.E. (1918). Service in WW1; with Territorials and guards; Mons, Givenchy, Somme, etc.   23

IRVINE, Lieut.Col. Andrew Alexander Land of No Regrets (1938). His career in the army in India 1891-1914;Indian politics, communism, riots, perils; & his views on independence.   24

IRWIN, Anthony Stuart. Infantry Officer (1943); Burmese Outpost (1945). Army life;experiences in WW2; Dunkirk and Battle of France;guerrilla war in Burmese jungles.   25

IRWIN, Eyles. Series of Adventures (1780). Travels in Red Sea area & the Arabian deserts; adventures; life and manners of Arabs from 1777.   26

ISAACS, Sir Henry. Memoirs of My Mayoralty (1890). Record of his year as Lord Mayor of London, 1889-90; the official functions, etc.   27

ISBEL MARY, Mother. From Theatre to Convent (1936). Her stage career and Shakespearean performances; religious life; social work in Fulham & work at Anglican convent in Wantage. 28

ISHERWOOD, Christopher. Lions and Shadows (1938). Public school & Cambridge;troubles of adolescence; beginnings as novelist;autobiography mixed with fiction. 29

IVES, Edward. Diary, 1754-58; journey to India; Arab and Indian peoples and scene; military operations under Clive. Voyage to India (1773). 30

JACKMAN,William. The Australian Captive (Auburn, N.Y., 1853). Devonshire boyhood; runs away to sea; adventures at sea; life in Australia. 1

JACKS,Lawrence Pearsall. Confession of an Octogenarian (1942). Nottingham boyhood;religious education; ministry in Birmingham,Liverpool; professor at Manchester College;Hibbert Review and scholarship; anecdotes. 2

JACKSON, Mrs. Annabel Huth. A Victorian Childhood (1932). Girlhood in 80's as Miss Grant-Duff, daughter of the Governor; Anglo-Indian life; her procession of governesses; education at Cheltenham Ladies College;a lively story of rebellious girlhood. 3

JACKSON, Anne. An Account of Anne Jackson(1832). Spiritual life in 17th Century; London life & the plague and the great fire; God's mercies. 4

JACKSON,Col. Basil. Notes and Reminiscences (1903).Staff-officer in the Waterloo campaign; service at St. Helena; Napoleon; a vindication of Sir Hudson Lowe. 5

JACKSON, Charles. Narrative of the Sufferings (Cambridge, 1803). Suffolk man's escape from Irish rebels; 1798 rebellion at Wexford; the barbarities of the Irish. Ipswich P.L. 6

JACKSON,Maj. Frederick George. Lure of Unknown Lands (1935). Warwickshire childhood; exploring in Australia and Africa; Polar expedition; his service in Boer War and WW1. 7

JACKSON, Sir Frederick John. Early Days in East Africa (1930). Career of governor of East African Protectorate and of Uganda; Lamu and Zanzibar; his work and diversions;1884-1900; Nubian Mutiny, Rider Haggard, etc. 8

JACKSON, Adm. George Vernon. Perilous Adventures, ed. H. Burrows (Edin. 1927). Naval officer's adventures in Napoleonic wars; capture and escape; horrors of ship life. 9

JACKSON, Nicholas Lane. Sporting Days (1932). Soccer,golf, lawn tennis Finchley; the Corinthians. 10

JACKSON,Thomas. Recollections of My Own Life (1874). Methodist ministry & circuit work; administration; editorial work for Wesleyan publications and his biographical work. 11

JACKSON, William Collins. Memoir of the Public Conduct (1812). Business and observations of a senior merchant for East India Company at Madras; end of 18th Century. 12

JACO, Peter. Lives of Early Methodist Preachers, ed. Thomas Jackson, I (1837). Cornish Methodist's ministry in South-West of England in the 18th Century. 13

JACOB, Alaric. Scenes from a Bourgeois Life(1949). Critical account of his education; hack journalism; socialism; his amours; views on bourgeois life; outspoken record of 40 years in a changing society. 14

JACOB, Naomi. Me (1933); Me in the Kitchen (1935); Me Again (1937); More About Me (1939); Me in War Time(1940) Me & the Mediterranean(1945); Me Over There (1947). Novelist's memories of things, people, and events which have influenced her since childhood;career as writer; the theatre; experience in wartime; ENSA work; travels. 15

JACOBS, Abraham. Life (Edin. 1769). Jew's conversion and spiritual life & troubles; 18th Century; autobiography not seen. 16

JACOBSON,Arthur. Huic Holloa (1935)
Country boyhood; Harrow; hunting and
riding in South; his military service
in WW1.   17

JACOMB, C.E. Torment (1920). Patriotic account of his service in France
in WW1; hospital experiences.   18

JACOMB-HOOD,George Percy.With Brush
and Pencil (1925). Victorian artistic
and social life; illustrator and portrait-painter;   sitters;   travels; and
clubs.   19

JACSON, Roger. Journal, 1847-8; the
travels, business, and paintings of a
merchant and artist in Hongkong. MS,
Lancashire County Record Office,Pres-
ton, 40 fos.   20

JAFFRAY,Alexander. Recollections of
public life and affairs;   2nd half of
18th Century; the Napoleonic wars. MS
Aberdeen Public Library.   21

JAGER,Harold. Brief Life (Liverpool
1934). Rugby; Oxford; law study; work
on northern circuit;   F.E. Smith and
other legal celebrities; conservative
politics.   22

JAMES,Adm.Bartholomew. Journal, ed.
J. K. Laughton (Navy Records Society,
1896).   Partly autobiography of naval
service during American Revolution and
in merchant service to 1828.   23

JAMES, Lieut. David.   A Prisoner's
Progress (Edin. 1947).   Naval service
with MGB's in WW2;capture; his escape
from Germany into Sweden; gay account
of adventures while disguised as Bul-
garian naval officer.   24

JAMES,Ernald. Unforgettable Country-
folk (Birmingham,1947). Reminiscences
of Staffordshire country life, people
and customs.   25

JAMES,Capt.Frank. Faraway Campaigns
(1934). Personal narrative of service
in WW1; with Hindu troops in Persia;
Persian life.   26

JAMES, Com.Henry. Life of, by E. G.
Festing (1892).   Begins with autobiography of his early life and adventure
in the navy to 1838.   27

JAMES,John. Memoirs of a House Steward (1949). His service with eminent
people from the 90's; Princess Louise
Marquis of Lansdowne, Lord Hardinge;
historical data.   28

JAMES,John Angell. Life and Letters
(1861); Autobiography (1864). Dorset
boyhood; draper's apprentice; conversion;ordination; Independent ministry
at Edgbaston; writings; work for Congregational Union.   29

JAMES, Colonel Lionel.High Pressure
(1929); Times of Stress (1929). Foreign and war correspondent for Times;
travels and observations; India; Far
East, America; Boer War.   30

JAMES,Montagu Rhode. Eton & King's
(1926). Scholastic and scholarly life
from 1875; pleasant, small details of
people and incidents.   31

JAMES, Norah C. I Lived in a Democracy (1939).   Novelist's childhood;
WW1 work in civil service; career as
writer; private life and loves.   32

JAMES, Lt. Robert Bastard. Autobiographical narrative of shipwreck and
captivity in France, 1804-14; adventures in France and Holland. MS, B.M.
Add. 38,886.   33

JAMES, Samuel. Abstract of the Gracious Dealings of God (1760). Hitchin
Baptist's spiritual life and ministry
in 18th Century.   34

JAMES, Stanley B. Becoming a Man(L.
1945). Adventures in England and USA
in search for religious truth; spiritual autobiography.   35

JAMES, Sydney Rhodes. Seventy Years
(1926). Haileybury; Cambridge; teaching at Eton and Malvern; educational
experiences;ministry and clerical affairs; Canon of Worcester.   36

JAMES,Winifred Lewellin. Out of the
Shadows (1924). Her family and domestic life in Panama from 1915.   37

JAMESON, Anna. Diary of an Ennuyée
(1826). Feminine interests;travel and
social life; France and Italy; mixed
with fiction.   38

JAMESON,Clarke. Man No Good (1936). Rough life as labour recruiter, plantation overseer,and nigger basher; the Solomons and New Guinea.   39

JAMESON, Storm.   No Time Like the Present (1933). Family life; University of London;development as novelist and reflections on work,life, war and people.   40

JAMIESON, Roger. The Siege Perilous (1897).Soldier's child; life in Scotland; attempts to enlist; work, in his uncle's business. A copy in Cambridge U.L.   41

JARCHÉ, James.   People I Have Shot (1934). Adventures and excitements of a newspaper photographer.   42

JARROTT, Charles. Ten Years of Motors (1906). Experiences in international motor races in England & on the continent.   43

JARVIS, Maj. Claude Scudamore. Yesterday and Today (L.1931); Desert and Delta (1938);The Back-Garden of Allah (1939); Scattered Shots (1942); Half a Life(1943); Happy Yesterdays (1948) Army career; Boer War; Ireland; WWl; 13 years as Governor of Sinai; Arab & Egyptian politics;Bedouin life; country life near New Forest;lighter side of WWl; anecdotes.   44

JARVIS, Col. Weston. Jottings from an Active Life (1928). Military experiences from 1880;work for Empire and travels; Boer War; WWl; Rhodes; sport and social; important friends.   45

JAY, Frank. Touch Lucky (1937). Irish soldier's adventures; WWl; with Sinn Feiners;scouting for Italians in Abyssinia; bombing for Franco; self-glorification.   46

JAY, William. Autobiography (1854). Series of letters to his children; a Methodist minister and revivalist and his work, travels, sermons, writings, and reading.   47

JEAFFRESON, John Cordy. Book of Recollections (1894). Oxford; career as novelist; London literary and social life; Cobden,Thackeray and Halliwell-Phillipps, etc.   48

JEANS, Adm. T. T. Reminiscences of a Naval Surgeon (1927). Work in hospital ships and naval hospitals; Boer War, Far East, Gallipoli; colleagues and friends;life at sea; chatty anecdotes.   49

JEANS, William. Parliamentary Reminiscences (1912). Work in Press Gallery from 1863;journalism; observation on important public and parliamentary affairs and trivia.   50

JEFFERIES, Richard. The Story of My Heart (1883). Naturalist's spiritual autobiography;confessional of thought and feeling; mysticism; classic. 51

JEFFERSON,Horace.Diary of a Governing Director(1934). Agreeable account of work of director of private limited company; humorous experiences of misfit soldier in WWl.   52

JEFFERY, Jeffery   (J. E. Marston). Servants of the Guns (1917). Service with artillery in France in WWl; capture; prisoner in Germany.   53

JEFFREYS, Keturah. Diary, 1821-25; pious account of her life in Mauritius and Madagascar; scenery; native life. Widowed Missionary's Journal (Southampton, 1827).   54

JEFFREY,William Frederick. Sunbeams Like Swords (1951). Army service WW2; training in India;with Wingate in the Burmese campaign;problems of guerrilla warfare;his reading; his leaves in India.   55

JEFFRIES, Joseph M. N. Front Everywhere(1935). Daily Mail correspondent 1914-33;largely his years as war correspondent in France in WWl.   56

JEFFRYS, John. A Serious Address to the People of the Church of England (Dublin, 1742).Prefixed with autobiography of the Connaught man's conversion to Quakerism. Harvard U.L.   57

JEFFS, Harry. Press, Preachers, and Politicians(1933). Fifty years in religious journalism; country journals; preachers,missionaries, the Christian world; public figures.   58

JELF,Col. Wilfrid. Hark Back (1935)

Adventures and incidents in military career; Boer War; WW1.   59

JELLARD, John. John Jellard's Journal, ed. A. G. Powell (Bristol, 1938) Master mariner's account of voyage on sailing ship into the South Seas;daily happenings, 1856-57.   60

JELLETT, Morgan Woodward. Autobiography of boyhood and schooling;Irish life in early 19th Century. Cora S. Gould, Great Trees from Little Saplings Grow (N.Y. 1931).   61

JEMMAT, Catherine. Memoirs (1762). Girlhood in Plymouth; courtships; her quarrels with tyrannical father, Adm. Yeo; unhappy marriage.   62

JENKIN , Arthur. A Tank Driver's Experiences(1922). Unpleasant career in tank warfare in France, WW1.   63

JENKINS, Com. C. A. Days of a Dogsbody (1946). Plain tale of adventures and humors of 22 years at sea;written for his children.   64

JENKINS, J. C. Autobiography of his boyhood in London; business in Hereford; brushes with military; work in West India trade; damaged. MS, Hereford City Library.   65

JENKINS,James. Quaker autobiography 1761-1821;work as a grocer; religious life and Quaker people; his reading & social life. MS, Friends' Soc.Library London, N. W.1; Yale Univ. Microfilm, 228-229.   66

JENKINS, John. Diary, 1824-25; work of Methodist missionary in Jamaica; & observations on plantations & slavery Memoir,by George Jackson (1832).   67

JENKINS,Richard Wade. Ceylon in the Fifties and Eighties (Colombo, 1886). Work as coffee and tea planter; problems of plantation work; living conditions; vicissitudes.   68

JENNINGS, Rev. Frank L. In London's Shadows (1926); Tramping with Tramps (1932). Experiences as temporary vagrant in refuges, workhouses, lodginghouses in East End; work at odd jobs; sociology and religion.   69

JENNINGS,Henry James. Chestnuts and Small Beer (1920).Journalism in Bristol and Birmingham; Birmingham Daily Mail;local life, entertainments, literature, public affairs, from 1870 to 1900.   70

JEPHSON, Arthur William. My Work in London (1910). Clergyman's life from 1876; Croydon, Waterloo and Walworth, crime and prostitution.   71

JEPHSON, Lady Harriet J. Notes of a Nomad(1918). Youth in Quebec; travels in England and Europe & society life; artists; literature.   72

JEPSON,Edgar. Memories of a Victorian (1933); Memories of an Edwardian (1937). Novelist's childhood; Oxford; London literary life and celebrities in 90's; club life, writers, artists; anecdotes of eminent friends.   73

JERDAN, William. Autobiography of (1852-3).Journalist's career with Sun and Literary Gazette; literary, political, social, public affairs; London scene and celebrities;authors; covers fifty years.   74

JERMY,Louise. Memories of a Working Woman (Norwich,1934). Excellent autobiography of working class life; milliner; servant; self-education; disappointment in love; London, Birmingham. Norwich P.L.   75

JERNINGHAM, Hubert E. H. Reminiscences of an Attaché (Edin. 1886). His life at Paris embassy in 60's; intellectuals and writers; Dumas, Dickens, Thiers, Gladstone; society.   76

JEROME, Jerome Klapka. On the Stage and Off (1886); My Life and Times (L. 1926).Experiences of a wouldbe actor; early poverty; work in journalism and his literary career; work in theatre; WW1 service in France; Shaw,Doyle and other literary friends.   77

JERROLD,Douglas. Georgian Adventure (1938). Lively account of his education and career in literature and the theatre;public affairs, WW1, politics and social scene.   78

JERSEY,   Margaret Elizabeth Child-

Villiers,Countess of. Fifty-One Years
of Victorian Life(1922). Girlhood and
society life;travels with her husband
in India, Australia, N.Z.; official &
society life.   79

JERVIS, Eustace. Twenty-Five Years
in Six Prisons(1925). Work and observations of prison chaplain; prisoners
and their ways, problems, language &c
sociological interest.   80

JERVIS-WALDY, W. T.   From Eight to
Eighty (1914); Marlborough; Sandhurst
and army life in Ireland, Crimean War
and India; the Mutiny; hunting, sport
and social life.   81

JESSOP, Gilbert L.   Cricketer's Log
(1922). His career in cricket; games
for Cambridge, Gloucester, & England;
famous games and players.   82

JESSOPP,Augustus. Trials of a Country Parson (1890). Loneliness, problems of country parish in East Anglia;
need for church reforms.   83

JOAD, Cyril E. M.   Under the Fifth
Rib (1934); Testament of Joad (1937).
Education;Oxford; intellectual, moral
and spiritual life, fancies, beliefs,
changes; his reactions to passing events and notions.   84

JOEL,John. Reminiscences(Eton, n.d.
1870?). Eton and Eton college in 30's
and 40's; masters, sports, etc.   85

JOHN,Owen. Autocar-Biography (1927)
Career as car owner and driver; work
as pioneer motor-journalist; Autocar;
anecdotes.   86

JOHN, Romilly. Seventh Child (1932)
Boyhood and youth at Alderney; family
and friends; rural life.   87

JOHNSON, Christopher. I Lived Dan-
gerously (1939). Nomad's adventures;
on stage in South America; banditry in
Mexico;tramping in USA: adventures in
Pacific and African jungle.   88

JOHNSON, Donald McIntosh. A Doctor
Regrets (1949).   Lancashire; medical
studies and practice; hospital work &
practice in Surrey; opposition to the
National Health Service; work on Arctic expedition and in Labrador.   89

JOHNSON,Sir Frank William Frederick
Great Days(1940). Empire pioneer; his
business and mining in South Africa &
military service, WW1; his travels in
India; imperial interests.   90

JOHNSON, Adm. George. Autobiography
and Memoir(1904). School; life at sea
to 1859;plain story of ships, sailors
and life under sail.   91

JOHNSON, George William. A Stranger
in India (1843). Work as advocate of
Indian Supreme Court; descriptions of
Indian life.   92

JOHNSON, H. H. Reminiscences of the
Near East (1914). Residence in Egypt,
1891-1913; politics; scandals; Egyptian life and scene.   93

JOHNSON, Samuel. An Account of the
Life(1805).Autobiography of the great
scholar's first eleven years.   94

JOHNSON, Ven. William Percival. My
African Reminiscences (1924). Work at
Universities Mission, Nyassaland, in
1875-95; native life and chieftains;
traders; slavery; pleasant, humorous
memories.   95

JOHNSTON,Ellen. Autobiography,Poems
and Songs (Glasgow,1867). Girlhood in
Glasgow; work in factories; her love
affairs and troubles;literary inclinations; her poems and publications; a
troubled life.   96

JOHNSTON, Sir Harry Hamilton. Story
of My Life (1923).Exploration and adventure in Africa; worldwide travels;
Liberal politics.   97

JOHNSTON, Margaret. Some Adventures
with a School (1934).   Foundation of
the Home School; curriculum; experiment; success.   98

⎣JOHNSTON,Charles F.⎦.Recollections
of Eton: by an Etonian(1870). A boy's
life at Eton; study and sport.   99

JOHNSTON, William.   Life and Times
(Peterhead, 1859). Scottish chemist,
gardener,cartwright;life in the Highlands and at Peterhead; local events;
changing manners.   100

JOHNSTONE, James, Le Chevalier de.

Memoirs (Aberdeen, 1870-71). Service
in the 1745 rebellion; adventures and
escapes; service in Canada; amours; a
lively record; translated.   101

JOHNSTONE, Major-Gen. Sir James. My
Experiences in Manipur (1896). Military and administrative affairs in Manipur and Naga Hills from 1873;   court
life.   102

JOHNSTONE, Julia. Confessions (1825)
Society woman's refutation of charges
made by Harriette Wilson; her seduction; anecdotes of Wellington, Byron;
upbringing at Royal Palace; court and
society.   103

JOHNSTONE, Nancy J. Hotel in Flight
(1939). Experiences while helping her
husband run a hotel on Catalan coast
during Spanish civil war; her guests;
local reactions to the war.   104

JOHNSTONE, Thomas M. U. The Vintage
of Memory (Belfast, 1943). Boyhood in
Ulster; Belfast University; career as
Presbyterian minister;temperance work
and persecutions.   105

JOLY, John. Reminiscences and Antic-
ipations(1920). Episodes in career of
a professor of geology;education; in-
specting lighthouses; Trinity College
during the troubles.   106

/JONES, Mr./. Life and Adventure in
the South Pacific (1861). Travels and
adventures of a roving printer.   107

JONES, Abel John. I Was Privileged
(Porthcawl,1943); From an Inspector's
Bag (Cardiff, 1944). Welsh life; his
own education; his career as a school
inspector; anecdotes of children and
teachers; foreign schools.   108

JONES, Captain Adrian. Memoirs of a
Soldier Artist(1933). Military career
in India; work as sculptor; Carlyle &
Whistler, royalty, actors.   109

JONES, Charles. History of Charles
Jones (1796). Childhood in Somerset;
work as a footman to a parson, and in
London; promotion to bailiff; temptations to gaming, lying, drinking, and
women; moral triumph; marriage.   110

JONES, Dennis. Diary of a Padre at

Suvla Bay (1916). Brief record of his
service as chaplain in WW1.   111

JONES,Doris Arthur. What a Life (L.
1932). Daughter of playwright & wife
of diplomat; travels in Mediterranean
countries; memories of famous writers
and actors.   112

JONES, E. E. Constance. As I Remember (1922). Girlhood and schooling in
Herefordshire;study at Girton;women's
education;teacher and head at Girton;
Cambridge life; rambling.   113

JONES, G. Hartwell. A Celt Looks at
the World (Cardiff,1946). Autobiography of Welsh life; travels to Moscow
and Rome; studies in Celtic Culture;
nationalism.   114

JONES, George Garro. Ventures and
Visions (1935). Service in WW1 in the
RFC; travels in USA and Africa; work
as journalist and businessman;Liberal
M.P.; politics.   115

JONES, Harry. Fifty Years (L. 1895)
Religious career; among poor and rich
in London; prebendary of St. Paul's;
comments on social reform.   116

JONES, Sir Henry. Old Memories (L.
1922).Inspirational story of struggle
for education;working his way through
university; philosophical studies and
his professorship at Glasgow; university and higher education.   117

JONES,Henry Bence. An Autobiography
(1929). Life of a 19th Century scientist and author (died 1873); physics,
medicine, etc.   118

JONES, Jack. Unfinished Journey (L.
1937); Me and Mine (L. 1946); Give Me
Back My Heart (1950). Working-class
life in Merthyr;education; mining and
other jobs; trade unionism and Labour
Movement; career as dramatist & work
for BBC;happy family life; Llewellyn,
Priestley, Hamish Hamilton; political
personalities; attractive.   119

JONES,James Ira T. An Air Fighter's
Scrap-Book (1938). Welsh boyhood; WW1
service with RFC, and later in Russia
and Iraq; flyers; sports.   120

JONES,John. Clergyman's autobiogra-

phy; life and work at Repton, Bolne-
ham and Welwyn;brief. MS, Dr.Williams
Library, London, W.C.1.   121

JONES, John Joseph. My Lively Life
(1930). Work in trade-union movement;
transport workers;life in East End of
London;local politics; career as M.P.
public figures.   122

JONES, Maj.Gen. John T. Journals of
Sieges in Spain (1824); The Military
Autobiography (1853).Military service
and details of campaigns, especially
of the Peninsular War.   123

JONES, John Daniel. Three Score
Years and Ten (1940). Welsh boyhood;
Owen's School, Manchester; congregational ministry,Lincoln, Richmond and
Bournemouth;religious movements, especially the reunion movement; friends
and travels.   124

JONES, Capt. Oliver John. Recollections of a Winter Campaign(1859). The
volunteer service of a naval officer
in the Indian Mutiny; marches; siege
of Lucknow; Colin Campbell.   125

JONES,Owen. Ten Years of Game-Keep-
ing(1909). Work of a keeper; problems
experiences of shoots and shooters; &
account of sporting life.   126

JONES, Richard Lambert. Reminiscences of the Public Life (1863). Member
of City of London Common Council,1819
to 1844; city life and celebrations ;
new bridges, railways, streets.   127

JONES,Richard Robert. Autobiography
of the Welsh scholar and linguist, to
1822. MS, Cardiff P.L.   128

JONES,Thomas.Autobiographical journal of Welsh painter;travels in Italy
dealings with patrons; foundation of
Royal Academy; artists of the day. MS
owned by Rev. J. Adams, Landulph Rectory, Saltash, Cornwall.   129

JONES, Thomas. Leeks and Daffodils
(1942). Student days at Aberystwyth;
Welsh preaching, life, character; his
broadcasts.   130

JONES,Thomas. Rhymney Memories(New-
town, 1938). Boyhood and youth in a
Welsh town, 1870-90; family, schools,

games, chapel life, factory work. 131

JONES, W.Bence. Life's Work in Ireland (1880). Affairs of landlord who
tried to "do his duty," 1865-90; Land
Acts, tenants, Fenianism.   132

JONES,William. Autobiography (1846)
Mostly devoted to his scholarship and
publications in church history.   133

JONES-PARRY, Capt. Sydney Henry. An
Old Soldier's Memories (1897). Career
in the army,1849-68; Dublin Fusiliers
Crimean War; Indian Mutiny.   134

JOPLING-ROWE, Louise. Twenty Years
of My Life (1925). Work as a painter,
1867-87; social life; her friendships
with painters, writers, actors.   135

JOSEPH, Michael. Sword in the Scab-
bard(1942). Experiences as an officer
in France in WW1; Home Guards in WW2;
beach battalion at Dunkirk.   136

JOSEPH, Shirley.   If Their Mothers
Only Knew (1946). Lively account of a
year in the Land Army in WW2.   137

JOSEPHINE, M. My Child-Life (1853).
Orphan living with maiden aunt in the
country; family life and piety; love
affairs, miseries; fiction?   138

JOURDAIN, Lt.Col. Henry F. N. Rang-
ing Memories (1934). Childhood; Sandhurst; service in Connaught Rangers;
Boer War, Ireland, Malta; WW1, Gallipoli, Bulgaria, France; Germany. 139

ANON. Journal of a Wanderer (1844).
Travels and residence in India, first
decade of 19th Century;general observations on Indian scene.   140

ANON. Journal of an Officer in the
King's German Legion (1827). Service
in army,1803-16; Peninsular War, England, Ireland, Denmark.   141

ANON. Diary, 1780-84; military service in Mysore;capture; sufferings as
prisoner of Hyder Ali at Seringapatam
Journal of an Officer of Col.Baillie's
Detachment(1788); A.W. Lawrence, Cap-
tives of Tibu (1929).   142

JOWITT, Jane.   Memoirs (Sheffield,
1844). Irish girl; marriage; life as

lodging-house keeper at seaside;later life in Sheffield;poetry reading; the poems of a distressed widow.   143

JOY, George W. The Work of (1904). begins with autobiography of his study of art in Paris; his paintings; notes on Victorian painters.   144

JOYCE, Matthias. Lives of the Early Methodist Preachers, ed. Thomas Jackson, II (1837). Dublin Methodist and his ministry in Ireland.   145

JUKES, Harriet Maria. The Earnest Christian(1858). Devon childhood; her posts as governess;marriage to minister and emigration to Canada;later in Ohio; American society; slavery.   146

JULIAN,Henry Forbes. Memorials, ed. Hester Julian(1914). Includes diaries of his travels in connection with his mining and metallurgical work.   147

JUPP, James. The Gaiety Stage Door (1923). Reminiscences of 30 years as stage door attendant at Gaiety Theatre with anecdotes and chitchat about actresses, George Edwardes, etc.   148

JUPP, William J. Wayfarings (1918). Spiritual autobiography; Fabian Society, New Fellowship and religious brotherhood movement; Congregationalist and Unitarian minister; work with Humanitarian League; pacifism.   149

JUVENIS. Suvla Bay and After (1916) Personal narrative of WW1 service; in the Gallipoli campaign.   150

KAHANE, Jack. Memoirs of a Booklegger (1939). Novelist's experiences in WW1;Paris after the war; Bohemia, literary exiles, sex; his writing.   1

KAIGH, Frederick. Ninety-Nine and All That (1946).Physician's recollections since boyhood in the 90's; his practice; service in WW1 and WW2.   2

KANE, Whitford. Are We All Met? (L. 1931). Actor's career; Ireland, England, USA; tours; period as professor at Univ. Washington; Benson, Tearle &

Barrymore, etc.   3

KARK, Leslie. The Fire Was Bright (1943).Personal narrative of squadron leader in RAF in WW2.   4

KATE, Miss. An Autobiography (1938) Catholic's devotion to poor;piety and devotion; forty years at Saint Mary's Home, Hammersmith.   5

KATHERINE, Sister. Toward the Land (1900).Educational and religious work of Anglican missionary in Burma 1894-1898; pleasant.   6

KATIN,Zelma. Clippie (1945). Experiences as tramcar conductress in WW2; a lively and thoughtful record of the life of workers.   7

KAVANAGH, Patrick. The Green Fool (1938). Irish childhood; catholicism; WW1; IRA; cobbling trade; interest in poetry; farming, "A.E."; impressions of London; literary criticism.   8

KAYE-SMITH, Sheila. Three Ways Home (1937).Education and career as writer Literature and Religion; Anglicanism; conversion to Catholicism & return to Anglicanism.   9

KEANE, John F. T. On Blue Water (L. 1883); Three Years(1887). His medical study in Edinburgh; poverty and later life at sea; dock work; travels, USA, China, India, New Guinea, Burma, Arabia; prospecting; journalism.   10

KEARTON, Richard (Cherry). At Home with Wild Nature (1922); Naturalist's Pilgrimage(1926); Adventures with Animals and Men (1935); Travels (1941). Boyhood in Swaledale; farming, shooting, natural history; hunting in Asia and Central Africa;photographing wild animals; Roosevelt and friends.   11

KEATING, Joseph. My Struggle for Life (1916). Welsh boyhood and work in mines; varied jobs and struggles; his reading; career as novelist and playwright; success story.   12

KEATS, Charles. Writings and Recollections of a Durnovarian (Dorchester (1894). County Treasurer of Dorset; a recollection of Dorchester and people and local events. Copy at Dorchester

County Library. 13

KEBBEL,Thomas Edward. Lord Beacons-
field and Other Tory Memories (1907).
Battle of Life(1912). Career as political journalist for The Standard and
memories of Tory politics and politicians; boyhood; Merchant Taylor's and
Oxford; his journalistic work; Bohemian life in London and country life at
Kirby; good. 14

KEEBLE,Sir Frederick William. Polly
and Freddie (1936). His childhood in
family of six boys;the six girls next
door; family life; games; social life
in the country; pleasant. 15

KEELAN,Alice Jeannetta. In the Land
of the Dohori (1929). Her travels and
adventures in New Guinea. 16

KEELING, Edward Herbert. Adventures
in Turkey and Russia (1924). Personal
narrative of WW1;capture at Kut; prisoner in Turkey; adventures in Russia
after the revolution. 17

KEEN,Edith.Seven Years at the Prussian Court (1916). Governess in Germany before WW1; with Princess Frederick Leopold; court gossip; work as a
court dresser and companion. 18

KEENE, Henry George. A Servant of
"John Company" (1897); Here and There
(1906). Haileybury; Oxford; his work
as a district officer and judge 1847-
1882; Indian public affairs; Mutiny;
social and literary life; retirement
in Jersey and London; good. 19

KEEP, Arthur William. Sixty Years in
Business(1936). Birmingham merchant's
rise from the bottom of the business
ladder; changing attitudes. Copy,Bir-
mingham P.L. 20

KEHOE, Thomas Joseph. Fighting Mas-
cot (N. Y. 1918). Boy-soldier in WW1;
heroic experiences in France;dictated
and used as propaganda. 21

KEIMER, Samuel. Brand Pluck'd from
the Burning (1718). London apprentice
and printer; conversion to Quakerism;
religious life in Southwark. 22

KEITH, Agnes. Land Below the Wind
(1939). Experiences of American wife

of British conservator of forests, in
North Borneo; domestic life; natives;
lively. 23

KEITH, Sir Arthur. An Autobiography
(1950). His boyhood in Aberdeen; education; career as an anthropologist;
intellectual controversies;a tolerant
record of scholarly pursuits. 24

KEITH,Charles. Circus Life & Amusements (Derby, 1879). Life, work, travels of a circus clown. 25

KEITH, Claude Hilton. Flying Years
(1937). Personal narrative of service
in RAF in Iraq,1926-29; life and ways
of Arabs; adventures. 26

KEITH, Eric A. My Escape from Germ-
any(1918). WW1 service in France; his
capture and imprisonment at Ruhleben;
escape to Holland. 27

KEITH, James F. E. A Fragment of a
Memoir (Spalding Club, Aberdeen,1843)
Field-Marshal's military activities,
1714-34; with James III; in Germany &
Russia; soldier-of-fortune. 28

KELLETT, Ernest Edward. As I Remember (1936); Ex-Libris (1940). People
and times he knew; religion, politics
business, literature, school, sport;
defence of Victorianism; his literary
and mental growth;books and their influence on him; good. 29

KELLY, Charles H. Memories (1910).
Life in Manchester; trials of Methodists in mid-19th Century; preachers;
religious life and work. 30

KELLY, Capt. D. V. 39 Months (1930)
Service with Leicester Regiment, WW1;
Somme, Arras, Ypres & 1918 offensive;
experiences and opinions of war. 31

KELLY, Ethel Knight. Twelve Mile-
stones(1929). Canadian actress's travels and tours in five continents;her
career in USA and England to 1924. 32

KELLY,Henry Warren. Prodigal of the
Seven Seas, ed. Rita F. Snowden(1949)
Boyhood in London; poverty and illit-
eracy;adventures at sea; his learning
to write;literal transcription of his
record; interesting language & spelling. 33

KELLY,Michael. Reminiscences (1825) Vocalist and composer;social, musical recollections; King's and Drury Lane; opera in Italy and Germany;his Mozart performances; amusing.   34

KELLY, Samuel. Autobiography of an Eighteenth Century Seaman(1925). Dour and courageous merchant seaman; rough life and dangers at sea; Anti-Papism; vigorous and good.   35

KELTY, Mary Ann. Reminiscences of Thought and Feeling(1852); Loneliness and Leisure(1866). Religious life and devotion; later life in Quaker family and removal from Cambridge to Ipswich; tragic love affair; fiction?   36

KEMBLE, Frances Ann. Record of a Girlhood(1878); Records of Later Life (1882); Further Records (1883). Education and social life in London; travels in Europe; theatrical and literary society; eminent writers; acting with her father; marriage and plantation life in USA: excellent.   37

/KEMBLE, T.7. Sporting Reminiscenses of an Old Squire;by T. K. (Chelmsford 1887). Life at Winchester and Oxford; High Sheriff for Herts; the Yeomanry; hunting and shooting.   38

KEMP,Dennis. Nine Years at the Gold Coast (1898). Work of superintendent of Wesleyan Methodist missions on Gold Coast, 1887-96; missionary problems; Ashanti War.   39

KEMP, John. A Memoir (1933). Early life in inns; experience of drunkenness; conversion; Baptist ministry at Biddenham. Maidstone Museum.   40

KEMPE,Sir John Arrow. Reminiscences (1928). St.Paul's; Cambridge; work at the Treasury from 1867;Comptroller of the Exchequer;public affairs from his Treasury viewpoint.   41

KEMPE, Margery. The Book of Margery Kempe(EETS, 1940); modernised version (1936). Dictated autobiography of the 15th Century mystic; life as wife of Lynn burgess and as mother; visions; travels to Italy and Holy Land; boisterous behavior; fanaticism and troubles; excellent.   42

KENDAL, Dame Madge. Dramatic Opinions (1890); Dame Madge Kendal (1933). Her career with husband; theatrical & social life in England & USA: Gilbert and Sullivan; anecdotes of actors and opinions on acting.   43

KENDALL,Guy. A Headmaster Remembers (1933); A Headmaster Reflects (1937). Prep school; Eton under Warre; Oxford and career as teacher and headmaster; Manchester, Charterhouse, University School, Hampstead; pedagogy; friends; associates; good.   44

KENDALL, Capt. H. G. Adventures on the High Seas (1939). Experiences under sail and steam; on merchantmen and liners; convoying in WW1; superintendent for the Canadian Pacific, Southampton; pleasant yarns.   45

KENDALL, John. Memoirs of the Life (1815). Brief account of a Quaker's religious life and charitable work at Colchester; remarks on stage.   46

KENDALL,Robert. A Brand Pluck'd out of the Fire: by W. P. Davies (Northampton, 1813). Convict's confession of sins and spiritual anguish; his 34 godless years; death sentence.   47

KENDALL, S. G. Farming Memoirs of a West Country Yeoman (n.d.). A farmer near Bath later 19th Century; work of dairy farming; social scene; changing customs and values. Bath P.L.   48

KENDON,Frank. The Small Years (Cambridge,1930). Poet's pleasant account of his childhood in the country at end of 19th Century.   49

KENEALY, Edward Vaughan. Memoirs of by Arabella Kenealy (1908). Includes autobiography to 1856; Irish boyhood; legal life and work in London; murder trials; literary friends.   50

KENNARD, Sir Coleridge. Farewell to Eilenroc (1934). Fragrant and nostalgic account of his childhood in South of France.   51

KENNEDY, Bart. Sailor Tramp (1902); Tramp in Spain (1904); Footlights (L. 1928). Travels on land and sea; hobo; writer; touring with plays and operas

in England and USA; experience in the
lower ranks of theatre.   52

KENNEDY, David. Kennedy's Colonial
Travel(1876). Four years' experiences
of a Scottish singer in Australia,New
Zealand and Canada.   53

KENNEDY, Rev. E. J. With the Immortal Seventh Division (1916). Personal
experiences of chaplain in France in
WWl.   54

KENNEDY,James. Life and Work in Benares (1884). Long career as missionary in Benares and Kumaon, 1839-1877;
work of London Missionary Society;the
Mutiny; Indian customs.   55

KENNEDY, John. Old Highland Days(L.
1901). Boyhood at Aberfeldy; school,
sport, missionaries, smugglers; student life and study for ministry,Edin-
burgh and Glasgow.   56

KENNEDY, Lt.Ludovic. Sub-Lieutenant
(1942). Simple narrative of experiences in navy in WW2.   57

KENNEDY, Richard Hartley. Narrative
of the Campaign(1840). Experiences of
a surgeon in India, 1838-9; campaign
in Sind and Kabul; epidemics.   58

KENNEDY, Sir William Robert. Sporting Adventures (1876); Sport, Travel,
and Adventure (1885); Hurrah for the
Life of a Sailor (1900). Travels and
cruises from 70's; South and Central
America and West Indies;his career in
the navy;climbing, hunting, pleasures
and social life.   59

KENNEDY-COX, Sir Reginald. Autobiography (1931); Through the Dock Gates
(1939). Boyhood; Malvern and Oxford;
WWl service;social work; his theatrical ventures and friends;thirty years
work in London Dockland Settlements &
work in slums; good.   60

KENNEDY-FRASER, Marjory. A Life of
Song (1929). Empire travels with her
singer-father; singing studies; life
as voice-teacher in Edinburgh;collec-
tion of Hebridean songs and recitals;
work with Kenneth MacLeod.   61

KENNET, Edward Hilton Young, Baron.
By Sea and Land (1924). Experience of

naval officer, WWl and after; Serbia,
Archangel,Zeebrugge, Scapa Flow, Russia; naval mission to Serbia.   62

KENNET, Kathleen Young,   Baroness.
Self-Portrait of an Artist (L. 1949).
The death of Captain Scott of the Antarctic,her husband; the rebuilding of
her life;work as a sculptress; second
marriage; politics; the Asquith circle; good.   63

KENNETT, Charles. Stormy Petrel (L.
1936). Service in RAF in WWl; travels
in Canada,California, Philippines and
Pacific; flying for Chinese; a lively
story of adventurous life.   64

KENNEY, Annie. Memories of a Militant (L.1924). Upbringing; her mother;
Christabel Pankhurst and suffragettes
her militant career for women's suffrage; arrests; hunger strikes; munitions work in WWl; lively.   65

KENNEY, Rowland. Westering (1939).
European travels;interest in politics
and Labour Movement; work at Foreign
Office from 1920.   66

KENNION, Lt.Roger Lloyd. Diversions
of an Indian Political (Edin. 1932).
Experiences of a political officer in
Northern India from 1892; opinions on
British Rule; sport in the Himalayas
and Persia.   67

KENNY, Louise. The Red-Haired Woman
(1905).Childhood on the west coast of
Ireland; Irish clans and family life;
love affair; marriage to an Englishman.   68

KENT, Madeleine. I Married a German
(1938). Experiences in Germany in the
30's;Nazi movement and persecution of
her socialist husband; exile in England.   69

KENT, William. Testament of a Victorian Youth (1938). Youth in nonconformist family in South London in the
late 19th Century; religion.   70

KENWAY,Philip. Quondam Quaker (Birmingham, 1947). Childhood in Birmingham Quaker family in 60's; education
at Bootham;later life in N.Z.; a good
picture of Quaker life and people during the 60's and 70's.   71

KENWORTHY, Lt.Com. Joseph M. (later
Baron Strabolgi). Sailors, Statesmen,
and Others (1933). Career in the navy
China;WW1 service; Parliamentary career as Labour M.P.;politics after the
war.   72

KENYON, Charles F. ("Gerald Cumberland"). Set Down in Malice (L. 1919);
Written in Friendship(1923). Journalist and author's reminiscences of intellectual life in London and Dublin;
famous writers; Shaw, Yeats, AE, Hall
Caine; actors, critics, etc.   73

KEPPEL, Henry. Expedition to Borneo
(1846);A Visit to the Indian Archipe-
lago(1853).Experiences on expeditions
with James Brooke; suppression of the
slave-trade and piracy; extracts from
diaries of Brooke and Keppel.   74

KEPPEL, Sir Henry. A Sailor's Life
(1899). Naval career 1822-76; at sea
and ashore; ships and cruises; social
life; sports; simple and lively.   75

KER,Hugh T. Dams, Diving and Diver-
sions(1938). Work of a civil engineer
from 90's; dams, docks & railways, in
Scotland,North, Folkestone, Palestine
South America,Canada, Africa; service
in WW1 in France.   76

KER, J. Journal, 1778; experiences
at sea of a surgeon's mate; fighting
in West Indies; loss of Royal George.
MS, National Lib. Scotland.   77

KER, John. Memoirs(1726). Adventure
of Scottish political agent, 1700-25;
in pay of both the government and the
Jacobites; England and abroad.   78

KER-SEYMER,Vere. Idle but Happy (L.
1930). Wild oats of youth; education;
life in South America, England, Paris
and adventures with beautiful women &
sportsmen; gambling; racing.   79

KERNAHAN, Coulson. Dead Man's Diary
(L.1892); Experiences of a Recruiting
Officer (1915). Soul's adventures and
retrospect of his life and attitudes
to the world and art during sickness,
when supposed dead; fiction? Work in
WW1; recruiting and recruitees.   80

KERR, Commander Charles L.   All in
the Day's Work (1939). His career in

the navy,1886 to 1922; WW1; his later
experiences in business.   81

KERR, Fred. Recollections of a De-
fective Memory (1930).Career as actor
and theatre manager, London and USA;
theatrical life and people.   82

KERR, John. Memories Grave and Gay
(Edin.,1902); Other Memories (Edin.,
1904).Forty years as school inspector
in Scotland; travels, schools, teachers; work with Edinburgh University &
training colleges.   83

KERR, Lennox. Back Door Guest (Indianapolis, 1930); The Eager Years(L.
1940). A Scottish writer's adventures
in USA; hobo, footballer & tramp; the
prohibition era; his travels and adventures on sea and land,Australia to
the Arctic, to 1915.   84

KERR, Adm. Mark Edward F. Land, Sea
and Air (1927). Career in navy, 1885-
1920;naval attaché; WW1 service; Jutland; work with air force & strategy;
social life; anecdotes.   85

KERSH, Gerald. I Got References (L.
1939). Candid and amused reminiscences of people he has known.   86

KERSHAW,John. Memorials of the Mercies of a Covenant God (1870). His 53
years' ministry at Hope Chapel, Rochdale.   87

KEYES, Nial O'Malley. Blubber Ship
(1939). Misfortunes at Eton; sent by
his family abroad;work on an American
whaler in Pacific; lively.   88

KEYES,Adm. Sir Roger. Naval Memoirs
(1934-35); Adventures Ashore & Afloat
(1939). Naval career,1910-18; submarine warfare in narrow seas during WW1;
Dardanelles, Zeebrugge; Scapa Flow; a
supplementary account of his boyhood
in India and Ireland; early career in
navy; birth of the New Navy.   89

KEYNES, Florence Ada. Gathering Up
the Threads (1950).Family history and
reminiscences; Girton; social life at
Cambridge as don's wife; Town & Gown;
local politics; work as Mayor; family
life; Cambridge worthies; good.   90

KEYNES, John Maynard.   Two Memoirs

(1949). His attempts to persuade the
Allies to lift blockade of Germany and
Central Europe after WW1; & his early
beliefs under influence of G.E.Moore;
the values of doing good.   91

KEYSER, Arthur. People & Places (L.
1922);Trifles and Travels (1923). His
long career as colonial official and
consul; Malaya, Java, Somaliland, and
Spain; business, sport, society.   92

KIDDER, Richard. The Life (Somerset
Rec.Soc., 1924). Life and work of the
Bishop of Bath and Wells;ecclesiasti-
cal and political affairs from 1633 to
1703.   93

KIERNAN, R. H. Little Brother Goes
Soldiering (1930). Simple account of
enlistment and service in France, WW1
battles; growth of fear.   94

KIFFIN,William. Remarkable Passages
in the Life (1823).Activities of 17th
Century puritan;struggles for religious liberty and persecutions; religious witness; London business.   95

KILBRACKEN, Sir Arthur Godley, Viscount. Reminiscences (1931). Aspects
of his life; boyhood and education at
Rugby, Oxford; scholarship; career in
Parliament; Liberal politics.   96

KILGOUR, William T. Twenty Years on
Ben Nevis(Paisley, 1905). His work at
a meteorological station; weather and
natural history; colleagues.   97

KILHAM, Alexander. Life (Nottingham
1799). Work and travels of Methodist
preacher;circuit work in Scotland and
North of England; mobs.   98

KILLEN, William Dool. Reminiscences
of a Long Life (1901). Presbyterian's
ministry in Belfast and Raphoe; work
as professor of church history.   99

KILLICK,Hallie(Miles). Untold Tales
(1930). London in WW1;organizing concerts in hospitals & recruitment centres; war news; refugees.   100

KILLICK, Joseph Morton. Scraps of
Seventy Years (Lewes, 1920). Boyhood
in Sussex; school; literary efforts;
business life; London entertainments;
patriotic poetry; WW1 memories.   101

KIMBER, Sir Sidney. Thirty-Eight
Years (Southampton, 1949). His public
life and work in Southampton; work as
Mayor; the development of Southampton
and local affairs.   102

KIMMINS, Anthony Martin. Half-Time
(1947). Osborne and Dartmouth; naval
service in WW1; film-making; with the
Admiralty Press Service in WW2; & his
broadcasts and lecture-tours.   103

KINCAID, Charles Augustus. Forty-
Four Years a Public Servant (L. 1934)
Career in Indian Civil Service, 1891-
1926; Bombay and Sind; administration
and law; historical studies; cricket
and racing.   104

KINCAID,Sir John. Adventures in the
Rifle Brigade (L. 1830); Random Shots
from a Rifleman (1835). Military career; mainly his service in Peninsular
War and Netherlands.   105

KING,Anna C. L. Reminiscences of My
Life (1931). Surrey childhood;religi-
ous life & vocation; journey to China
as missionary when fifty;her work and
travels; retirement to England.   106

KING,Capt. Bastien. Diary of a Dug-
Out(1901). His recall from retirement
and observations on army and War Office procedures and red tape.   107

KING, Paul H.In the Chinese Customs
Service(1924). Chinese customs, trade
and public affairs; Shanghai, Canton,
Pekin;Boxer Rebellion; 1874-1920; and
social life and sport.   108

KING,Mrs. Robert Moss. Diary, 1877-
1882;domestic and family life of wife
of judge in India; the picturesque in
India. Diary of a Civilian's Wife (L.
1884).   109

KING, William. Fragment of autobiography; education; religious training
and church career in Ireland in 17th
Century.   Translated in: Sir Charles
S. King, A Great Archbishop of Dublin
(1906).   110

KING, William. Political and Literary Anecdotes (1818). Antiquarian and
scholarly interests and anecdotes and
church and politics, 1715-58; principal of St. Mary's Hall.   111

KING, Dr. William. Incomplete autobiography;Ipswich youth; medical studies and work at Brighton;the cooperative movement; editor of The Cooper-
ator; friend of Byron's widow; mostly
life in Ipswich in later 18th Century.
MS, Ipswich Public Library.   112

KING-HALL, Sir Herbert. Naval Memories (1926). Admiral's naval service,
1874-1919; cruises, traditions, anecdotes; WW1 service.   113

/KING-HALL, William Stephen/. Naval
Lieutenant, by Etienne (1919).Person-
al narrative of naval service in WW1;
Jutland, Scapa Flow.   114

KINGDON,Frank. Jacob's Ladder (N.Y.
1943). Poverty in London; a religious
life in early 20th Century; Methodist
ministry; later in USA.   `115

ANON. Kings, Courts and Society (L.
1930). Anecdotes of society; scandals
blackmail, social climbers.   116

KINGSCOTE, Henry Robert. Memoir and
Autobiographical Notes (Cirencester,
1882?). Public and philanthropic work
in Gloucestershire; public affairs; &
religion, sport & social. Gloucester
City Library.   117

KINGSFORD, A. R.   Night Raiders of
Air (1930). Personal narrative of WW1
service; RFC pilot; accounts of night
raids on Germany.   118

KINGSMILL, Hugh. Behind Both Lines
(1930). Personal narrative of service
in France, WW1; capture; experiences
in Karlsruhe and Mainz camps. His real
name is H. K. Lunn.   119

KINGSTON, Gertrude.   Curtsey While
You're Thinking (1937). Actress's career; theatrical and social life; her
political interests.   120

KINNAIRD, Emily. Reminiscences (L.
1925). Childhood and society life in
London; social work; Y.M.C.A.; religious and educational work in India;
with Y.M.C.A. in WW1.   121

KINNEAR, Alfred. Across Many Seas,
(1902). Life of newspaper correspondent; Crimean War; American Civil War;
Boer War; travels throughout world; &

notes on celebrities.   122

KINNEAR, Sir Norman. The One Thing:
by Alfred Norman(1923). Autobiography
of an industrialist; youth in Staffs.
industrial life in North; a leader in
Free Church and Liberal Party; original and frank.   123

KINROSS, Albert. An Unconventional
Cricketer (1930). Youth in Hampstead;
business life;writing; cricket; anecdotes of cricketers & writers.   124

KINROSS, James. No Longer Wings to
Fly (1949). Returned prisoner of war;
two years of suffering in tuberculosis
sanatorium;surgery; pains, fears, and
despairs; depressing.   125

KIPLING, Rudyard. Something of Myself (1937). Essays on his boyhood in
India; journalism; travels in Canada,
USA,South Africa; social and domestic
life in Sussex;working habits and his
writing.   126

KIRBY, Mary (Gregg). Leaflets from
My Life (Leicester, 1887). Childhood
and education at Market Harborough; &
social life in Leicestershire; marriage and clerical life at Brooksby;the
humors of parish life. Copy,Leicester
P.L.   127

KIRK,Francis J. Reminiscences of an
Oblate of St.Charles (1905). Catholic
progress in Bayswater and West End of
London from 1857;his part in development of new churches.   128

KIRKALDY,Andra. Fifty Years of Golf
(1921). Dictated; his career in golf
at St. Andrews; great golfers.   129

KIRKE, Henry. Twenty-Five Years in
British Guiana (1898). Administration
as Sheriff of Demerara; police, crime
and law; native life and culture; the
whites; social life.   130

KIRKMAN, Francis. The Unlucky Citizen (1673). Bawdy, picaresque adventures; includes several novella; and
apparently fictional.   131

KIRKWOOD, David. My Life of Revolt
(1935). Working-class life on Clydeside; engineer in Glasgow; socialism
and Labour Party; career as M.P.; ac-

tivities of Clydeside Group.   132

KISCH, Lt. Col. Frederick Hermann. Diary, 1923-31; public affairs in Palestine; Zionism; Arabs; politics and conflicts; valuable record. Palestine Diary (1938).   133

KITCHEN, Fred. Brother to the Ox(L. 1940).An excellent account of life of a farm labourer;rural work before the coming of railways; old ways.   134

KITCHIN, Darcy Butterworth. Days of My Youth (1936). Worcestershire boyhood; Harrow; Cambridge; teaching and publishing;scholarly work; sports; to 1899; pleasant.   135

KLEIN,Hermann.Thirty Years of Musical Life in London (1903). Boyhood in Norwich; musical journalism in London critic for Sunday Times; anecdotes of opera singers, virtuosi, etc.   136

KNAPPETT,Rachel. Pullet on the Midden(1946). Five years' farming in the Land Army in WW2; Lancashire life and mixture of town and country; varied & human record.   137

KNATCHBULL, Lady Lucy. Life: by Sir Tobie Matthew(1931). Includes her own narrative; excellent picture of nun's life at beginning of 17th Century; an abbess at Ghent.   138

KNATCHBULL-HUGESSEN,Sir Hughe. Diplomat in Peace and War (1949). Career in Foreign Office and as ambassador in Turkey and China; WW1 and WW2; international politics;statesmen and celebrities.   139

KNIGHT, Captain. Brother Bosch (L. 1919). Personal narrative of service in WW1; airman; captured, escaped and recaptured; adventures.   140

KNIGHT,Charles. Passages of a Working Life(1864-65). Printer, publisher editor, social reformer; a pioneer of Society for Diffusion of Useful Knowledge;valuable account of social history;reminiscences of celebrities and most eminent writers.   141

KNIGHT, Cornelia. Autobiography (L. 1861).Companion to Princess Charlotte her life at court; travels in France

and Italy; anecdotes of court.   142

KNIGHT, Edward Frederick. Reminiscences (1923). Activities of yachtsman and war correspondent;sailing in many seas; reporting, from Franco-Prussian war to Spanish-American war.   143

KNIGHT, Esmond. Seeking the Bubble (1943). Actor's experiences in films between wars;naval service and adventures in WW2.   144

KNIGHT, Francis. Relation of Seaven Years Slaverie (1640). Captivity and sufferings of an English merchant, in Algiers.   145

KNIGHT, Dame Laura.   Oil Paint and Grease Paint(1936). Career as painter theatrical, ballet & circus subjects; travels; social life.   146

KNIGHT,Thomas. British Battalion at Oporto(1834). Corporal with the Rifle Brigade, 1811-33; Peninsular War and Waterloo; expedition to Portugal; the campaigns; military life.   147

KNIGHT,William A. Retrospects(1904) Anecdotes and reminiscences of literary men by St. Andrew's professor of philosophy; Carlyle, Browning, Arnold Tennyson, etc.   148

KNIGHTON,William. Tropical Sketches (1855).Work as journalist in Calcutta and Ceylon;public affairs;Indian life before the Mutiny.   149

KNOBLOCK, Edward. Round the Room(L. 1939). New York childhood; career as playwright in English theatre;his experiences intended as a guide to hopeful dramatists.   150

KNOTT, Middleton O. Gone Away with O'Malley(1946). Ireland and USA; life of a man devoted to horses; hunting, riding, etc.   151

KNOWLES, Richard G. Modern Columbus (1915). Comedian's life in vaudeville his tours in Australia, Far East, USA determinedly humorous.   152

KNOX,Collie. It Might Have Been You (1938); It Had to be Me (1947). Rugby School;WW1 military service; on staff of Lloyd in India; work as journalist and travel for Express and Mail. 153

KNOX, Edmund Arbuthnot. Reminiscences of an Octogenarian (1935). Family
life; St. Paul's and Oxford; clerical
career in country parish, Birmingham,
and as Bishop of Manchester;religious
life and people from 1847.   154

KNOX, Louisa Isabel. Leaflets from
My Past (1934). A lonely aged woman's
recollections of old loves, incidents
friends, dreams, moods.   155

KNOX, Robert. A Historical Relation
of Ceylon (Glasgow, 1911; first published in 1681). Adventures of a merchant seaman;long life in East Indies
and Africa; activities as pirate and
slaver; captivity in Ceylon. Used by
Defoe in Captain Singleton.   156

KNOX, Ronald Arbuthnot. A Spiritual
Aeneid(1918). Childhood; education at
Eton and Balliol in early 19th Century
his spiritual life;influence of Tractarian Movement.   157

KNUTSFORD, Sydney Holland, Viscount
In Black and White (1926). Education;
legal career; business with East and
West India Dock Co.; work for London
Hospital;champion fund-raiser; volun-
tary hospital system; London life and
society; interesting.   158

KORNITZER,Louis. Trade Winds (1933)
Pearls and Men (1935); Bridge of Gems
(1939); Jewelled Trail (1940). Dealer
in diamonds and pearls; his business;
adventures; travels; cheats, crimes &
tricks of the trade.   159

L., M. Sunny Memories(1880). Social
encounters, anecdotes & recollections
of Turner, Faraday, etc.   1

LACEBY, Arthur. Stage Struggles of a
Bad Actor (Edin.1904). Work about the
theatre and acting, Scotland and London; anecdotes; no distinction.   2

LACKINGTON, James. Memoirs of the
First 45 Years (1792); Confessions of
(1804). His early life; Wesley; life
as a Methodist;career as a bookseller

in London; social and religious opinions; working-class culture; good.   3

LACY, John. A Relation of the Dealings of God(1708). Activities of 17th
Century religious prophet and healer;
records of his healings;his religious
musings.   4

LADDS, Charles. I'll Go No More A-
Roving (1934). A boy at sea on windjammer;ranching in Mexico; world-wide
travels and varied jobs.   5

ANON. Ladies Must Live (1939). Career as dancer;Isadora Duncan, Pavlova
etc.; her love affairs.   6

LAILEY,Bernard. Jottings from a Fee
Book(Portsmouth, 1932). Reminiscences
of a lawyer and judge; his career and
cases.   7

LAKE, Harold. In Salonika (1917). A
personal narrative of WW1 service; in
Gallipoli campaign.   8

LAKE, William Charles. Memorials of
ed. K. Lake (1901). Reminiscences of
the Dean of Durham from 1869; Rugby &
Arnold;Oxford and Newman; his life at
Oxford.   9

LAMB, Col. Dean Ivan. The Incurable
Filibuster (1934). Lively adventures
of a soldier-of-fortune in Central and
South America;goldmining; war and revolution.   10

LAMB, George R. Roman Road (1951).
Grammar school and Cambridge; family;
his mother; emotional troubles; pacifism; conversion to Catholicism. 11

LAMB,Robert. Saints and Savages (L.
1905). Five years' adventures in New
Hebrides; missionaries; natives. 12

LAMB, Roger. Memoir of His Own Life
(Dublin, 1811). Military service as a
sergeant in Welch Fusiliers;experien-
ces in America during the revolutionary war; good.   13

LAMBERT,Arthur. Over the Top (1930)
Service with Hon.Artillery Company in
France and Italy in WW1; bitter,rail-
ing account of miseries.   14

LAMBERT, Charles William. Journal,

1888-95; missionary's religious, medical and educational labours in Upper Burma;religious rivalries. Missionary Martyr of Thibaw (1896).   15

LAMBERT, Richard S. Ariel and All His Quality(1940). London boyhood and workingclass life; work for BBC; editor of The Listener;troubles with Sir John Reith; criticisms.   16

LAMBTON, Arthur. My Story (L. 1925) Salad Bowl (1927). Rambling anecdotes of social life, literature & writers, sport and sportsmen, soldiers.   17

LAMBTON, George. Men and Horses (L. (1924).Famous trainer's reminiscences of horses, races, riders, owners, and social celebrities.   18

LAMOND, Henry. Days and Ways of a Scottish Angler (1932). Reminiscences of trout, pike & salmon fishing; from his boyhood.   19

LAMONT, E. H. Wild Life among Pacific Islanders (1867). Activities of a trader in South Pacific; residence in California; business, travels, wives, kingdom; missionaries & natives.   20

LAMONT, James. Seasons with the Sea Horses (1861); Yachting in the Arctic Seas (1876). Cruises around Spitzbergen and in Arctic;geographical observations; hunting and observation of seal, walruses, bears, etc.   21

LAMP,Henry. Curriculum Vitae (1895) Life of 17th Century Quaker;education and work as apothecary-physician;life at Ulverstone, Lancs; conversion and Quaker religious life,persecution and adventures; varied and good.   22

LAMPLUGH, Lois. Stream Way (1940). Four years as child in village; Combe life and people; delicate. Cambridge U.L.   23

LANCASTER, Joseph. Epitome (New Haven, 1833). Career of English educational reformer; Lancasterian system and its reception in England, USA and S. America.   24

LANCELEY, William. From Hall-Boy to House-Steward (1925). Work as servant in noble households from 1870; below-

stairs view of society and royalty; & commentary on a servant's lot.   25

LANCHESTER, Elsa. Charles Laughton and I (N. Y. 1938). Comedienne's career on the stage and in films, with & without her husband.   26

LANCUM, F. Howard. Press Officer, Please! (1946). WW2 work as press officer to Ministry of Agriculture; the War and British farming.   27

LANDAU, Rom. The Wing (1945); Personalia (1949). Service with RAF in WW2 as gunner, administrator, liaison officer with Poles; family and society life;Lady Oxford; Patrick Campbell etc.   28

LANDER, Richard Lemon. The Journal (1829); Travels & Discoveries (1831); Adventures on the Niger (1856). With Clapperton in Central and N. Africa; travels and exploration in 30's. 29

LANDERY, Charles. So What? (1938). Adventures of Scottish tramp, drifter and ne'er-do-well.   30

LANDMANN, Col.George. Recollections of My Military Life(1854); Adventures and Recollections (1852). Career with Royal Engineers;light-hearted account of adventures in Spain and Portugal in the Peninsular War.   31

LANDOR, Arnold Henry Savage. In the Forbidden Land (1899); Everywhere (L. 1924). Travel and adventure in Tibet; many jobs and world-wide travel; work as painter,lecturer, inventor, explorer; Far East and South Seas.   32

LANDSHEIT, Norbert. The Hussar, ed. G. R. Gleig(1837). Military career of sergeant in York Hussars and the Light Dragoons; not seen.   33

LANE, Edward William. Life: by S.L. Poole (1877). Includes extracts from his journals of exploration in Egypt in early 19th Century.   34

LANG, Lt. Andrew Moffatt. Military diary, 1857-58; his service in Indian Mutiny;siege of Lucknow; good, lively details. Journal Society Army Historical Research IX-XI (1930-2).   35

LANG, Matheson. Mr. Wu Looks Back
(1940). Career as actor; with Benson
company;Shakespearean roles; tours in
Far East and the Empire; anecdotes of
theatrical life and people.   36

LANG, William. A Sea-Lawyer's Log
(1919).Personal narrative of a seaman
and his service with the Grand Fleet
in WW1; navy life; humorous.   37

LANGDON, Roger. The Life of (n.d.)
Hard boyhood on a Dorset farm in 30's;
runs away;work in Jersey; his life in
Somerset cloth factory;marriage; very
good account of working-class life in
mid 19th Century. Exeter P.L.   38

LANGLEY,Edward Archer. Narrative of
a Residence (1860). Work as secretary
to ruler of Upper Sind, Meer Ali Moo-
rad; court life,politics, British policy, economy; hunting.   39

LANGLEY,Frederick Oswald. Singapore
to Shoreditch (1943). Experiences as
London magistrate;working of a police
court; lives of the poor.   40

LANGLEY, Gilbert.   Life and Adventures (1710). Highwayman's account of
crimes & amours; written in Maidstone
Gaol.   41

LANGMAID, Rowland. "The Med" (1948)
His work and adventures while official artist to the Mediterranean Fleet
during WW2.   42

LANGTON,Richard. The Narrative of a
Captivity (1836). Seaman captured by
French in 1809;prison experiences and
escape; fairly good.   43

LANGTRY, Lillie. Days I Knew (1924)
Her career as an actress; her roles &
fellow players; literary celebrities;
society life as Lady De Bath.   44

LANKTREE,Matthew. Biographical Narrative (Belfast,1836). Methodist ministry in early 19th Century; travels
on Irish circuits;Irish congregations
and conferences. New York P.L.   45

LANSBURY, George. My Life (L. 1928)
Looking Backwards(1935); My Quest for
Peace (1938). Working-class life from
60's; East End of London social life,
customs, attitudes; the Labour Party,

women's suffrage, social reform; his
work in Poplar and Parliament;travels
carrying message of pacifism in 30's;
activities of great humanitarian and
mirror of socialist reform.   46

LANSBURY, Violet. Englishwoman in
the U.S.S.R. (1940). Typist at the
Soviet Embassy;office work and domestic life in Moscow;university, social
and women's life in Russia;sympathies
with Labour Movement.   47

LANSDOWNE, Andrew. A Life's Reminiscences (1890). Police work in London
and his work as a C.I.D. inspector at
Scotland Yard.   48

LARDEN, Walter. Recollections of an
Old Mountaineer (1910). A lifetime of
climbing in Swiss Alps.   49

LARDNER, Captain Edgar George Dion.
Soldiering and Sport (1912). Service
with King's African Rifles;travel and
sport in Uganda.   50

/LATHROP/, Annie Wakeman (editor).
Autobiography of a Charwoman (1900).
Interesting account of experiences of
girl as a charwoman; written in Cockney dialect.   51

LARKINS, William. Steeplejacks and
Steeplejacking (1926). His work as a
steeplejack; churches and monuments;
life in a sporting trade.   52

LARKWORTHY, Falconer.   Ninety-One
Years (1924). Career as a banker; an
apprenticeship in London; accountant
and banker in Australia and N.Z., and
representative of N. Z. banks in London; the Ionian Bank.   53

LARYMORE, Constance.   A Resident's
Wife in Nigeria (1908). Everyday farm
and domestic life,1902-7; customs and
life of natives of Nigeria.   54

LASCELLES,Francis. Reminiscences of
an Indian Judge (Guernsey, 1880). His
administrative and judicial work 1825
to 1865; troubles with the government
and self-justification; Macaulay. 55

LASCELLES, Gerald William. Thirty-
Five Years (1915). Life and work as a
surveyor of Crown forests in the New
Forest; hunting, shooting & falconry;

natural history; forestry.   56

LASERON, Charles F. South with Mawson (1947). Biologist with Australian Antarctic expedition, 1911-14; daily life, hardships; scientific work; and adventures.   57

LASKIER, Frank. My Name is Frank(L. 1941). Merchant seaman's broadcasts; life at sea in WW2;German raiders and submarines; torpedoed; wounded.   58

LA TERRIÈRE, Bulmer de Sales. Days that are Gone (1924). Lowestoft, Eton and Oxford; sport in Ireland; society in London;service with Hussars, Egypt and S. Africa; pleasure; sport.   59

LA TROBE-BATEMAN, William Fairburn. Memories Grave and Gay (1927). Life & work of a Catholic priest; his ministry at Norwood.   60

LATYMER, Hugh Burdett Money-Coutts, Baron.Chances and Changes (Edin.1931) Schools in 90's; Oxford; country life and sport; military service in France in WW1.   61

LAUD, William. History of the Troubles and Trial (1695). Summary of the chief events in his career;the events leading up to his trial;an account of the trial. The Autobiography (Oxford, 1839) is made up from various sources apart from the above.   62

LAUDER, Sir Harry. Harry Lauder at Home and on Tour (1907); Between You and Me(1919); Roamin' in the Gloamin' (1928); Wee Drappies (1931). Boyhood in Scotland; work as a miner; concert and music-hall career;tours in Empire and USA:many anecdotes of theatre and celebrities.   63

LAURENCE, Thomas Benson. Six Years in the Northwest(Calcutta, n.d.). His work for British officers in Northwest India;odd jobs;travels, 1854-60. Copy India Office Library.   64

LAURIE,Arthur Pillans. Pictures and Politics (1934). Scottish youth;Edinburgh and Cambridge universities; his social work in London; reminiscences of Pre-Raphaelite painters; principal of Heriot-Watt College; Liberal politics.   65

LAURIE, David. Reminiscences of a Fiddle Dealer (1924). A Glasgow man's thirty years dealings with great violins; Strads; violinists; travels of a collector.   66

LAURIE, James. Reminiscences of the Town Clerk of Edinburgh, 1808-56; his work;public affairs and personages in Edinburgh. Book of the Old Edinburgh Club, XIV (1925).   67

LAVER, Fred G. Memoirs of a Christian Endeavour Secretary (1900). His social work in London;work for fallen women; Christian Endeavour Movement; influence of Clement Dare. Copy, Bodleian Library.   68

LAVERACK, Alfred. Methodist Soldier in the Indian Army (1885). Sergeant's conversion; religious work in India & in Yorkshire; army life; experiences in Indian Mutiny. Copy,Methodist Book Room.   69

LAVERTY,Maura. Never No More (1942) Life of girl in village near the Bog of Allen; farming and domestic life; romantic and sensitive.   70

LAVERY, Sir John. Life of a Painter (1940). Education;art study; successful career as portrait-painter; exhibitions,sitters, models; Whistler and other contemporary painters.   71

LAWFORD,Stephen (Stephen L. Childs) Youth Uncharted (N. Y. 1935). Work in diplomatic and military affairs, 1914 to 1930;India, Russia, Balkans, Geneva; work for League of Nations; labor and economic problems.   72

LAWLESS, Emily. Garden Diary (1901) Daily work and observations in garden and comments on life in general.   73

/LAWRENCE, Alfred Henry/. Reminiscences of Cambridge Life: by O. C. (L. 1889). University life in 80's;study; the Union; cricket; personalities and university celebrations.   74

LAWRENCE, Dorothy. Sapper Dorothy Lawrence (1919). WW1 experiences of a woman serving with Royal Engineers until her discovery and deportation;her treatment by the men.   75

LAWRENCE, Lieut-General Sir George. Reminiscences of Forty-Three Years in India(1874). His military career from 1821; public and military affairs;the Afghanistan expeditions; Mutiny.   76

LAWRENCE, Gertrude.   A Star Danced (N. Y. 1945). Her career in the theatre; plays, musical comedies, Coward; work in London & New York; France in WW1; her life and loves.   77

LAWRENCE, Maj. Sir Henry Montgomery Some Passages in the Life of an Adventurer (Delhi, 1842); Adventures of an Officer(1845); Adventures in the Punjaub(1846). Experiences in the Punjab as political agent to Prince Runjeet Singh; court life at Lahore; military affairs, public events, and politics; his marriage and love affair.   78

LAWRENCE, Lady Rosamond. Indian Embers (1949). Her life with Sir Henry Lawrence in India; civil service, domestic life, Anglo-Indian society in Sind etc.; Indian leaders; based on a diary.   79

LAWRENCE, Thomas Edward. Revolt in the Desert (1926). His work inspiring and organizing the Arab revolt during WW1;guerilla warfare in the desert; a fine narrative.   80

LAWRENCE, Sir Walter Roper. The India We Served (1928). His administrative work in India; his ideas, ideals and personal life.   81

LAWRENCE, Sgt. William. Autobiography (1886). Military career in infantry; service in S. America and Peninsular War; Waterloo; good account of life of a soldier.   82

LAWRY, Walter. Friendly and Feejee Islands (1850);   A Second Missionary Visit (1851). Work and travels of a missionary in the South Seas, in 1847 and 1850.   83

LAWS, Robert. Reminiscences of Livingstonia (Edin.1934). Religious work at the Livingstone mission in Nyassaland, 1875-1927; negro life.   84

LAWSON,John James. A Man's Life (L. 1932). Working-class life; sailor; in Durham mines;   trade-union work; M.P.

for Chester-le-Street; his Parliamentary career;service in Labour government; undetailed and poor.   85

LAWSON, Sir Wilfrid. A Memoir, ed. G. W. E. Russell (1909). Mostly diary and autobiography, 1856-98; political career as Liberal M.P.; Reform Movement; his work for teetotalism.   86

LAWSON, William. The Life(1917). A Canadian's early life in Cumberland; education and religious life; Primitive Methodism; to 1829. Copy, Harvard U.L.   87

LAX,William H. Lax, His Book (1937) Life and work of a popular Methodist; childhood in Lancs village; ministry in Yorks and Poplar; a jolly view of life of the London poor.   88

LAYARD, Sir Austen Henry. Early Adventures (1887); Autobiography (1903) Childhood; education; career as diplomat in Turkey, Persia, Spain; travels in Near East; archaeological studies and diggings.   89

LAYTON, Dr.Frank George. Behind the Night Bell (1938). Medical studies in London; general practice in the Black Country; sympathetic account of working class life.   90

LAYTON, T. A. Table for Two (1942); Restaurant Roundabout (1944). Education; work as owner of small restaurant in Bloomsbury and reminiscences of his customers; Stephen Gaselee.   91

LAZAROVICH-HREBELIANOVICH, Princess (Eleanor Calhoun). Pleasures and Palaces (N. Y. 1915). Her career in the theatre; marriage; society in London and Paris; social life in the Balkans in later 19th Century.   92

LEACH, Charles E. On Top of the Underworld (1933). Work and adventures of a policeman and detective.   93

LEACH,Col. Jonathan. Rough Sketches (1831);Rambles along the Banks of the Styx (1847). Military career in Rifle Brigade; service in the W. Indies, at Copenhagen, in Peninsular War; Waterloo; army of occupation.   94

LEAF,Walter. Some Chapters of Autobiography (1932). Education at Harrow and Cambridge;work as banker; classical scholarship; mountaineering, botany, psychic research;work for League of Nations; his travels.   95

LEAKEY, Louis Seymour Bazett. White African (1937). Childhood on an African mission station; Cambridge; archaeological exploration in Kenya; work among Kikuyus;anthropological study & research at Cambridge.   96

LEASK, William. Struggles for Life (1854). Religious autobiography; his fearful youth in Edinburgh; ministry as village pastor; theology; sins and self-analysis.   97

LEATHES,Edmund John.An Actor Abroad (1880). An actor's tours in Australia N.Z., USA; adventures and social life on the frontiers.   98

ANON. Leaves from a Lady's Diary(L. 1850). Notes of travel along Barbary coast in 1847-8; scenery; antiquities and travel conditions.   99

ANON. Leaves from the Diary of an Officer of the Guards(1854). Personal narrative of the Peninsular War; battles and campaigns; his own experiences.   100

ANON. Military journal, 1848-1849; lively account of campaign in Punjab; service with the Guards. Leaves from the Journal of a Subaltern, ed.George R. Gleig (Edin. 1849).   101

LE BLOND, Mrs. Aubrey. Day In, Day Out (1928). Victorian youth; amazing travels and adventures of her husband Fred Burnaby; mountaineering, skiing, photography; Switzerland, Morocco and Egypt; lively.   102

/LE BRETON,Anna Letitia Aikin7. Memories of Seventy Years (1883). Life in Hampstead;literary society and literary ladies; Mrs. Aikin, Barbauld & Baillie; Sydney Smith.   103

LE CARON, Maj. Henri (Thomas Miller Beach). Twenty-Five Years in the Secret Service (1892). Military life and espionage from 1865; work among Irish nationalists in Canada and USA.   104

LECKIE, Col.Victor C. Centaur Looks Back (1947). Career in the Veterinary Corps, mostly Lahore and United Provinces.   105

LECKY, Peter. Peter Lecky (L. 1935) Education; agricultural training and art training; ranching in Canada; WW1 service; trading in Australia; journalism for Sunday Times.   106

/LE CONTE, Honore Lazarus7. A Short Account of the Extraordinary Life and Travels (n.d.). Sorry childhood Santo Domingo end 18th Century;education in France; life as sailor; captured and imprisoned in Derbyshire. Copy, Derby P.L.   107

LEE,Arthur S. G. Special Duties (L. 1946).Work of Air Vice-Marshal; military flying; staff work in Turkey and Middle East; politics and war in Near East and Balkans.   108

LEE, Frederic. Manufacturer (1938). Picture of life and work of business man; problems of competition, finance trade-slumps; military service in WW1 and conservative politics.   109

LEE, Harry W.Forty Years of English Cricket (1948). Career and games of a professional cricketer; Middlesex and England; tours to dominions.   110

LEE, Henry. Memoirs of a Manager (Taunton, 1830). Life of a provincial theatre manager from 1780's; Taunton and Barnstaple; difficulties; anecdotes of famous actors.   111

LEE,James S. Underworld of the East (1935).Work as draughtsman and engineer;addiction to drugs; investigation of drug traffic in India, China, Sumatra, Malaya; effects of drugs.   112

LEE, Jennie. Tomorrow is a New Day (1939);This Great Journey (1942). Her childhood in Fifeshire;schools; union work; ILP and Labour Party; career as M.P. for N. Lanark; politics and public affairs between wars; life,values of Scottish mining areas. Single book with two titles.   113

LEE,Sir John Theophilus. Memoirs of the Life and Services (1836). Life as

midshipman in 1790's; Battle of Nile;
later government posts, honors, family life, social events.   114

LEE, Lt. Joseph. Captive at Carls-
ruhe (1920). Personal narrative, WW1;
capture; prison experiences; a lively
account.   115

LEE, Norman. Landlubber's Log (1945)
My Personal Log (1947); Log of a Film
Director (1949). Service as a sailor
in WW2; work as writer, playwright and
scenarist and as film-director; anecdotes of films and actors; experience
as an amateur sailor; poor.   116

LEE, Rachel F. A. Memoirs (1812). A
literary and social career; wrote under name of Baroness Despenser.   117

LEE, Dr. Robert. Extracts from the
Diary(1897). Kept while resident with
Viscount Melbourne, 1821-22; his din-
ner conversations; society, politics,
gossip, anecdotes.   118

LEE, Thomas. Lives of Early Methodist Preachers, ed. Thomas Jackson, II
(1837). Life, religious work, travels
on circuit of a Yorkshire Methodist &
preacher in 18th Century.   119

LEE, William. Journal, 1807-21; his
religious work at independent missions
in Bengal and Orissa; later ministry
at Newmarket. Memoirs, By Henry Lacey
(1825).   120

LEECH, Samuel. Thirty Years from Home
(Boston, 1844). Six years in British
and American navies; twice captured;
cruelties on shipboard; naval engagements; may be American.   121

LEEDS, Francis Godolphin Osborne,
5th Duke of. Political Memoranda (Camden Soc., 1884). Political, Parliamentary and Court activities, 1774-96; &
some social matters.   122

LEEMING, John F. Airdays (1936). Experiences flying light planes around
Manchester.   123

LEESON, B. Lost London (1934). Work
as policeman and detective from 1890;
Whitechapel and East End; Sidney St.
and Jack the Ripper murders.   124

LEESON, Margaret. Memoirs (Dublin,
1797). Reminiscences of society life
and scandals in England and Ireland;
18th Century. Not seen.   125

LE FANU, W. R. Seventy Years of Irish Life(1893). Boyhood in Dublin and
later life in Limerick; Irish social
life and its humours.   126

LEFEVRE, Sir George. Life of a Travelling Physician (1843). His work as
physician to noble families in France
Germany, Russia; high society abroad;
and the poor.   127

LEFROY, Anne (Rickman). Good Company
in Westminster: by Constance Hill (L.
1925). Girl's life in London in early
19th Century; Westminster and Temple;
literary society and friends; Burneys
the Lambs, Hazlitt, etc.; musicians &
painters; very good.   128

LE GALLIENNE, Eva. At 33 (1934). Her
career as actress and producer; childhood; theatrical life and repertory in
London, Paris, New York; Bernhardt and
other great actresses.   129

LE GALLIENNE, Richard. The Romantic
90's(1925). Literary life and friends
Wilde, Stevenson, Meynells; anecdotes
and criticism.   130

LEGGATT, Ashley. Stalking Reminiscences (1921). Experiences deer-stalking at Farley. Cambridge U.L.   131

LEHMANN, Liza (Elisabetha Nina Mary
Frederica Lehmann). The Life (1919).
Career as a musician; piano studies &
concerts; tours; her compositions; and
family and social life.   132

LEHMANN, Rudolph. Artist's Reminisc-
ences(1894). Work as painter; travels
and people he met; painters, musicians
writers; Dickens, Thackeray, Browning
Landseer, etc.   133

LEHMANN, Rudolph C. Memories of Half
a Century(1908). Literary and musical
life in England and abroad; Thackeray
Dickens, Sullivan, etc.   134

LEIFCHILD, John. John Leifchild: by
J. R. Leifchild (1863). Largely autobiography of his nonconformist minis-

try in Kensington, Bristol, Brighton, and London.   135

LEIGH, Sir Edward Chandos. Bar, Bat and Bit (1913). Warwickshire; Harrow and Oxford; work at the Parliamentary Bar and as Recorder of Nottingham;his social work, social life, cricket and hunting; celebrities he knew.   136

LEIGH,James. My Prison House (1941) Walnut Tree (1941). Vivid, thoughtful account of his term in prison;routine discipline, gaolers, prisoners; after care; psychological methods.   137

LEIGH, James Wentworth. Other Days (1921).Oxford studies; travels in USA W.Indies and Near East; his religious career; Dean of Hereford; teetotalism sport.   138

LEIGH,Margaret Mary. Highland Home-spun (1936); Harvest of the Moor (L. 1937); Spade among the Rushes (1949). Novice farmer, cattle-raiser, crofter in Western Ross, Bodmin Moor & Inver-nessshire; country life & work.   139

LEIGH, Medora. History and Autobio-graphy (1869). Her family life & dis-tresses of "Byron's child by his sis-ter"; finance; Lady Byron's tyranny; Miss Leigh's disappointment.   141

LEITCH,Mary & Margaret. Seven Years in Ceylon (1890). Work and travels of medical missionaries in North Ceylon, 1880-6; mostly about Jaffna College & the medical mission.   142

LEITH, W. Compton. Apologia Diffi-dentis (1908). His shyness; attempts to escape into active life & vindica-tion of contemplative life;London and books; mental analysis.   143

LEITH-ROSS, Sylvia.   Cocks in the Dawn(1944). Her experiences in France before and during WW1, between wars, and in WW2;French life, character and reactions to war.   144

LELAND, Lt.Col. F. W. With the M.T. in Mesopotamia(1920). WW1 service in mechanical transport,1916-18; Mesopo-tamian campaign.   145

LEMERLE, F. Franz. Diary, 1887-91; Catholic layman's record of religious experiences and feast days near Madras My Diary (Madras, 1891). India Office Library.   146

LE MESSURIER, Col. Augustus. Diary, 1878-79;military and engineering work with the Quetta column on the Afghan border. Kandahar in 1879 (1880).   147

LENNOX,William Pitt, Lord. Story of My Life (1857); Pictures of Sporting Life(1860); Recreations (1862); Fifty Years' Biographical Memories (1863); Adventures of a Man of Family (1864); Drafts on My Memory (1866); My Recol-lections (1874); Plays, Players, and Playhouses (1881), etc. Untiring gos-sip of man about town; society, army life,politics, theatre, sport, social life; celebrities he knew; court and clubs; England, France, Germany; the Victorian scene.   148

LENO, Dan (George Galvin). Dan Leno Hys Book (1899-1904). His work in the musichalls and theatre;pantomime; re-miniscences of theatrical life; anec-dotes of players; reported.   149

LEONARD, Gladys Osborne. My Life in Two Worlds (1931). Life and work of a medium; psychic experiences.   150

LEONOWENS, Anna Harriette. English Governess at the Siamese Court (1870) Life and Travel in India (1884). Life at Bombay and travels in India; Hindu life and customs; six years at Bang-kok as teacher of English to children of the king; lively detail of Siamese life and customs and court.   151

LE QUEUX,William. Things I Know (L. 1923). His career as a journalist and novelist;clubs and Bohemian life; his travels;acquaintance with celebrities spies, crooks.   152

LESLIE,Col. Military Journal (Aber-deen, 1887). Military career from 1807 Service in Peninsular War; later life in Canada. Bibliothèque St. Sulpice, Montreal.   153

LESLIE, Anita. Train to Nowhere (L. 1948). Flippant narrative of service as ambulance driver in Africa, Italy, and France during WW2.   154

LESLIE, Charles Robert. Autobiographical Recollections(1860). Career as painter; Royal Academy; artistic life in London; anecdotes of his painter & writer friends; Turner, Ruskin, Haydon Willkie, Coleridge, Scott.   155

LESLIE, George Dunlop. Our River (L. 1881). Artist's life on Thames; Hampton Court and Staines; boating; natural history; painting.   156

LESLIE, Henrietta (Gladys Henrietta Schütze). More Ha'pence than Kicks(L. 1943); Harlequin Set(1945); Go as You Please(1946). Life in prosperous Jewish family in London; social life and social controversies; work as journalist and novelist; social work; PEN; & travels in Europe.   157

LESLIE, Robert Charles. A Sea-Painter's Log (1886); Water-Biography (L. 1894). Career as a painter; activities relating to water; painting; sailing; swimming; voyages.   158

LESLIE, Shane. The End of a Chapter (1919); American Wonderland (L. 1936) Film of Memory(1938). Memories of his education at Eton and Cambridge; Ireland and politics; humours of lecture tours in USA: education; life in Latin Quarter and London East End; career as novelist; Irish life.   159

LESLIE, Col. Stephen. Military Journal (Aberdeen, 1887). Military career from 1807; service in Peninsular War; later life in Canada.   160

LESTER, Muriel.   It Occurred to Me (1937). Life of Christian social worker in Bow; schooling; work at Kingsley Hall; poverty, housing, working-class life; visits to USA and India; Gandhi and the untouchables; good.   161

L'ESTRANGE, Sir George B. Recollections (1874). Military service in the infantry; service in Peninsular War; campaigns; and urbane account of personal activities.   162

LETCHER, Owen. Big Game Hunting in North-Eastern Rhodesia (L. 1911). The exploits of a hunter.   163

LETHBRIDGE, Mabel. Fortune Grass (L. 1934); Against the Tide (L.1936). Her life in London; nursing, hospital work

charwoman, down and out, estate agent, struggles with illness; the seamy side of life.   164

LEUPOLT, C. B. Recollections of an Indian Missionary (1846); Further Recollections (1884). His work as a missionary in Benares; Hindu religion and customs.   165

LEVERTON, W. H. Through the Box-Office Window (1932). Fifty years' work at the Haymarket Theatre; anecdotes of actors, playwrights, shows.   166

LEVESON-GOWER, Edward Frederick. Bygone Years (1905). Amiable recollections of Victorian society, politics, diplomacy, legal affairs, literature; anecdotes of Ruskin, Thackeray, Dickens, Lady Holland, etc.   167

LEVESON GOWER, Sir George. Years of Content (L. 1940); Years of Endeavour (1942); Mixed Grill (1947). Northants childhood; Eton and Oxford; London society and clubs; political work with Morley; government; court; anecdotes of the Age of Privilege; good.   168

LEVESON-GOWER, Ronald Charles Sutherland, Lord. My Reminiscences (1883); Old Diaries (1902); Records and Reminiscences (1903). Schools; Cambridge; life at Cliveden; court life and the reign of Victoria; political and diplomatic life and personages; society; travel; Paris in war and peace; last book is a compilation.   169

LEVI, Leone. Story of My Life (1888) Life in England, 1845-55; lecturer on commercial law; professor at University of London; business and political figures.   170

LEVINSON, Maurice. The Trouble With Yesterday(1946). Orphanage and family life; work in furniture factory; unemployment; communism; tough and sordid account of London slum life.   171

LEVY, E. Lawrence. Autobiography of an Athlete (Birmingham, 1913). Weight lifter and gymnast; Olympic Games; his journalism work for Birmingham Daily Times. Birmingham P.L.   172

LEWES, Charles Lee. Memoirs (1805). Actor's anecdotes of English and Scottish stage; provincial theatres; famous players; good dialogue.   173

LEWIN, Lt. Col. Thomas Herbert. Fly on the Wheel (1885). Military, police and administrative service in India, 1857-72.   174

LEWIN, Maj. Thomas Ross. Life of a Soldier (1834). Military service; St. Domingo rebellion;Ireland; Peninsular War; Greece; mostly his campaigns and descriptions of places.   175

LEWIS,Cecil. Sagittarius Rising (L. 1936). An airman's life;combat flying in WW1; civil flying; teaching flying in China; good.   176

LEWIS, Edith Nicholl. (E.N. Ellison) As Youth Sees It (Boston, 1935). Victorian society from 1870; with father at Marlborough School and Oxford; the Eminent Victorians; Tennyson, Arnold, Grove, Lang; sentimental.   177

LEWIS, Edward Broad. A Brief Memoir (1931). A Bristol man's adventures at sea, 1799-1809; merchantmen and privateers during Napoleonic wars; lively account of rough life below decks and work of ship's carpenter. Copy, Bristol Central Library.   178

LEWIS, Frederick. Sixty-Four Years in Ceylon (Colombo, 1926). Boyhood in Ceylon; life on coffee & rubber plantations;work in forestry service; and Singalese life and customs; opinions on government.   179

LEWIS,Georgina King. Autobiographical Sketch(1925). Childhood of London minister's daughter in 50's; mission and temperance work; Quaker education and religion; relief work in Serbian and Boer wars.   180

LEWIS, John. Clergyman's life; his education and study at end of the 17th Century;work as Kentish parson; theological writings; Cambridge life; his friendship with Hickes and other scholars. MS, B.M. Add. 28651.   181

LEWIS, Mathew Gregory. Diary, 1815-1817;excellent details of the life of a planter in Jamaica; negro life and customs; slavery. Journal of a West India Proprietor (1834).   182

LEWIS, Percy Wyndham. Blasting and Bombadiering (1937); Rude Assignment (1950). Service as Bombadier in WW1; painting,writing, artistic controversy; writings and ideas; mental activities; Joyce, Eliot, Pound, John etc. politics and social tendencies; writing and art movements.   183

LEWIS, Rosa. Queen of Cooks (1925). Dictated autobiography of her career; scullery maid to society cook.   184

LEWIS, Thomas. These Seventy Years (1930). Work and life of Baptist missionary in Cameroons and at Kibokolo, Congo, 1883-93; natives and traders; pleasant.   185

LEWIS, William. Memoirs of the Life (Bristol, 1820). Quaker's spiritual autobiography; conversion; his ministry around Bristol;rivalry with Methodists.   186

LEY, Dr. John William. From Youth Onwards (Newton Abbot, n.d.). Devon boyhood; Epsom College; medical study in London and work there; his general practice at Newton Abbot; Devonshire life and sport; pleasant. Copy,Exeter P.L.   187

LIDDELL, Adolphus G. C. Notes from the Life (1911). School; Balliol; Oxford dons and students;career as lawyer and as a civil servant; political and parliamentary affairs;life in society and literary circles; sport and country life; Jowett, Carlyle, Arnold George Eliot,etc.; varied record covering 1846-1906.   188

LIDGETT, J. Scott. Reminiscences(L. 1928); My Guided Life (1936). Boyhood at Blackheath; London University; his Methodist ministry;foundation of Bermondsey Settlement & life work there; LCC alderman; Free Church Council and work for Christian Unity; varied career of influential churchman.   189

LIECK, Albert Henry. Narrow Waters (1935); Bow Street World (1938). His boyhood in Hackney; lower middleclass life; London scene; civil servant and journalist; chief clerk at Bow Street Police Court; forty years in courts & views on magistrates;lawyers, police; a good, thoughtful account.   190

ANON. Life Amongst the Colliers (L. 1862).Society woman's missionary work among colliers at Brentwood;religious and educational work; their customs & superstitions.   191

ANON. Life as I Saw It (1924). Good account of life devoted to social work mostly in London East End; missions & settlements at Wapping,etc.; visitors and preachers; education.   192

ANON. Life in a Lunatic Asylum (L. 1867).Experiences of a husband & wife prison-like life; patients; treatment and routine; temperate account.   193

ANON. "Life of an Architect" (Bentley's Miscellany (1852-54). Education and his training and practice; social artistic, literary life and personalities in London from 1817.   194

LIGHTOILER, Com. Charles H. Titanic and Other Ships (1935). Sailor's career in sailing ships and in the White Star Line; Atlantic service; the loss of the Titanic.   195

LILLEY, Arthur A. Twenty-Four Years of Cricket(1912). Memories of wicketkeeping for Warwick and England, from 1888; games; tours; players.   196

LILLY, William. History of His Life (1715). Life of 17th Century astrologer; studies; consultation by statesmen, aristocracy, scholars; his scholarly controversies; the Civil War; a very lively record.   197

LIMMER, Raymond. Reminiscences of a Year's Captivity (Salisbury, 1919). A personal narrative of WW1 service;his life as prisoner of Turks.   198

LINCOLN, Ignatius Timothy Trebitsch Autobiography of an Adventurer (1931) Hungarian Jew converted to Christianity;mission work in Canada and curacy in Kent; Liberal M.P.; suspected as a spy in WW1;plots and politics; stormy career.   199

LINDGREN,Oscar. Trials of a Planter (Kalimpong, 1933). Work and travel in Assam from 1877; work on tea-plantation and sawmills; making tea-boxes; labour problems. Copy in India Office Library.   200

LINDLEY, Sir Francis O. A Diplomat Off Duty (1928). Mostly sporting diversions in Bulgaria, Norway, and Korea hunting, fishing, natural history.201

LINDSAY, Hector. Jungle Lindsay (L. 1936). Scottish youth; herring fishing; life of high adventures and tall stories in Central Africa;animals and natives; circus life.   202

LINDSAY,James. Autobiography (1924) Spiritual and intellectual development of clergyman, philosopher, theologian and author.   203

LINDSAY, Martin. So Few Got Through (1946); Three Got Through (1947). His WW2 service in Gordon Highlanders; in North African and Normandy campaigns; happenings in the field;memoirs of an arctic explorer.   204

LINDSAY, Patricia. Recollections of a Royal Parish (1902). Queen Victoria and her entourage; Hopewell, Balmoral and the Highlands.   205

LINDSAY, Philip. I'd Live the Same Life Over (1941). Larrikin upbringing in Australia; journalism and publishing in London; Bohemian life in Hampstead.   206

LINDSAY, Robert. Autobiography of a military and trading life in India in early 19th Century;Hyder Ali war. The Lives of the Lindsays,by Lord Alexander Lindsay (1858) III.   207

LINDSAY-BUCKNALL, Hamilton. Search for Fortune (1878). Travel, prospecting, adventure from 60's; Australia, N.Z., S. America.   208

LINDSEY, John (John St. Clair Muriel). Still Eastward Bound (1940). His schools and career as schoolmaster in prep schools;literary career; socialism; beginning of WW2.   209

LINES, Samuel. A Few Incidents in the Life (Birmingham, 1842). Youth on Warwick farm; foundation of Art Academy in Birmingham; its growth and his honours. Birmingham P.L.   210

LINKLATER, Elizabeth. A Child Under Sail (1938). Her childhood in sailing ships with captain-father; travels in

South Seas and S.America; adventurous life of child among seamen.　　211

LINKLATER, Eric. The Man on My Back (1941). Military service, WW1; education and teaching in Scotland; travel in America and Asia; Scottish Nationalist politics;his career as a novelist; lively.　　212

LINNELL, J. E. Old Oak (L. 1932). A Beds. parson's work and life in village of Silson; amusing picture of the villagers and their life.　　213

LINTON,Eliza Lynn. My Literary Life (1899).Career as a novelist; literary life and friendships; Landor, Dickens Thackeray, George Eliot.　　214

LINTON, William James. Memories (L. 1895). Work as an engraver; work for Chartists and social reform; journalism; reminiscences of most of the important Victorian writers, painters, actors, etc.　　215

LION, Leon M.　Surprise of My Life (1948).Effervescent account of career as actor, playwright, manager, producer; anecdotes.　　216

LIPTON, Sir Thomas J.　Leaves from the Lipton Logs (1931).　Glasgow boyhood;trip to USA; grocery business in Glasgow & growth of his tea business; salesmanship; yachting.　　217

LISLE, Mary. Long, Long Ago (1856). Childhood and youth in country vicarage of Mitchelmore;social life; girls and young officers; done in the style of Edgeworth and Austen.　　218

LISSACK, Moses. Jewish Perseverance (1851). Relation of Jews & Christians his life in Poland & Germany; settlement in Bedford.　　219

LISTER,Joseph. Autobiography (Bradford, 1860). Life in Bradford in 17th Century; in the civil wars; defence of Bradford; capture of Leeds.　　220

LISTER, Roma. Reminiscences (1926); Further Reminiscences (1927). Society in England and Italy from 70's; literary and artistic life;　the Italian court;　Arnold and other celebrities; folk-lore and the occult.　　221

LISTER, Stephen. Savoy Grill at One (1939). Mistral Hotel (1940). Work as representative of appliance company in France;advertising; escape into hotel keeping in South of France;hotel business; French life.　　222

LISTOWEL, Judith, Countess of. Our Betters (1941). Society life; reminiscences of royalty and celebrities; Nuffield, Reith, M. Norman etc.　　223

LITHGOW,William.The Total Discourse (1632). Scotsman's extensive travels; European countries, Asia, Africa; and his sufferings from Inquisition;religion, politics, customs.　　224

LITTLE, Archibald.　Gleanings from Fifty Years in China (1910). Life and work of a scholarly merchant at Shanghai; trade, war, politics, 1859-1909; drama, religion, philosophy.　　225

LITTLE, Mrs. Archibald, Diary,1893; details of her life in a farmhouse in the far West of China;domestic, farming and social affairs. My Diary in a Chinese Farm (Tokyo, 1898).　Copy in Cambridge U.L.　　226

LITTLE,Thomas (ed.). Confessions of an Oxonian (1826). A lurid account of student life, drinking, eating, love, at Oxford; fiction?　　227

LITTLEFAIR, Mary. An English Girl's Adventures(1915). Experiences in Germany just before outbreak of WW1;hostility; escape.　　228

LITTLEFIELD, Chief Inspector. Reminiscences (1894). Work as policeman & detective;his cases on two continents smugglers and swindlers.　　229

LIVESEY, Joseph. Life and Teachings (1886). Early poverty;Lancashire weavers and their hardships;his fighting against Corn Laws and Poor Law; temperance; hydropathy; life in the Preston area.　　230

LIVINGSTON, Gen. Guy.　Hot Air in Cold Blood(1933). Military career and Boer War and WW1 service;early interest in flying;　director of air-force organization; USA liaison work.　　231

LIVINGSTONE,David. Missionary Travels (1857); Last Journals (1874). His travels and work as missionary in Central Africa; scientific observations; exploration;lives of natives; slavery and adventures.   232

LIVINGSTONE, John. Select Biographies, ed. W. K. Tweedie (Wodrow Soc. Edin., 1845) I, 127-348. Autobiography of Scottish minister to 1666; his education and ministry; difficulties as a covenanter; exile to Holland; a record for his children.   233

LIVINGSTONE, Patrick. Selections from the Writings (1847). Includes a short autobiography; ministry & hardships of a Scottish Quaker; imprisonment in Aberdeen, 1678.   234

LLEWELLIN,Frederick G. Lighter Side of a Parson's Life (Hereford, n.d.). Prison chaplain; work in a Herefordshire parish; mission work among bargees and miners; 19th Century. Copy, Hereford P.L.   235

LLEWELYN, Michael Gareth (Frederic Evans). Sand in Glass (1943). Village life in South Wales,early part of the century; schools, mines, village ways and people;his education; career as a teacher.   236

LLOYD,Albert Bushnell.In Dwarf Land (1907); A Life's Thrills (1948). Work and travels of a missionary in Uganda anti-slavery activities; development of Uganda; adventures with animals; & Sudanese rebellion.   237

LLOYD, Charles. Particulars of the Life (1812). Academic and religious training;work as General Baptist minister; farming.   238

LLOYD, Charles D. C. Ireland Under the Land League (1892). Life and work of a resident magistrate in Ireland; politics, the Land League, riots, and law in the 80's.   239

LLOYD,Gladys. An Englishwoman's Adventures (1914). Journalist caught in Luxembourg at outbreak of WW1; arrested as spy; released.   240

LLOYD, James. My Circus Life (1925) Career as circus performer and owner; Astley's London amphitheatre in 40's;

touring in British Isles.   241

LLOYD, Llewellyn. Field Sports in the North of Europe (1830); Scandinavian Adventures (1854). Thirty years' residence in Sweden and Norway; Scandinavian life and sport.   242

LLOYD, R. A. Trooper in the "Tins" (1938). A military career; service in the Life Guards.   243

LLOYD, Samuel. Reminiscences (Birmingham, 1913). Education at Wednesbury in 30's; Quaker life and religious practice; work as a manufacturer in Birmingham area; social work, and philanthropy.   244

LLOYD, Major Sir William. Journal, 1821-2; exploration on the North-West Frontier of India; political and historical matters. Narrative of a Journey from Cawnpoor (1840).   245

LLOYD GEORGE, Right Hon. David. War Memoirs (1933-37) 6v. Detailed story of conduct of WW1; military, political,strategic; problems, events, personages, decisions & progress of the great struggle; a vindication of his own activities.   246

LLOYD-JONES, Maj. William. Havash! (1925). Military service in Kenya;patrols, settlers, natives, and hunting from 1910.   247

LOCK, Major H. O. With the British Army (1919). Military service in WW1; the Palestine campaign; mostly historical and impersonal.   248

LOCK,Walter. Oxford Memories (1932) His career at Keble 1870-1920;professor of Divinity; ecclesiastical, academic, scholarly memories; Newman and Church.   249

LOCKE, James. Tweed and Don (Edin. 1860). Recollections of trout fishing in Scotland and North.   250

LOCKER, Arthur. Village Surgeon (L. 1874-5). Life and work of a physician in the 60's;patients; local affairs, may be fiction.   251

LOCKER-LAMPSON, Frederick. My Confidences (1896). Family life in 30's;

social and domestic scene; work as a clerk of the Treasury;his poems; literary interests and friends;anecdotes of Dickens, Thackeray, Eliot, Landor, Brownings, etc.; lively and personal picture of Victorian scene. 252

LOCKER-LAMFSON, Godfrey T. L. Life in the Country (1948). Nostalgic memories of vanished country house life; country estates, society, sports, and natural history; the decay of country and English virtues. 253

LOCKERBY, William. Journal (1925). Narrative of the adventures of sandalwood trader in the Fijis,beginning of 19th Century; trading success; cannibals and his relation with them. 254

LOCKHART,Robert Hamilton Bruce. Memoirs of a British Agent (1932); Retreat from Glory (1934); My Scottish Youth (1937). Life in Malaya; political agent in Russia in WW1;adventures in Russian revolution; with legations in Poland and Czecho-Slovakia; school and boyhood in Fifeshire; historical and romantic background; good. 255

LOCKHART, William. The Medical Missionary in China (1861). A somewhat impersonal account of work of medical missionary based on twenty years work in China; siege of Shanghai. 256

LOCKLEY, Ronald M. Dream Island (L. 1930); Island Days (1934); I Know an Island (L.1938); The Way to an Island (1941); Dream Island Days (1943); The Golden Year (1948). Life at Skokholm off Pembroke coast;goatherding, fishing,natural history; romantic idyllic life; earlier years in Cardiff & Monmouth; life on Welsh farm; nature and literature; pleasant. 257

LOCKWOOD, Edward. The Early Days of Marlborough College(1893). Schooldays there; teaching at Haileybury; & life at Patna; Indian scene. 258

LOCKWOOD, Mrs. Josiah. An Ordinary Life (1932). Daughter of naval doctor in Devonport; art study; marriage to Yorkshire manufacturer; work in Suffragette and Pacifist movements; dull but useful. 259

LODGE, Eleanor C. Terms and Vaca-

tions (1938). Her studies, teaching & scholarship;Lady Margaret Hall; Westfield College; good. 260

LODGE,Sir Oliver Joseph. Past Years (1931); Advancing Science (1932). His career as a physicist; British Association and progress of science; education and teaching at Universities of London, Liverpool, Birmingham; famous scientists and discoveries; experiences in psychic research. 261

LOFFT,Capell. Autobiography, Monthly Mirror (June, 1802). Eton and Cambridge; law studies; work for constitutional reforms; estate in Suffolk; interest in abolution of slavery;18th Century humanitarianism. 262

LOFFT,Capell. Self-Formation (1837) Eton and Cambridge; mental and moral development;struggles with temptation of gambling and idleness; his religious convictions. 263

LOFTUS,Augustus W. F. Spencer, Lord Diplomatic Reminiscences(1892). Early life, Brighton; diplomacy in Germany, Turkey, Austria, Russia; the history of Europe from 1837 and his part; society; celebrities; peoples. 264

LOFTUS, Major Charles. My Youth by Sea and Land (1875); My Life (1877). Service in Navy and Coldstream Guards; garrison service; life in navy; social,sport, adventures and gallantries; service in Peninsular War;with Guards at Waterloo; good. 265

LOGAN,William Barnett. Dress of the Day (1930). Medical student interrupted by war; naval service in destroyers and battleships in WW1;indictment of war. 266

LOGIN, Lady E. Dalhousie. Lady Login's Recollections (L. 1916).Memories of army, society, and court life from 1820 to 1904; Scottish youth; India & the Mutiny;life at Indian courts with physician husband; Court of St.James; retirement to Kent. 267

LOMAS, George. Autobiography, Methodist Magazine (July, 1811). His work as calico printer in Manchester, from 1776; Methodist life and observances; God's providences. 268

LOMAS, Robert. Autobiography, Methodist Magazine (1811). His business
in Manchester and London; conversion;
Methodist ministry, Manchester.   269

LONDONDERRY, Charles Stewart Henry
Vane-Tempest-Stewart, 7th Marquis of.
Wings of Destiny (1943). Work in Air
Ministry, 1918-1935; expansion of air
force;Versailles Treaty; politics and
defence; firm self-justification. 270

LONDONDERRY,Edith Helen Vane-Tempest
Stewart, Marchioness of.   Retrospect
(1938). Childhood; court and society;
life in Ulster;with husband in India,
women's work in WW1; politics, society, celebrities.   271

LONERGAN, Walter F. Forty Years of
Paris (1907). Experience of an author
and journalist; chief events; celebrities in literature, society, church,
politics, theatre.   272

LONG, G. T. The Handy Man (1901?).
Surrey man's twenty years in the navy
from boy to chief petty officer; master at arms. Croydon P.L.   273

LONG,Gabrielle Margaret Vere (Campbell; "Marjorie Bowen").   The Debate
Continues,by Margaret Campbell (1939)
Childhood,education, marriage, domestic life,travels and career as novelist and author.   274

LONG, P. Walter. Other Ranks of Kut
(1938). Sergeant in R.A.F.; WW1 service; capture at Kut; experiences in
Turkish prison.   275

LONG,Veritas. Confessional Autobiography (187?). Son of a clergyman in
Wales; longing to become priest; confession of teaching Catholicism in the
schools; return to Anglicanism. Copy
Cambridge U.L.   276

LONG OF WRAXALL, Walter Hume Long,
Viscount. Memories (1923). Career as
Conservative M.P. from 1878; the Home
Rule struggle; work in cabinet as 1st
Lord of Admiralty; activities in WW1;
politics and public affairs.   277

LONGBOTTOM, Eva H. Silver Bells of
Memory (1933). Blind musician; childhood in Liverpool and Bristol; training as singer; her poetry and stories

and work as teacher.   278

LONGDEN,Henry. The Life (1846). His
life as an apprentice; his conversion
to Methodism; ministry in Yorkshire;
18th Century; pleasant.   279

LONGHURST, Henry. It Was Good While
It Lasted(1941);I Wouldn't Have Missed
It (L. 1945).Journalist on Sunday Express and Daily Express in good old
days of 20's and 30's, social, sport,
schools; military service in WW2; his
political work as M.P. for Acton from
1943.   280

LONGMORE, Sir Arthur.   From Sea to
Sky (1947). Naval career; WW1 service
at Jutland and in anti-submarine work;
development of air power; RAF College
and Imperial Defence College;with RAF
in Middle East in WW2.   281

LONSDALE,Sir John Lowther, 1st Lord
Memoir of the Reign of James II (York
1808); continuation in, English Hist.
Rev. XXX(1915). Two narratives relating what happened to him in political
and court life, 1688-99.   282

LONSDALE,Lady Sophia. Recollections
(1936). Schools, family, social life,
theatres, religion, from 50's; Newman
and Ainger; clerical life; her church
and social work; local government and
poor law; family life.   283

LORD, William R.   Real Life at Sea
(Glasgow, 1896). Life and adventures
of a sea-captain;voyages in many seas
and adventures in shipwreck, smuggling, etc. Copy, Bibliothèque St. Sulpice, Montreal.   284

LORENZ, Adolf. My Life and Work (L.
1936). Boyhood in Silesia; pioneer in
orthopoedic surgery; his struggle and
success in England; hobbies, domestic
life,troubles, philosophy; modest and
interesting.   285

LORRAIN,Reginald Arthur. Five Years
in Unknown Jungles (1913). Missionary
work among the Lakhers in Further India;linguistic work; anthropology and
folklore in Assam.   286

LORT-PHILLIPS, Frederick (Frederick
Gillett). Wander Years (1931). Travel
and big-game hunting in Africa, Asia,

Canada, Europe; adventures.   287

LOUTHE, John. Narratives of the Reformation (Camden Soc., 1859). Anecdotes of his religious experience and
persecution, addressed to James Foxe,
in 1579, as Archdeacon of Nottingham's
protestant witness.   288

LOVAT, Simon Fraser, Lord. Memoirs
of the Life (1902). Sufferings of the
17th Century Jacobite at hands of the
Athol family;life at the court of St.
Germains in exile;translated, from the
French edition of 1747.   289

LOVE, David. Life, Adventures, and
Experience (Nottingham, 1823). Scottish boyhood; itinerant ballad poet;
his poems; life in and out of prison
and workhouses; interesting. Nottingham P.L.   290

LOVE, William. Autobiography (Paisley, 1857). Humorous account of travels, love adventures, and observation
of a roving Scotsman. Copy, Harvard
U.L.   291

LOVELL, Adm. William Stanhope. Personal Narrative (1879). Naval career;
service in Mediterranean and the West
Indies; engagements at Trafalgar; and
in war of 1812.   292

LOVERIDGE, Arthur. Many Happy Days
I've Squandered (1949). His life as a
naturalist from boyhood; his passion
for animals & insects; Curator at the
Nairobi Museum and game warden in Tanganyika; military service in East Africa in WW1; good.   293

LOVETT, William. Life and Struggles
(1876). His youth; working-class life
and unemployment; journalism; propaganda for Chartists and London Working
Men's Association; leader of moderate
Chartists; valuable record of working
class politics.   294

LOWDER, Charles Fuge. Ten Years in
St. George's Mission (1867). Clergyman's mission work in London East End
working-classes,religion, conditions;
a devoted life.   295

LOWE, Charles. Tale of a Times Correspondent (1927). Edinburgh University; law study; European travel; cov-

ering politics and public events, and
wars from 1878; Germany, Russia, Near
East, etc.   296

LOWELL, Joan. Child of the Deep (L.
1929). Childhood on sailing ships in
South Seas and Australian waters; unusual happenings.   297

LOWELLIN, David. Life, Voyages, and
Travels (1792). Robinson-Crusoe-like
account of his experiences,1770-1784,
while marooned on the Slave Coast of
Central Africa.   298

LOWNDES, Marie Adelaide (Belloc). I
Too, Have Lived in Arcadia (L. 1941);
Where Love and Friendship Dwelt(1943)
The Merry Wives of Westminster(1946);
The Passing World (1948). Early life
in France; people who influenced her;
Zola,Anatole France; her marriage and
life in Westminster; literary and political friends;her writing; vanished
society and social life; WW1, and its
effects; a charming record.   299

LOWRY, Captain Gerald. From Mons to
1933 (1933); Helping Hands (1935). A
blinded soldier's recollection of his
service in WW1; hospital experiences;
rehabilitation;his later career as an
osteopath.   300

LOWTHER, Sir Henry Cecil. From Pil-
lar to Post (1911). Ranching in U.S.A.
lion-hunting in Africa;his service in
the Scots Guards in Boer War;military
attaché in Morocco and Paris.   301

LUARD, G. D. Fishing Fortunes and
Misfortunes (1942). Trout and salmon
fishing from boyhood, mostly Ireland,
before and after WW1.   302

LUBBOCK, Alfred. Memories of Eton
(1899).Ten years as student from 1854
and ten years cricket with I Zingari;
study, sport, masters, boys.   303

LUBBOCK, Percy. Earlham (1922); and
Shades of Eton(1929). Childhood holidays on a Norfolk estate; Eton thirty
years before; Warre, Cornish, masters
boys, and sports.   304

LUBBOCK,Lady Sybil. A Page from the
Past (1936); The Child in the Crystal
(1939).Her childhood; marriage to the
Earl of Desart(co-author of the first

book); London society & Irish country
life; her father and his public work;
childhood, education, society, court;
London and Ireland in 70-80's.　　305

LUCAS,Edward Verrall. Reading, Writing and Remembering (1932); Old Contemporaries (1935). Career as writer;
Punch;literary friendships and social
life; family and early influences and
life in Sussex.　　　　　　　　306

LUCAS,Margaret. Account of the Convincement (1797). Conversion; Quaker
spiritual life;sufferings; Manchester
and Staffs. early 18th Century.　　307

LUCAS, Netley.　Autobiography of a
Crook (1925); My Selves:by Netley Lucas and Evelyn Graham(1933). Criminal
youth;crime and prison; schizophrenic
life; drugs and sex; work as journalist; life in Borstal and gaol.　　308

/LUCATT, Edward/.Rovings in the Pacific (1851). Experiences of resident
trader at Tahiti, 1837-49; business &
adventures; native life; travels; and
visit to California.　　　　　　309

LUCKMAN,A.Dick. Sharps, Flats, Gamblers and Racehorses (1914). Sporting
journalist for Daily Express; theatre
sport, newspaper worlds; travel; good
humored reminiscences.　　　　310

LUCY, Sir Henry. Sixty Years in the
Wilderness (L.1909-16) 3v; Diary of a
Journalist (1922). Work for the News,
Observer & Punch;　Parliament, public
affairs,politics; eminent writers and
artists, explorers, celebrities; the
Punch authors; largely anecdotes.　He
also wrote numerous parliamentary diaries of an impersonal kind.　　311

LUCY, John Frederick. There's a Devil in the Drum (1938).　Army life in
Ulster; WW1 service in France in the
early days.　　　　　　　　312

LUDLOW, Edmund. The Memoirs (Oxford
1894). Military and political activities in 1625-72 and history of times;
general in Commonwealth army; service
in Wales and Ireland;adventures after
the Restoration.　　　　　　313

LUDOVICI, Anthony. Artist's Life in
London and Paris (1926). Study in Pa-

ris;work as painter; art and fashions
in art from 70's; Whistler, Rodin, H.
James, and others.　　　　　314

LUFF, William. Autobiography (Good-
mayes, 1930). Bible teacher in London
and missionary work among the poor in
Home Counties; family life; religious
poems.　　　　　　　　　315

LUKE, Sir Harry Charles Joseph.　An
Eastern Chequer-Board (L. 1934); More
Moves on an Eastern Chequer-Board (L.
1935); From a South Seas Diary (1946)
His administrative work in Mediterranean and Pacific; Levant; Governor of
Malta and of the Fijis;administration
politics, history, official and private social life; natives; and the local scenes; mélange.　　　　316

LUKE,Jemima. Early Years of My Life
(1900). Life in Brixton in early 19th
Century;general conditions and public
events;Victoria's coronation; mission
work; religious life. Bodleian.　317

LUMFORD, Richard.　My Father's Son
(1949). Psychological history; eccentric father and neurotic mother;　his
troubled youth in South-West counties
Ireland and France;　schools; Oxford;
welfare work, journalism, and service
in RAF as pilot; metaphysics and aesthetics; well-written.　　　318

LUMLEY, Benjamin.　Reminiscences of
the Opera(1864).Work at His Majesty's
Theatre from 1842; direction of opera
& notes on musical life, singers, and
professional matters.　　　319

LUMSDEN, Dame Louisa Innes.　Yellow
Leaves (Edin. 1933).　Scottish childhood; religious life; study at Girton
later teaching there;work as Mistress
of Girton; travels.　　　　320

LUMSDEN, Lt.Thomas. Diary, 1819-20;
journey overland from Meerut to London
via Persia, Arabia, Armenia; sights &
adventures. A Journey from Meerut (L.
1822).　　　　　　　　　321

LUNDIE,George Archibald. Missionary
Life in Samoa (Edin. 1846).　His work
with the London Missionary Soc., 1840
to 1841;　native life and ways; evangelism and revivals; his health;　extracts from diary.　　　　322

LUNN, Arnold. Now I See (1933); Come What May (1940); And the Floods Came (1942); Mountain Jubilee(1943); Mountains of Memory (1948). Conversion to Catholicism;Ronald Knox and his other teachers; work for Catholicism; pioneer work in ski-ing, touring, climbing; climbs; mystical love for Alpine life and mountains; WW2 and Catholic views of war;a blend of mysticism and religion with sport and business. 323

LUNN, Sir Henry Simpson. Chapters from My Life (1918); Nearing Harbour (1934). Career as Wesleyan minister & Liberal politician; work for Reunion; development of travel clubs and tourist movement.   324

LUPINO, Stanley. From the Stocks to the Stars (1934). Comedian's career; clown, revues, musical comedy, Hollywood; his family.   325

LURTING,Thomas. The Fighting Sailor (1711). Quaker life, 1646-66; in navy with Blake; warfare and naval adventures; conversion; and militant Quaker pacifism; a lively and unusual spiritual autobiography.   326

LUSHINGTON, Franklin. Portrait of a Young Man (1940).Youth in Ireland and England before WW1.   327

LUSHINGTON, R. F. Prisoner with the Turks (Bedford, 1923). A narrative of military service, WW1; capture & prison and hospital life in Taurus; escape; lively story.   328

LUTTON, Anne. Memorials of a Consecrated Life (1882). Youth in vicarage in County Down; schools; social life; reading and writing;conversion to Methodism; entertaining picture of early 19th Century life.   329

LUTTRELL,Claude. Sporting Recollections (1925). Hunting and fishing in Oxon, Somerset, Leicester; & Yeomanry service in England, WW1.   330

LUTY, Mary. Penniless Globe Trotter (Accrington, 1937). Youth on a farm; Lancs factory work; travels in Canada Australia & New Zealand, working as a maid. Manchester P.L.   331

LYALL, J. G.   Round Goes the World

(Stamford, 1947). Lincs horsebreeder; horses,hunting, racing in England and USA before WW1; his deals.   332

LYBURN, Dr. E. F. St. John. Fighting Doctor (Dublin, 1949). Careers as a boxer and a doctor; his fights; his practice; medical reforms; colleagues described under fictitious names. 333

LYDALL,Edward. Enough of Action (L. 1949). Lighthearted reminiscences;his education at Marlborough, Cambridge & in Germany and Austria; work as Civil Servant in Assam and Afghanistan; administration in Manipur; amusing. 334

LYDE,Richard. Narrative of the Life (1731). Hereford man's religious life and adventures in 17th Century;family life; civil wars; attempts to convert French merchants. Hereford P.L.   335

LYELL, Denis D. Memories of an African Hunter (1923). Early work as a tea-planter in Assam;big-game hunting in Central Africa; natural history; & adventures.   336

LYNCH, Arthur. My Life Story (1924) Australian childhood;fighting in Boer War on Boer side; journalism; politics in Ireland; M.P., West Clare.   337

/LYNCH, Hannah7. Autobiography of a Child (Edin. 1899). Irish childhood; family troubles; girlhood in English convent; misery and revolt; return to Ireland about 1870.   338

LYNCH, Patricia.   A Storyteller's Childhood (1947). Childhood in Bantry Bay, Cork, London; eccentric family; delighted life on small farm; convent schools; charming to excess.   339

LYNCH, Theodora Elizabeth. Story of My Girlhood (1857). Sentimental story of her family life in country;sisters and nurse; heart affairs.   340

LYNCH, Thomas Toke. Memoirs (1874). Life and work of a nonconformist parson and writer.   341

LYNE, Admiral Sir Thomas J.S. Something About a Sailor (1939).Career in navy from sailor boy to admiral; Boer War, China Station, WW1; adventures & events from the eighties.   342

LYNN, Andrew. Methodist Records (L. 1858). Methodist ministry in Northumberland and the North; local life and customs; his personal religious life; travels in ministry.   343

LYON, Capt. George Francis. A Narrative of Travels in Northern Africa (1821); Private Journal (1824); Journal of a Residence and Tour (1828). A naval officer's travels and observations; North Central Africa; Parry's voyage of discovery on the Hecla; and travels in Mexico in 1828.   344

LYSAGHT, S. R. My Tower in Desmond (1925).Country life in Ireland; Irish nationalism and politics;his literary interests.   345

LYSONS, Sir Daniel. Early Reminiscences (L.1896). School; life in Bath; travel and social life; soldiering in Canada,West Indies, Crimea; sport and society.   346

LYTTELTON,George Lyttelton, 1st Baron. A Modest Apology (1748). Patriotic,partisan, political activities in early 18th Century. Harvard.   347

LYTTLETON, Rev.Edward. Memories and Hopes (1925). Eton and Cambridge; his work as teacher at Eton and Haileybury and as country parson; his literary & musical recollections.   348

LYTTLETON, Gen. Sir Neville. Eighty Years' Soldiering(1927). His military career up to the Boer War;Ireland and South Africa; War Office; political & public activities; sports.   349

LYTTON, Lady Constance, and WARTON, Jane. Prisons and Prisoners (1914). A lively story of agitation for women's suffrage; periods in various prisons; hunger strikes; success of movement ; Jane Warton is Lady Lytton's assumed name.   350

LYTTON, Sir Henry A. The Secrets of a Savoyard (1920); Wandering Minstrel (1933). His early days & his friends; mostly his career,roles, tours in the Gilbert and Sullivan operas.   351

LYTTON,Neville Stephen. Life in Unoccupied France (1942). Flight before German invasion in WW2; life and work

as painter in Lyons;first hand observation of life in France.   352

LYTTON,Lady Rosina. Life; by Louisa Devey (1887). Contains partial autobiography; life of Bulwer-Lytton's unfortunate wife.   353

LYTTON,Victor A.G. R. Bulwer-Lytton 2nd Earl of. Pundits and Elephants(L. 1942).Administration, public and personal life of the Governor of Bengal, from 1921; Indian politics, nationalism, terrorism; travel; sport.   354

M., I. E. Confessions of an Etonian (1846). At Eton under Keate; ordination and country parish; wandering in France and Alps;retirement to a Trappist monastery.   1

M. M. M. A Highland Conscript(1912) His thirty-four years'service in army in India and Burma;details of life in the ranks.   2

M. R. C. S. Confessions of a Hypochondriac (1849). Early troubles; retirement with inheritance; travel and discontents; search for health; spas, cures, doctors; fiction?   3

McALMON, Robert. Being Geniuses Together(1938). His literary career and literary world of 20's;the chief writers of the time.   4

McALPINE, John. Genuine Narratives (1788). Scotsman's adventures in 70's emigration to America; experiences in Canada and Nova Scotia.   5

MACARA,Sir Charles W. Recollections (1921). Career of cotton spinner; his experiences with labour-employer relations, strikes,free trade, National Health Act,international conferences; work for Lifeboat Association.   6

MACARTNEY, Lady Catherine Theodora. An English Lady in Chinese Turkestan (1931). Life of consul's wife, 1900-1912;family, friends, and social life in Kashgar; 1912 Revolution.   7

MACARTNEY, George, Earl of. Diary,

1793-94; experiences in first embassy
to China; detailed account of Chinese
life, court, and entertainments. Our
First Ambassador to China, by Helen H.
Robbins (1908).   8

MACARTNEY, Wilfred F. R. Walls Have
Mouths (1936); Zigzag (1937). His ten
years in prison as communist spy; the
penal system at Parkhurst; boyhood in
Malta; life of adventure; WW1 service
in Mediterranean.   9

MACAULAY, Zachary. Diary, 1793-99;
a very interesting account of his work
as governor of Sierra Leone and of his
efforts to suppress slave-trade. Life
and Letters, edited by Lady Knutsford
(1900).   10

MacBRIDE, Maud Gonne. Servant of the
Queen (1938). Social work in Donegal;
work for independent Ireland; National
League; Home Rule; literature.   11

McCABE, Joseph.   Twelve Years in a
Monastery (1907). Novitiate; student;
work as priest; Louvain; ministry in
London; critical, rationalistic record
of apostate monk.   12

McCALMONT, General Sir Hugh. Memoirs
(1924). Military career and campaigns
1865-1902; Red River; Ashanti; China;
Turkey; S. Africa; Egypt.   13

McCARTHY, Edward T. Incidents in the
Life (1918); Further Incidents (1920)
Career of mining engineer; training in
England; work in USA, S.America, Afr-
ica, Asia.   14

MacCARTHY, Justin. Reminiscences (L.
1899); Story of an Irishman (L. 1904);
Irish Recollections (1911). Life and
work of Irish journalist-politician in
England and Ireland; work for Morning
Star; M.P. for Longford; Parliament &
Irish Members; social life, literature
and friends.   15

McCARTHY, Lillah (Lady Keeble).   My
Monte Carlo Indiscretions (1930); Myself and My Friends (1933). Pleasures
of a widow of means; her career in the
theatre from 1895; poetical and artistic drama; Shakespeare, Masefield and
Drinkwater; Poel; Shaw.   16

MacCARTHY, Mary. Nineteenth Century

Childhood (1924). Family life in 80's
and 90's; religion, music, literature
and romance; H.James, O. Browning, C.
Shorter, etc.; a nostalgic picture of
life at Eton.   17

M'CLELLAND, James. Diary, 1875-1876;
travels in Egypt and India; Calcutta;
Madras; descriptions. Journal of a Visit to India (Glasgow, 1877).   18

McCLURE, Herbert R. Land-Travel and
Seafaring (1924). Naval cadet in the
Far East; work as resident commissioner in Ellice and Gilbert Islands, and
as administrator in Kenya; native life
light and humorous.   19

MacCOLL, Rene. Flying Start (1939).
Schooling; stage and secretarial work
reporter for Baltimore Sun; odd jobs;
concentrated on his career in flying;
journalism.   20

MacCORMAC, William. Notes and Recollections (1871). Surgeon's work for
Red Cross in Franco-Prussian War; his
ambulance and hospital work in field;
Sedan.   21

MacCORMICK, Robert. Voyages of Discovery (1884). Appended autobiography
of career of naval surgeon; exploration in Arctic and Antarctic.   22

McCOSH, James. Life, ed. W.M. Sloane
(Edin.1897) Scottish childhood; Edinburgh University; ministry in Arbroath
and his later career as professor of
psychology at Princeton.   23

McCRACKEN, R. F.   Earnest Playgoer
(1933). Over fifty years' experience
of London stage and musichalls; serious views of plays and players.   24

McCRAITH, Sir Douglas.   By Dancing
Streams (L.1929); Dancing Streams in
Many Lands (Nottingham, 1946). Lawyer
fishing and sport at home and abroad;
country pleasures from 90's.   25

McCUBBIN, Louis. I Licked the Plat-
ter Clean: by Kelman D. Frost (1947).
McCubbin's lurid adventures as part-
ner to American gambler in S. Africa;
Boer War; hotel porter in USA.   26

McCUDDEN, Maj. James Thomas Byford.
Five Years in the Royal Flying Corps

(1919). Training, patrol work, combat work in France in WW1.   27

McCULLAGH, Francis. Prisoner of the Reds (1921). With Koltchak in retreat through Siberia; military adventures; capture by Bolsheviks; release.   28

McCURE, John Bunyan. Life in England and Australia (1876). Travel and work of clergyman during 40 years.   29

MacDIARMID,Hugh (Christopher Murray Grieve). Lucky Poet(1943). A rambling account of his literary and political career;ideas; his troubles; Germanism and Scottish nationalism;the problems of poetry.   30

MacDONALD OF THE ISLES, Lady Alice Edith. All the Days of My Life (1929) Childhood & family and social life at Kinfauns; marriage and family life in East Riding;life in the Isles; changing social customs; pleasant.   31

MACDONALD, Colin. Highland Memories (1949). His life in the mountains and islands of Scotland; in form of diary and stories.   32

MACDONALD, Capt. David. A Narrative of the Early Life (Weymouth, 1840). A cadet's military service in India,Java and Malaya; Raffles; later work as officer in Indian Navy,1799-1841; imperial affairs.   33

MACDONALD, David.   Twenty Years in Tibet (Philadelphia,1932). Experience of a trade agent of mixed blood in Tibet. Harvard U.L.   34

MacDONALD,Frederic W. Reminiscences of My Early Ministry(1912); As a Tale that is Told (1919). Methodist family life;ministry in Lancs, Potteries and London; Methodist administration and teaching;work in Leeds; his study and work for the poor.   35

MacDONALD, Greville. Reminiscences of a Specialist (1932). Medical study at King's College Hospital; assistant to Lister; work as throat specialist; Ruskin; friends.   36

MacDONALD, Sir J. H. A. Fifty Years of It (1909); Life Jottings (1915). A career in the law in Edinburgh as Lord

Chief Justice Clerk; legal scene; and Edinburgh religious and social affairs from the forties.   37

MacDONALD, Maj. James Ronald Leslie Soldiering and Surveying (1897). Work as army engineer;railway surveys from Mombasa to Victoria Nyanza in nineties Uganda Protectorate and its establishment.   38

MacDONALD,John. Life: by William K. Tweedie (Edin. 1849). Contains diary of missionary work in Calcutta in the period 1825 to 1847.   39

MacDONALD,John. Travels (1790), reprinted as, Memoirs of an Eighteenth Century Footman (1927). Childhood in Highlands; work as postilion, groom & valet with various masters; travel in England,India, Africa, Europe; adventures a-la-Sterne.   40

MacDONALD, M. Under the French Flag (1917). Simple narrative of a British soldier's service in the French army; WW1 experiences.   41

MacDONALD,Mina. Some Experiences in Hungary (1916). Personal narrative of adventures in enemy territory, during first months of WW1.   42

MacDONALD, Robert. Personal Narrative of Military Travel and Adventure (Edin.1859). Poverty in Highlands and London; enlistment; service in Rifle Brigade;work with Persian and Turkish armies and politics in East in 30's & 40's; humble record.   43

MacDONALD, Violet M.   Up the Attic Stairs (1933). Pleasant story of her childhood and schooldays in Switzerland.   44

McDONALD, Walter. Reminiscences of a Maynooth Professor (1925).Education and teaching at Maynooth; philosophy; educational reforms; Irish politics & Catholicism.   45

MacDONALD,Yvonne. Red Tape Notwithstanding (1941). WW2 service with the transport in Paris; invasion & escape via Bordeaux; red tape.   46

MacDONELL,Lady Anne. Reminiscences of Diplomatic Life(1913). Her childhood in Argentina;marriage; diplomatic and society life in Spain, Germany, Italy Brazil, Denmark, Portugal.   47

M'DONELL, Colonel John. Spanish John (Edin. 1931). Lively adventures of a Jacobite after Culloden; service with King of Spain.   48

McDONNELL, Ranald. And Nothing Long (1938). Victorian childhood;the Wilde set;work on tea estate in Ceylon; his work as vice-consul in Baku; services as courier in Armenia in WW1.   49

McDOUGALL, Harriette. Sketches of Our Life(1882). Missionary work among Dyaks in Sarawak in 50's; educational and civilising work.   50

MacDOUGALL, Sylvia. Let's Light the Candles, by "Paul Waineman" (1944). A childhood in Finland; Russian travels and friendship of Russian royal family; her first book and beginnings of literary career; adventures.   51

/MacDUFF, John Ross7. Reminiscences of a Long Life (1896). Scottish youth Edinburgh University; his ministry in Glasgow;retirement to Kent; poems and books on religion.   52

McEVOY,Patrick A. The Gorse and the Briar(1938). Tramp-writer's life with gypsies in the west country.   53

MacFARLANE, Charles. Reminiscences of a Literary Life (1917). His literary career in first half of 19th Century; artistic and literary society; Scott, Coleridge, De Quincey, Shelley Keats, etc.   54

MacFARLANE,Samuel. Among the Cannibals of New Guinea (1888). Work with London Missionary Society;New Guinea; Chalmers; adventures.   55

McFARREN, Walter. Memories (1905). Chorister at Westminster; student and a professor at R.A.M.; work in choral music;his concerts and tours; musical life in Victorian era.   56

McFEELY, Joseph Daniel. Recollections (1931). Childhood;education and medical study;practice in Ireland and Liverpool;reflections and opinions on medicine. Cambridge U.L.   57

MacFIE,John William Scott. An Ethiopian Diary (Liverpool, 1936). Record of his service with British Ambulance unit in Abyssinian War, 1935-6.   58

M'GAURAN, Major Edward. The Memoirs (1786). Military career; ensign with Austrian infantry;cadet with the East India Co.; service with British army in American Revolution;adventures and amorous intrigues; Irishman.   59

MacGILL, Patrick. Children of the Dead End (1914). Childhood; hand-to-mouth struggles in Irish countryside; poverty and hunger.   60

MacGILLIVRAY, George John. Through the East to Rome (1931). Training in Free Kirk;missionary work in the Near East;mystical studies; spiritual life and conversion to Catholicism.   61

MacGILLIVRAY, William. Memories of My Early Days (1912). Youth in Scotland;reminiscences of old customs and people.   62

McGILVARY, Daniel. Half a Century (1912). Autobiography of his life in East; the Siamese and Lao.   63

McGOVAN,James. Brought to Bay(Edin. 1903); Hunted Down (1903); Invisible Pickpocket (1922). Stories of crime & detection in Scotland by an Edinburgh policeman and detective.   64

McGOVERN,John Terence.It Paid to be Tough (1939). Travels, varied jobs in USA, S. America, South Seas & Canada; hobo,animal trainer; with IRA in Dublin; rum-running in USA.   65

MacGREGOR, Alasdair Alpin. Vanished Waters (1936); Auld Reekie (L. 1943); Turbulent Years(1945). His boyhood in western Highlands and in Edinburgh in early century; family, neighbours and friends; lively record of social life and manners in Scotland.   66

MacGREGOR,Major-Gen. Sir Charles M. Diary, 1879-80; military affairs; his work as chief of staff in Afghan War. Life and Opinions (Edin. 1888).   67

McGRIGOR, Sir James. Autobiography and Services (1861). His career as an army surgeon and director of the army medical department; Netherlands,India and Peninsular War; a good account of medical conditions in war. 68

McGUFFIE, Duncan. Spring Onions (L. 1942). Life and work of a progressive market-gardener in the Vale of Evesham; his opinions. 69

MacGUINNESS,Charles John. Nomad (L. 1934). Adventurous life; pearl fisher in South Seas; service in Navy; IRA; with Byrd's Antarctic expedition. 70

McHARDIE,Douglas. On the Run (1936) Travels and adventures of a tough guy in America,Canada, Asia; cowboy, miner,gunrunner, sailor, barkeeper, spy; raucous. 71

MACHEN, Arthur. Far Off Things (L. 1922); Things Near and Far (1923). An attractive story of Welsh boyhood and childhood enchantment;nature and romance; the spell of De Quincey and the medieval writers;work as clerk, actor and author; failures, hardships, and growing reputation. 72

McHUGH,Mary Frances. Thalassa(1931). A sensitive story of girlhood on west coast of Ireland and in Dublin;nature people and animals. 73

MacINTYRE, Dugald. Highland Game - keeper (1941). Life and work in Kintyre; sport; observations of animals and birds. 74

McIVER, Evander. Memoirs of a Highland Gentlemen (Edin.1905). Education in Edinburgh; banking work in Dinwall and factor for Duke of Buchan;farming at Scourie; social life and Scottish celebrities. 75

MacIVER, Col. Henry R. H. Experiences of the Servian War(1876). Enlistment with Serbs in 1876; organization of cavalry; Turkish atrocities. 76

MACK, Marjorie (Dixon). Hannaboys Farm (1942). Farming and country life in Norfolk between wars. 77

MACK, Max. With a Sigh (1943). Random recollections of life on the stage and the movies in Germany and Central Europe; early days of screen. 78

MACKAIL, Denis. Life with Topsy (L. 1942); Where Am I? (1948). Social and literary life in London; family life; his Pekingese; impressions of life in 40's and comparisons with life before WW2. 79

MACKAY,Charles. Forty Years' Recollections(1877); Recollections of Life (1878); Through the Long Day (1887). Life of journalist,1830-70; political affairs; Corn Laws, Chartism & Reform Movement; Crimean War; education and social changes; Wordsworth, Scott and Thackeray; Victorian scene. 80

MACKAY, Helen. A Journal of Small Things (1916). Her life in France;the spiritual values of France. 81

MACKAY, James. Diary, 1857-58; work and adventures of a chaplain in Indian Mutiny; marches; the siege of Lucknow. From London to Lucknow (1860). 82

MACKAY, William. Bohemian Days in Fleet Street (1913). Work as journalist in 70's and 80's; newspaper world theatre,clubs, sport; celebrities and eccentrics. 83

MacKELLAR, Patrick. Journal, 1762; artillery and engineering details of siege of Havana. A Correct Journal of the Landing (1762). 84

MacKELLOW, John. Autobiography (L. 1863). Orphan; childhood hardships in 1770's; enlists; wickedness of military life; his conversion to Methodism religious work; business; activities for temperance. 85

McKENNA, Stephen. While I Remember (1921).Westminster School and Oxford; his career in politics; Liberal Party and its fortunes; work in WW1. 86

MACKENZIE, Sir Alexander Campbell. Musician's Narrative (1927). Musical career,Edinburgh and London; teaching at R.A.M.; work with Royal Choral Soc and his compositions; festivals; the English musical scene from the 60's; Empire tours. 87

MACKENZIE, Charles. Notes on Haiti (1830). Experiences and work of consul in 1820's; plantation life; conditions and society in Haiti.   88

MACKENZIE, Lt. Col. Colin. Journal, 1811-13; expedition to Batavia; work on engineering inspection of Java and strategical notes. MS, India Office; Mackenzie Collection.   89

MACKENZIE,General Colin. Storms and Sunshine(1884). Military career from 1825, mostly in India; his campaigns; the Mutiny; embassies; marriage; social life in India.   90

MACKENZIE, Compton. Gallipoli Memories (1929); First Athenian Memories (1931); Greek Memories (1939); Aegean Memories (1940); Reaped and Bound (L. 1933). Four volumes of WW1 memories; naval intelligence work in Greece and Mediterranean; essays, including one on his musical life.   91

MACKENZIE,Faith Compton. As Much as I Dare (1938); More than I Should (L. 1940); Always Afternoon(1943). Childhood at Eton and Stonehouse, with her teacher-father; music and her career in theatre; travels in Italy and Mediterranean with her husband; country life at Herm; his literary & artistic friends.   92

MACKENZIE, Helen. Diary, 1846-1851; missionary life and work in India;the Punjab campaign and military affairs; Anglo-Indian relations;teaching. Life in the Mission (Redfield 1853).   93

MACKENZIE, James. Life and Adventures (Glasgow, 1825). Scottish thief transported to Botany Bay;his criminal career and reform.   94

MACKENZIE, Kenneth. Been Places and Seen Things (1935); Living Rough (L. 1936).Odd jobs and wide travels; hobo seaman,docker, unemployed; Canada and USA, S. America, Siberia; experiences of people at street corners;an honest picture of working life.   95

MACKENZIE,Osgood Hanbury. A Hundred Years in the Highlands(1921). His own memories and earlier ones of Dr. John Mackenzie; country life, agriculture, social,religion, sport, folk-lore and smuggling; attractive.   96

McKENZIE, Srgt. Thomas. My Life as

a Soldier (St. John N.B. 1898). Boyhood in army; service in India; Mutiny; settled in New Brunswick; activities of the Fenians. Copy in Ottawa Archives.   97

MACKENZIE-ROGAN,Lt.Col. James. Fifty Years of Army Music(1926). Musical career from a bandboy to conductor of Coldstream Guards band; S.Africa, India, Ireland, Kneller Hall.   98

M'KEOWN,Robert L. Twenty-Five Years in Qua Iboe (Belfast, 1912). Life and work of a missionary in Nigeria; life and customs of natives.   99

McKERLIE, E. Marianne H. Rome via Whithorn (1934). Free Kirk background her social and artistic work; Catholic friends; her conversion.   100

M'KERLIE, Robert. Two Sons of Galloway: by E. M. M'Kerlie (Dumfries, 1928). Military career,1796-1803; the Irish rebellion; & his service in the Netherlands.   101

MacKICHAN, Dugald. Forty-Five Years in India (1934). School;University of Glasgow; administration and teaching, University of Bombay; Indian life and celebrities; anecdotes.   102

McKIE, R. C. H. This Was Singapore (1950).Experiences of a journalist in Singapore in 1937-39; Chinatown & the miseries of the Chinese; indifference of Europeans; one-sided.   103

McKIERNAN, Thomas. Experiences of a British Veteran Soldier (Port Talbot, 1892).Irish sergeant's service in the Crimea and in New Zealand.   104

MacKINNON, C. Journal, 1830; travel from England to India. MS, Royal Empire Soc., 86/30300 Case.   105

McKINNON, Clarence. Reminiscences (Toronto, 1938). Boyhood in Highlands; education at Edinburgh University;his later career as a clergyman, Nova Scotia and Saskatchewan.   106

McKINNON, D.H. Military Service and Adventures(1847). Service and life of an army officer in India in 30's and 40's; Afghan and Sikh campaigns; travel notes; good. Copy in India Office

Library.   107

MacKINNON, Sir Frank D. On Circuit (1940). His legal career, cases, and travels on circuit, 1924-37; the Lord Chief Justice of Appeal.   108

MacKINNON,General Henry. Journal of the Campaign in Portugal and Spain(L. 1812). Marches and battles of Peninsular War, 1809-12.   109

McKINNON, Ian. Garrott (1933). Adventures of a Clydeside apprentice in Syria and Near East, W.W.1 and after; Arab warfare; business.   110

MacKINNON,Lachlan. Recollections of an Old Lawyer (Aberdeen,1935). Education in Aberdeen;legal career; social life, institutions, sport, university in Aberdeen.   111

MACKINTOSH,Sir Alexander. Echoes of Big Ben (1945). Work and memories of a Parliamentary journalist from 1881; view of statesmen and politicians and events.   112

MACKINTOSH,Matthew. Stage Reminiscences (Glasgow, 1866). Actor's career and memories of great actors; Mathews Kean, Alexander & Vestris; entertainingly written.   113

MACKNESS, Reginald Courtney. Autobiography of his career as organist; Wandsworth; church music. MS, Battersea Public Library.   114

MACKNIGHT, Thomas. Ulster As It Is (1896). Journalist and editor of Northern Whig; Irish political affairs & figures from 1866.   115

MacKRABIE, Alexander. Diary, 1774-1776; his service as secretary to Sir Philip Francis in India. MS,India Office Library, Eur. E.25.   116

MACKY, John. Memoirs of the Secret Services (1733). Government agent under William and Anne and George I;his missions; activities at St. Germain's ill-treatment by court.   117

McLAGLEN, Victor. Express to Hollywood (1934). Odd jobs and travels; a trooper in Boer War,prospector in Canada,policeman, wrestler, boxer, circus performer, actor, film-star; early days of Hollywood.   118

McLAREN, Jack. My Odyssey (1923). A lively record of trading, goldseeking and pearling in New Guinea, Solomons, Torres Straits; primitive life.   119

MACLEAN, Brig.Gen. Fitzroy. Eastern Approaches(1949). Career of a brilliant young soldier, diplomat, M.P. and leader with Yugo-Slav guerrillas during WW2; his experiences in Russia in 30's and the 1938 trials; Mihailovic, Tito and the war in Jugo-Slavia; excellent.   120

MACLEAN, James M. Recollections of Westminster & India (Manchester 1901) Journalist and politician; member for Oldham and Cardiff; public affairs in England and India.   121

MACLEAN, Norman. Former Days (1945) Childhood and schooling on West coast of Scotland; Gaelic and Nationalistic movements in 80's; country life & the old ways.   122

MacLEOD,Sgt. Donald. Memoirs of the Life (1791, 1933). Long career in the army from boyhood;service under Marlborough and in American Revolution; a soldier's view of most of the battles of 18th Century; lively.   123

MacLEOD, Donald. Nonagenarian's Reminiscences (Helensburgh, 1883). Life at Garelochside and Helensburgh; local customs and people.   124

MacLEOD, J. Reminiscences (Elgin, 1910). Inspector of schools in Scotland;teaching in Nova Scotia, Glasgow University,and Royal Military Academy at Woolwich; trivial.   125

McLEOD, John. Narrative of a Voyage (1817); A Voyage to Africa (1820).His life as ship's surgeon;Korea; Africa; work on slaver;slave-trade in Dahomey his own slavery; revulsion from trade later experiences in West Indies; the early 19th Century; good.   126

MacLEOD, Joseph. Job at the B.B.C. (Glasgow, 1947).Years in broadcasting during WW2; his work; events leading to his resignation.   127

McLEOD, Lyons. Travels in Eastern Africa (1860). Work as consul in East Africa and Mozambique in 50's; business; economics; slavery and his work to suppress it.   128

McLEOD, Norman. Recollections of a Highland Parish (1867). Impersonal account of Scottish social life, sport, customs.   129

MacLEOD, Roderick Donald. Impressions (1938). Work in ICS; district officer at Agra and Oudh, 1910-34; society and politics in India.   130

MacLIAMMÓIR, Mícheál. All for Hecuba (1946). Actor's career in England and Ireland; tours in Egypt and Balkans; work at Gate Theatre in 30's; theatre life; well-written.   131

M'MAHON, Benjamin. Jamaica Plantership (1839). His eighteen years as a planter; plantations, planters, and slavery in Jamaica; his anti-slavery activities.   132

MacMAHON, Ryan. Tramp Royal (1948). Irishman's travels and various jobs on four continents; jackaroo, trapper, & cowpuncher; soldier, doctor, prospector, etc.; colloquial.   133

MacMANUS, Seumas. The Rocky Road to Dublin (N. Y. 1938). Childhood; peasant life in Donegal; Irish life; the beginning of his success as author and poet.   134

MacMILLAN, Norman. Into the Blue (L. 1929); Freelance Pilot (1937). Service in RFC in France and Italy during WW1; flying in Spain; flight to India, after the war.   135

MacMULLEN, Sergeant John. Camp and Barrack-Room (1846). Experiences of an Irish soldier in India; life in ranks; critical view of soldier's lot.   136

McMULLEN, R. T. Down Channel (1903) Cruises and adventures of a persistent yachtsman, from 50's.   137

MacMUNN, Gen. Sir George F. Behind the Scenes (1930). Military service; India, Boer War, WW1, Mesopotamia; his work at Indian Staff College and the War Office; a personal and historical account of wars.   138

MacNAGHTEN, Hugh. Fifty Years of Eton (1924). Life at Eton; memories of famous Etonians.   139

MacNAGHTEN, Sir Melville L. Days of My Years (1914). Eton; business life in Bengal; career with police and the CID from 1889; famous crimes; the work of detection; Scotland Yard.   140

MACNAMARA, Maj. J.R. J. The Whistle Blows (1938). Perturbed account of his career in the army and in Parliament, as Conservative member; affairs of the troubled world.   141

McNAUGHT, Thomas P. Recollections of a Glasgow Detective Officer (1887). A Glasgow detective's work, duties, and reflections on crime, human nature and ways of criminals.   142

MacNAUGHTON, S. Us Four (1909); Woman's Diary of the War (1915); My War Experiences (1919). Childhood in the western Highlands; nursery life, with her sisters; tourist's experiences in Belgium in 1914; German invasion; her WW1 experiences.   143

McNEIL, Capt. Samuel G. S. In Great Waters (1932). Life at sea; sailing ships; in tramp steamers; with Cunard Line; minesweeping in WW1; Mauretania and other liners; personalities at the captain's table.   144

MacNEILL, John Gordon Swift. What I Have Seen and Heard (1925). Education in Dublin and Oxford; legal studies & career; work as Irish M.P.; Irish affairs and politicians; Parnell; anecdotes of social life, clubs, writers, politicians.   145

MacNIE, J. Work and Play in the Argentine (1925). Life as a cattleman in Argentina, 1899-1924; station life at Venado Tuerto; economics, business and general conditions.   146

McNIEL, James B. The Contrabandits (1940). Adventurous life of an amateur gun-runner in South America.   147

MACONOCHIE, Sir Evan. Life in the Indian Civil Service (1926). Career in ICS, 1889-1921; Bombay, Mysore, Kathiawa; administration; Indian life and society.   148

MacPHAIL,James M. Five Years' Practice (Pokhuria, 1895). Work and life of medical missionary at Manbhoom and in Bihar in 90's; native living conditions; disease. Copy in India Office Library.   149

McPHEE, Colin. House in Bali (1948) His life and musical studies during a five years' stay in Bali.   150

MacPHERSON, Lt.Col. Allan. Diaries, 1770-76;military service for the East India Company;Dinapore, Oudh and Fort William; French wars. Soldiering in India, ed. W.C. Macpherson (Edinburgh 1928).   151

MacPHERSON, Charles. Memoirs of the Life (Edin. 1800). Travel and adventures in Asia, Africa, America, West Indies; life among French settlers in West Indies; his amours.   152

McPHERSON,Duncan.Two Years in China (1842).Experience and observations as surgeon with Madras army and the Grenadiers during an expedition to China, 1840-42.   153

MacPHERSON, Lt. Col. John. Journal, 1778-81;military service for the East India Company;Fort William, etc.; the French wars. Soldiering in India, ed. W. C. Macpherson (Edin. 1928).   154

MacPHERSON, Major Samuel Charters. Memorials of Service in India (1865). Cambridge; military service with East India Co. in 30's to 60's; political agent in Gwalior; the Mutiny; scientific and sociological interests; his efforts vs. human sacrifice.   155

MACPHERSON, Sandy. Sandy Presents (1950). His career as an organist and his work for the BBC; anecdotes. 156

MacPHERSON, Stewart. The Mike and I (1948). Career with the B.B.C. of the Canadian radio reporter; sports commentaries.   157

McQUEEN,James Milroy. Our War (Worcester, 1931). Service as a sanitary officer with Highland division in WW1; army life and its humours.   158

MACQUEEN-POPE, W. Twenty Shillings in the Pound (1949). Nostalgic memories of his youth at end of the 19th Century; social life, sport & boyhood activities; Diamond Jubilee.   159

MACRAE, David.   Quaint Sayings of Children (Glasgow, 1895). Reminiscences of his childhood in Scotland; the games and language of children. 160

MACRAE, Ian. Next Please! (1941). A barber's life story; training; saloon in Mayfair;his clients; tricks of the trade.   161

MACREADY,William Charles.Macready's Reminiscences, ed. Sir F. Pollock (L. 1875). Contains autobiography of his education, training in the theatre, & his early career up to 1833; theatrical life; Siddons and others.   162

MACREADY, Gen. Sir Cecil Frederick Nevil. Annals of an Active Life(1924) Army career in Gordon Highlanders;his campaigns in Egypt and South Africa; India; commander in chief in Ireland; WW1 service;later work as Commissioner of Police; work of keeping law and order; police and strikes.   163

M'TAGGART,Ann. Memoirs of a Gentlewoman of the Old School; by a Lady(L. 1830). Family and domestic life; social life; travels.   164

MacVINE, John.   Sixty-Three Years' Angling(1891). Trout and salmon fishing in Scotland and North of England, from his boyhood.   165

ANON. Mad Mike, ed.George Goodchild (1934). Dictated life of a pedlar who had once been in grand opera and travelled in the South Seas; adventures and romance; fiction?   166

/MADDEN, Charles Horace/. Recollections of an Eton Colleger: by C.H.M. (Eton, 1905). Life at Eton; sport and pleasures, about 1900.   167

MADDEN,Dr. Richard Robert. A Twelve Months' Residence in the West Indies (1835); Memoirs (1891). Irish boyhood medical education; practice in Turkey Egypt; residence in West Indies; anti slavery work;Ireland during the great famine; colonial secretary in Australia; poetical and historical writings covers 1798-1886.   168

MADOX, Richard. Journal, 1582; the observations of a chaplain on Fenton's expedition to discover route to Cathay MS, B. M. Cotton App. XLVII.   169

/MAIKWORTH, Major/. Diary, 1820-22; travels of a cavalry officer in India Hindu religion;missionary work. Diary of a Tour through Southern India;by a Field Officer of Cavalry (1823).   170

MAIN ROYAL. Second Dog Watch (1949) Reminiscences of his life at sea told to soldiers of WW1.   171

MAINE, Basil. The Best of Me (1937) People Are Much Alike (1938). Author and broadcaster; society and celebrities; sketches of people, places, and conversations.   172

MAINWARING,Arthur. Fishing and Philandering (1914). Fishing, sport, the open air, social life, friends; Scotland, Ireland, India.   173

MAIR, Elizabeth H. Recollections of the Past(Edin.1877). Reminiscences of the theatre and literature by a granddaughter of Mrs. Siddons; Scott, Kemble, Thomas Campbell; Scottish social life and people.   174

MAIR, William. My Life (1911). Career of a Scottish minister from 1869; parish work at Earlston; Moderator of General Assembly;legal and church affairs.   175

MAIS, Stuart Petre Brodie. All the Days of My Life (1937). English country life;his career as journalist and author; travels.   176

MAITLAND, John. Savages and Sinners (1933).Experiences in New Guinea during German occupation;crime; ruthless rulers; violence.   177

MAJOR, J. W. Quayside Crooks (1941) Thirty years as detective at the London docks and in CID: work for shipping company; smuggling, pilfering and dope traffic; life of East End.   178

MAKINS, Sir George. Autobiography of a surgeon, 1853-1933. MS, typewritten, Royal College of Surgeons.   179

MALAN,Charles H. A Soldier's Experience (1874). Military career; Crimea India, China expedition & Africa; his conversion;God's mercies; evangelistic work.   180

MALBON, Thomas. His experiences in the civil war, 1642-48; activities in Cheshire;sometimes day to day. Record Soc. Lancs & Cheshire XIX (1889). 181

MALCOLM, Sir Ian. Trodden Ways (L. 1930).His military career and work in Parliament; European travels with eye to military & public interest.   182

MALCOLM, Lt. John. Memorials of the Late Wars (Archibald Constable's Miscellany, XXVII, 1828). Reminiscences of the Peninsular War; his campaigns in Pyrenees and S. France.   183

MALCOLM,Napier.Five Years in a Persian Town (1905). Missionary work in Persia; Persian customs.   184

MALET, Sir Edward. Shifting Scenes (1901). His diplomatic career, 1854-1870; America, Egypt & Turkey; ambassador to Germany; Franco-Prussian War and the political scene.   185

MALET, Rawdon. Unforgiving Minutes (1923). Adventures of a big-game hunter in Central Africa.   186

MALINS, Lt.Geoffrey H. How I Filmed the War(1920). Work of official cinematographer during WW1;adventures and triumphs; the Somme battles.   187

MALLESON, Lady Constance. After Ten Years (1931); In the North(1947). Her youth in Ireland; stage career; marriage; work for Labour Party; life in Scandinavia from 1936.   188

MALLOCK,William Hurrell. Memoirs of Life and Literature (1920). His youth in Devon; Oxford; literary life, London; travels in Europe and America; & his novels and religious and sociological writings.   189

MALMESBURY, James Howard Harris,3rd Earl of. Memoirs of an Ex-Minister(L. 1884). Education at Oxford; political career; Foreign Minister in the Derby cabinet;Reform Movement and political affairs 1832-69; largely in form of a diary.   190

MALONE, Desmond. The Last Landfall (N. Y. 1936). Training as priest; expulsion;clerk, sailor on tramp steamers; capture by German submarine WW1; imprisonment in Germany; good narrative of adventures.   191

MALTBY, Edward (ed.). Secrets of a Solicitor (1929). Forty years in the law; curious cases; Oscar Wilde case; Baccarat case; famous lawyers.   192

MALTBY, Henry Francis. Ring Up the Curtain (1950). His career as a playwright;memories of the London theatre cinema and films;theatre life, actors Patrick Campbell.   193

MALTBY,Private Isaac. Adventures of a Private Soldier (Skipton,1886). His military service in Egypt and Soudan; Nile expedition; life in ranks.   War Office Library.   194

MALVERY,Olive Christian. A Year and a Day (1912). Social work for women; industry and the poor; philanthropy; success as author; goat farmer.   195

MANACORDA, Harold.   Notes from the Diary (1931). Travel and diplomacy of a minister-plenipotentiary of King of Italy; Rhodes, Cyprus, Syria.   196

MANBY,Capt. George William. Reminiscences (Yarmouth, 1839). Life and friendships in the navy in early 19th Century. MS, B. M. Add. 29893.   197

MANCHESTER, William A. D. Montagu, Duke of. My Candid Recollections (L. 1932). Childhood in Ireland and USA; Cambridge;society, sport, travel, India and America; observation on politics of 20's.   198

MANGAN, James Clarence. Early life of poet;life in Ireland in early 19th Century; somewhat imaginative. MS, in Royal Irish Academy; extracts in Life and Writings of James Clarence Mangan by D. J. O'Donaghue (Edin.1897).   199

MANINGTON, George. A Soldier of the Legion (1907). English adventurer in French Foreign Legion in 90's; fighting in Algeria and Tonquin.   200

MANN,John. Recollections of My Early and Professional Life (1887). London childhood; Napoleonic wars; work as printer; medical study in London & medical practice. Copy in Gloucester City Library.   201

MANN,Thomas. Tom Mann's Memoirs (L. 1923). Working-class life in Warwickshire; work for trade unions and Labour Party;secretary ILP; M.P.; organization of General Workers; Dockers' Strike; struggles and difficulties; a representative life.   202

MANNIN, Ethel. Confessions and Impressions(1930); All Experience(1932) Privileged Spectator(1939); Connemara Journal(1948). London; education; her career in journalism and as novelist; marriage; free love; pacifism; political activities; social, literary and political scene; Yeats, Housman, and other celebrities; travels; residence in Ireland.   203

MANSBRIDGE,Albert. The Trodden Road (1940). Gloucester & London; his work as clerk and civil servant; a teacher in Cooperative Movement & lecturer in Adult Education; founder of Workers' Educational Association.   204

MANSFIELD,Robert Blatchford. School Life (1870). Experience at Winchester College as pupil in 30's; studies and educational system; life of the boys; customs; slang, etc.   205

MANT, Frederick Woods. The Midshipman(1854). Training as midshipman and life and travels in the navy,1825-37; places and people he saw.   206

MANTON,Henry. Reminiscences of life and work of a Birmingham brass-founder from early 19th Century;religious and public life of the town;& service on the Council and as alderman. Cuttings from Weekly Mercury, 1902-3, Birmingham Public Library.   207

MAPLES, Rt. Rev. Chauncy. Journals, 1881-87; religious work and travel in Nyassaland; Bishop of Likoma; native life and culture. Journals and Papers (1899).   208

MAPLESON, J. H. Mapleson Memoirs
(1888). Musical agent and impressario
from 40's; concerts, singers & shows;
Drury Lane, Covent Garden etc.   209

MARCY, William Nichols. Reminiscences of a Public School Boy(1932); Adventures of a Schoolmaster (1925). A
student at St.Paul's in the 90's; the
teachers,boys, sport; his own life as
a teacher.   210

MARETT, Robert Ranulph. A Jerseyman
at Oxford (1941). Life as student and
don;rector of Exeter College; anthropological and archaeological studies;
social and academic life and persons,
at Oxford; good.   211

MARGRIE, William. A Camberwell Man
(1926);Cockney's Pilgrimage in Search
of Truth (1927). Working man's life &
self-education; mental adventures and
membership in political, ethical, and
literary societies;life in South London; thin.   212

MARINUS, D. Alloquia (1928). Simple
reminiscences of medical training and
practice as doctor.   213

MARION, Frederick (Josef Kraus). In
My Mind's Eye (1949). Memories of his
strange psychic powers and his theory
about them.   214

MARK, William.   At Sea with Nelson
(1929). Scottish purser's service on
the Victory; adventures and battles;
earlier account of business life and
failure at Bath.   215

MARK VII. A Subaltern on the Somme
(1927). Personal narrative, army service in France, WW1.   216

MARKHAM, Beryl. West with the Night
(1943).Adventures of woman free-lance
pilot in Kenya; the Mwanis.   217

MARKHAM, Francis. Markham Memorials
ed. Sir C.Markham (1913). Autobiography of antiquary's military life and
misfortunes to 1616; brief.   218

MARKHAM, Francis. Recollections of
a Town Boy (1903). Life as a student
at Westminster School in 50's.   219

MARKHAM,Col. Frederick. Shooting in

the Himalayas(1854). Travel and hunting in India, Tibet and Chinese Tartary from 1846.   220

MARKHAM, Violet R. A Woman's Watch
on the Rhine(1921). Journalist during
Rhineland occupation after WW1.;German
life and people.   221

MARKS, Henry John. Narrative (1838)
Jew's conversion to Christianity; his
family and social troubles.   222

MARKS, Henry Stacy. Pen and Pencil
Sketches (1894). Childhood; art study
at Leigh's and inParis and Belgium in
50's; painting in Dublin and London;
Royal Academy, Victorian artists, and
London social life; Punch, Spectator,
Ruskin; art criticism.   223

MARKS,John Ebenezer. Forty Years in
Burma (1917). Missionary work in Ran-
goon; educational work at St. John's
School;medical work; King Mindon; and
Burmese customs.   224

/MARKS,Richard/. The Retrospect: by
Aliquis (1820). Service in navy; work
as minister of the established church;
God's mercies.   225

MARLING,Col. Sir Percival. Rifleman
and Hussar(1931). His military career
1880-1918;service in S. Africa, Egypt
Boer War and WW1; social life, sport,
country life.   226

MARLOWE,Dave (A.H. Timmins). Coming
Sir! (1938). Life and work in London
pubs and taverns; life as a waiter on
Queen Mary; life at sea; lively story
and exposé.   227

MAROCHETTI, George.   Rich in Range
(1941). Naturalized soldier's service
in WW1; with military mission to Austria after the war; changes in social
and political life.   228

MARRIOTT,Sir John.Memories of F o u r
Score Years (1946). His life in scholarship, education, and politics; the
social and public scene.   229

MARSDEN, Joshua.   Grace Displayed
(N. Y.1813). Good account of his early
life as a sailor;conversion; ministry
and travels as a Methodist evangelist
preacher.   230

MARSDEN, William. A Brief Memoir of the Life (1838). Scientist's travels and adventures in Sumatra and the Far East; literary and historical work on Sumatra.   231

MARSH, Edward.   A Number of People (1939). His career as political private secretary from 1900; his literary and artistic interests and friends; & anecdotes of celebrities in the arts and public life; good.   232

MARSH,Richard. Trainer to Two Kings (1925). Work at Newmarket, Banstead & Egerton; his great horses; turf life; sporting celebrities.   233

MARSHALL, Archibald. Out and About (1933). Cambridge; work for literary magazines; literary editor for Daily Mail;travels as special correspondent and notes on Peace Conferences; anecdotes of literary men.   234

MARSHALL,Charles. Sion's Travellers Comforted(1704). Life at Bristol; his conversion; ministry, sufferings, and public testimony of a Quaker physician and early Quaker life.   235

MARSHALL, Herbert.   Memories of a Private Detective(1925). His work and adventures; career of righting wrongs and tall stories.   236

MARSHALL, John. Diaries, 1668-1671; journeys in Bengal, on behalf of East India Company;descriptions; astronomy and medicine; folklore and culture of India. John Marshall in India, edited Shafaat Ahmad Khan (1927).   237

MARSHALL, Mary Paley. What I Remember(1947). Newnham; Women's education movement at Cambridge and Sidgwick's part in it; university life at Oxford Bristol & Cambridge with her husband; entertaining and high-minded.   238

MARSHALL, Matt. Tramp-Royal on the Toby(1933). Travels and adventures of a tramp in England, Wales, Scotland; casual wards and doss-houses; amusing account of the life.   239

MARSHALL,Samuel. Life of a Successful Farmer (Farnham, 1942). Farm-boy, labourer, and farmer in Surrey; work, social life, old ways, ballads; short and interesting. Croydon P.L.   240

MARSHALL, W.H. Four Years in Burmah (1860). Work as editor of the Rangoon Chronicle in 50's;trade and business; Burmese life and customs.   241

MARSHALL,Gen. Sir William. Memories of Four Fronts (1929). Service in WW1 with infantry; India, France, Gallipoli, Macedonia, Mesopotamia, Baghdad and Mosul.   242

MARSON, T. B. Scarlet and Khaki (L. 1930). Simple story of soldier's life in Boer War and WW1;Leicester country life and sport;foxhunting with famous packs between wars.   243

MARSTON, Edward. After Work (1904); Easy-Chair Memories (1911). Publisher in London; his work; memories of writers; fishing in the South of England especially for trout.   244

MARTHA. Memoirs of Martha (L. 1933) Dictated experiences;girlhood in East Anglia; emigration and work as a maid and cook in Australia; later in USA & England; frank and amused.   245

MARTIN, Alexander G. Mother Country Fatherland (1936). Englishman's boyhood in Germany;service in the German army from 1894; WW1 service in France with German forces.   246

MARTIN, Arthur Anderson. Surgeon in Khaki(1915). Vivid account of service with New Zealand troops in WW1;medical work; mainly impersonal.   247

MARTIN, Basil. An Impossible Parson (1935). London youth; business life; study for ministry; New College; social work in East End and Kentish Town and ministry at Hereford and Finchley; good, straightforward spiritual autobiography.   248

MARTIN, Frank A. Under the Absolute Amir(1907). Work as chief engineer in Kabul from 1895;geology; politics and court life;Abdur Rahman; religion and customs of Afghans.   249

MARTIN, Frederick Townsend. Things I Remember (1913). American who adopted England; society in London, country house life, sport.   250

MARTIN, John. <u>Some Account of the Life</u> (1797). Baptist minister's story of ministry and travels in England and his sermons and numerous writings in defence of Baptist practice.   251

MARTIN, John W. <u>My Fishing Days and Fishing Ways</u> (Plymouth,1906). Fishing from boyhood; Lincs and Notts; River Trent; Walton style. Cambridge.   252

MARTIN, Sarah. <u>Brief Sketch of the Life</u> (Yarmouth, 1844). Orphan; dressmaker; religious and social labour in workhouses and prisons; sincere, earnest work of a poor Christian.   253

MARTIN, W. W. <u>Chequers Inn</u> (1929). Old man's memories; mainly his childhood in Kent; village life; visits to the inn; sport; pastimes.   254

/MARTIN, William/. <u>At the Front</u>: by One who was there (Paisley, 1915).His army career; service in Crimean War & Indian Mutiny; garrison life; adventures at Lucknow; humours.   255

MARTIN, Adm. William Ernest Russell <u>Adventures of a Naval Paymaster</u>(1924) Career in the navy from 1867; service in West Indies; WW1.   256

MARTIN-HARVEY,Sir John. <u>Autobiography</u> (1933). Boyhood at Wivenhoe; his career as an actor;at the Lyceum with Irving; roles, productions, tours in America;troubles with unions; stories of actors and theatre life.   257

MARTIN-NICHOLSON,Mary E. <u>My Experiences on Three Fronts</u>(1916). Personal narrative of service as nurse in WW1; Belgium, Russia, France.   258

MARTINDALE, Adam. <u>The Life</u> (Chetham Soc., 1845). Childhood; school; work as tutor and teacher,Presbyterian minister and chaplain; imprisoned as a nonconformist in 1684; excellent picture of his life in Lancashire, religious movements, social, economic and public life of 17th Century.   259

MARTINDALE, Hilda. <u>From One Generation to Another</u> (1944). Her career in social work for children and as civil servant, 1895-1937; inspector of factories and Treasury official.   260

MARTINEAU, Lady Alice Margaret. <u>Reminiscences of Hunting</u> (1930). A fond record of foxhunting, hunts & horses; Pytchley and other hunts.   261

MARTINEAU, Harriet. <u>Autobiography,</u> ed. M. W. Chapman (1877). Career as a scholar, journalist, author; literary and economic writings; travel in USA; friendship with eminent scholars,writers, politicians; good.   262

MARTYN, Frederic. <u>A Holiday in Gaol</u> (1911); <u>Life in the Legion</u> (1911). A narrative of 18 pleasant months spent in gaol; five unpleasant years in the French Foreign Legion; service in Nth Africa.   263

MARTYN,Henry. Journal, 1802-12; his missionary work in India and Persia; language study; biblical translation; his spiritual life; the struggles of a Christian hero. <u>Journals and Letters,</u> ed. Samuel Wilberforce (1839).   264

MARTYR, Weston. <u>The Wandering Years</u> (Edin. 1940). Youth at sea; mining in S.Africa and Japan; buccaneering life and adventures; military service,WW1; confessional.   265

MARWICK,Sir James David. <u>Retrospect</u> (Glasgow, 1905). Legal studies, Edinburgh; work as Writer to Signet; his work as Town Clerk of Glasgow and municipal affairs from 1873.   266

MARY II, Queen of England. <u>Memoirs of Queen Mary of England,</u> ed. Richard Doebner (1886). Court life in Hanover and her health and travel;business of the King; British politics.   267

MASEFIELD, John. <u>In the Mill</u> (1941) <u>New Chum</u> (1944). The poet's work in a cloth-mill in USA at end of 19th Century; his early life in the navy and merchantmen;some details of his reading and literary interests.   268

MASKELYNE, Jasper. <u>Magic - Top Secret</u> (1949). His WW2 activities; providing illusion and bluff in connection with the Desert campaigns and the Normandy invasion.   269

MASON, Arthur. <u>Come Easy, Go Easy</u> (1933). A seaman's adventures seeking for gold in Nevada about 1900;life in Wild West. 270

MASON, Charles Welsh. Chinese Confessions (1924). His work in Chinese customs service; adventures; attempt to become Emperor of China. 271

MASON, G. Finch. Sporting Recollections (1885). Varied sports; cricket; hunting; steeplechasing; horseracing; shooting; hunting. 272

MASON, Captain James. Twelve Years' Residence(1894). Shooting and fishing on the west coast of Scotland;country life and neighbours; slight. 273

MASON, John. Lives of Early Methodist Preachers, ed. Thomas Jackson, II (1937). Ministry and travels of 18th Century Methodist in Hampshire and the South of England. 274

MASON, John. Journal, 1846-49; work of Newcastle medical missionary among Jews in Turkey; religious conflicts; Moldavia. Three Years in Turkey(1860) 274 A

MASON, John Henry. Autobiographical Notes(1936). Printer's account of his jobs and work as director of printing classes for L.C.C.; the books that he designed and printed;editor and founder of Imprint. 275

MASON, Richard. Angling Experiences (Grimsby, 1901). Fishing and fishermen in Lincs; gentlemen and yokels; & dialect humour. 276

MASON, Simon. Narrative of the Life (Birmingham, 1754). London apothecary relations with doctors and patients; failure;later business at Market Harborough; family life; simple and colloquial story; good. 277

MASSEY, Gertrude. Kings, Commoners, and Me (1934). Artist's career; noble sitters; dog-sitters; fellow artists; sketching tours from 90's. 278

MASSEY, Montague. Recollections of Calcutta (Calcutta, 1918). Business, administration, and social life; Calcutta from the sixties. Royal Empire Society Library. 279

MASSIE, Chris. The Confessions of a

Vagabond (1931). Soldier's life after WW1; tramp,costermonger, jack-of-all-trades; journalist for the Daily Herald; adventures of rough life. 280

MASSINGHAM,Harold John. Remembrance (1941). Childhood; Oxford; career as journalist; Daily Chronicle; country life and religion; regional life and arts; study of primitive man and natural history;mental autobiography and lifetime quest of values. 281

MASSINGHAM, Hugh. I Took Off My Tie (1936). Residence in London East End; his life among the poor and criminals sociological interest. 282

MASSON, Charles (i.e. James Lewis). Journals, 1828-40; travels in Punjab, Afghanistan, Sind, Persia etc.; notes for his travel books. MS,India Office Eur. B. 61, E. 163-165. 283

MASSON, David. Memories of London (Edin.1908). Social and literary life in the forties; clubs, literature,and friends; Carlyle, Mazzini etc. 284

MASSY,Col. Cromwell, Diary, 1780-4; service with Baillie's regiment; his capture by Hyder Ali and sufferings in prison. Diary (Bangalore 1876). 285

MASSY, Percy H. H. Eastern Mediterranean Lands (1923). Twenty years in Turkey, Palestine, Greece; a military consul; social, sport, travel. 286

MASTER,Sir Streynsham. Diary, 1675-1680; trouble-shooter for East India Company;travels in Bengal; inspection of factories;wonders of the East. The Diaries, ed. R. C. Temple (1911). 287

MASTERMAN, George Frederick. Seven Eventful Years in Paraguay(1869). The experiences of a medical apothecary in the 60's; medical and military; Brazilian war;exploration; South American life and customs. 288

MASTERS, John Neve. A Second Book of Reminiscences (Rye, 1925). Life in Sussex; social gossip; slight. 289

MATHER, Alexander. Lives of Early Methodist Preachers, ed. Thomas Jackson,I (1937). Ministry and travels of 18th Century Methodist in Wales & the

West of England.   290

MATHESON, Com. Sir Charles G. Fifty Years of Ocean Hazard (1939). Career at sea; sailing ships, steamers, liners;with Q-ships in WW1; commodore of Orient Line; humours of liners.   291

MATHESON, Hugh. Puritan's Progress (1943). Spiritual autobiography of a latter-day puritan; mostly deals with his youth and WW1 experiences.   292

MATHEWS, Charles James. The Life of (1879). London boyhood; architectural study;work as builder in Wales; stage experiences as writer, painter, actor and financial vicissitudes; completed by Dickens.   293

MATSON, John. Indian Warfare (1842) Experiences of a soldier in India in 1780's; expedition against Hyder Ali; capture; prison experiences.   294

MATTHEW, Sir Tobie. True Historical Relation, ed. A.H. Mathew (1904). His conversion to Catholicism; life as a priest and Jesuit; his intellectual & spiritual autobiography;the episode begins in 1605.   295

MATTHEWS, Caroline. Experiences of a Woman Doctor (1916). Service in WW1 with Red Cross in Serbian Army field unit; adventures; prisoner of Germans lively.   296

MATTHEWS, Edward D. Diary,1874-75; engineer's travels in Brazil, Bolivia and Peru;Indians and settlers; industry; travel notes. Up the Amazon (L. 1879).   297

MATTHEWS, Ernest C. A Subaltern in the Field (1920). Military & hospital experiences in France, WW1.   298

MATTHEWS, Ike. Full Revelations of a Professional Rat-Catcher(Manchester 1898). His career;methods of working; anecdotes about rats.   299

MATTHEWS, Thomas T. Notes of Nine Years' Mission Work (L. 1881); Thirty Years in Madagascar (1904). Medical & missionary work in Central Madagascar education; anti-slavery; linguistic & translation work;difficulties; native paganism in Vonizongo province.   300

MATTHISON, Arthur Llewellyn. Art, Paint and Vanity (1934); Less Paint, More Vanity (1937). Work in Post Office;dramatic critic for The Clarion; Blatchford and socialism; business as paint-seller; social conditions, Birmingham; theatre there.   301

MAUDE, Cyril. The Haymarket Theatre (1903); Behind the Scenes(1927); Lest I Forget (1928). Career as actor and manager; Haymarket; theatre life and people in England and America; Hollywood; famous players.   302

MAUDE,Col.Edwin. Oriental Campaigns and European Furloughs (1908). Career in army in India, 1843-66; from cadet to colonel; the Mutiny; Persian campaign; hunting, social life, holidays in Europe.   303

MAUDE, Colonel Francis Cornwallis. Memories of the Mutiny (L.1894); Five Years in Madagascar(1895). Service in the artillery in Indian Mutiny; experiences with Havelock's column; later administration in Madagascar;opinions and social life.   304

MAUDSLAY, Alfred Percival. Life in the Pacific(1930). Harrow; Cambridge; work as proconsul in Fijis and Samoa, in 80's; archaeology.   305

MAUGHAM, Reginald C. F. Africa as I Have Known It (1929). His experiences as colonial administrator; Nyassaland Liberia, Senegal; education; slavery; native life; travel; sport.   306

MAUGHAM, Robin. Come to Dust (1945) Military service in WW2;with armoured division in North Africa.   307

MAUGHAM, William Somerset. Summing-Up (1938); Strictly Personal (1940). Survey of life-experiences and lessons he drew from them; largely literature and style; his writing career, ideas, incidents in his life;his life at the beginning of WW2.   308

MAURICE, Henry G. Sometimes an Angler (1947). Work in Ministry of Agriculture & Fisheries; the President of Zoological Society; fishing;pollution of southern rivers.   309

MAURICE, Thomas. Memoirs (1819-22).

His education and work as antiquarian and Orientalist; thirty years of Oriental studies in England; memories of famous scholars and poets.   310

MAVOR,James. My Windows (1923). His youth in Scotland; education; travels and studies in Europe, America, Asia; work of historian and economist; professor at Toronto; partly history and partly personal.   311

MAVOR, Sam. Memories of People and Places (1940). Engineer's life in St. Petersburg before the revolution; the technical developments of his period; world-wide travels;Kropotkin; eminent scientists.   312

MAW,Henry Lister. Journal of a Passage from the Pacific to the Atlantic (1829).Experiences of a naval officer exploring a river route across Peru & down the Amazon on behalf of British merchants.   313

MAWSON,Thomas Hayton. Life and Work (Manchester,1927). Life and career of landscape architect; gardening in the Lake District and Lewis; work for the disabled.   314

MAXWELL, Donald. A Dweller in Mesopotamia (1921). Expedition on behalf of Imperial War Museum; seeking official paintings; local scene.   315

MAXWELL,General E. H. With the Connaught Rangers(1883). Military career from 1839;West Indies, Crimea, India; campaigns, social sport.   316

MAXWELL, Henry.   Book of the Words (1939). Childhood memories;his family and teachers; fascination of sea and boats; study of the occult; wordy and grandiloquent.   317

MAXWELL, Sir Herbert. Evening Memories (1932). Scottish boyhood; Eton & Oxford;country life and sport; career in Parliament; Conservative politics; Scottish interests and Scottish life, sport, literature from 1880.   318

MAXWELL, James.   A Brief Narrative (Paisley, 1795). Poet's childhood and marriage; various jobs; travels; poverty and distress; work as writer of books & pamphlets at Paisley; written

in verse.   319

MAXWELL, Katherine. History of Miss Katty M*** (1757). Orphan; maltreatment by her noble relations; her love affairs; life in nunnery; emigration to Jamaica; her distress & cruelty of her family;publication of her memoirs as means of support; fiction?   320

MAXWELL, Col. Montgomery. My Adventures (1845). Experiences in Italy in 1814-15;society and love affairs; visit to Napoleon at Elba; meeting with Mme de Stael, Murat, and other celebrities; his scrapes.   321

MAXWELL, William B.   Time Gathered (1938).Memories of elegant society in London and Richmond; military service in WW1; work as a writer; the Society of Authors.   322

MAY, Betty. Tiger-Woman (1929). Low life in London slums; the underworld of Paris, Sicily and USA; night clubs and their habitues; drugs, crimes and society; a lively shocker.   323

MAY, C. Austen N. Wheelspin Abroad (1949); More Wheelspin (1949). Experiences of a racing motorist;competing in races and rallies in England, Portugal, and France.   324

MAY,Capt. Daniel. Diaries, 1854-99; travels of a surveyor in Central Africa; Livingstone;suppression of slave trade. MS, Bay May, 5 Kloof Mansions, Sea Point, C.P.   325

MAY, Maj.Gen. Sir Edward S. Changes and Chances (1925). Education and his military career from 1875;his service in India, Boer War & WW1; War Office; travel, hunting, social.   326

MAY, Col. H. A. R. Memories of the Artists' Rifles (1929). Work as commanding officer; building up Artists' Rifles; service in WW1.   327

MAY, Henry John. Red Wine of Youth (1946). Boyhood and legal studies in S.Africa; journalism in Australia and N. Z.; travels in Far East & the Near East; WW2 service with South African forces; politics; celebrities.   328

MAY,Jacques Meyer. A Doctor in Siam

(1950). His work as a physician; Siam and Indo-China;practice and teaching; School of Medicine in Bangkok; tropical diseases and problems.   329

MAY, James Lewis. Path through the Wood(1930); Thorn and Flower (1935). Childhood in Devonshire; pretty details of boyish pleasures; family life and his schools; his work as a writer and his literary friends.   330

MAYBRICK, Florence Elizabeth. Mrs. Maybrick's Own Story(1904). Trial and prison experiences; criticism of the proceedings against her.   331

MAYER, Sylvain. Reminiscences of a K. C. (1924). His career at the bar; legal anecdotes; mainly reminiscences of theatre and opera; Bernhardt, Irving, Patti, etc.; scrappy.   332

MAYNARD, John. Remarkable Incidents in the Life (1900). Devonshire youth; conversion to Methodism; preaching in Cornwall, Devon, Jersey; his campaign against tobacco, drink, Bradlaugh and other vices. Exeter P.L.   333

MAYNARD, Theodore. The World I Saw (Milwaukee, 1938). Boyhood in India; Salvation Army; education in England; work as congregationalist minister and later poetical career in USA.   334

MAYO, C. H. P. Reminiscences of a Harrow Master(1928). Career as teacher from 80's; school life, work, customs, etc.   335

MAYO, Isabella Fyvie. Recollections during Fifty Years (1910). Career as journalist and author; childhood and social life in London; religion, social problems, literary life and memories of eminent writers.   336

MEAD, Isaac. Life of an Essex Lad (Chelmsford, 1923). Labourer, farmer, miller, landowner; cottage life; farm work; doctrine; simple.   337

MEADOWS, Lindon. College Recollections (1879). Life and work at theological training college; ordination; curate at Stanmore and Cheriton; parish life, ladies, work, social; humor of clerical life.   By Charles Butler Greatrex.   338

MEADOWS, Mary Jane. Life, Voyages, and Surprising Adventures (1802). Her London business;bankruptcy; ships for India;shipwrecked; castaway in Africa and adventures in deserts;Crusoe-like life on island;later adventures among the Iroquois; Defoe-like.   339

MEAGHER,Thomas Francis. Autobiography of a young Irelander; youth, manhood, political career, earlier 19th Century. MS,Royal Irish Academy, Dublin.   340

MEANEY, Joseph. Clipperty-Clop (L. 1943); Scribble Street (1945). London journalist;himself and horses; adventures and stunts getting news of murders and sensations.   341

MEATH, Reginald Brabazon, 12th Earl Memories of the Nineteenth Century(L. 1923); Memories of the Twentieth Century (1924). Germany; his career in diplomacy; Germany, France; society & political life in England and Ireland; travels; celebrities.   342

MEDLEY,Capt.Julius George. A Year's Campaigning (1858). Experiences of an engineer in the Indian Mutiny; siege of Lucknow; Doab campaign.   343

MEDWIN, James. Memoirs of William West Medwin(1882). The son's autobiographical notes appended; early life near London;country life in Bucks and events of earlier 19th Century.Aylesbury Archaeological Society.   344

MEDWIN,William West. Memoirs (1882) Life at sea in later 18th Century;his business trips to South America,Spain and France;work as corn merchant; his life in Aylesbury; good.   345

MEE, Patrick. Marine Gunner (1935). Career in Marine Artillery;lower deck life and sport; service in WW1; Dardanelles. Suvla Bay, Jutland.   346

MEEK, A.S.A Naturalist in Cannibal-Land(1913). Early interest in natural history;travels to New Guinea and Solomons; butterfly-hunting.   347

MEEK, George. George Meek (1910). A bathchairman's account of his life and work at Eastbourne; casual work, poverty, marriage, political aspirations and socialist work; good.   348

MEETWELL, James. Incidents, Errors, and Experiences (Edin. 1866). Life of a Scottish merchant; family life, and business ups and downs.   349

MELBA,Dame Nellie. Melodies and Memories(L.1925). Early days in Australia; music studies in Paris; concert and operatic career in England and the Empire;celebrities in society and the arts.   350

MELFORD, Mark. Life in a Booth (L. 1913). Theatrical career; mostly life as a strolling player.   351

MELHUISH, Thomas. An Account of the Early Part of the Life(1805). Conversion of a Taunton man; forty years of travel in the Quaker ministry;religious work and experiences. Copy,Exeter P.L.   352

MELLOR, Maj. Anthony Henry Seymour. Machine-Gunner(1944). His WW2 service in N. Africa; war in the desert; capture by Italians and escape.   353

MELLOR, Capt. Francis Horace. Sword and Spear (1934). Military service in India and Persia from 1918; policeman in S. Africa and N. Nigeria; administration, sport, adventure.   354

MELLY, George. School Experiences (1854); Recollections of Sixty Years (Coventry,1893). Critical memories of life,work, methods of prep school and public school;Rugby; memories of public, political, social events of Victorian age;his parliamentary work and social and sporting life.   355

MELTON ROUGHRIDER. Rum 'Uns to Follow (1934). Childhood, country life, and hunting in Leicester and Midlands seventy years in the shires; dialect; good.   356

MELVILL,Sir Andrew. Memoirs (1918). Scottish soldier-of-fortune with the French army in Flanders, Sweden, Germany,1650-80; battles and adventures; lively;translated from French edition of 1704.   357

MELVILL, Colonel Teignmouth Philip. Ponies and Women (1932). Wellington &

Sandhurst;army career; Gibraltar, India,WW1; association with the Spanish royal family;polo-playing; his international games.   358

MELVILLE, Sir James. Memoirs (1683; 1929). Scottish diplomat of Sixteenth Century; public affairs and diplomacy at court of Mary and James VI; international relations;embassies to Elizabeth; vivid scenes; excellent.   359

MELVILLE, Lewis (Lewis S. Benjamin) Not All the Truth (1928). His life as actor, journalist, author; WW1 work; censorship; anecdotes of celebrities; correspondence.   360

ANON. Memoirs of a Lady of Quality (1926). Reprint of the section of society memoirs and scandals that Smollett inserted in Peregrine Pickle.361

ANON. Memoirs of a Norfolk Lady (L. 1733).Childhood and schooling in Lynn and Norwich;joins gypsies; her amours with the gentry and her downhill career; picaresque and bawdy; probably a fictional work. Bodleian.   362

ANON. Memoirs of a Printer's Devil (Gainsborough, 1793). Boyhood, education, work as printer, travels, love life, etc.   363

ANON. Memoirs of a Sergeant (1835). Irish youth's service in the infantry in the Peninsular War; conversion to Methodism; religious work; detailed & good account of soldier's life. Methodist Book Room.   364

ANON. Memoirs of a Younger Brother (1789). Boyhood on East Anglian farm; apprentice and shopkeeper in London; finances; his interests; escape from the country.   365

ANON.Memoirs of an Unfortunate Young Lady (Bristol, 1710,1790). A Bristol girl's fall; bad company; licentious living; life as prostitute; brothels and street-walking; disease; hopeless contrition;appeal to philanthropists; fiction?   366

ANON.Memoirs of the Life of a Country Surgeon(1845). His apprenticeship and later success in his own practice criticism of College of Surgeons; and suggestions about its charter.   367

ANON. Memories: A Life's Epilogue
(1872). Devon man; boyhood at sea and
life on moors;interests in literature
history and science;philosophical reflections; public events.   368

ANON. Memories and Music(1908). His
reminiscences of opera,music, foreign
travel, in letters addressed to woman
seen at the opera.   369

ANON.Memories and Musings of a Hospital Surgeon (Glasgow, 1920). Student
and doctor in London hospitals; work
and routine of large general hospital;
particular cases. Copy in Cambridge
U.L.   370

ANON. Memories of a Lady's Maid (L.
1938). Lurid experiences of a girl in
noble families in 19th Century; work
as maid; amours and scandals.   371

ANON. Memories of a Sister of Saint
Saviour's Priory (Oxford, 1903). Work
among London poor in mid-19th Century;
Catholic religion and social work in
Soho, Haggerston, Bethnal Green. 372

MEMORY, F.W. Memory's (1932). Daily
Mail reporter's work as leg man & his
adventures; searching out sensational
crimes, etc.   373

MENDOZA,Daniel. Memoirs of the Life
(1816). Life and fights of the famous
18th Century pugilist; his opponents;
his noble patrons; fair.   374

/MENZIES, Amy Charlotte (Stuart)/.
Memories, Discreet and Indiscreet(1917)
Further Indiscretions (L. 1918); Sir
Stanley Maude & Other Memories (1920)
Recollections and Reflections (1921);
Joys of Life (1927). All except third
written under pseudonym, "A Woman of
No Importance." Piquant memories and
anecdotes of society, statesmen, soldiers, churchmen, fine ladies, men of
letters;country life, politics, sport
and literature; England,Europe, India
from 1870's.   375

MENZIES, Sgt. John. Reminiscences of
an Old Soldier (Edin. 1883). Military
service,1834-67; India and S. Africa;
recruiting at Nottingham; instructor
in drill at Perth.   376

MERCER,Gen. Cavalié. Journal of the
Waterloo Campaign(1927). Detailed and
personal account of service in Artillery in the campaign.   377

MEREDITH, Anne   (Anthony Gilbert).
Three-a-Penny (1940). Her childhood &
schooling;development of her literary
interests; writing of detective stories; Sayers,Chesterton; pleasant life
of a popular writer. Real name, Lucy
B. Malleson.   378

MEREDITH, Isabel. A Girl among the
Anarchists(1903). London girlhood and
idealism;work with foreign anarchists
and for the journal Tocsin;encounters
with police; disillusionment.   379

MEREDITH,John B.Fragmentary Records
(1910). Boyhood in Woolwich;the first
railways; work as railway engineer in
England, Canada, India, S. America; &
work for teetotalism.   380

MERIVALE,Charles. Autobiography and
Letters (Oxford, 1899). Education at
Harrow; teaching at Haileybury; study
for ministry; work as rector in Essex
and as Dean at Ely;antiquarian, architectural, historical studies; literary friendships.   381

MERIVALE,Herman Charles. Bar, Stage
and Platform(1902). Harrow & Balliol;
legal studies; work as a lecturer and
author; life in literary and theatrical circles; Thackeray, Kean, Palmerston, etc.   382

MERIVALE, John Herman. Leaves from
the Diary (1910). Work as lawyer and
commissioner in bankruptcy in the 1st
half of the century; scholar, translator, poet; literary society; Irving
Coleridge, Lockhart, Mallet, Sharpe &
others.   383

MERSEY,Charles Bigham, 2nd Viscount
A Picture of Life (1941). Career as a
diplomat from 1895; China,Turkey; his
later career in House of Lords;public
affairs, society, business.   384

MERSON, Billy. Fixing the Stoof Oop
(1925).Career and life of a comedian;
musichalls and revues;experiences and
anecdotes.   385

MESSENT, Charles. Autobiography of

a Sunday School Teacher (1856). Vague and pious account of his work, ideals and beliefs.   386

METCALF, H.E. On Britain's Business (1943).Work and travels of a ship engineer from later 19th Century; business in Russia, China, Japan.   387

METCALF,John. The Life (York, 1795) Tricks and adventures of Blind Jack of Knaresborough; poacher and thief; reported in Yorkshire dialect.   388

METCALFE, Francis James.   Colliers and I (Manchester, 1903). Ordination and ministry in Litchfield; rector of Killamarsh;parish life;religious work among Midlands miners. Copy in Derby P.L.   389

METCALFE, Thomas Washington. A Sea-Lover's Memories (1934); Memorials of the Military Life (L.1936); A Country Bloke's Chronicle (1940). Experiences at sea in sailing ships; education at Sandhurst; WW1 service RFC; life in a Somerset village as country squire and writer; army celebrities.   390

METFORD, Joseph. Autobiography of a Glastonbury Quaker;business life as a hosier in early 19th Century; Quaker life and religion; abridged. Journal Friends' Hist. Soc. XXV (1928).   391

METHUEN,Thomas Anthony. Autobiography (1870). Boyhood in 1780's; Eton & Oxford; ordination; life as a country curate;vicar of Garsdon; domestic and social life in Wilts; sorrows.   392

MEYER, Frederick B. The Bells of Is (1894). A Leicester clergyman's work for discharged prisoners in the 80's; fight for temperance.   393

MEYNELL, Esther Hallam. Woman Talking(1940). Author's memories of country life and influences of books and music; literary and artistic circles; friends and celebrities.   394

MEYNELL, Lady Mary.   Sunshine and Shadows(1933). Childhood in 50's; her family and life in country;London and court; country house life; travels; & public events from Crimean War to WW1; celebrities.   395

MEYRICK, Mrs. F. R. (Kate). Secrets of the 43 (1933). Proprietor of night club in Soho; celebrated clients; the underworld; prostitutes, gamblers and crooks; experiences in gaol.   396

MEYRICK,Frederick. Memories of Life at Oxford(1905). Academic life at Oxford,1847-54; work at Maynooth and as school inspector;parish life and work as the rector of Blickling; Manning & Anglo-Catholicism.   397

MEYSEY-THOMPSON, Col. Richard Frederick. Reminiscences of the Course(L. 1898). Eton in 60's; army career and service in Ashanti war;hunting in Devon; horseracing in Ireland; horses & hunts, mostly in Yorks.   398

MIDDLETON,Cecil H. Village Memories (1941). Childhood and village life in late 19th Century; charming.   399

MIDDLETON, Edgar. I Might Have Been a Success (1935). London childhood; & his varied career and travels; journalist,playwright, Parliamentary candidate, filming; WW1 service in RNAS; adventures.   400

MIDLETON, W. St.John Brodrick, Earl Records and Reactions (1939).Eton and Oxford;Parliamentary career.from 1880 and work in the War Office;activities in Boer War and WW1; Lord Lieutenant of Ireland; conservative politics and public events.   401

MIEVILLE,Sir Walter Frederick.Under Queen and Khedive (1899). His career in Egypt, 1874-95; consular officer & quarantine officer; plagues; sanitary work; Sudan War; Egyptian society and his travels.   402

ANON.Military Service and Adventure in the Far East(1847). Experiences of a cavalry officer; Afghan campaign of 1839; Sikh campaign, 1845.   403

MILL, John Stuart. Autobiography of (1873). Education; moral influences; travels;work with East India Company; utilitarian propaganda and writings; philosophy and intellectual development; Liberalism; books and friends; his achievement; good.   404

MILL,William Hodge. Diary, 1820-22,

1828-29, 1837-38; clergyman's travels to, from, and in India; work as principal of Bishop's College, Calcutta. MS, Bodleian, Mill 203-212.　　405

MILLAIS, John G. Wanderings & Memories (1919). Surrey naturalist's travels and sport; big game and natural history in the Highlands, Africa, and the Arctic; adventures.　　406

MILLAR,George Reid. Maquis (1945); Horned Pigeon(1946). With the Maquis in WW2;French resistance and guerilla warfare; retreat of 8th Army; capture and escape from Germany in a nightmare journey; vivid story; excellent. 407

MILLER, David Prince. The Life of a Showman (1849). Life and difficulties of manager of Adelphi Theatre, Glasgow; earlier poverty in London; work as conjurer; circus life; tricks and frauds; good for low life.　　408

MILLER, Edward Dailey. Fifty Years of Sport (1925). Harrow and Cambridge military service in India,Egypt, Boer War and WW1; football, riding & polo; games in India and USA.　　409

MILLER, George. Latter Struggles in the Journey of Life (Edin. 1833). His religious life and moral reflections; publisher of tracts in Dunbar; bookselling at turn of century;written in turgid style.　　410

MILLER,Hugh. My Schools and Schoolmasters (1854). His education and the things and people that influenced him; school, teachers, early jobs, people; his geological studies and writings ; politics, Reform Bill, society; written for working men.　　411

MILLER, James. Autobiography; with Highland army at Preston in 1745; enlisted as alternative to execution; & served in India; siege of Pondicherry return in 1750; may be by Roger Fulton. Journal Soc. Army Hist. Research III (1924).　　412

MILLER, Gen. John. Memoirs (1828). Young soldier's military service with Peruvian forces during War of Independence, 1820-29.　　413

MILLER, Walter R. S. Reflections of

a Pioneer(1936); Yesterday and Tomorrow (1938). Work and life of a Church of England missionary in Northern Nigeria,1900-35; Hausa life and customs and modern tendencies.　　414

MILLICAN,Albert. Travels and Adventures(1891). Travels in South America and Andes; work as orchid-collector; Colombian life.　　415

MILLIGAN,Kenneth. Alone (1950). His work as an electrical engineer; romantic longings; purchase of cottage in Welsh mountains & life there; discovery of himself and his world.　　416

MILLIE, P. D. Thirty Years Ago (Colombo(1878). Work as a coffee-planter in Ceylon; labour,work and economics; social life of planters.　　417

MILLING, John M. Great Days (1935). Country life and sport; army service in Hants, Bermuda, Ireland, India and WW1; mostly fishing.　　418

/MILLINGEN,John Gideon7. Adventures of an Irish Gentleman(1830). An Irish adventurer's tricks and amours in England and on the continent;may be fiction.　　419

MILLS,Lady Dorothy. Different Drummer(1930). Her travels and adventures in Africa; a woman in a man's world; relations of sexes.　　420

MILLS, Freddie. Twenty Years (1950) The career of the British light-heavy weight boxing champion;his fights and his background.　　421

MILLWARD, Jessie. Myself and Others (1923). Actress's career in theatre; her roles; theatrical society; Terry, Irving, etc.; criticism.　　422

MILN, Louise Jordan. When We Were Strolling Players (1894). Theatrical tour with her husband in India, China and Japan.　　423

MILNE, Alan Alexander. It's Too Late (1939). Childhood; school; Cambridge; freelance journalism; editor of Punch and work as literary journalist; army service in WW1; literary and theatrical society; books and writers; whimsical and pleasant.　　424

MILNE,James. Window in Fleet Street
(1931); Memoirs of a Bookman (1934);
Over the Hills (1945). His boyhood in
Scotland; London from the 90's; journalism; travels; social; celebrities;
Butler, Smiles, Hardy, Meredith, Kipling, etc.; nostalgic.　　　　　425

MILNE,Thomas Ferris. This World and
That(1934). Boyhood at sea; adventure
among savages in Far East;his work as
a diver in the navy from 1891.　　426

MINCHIN, J. G. Cotton.　Old Harrow
Days (1898).His life as a boy at Harrow in the 60's; boys, masters, sport
institutions, pleasures.　　　　427

MINSHALL,Ebenezer. Fifty Years' Reminiscences (1910). Religious life in
Free Church; musician and organist in
the church.　　　　　　　　428

MITCHEL,John. Jail Journal (Glasgow
1876). Irish writer and patriot; his
arrest as an alleged felon & deportation to Bermuda and Tasmania; life on
a Tasmanian farm; convicts and kanga-
roos; escape to America.　　　　429

MITCHELL, C. Ainsworth. A Scientist
in the Criminal Courts(1945). A hand-
writing expert's experiences as a witness in the courts.　　　　　430

MITCHELL, Ernest Pryce. Deep Water
(1933).　At sea from boyhood; captain
on steamers;　interlude as a cockatoo
sheepfarmer, Australia.　　　　431

MITCHELL,James. Brief Autobiography
of religious life; written in 1678 as
he was about to be executed for shooting the Bishop of Orkney. MS, University of Edinburgh, Laing 269.　　432

MITCHELL, Mrs. John Murray.　A Missionary's Wife (Edin. 1871); In India
(1876); In Southern India (1885). Her
missionary work, life and travels; in
Southern Bengal; educational work;and
zenanas.　　　　　　　　　433

MITCHELL, John Murray.　In Western
India (Edin. 1899). Scottish boyhood;
education in Aberdeen;his theological
study;missionary career in India; the
castes; government; missionaries. 434

MITCHELL,Sir Peter Chalmers.My Fill

of Days (1937). Family and education,
from 60's;his work in natural history
and travels in Asia and Africa;　work
at London Zoo and Whipsnade.　　435

MITCHELL,Thomas. Lives of Early Methodist Preachers, ed. Thomas Jackson
I (1837).　Life, ministry and travels
of 18th Century Methodist preacher in
Yorks and North of England.　　436

MITCHELL, William. Reminiscences of
a Professional Billiard Player(1902).
Billiards champion;　the game, mostly
in London and Sheffield,　in 70's and
80's; games, players, sportsmen; gambling and sharp practices.　　437

MITCHELL-HEDGES, Frederick Albert.
Battles with Giant Fish(1925). Adven-
tures with big fish, sea monsters and
Lady Richmond Brown.　　　　438

MITFORD,Mary Russell. Recollections
of a Literary Life (1852).　Childhood
in the country; London education; her
travels; literary career; writers and
books that influenced her.　　439

/MOFFITT,William/. Autobiography of
the Sark M. P. (1910).Boyhood in Cumberland; a draper's assistant in Manchester; draper in Carlisle; his shirt
making; Methodism; philanthropy; Carlisle social life and friends.　440

MOISTER, William. Memorials of Missionary Labours (1866);　The Story of
My Life (1886).　Career as missionary
in West Africa, West Indies and South
Africa; work of missions; travels and
native life; slavery.　　　　441

/MOLE, Sgt.Maj. Edwin/. King's Hussar, ed. Herbert Compton (1893).　His
military service and life in camp and
on the march; England, Ireland, India
and S. Africa, 1862-88;　good, lively
narrative.　　　　　　　　442

MOLLISON,James A. Death Cometh Soon
or Late(1932); Playboy of the Air (L.
1937).　Adventures and triumphs of an
airman; in RAF; India; Australia; his
record flights; marriage to Amy Johnson; celebrities he met.　　　443

MOLONY, William O'Sullivan. New Ar-
mor for Old (N.Y. 1935); Victims Vic-
torious (1937).　Oxford; WW1 service;

travels; his neurosis and mysticism; reactions against war, capitalism and religion; work and creed of a communist; from Buddha to Marx.   444

MOLYNEUX, Jack. Thirty Years a Hunt Servant (1935). Kennel boy and huntsman from 1901; foxhunting; work with Quorn and other hunts;breeding hounds and work of the hunt.   445

MOLYNEUX, Gen. William Charles Francis. Campaigning (1896). His military career; Kaffir and Zulu wars; Soudan; personal experiences.   446

MONCKTON, Charles Arthur Whitmor e. Some Experiences (1921); Last Days in New Guinea (1922); New Guinea Recollections (1934). Career and experiences as resident magistrate; natives & traders and missionaries; New Guinea; social life.   447

MONEY, R. R. Flying and Soldiering (1936). Service as flyer in WW1; subsequently with RAF to 1928.   448

MONEY,Walter B. Humours of a Parish (1920). Clerical life, 1870-1900; his work, mostly at Weybridge; people and natural history; fond record.   449

MONKHOUSE,Muriel J. Ancient History (1938). Childhood in Edinburgh in the 80's;school in Liverpool; family life holidays and sport.   450

MONMOUTH,Robert Cary, Earl of. Memoirs, ed. G. H. Powell (1903). Gilded youth at court of Elizabeth; courtier and diplomat; Warden of the Marches; military service; the Armada; lively and valuable; 1st ed., 1759.   451

MONSARRAT, Nicholas. H. M. Corvette (1942); H. M. Frigate (1946). Naval service in WW2;medical officer aboard a corvette in Atlantic service; later commander of a frigate; adventure and heroism.   452

MONTAGU, Edwin Samuel, Travel diary 1917-18; visit to India; politics and official life and society; receptions and hunting;dictated. An Indian Diary (1930).   453

MONTAGU,Lilian Helen. My Club and I (1943). Life in London Jewish family;

foundation of a Jewish girls' club in East End of London; her life and work there.   454

MONTAGU,Adm. Victor Alexander. Middy's Recollections(1898); Reminiscences (1910). His life in navy in 50's; Crimean War;China War; adventures and midshipman's life;his later career in the navy; social life; sport.   455

MONTAGUE, Charles W. Recollections of an Equestrian Manager (Edin. 1881) Circus life in mid-century; shows and adventures in provinces; the language of the circus.   456

MONTAGUE,Nell St. John. Revelations (1926). Experiences of a clairvoyante her psychic experiences;her clientèle in high society.   457

MONTEFIORE,Dora B. From a Victorian to a Modern (1927). Childhood in Kenley Manor;emigration to Australia and her family life there; women's suffrage movement, socialism, communism in England from 1892.   458

MONTGOMERY, Bernard Law Montgomery, 1st Viscount. Ten Chapters (L. 1946); Military Leadership(1946); Forward to Victory(1946); Normandy to the Baltic (1947);El Alamein to the River Sangro (1948); Forward from Victory (1948). Military career of WW2 general;record of campaigns and victories; the North African and Italian campaigns; historical and personal.   459

MONTGOMERY, D. H.   Down the Flare Path (1937). Personal narrative; WW1 service in RFC in France.   460

MONTGOMERY, William. The Montgomery Manuscripts (Belfast, 1869). Contains autobiography of the compiler;life in Ireland in 17th Century; social life in County Down; antiquarian and historical studies.   461

MONTGOMERY-CUNINGHAME, Sir Thomas Andrew. Dusty Measure(1939). Military career; India,Boer War, Ireland, WW1; military attaché in Vienna and Athens before WW1; Dardanelles; Central Europe after the war, public and private affairs.   462

/MONTRESOR, C. A., editor/. Leaves

from Memory's Log Book: by an Ancient Mariner(1887). Naval life in 20's and 30's; Far East; West Indies.   463

MOODIE, J. W. A Soldier's Life (Ardrossan, 1887). Pamphlet; his life in the army; conversion; religion, temperance, evangelism.   464

MOODIE, John W. D. Memoirs of the Late War(1831); Scenes and Adventures (Montreal,1866). Service in Fusiliers in 1814 campaign in Holland; a lively account of attack on Bergen-op-Zoom; later service in S. Africa and Canada and his settlement in Ontario.   465

MOODY, A. F. Memories and Musings (1938). Work of Presbyterian minister in Ulster;work as Moderator; opinions on Irish life.   466

MOONEY, Nicholas. The Life (London, 1752). Early life in Ireland;army and navy service; his robberies; conversion; dictated before hanging.   467

MOORCROFT, William. Diary, 1820-25; travels in India; commercial investigations for East India Co. MS, India Office, Eur. D.236-253.   468

MOORE, Bob. Don't Call Me a Crook (1935). Glasgow man's life of crime & wandering; adventures in China, USA & England; amoral adventuring.   469

MOORE, Eva. Exits and Entrances (L. 1923). Her career in the theatre from the 90's; roles, plays, theatre life; suffragette movement; WW1.   470

MOORE,Francis. Travels into the Interior Parts of Africa (1738). Travel in Gambia as factor for Royal African Company, 1723-4, 1730-5; exploration; trade; natives.   471

MOORE,Frank Frankfort. Journalist's Note-Book (1894); Mixed Grill (1930). Life and work as journalist in London and Ireland; social life; amusements; late Victorian and Edwardian literature, music, art, theatre.   472

MOORE,George.Confessions of a Young Man (L.1888); Memoirs of My Dead Life (1906); Hail and Farewell(1911); Communication to My Friends(1933). Early years in London and Paris; literature

and art studies; his writings; criticism of his time;youth in Ireland and personal reminiscences of Irish writers; French painters; repudiation of Catholicism;his writings, circumstances of their publication and struggle with censorship.   473

MOORE, George Greville. Memories of an Old Etonian (1919); Society Recollections (1908); More Society Recollections (1908). Life at Eton; military service in India;travels, society theatre and music; England,France and Austria; from 1860's.   474

MOORE, Henry. Life: by Mrs. Richard Smith (1844). Includes autobiography, 1751-90;Dublin boyhood; conversion to Methodism; ministry in Ireland; Irish social life and conditions.   475

MOORE, Henry Kingsmill. Reminiscences and Reflections (1930). Ministry in Dublin; sixty years of education & church work in Ireland.   476

MOORE, Jane Elizabeth. The Genuine Memoirs (1786). Travels and sentimental adventures through England; trade and industry; moralisings.   477

MOORE, Mark. Memoirs and Adventures (1795). Naval officer's service with British, Portuguese, Tuscan, Imperial navies; theatrical tours; his debts & prison experiences;poverty in his old age; very good.   478

MOORE, Rev. Thomas. Diary, 1857-58; his experiences and events at Lucknow and Cawnpore during the Mutiny. MS, B. M. Add. 37151.   479

MOORHOUSE, Michael. The Defence of (Leicester, 1789). Abandonment of his business to become Wesleyan preacher; travels in Ireland and England;Wesley and himself; criticism of the Methodist organization.   480

MORAN, Herbert M. In My Fashion (L. 1946). Last ten years of cancer specialist; RAMC service; human weakness as seen from a Medical Board; medical corruption and inadequacy.   481

MORAY, Alastair. The Diary of a Rum Runner(1929). Smuggling liquor during Prohibition period; adventures; associates; New York area.   482

MORDAUNT, Elinor. Sinabada (1937).
Family and childhood; literary life &
her writing;her travels; psychological strain of continued writing; self
deprecating and self-conscious account
of a writer's life and mind.   483

MORE,John. With Allenby's Crusaders
(1923). Cheerful narrative of service
in Sinai and Palestine campaigns,WW1;
desert warfare.   484

MORE, Martha. Mendip Annals, edited
Arthur Roberts (1859). Autobiography,
based on diary for 1789-98;charitable
labours; foundation of schools in the
mining villages of Somerset;influence
of Wilberforce; her ideals.   485

MOREHEAD, Robert. Memorials of the
Life and Writings (Edin. 1875). Youth
of the Dean of Edinburgh to 1795; his
education and reading; social life in
Scotland.   486

MORESBY, Adm.John. Two Admirals (L.
1909).Consists mostly of his memories
of his own career and life in the navy
1847-81.   487

MORGAN, Guy. Only Ghosts Can Live
(1945). Personal narrative, WW2; life
in German and Italian camps for wounded prisoners.   488

MORGAN, J. Ministerial Experiences
(1870?). Family life; religious work
and ministry in Thornbury,Gloucester-
shire.   489

MORGAN, James. Recollections of My
Life (Belfast, 1874). Religious education and career in church; ministry
in Lisburn and Belfast; Presbyterian
life and beliefs.   490

MORIER,James Justinian. Diary 1808-
1815; writer's travels in Persia and
Asia Minor, India and Persian Gulf as
secretary to British Embassy and minister to Persia; author of Hajji Baba
A Journey through Persia (1812); Second Journey (1818).   491

MORLEY,Henry. Early Papers and Some
Memories (1891). Critic's memories of
social, club, literary life, books in
London.   492

MORLEY, Sgt. Stephen. Memoirs of a
Serjeant (Ashford,1842). His military
career; service in Hanover and South
America; mostly his adventures in the
Peninsular War.   493

MORLEY OF BLACKBURN,   John Morley,
Viscount. Recollections(1917). School
and Oxford; literary and intellectual
influences;work for Liberal Party and
his career in Parliament; politics and
public events and personalities. 494

MORRIS, Marmaduke C. F.   Yorkshire
Reminiscences(1922). Boyhood in Yorks
and coming of railways; Oxford; life
as clergyman in East Riding;rector of
Nunburnholme; Yorkshire life, people,
customs, sport; excellent.   495

MORRIS,Maurice O'Connor. Memini (L.
1892). Irish society, sport, industry
and personalities from the 40's; work
as civil servant; visits to England,
West Indies, Germany.   496

MORRIS, Sgt. Thomas. Recollections
of Military Service (1845). Campaigns
of the Peninsular War; Holland,France
and Waterloo; infantry view.   497

MORRIS, William O'Connor. Memories
and Thoughts (1895). Ireland and its
history from 1845;legal career; county court judge; society, church, Land
League,National League, local government; political movements.   498

MORRISON,Pearse. Rambling Recollec-
tions(1905). Boyhood at Banff; London
life and business; member of the City
Corporation; City of London School; &
commercial education,city life, clubs
and conservative politics.   499

MORRISS, Henry F. Minister, Mayor &
Merchant (1914); Cinderella Christian
(Woldingham, 1936?). His business in
London metal trade;his work in Sunday
schools & missions; Mayor of Bermondsey;municipal politics; lively record
of London life from 60's. Copy of the
second book, Croydon P.L.   500

MORSE, John. Englishman in the Russian Ranks (1915). Military service,
WW1;fighting in Poland against German
invaders; vivid.   501

MORSE-BOYCOTT,Desmond. Ten Years in

A Slum Parish(1929); We Do See Life!
(1931); Fields of Yesterday (1932). A
pleasant childhood;religious training
and ministry in slum parish of Somers
Town; Edward Irving and the Apostoli-
cal Movement; Manning and Anglo-Catholicism; social work among the London
poor;life of a clerical Micawber. 502

MORTENSEN, Stanley. Football Is My
Game (1949). Career of a celebrated
association football player; boyhood
games in South Shields; playing for
England; simple.   503

MORTON, Charles. My Sixty Years of
the Turf(1930). Work of a trainer and
stories of the turf; his successes in
the Derby and other races.   504

MORTON, William. I Remember (Hull,
1934). Printing in Yorks in 70's;work
for solicitors;book and music seller;
commercial work in theatre,London and
Hull; Maskelyne and Cooke.   505

MORYSON, Fynes. An Itinerary (1617)
Ten years of travel in British Isles
and all countries of Europe at end of
16th Century; Irish affairs; customs;
social life; valuable.   506

MOSCHELES,Felix. In Bohemia (1896);
Fragments of an Autobiography (1899).
Early life in Germany;work as painter
in Germany and England;reminiscences,
Mazzini, Rossini, Browning,etc.   507

MOSELEY, Benjamin. Family Memoirs,
edited Sir Oswald Moseley (1849).This
includes diary, 1781; voyage from Jamaica to England; brief. William Salt
Library, Stafford.   508

MOSELEY,Sydney Alexander. The Truth
About a Journalist(1935). His work on
provincial and London newspapers; ups
and downs;journalists, editors, celebrities; truth about schools of journalism.   509

MOSLEY, Leonard Oswald. So Far, So
Good (1937); Down Stream (1939). Work
and travels as journalist in the 30's;
Hollywood, Palestine, Spain, Germany;
the political scene and movements for
war; public events.   510

MOSS, Fletcher. Fifty Years of Public Work (Didsbury,1915). His work on

the Didsbury Council; Lancs politics,
sports,quarrels, antiquities; amusing
local record.   511

MOSS, Herbert James. Windjammer to
Westminster(1941). His forty years at
sea; military service in WW1; Parliamentary service as Member for Ruther-
glen; Conservative politics.   512

MOTHER SUPERIOR.Life of an Enclosed
Nun (1910). Life as novice and nun in
a Belgian convent in 80's; observance
and spiritual life.   513

MOTT, Lt. Edward Spencer. A Mingled
Yarn (1898). Misdeeds at Eton; military service in India; social life and
sport; playwriting and acting in England; horseracing; sports journalism;
Nathaniel Gubbins of the Pink Un; his
life as a Victorian blood; good. 514

MOTTISTONE,John Edward Bernard See-
ly, Baron. Adventure (1930); Fear and
Be Slain (1931).Former War Secretary;
adventures by land, sea and air; his
school;Cambridge; service in Boer War
and WW1; Peace conferences; Conservative M.P.; politics.   515

MOTTRAM, Ralph Hale. Three Personal
Records (1929); Autobiography (1938);
Bowler Hat (1940). Personal narrative
of WW1 service in France; people and
places and his relation to them; work
in a Norwich bank;the routine as seen
by a clerk.   516

MOULE, Ven. Arthur Evans. New China
and Old (1892); Half a Century (1911)
Recollections of his life and work as
a missionary,1861-1911; Archdeacon of
Mid-China;educational work; T'aip'ing
rebellion.   517

MOULE,George Evans. A Retrospect of
Sixty Years (Shanghai, 1907). Education at Cambridge; missionary work in
China;Bishop of Shanghai;Chinese life
and rebellions.   518

MOULE, Handley Carr Glyn. Memories
of a Vicarage (1913). Bishop of Durham's memories of clerical life at his
old home in Dorset.   519

MOUNT EDGCUMBE,Richard Edgcumbe,2nd
Earl of. Musical Reminiscences (1827)
Memories of opera and music since his

childhood; travels in Germany, France and Italy; rather impersonal.   520

MOUNTAYNE,Thomas. Narratives of the Reformation (Camden Soc.,1859). Lively story of sufferings of London protestant minister during Mary's reign; interesting language.   521

MOUNTEVANS,Sir Edward R.C.R. Evans, Baron. Keeping the Seas (1919); Evans of the Broke (1941); Adventurous Life (1946). Life of a modern hero; patrol and minesweeping work in WW1; work on China, Australia, Africa stations and as Commander of Nore;civil defence in WW2; lively adventures.   522

MOUNTJOY,Timothy. Life, Labours and Deliverances (1887). Work as miner in Forest of Dean;working conditions and miners,managers, owners, strikes; his work as Methodist and lay-preacher;and experiences of religion and working-class life. Gloucester City L.   523

MOUSLEY, Capt. Edward O. Secrets of a Kuttite (1921). Service with RAF in siege of Kut; Mesopotamian campaign; capture and experiences in the Turkish prisons.   524

MOWATT,James Alexander. Autobiography of a Brewer's Son(1869). A Dublin man's career of drinking; temperance meetings; teetotalism.   525

MOWBRAY, Sir John Robert. Seventy Years at Westminster (Edin. 1900). At Westminster and Oxford; his career in law from 1837; Parliamentary service from 1857; work of Parliament; famous politicians and events.   526

MOYNE,Walter Edward Guinness, first Baron. Walkabout (1936). The travels and observations of an ethnographer & animal collector in New Guinea, Malaya, etc.; studies of cannibals, aborigines, anthropology.   527

MOZART, George. Limelight (L.1938). Comedian's career;busking; vaudeville and revues; tours in USA and Empire; anecdotes of performers and musichall life, from 1880's.   528

MOZLEY, John Rickards. Clifton Memories (Bristol,1927). Life in Clifton and sketches of Henry Sidgwick and of other Clifton celebrities.   529

MOZLEY, Rev. Thomas. Reminiscences of Oriel College (1882); Reminiscences Chiefly of Towns (1885). Academic and religious life at Oxford;Oxford Movement; Newman; Anglo-Catholic journalism;family life from beginning of the century; his schools; work as curate, rector and dean in Northants, Wilts & Devon; good and valuable.   530

MUDDIMAN, Sir Alexander P. Memoirs (Allahabad, 1930). Career as a civil servant in Bengal; work with Calcutta Historical Society;social life; sport Tibetan War.   531

MUDDOCK, J. E. Preston. Pages from an Adventurous Life (1907). Travels & adventures in India and the East; his work as journalist and author ("Dick Donovan" of Daily News); Savage Club, literary and theatrical circles.   532

MUELLER, Friedrich Max. Auld Lang Syne (1898); My Autobiography (1901). Musical, literary, society recollections; philology and Indian friends; life of a scholar at Oxford; linguistic studies and friends; good.   533

MUELLER, George. Narrative of Some of the Lord's Dealings (1837); Autobiography (1905). German youth; emigration to England as young man; work for orphans in Bristol; ministry and mission work.   534

MUGGLETON,Lodowick. The Acts of the Witnesses (1699). Exemplary child and apprentice;London tailor; his gift of prophecy; founding Muggletonians; his experiences in prison and pillory;the religious life and propaganda of harsh and earnest Puritan.   535

MUIR,Edwin. The Story and the Fable (1940). Boyhood in Orkneys and North of Scotland; farming, social, reading and intellectual development; work as Glasgow clerk;political interests and work as journalist and author; strong Freudian element; good.   536

MUIR, Major H. J. Hoo Hooey (1947). His travel and work in Argentina from 1918; railroads, estates, sugar plantations; lively adventures; variety of jobs.   537

MUIR, Surgeon-Adm. John Reid. Years of Endurance (1936); Messing About in Boats(1938). WW1 service; surgery and naval war in the North Sea; lifelong experiences with small boats;yachting and racing.   538

MUIR,Ramsay. An Autobiography(1943) Oxford; teaching at Liverpool University; historical studies; philosophy; Liberal politics;travels in India and Germany; very interesting for intellectual interests.   539

MUIR, W.and E.H. Agra in the Mutiny (1896).Experiences at Agra during the Mutiny; work in the Intelligence Department.   540

MUIR, Ward. Observations of an Orderly (1917). WW1 service with RAMC; service at a Wandsworth hospital; his chores and patients.   541

MUIRHEAD,J.T. Ivory Poaching (1933) Thirty years' experiences in S.Africa Abyssinia and the Sudan; diamond mining; elephant hunting.   542

MUIRHEAD, John Henry.   Reflections (1942). Glasgow and Oxford education; professor at Birmingham; his life as student and professor of philosophy; philosophers of his time.   543

MUIRHEAD, Thorburn. Strange to Relate (1937). Travels in Canada, West Indies,Africa, Ceylon, Australia, big game hunting, jungle life, folk-lore and anthropology; pleasant.   544

/MULGRAVE, Helen/. Jesuit Executorship(1853). Her childhood at Mulgrave Castle and revolt against her catholic upbringing; marriage; Protestantism; tyranny of Jesuit executors of estate of her husband.   545

MULHALL, Mrs. Marion.   Between the Amazon and the Andes (1881). Her ten years as missionary in Argentina and Paraguay;Pampas, Gran Chaco and Matto Grosso; Jesuit missions; Indians; and her travels.   546

MULLEN,Pat. Man of Aran(1934); Come Another Day (1940). Life of fisherman and peasant in Aran Isles;life of the islanders; filming with Flaherty; his lessons in shark-hunting; his work as

labourer in USA; trade-unions; Irish-American life.   547

MULLIN, James. Story of a Toiler's Life (1921). His work for the United Irish League in Ireland and Wales;education, reading, politics, Fenianism to 1890.   548

MULLINS, Claud. Fifteen Years' Hard Labour (1948). Candid account of his work and experiences as a Metropolitan police magistrate; wise,humane record of crime and punishment.   549

MUNCASTER,Claude. Rolling Round the Horn (1933). Journalist's experiences on a Finnish barque.   550

MUNDAY, John. Reginald Blunt's Red Anchor Pieces(1928) contains Munday's story of his life as a poor boy, early 19th Century; hardships; his life in Chelsea.   551

MUNDAY,Luther. Chronicle of Friendships (1912). London in 70's; coffee-planting in Ceylon; philanthropic and hospital work; society, clubs, literary,theatrical, artistic friends, and sport; pleasant.   552

MUNDAY, Madeleine C. Rice Bowl Broken (1946). Fifteen years of teaching and journalism in Shanghai; Japanese invasion and Chinese reaction.   553

MUNDY, Louisa. Diary, 1822-42; her life and work as a missionary in Bengal; marriage and domestic life; her own religious life. A Brief Memoir,by George Mundy (1845).   554

MUNN,Thomas. The Life (1750). Highwayman who robbed the Yarmouth mail; confessions of a gentleman bricklayer before his hanging.   555

MUNNINGS, Sir Alfred J. An Artist's Life (1950). Nostalgic but lively account of his life to 1918; boyhood in East Anglia, schooling, family life & sport;commercial drawing & art training; painting of country life and animals; reading and literary tastes.556

MUNRO, Sir David.   It Passed Too Quickly(1941). Scottish childhood and education in Scottish universities; a career in army and air-force from 1902

India, WW1 & Mesopotamia; work as Air Vice-Marshal.   557

MUNRO, Donald John. Roaring Forties (1929). Highland boyhood; apprentice on clipper-ship; experiences as captain in the navy; Burmese War; interesting account of Burma.   558

MUNRO, Neil. Brave Days (Edin. 1931) Reminiscences of Scottish life; work as law clerk; reporter on the Glasgow Evening News.   559

MUNRO, Robert. Autobiographic Sketch (Glasgow, 1921). Education; effect of Darwin on him; medical study in Edinburgh in 60's; archaeological studies travels and writings.   560

MUNRO, Gen. William. Reminiscences of Military Service (1883);Records of Service (1887). Military career, 1844 to 1881; Kaffir Wars; Indian Mutiny; Crimean War; campaigns and service as surgeon-general.   561

MUNSTER, Wilhelmina, Countess of. My Memories (1904). Childhood; court of William IV; Kensington Palace and Queen Adelaide; life at court of Victoria; court and society.   562

MURE, Elizabeth. Extracts in J. G. Fyfe, Scottish Diaries (1942). Some observations of Ayrshire life in the 18th Century; changes of manners; a good picture of social life.   563

MURLIN, John. Lives of Early Methodist Preachers, ed. Thomas Jackson, II (1837). Life and ministry of itinerant Cornish preacher; Methodism in the South-West.   564

MURPHY, Arthur. Life, by Jesse Foot (1811) contains brief autobiography of family, education, legal practice and work as writer and playwright in 18th Century; modelled on Hume.   565

MURPHY, Captain John Richard. Storm Along (1936). Lifetime at sea in sail and steam; voyages all over world and yarns of the sea.   566

MURPHY, John T. New Horizons (1941) Poverty and working-class life in Manchester; trade union work; Russia in the 20's; work with Communist Party &

his resignation; socialist work; life and politics.   567

MURRAY, A. W. Forty Years' Mission Work (1876). His life and work as a missionary in Samoa and New Guinea in 1835-75; missions, conversions, Bible translation.   568

MURRAY, Capt. Alexander. Doings in China (1843). Experiences during the Chinese expedition to Chusan, 1841-2; Peace of Nankin.   569

MURRAY, Amelia Matilda. Recollections(1868). Life at court in time of George III,to coronation of Victoria; court personages.   570

MURRAY, David Christie. Making of a Novelist (1894); Recollections (1898) Experiences contributing to his writing; army, travel, poor law, theatre; boyhood in printing office; journalism in Midlands and for the Times and the Scotsman; a Parliamentary and War Correspondent; London literary life & friends; his novels.   571

MURRAY, Elizabeth. Sixteen Years of an Artist's Life (1859). Her travels in Morocco,Spain, Canary Islands; art travel books, social life.   572

MURRAY, Harold. Press, Pulpit, and Pew (1934); Kaleidoscope (1946). Work as religious journalist; English nonconformity; travels reporting religious events; reminiscences of people & places.   573

MURRAY, Henry. A Stepson of Fortune (1909). Career of journalist and novelist; Harmsworth papers; London edition of N. Y. Herald; dramatic criticism; literary amanuensis; his books; literary friends.   574

MURRAY, Sir John. Memorials (1747); ed. R.F. Bell (Edin. 1898). Secretary to Prince Charles Edward;negotiations with Jacobites; the rebellion; Culloden; his later travels.   575

MURRAY, Lindley. Memoirs of the Life (York, 1826). Youth in Pennsylvania; Quaker religious life in America and England; legal work; studies in science and grammar; autobiography mixed with reflections.   576

MURRAY, Thomas. Reminiscences of a journey from Edinburgh to London 1840; notes on M'Culloch the economist; his upbringing,education, teaching, writing in Scotland;Edinburgh life._Trans. Dumfriesshire and Galloway Nat. Hist. and Antiq. Soc. XXII-XXIII._   577

MURRY, John Middleton. Between Two Worlds (1935). London; Christ's Hospital;Oxford; literature and sex; his reading and writing;literary and artistic society;Katherine Mansfield and D.H. Lawrence; literary friends, criticism, literary enthusiasms.   578

MURSELL,Arthur. Memories of My Life (1913). Leicester boyhood;his Baptist ministry in Glasgow, London, Manchester,Birmingham; social life and changes; friends; pleasant.   579

MUSPRATT, Edmund Knowles. My Life and Work (1917). The work, travel and friends of an engineer and chemist in later 19th Century.   580

MUSPRATT,Eric. Fire of Youth (1948) Romantic account of a lifetime of travels in England, America, Australia, S. Africa, Europe, Russia; work as a writer.   581

MUSTARDE, John Clark. The Sun Stood Still (1944). Doctor in British Army; North African campaign;capture at Tobruk; prison experiences.   582

MUSTERS, George C. At Home with the Patagonians (1871). Travels among the Indians in Patagonia;from the straits to the Rio Negro.   583

MUTER, Mrs. Dunbar Douglas (Elizabeth). Travels and Adventures (1864); My Recollections of the Sepoy Revolt (1911).   Experiences of an officer's wife in India, China and New Zealand; Indian Mutiny; social life in China & pioneer life in New Zealand.   584

MYALL,Laura Hain (Friswell). In the Sixties and Seventies(1906). Youthful memories of social life and literary society; Dickens and others.   585

MYERS, Arthur Wallis. Twenty Years of Lawn Tennis(1921); Memory's Parade (1932). Tennis, games, players; Wimbledon, Davis Cup; travels for game;

work as journalist; public scene from Boer War; propaganda work in WW1; energetic and shrewd.   586

MYERS, Bessy. Captured (1941). Her work as ambulance driver in WW2; German blitz in France; captured; prison life at Cherche-Midi; good.   587

MYERS, Frederic W. H. Fragments of Prose and Poetry (1904). Six chapters on the phases of thought through which he passed;Hellenism,Christianity, agnosticism,spiritualism; his spiritual pilgrimage; good.   588

ANON.   My Father's Friends (1833). Childhood and schooling in Derby; his games;religious training. Copy, Derby P.L.   589

ANON. My Name is Million (1940). An Englishwoman married to a Pole; life in Warsaw;Nazi and Russian activities and the political scene;her escape to England; knowledgeable.   590

MYSON, Sonia.   My Desert Adventure (1940). Trip to India as lady's companion;adventure in Syria as a dancer and foster-mother to a Sheik's son; a love-affair, marriage, and settlement in Syria.   591

N., H. R.   Here and There Memories (1896). Dublin life; Trinity; service in army; Irish theatre, politics, elections; his travels.   1

NAISH, Percy Llewellyn. Rollings of a Mossless Stone (1913).   Foxhunting in Wilts,Cheshire, Shropshire; motoring;travels; lively incidents at home and abroad.   2

NAPIER,Archibald, 1st Lord. Memoirs (Edin. 1793). Public life in Scotland in early 17th Century;work as Treasurer-Depute;rivalries of courtiers and his own complaints.   3

NAPIER, David. An Autobiographical Sketch (Glasgow,1912). Work as engineer and shipbuilder, Glasgow and London; inventions and patents; 1st half of 19th Century.   4

NAPIER, Elma. <u>Winter Is in July</u> (L. 1949). Her two marriages and family; social life;residence in Australia in 1914-22; nostalgia for pre-war life & society; anecdotes.   5

NAPIER,Gen. Sir George Thomas. <u>Passages in the Early Military Life</u> (L. 1884). His service as a youth in Peninsular War; battles and adventures & hero-worship;   told chattily for his children.   6

NAPIER,Henry Dundas. <u>Experiences of a Military Attaché</u> (1924). Service in WW1; Bulgaria, Serbia, Rumania; politics and military affairs.   7

NARES,Edward. <u>A Versatile Professor</u> ed. G. C. White (1903). Political and social life in late 18th and the early 19th Century;clerical work; career as professor of history at Oxford;historical and antiquarian studies.   8

NARES, Owen. <u>Myself and Some Others</u> (1925). His career as an actor; anecdotes of theatrical life.   9

ANON. <u>Narrow Waters</u> (1935). Service in Post Office; life with poor in the East End of London, with unusual details of their lives; wide reading in several languages; good.   10

NASH, Eveleigh. <u>I Liked the Life I Lived</u> (1941). His business as a book publisher from 1892; anecdotes & gossip about writers.   11

NASH, Paul. <u>Outline</u> (1949). Boyhood in London and Slough; schooling; his discovery of artistic talent;training with Rothenstein and Richmond;service in WW1 and work as war artist; sensitive story of youth.   12

NASMYTH,James. <u>Autobiography</u> (1883) Boyhood in Edinburgh; manufacturing & engineering there; engineering study; work with Maudsley; business in Manchester;engineering, machinery, foundry work; Free Trade; study of astronomy; good and valuable.   13

NATHAN,Charles Frederick. <u>Schoolmaster Glances Back</u> (Liverpool, 1946) Career as teacher in Liverpool area; curriculum and changing ideas in education; colleagues; holidays.   14

A NATIVE. <u>Recollections of Dublin Castle</u> (1902). Forty years of Dublin society; noblemen, clergy, soldiers & lawyers; fond memories.   15

A NAVAL WIFE. <u>My Deeds and Misdeeds</u> (1931). Gay life and longings of wife of a navy officer; fiction?   16

NEALE, Dennis. <u>Memoirs of the Life</u> (1754). Confessional life of a highwayman executed at Tyburn; his crimes thieves' jargon. Copy in the Harvard U.L.   17

/NEALE, Erskine7. <u>Experiences of a Gaol Chaplain</u> (1847). Work in prisons and accounts of criminals,their lives and crimes; lively account of prison system; needed reforms.   18

NEALE,Frederick Arthur. <u>Eight Years in Syria</u>(1851); <u>Narrative of a Residence</u>(1851). Experiences in service of King of Siam in 40's;later career and travels in consular service in Syria, Palestine, Asia Minor.   19

NEALE, Samuel. "Some Account of the Life," <u>Friends Library</u>, XI (Philadelphia, 1847). Life of a Cork Quaker; a ministry in Ireland in 18th Century & visit to America.   20

NEAME, Lt.Col. Sir Philip. <u>Playing With Strife</u> (1947). Army career; WW1 and WW2 service; earning V.C.; Governor of Guernsey;mission to Tibet; his sports; hunting; mountaineering.   21

NEAVE,Dorina Lockhart, Lady. <u>Twenty Six Years on the Bosphorus</u>(1933); <u>Romance of the Bosphorus</u> (1949). Childhood in Turkey where her father was a judge; European and Turkish society & customs; Turkish life before time of Kemal; politics; Turko-British relations; rather dull.   22

NEAVE,Joseph James. <u>Leaves from the Journal</u> (1911). Suffolk man's travels in Quaker ministry in 2nd half of 19th Century; Russia, Australia, N.Z., and South Seas.   23

NEELD,Reginald Rundell. Naval diary 1893-94; experiences in naval revolution at Rio de Janeiro. <u>Diary of the Revolution</u> (Portsmouth, 1895).   24

NEELE,George P. Railway Reminiscences(1904). Career with London & North Western from 1847;railway development and personages.   25

NEILD,Alfred. Autobiography and reminiscences of his life in Manchester and Mayfield in 19th Century. MS,John Rylands Library, Eng. 872.   26

NEILD,James. Memoirs of..John Coakley Lettsom: by J.C. Pettigrew (1817) contains Neild's autobiography of his philanthropic work in late 18th Century; work for relief of small debtors in prison;work with Howard. Cambridge U.L.   27

NEILL, Alexander Sutherland. That Dreadful School (1937). His teaching career and experiments at the Summerhill School;love in education; enfant terrible style.   28

NEILL,John Martin Blader. Recollections (1845). Military service, 1839-1842 in Sind,Kandahar and Afghanistan campaigns with Nott.   29

NEILSON, Harry B.   Auld Lang Syne (Birkenhead,1935). Scenes, people and ways of Old Claughton, Birkenhead and Bidston;experiences as soldier in India; work as an engineer. Cambridge, U.L.   30

NEILSON,Julia. This for Remembrance (1940). Her career as an actress; the Haymarket; Tree; Fred Terry; favorite plays.   31

NEISH, Rosalie (Galsworthy), Lady. My Scottish Husband (1940). Life with her husband in London, Scotland, Ireland, Southcombe; fond reminiscences of their life.   32

NELSON, Edith Halford. Desert Sanctuary (1946). Astonishing life of the English wife of an Arab sheik.   33

NELSON, Horatio, Lord. Dispatches & Letters (1844) I, Pref. Brief outline of his naval career; cruises; diplomatic receptions.   34

NELSON, John. Memoirs (Birmingham, 1807).Violent bouts of conscience inspired by Wesley;conversion; ministry and travels to 1745; sufferings from

the mob; lively narrative.   35

NESBIT,Evelyn. Prodigal Days (1934) Candid and lively story of gaieties of early century; the Harry Thaw & Stanford White murder.   36

NESBIT, Robert. Diary, 1825-30; his life and work at the Scottish Mission at Bombay; his own religious life. A Memoir, by J. M. Mitchell (1858). 37

/NESFIELD, W.J./. A Chequered Career (1881). Schooling at Eton; clerk to a shipbroker; early scrapes; adventures in Australia; seamy side of life,told by a ne'er-do-well.   38

NEUFELD, Charles. A Prisoner of the Khaleefa(1899). Account of his twelve years' captivity at Omdurman;Egyptian life.   39

NEVE, Arthur. Thirty Years in Kashmir (1913). Missionary's work, life & travels in India from 1881.   40

NEVILL, Lady Dorothy. Reminiscences (1906); Leaves from the Note-Books of (1907); Under Five Reigns (1910); My Own Times (1912). Society and social life in Victorian period; London and country houses; politicians; fashions and social changes.   41

NEVILL,Col. Park Percy. Some Recollections (1864). Career in the army; service in the Peninsular War and in India; social and sport.   42

NEVILL, Ralph. Sporting Days (1910) Yesterday and Today (1922); Unconventional Memories (1923). Country life, hunting, boxing; society, social life and personalities; travel in Europe, Persia, Japan; diplomacy.   43

NEVILLE, Hippo. Sneak-Thief on the Road(1935). Hawker, tramp,ne'erdowell on the road and in casual wards; affected but amusing,and written in the style of James Joyce.   44

NEVINSON, Christopher R. W. Paint & Prejudice (1937). School; the Slade; Paris; military service in WW1; work as a painter; friendship with writers and painters; personal life.   45

NEVINSON,Henry W. Changes and Chan-

ces (1923;More Changes, More Chances,
(1925); Last Changes, Last Chances(L.
1928); combined as, Fire of Life (L.
1935).Youth in Midlands; teaching and
social work in London; work and travels as foreign correspondent; Liberal
politics and journalism; chief events
and movements of his time; excellent
account of his life and times and the
Liberal Movement.   46

NEVINSON, Margaret Wynne. Life's
Fitful Fever(1926). Childhood; teaching and social work in Whitechapel and
activity in suffragism;Justice of the
Peace;the probation system; her writings.   47

NEW, Charles. Life, Wanderings, and
Labours (1874). Work and travels as a
missionary in Zanzibar and Central Africa; Livingstone relief expedition;
native life and religion.   48

NEWBOLT,Sir Henry John. My World as
in My Time (L.1932); Life and Letters
(L. 1942). Staffs; Clifton and Oxford;
career as writer and poet; literary &
social life in London;review of writers; politics and WW1.   49

NEWBOLT, William C. E.   Years That
Are Past (1921). Uppingham and Oxford
his clerical work in country parishes
and as canon of St. Paul's.   50

NEWBOULD, C. E. A Padre in Paraguay
(1929). Twenty years of clerical work
in Argentina, Brazil, Paraguay; chaplain of Australian colony in Paraguay
settlers and natives.   51

NEWCASTLE,Margaret Cavendish, Duchess of."A True Relation of the Birth"
in Nature's Pictures (1656); appended
to her Life of the Duke of Newcastle;
ed. C.H. Firth (1906). Garrulous character sketch of herself; her family;
effects of civil war on them and her;
her husband.   52

NEWCOME,Henry. Autobiography (Chetham Soc., 1852). Life of a Puritan &
nonconformist clergyman in Lancashire
(Gawsworth and Manchester);abstracted
from lost diaries; 1627-95.   53

NEWELL, Edward John. Life and Confessions (1798). Not seen. Activities
of Irish informer during the rebellion

of 1798.   54

NEWLANDSMITH,Ernest. Minstrel Friar
(1928); Musician's Pilgrimage (1932).
Career as violinist and conductor and
later as an Anglican missionary friar;
New Life Movement; evangelism; drama
and music services.   55

NEWMAN, Bernard. Spy (1935); Secret
Servant (1935); One Man's Year (1941)
Work in intelligence and espionage in
Germany in WW1; with German Command;
lecturing to troops in WW2; education
in army; France before the German invasion.   56

NEWMAN, Francis William. Phases of
Faith(1850). Development of religious
creed through various phases;Anglican-
ism to Independence; brother of Cardinal Newman.   57

NEWMAN, Henry. A Roving Commission
(1937); Indian Peepshow (1937). Work
and travels of a war correspondent in
China, India, Afghanistan; Boxer rebellion, Afghan War, WW1.   58

NEWMAN, Cardinal John Henry. Apologia pro vita sua (1864); "Autobiographical Memoir" in Letters and Correspondence (1891) Vol. I. Record of his
religious opinions and spiritual life
from childhood to 1864;early years at
Oxford; scholarship and theology; his
curacy; development of his religious
thought; work as tutor.   59

NEWMAN, Thomas Charles. Many Parts
(1935). Work for solicitor, law stationer, stockbroker & banker; social
work in Kensal; London life and theatre in 80's.   60

/NEWMARCH,Charles Henry7. Recollections of Rugby: by an Old Rugbean (L.
1848). His life there; traditions and
customs; Dr. Arnold.   61

NEWSHOLME, Sir Arthur. Fifty Years
in Public Health(1935). Medical study
and work in medicine & public health;
largely an account of the public work
in health.   62

NEWTE,Frederick. Twenty Years' Wan-
derings(1869). Family life and travel
in France and Italy as a boy with his
parents; people and places.   63

NEWTON, Bertha. My Life in Time (L. 1938). Spiritual autobiography; fantastic account of mystical experience in space-time.   64

NEWTON, Frances E. Fifty Years in Palestine (Wrotham, 1948). Derbyshire girlhood; missionary work, teaching & medical work in Haifa; Arab life and customs.   65

NEWTON, Henry Chance. Cues and Curtain Calls (1927); Idols of the Halls (1928). Journalist's memories; theatre and music-halls; famous players, comedians, chairmen, acts; lively, varied details.   66

NEWTON, John. The Life (1764); many later editions. Early life and adventures; slave in Africa; work and ministry at Olney and in London in mid-18th Century; spiritual experiences & beliefs.   67

NEWTON, Montague Noel. My Confessions (1925). Lifetime of graft; gambles in pre-WW1 Europe, China, South America; relations with aristocracy, bankers & crooks.   68

NEWTON, Thomas. The Works of (1782) Vol.I. Formal account of education of the Bishop of Bristol; Westminster and Oxford; career in church.   69

NEWTON, Thomas Wodehouse Legh, 2nd Baron. Retrospection(1941). Career as diplomat and in Parliament 1887-1919; public events, politics, life in the Paris embassy.   70

NEWTON, William. A Full and True Account (Salisbury, n.d.). Confessional autobiography of highwayman; descent from servant to criminal; executed in 1777. Devizes Archael. Soc.   71

NICHOL, John. Memoir: by W. Knight (Glasgow, 1896). Begins with autobiography of the early life of the Glasgow professor, to 1861; education and religion; good.   72

NICHOLAS, Sir Edward. The Nicholas Papers (Camden Soc., 1886) contains an autobiography of his public service as secretary to Charles I.   73

NICHOLLS, Ernest. Crime Within the

Square Mile (1935). Policeman and detective in City of London; his cases; forgeries, bucket-shops, swindlers and fences.   74

NICHOLLS, John. Recollections and Reflections (1820-22). Public affairs and personalities during the reign of George III; mostly impersonal, but has some details of his life as a courtier and Member of Parliament.   75

NICHOLS, Beverley. Twenty-Five (L. 1926); Down the Garden Path (L. 1932) Thatched Roof(1933); All I Could Never Be (1950). Oxford days; travels in USA, Australia, Europe; village life in Hunts; gardening; London journalism in 20's; Bright Young Things; search for God and Peace; Buchmanism.   76

NICHOLSON, Hamlet. Autobiographical and Full Historical Account (Rochdale 1892). His opposition to ritualism at Rochdale parish church; fight with the vicar; work for conservatives, 1832 to 1892; social work; life and opinions of an old-style protestant. Manchester P.L.   77

NICHOLSON, Henry Whalley. From Sword to Share (1881). Experiences of business man in Hawaii; making a fortune in five years.   78

NICHOLSON, Hubert. Half My Days and Nights (1941). Work as a reporter; a journalistic picture of himself & his times; art, sex, Bohemia, Freud, and Marx; somewhat squalid.   79

NICHOLSON, Phyllis. Norney Rough (L. 1941); Family Album (1943); Country Bouquet (1947). Experiences of retired soldier and his wife as novice farmers near London; her life in India and Oxford; family affairs; happenings and thoughts on a Sussex farm.   80

NICHOLSON, Renton. Autobiography of a Fast Man (1860, 1863). Journalism & Bohemian life in London, 1845-60; his work as editor of The Town; sporting life, theatre, society, gossip.   81

NICHOLSON, Col. Walter N. Behind the Lines (1939). Military service in WW1 in France; experiences of billetting; transportation.   82

NICKALLS, Guy. Life's a Pudding (L. 1939). His sporting career; rowing at Eton and Oxford; shooting and fishing and WW1 service.   83

NICKALLS, Major Vivian. Oars, Wars, and Horses (1932). Eton in the 80's; rowing; Oxford; social life; hunting; Stock Exchange; WW1 service.   84

NICOL, John. Life and Adventures of (Edin. 1822; 1937). Sailor's life in late 18th Century; voyages to Australia and South Seas; battles of Aboukir and Cape St. Vincent; steward on female convict ship; life of sailors and love of sea; excellent.   85

NICOLL, Lady Catherine Robertson. Bells of Memory (1932); Under the Bay Tree(1934). Childhood in Herts in the 70's; country life; family; Victorian education; Hitchin scene; marriage and life with husband, a canon and professor of Hebrew, at Oxford and Hampstead Barrie and other friends.   86

NICOLSON, Harold. Helen's Tower (L. 1937). Autobiography of his boyhood; fitted into life of Marquess of Dufferin and Ava and his nurse; himself and celebrities.   87

NIGHTINGALE, Thomas. Some of the Reminiscences (1891). Life, ministry and travels of Rotherham Methodist in the 19th Century; London, Lancs and Yorks; includes diary.   88

NIGHTINGALL, Arthur. My Racing Adventures (1907). Career as jockey and Epsom trainer; Grand National wins and turf life and people.   89

NIMMO, James. Autobiography of Scottish covenanter in 17th Century; religious life and troubles; domestic life and church-state affairs. Acad. Edin. Scottish Hist. Soc. VI (1887).   90

NISBET, Hugh. Experiences of a Jungle Wallah (St. Albans, 1936). Thirty seven years with Bombay-Burma Trading Corporation; teak industry; hunting; social life; colonial life and trade; entertaining.   91

NISBET, James. Private Life of the Persecuted (Edin. 1827). Life of an Ayrshire covenanter in 17th Century;

military engagements with Cameronians and his religious life.   92

NIVEN, Frederick J. Coloured Spectacles (1938). Author's travels and impressions in England, Canada, Honolulu etc.   93

NOAKES, Ernest E. Mirthful Memories (1920). Genial account of the work and experiences of a magician; public and private entertainments.   94

NOBLE, Algernon. Siberian Days(1928) Work and travel as a gold assayer and mining engineer in the Khirgiz country from 1905.   95

NOBLE, Margery Durham, Lady. A Long Life (Newcastle, 1925). Quebec childhood; marriage to army officer; social and army life in England. Copy, McGill U.L.   96

NOBLE, Sam. 'Tween Decks in the Seventies (1925). A Dundee man's life at sea in 1870's; Africa & South America; a good account of life of an AB, told in affable style.   97

NOEL, Conrad. Autobiography (1945). Life and activities of the minister of Thaxted; Christian-Socialism; social work in slums of N. London.   98

NOEL, Major E. M. Military journal, 1919; political tour in Kurdistan and reports on Turks and German military works. Diary...in Kurdistan (Basrah, 1920).   99

NOMAD. Reminiscences of Many Lands (1905). Travels and adventures in the Pacific, China Coast, Australia, South Africa.   100

NORMAN, H. N. Tattered Shuttlecock (1937). Army service in WW1; Mesopotamia, France, India; farming in Kenya; travels as secretary to American millionaire; salesman; farmer.   101

NORMAN, Norman. Recollections of a Rolling Stone (1932). Lifetime travel and adventure; pioneering in Australia and Canada; WW1 service; many jobs of a hardy soul.   102

NOR NALLA. A Yellow Sleuth (1931). Experiences of a native detective with

Malay States Police; criminals, drug-
pedlars, communists; in France in WW1
with Chinese Labour Corps.   103

NORRIS,Samuel. Manx Memories (Douglas,1938). Public work in the Isle of
Man; member of House of Keys; social
and public life, from 1880.   104

NORROY, Muriel. I Robbed the Lords
and Ladies Gay (1939). Activities of
a thief; underworld; prison life; low
life related vividly.   105

NORTH, Charles Napier. Diary, 1857-
1858; military service in the Indian
Mutiny; with Havelock's force to the
relief of Lucknow. Journal of an English Officer (1858).   106

NORTH, Marianne. Recollections of a
Happy Life (1892); Further Recollec-
tions (1893). Travels in the Americas
Japan,Borneo, India, Australia, South
Africa,Europe, Near East; social life
places and people.   107

NORTH, Roger. Autobiography (1887).
Boyhood in East Anglia in 1650's; law
study at Cambridge and legal practice
in London;career and honours; Parliamentary career to 1685; many hobbies;
intellectual interests; a very lively
record.   108

NORTHCOTE, James.   Memorials of an
Eighteenth Century Painter,by Stephen
Gwynn(1898) includes autobiography of
his apprenticeship with Reynolds and
his painting career; Fuseli, Reynolds
circle, etc.   109

NORTON, Caroline Elizabeth (editor)
A Residence at Sierra Leone,by a Lady.
Diary of her life in Sierra Leone, in
1841-46;domestic and social life; the
slave trade.   110

NORWOOD, Richard. The Journal (N.Y.
1945). His adventures, 1613-53; Puritanism; religion; travels; surveying;
education; plantations; pearl-seeking
in Bermudas.   111

NOTT-BOWER, Sir William. Fifty-Two
Years (1926). Career with the City of
London Police from 1873,after serving
in army and in Leeds and Liverpool police; crimes, police methods.   112

NOVELLO, Clara Anastasia. Reminisc-
ences(1910). Career as a singer; concerts,opera, music, musicians; social
life; literary circles; Lamb, Hazlitt
and society celebrities.   113

NOVELLO-DAVIES, Clara.   The Life I
Have Loved (1940). Welsh childhood in
60's;career and tours as a singer and
her teachers, friends and family, especially Ivor.   114

NOYES, H. E. Seventeen Years (1909)
Chaplain to British Embassy in Paris;
Franco-British relations; religious &
social reminiscences.   115

NUGENT, Lady Maria. Diary, 1801-14;
in Jamaica with her husband the governor;social and family life; politics;
negroes; later life in England and in
India;sympathetic; with good details.
Journal of a Voyage (1839); ed. Frank
Cundall (1907, 1934).   116

NO. 7.   Twenty-Five Years in Seventeen Prisons (1903). Life story of a
convict; experiences and impressions
of a variety of prisons.   117

NUNN,Lindley. Musical Recollections
(Ipswich, 1899). Bury-St.Edmunds; his
musical study at Royal Academy;London
musical life in 50's; career as pianist and organist in Ipswich;festivals
in Norwich. Ipswich P.L.   118

NUNN, William. Memoirs (1842). Preparation for ministry at beginning of
19th Century; parish work in Manchester; religious life.   119

ANON. Nursing Adventures(1917). Her
WW1 service with FANY in France, WW1;
hospital work.   120

NUTTALL, Rt.Rev. Enos. Diary, 1878-
1915; his parish and diocesan work in
Jamaica; Archbishop of Jamaica; local
life and society. The Life, by Frank
Cundall (1922).   121

OAKE, Mary Elisabeth.   No Place for
a White Woman (1933). Experiences in
the Cameroons; wife of government of-

ficial;domestic and social life; role
of women in the tropics.   1

OAKELEY, Sir Charles. Some Account
of the Services (1836). Career as an
official with the East India Co. from
1770's; administration; finance; social life; travels.   2

OAKELEY, F. "Personal Recollections
of Oxford," Time (March,1880). Covers
1820-45; student and fellow of Christ
Church; Tractarian Movement; general
reminiscences.   3

OAKELEY, Hilda D. My Adventures in
Education (1939). Work of teacher and
philosopher;education teacher, McGill
Manchester and London universities and
research in pedagogy.   4

OAKLEY, Capt. Richard R. Treks and
Palavers (1938). Work as a political
officer and magistrate in Northern Nigeria from 1921; personal life.   5

O'BRIEN, Brian. Beating about the
Bush(1938). Work, travels, adventures
and amusements of a trader in the Cameroons.   6

O'BRIEN, Capt. Donat Henchley. The
Narrative (1839; 1932). His shipwreck
in 1804; capture and imprisonment in
France; escape and adventures; lively
story.   7

O'BRIEN,Lt. Pat. Outwitting the Hun
(1918). Flying with RFC in WWl; capture;life in German prison; thrilling
escape.   8

O'BRIEN, William. Recollections (L.
1905); Evening Memories (Dublin 1920)
Irish journalist and M.P.; Fenianism;
Irish nationalist and political activities to 1910.   9

O'BRIEN OF KILFENORA, Peter, Baron.
Reminiscences (1916). Legal career in
Ireland; Solicitor-General and L.C.J.
politics, Land League, politics, social life, literature, sport, personalities, to 1911.   10

O'CALLAGHAN,Sir Desmond. Guns, Gunners and Others (1925). Military career from 1858; Woolwich, Canada, West
Indies, Roumania, South Africa; work
in ordnance; social; sport.   11

O'CASEY, Sean. I Knock at the Door
(1939);Pictures in the Hallway (1942)
Drums under the Window (1945); Inish-
fallen(1947). Childhood in Dublin and
schooling; family and personal difficulties;political troubles; hates and
enthusiasms; Yeats, Lady Gregory, and
the Dublin literary circle; his first
writings; farewell to Ireland.   12

O'CONNELL, James F. A Residence of
Eleven Years (Boston, 1836). Boyhood
in circus and at sea;experience among
convict settlers in New Holland;ship-
wreck in Carolines;life among natives
adventures; dictated.   13

O'CONNELL, John. Recollections and
Experiences(1849). Parliamentary career from 1833;Irish affairs; politics
and H. C. debates.   14

O'CONNOR,Batt. With Michael Collins
(1929).Revolutionary activities 1900-
1922; Irish republicans,Sinn Fein and
Collins; the troubles; adventures out
and in jails.   15

O'CONNOR, Daniel. Diary and Other
Memoirs (Ottawa,1901). His early life
in Ireland at beginning of 19th Century; emigration to Canada.   16

O'CONNOR,Elizabeth. I Myself (1910)
Childhood and youth in Ireland;marri-
age to T.P. O'Connor; his career as a
journalist and politician; social and
literary life in London.   17

O'CONNOR,Gerald. Memoirs (1903). An
Irishman's war service, 1689-91; defence of Limerick; later service with
the French; Blenheim, Ramillies, Oud-
enarde;lively and interesting for his
meeting with Swift.   18

O'CONNOR, Thomas Power. Memoirs (L.
1929). Work as a journalist and M.P.,
1870-1922; Home Rule and Irish interests and politics; Parnell; literary
and social life in London.   19

O'CONNOR,Vincent Clarence Scott.The
Silken East (1904). Life and work as
Comptroller of Assam; politics, history,economics, local customs; his own
personal affairs.   20

O'CONNOR, Lt.Col. Sir William F. T.
On the Frontier and Beyond (L. 1931);

Things Mortal (1940). Education; army career; in service of the government of India, 1895-1925; Kashmir, Tibet, Nepal, Persia; frontier life; war and sporting and social life.   21

O'CROHAN, Tomás. The Islandman (L. 1934). Seventy years in the Blaskets; peasant and fishing life on west coast of Ireland;local customs and beliefs; pleasant; translated from Irish.   22

O'DAZI, Jack. Coaster at Home, ed. J.M. Stuart-Young (1916-18). Life and work of a Scottish trader on the River Niger;missionaries; natives; religion and trade; a candid and amoral story; lively.   23

ODDIE, Samuel Ingleby. Inquest (L. 1941). Education; early life in navy; career as a coroner in London; famous cases; London life.   24

ODHAMS,William J. B. Business and I (1935). Work as publisher of journals and newspapers from 1873; the People; the Herald; work and problems and his philanthropic activities.   25

ODOM, W. Fifty Years (1917); Memories and Musings(1932). His boyhood in Sheffield; work in law office; curate and vicar in Sheffield from 1877;parish work; his writings; reminiscences of Sheffield life.   26

O'DONNELL, Josephine. Among the Covent Garden Stars (1936). A secretary at Covent Garden from 1925; anecdotes of singers.   27

O'DONNELL, Peader. The Gates Flew Open (1932). Experiences of an Irish rebel in Mountjoy Prison.   28

O'DUFFY, Eoin. Crusade in Spain (L. 1938).Military service in the Spanish civil war; general for Franco's Irish volunteers.   29

O'DWYER, Sir Michael Francis. India as I Knew It (1925). His administrative work in Punjab and native states and military affairs;WW1 service; the Punjab rebellion and his role.   30

O'FLAHERTY, Liam. Two Years (1930); Shame the Devil(1934). His travels in America and Turkey; hobo, lumberjack,

miner in Canada; left-wing political activity; career as a novelist; Bohemian life in England and Paris;people who interested him; good.   31

O'FLANAGAN,James R. An Octogenarian Literary Life (Cork, 1896). Career as lawyer in Ireland; work as a writer; social life.   32

OGILVIE, Eain G. Libyan Log (1943). Squadron-Leader in RAF in WW2; North African campaign.   33

OGILVIE, John. Relatio incarcerationis (Douai,1615) translated, C. J. Kerslake (1877). Trial and imprisonment of a Jesuit priest, executed at Glasgow in 1615.   34

OGILVIE, William H. My Life in the Open (1908). Farming in Australia, S. Africa, USA; sheepfarming on Scottish border; farming conditions.   35

OGSTON,Sir Alexander. Reminiscences (1919). Military career of a surgeon; Egyptian War, Boer War, WW1 in Serbia and Italy; medical work.   36

O'HAGAN, H. Osborne. Leaves from My Life (1929). Career as financier from 1869; Stock Exchange; development of joint stock companies; industry; work for consumptives.   37

O'KEEFFE,John. Recollections (1826) Boyhood in Ireland in 1750's; career as a playwright;theatres and theatrical life in London and Dublin; social and club life; good.   38

OKEY, Thomas. Basketful of Memories (1930). Basketmaker in Spitalfields; workingclass life and education;night schools and university extension; socialism; professor of Italian at Cambridge; scholarship.   39

OLD CALABAR. Experiences of Sport (1873). Mostly fishing experiences in England and France.   40

OLD COLLEGER. Eton of Old(1892). An account of his days as pupil in period 1811-22; curriculum, sport; Keate and masters and boys.   41

OLD ETONIAN. Life at Home,at School and at College (1882).Boy's experiences at Eton and Cambridge; love life; may be fiction. 42

OLD ETONIAN. Eton Memories (1909). His days as a student in the days of Keate. 43

OLD FOLKESTONER. Reminiscences of Folkestone Smugglers(Folkestone 1888) Smuggling,police, trials in the early part of the century. Copy, Maidstone Museum. 44

OLDMIXON,John. Memoirs of the Press (1742). Work as journalist and writer and his public career, 1710-40; chief writers of the time. 45

OLD PLANTER. Reminiscences of Behar (Calcutta, 1887). Life in India from 1847; work as an indigo planter; the Mutiny; hunting; social life. Copy in India Office Library. 46

OLD POTTER. When I Was a Child (L. 1903). Wretched condition of children in the potteries of 1840's; industrialism and its victims; strikes, pubs, workhouses; Pottery Riots; work as a local preacher and his pursuit of an education; excellent. 47

OLD PRINTER. A Few Personal Recollections(1896). Schooling; apprentice and printer;work with Cassell's; London in 50's and 60's; theatres; Workmen's institutes; Quakers. 48

OLD STALKER. Days on the Hill(1926). Work and sporting and nature experiences of a Scottish deerstalker. 49

O'LEARY, John. Recollections (1896) Legal and medical studies, Dublin and Cork; Grattan Club; work for Fenians; editor of The Irish People; imprisonment; famous Fenians. 50

OLE MAN RIVER. Beloved Ghosts(1936) School and medical education in 60's and 70's;his practice in Midlands and London; medical conditions; theatre & social life; entertaining. 51

OLIPHANT, Sir Lancelot. Ambassador in Bonds (1946). Diplomatic experiences in Hitler's Germany; internment; release; later visit. 52

OLIPHANT, Laurence. Episodes in a

Life (Edin.1887). Author's travels in the Americas, Asia, and Europe; sport politics and war. 53

OLIPHANT,Margaret Oliphant. Days of My Life(1876); Autobiography and Letters (Edin.1899). Domestic and social life in Edinburgh and London; writing career;Blackwood's Magazine; literary society and celebrities. 54

OLIPHANT, Nigel. Diary, 1900; work in Chinese postal service; the siege of Pekin;Chinese life. A Diary of the Siege of the Legations (1901). 55

OLIVER, Samuel Pasfield. Rambles of a Gunner (1879); On and Off Duty (L. 1881). Military life and travels in South America from 1867; in Nicaragua Turania, Lemuria, Colombia. 56

OLIVERS,Thomas. Account of the Life (1789). Welshman converted by Wesley; his travels and adventures in Methodist ministry; one of the liveliest of the early Methodist lives. 57

OLIVIER, Edith. Without Knowing Mr. Walkley (1938). Rectory childhood at Wilton and Salisbury;charming account of clerical social life; her literary friends and her own writing; herself and her home. 58

OLLEY,Capt. Gordon P. Million Miles in the Air (1934). Career and adventures of an air transport pilot, 1915 on; pilots and passengers. 59

O'MALLEY, Ernie. On Another Man's Wound(1936). Work in the Irish rebellion, 1916-21; organising in country districts; folk-lore and ballad collections; rather literary. 60

O'MALLEY, James. The Life (Montreal 1893).Irishman's service in the British army; Crimean War; his emigration to Canada. Ottawa Archives. 61

O'MALLEY, Raymond. One Horse Farm (1948). Novice farmer on small croft, Western Highlands; primitive life and people; farming methods. 62

O'MALLEY,William. Glancing Back (L. 1933).Seventy years as journalist and M.P.; writing, parliamentary and political work; Sinn Fein and the rebellion; Irish social life, literature & sport. Cambridge U.L.   63

OMAN, Sir Charles. Memories (1941). Cheltenham;Winchester and Oxford; his studies with Stubbs;work and scholarship as professor of history, Oxford; students and dons; All Souls; Oxford life, politics, amusements.   64

OMANNEY, F.D. The House in the Park (1944). Boyhood in Richmond Park; his family, friends, schools, sports, and amusements, 1900-1916.   65

O'MARA, Patrick. Autobiography of a Liverpool Irish Slummy (1934); Irish Slummy in America (1935). Life in the slums and workhouses; dock labourer & sign painter; emigration and work as taxidriver in Baltimore.   66

O'MEARA, Lt. Col. Eugene John. I'd Live It Again (1935). His career in the Indian Medical Service, 1898-1918 plagues,hospitals, medical conditions and jails; sport; travels.   67

O'NEILL, Ellen. Extraordinary Confessions (Preston, 1850). Poverty in Stockport; pickpocket at fifteen; her marriage to a thief; work in Manchester factory; prison life.   68

ONIONS,Maude. A Woman at War (1929) Army signaller in France in WW1; horror of war; courage.   69

ONSLOW,Arthur. Autobiography of his childhood, education, political work, life as Speaker of House of Commons in 18th Century. H.M.C. 14th Rep. App. Pt. IX (1895).   70

ONSLOW, R. W. A.Onslow, 5th Earl of Sixty-Three Years (1944). Eton;career in Foreign Office from 1901;Spain and Tangier,Russia, Germany; WW1; work in House of Lords; social, travel, sport etc.   71

ANON. On the Road from Mons with an Army Service Corps Train: by Its Commander(1916). WW1 service with supply train attached to 19th Infantry; Mons to the Aisne; vivid.   72

OPIE, Peter. I Want to be a Success (1939); Case of Being a Young Man (L. 1946). Schooldays at Eton; experience

in Bombay, Poona, Egypt; analysis of his traits,talents, hopes; officer in WW2; work for BBC; his life.   73

OPPENHEIM, Edward Phillips. Pool of Memory (1941). Career as journalist & novelist from 80's;travels in America and Riviera; social life, sport, and celebrities.   74

ORCHARD, William Edwin. From Faith to Faith(1933). Religious development up to adoption of Catholicism; pious upbringing; Presbyterian ministry at Enfield;ministry at King's Weighhouse Chapel;pacifism; religious trends and movements; good.   75

ORCZY, Emmuska, Baroness. Links in the Chain (L. 1947). Her career as a popular novelist;excellent account of the contemporary scene and of literary fashions.   76

ORD,Hubert. Adventures of a Schoolmaster (1936). Long career in private schools as boy and master; Cambridge, Sorbonne,literary research; coach and tutor;work at Blackheath School; educational methods and exams.   77

/O'REILLY, Andrew?/. Reminiscences of an Emigrant Milesian (1853). Irish rebel's life in France.   78

O'REILLY,Septimus. The Tiger of the Legion (1936). London childhood; runs away from home with blacksmith-father and joins circus; odd jobs; adventure in USA;service with Foreign Legion in 20's; hardships; escape.   79

ORMATHWAITE,Arthur Henry John Welsh, Baron. When I Was at Court(1937). His work as master of ceremonies to Edward VII and George V; childhood, life at Windsor and in Royal Household; early life in Guards; sport; social.   80

ORMEROD, Eleanor. Autobiography and Correspondence (1904). Education, research work and travels of an economic entomologist.   81

ORPEN, Sir William. An Onlooker in France (1921). Work as official painter in France during WW1; adventures; battle scenes; personal life.   82

ORWELL, George. Down and Out (1933)

Writer's early life; unemployment and odd jobs in France and England; tramp and washer-up; life in workhouses and lodging-houses.   83

OSBALDESTON, Squire George.Autobiography(1926). Life of a sportsman and patron of prizefighters in first half of 19th Century;hunting, racing, Leicestershire country life and society; interesting and valuable.   84

OSBORN,Charles. Memoirs of the Life (1752). Nobleman's bastard; education and adventures as highwayman and lover courtship of old maids and widows;his fond recollections written in decline of life.   85

OSBORN,Edward Bolland. E.B.O. (L . 1937).His work as a literary journalist; Observer and Morning Post;literary society; books; travels.   86

OSBORN, Elias. A Brief Narrative of the Life (1723). Life, ministry, travels and sufferings of a Somerset Quaker in 17th Century.   87

OSBORN, Sherard. Stray Leaves from an Arctic Journal (L. 1852); Quedah (1857); My Journal (1860). His naval and military life and adventures; the search for Franklin's expedition; the siege of Quedah and life and adventure in Malaya.   88

OSBURN, Arthur Carr. Unwilling Passenger (1932). Army service in France in WW1;Mons; Western Front; moral and psychological changes.   89

OSCAR, Alan (W. B. Whall). School & Sea Days (1901). Boyhood in Cambridge choirboy at Magdalene; experiences as midshipman and seaman;his first steamer; written for children.   90

O'SHAUGHNESSY, Capt. Terence. Capt. O'Shaughnessy's Sporting Career(1873) Munster Castle;family life and sport; army service in Peninsular War and in India;work on staff of Viceroy and of Governor of Victoria; society, sport, marriage; anecdotes.   91

O'SHEA, John Augustus. Leaves from the Life (1885); Roundabout Recollections (1892). Life and work of Irish journalist and special correspondent;

siege of Paris; travels in Spain and Italy;Irish life, theatre, circus and amusing tales of his adventures.   92

O'SHEA, Laurence.   Three Campaigns (1918).Simple story of military service; frontier wars in India; two Boer wars.   93

O'SULLIVAN, Maurice.   Twenty Years A-Growing (1933). Peasant and fishing life on the Blasket Islands;primitive life and ideas;folk-lore and fantasy; translated from Irish; a work of much charm and poetry.   94

/O'SULLIVAN,Samuel/. College Recollections(1825). Student days at Trinity College, Dublin; his friends and their experiences.   95

OSWALD,Eugene. Reminiscences (1911) German exile-scholar in England; his teaching and journalism;Working Men's College & Cheltenham Ladies' College; Ellis, Furnival; Carlyle, Goethe, and Ethical societies.   96

OSWALD,Henry Robert. Memoirs (1936) Medical and legal studies;thirty-five years as coroner in South London;famous crimes and sudden deaths.   97

OSWALD, Gen. O. C. Williamson. "61" (1929).Career as an officer in artillery; WW1 service in France, Salonika and Palestine.   98

OTHEN,Nathaniel. A Short Account of the Life (Bristol, 1775). Short life of a sailor, soldier and sinner; converted to Methodism, but shot as deserter.   99

OUDENYK,Sir William J. Ways and By-Ways in Diplomacy (1939). Career as a diplomat from 1894, mostly in China; politics,war, Russian revolution; his official work; society.   100

OULD, Hermon. Shuttle (1947). Playwright's childhood in 90's; pacifism; conscientious objector in two wars; a picture of European political scene & his work as international secretary of P.E.N.   101

OUSELEY,Sir William. Travels (1819-1823).His travels in India and Persia 1810-12;historical, antiquarian, linguistic interests and studies.   102

OUTRAM, Sir James. Journal, 1838-9; military activities; campaign in Sind and Afghanistan; staff details. Rough Notes of the Campaign (1840).   103

OUVRY, Mrs. M. H. Diary, 1854-1858; life with her soldier-husband in India station social life and travel;Mutiny good details. A Lady's Diary (Lymington, 1892).   104

OWAIN, Dan. Pot of Smoke (1940). An old Welshman's rovings and adventures in Boer War; Nigeria, Egypt & Canada; work as miner and farmer.   105

OWEN,Arthur. Recollections (Lucknow 1916). Sixty years in army and police in India; Lucknow police and crime; & siege of Lucknow; anecdotes. Copy in India Office Library.   106

OWEN,Lady Edmée. Flaming Sex (1934) Widow of a Ceylon tea-planter;society life in France;imprisonment for crime passionelle.   107

OWEN, Maj. Edward Roderic. Journal, 1892-1894;army service in West Africa and in Jebu campaign and Uganda & Unyoro War. Mae Bovill, Roddy Owen (L. 1897).   108

OWEN, Sir Hugh. Brief autobiography of his work in poor law and local government in Wales in mid-19th Century in: North Wales Chron., 1881.   109

OWEN, Robert. The Life (L. 1857-58) Early work as a draper; work as manufacturer and factory owner; development of his religious, social, educational ideas;the cooperative movement and his philanthropic work.   110

OWEN, Robert Dale. Threading My Way (1874). His family and his father;the New Lanark social experiment and his work as manager there after schooling in Switzerland; marriage; experiences of community life at the New Harmony settlement; Lafayette, Mary Shelley, Frances Wright; excellent.   111

OWEN, Rosamund Dale (Oliphant). My Perilous Life in Palestine(1928). Her life and experiences as owner of Armageddon; religion; mysticism.   112

OWEN,Thomas. Personal Reminiscences (Oswestry, 1904). Work as stationer; life in Oswestry and Shropshire in the mid-19th Century.   113

OWENSON, Sydney (Lady Morgan). Passages in My Autobiography (1859). Her childhood in Ireland; social life in Dublin and London; work a s an author; literary society in England & France; Byron, etc.; good and useful.   114

OXENDEN, Ashton. History of My Life (1891). Kent boyhood; Harrow and Oxford;ministry at Barham and Pluckley; work as Bishop of Montreal.   115

OXFORD AND ASQUITH, Herbert Henry Asquith, Earl of. Fifty Years of Parliament(1926); Memories & Reflections (1928).Education and political career from 1852; Liberal politics, cabinets and statesmen; Gladstone; Parliament, reform, public events; intellectual & religious and literary interests;semi historical.   116

OXFORD AND ASQUITH, Margot Asquith, Countess of. Autobiography (1920-22); Places and Persons (1925); More Memories(1933); More or Less about Myself (1934); Off the Record (1935). Gossip and anecdotes of society and politics and celebrities in public life;travel literature and theatre;travels; Scottish upbringing.   117

OXFORD AND ASQUITH, Margot Asquith, Countess of (ed.). Myself When Young (1938). Autobiographies of childhood and youth by prominent women; herself Marjorie Bowen,Elizabeth Chesser, Amy Johnson,Caroline Haslett, Marchioness of Londonderry, Ethel Levey, Countess of Minto,Edith Picton-Turbeville,Sylvia Pankhurst,Maude Royden,Irene Vanbrugh, Ellen Wilkinson.   118

OXFORD SCHOLAR. Memories of an Oxford Scholar (1756). Love affairs of a student; affaire with the beautiful Miss L.; fiction?   119

OXLEY, Joseph. Joseph's Offering to His Children (1837). Norwich man's religious life in first half of 18th Century; travels in the Quaker ministry, England, Ireland, America.   120

OYLER, T. H.   Fifty Years of Lawn

<u>Tennis</u> (Maidstone, 1925). Beginnings of the game; life as player and referee; Queens Club.   121

P., M.   <u>Reminiscences of Travel</u> (Bournemouth, 1872). Travels in England and on continent in first half of the century; tourist notes.   1

P., Philip. <u>Life of</u> (1830). Religious life of a Birmingham man; conversion of a counterfeiter.   2

PACKER, Joy. <u>Pack and Follow</u> (1945) <u>Grey Mistress</u> (1949). Girlhood in Sth Africa;life as admiral's wife in England, Germany, Shanghai, the Balkans; partings and reunions; WW2.   3

PACY, Joseph. <u>The Reminiscences of Gauger</u> (Newark, 1873). His childhood in Lincs;schoolmaster; whiskey gauger in Lancashire, Scotland & London; his adventures with smugglers.   4

PADRE.   <u>Fifty Thousand Miles on a Hospital Ship</u> (1917). Anglican chaplain's service in WW1.   5

PAGE, Edward. <u>Escaping from Germany</u> (1919). Marine infantryman's life in German prisons in WW1; three attempts to escape.   6

PAGE, I. E. <u>Long Pilgrimage</u> (1914). A Nottingham man's life as a Methodist minister, mostly in Midlands; friends celebrities and books. Methodist Book Room.   7

PAGET, Clarence Edward, Lord. <u>Autobiography and Journals</u> (1896). Career in the navy, 1823-70; political work, as M.P. for Sandwich and Secretary of the Admiralty; Crimean War.   8

PAGET, Sir James. <u>Memoirs & Letters</u> (1901). Boyhood and education in 20's his apprenticeship as a physician and his work at Barts, to 1851. MS, Royal College of Surgeons.   9

PAGET, John Otho. <u>Memories of the Shires</u> (1920). Sports journalist for The Field;foxhunting in Northants and Leicestershire; Quorn, etc.   10

PAGET,Mrs. Leopold Grimston. Diary, 1857-58; life in Central India with a soldier-husband; experience in Mutiny <u>Camp and Cantonment</u> (1865).   11

PAGET,Lady Walpurga. <u>Scenes and Memories</u>(1912); <u>Embassies of Other Days</u> (1923); <u>In My Tower</u>(1924); <u>Linings of Life</u> (1928). Society, court, diplomatic life from 1840's; Copenhagen,Lisbon, Florence, Rome, Vienna & Berlin; international affairs and celebrities and the Victorian social scene; quite lively.   12

PAIN, C. Ernest. <u>Fifty Years on the Test</u>(1934). Experiences and anecdotes of trout fishing on the R. Test.   13

PAKENHAM, Lady Mary K. <u>Brought Up & Brought Out</u> (1938). Social life, London, Oxon & Ireland; Irish rebellion; literary interests; business and domestic studies; her work as newspaper gossip columnist.   14

PAKENHAM-WALSH, William S.   <u>Twenty Years in China</u> (Cambridge, 1935). His life as missionary from 1897;evangelical work at Fukhien; education; politics; Boxer rebellion.   15

PALGRAVE, Francis Turner. <u>Journals and Memories</u> (1899). Social, domestic and literary life of poet and critic; Lyme Regis, London, Italy; literature and literary friends.   16

PALMER, Bessie.   <u>Musical Recollections</u> (1904). Family life in London; training in singing; her career as an opera and oratorio singer.   17

PALMER, Frederick. <u>With My Own Eyes</u> (1934). Travels and adventures of war and foreign correspondent; Klondyke, China,Russo-Japanese War, Balkans and WW1; dangers and escapes.   18

PALMER, Com. George. <u>Kidnapping in the South Seas</u> (Edin. 1871). Service with 1869 naval expedition, investigating blackbirding in New Caledonia & New Hebrides.   19

PALMER,Herbert E. <u>The Roving Angler</u> (1933); <u>Mistletoe Child</u> (1935). Fishing memories from boyhood; life as child; nursery, education, dreams, Methodist home life in North of England; psyche and ego; good.   20

PALMER, Joe. Recollections (1927). Thirty years in sport; boxing; training; fight referee; Pedlar Palmer and other fighters and managers.   21

PALMERSTON, Henry John Temple, Viscount. Autobiographical sketch,in The Life: by Sir Henry Lytton Bulwer (L. 1870) Vol.I. Education; Parliamentary career; Napoleonic Wars & his government posts to 1830.   22

PAMPLIN,E.L. My Reminiscences (Winchester, n.d.). Childhood and family; governess, bookshop keeper; proprietor of hotel; brief;religious. Copy in Winchester P.L.   23

PANKHURST, Emmeline. My Own Story (1914) Growth of her belief in women's rights; career as a militant suffragette; good narrative of politics and agitation.   24

PANTON, Jane Ellen (Frith). Leaves from a Life (1908); More Leaves from a Life(1911); Most of the Game(1911). Childhood in 50's; career as writer; domestic and social life; theatrical and literary circles; Dickens, Sala, Brooks, Yates; painter-father.   25

PAPENDIECK, Charlotte L. H. Court and Private Life(1887). Keeper of the Wardrobe and reader to Queen Charlotte 1768-92;social life and ceremonies at court; gossip; personalities.   26

PARES, Sir Bernard. My Russian Memoirs(1931). Official correspondent in Russia during WW1; the Revolution,and later; war scenes; Menshevik and Bolshevik leaders and activities; valuable.   27

PARK,Mungo. Travels in the Interior Districts of Africa(1799); Journal of a Mission (1815). Explorations in the African interior in 1795-7 and 1805; scientific observations; work for the African Association.   28

PARK,Mrs. Rosamund E. Recollections (1916). Missionary work in Burma and Andaman Islands 1912-15;domestic life

and adventures;pleasant. India Office Library.   29

PARKE,Thomas Heazle. Diary, 1887-9; military service on Emin Pasha Relief expedition;medical officer. My Experiences in Equatorial Africa (1890).30

PARKE, William Thomas. Musical Memoirs (1830). Career as oboist, 1784-1830; orchestral and instrumental music in London; Covent Garden; opera; festivals;social, musical and general anecdotes; interesting.   31

PARKER, Eric. Eton in the Eighties (1914); Memory Looks Forward (1937). Boys, masters, study, sport, fagging; journalism career from 1899; St.James Gazette,Country Gentleman, The Field; country life and sport;his novels and other writings.   32

PARKER, Dr.Ernest. In and Out of My Consulting Room (1933); Doctor Tells (1938). Life of general practitioner; his patients and cases;fairly amusing anecdotes.   33

PARKER,James L. Reminiscences(Edin. 1886). Boyhood on estate in Honduras in 40's; religion;later missionary in Scotland.Copy in Royal Empire Society Library.   34

PARKER, Joseph. Tyne Childe (1886); Preacher's Life(1899). Norfolk youth; religious life and work as minister of Holborn City Temple;his preaching and writing and critics;Gladstone; Huxley and the evolutionists.   35

PARKER, Louis Napoleon. Several of My Lives (1928). His life in theatre; composer and performer; playwriting, managing and producing.   36

PARKER, Ralph. Moscow Correspondent (1949). Journalist's experiences in Russia after WW2; impressions of Russian life.   37

PARKER, Samuel. History of His Own Time (1727). Bishop of Oxford's history of the years 1660-1678; religion and politics and his part.   38

PARKER, Capt. Walter H. Leaves from an Unwritten Log-Book (1931). Boy on a windjammer; clipper ships, steamers and liners; work on Orient,Royal Mail and Cunard lines; captain of Olympic; secret service work in WW1.   39

PARKIN,Cecil. Cricket Reminiscences (1923); Parkin Again (1925). Life and anecdotes of Lancashire bowler; Test, County and League cricket; the life & difficulties of pros.   40

PARKINSON, Joseph Charles. Journal, 1870;his experiences laying telegraph cable from Suez to India. The Ocean Telegraph to India (Edin. 1870).   41

PARKS(or Parkes), Fanny. Wanderings of a Pilgrim (1850). Wife of official in Calcutta and Allahabad from 20's to 40's; official life, society, hunting and Indian life and troubles.   42

PARKYNS,Mansfield.Life in Abyssinia (1853). Travel and residence there in 40's; scenery; social life and sport; Abyssinian customs.   43

PARMOOR, Charles Alfred Cripps, Baron. Retrospect(1936). Winchester and Oxford; legal career at Parliamentary Bar and in ecclesiastical law; political career in Labour Party;in office as Lord President of Council;work for Church Assembly and League of Nations; excellent.   44

PARR, Gen. Sir Henry. Recollections (1917). Eton and Sandhurst; military career 1877-1903; South Africa, Sudan and India and in War Office;sport and social life.   45

PARRISH, Maud. Nine Pounds of Luggage(1940). Wanderer's life in Alaska South Seas,South America; her work in the Klondyke dance-halls, clubs, and gambling-houses; genial.   46

PARRY, Sir Edward A. What the Judge Saw(1912); What the Judge Thought (L. 1922); My Own Way(1932). Legal career in Manchester; Northern circuit; Manchester County Court judge;Manchester social life and theatre; work for the poor; journalism and scholarship; his edition of Dorothy Osborne.   47

PARRY, James. The True Anti-Pamela (1742). A poor Welsh boy's love for a rich Monmouth girl; racy story of an organist and singer.   48

PARSLOE, Muriel Jardine. A Parson's Daughter (1935). Essex childhood and county society and sport; life after WW1 in Australia, Canada & Herts; her travels and adventures.   49

PARSONS, George Samuel. Nelsonian Reminiscences (1843; 1905). Midshipman and lieutenant 1795-1801; service under Nelson; Cape St. Vincent, West Indies and Copenhagen; good narrative and dialogue.   50

PARSONS, William. Memories of the Life (1751).Baronet's son's crime and exploits;thieving, seduction, forgery and gambling;debts, imprisonment, deportation, hanging.   51

PARTRIDGE, E.H. Journey Home (1946) Country life; farming, sport and life of nature; natural beauty and release from industrialism.   52

PARTRIDGE, Eric. Three Personal Records of the War (1929). Writer's WW1 service in France as private with the Australian forces.   53

PASCO,Com. Crawford. Roving Commission(1897). Boyhood at sea and career in navy;Portuguese War of Succession; surveying West Australia and service in Malayan and Chinese waters;work in Tasmanian Water Police.   54

PASKE, Charles Thomas. A Retrospect of Life and Travel (1892). Military & medical work of an army surgeon;Lower Burma in 50's; social life.   55

A PASSIONATE PILGRIM. Up and Down the World(1915). Woman's early days in Scotland;travels in East; memories of Arnold, Ruskin, etc.   56

PAT. Thirty Seasons at Monte Carlo (1924). Experiences and systems of a moderate gambler.   57

PATERSON, Herbert John. A Surgeon Looks Back (1941). Glasgow childhood; Cambridge and Barts;his practice as a specialist in Harley Street; hospital work in WW1; visits to USA.   58

PATERSON, James. Autobiographical Reminiscences (Glasgow,1871). Life of a Scottish journalist and radical;the years 1819-20 in Kilmarnock; work on

Kay's Edinburgh portraits.   59

PATMORE, Peter George. My Friends &
Acquaintance(1864). Literary life and
friends; Lamb, Plumer Ward, Hazlitt,
the Smiths,the Sheridans, etc.; mostly biographical reminiscences.   60

PATON, John. Proletarian Pilgrimage
(1935); Left Turn(1936). Childhood in
Scotland; intellectual influences and
work for trade unions and ILP; career
as Labour politician; editor of "New
Leader"; divergent interests in Labor
Party; Labor Government; good.   61

PATON, John Gibson.   Autobiography
(1891). Scottish boyhood; missionary
work in Scotland & religious life and
work in New Hebrides; native life and
customs; covers 1824-85.   62

PATON, William A. Down the Islands
(1888). Travel and residence in Windward Islands in 80's; scenery, people
and mixture of races.   63

PATRICK, Rt.Rev. Simon. Autobiography (Oxford, 1839); MS, Cambridge University, Add. 36. Education; student
at Cambridge; ministry in London; his
advancement; religious and court matters to 1686; his change of religion;
good.   64

PATTERSON, A. H. Autobiography of a
Norfolk naturalist and author,written
in 1916. MS, Norwich Public Library,
2 vols.   65

PATTERSON, J. Brunlees. Life in the
Ranks (1885). Ranker's experiences on
troopship and in India;army life and
routine; advice to recruits.   66

PATTERSON, Captain John. Adventures
(1837); Camp and Quarters (1840). His
military service from 1807; campaigns
of Peninsular War and in West Indies;
army life and sport.   67

PATTERSON,John Edward. My Vagabondage (1911). Adventures of a Yorkshire
rolling stone and Johannes Factotum;
orphan, tramp, seaman, journalist, in
India,London, etc.; lively, especially for his childhood.   68

PATTERSON, Lt.Col. John Henry. With
the Zionists in Gallipoli (1916). An

account of service in Egypt during WW1
raising a unit from Russian—Jewish refugees; lively.   69

PATTISON, Mark. Memoirs (1885). His
intellectual and spiritual life, from
his arrival at Oxford in 1832 to 1860;
Newman and theTractarian Movement and
their effects at Oxford. MS notes for
this in the Bodleian include material
on other people's autobiographies and
diaries.   70

PAUL,Brenda Dean. My First Life (L.
1935). Rackety social life in London
society; life as a drug addict; trial
and imprisonment.   71

PAUL,Charles Kegan. Memories (1899)
Childhood;Eton and Oxford in forties;
his clerical life and his career as a
publisher to 1890;books, business and
writers.   72

PAUL, Leslie. Living Hedge (1946);
Heron Lake (1948). Boyhood in suburbs
of London; elementary school; work in
office; religion, sex, socialism; his
year on a Norfolk farm while sergeant
in army in WW2.   73

PAUL, Robert Bateman. Autobiography
of a Cornish Rector: by J.H. Tregenna
(1872). Childhood on Bodmin moor; education at Truro and Oxford; work as
tutor; curacies in Devon and London;
ministry in Cornwall.   74

PAULING, George.   Chronicles of a
Contractor (1926). Work as a builder,
miner,trader, railroad man; mainly S.
Africa but also England, India & Near
East; self-satisfied story of his own
ruthlessness.   75

PAWLEY, Tinko (Edith M.). My Bandit
Hosts (1935). Dictated account of her
Manchurian childhood; marriage; cap-
tured by bandits; rescue.   76

PAWSON, John. Short Account of the
Lord's Gracious Dealings (Leeds 1801)
Ministry and journeys of an itinerant
Methodist preacher, mainly in Lancs &
Yorks.   77

PAXTON, Sydney. Stage See-Saws (L.
1917). An actor's career in provinces,
London and America;anecdotes of players and theatrical life.   78

PAYEN, James Thomas. A Tangled Yarn (1891). London boy at sea in 20's and voyages to India and Africa; California Gold Rush; work in logging business in Australia; good.   79

PAYN, James. Some Literary Recollections (1884); Gleams of Memory (1894) His career as a journalist and writer; social and literary circles in London anecdotes of Mitford, Martineau, Dickens, Thackeray, Trollope etc.   80

PAYNE, George. Experiences at Darenth (Rochester, n.d.). Archaeological work in Kent; social life; general observations; slight. Pamphlet, Maidstone Museum.   81

PAYNE, Jack. This Is Jack Payne (L. 1932); Signature Tune (1947). Career as dance band leader; entertainment; broadcasting; his love affairs; & his heroes and admirers.   82

PAYNE, John. Autobiography (Olney, 1926). Life of poet and scholar; his schools in 50's; his translations and other works; poets of his time.   83

PAYNE, Pierre Stephen Robert. Chungking Diary (L. 1945); Journey to Red China (1947). Work and travels of a Times correspondent and teacher, from 1941; Chinese war and politics; university life at Chungking.   84

PAYNE, Thomas. Lives of Early Methodist Preachers, ed. Thomas Jackson (1837) I. Ministry and circuit work of an 18th Century Methodist preacher in Gloucestershire and the West.   85

PAYTON, Sir Charles A. Moss from a Rolling Stone (1879); Days of a Knight (1924). Sport in Mogador; fishing in England and abroad; early travels in California, S. Africa, Europe; diamond mining; work as consul in Morocco and Genoa; fishing and sport.   86

PEACOCK, Arthur. Yours Fraternally (1946). Twenty-five years in the Trade Union and Labour Movement, England and dominions; with medical mission during Spanish Civil War.   87

PEACOCK, Mabel R. A Nurse's Indian Log Book (1924). Training as a nurse; missionary and medical work, in India

from 1919. India Office.   88

PEACOCK, Thomas Love. "Recollections of Childhood," in Tales from Bentley (1859). House, garden, country town in which he spent his childhood.   89

PEAKE, Arthur Samuel. Recollections and Appreciations (1938). His scholarly studies and academic life; by the professor of Biblical Exegesis at the University of Manchester.   90

PEAL, Fred. War Jottings (Calcutta, 1916). Jesuit chaplain with Connaught Rangers in WW1 and with Indian forces in France and Mesopotamia. Copy, India Office Library.   91

PEARCE, Nathaniel. Life and Adventures (1831). Life as sailor; service with the ruler of Abyssinia, 1810-19; civil war; lively adventures of a chequered career.   92

PEARCE, Stephen. Memories of the Past (Edin. 1903). Boyhood and school in London in 30's; career as painter; Royal Academy; sitters and painters of the time. Cambridge U.L.   93

PEARCE, Zachary. A Commentary (1777) Prefaced by an autobiography and character study; clerical career of Bishop of Rochester to 1769.   94

PEARS, Sir Edwin. Forty Years (1915) Experiences of lawyer, journalist and author in Constantinople; diplomatic, legal, and historical work in Turkey, anecdotes.   95

PEARSE, A. W. Windward Ho (Sydney, 1933). Boyhood; life at sea from 60's; work with RMSP Company and Orient Line and later years in Australia.   96

PEARSE, Mrs. Godfrey. Enchanted Past (1926). Life to WW1; her Italian singer parents; life in Italy, Russia and London; stage life; anecdotes of royalty and celebrities.   97

PEARSE, Richard. Three Years in the Levant (1949). Life in Arab villages; work for intelligence corps; troubles with French; native life, and Palestine question; Russian propaganda.   98

PEARSON, Alexander. The Doings of a

Country Solicitor (Kendal, 1947). His
life in Kirkby Lonsdale; a delightful
account of life and manners in Westmoreland;the great house and the villagers.   99

PEARSON, Charles Henry. Memorials
(1900). Boyhood and education; Rugby,
Oxford;studies and work as a lecturer
on history in London,Manchester, Liverpool,Cambridge; emigration to South
Australia; to 1871.   100

PEARSON,Emma Maria, and McLAUGHLIN,
Louisa Elizabeth. Service in Servia
(1877). Their experiences while working for Red Cross in 1876 during the
Servo-Turkish War.   101

PEARSON, Francis. Memories (1935).
Work of a barrister's clerk;his eminent employers; famous cases.   102

PEARSON, Hesketh. Thinking It Over
(1938). Work as a clerk;career in the
theatre and as a critic and biographer;musical and literary acquaintances
and friends.   103

PEARSON, S. Vere. Man, Medicine and
Myself (1946). A London physician who
developed TB;life and work in a sanatorium; social and environmental fac-
tors in TB; interesting.   104

PEARSON, Scott. To the Streets and
Back (1932). Soldier down on his luck
after WW1; wanderings and odd jobs in
America and England; the struggles of
an unemployed man.   105

PEART,Barbara. Tia Barbarita (1933)
Her marriage;domestic and social life
on cattle-ranches in Mexico and Argentina; lively.   106

PEASE, Sir Alfred. Cleveland Hounds
(1887); Hunting Reminiscences (1898);
Half a Century of Sport (1932); Elections and Recollections (1932). Runs
and hunting with Cleveland; steeplechasing; big game hunting in Africa &
India; Parliamentary career to 1903;
Home Rule debates.   107

/PECHEY, Archibald Thomas/. Leaves
of Memory, by Valentine(1939). School
at Repton; insurance clerk, novelist,
and playwright; English life from the
70's; celebrities he knew.   108

PEEKE, Richard. Three to One (1626)
Devonshire man's exploits at Cadiz in
1625; the siege; his duels with three
Spaniards.   109

PEEL, Dorothy Constance. Life's Enchanted Cup(1933). Childhood in country house;Victorian mores; society in
London; women's life and work in WW1;
editor, women's page of "Daily Mail";
women's role.   110

PEEL, Lady Georgiana. Recollections
(1920). Her childhood and education;
court,society, celebrities of Victorian period;memories of her family and
social life.   111

PEEL, Sir Robert. Memoirs (1856). A
narrative of political events and defence of his decisions; Roman Catholic
question; the New Government; Repeal
of Corn Laws.   112

PEEL, Sir William. Journal, 1851;
travels in the Sudan for the purposes
of a Christian mission.A Ride through
the Nubian Desert (1852).   113

PEET, G. L. Malayan Exile (1934). A
series of newspaper sketches; life in
Malaya in 30's; Kuala.   114

PEILE, Frederick Kinsey.   Candied
Peel (1931). Military life in India &
Ireland at end of 19th Century;career
in the theatre as actor & playwright;
anecdotes.   115

PELHAM, Angela.   Young Ambassadors
(1944).A girl's account of her experiences in America.   116

PELHAM,Edward. God's Power and Providence (1631). A sailor's account of
experiences in Greenland,where he and
seven others were left by mischance in
1630; sufferings; God's mercy.Copy in
Cambridge U.L.   117

PELL, Albert. Reminiscences (1908).
Schooling,sport, social life; farming
in Middlesex and Fens;London in 60's;
Parliamentary career as M.P.for South
Leicester to 1885;agricultural inter-
ests.   118

PELLATT, Thomas. Boys in the Making
(L.1936). Sussex boyhood; Lancing and
Oxford; schoolmaster,Marlborough and

Eton;a wise and amused account of education, fashions, teachers, boys and school life.   119

PELLOW, Thomas. Adventures (1890). Captured by Sallee pirates as boy and twenty-three years prisoner of Moors; military service; adventures; earlier 18th Century.   120

PELLY, Adm. Sir Henry. 300,000 Sea Miles (1938). Gossippy account of his career and cruises, social life, adventures, in the navy.   121

PEMBERTON, Charles Reece. Autobiography of Pel. Verjuice (1929). Lively account of his early life in navy; and adventures to 1808.   122

PEMBERTON, Sir Max. Reminiscences (1935); Sixty Years Ago (1936). Anecdotes of literature, Bohemian social life, travel and sport; education in Birmingham and Cambridge; journalism; literary and social life in London and reminiscences of sport, celebrities & his novels.   123

PEMBERTON-BILLING,Noel. P.B. (Hertford,1917). His varied career and his Parliamentary activities as member for East Herts.   124

PENINGTON, Mary. Experiences in the Life (1911). Spiritual autobiography; religious life,ministry, hardships of a Kentish Quaker to 1681.   125

PENLEY, William Sidney. Penley on Himself (Bristol, n.d.). Rambling and wouldbe humorous experiences of actor 1883-90. Harvard U.L.   126

PENNANT, Thomas. The Literary Life (1793). His travels and travel books; scholarly and antiquarian studies and his honours at home and abroad;a personal report.   127

PENNELL, Elizabeth Robins & Joseph. Whistler Journal (1921). Their activities relating to Whistler;art,travel and social life; Whistler's conversations; art institutions.   128

PENNELL, Theodore L. Among the Wild Tribes of the Afghan Frontier (1909). Missionary work in late 19th Century; 16 years on frontier;travel disguised

as pilgrim;sympathetic account of native life and customs.   129

PENNINGTON,Arthur Robert. Recollections (1895). Clapham Common and its residents from 30's;his reading, politics, religion, literature; events & celebrities of Victorian era.   130

PENNINGTON, W. H. Sea, Camp & Stage (1906). Army life; survivor of Charge of Light Brigade;mostly his career in the theatre from 1862.   131

PENN-SMITH, Frank. The Unexpected (1933).Boyhood in France and England; and his travels in Tasmania, Queensland, Swaziland, Rhodesia, & Nigeria; work as pioneer,miner, farmer; a good and sensitive account of scenes, people, and nature.   132

PENNY, Alfred. Ten Years in Melanesia (1887). Missionary experiences in 70's;conversions; native life; tours; whales and traders.   133

PENNYMAN, John. A Short Account of the Life (1696).A Yorkshireman's life and ministry; Quaker travels, preaching and hardships.   134

PENROSE, Llewellin. Journal (1815). A Welsh sailor's shipwreck and adventures in mid-18th Century; one of the better examples of the kind.   135

PERCIVAL, Robert. Diary, 1800; army life; journey to court of Candy; descriptions of Ceylon.An Account of the Island of Ceylon (1805).   136

PEREIRA,Capt. Jocelyn. Distant Drum (Aldershot, 1948). Intelligence officer in WW2; campaign from Normandy to Germany; his emotions and thoughts in the advance.   137

PERRY, Frederick J. My Story (1934) His career as a tennis player; Davis Cup and Wimbledon; championships; and famous players.   138

PERRY, Sir Thomas Erskine. Journal, 1850-51;Bombay judge's travel through Northwestern Provinces and Nepal;full detail of courts, public life, sights A Bird's-Eye View of India (1855).139

ANON. Personal Narrative of a Private Soldier (1821). Twelve years from boyhood in a Highland regiment; service in Peninsular War; simple narrative; good for soldiers' life.   140

PERSONS, Robert. His brief autobiography of adventures and sufferings as a Jesuit in England during the reign of Elizabeth. Catholic Record Society Misc. II (1905), IV (1907).   141

PETERS, John. A Brief Narration of the Life(1709). Cornish Quaker; religious life and ministry;imprisoned at Lancaster.   142

PERTWEE, Roland. Master of None (L. 1940). Whimsical account of boyhood, education, WW1 army service, theatrical career as an actor and playwright his travel and sports.   143

PESTER, Maj. John. Journals, 1802-6 and 1812-23; military activities, and social life and travels in India;service in Lake's campaigns. MS, India Office Library, Eur. D. 434-439; part of them published in J. A. Devenish's War and Sport (1914).   144

PETERS, E.W. Shanghai Policeman (L. 1936). His service in Shanghai Police 1929-36; organization of force; crime and his own trial for murder.   145

PETERSON,Sir Maurice Drummond. Both Sides of the Curtain (1950). His diplomatic career; secretary to Balfour; ambassador in Sofia, Baghdad, Madrid, Moscow; foreign affairs from 1936 and notes on British and European statesmen; Parliament and foreign affairs; outspoken.   146

PETHICK-LAWRENCE, Emmeline. My Part in a Changing World (1938).Her social work in West London; work in women's rights movement; her husband and the Pankhursts; history of suffrage movement and her part in it; Labour Party politics.   147

PETHICK-LAWRENCE, F. W.   Fate Has Been Kind (1942). Eton and Cambridge; journalism; work in Women's Suffrage; Labour Party politics and development of the party; work as M.P. and Labour Minister;Union of Democratic Control; good.   148

PETRE, Maude D. M. My Way of Faith (1937). Childhood; education; religious life of a woman of deep faith;the Catholic Modernist movement; Tyrrell, Bremond, Von Huegel.   149

PETRIE, Sir Charles A. Chapters of Life (1950).   Political career of a right-wing conservative; politics between wars;Oxford Union, Carlton Club and Parliament; Baldwin; Churchill; a vigorous record.   150

PETRIE,Sir William Matthew Flinders Seventy Years in Archaeology (L.1931) Childhood;education; study of archaeology; surveying and research, Egypt, Palestine; publications; his relation with eminent scholars.   151

PETROVA, Olga. Butter With My Bread (Indianapolis, 1942). Early life and odd jobs in North of England; career as an actress; later work in theatre and films in USA.   152

PETT, Phineas. Autobiography (1918) His life at sea and as a shipwright, to 1638; his religious and spiritual life; good.   153

PETTIFER,Ernest W. Court is Sitting (Bradford, 1940).   Clerk to the West Riding Justices;police courts, police criminals, people in the dock.   154

PETULENGRO,Gypsy. A Romany Life (L. 1935); Gypsy Fiddler (1936).Life and travels of a gypsy; Roumania, England USA,Australia; fairs; music.   155

PHELAN, James Leo. Jail Journal (L. 1940); The Name's Phelan (1948); We Follow the Roads (1949). Experiences in Maidstone Jail while serving a life term;early career as tramp, actor and drifter;lodging-houses; ways & tricks of tramps; Borrow-style.   156

PHELPS, Anthony.   I Couldn't Care Less (Leicester, 1946). His experiences with Air Transport Auxiliary during WW2.   157

PHILBY, Harry St. John B. A Pilgrim in Arabia (1943); Arabian Days (1948) Education; career in the Indian Civil Service; political and military work in Iraq; Ibn Saud, Lawrence, Doughty,

Blunt, Burton; conversion to Islam; a revealing record.   158

PHILIP, Hugh.   Two Rings and a Red (1945). Naval surgeon's WW2 service; on depot ship and stone frigate, with commandos in Arctic and Near East; an amusing, light record.   159

PHILIPS, Francis C. My Varied Life (1914). His early career as a soldier in 70's; work as actor and theatrical manager; legal work with memories of judges and trials;journalism; fiction writing.   160

PHILIPS, Miles. Voyages and Adventures (1724).   West country sailor's travels to New World in 1570's; sufferings from Spaniards in Mexico and Indians in Canada; first published in Hakluyt.   161

PHILLIMORE, Godfrey Walter, Baron . Recollections (1930). His WW1 experiences in German and Austrian prisons; captors; attempted escapes.   162

PHILLIPS, A.H. I Shall Die Laughing (1948).Travels and observations of an amateur naturalist in Europe and South America; strange people and ways seen in strange circumstances.   163

PHILLIPS, Catherine. Memoirs of the Life,in Friends Library XI (Philadelphia, 1847). A Worcestershire woman's Quaker ministry and travels in the 2nd half of 18th Century; England and America.   164

PHILLIPS, G. Purssey.   Two Million Miles (1939). Life at sea;early years in sailing ships and cargo vessels including Cutty Sark;later commodore of the Clan Line.   165

PHILLIPS, Henry. Musical & Personal Recollections (1864). A singer's memories of opera, oratorio, concerts and performers;his songs and compositions anecdotes.   166

PHILLIPS, J.S. Coconut Quest (1940) Scientist's lively account of work and life in Solomons and East Indies;work on coconut disease.   167

PHILLIPS, Margaret Mann. Within the City Wall (1943). A young girl's life

in a York slum during WW1; emotional pressure of war; her thoughts about a historical novel; happy, intelligent child; very good.   168

PHILLIPS, Phebe; alias, Maria Maitland. Woman of the Town (1801). Memoirs of a courtesan; family troubles; sexual urges, lovers, brothels, and street-walking; prosperity, marriage; works of charity.   169

PHILLIPS, Teresia Constantia. Apology for the Conduct (1748). Splendour and misery of a courtesan;her amorous adventures;life with a Dutch merchant in Roxana-style.   170

PHILPOT, Benjamin. Our Centenarian Grandfather, by A. G. Bradley (1922). Suffolk boyhood; Cambridge; ministry in Isle of Man and at Great Cressingham to 1858;scholarship, study, local events and folk-lore,social; pleasant story of country life.   171

PHILPOT,Oliver L. S. Stolen Journey (1950). Airman's escape from a German prison camp into Sweden; a supplement to the famous wooden-horse escape, in which he took part.   172

/PHILPS, Arthur Carlton7.   Twenty Years of Spoof and Bluff, by Carlton (1919). Work and travels of an entertainer; conjuring; Mesmerism; debunking and revealing tricks of card-sharpers; tours in USA, Australia.   173

PHIPSON, T. Lamb. Voice and Violin (1898);Confessions of a Violinist (L. 1902). Musical study; career as violinist; Bohemian Orchestral Society; family life.   174

A PHYSICIAN. Seventy Years of Life in the Victorian Era (1893). Medical study and practice;country hospitals, service in Crimea; travels in America Australia and N.Z.   175

PICK,John B. Under the Crust (1946) His experiences as a Bevin Boy in WW2 coalmining in Yorkshire; the work and the attitudes of the workers.   176

PICKERING,R. Memoirs (Wellinborough 1837).Religious autobiography and diary of Independent minister of Brigstock, Yorks., in early part of 19th

Century; Yorkshire affairs.   177

PICKERING, William Alexander. Pioneering in Formosa(1898). Protector of Chinese in Malaya;his adventure among mandarins and savages, 1860-72; work in Chinese customs service.   178

PICKFORD, Elizabeth. Love Made Perfect (1858).   Wife of a sea captain; her distress in London during her husband's absence; religious preoccupations and social work at Bridewell and her life in Bristol; voyages with her husband.   179

PICKLES,Wilfred. Between You and Me (1949). Life, work, and anecdotes of a radio commentator and entertainer; work with BBC.   180

PICTON-TURBERVILL, Edith.   Life Is Good (1939). Brighton childhood; missionary work in India and settlement work in London; career as Labour M.P. and travels and incidents in her parliamentary career.   181

PIDGEON,Nathaniel. Life, Experience and Journal (1837).Early life in Ireland and his troubles there as Methodist; emigration to Australia and his ministry there.   182

PIERCE, Robert. Bath Memoirs (1697) Medical practice   at the Bath in second half of 17th Century.   183

PIERCE,Samuel Eyles. A True Outline (1822). Religious and spiritual autobiography; ministry in Devonshire and Cornwall and seventeen years at Shoe Lane; his palsy.   184

PIGACHE, Daniel Nichols. Cafe Royal Days (1934). Reminiscences of life at Cafe Royal from late 19th Century;Bohemian life and celebrities.   185

PIGGOTT, Major-Gen. Francis Stewart Gilderoy. Broken Thread (1950). Boyhood and education; early interest in Japan; military career and experience in Tokyo;WW1; Anglo-Japanese politics and his Japanese friends.   186

/PIGGOTT, Harriett7.Private Correspondence of a Woman of Fashion (1832) Records of Real Life (1839). Travel & writing; fashionable life in England,

Holland, Belgium, France, Switzerland and Italy; amusing.   187

PIGGOTT, Sir Theodore Caro. Outlaws I Have Known (Edin. 1930). Career as a judge in Allahabad;reminiscences of police, dacoits, law, crime.   188

PIGOT, Gen. R.   Twenty-Five Years Big-Game Hunting (1928). Hunting from Norway to Sardinia;India; New Zealand etc. India Office Library.   189

PIGOTT, Richard. Personal Recollections (Dublin, 1882).Work of an Irish journalist from 1848; Fenianism, Land League, Irish troubles, Parnell, etc. somewhat impersonal.   190

PIGOU, Francis.   Phases of My Life (1898); Odds and Ends (1903). Boyhood and schools; Ripon, Cheltenham, Edinburgh, Dublin; curacies in Yorkshire; fashionable preacher in London; Dean of Bristol; cathedral life; literary, society, social reminiscences; Sunday schools and missions.   191

PIKE, Joseph.   Some Account of the Life (1837). Cork man's religious and spiritual life; Quaker ministry, Ireland, England, Holland, in later 17th Century and after.   192

PILKINGTON, Ernest M. S. Eton Playing Field (1896). His social work at Eton Mission in Hackney Wick;muscular Christianity and public school humanitarianism in London slums.   193

PILKINGTON, John Carteret. The Real Story(1760). Adventures of the son of Laetitia Pilkington;travels and picaresque adventures in Great Britain and Ireland;memories of his mother and of theatrical celebrities.   194

PILKINGTON,Laetitia. Memoirs (1748) Chroniques scandaleuses of first half of 18th Century;the polite world, the theatre, and the City.   195

PINDAR, John (Peter Leslie). Autobiography of a Private Soldier (Cupar 1877). Youth as miner; enlists; army service in India; Edinburgh, Ireland, Gibraltar, Malta; promotion; account of army conditions.   196

PINNEGAR, Eira Gwynneth. The Great

Awakening (Newport, 1948). Life as a singer and entertainer; her loves and troubles;religious promptings; mysticism; spiritual advice.Copy, Cambridge U.L.   197

PINNOCK, James. Journal, 1758-1794; study at Cambridge and Lincoln's Inn; work on a cocoa plantation in Jamaica and details of social life, negroes & Jamaican affairs. MS, British Museum, Add. 33316.   198

PITCAIRN, W. D. Two Years among the Savages of New Guinea (1891). Travels 1887-9; exploration; natives.   199

PITMAN, Charles Robert Senhouse. A Game Warden among His Charges (1931); Game Warden Takes Stock (1942). Work as a game warden in Uganda and Kenya, and partly in India; observations of animals; zoology.   200

PITMAN, Emma Raymond. My Governess Life (1883). Daughter of a Methodist minister; turns to teaching after his death; school and Sunday School work; Methodist observances.   201

PITMAN,Henry. Relation of the Great Sufferings(1689). Surgeon to the Duke of Monmouth; imprisonment and deportation after Duke's defeat;escape from Barbados, life on desert island, and return to England.   202

PITMAN, Major Stuart. Second Royal Gloucestershire Hussars (1950). Contains his diary, 1941-42; activities of his regiment and himself in desert warfare of WW2.   203

PITT, Billy (pseud.). The Cabin Boy (1840). Personal experiences in navy, 1790-1837; cabin boy; officer in the civil department.   204

PITT, Frances. Hounds, Horses, and Hunting (1948). Activities as Master of Wheatlands Hunt; pleasant memories of hunting and hunters in Shropshire; natural history.   205

PIXLEY, Capt. William. Short Autobiography (1916). Shipbuilder's son; schooling in Dunkirk;adventures while detained in France during Napoleonic Wars;later life at sea; shipwreck and other adventures. Copy, Bucks Museum,

Aylesbury, Buckinghamshire.   206

PLACE,Francis. Autobiography of the early 19th Century reformer; notes on public affairs,reform, social change, together with letters,essays, miscellanea. MS,B.M.Add. 35142-35147 (Place Papers I-VI); used in Graham Wallas's Life.   207

PLAISTED, Bartholomew. Diary, 1749-1756; his travels and observations in Bengal;   journey overland to England. A Journal from Calcutta (1757).   208

PLANCHE, James Robinson. Recollections and Reflections (1872). Professional life of Somerset Herald; mostly his work in the theatre as dramatist; Covent Garden; theatrical life, entertainment, actors, costumes, etc. and travels in Europe.   209

/PLANT, D./.   Life's Realities, by T. C. T.(Wolverhampton, n.d.). Education and college life in 60's; social life, public events in West Bromwich, in mid-century. William Salt Library, Stafford.   210

PLATT, William. Man's Day on Earth (1925). Man of many talents, artistic and commercial; lecturing for League of Nations Union; poet and author; in love with life.   211

PLAYFAIR,Giles William. My Father's Son (1937). Home, Harrow and Oxford, and his father; youth in theatrical & literary society; Milne, Bax, Herbert, Drinkwater;Oxford in thirties; a good story of himself and his setting. 212

PLAYFAIR, Lyon Playfair, 1st Baron. Memoirs and Correspondence(1899). His private and public life; Lancashire & London;career as Liberal M.P.; office of Vice-President of Council; Parliamentary affairs.   213

PLAYFAIR,Sir Nigel. Hammersmith Hoy (1930). Harrow and Oxford; career as lawyer;his theatrical career as actor and manager;productions at the Lyceum Hammersmith; literary and theatrical life and people; good.   214

PLESS,Mary Theresa Olivia, Princess of. From My Private Diary (1931). Her life in England, Germany, and Austria from 1895 to WW1; court and society; travels; personalities.   215

PLOMER,William. Double Lives (1943) Life to 25; bourgeois family; education at Rugby;literary interests; his life and work in S. Africa; travel in Japan & university life, art, friends there; writing.   216

PLOWDEN, Alfred Chichele. Grain or Chaff(1903). Boyhood in India; school in England and Oxford; legal career; law reporter,barrister on circuit,Recorder,magistrate; work in the London police courts.   217

PLOWMAN, Thomas F. In the Days of Victoria (1918); Fifty Years (1919). Journalism; public affairs and social life, art, education, theatre and old entertainments; the Victorian scene; his life as an agricultural showman in Somerset and the South-West; farming; work for agricultural societies;anecdotes of shows.   218

PLUMMER, Priv. Samuel. Diary, 1800-1819; army service in India and Java; work as a Methodist missionary; pagan practices. The Journal (1821).   219

PLUMPTRE, Anne. Narrative of Three Years' Residence in France (L. 1810); A Narrative of a Residence in Ireland (1817). Life abroad;travels; descriptions of places, society,theatres and people she met.   220

POCOCK, Robert. Life, by George M. Arnold (1883). Gravesend antiquarian, historian, naturalist, printer; work; extracts from diary 1811-23.   221

/"POCOCKE, Captain"/. Journal of a Soldier of the 71st or Glasgow Regiment (Edin. 1819). Military service, 1806-15; campaigns and battles of the Peninsular War and a vivid account of Waterloo.   222

PODMORE, St.Michael. Rambles and Adventures(1909). Experiences in India, Australia, Canada, etc.   223

POLAND, Sir Harry Bodkin. Seventy-Two Years at the Bar, by Ernest Bowen Rowlands (1924). Reported reminiscences of legal life from 1851; celebrated cases,crimes, trials; memories of

judges and lawyers.   224

POLE, John L. When (1929). Schools; notes on social life and politics;his mental difficulties; died in a mental home; fiction?   225

POLE, William. Some Short Reminiscences (1898). Career and travels of a civil engineer; railways, bridges and water-supply in India,Japan, England; scientific work;service on government boards;amateur music. Copy, Cambridge U.L.   226

POLEHAMPTON, Emily. Diary, 1857-58; experiences in Indian Mutiny; evacuation from Lucknow. A Memoir..of Henry Polehampton (1859).   227

POLEHAMPTON, Henry Stedman. Diary, 1857; details of the siege of Lucknow by the chaplain. A Memoir (1859). 228

POLLARD, Capt. Alfred Oliver. Fire-Eater (1932). Military service on the Western Front in WW1; adventures; his exploits; won V.C.   229

POLLARD, Samuel. Tight Corners in China (191?); In Unknown China (1921) Life and work of a pioneer missionary among the Nosu Tribe of Western China and observations of Nosu culture;travel and adventure.   230

POLLITT, Harry. Serving My Time (L. 1940). Family life; early years as a political speaker in Lancs and work as a plater; work in Communist Party and international congresses; activities and troubles in politics; poor.   231

POLLOCK,Col. Arthur J. Incidents of Foreign Sport (1894). Fishing and big game hunting in England, India, Syria and Africa from boyhood.   232

POLLOCK, Bertram. Twentieth Century Bishop(1944). Education; religion and his ordination; work as headmaster of Wellington; career in church; work as Bishop of Norwich.   233

POLLOCK,Sir Frederick. Personal Remembrances (1887). His career in law and politics; reminiscences of social life, literature, theatre, music, and celebrities; useful.   234

POLLOCK,Sir Frederick.For My Grandson (1933). Boyhood; Eton, Cambridge; career as a lawyer; literature, philosophy, music, mountain climbing; his friends in the law, scholarship, theatre, literature; pleasant.   235

POLLOCK, James M. Unvarnished West (1907). Recollections of British army officer; farming and ranching experiences in Texas in 80's.   236

POLLOCK, James S. Vaughton's Hole (Oxford, 1890). Birmingham minister's twenty-five years in St. Alban's mission;religion and social work; finances and difficulties.   237

POLLOCK, William. Cream of Cricket (1934). Forty years as cricket journalist; the game, players, controversies; body line bowling; etc.   238

POLLOK, Colonel Fitzwilliam Thomas. Incidents of Foreign Sport and Travel (1894); Fifty Years' Reminiscences(L. 1896). Schooling in 30's; army career as cadet in Egypt and later in India, Burma, etc.; 2nd Burma War; travels & adventures; social life.   239

POLWARTH, Walter G. Hepburne-Scott, Baron. Lord Polwarth, by George Barbour (Edin. 1947) is based on reminiscences; public life and administration of a Scots laird;Border life and people; relation of Scott.   240

POLWHELE, Richard. Traditions and Recollections (1826). Education, work as curate and vicar of Newlyn; historical and antiquarian work, literary scholarship, poetry; mainly reminiscences of chief writers of late 18th & early 19th Century.   241

PONDER,Stephen Ernest Gilbert. Soldier in the Sun (1935); Mediterranean Memories (1937);Seven Cantonments (L. 1938). Interesting records of life of soldier after WW1; Aden, India, West Africa, China, Salisbury, Malta, Sind and N.W. Frontier; army work, sport, travel.   242

PONSONBY,Mary. A Memoir (1927). Her life and work as Maid of Honour to the Queen in 60's; court life; marriage & friends; books; travels; George Eliot, A. C. Benson, etc.; good.   243

POOLER, Harry William. My Life in General Practice (1948); My Life in Three Counties (1950). Upbringing in Shropshire; medical work in Birmingham as family doctor; work in welfare centres in Derbyshire;service on Medical Council.   244

POORE, Lady Ida. Recollections of an Admiral's Wife (1916); Admiral's Wife in the Making(1917). Social life ashore from 1903; Australia, England; Irish girlhood with her Bishop-father and life with sailor-husband in many parts of world; interesting.   245

POPE, Douglas. Now I'm Sixteen (L. 1937). Country life in Sussex village and his hobbies and interests; local ways and people.   246

PORRITT,Arthur. The Best I Remember (1922); More and More of Memories (L. 1947).Lifetime as journalist in Fleet Street;editor of Christian World; religious movements;famous preachers in Free Churches; Liberal politics; social reform; interesting.   247

PORTEOUS, Crichton. Farmer's Creed (1938); Land Truant (1940). Incidents in life of a Cheshire farmer; his later work as a journalist in North of England; Daily Awakener.   248

PORTER, Frank Thorpe. Gleanings and Reminiscences (Dublin, 1875); Twenty Years' Recollections (1880). Life and work as a magistrate in Ireland, from the 40's;police, crime, prisons, legal life, circuit travels.   249

PORTER, John. Kingsclere (1896); An Autobiography (1919).Life and work as jockey and trainer from 50's; training at Kingsclere; his horses, owners and successes; Turf life, jockeys and gamblers.   250

PORTER,Josias Leslie. Five Years in Damascus (1855). Life in Damascus and travels from 1849; Arab life, customs and e conomy.   251

PORTER, Rose. Years That Are Told (1870). Sentimental account of childhood, family and friends; fifty years of married life.   252

PORTLAND,William John A. C. J. Cav-

endish-Bentinck, 6th Duke of. Fifty
Years and More(1933); Memories (1935)
Men, Women and Things (1938). Account
of stag-hunting and fishing in Highlands; association with Jockey Club &
horse-racing; famous trainers, horses
and jockeys; childhood at Welbeck and
at court; London society and nobility
and celebrities in the arts, services
church and politics.   253

PORTMAN,Lionel. Station Studies (L.
1902). Life and work of a government
official in Kenya and Uganda; hunting
and social life.   254

POSTLETHWAITE, John Rutherford Parkin. I Look Back (1947). Haileybury;
colonial administration in Buganda and
nutria farming in retirement;Ministry
of Food; work for Royal African Society; simple and informative.   255

POTENGER, John. Private Memoirs (L.
(1841). His education at Winchester &
Oxford;classical studies and reading,
law studies at Temple and practice in
Wilts; work as Comptroller of Pipe in
Wilts; London clubs; literature; marriage, wife, and family; second half
17th Century; excellent.   256

POTTER, Louisa. Lancashire Memories
(1879). Country life and people, early 19th Century; home at Riverton and
school in London.   257

/POTTER, Richard7. From Ploughshare
to Parliament, by Georgina Meinertz-
hagen (1908). Extracts from his diary
from 1793; farming and shopkeeping in
Tadcaster;country life and work; M.P.
for Wigan in Reform Parliament, 1832;
excellent picture of the rise of middle-class family.   258

POTTS, W. H. Wind from the East (L.
1940). Business man's escape; apprentice on a windjammer; work on tramp-
steamers; prospector in Australia and
travel in China; extraordinary adventures poorly described.   259

POULTER (alias, Baxter), John. Discoveries (Sherborne,1761). A highwayman's account of his robberies during
period 1749-52.   260

POULTON, Prof. Edward Bagnall. John
Viriamu Jones (1911).Reminiscences of

Jones,the Oxford Union, academic life
and personalities at Oxford, by Professor of zoology.   261

POUND, Reginald. Their Moods & Mine
(1937); Pound Notes (1940); A Maypole
(1948). Work as journalist; editor of
Strand Magazine; everyday and intellectual life; theatre, literature and
gardening; people he interviewed; impressions; quite good.   262

POURIE,John. Memorials of (Calcutta
1869). Education at Edinburgh University;ministry in Free Church of Scotland; thirteen years in Calcutta; diary extracts. Bodleian.   263

/POWEL-BROWN, Mrs. E.M.7. A Year on
the Irrawaddy (Rangoon, 1911). Experiences and domestic life of the wife
of a captain of an oil-tanker plying
on the river. India Office.   264

POWELL, Ellen. One White Woman, by
Maude Dicker Simms (1925). Domestic &
social life in Assam; husband working
on railway construction.   265

POWELL, Joseph. Two Years (L. 1871)
Service in Pontifical Zouaves 1868-70;
siege of Rome;travels in Papal States
and notes on life and work.   266

POWELL, Lacy.   Memoirs of the Life
(Manchester, 1801). Irish boyhood and
work in a Manchester cotton-mill;rob-
beries and other crimes; confessional
autobiography written before hanging,
at Derby Gaol. Derby P.L.   267

POWELL, Vavasor. The Life and Death
(1671). Welshman's religious life;his
conversion and ministry.   268

POWELL,Wilfred.Wanderings in a Wild
Country (1883). Travels and adventure
during three years among the cannibals
in New Britain group.   269

POWER,William. Should Auld Acquaintance (1927). Scottish boyhood; bank
clerk; journalist on Glasgow Herald;
public events; good account of Scotch
newspaper world.   270

POWER, Sir William T. Recollections
of a Three Years' Residence in China
(1852).Travels in Mediterranean lands
Egypt, India, Australia; residence in

China; Chinese customs.   271

POWLES, Louis Diston. Land of the
Pink Pearl(1888). His career as judge
in the Bahamas;local economy; slavery
and his work for reform;Bahaman scene
and Nassau society.   272

POWYS, John Cowper. Autobiography
(1934). Childhood in Dorset; school &
Cambridge; Southwick court house and
Burpham; travels and WW1 experiences;
eccentricities, love affairs, mysticism, emotions; and his career in literature.   273

POWYS, John Cowper, and Llewellyn.
Confessions of Two Brothers(Rochester
1916).First analyses his emotions and
soul as an artist in relation to literature, society and nature; miseries
in adapting to circumstances;   second
gives experiences at Cambridge, life
as tutor and teacher, travels in USA
and Europe; life in Swiss sanatorium;
sharp sketches of people.   274

POWYS, Littleton C.   The Joy of It
(1937).Pleasant boyhood in a clerical
household;   Cambridge days; work as a
schoolmaster at Bruton,Llandovery and
Sherborne; attractive.   275

POWYS, Llewellyn. Skin for Skin (L.
1926). Childhood and youth in Dorset;
country life and scenes;   reading and
writing; mysticism and nature; mainly
his experiences of tuberculosis & his
convalescence.   276

POYNDER, John. Fragment of Autobio-
phy (1847), orig. published in Chris-
tián Observer, July, 1847. Religious
life; material influence; Dissent and
his loyalty to Church of England; his
work as sheriff at Newgate;   interest
in Church Missionary Society. Copy in
Cambridge U.L.   277

POYNTZ, W. H. Per Mare, Per Terram
(1892). Officer's career in marines;
China expedition; South Africa; Japan
Chief Constable of Notts and Essex; &
social, sport, personal life. Copy in
Cambridge U.L.   278

PRAEGER, Robert Lloyd. A Populous
Solitude (1941). Work of a naturalist
in Ireland; devotion to the beauty of
nature; country life and people; fel-

low-scientists; interesting.   279

PRAGNELL, Vera G. The Story of the
Sanctuary (1928). Her work at retreat
in South Downs; quietism, meditation,
Christian communism.   280

PRATT,Antwerp Edgar.Two Years among
New Guinea Cannibals (1906). Travels;
scientific and anthropological observations of a naturalist.   281

PREMIUM,Barton(pseud.). Eight Years
in British Guiana (1850). Life & work
of a sugar planter in Guiana from the
40's; administration, labour, outlook
for planting; native affairs.   282

PRENTICE, Archibald.   Historical
Sketches (1851). Journalist's work in
Manchester to 1848; industry, trade &
economics; Bentham,working-class life
and factories in Manchester & strikes
and troubles; Corn Laws; Reform Act;
Manchester scene.   283

PRESCOTT-WESTCAR, Lieut.Col. V. Big
Game, Boers, Boches (1937). Military
career in Rifle Brigade; Boer War and
WW1 service; hunting in Africa; blunt
and cheerful record.   284

PRESTON, Sir Harry John.   Memories
(1928);Leaves from My Unwritten Diary
(1936). Seventy years of sport;boxing
and football;theatre and Bohemian social and club life in Brighton & London; celebrities he knew.   285

PRESTON, Raymond. Raymond Preston,
by W.K. Greenland (1930). Autobiographical sections on poor early life in
Yorks in 60's;factory life; converted
and worked as a Methodist minister in
North of England and later in Australia.   286

PRESTON, Thomas Hildebrand. Before
the Curtain (1950). Education at Cambridge; mining engineer in Russia and
consul at Ekaterinburg in WW1;Russian
Revolution; missions to Russia; work
as consul in Lithuania;interpreter at
political conferences;musical compositions and work for ballet; good. 287

PRESTON-THOMAS, Herbert.   Work and
Play (Edin. 1909). Career with Local
Government Board from 1859; poor law,
workhouses, sewerage, lunacy; inter-

esting sociologically.   288

PRETYMAN, Lt.Herbert Edward. Diary, 1890-91; exploration and observations in Kittar Mountains in Lower Egypt. A Journal of an Expedition (1892).   289

/PRICE, Maj. David/. Memoirs of the Early Life and Service of a Field Officer (1839). Welsh boyhood; service with East India Company;activities in war with Tippoo; work a s judge-advocate; adventures, 1780-1806; a lively record.   290

/PRICE, Mrs. Hamlyn/. Diary, 1909; travels in Northern Ceylon; with her husband on tours of inspection; economy, schools, missions.   A Diary of Three Tours (1909). Copy in Colonial Office Library.   291

PRICE, Harry. Leaves from a Pyschist's Case Book (L.1933); Confessions of a Ghost Hunter (1936); Search for Truth(1942). Lifetime interest in and study of psychical phenomena; ghosts, poltergeists, mediums, spiritualists; Ghost Club; Mongoose affair; research at London University; scientific approach to supernatural.   292

PRICE,Henry. Autobiography and diary,1824-1904; poor-law boy in West of England;work in New York; cabinet maker in Islington from 1849; workingman and his life and conditions;very good sociological material. MS, Islington Public Library.   293

PRICE,Hereward T. Boche and Bolshevik (1919). English scholar naturalised as German; service in the German army in WW1 on Eastern Front; capture by Russians; experiences in prisons & in revolution; escape.   294

PRICE, Howell ap David. A Genuine Account of the Life (L.1752). A Welsh sailor captured and sold as a slave in Algeria; escape with Cleone; his love affairs; fiction?   295

PRICE, Julius M. From Arctic Ocean (1892); My Bohemian Days in Paris (L. 1913); My Bohemian Days in London (L. 1914); On the Path of Adventure(1919) Journalist and foreign correspondent; work for Illustrated London News; his travels in Siberia and China; life in

Paris and London; art, love, and vie de Boheme; frothy.   296

PRICE, William. Travel diary, 1810-1812; embassy to Persia; descriptions of Persian life,culture, architecture Journal of the British Embassy to Persia (1832).   297

PRICE,William Salter. My Third Campaign (1890). Life and work of a missionary in East Equatorial Africa;his teaching; Arab slavery.   298

PRICHARD, Augustin. A Few Medical & Surgical Reminiscences (Bristol,1896) Medical training in 30's; practice in Bristol; his teachers & friends; John Addington Symonds.   299

PRICHARD, Iltudus Thomas. Mutinies in Rajpootana (L.1860); Chronicles of Budgepore (1870).Experiences in Jodhpore; the Mutiny; social and official life in upper India;army and business life; fictional setting.   300

PRIDE,David. Reminiscences (Paisley 1914). Education,medical training and practice in Scotland; Scottish life & local events; Dundee,Glasgow, Paisley and Neilston; social history.   301

PRIESTLEY, Lady Eliza.   Story of a Lifetime (1908). Her life from 1850; social work; literary and social life and politics.   302

PRIESTLEY, John Boynton. Midnight on the Desert (1937); Rain upon Gadshill(1939). Writing plays and reflections upon art and life while wintering in Arizona; theatrical life,writing, reflections on time, social system and himself, in England.   303

PRIESTLEY, Joseph. Memoirs (1806). Upbringing as nonconformist;religious education & training for the ministry; ministry in London;his scientific and philosophical studies and research; & travels in America,etc.; valuable account of life of the great theologian scientist.   304

PRIESTWOOD, Gwen. Through Japanese Barbed Wire(1943). Personal narrative of WW2 experiences; interned by Japanese in Hong Kong; adventures related with good humour.   305

PRINCE, John Henry. The Life (1806)
London bookseller's reminiscences, of
his family, their poverty, his early
jobs and love affairs; his writings &
religious work.   306

PRINGLE, Walter. Memoirs (1723). A
Covenanter's account of his religious
life and God's mercies in the mid-17th
Century; Scottish religious affairs &
politics.   307

PRINSEP, Valentine Cameron. Diary,
1876-77; travels and work of official
painter in India; Indian princes and
courts. Imperial India (1879).   308

PRIOR,Charles. So I Wrote It (1937)
Life in the army;travels in Spain and
France;his career as a burglar; tech-
niques; prison experiences.   309

PRIOR, Melton. Campaigns of a War
Correspondent (1912). Travels and adventures of a journalist, 1873-1905;
Illustrated London News; Ashanti,Tur-
kish, Zulu wars; the Boer Wars; Egypt
and Soudan; Russo-Japanese War.   310

PRITCHARD, John. Lives of Early Methodist Preachers, ed. Thomas Jackson
(1838) III.   Life and travels in the
ministry of an Irish Methodist; later
18th Century.   311

PRITCHARD, William Thomas. Polynesian Reminiscences (1866). Experiences
in Tahiti,Samoa, Fijis from 1848; his
work as British consul; history; native life and customs.   312

PRIVATE No. 940.On the Remainder of
Our Front (1917). Personal narrative
of military service in France in WW1;
good details of life of men.   313

PROCTER,Bryan Waller. Autobiographical Fragment (1877). Literary life &
friends of Barry Cornwall, poet; the
chief poets and prose-writers of his
time from Wordsworth to Carlyle; familiar anecdotes; useful.   314

PROCTER, Richard Wright.   Literary
Reminiscences (Manchester, 1860). His
social and literary life in Manchester in mid-19th Century; writers, eccentrics,and the Manchester scene and
antiquities.   315

PROTHEROE,Charles. Life in the Mercantile Marine (1903). A lifetime at
sea under sail and steam; Australia &
New Zealand; adventures;conditions of
life; nautical customs.   316

PROTONIUS. Personal Pie (1938). His
upbringing in Glasgow; intellectual &
religious life; reading; his defence
of scepticism; journalism.   317

A PROVINCIAL SURGEON.My First Grief
(Bath, 1852). Childhood in a clerical
home of sweetness and light; training
as doctor; death of favourite sister;
God's mysteries and mercy;his work in
hospitals. Bath P.L.   318

PRYDE, David. Pleasant Memories of
a Busy Life (Edin. 1893). His boyhood
in Fifeshire; education; work for En-
cyclopoedia Britannica;career as teacher and principal of Edinburgh Ladies
College; Edinburgh life.   319

PRYME, George. Autobiographical Recollections (Cambridge, 1870). Education at Cambridge; fellowship at Trinity & his professorship of political
economy; M.P. for Cambridge; politics
and Parliament; travels; the notes go
up to 1866.   320

PULESTON,Fred. African Drums (1930)
Life as an African trader, 1882-1896;
Benin River, Cacongo, Loanga; trading
routes; Emin Pasha relief expedition;
native life; adventures.   321

/PULMAN,George Philip Rigney7. Rambles, Roamings and Recollections, by
John Trotandot (1870). Travels, local
events, folk lore, rambles, in Dorset
Devon, Somerset.   322

PURCELL, Edmund D. Forty Years at
the Criminal Bar (1916). Career as a
lawyer; cases, clients, judges, criminals; famous crimes; boxing.   323

PURDOM, Charles Benjamin (editor).
Everyman at War (1929). Personal narratives of WW1 related by sixty men &
women of all ranks and all services &
reflecting war service on all sectors
and phases of the war.   324

PURVES-STEWART, Sir James. Sands of
Time (1938); Over Military Age (1942)

Training and career of a mental specialist;human aberrations in peace and
war; medical life; anecdotes; service
in Home Guard and missions abroad for
Red Cross in WW2.   325

PYCROFT, James. Twenty Years (1859)
Oxford Memories(1886). Life and work
in Church of England; parish life and
church celebrities; study at Trinity
in 30's; students and scholars; sport
Town and Gown; Tractarian Movement; a
comparative retrospect.   326

PYKE, Richard. Men and Memories (L.
1948). Boyhood in Devon village;Meth-
odist life; reading; spiritual development & Methodist ministry in London
and Devonshire; bookish life.   327

PYM, Dorothy. Houses as Friends (L.
1936). Her life in five houses;domes-
tic life, chicken farming, gardening,
literary associations.   328

PYPER, Lt. H.C. Hounds First (1937)
Otter-hunting;sheep-farming and sport
in Australia; service with RFC during
WW1 in Egypt and Suvla Bay; fox-hunting and point-to-point racing, Devonshire and New Forest.   329

.QUEKETT, William. My Sayings and
Doings (1888). Somerset boyhood; Cambridge; curacies in Somerset and London;social work in East End; ministry
in Warrington; photography.   1

QUELCH,Stephen. Early Recollections
(1900). Printer's memories of Oxford
in 19th Century; Town and Gown; local
events;work as apprentice printer and
later associations with Parker's, the
Oxford booksellers.   2

QUICK, Robert Herbert. Life and Remains (1899). Notebooks and diaries,
arranged under life and subjects; education and work as school inspector;
morals, religion, travel, etc.   3

QUILLER-COUCH, Sir Arthur. Q: Memories and Opinions (1944). Unfinished
autobiography to 1887; his boyhood at
Polperro and Newton Abbott; Clifton &
Oxford;beginning of his literary car-

eer; a pleasant fragment.   4

QUIN,Malcolm. Memoirs of a Positiv-
ist (1924). Thirty years' search for
religious truth; founding of Positiv-
ist Church and priesthood; preaching,
Catholicism, politics.   5

QUINAIN, Louis. Country Beat (1946)
Policeman on the Green (1948). Training as policeman;his beat and work as
policeman at Gayford & at Fittlewick;
humours of country life.   6

QUINTERLEY, Esmond. My Airman Days
(1948). Middle-aged soldier's account
of service in WW2; with the RAF mostly in Middle East; dull.   7

QUIRKE, William Michael. Recollections (1914). Career of Irish violinist; concerts and lessons; visits to
Ireland; English musical and literary
scene; Wilde, the Schumanns.   8

RACE, G. Forty Years a Master(1911)
Experiences as Master of foxhounds; &
notes on runs and hunters.   1

RADCLIFFE, Mary Ann. Memoirs (Edin.
1810). Family life and its cares told
in letters to a friend.   2

RADNOR, Helen Matilda Pleydell-Bou-
verie, Dowager-Countess. From a Great
Grandmother's Arm-Chair (1926). Life
at Longford Castle and Armitage Hill;
her old age; society, politics, art &
literature; Victorian era.   3

RADZIWILL,Princess Catherine. Those
I Remember (1924). Memories of court
and society in England and Germany in
pre-WW1 period; nobility, politicians
writers, celebrities; impersonal.   4

RAGG,Thomas. God's Dealings with an
Infidel(1858). Work as journalist and
lace-worker in Nottingham; his sins;
conversion; work as minister.Birming-
ham P.L.   5

RAGLAN,The Dowager Lady Ethel. Memories of Three Reigns (1928). Society
and court,Victorian, Edwardian, Georgian;manners and customs; her life in

Isle of Man; contemporary ideas.   6

RAIGERSFELD,Jeffrey, Baron de. Life of a Sea Officer (Maidstone, 1831). A sailor's life from late 18th Century; admiral of the red; valuable details of ship life. Edited L.G. C. Laughton (1929).

RAIKES, Charles. The Englishman in India (1867). Career as judge in Lahore from 30's; legal life; official work and administration;Indian Mutiny and events; personalities.   8

RAIMBACH, Abraham. Memoirs and Recollections (L.1843). Life of a Swiss engraver in France and England; memories of art & artists; Willkie, etc.; influence of Paine.   9

RAINOW, G. K. G. P. (1939). Medical study;London hospitals; work as locum tenens and general practitioner; medical practice and fashions.   10

RAINSFORD,William Stephen. Story of a Varied Life (N. Y. 1922). Irish boy in slums of London East End;Cambridge education; work as curate in Norwich; later life in USA.   11

RAMKINS, Maj. Alexander. Memoirs of (1719). Life of a Scottish soldier of fortune; 28 years service in Scotland Germany,Italy, Flanders, Ireland; and his amours and gallantries.   12

RAMSAY,Balcarres Dalrymple W. Rough Recollections (Edin. 1882). Military career, travel and social life; Malta India;Indian Mutiny; residence in Italy and Spain.   13

RAMSAY, Edward Bannerman. Reminiscences (Edin.1892). Life in a Scottish episcopal family from 1810; career in church; Dean of Edinburgh; & Scottish life and character.   14

RAMSAY,Capt. Robert. Rough and Tumble(1931). Life on sailing ships from boyhood; fifty years on Great Lakes & Seven Seas; work and adventures of a Glasgow man; famous clippers.   15

RAMSDEN, A. R. Assam Planter (1945) Life and work of manager of tea-plantation in Assam; the jungle; hunting; social life.   16

RANDALL, Harry.   Old Time Comedian (1930). Career as entertainer; music-halls and pantomime in London and the provinces; old time comedians.   17

RANDALL, Mary. In the Keeping of a Vow(1937). Service with the Salvation Army in China; training,education and social work in Shanghai. Copy, Worthing P.L.   18

RANDELL,Capt.Jack. I'm Alone (1930) Bridport man's life at sea; anti-submarine work in WW1; rum-running in US waters during prohibition.   19

ANON.Random Recollections of a Commercial Traveller(1909). His business and travels around England and Wales, late 19th Century; hotels, inns, people, customers, travellers.   20

RANGARD, Ellen.   Light Amid London Shadows (1906). Experience in pedling the Bible through London slums;founding of Bible Women's Mission 1857 and her work for it; social work, nursing and working-class life. By Rose Emily Selfe.   21

RANKEN, George. Canada and the Crimea (1862). Military service; Crimean War; garrison life in Canada.   22

RANKIN, Thomas. Lives of Early Methodist Preachers, ed. Thomas Jackson (1838) III. Dunbar man's travels and adventures in the Methodist ministry, later 18th Century;one of the best of its kind.   23

RANNIE, D. My Adventures(1912). His life and work as a government official in the New Hebrides; native life; and adventures.   24

RANSOME, Jessie. Journal, 1900; the experiences of a missionary in siege of Pekin. Story of the Siege Hospital in Peking (1901).   25

RAPER, Fred. Klondyke to Kenya (L. 1938). Work as manager for the Singer Company in South Africa; prospecting for diamonds; farming in Kenya.   26

RATCLIFFE, Dorothy Una. Delightsome Land (1945). Impressions of a child; life in Yorkshire; moorlands,pleasure of childhood; nursery life; vivid and affectionate story of 10-year old. 27

RATCLIFFE,George. Sixty Years of It (1935).His rise from butcher's boy to Mayor of Leeds in 1927;public and social life in Leeds & work of Council; Liberalism.   28

/RATCLIFFE, S.K./. Middle Age(1935) Woman's life 1885-1932; her emotional reactions to nonconformist family life in Hampstead; love life, unhappy marriage,and unhappy love affair; intellectual's dilemmas; V. Woolf.   29

RATER,Justice Chumley. How I Became a Judge (1905). Boyhood; training and life in Inns of Court; career as barrister and judge; Parliamentary candidacy; chatty. Bodleian.   30

RATHBORNE,Ambrose B. Camping (1898) Travel, exploration, pioneer life; 15 years in Malaya.   31

RATHCREEDAN, Cecil Norton, Lord. Memories (1931). Irish boyhood in the 50's; Trinity College; army career in India in 70's;career in Liberal Party and Parliament; Government Whip; public affairs; rather slight.   32

RATTENBURY,John. Memoirs of a Smuggler (Sidmouth, 1837). A Beer man's life at sea to 1831; fishing; smuggling between France and Devon;a simple and interesting narrative.   33

RATTIGAN, Frank. Diversions (1924). Career in the diplomatic service from 1904; Tangier,Egypt, Roumania; social life and general observations.   34

RATTRAY, James. Round and Round in the World (Glasgow, 1870). Adventures, mining;many parts of the world, especially Australia.   35

RAVEN, Charles Earle. A Wanderer's Way (1929). Schooling; Cambridge; his educational work and career in church, Canon of Liverpool;religious life and devotion.   36

RAWLINS, Anthony. This Petty Pace (Ilfracombe, 1943). Military service, WW2;barrack routine; life in military hospital; frustrations.   37

RAWLINS, J. P. Under the Indian Sun (Lahore, 1898). Life of a soldier in Baluchistan; travels; Indian life and search for antiquities.   38

RAWLINSON, Col. Alfred. Adventures in the Near East(1923); Adventures on the Western Front(1925). His military service in WW1; Mesopotamia, Caucasia and Turkey; intelligence work; adventures with Bolsheviks;earlier service in France; driving for GHQ; the early battles in France.   39

/RAWSTON, George/. My Life, by an Ex-Dissenter(1841). Satirical account of life and work in Independent Church and the delights of theological hairsplitting among congregations,deacons and ministers; fiction?   40

RAY, Com. Joseph. Captain's Yarns (1886).Service in navy and coastguard, 1809-60;Peninsular war; China; Indian Mutiny; good yarns of adventure.   41

RAYMOND,Ernest (ed.). Autobiography of David (1946). Mental disorders and life in institutions; agrophobia and sex compulsions;efforts to adjust and work as newspaper editor.   42

RAYMOND, Thomas. Memoirs of the Family of Guise (Camden Soc., 1917). A soldier's account of his military service in the Netherlands in the middle of 17th Century.   43

RAYNE, Maj. H. Sun, Sand and Somals (1921). Administrative work of a district commissioner in Somaliland; experiences with natives, traders, and in court; WW1 campaigns.   44

REA, S.J. I Sought Adventure (1940) Life at sea as a brass-bounder in the 70's; later work as journalist.   45

READ,Herbert E. Annals of Innocence (1940). Childhood in Yorkshire; country life, sport, nature; poet's first impressions; discovery of literature and art; war and its effects on him & development of his mind and beliefs; poetry and criticism; good.   46

READE,Edward Anderson. Diary, 1825-1831; education at Haileybury; travel in India and Far East; brother of the novelist.   MS, Bodleian, Eng. Misc. d. 261-264.   47

READY, Oliver G. Life and Sport (L. 1910). Country life and sport;boyhood in Norfolk Broads; fishing, shooting, bird-nesting, sailing; country folk, folk-lore, dialects; nostalgic.   48

RECKITT, Maurice B. As It Happened (1941). School and Oxford; WW1; religious life and social crises; work in Social Credit Movement, Anglo-Catholicism, and Christian social reform; a life of social endeavour.   49

RECKITT, William. Some Account of the Life (1776). A Lincs man's Quaker ministry in England; his captivity in France and travels in America; lively adventures in 1750's.   50

ANON. Recollections of a Blue-Coat Boy (Swaffham, 1829). Eight years at Christ's Hospital in Hertford and London,at beginning of century; colloquy form; dedicated to Elia.   51

ANON. Recollections of a Country Pastor(1839). Life and work as curate in the Midlands;church ritual; people he met and worked with.   52

ANON. Recollections of a Royal Governess (1915). Work at Austrian Court and in Rome; teaching English; social life and sport; Catholicism; personalities; good.   53

ANON. Recollections of a Sailor (L. 1876).Childhood in Scottish manse and cabin-boy on a brig; Glasgow in early 19th Century; cruises; shipwrecked in Hebrides & experiences with wreckers; adventures.   54

ANON. Recollections of a Service of Three Years (1828).Service of British officer in Colombian navy; Venezuelan War; transport of Irish volunteers; & Simon Bolivar.   55

ANON. Recollections of a Society Clairvoyant (1910). Fortune-telling & spiritualism; society and celebrities in many parts of world.   56

ANON. Recollections of An Old Soldier (Birmingham, 1886). His boyhood; enlistment in artillery; Crimean War; Indian Mutiny;discharge; reenlistment and promotion to sergeant; army life and morals; good.   57

ANON. Recollections of Four Years' Farming(1905). Retired soldier's life and work as farmer; experiences with crops and livestock.Copy in Cambridge U.L.   58

THE RECTOR. Reminiscences of a Private Tutor (1927). A rector's work as examination tutor; advice to crammers and some religious comment.   59

RED COLLAR MAN. Chokey (1937). His experiences as a trusty in Wandsworth and Parkhurst prisons in 30's, during a seven year sentence; discipline and routine; brutalities; inspired by the current reform movement.   60

REDDING, Cyrus. Fifty Years' Recollections (1858); Yesterday and Today (1863); Past Celebrities (1866). His work as London journalist; literature art, theatre, music, politics; anecdotes of celebrities.   61

REDESDALE,Algernon Bertram Freeman-Mitford, Lord. Memories (1915); Further Memories (1917). Family; Eton and Oxford; diplomatic career and posts, Russia, China & Japan; Parliamentary career and service in Office of Works; society, theatre, music; intellectual interests and reflections; politics & public affairs; good.   62

REDFERN,James. Looking for Luck (L. 1937). Adventures of a rolling stone in Australia, Malaya and Borneo; gold mining, pearl-diving, debt-collecting and other jobs.   63

REDFERN, Percy. Journey to Understanding (1946). Work in a Leicester draper's and as commercial traveller; writing for Free Thinker; conversion; writing for The Clarion;socialism and spiritual life.   64

REDGRAVE, Richard. Memoir, by F. M. Redgrave (1891). Art study and career as painter;work at Royal Academy; social and country life;art and artists of Victorian period.   65

RED HEATHER. Memories of Sporting Days(1923). Hunting deer and big game in India;staghunting in Scotland; his hunts and adventures.   66

REDMAYNE, Sir Richard A. S.   Men,

Mines and Memories (1942). Work of a mining engineer from 1894;Northumberland coalmines; S.Africa; Birmingham University;Inspector of Mines; mining safety and conditions; trade unions & labour troubles; good.   67

REDWOOD, Hugh.   God in the Shadows (1932); Bristol Fashion (1948). Work of Salvation Army; conversion; life & happiness in the Army;work as Bristol journalist from 1876; later with Central News in London; Foreign Editor; WW1; development of press and radio; pleasant record.   68

REECE,Tom. Cannons and Big Guns (L. 1928). His career as billiards player travels, players, games, Thurston's & anecdotes.   69

REED, Andrew.   Memoirs of the Life (1863). Work of an independent minister;East London Orphan Asylum; social work and philanthropy; spiritual life and reflections; diary.   70

REED, Thomas Allen. Leaves from the Note Book (Bath, 1884). His career as a shorthand-writer and a journalist in Norwich and London;government reporting;Isaac Pitman; written in Pitman's shorthand.   71

/REED, William Henry McLeod7. Play and Politics, by Old Resident (1901). His experience in Singapore from 1841 official life and society; uprisings; visit to Hong Kong in 1860.   72

REES,L.E. Ruutz. Personal Narrative (1858).A full but somewhat impersonal account of siege of Lucknow.   73

REES,Maj. Robert Tait. Schoolmaster at War (1936). Personal narrative of military service in France in WW1; at Messines, Passchendaele, Bapaume, and in Hindenburg push.   74

REEVES,Edward A. Recollections of a Geographer (1935). Service in maproom of Royal Geog.Soc. from 1878; surveying instructor; geographical work and his psychical experiences.   75

REEVES, Jeanie Selina.   St. Mary's Convent (1899). Protestant girl in an Irish convent following her father's conversion; sufferings, release, and

later marriage; fiction?   76

REEVES, John Sims. Sims Reeves, by Himself (1888); My Jubilee(1889). The great singer's study in Paris and his career in opera and oratorio;triumphs and anecdotes of musical world and of musical colleagues.   77

REID, Alexander. Life of a Scottish Covenanter (Manchester,1822). Religious and military protest in Scotland, from 1660's; life of covenanters; military activities; defeat by Monmouth and hardships.   78

REID, Douglas Arthur.   Memories of the Crimean War (1911). Service as a surgeon with 9th Infantry; military, medical, camp affairs.   79

REID,Forrest. Apostate (1926); Private Road(1940). Childhood resistance to religion & youthful pantheism; his dreams and stream of memory; literary career; novels; literary society; his spiritual life and psyche.   80

REID,Capt. Ian Douglas. Prisoner at Large (1947). With the Black Watch in WW2; capture in North Africa; escapes and recapture five times; adventures in Southern Italy.   81

REID, Robert ("Senex"). Autobiography (Glasgow, 1865). Chief events in his life,1773-1820; Glasgow education and inheritance; trade and business; marriage and residences;work on antiquities of Glasgow.   82

REID, Sir Thomas Wemyss. Memoirs of (1905). Boyhood in Newcastle; collieries; reporter in Newcastle; publishing in Preston and Leeds; provincial press; public events, politics, politicians;work on Bronte and his novels to 1885; literary society.   83

REILLY,Charles Herbert. Scaffolding in the Sky(1938). School & Cambridge; work in London architect's office and teaching architecture in Universities of London and Liverpool;his architectural work;friends; celebrities; culture of Liverpool; good.   84

REILLY,John Edward. I Walk With the King, by Sarah Reilly(1931). Includes autobiography;poor boy in Yorks; work

as coalminer; conversion; his Methodist ministry in Yorks.   85

REILLY, Sidney George. Adventures
(1931). Adventures of a British agent
in Communist Russia; espionage; also
personal narrative of his wife.   86

REITH, John Charles Walsham Reith,
Baron. Into the Wind (1949). Scottish
education; subaltern in WW1; his work
as manager and director of BBC; radio
and public figures;later work in politics and business.   87

/RELPH, Harry7. Little Tich (1911).
Famous comedian's career in vaudeville
in England,dominions, USA; theatrical
life and people; tours.   88

ANON. Reminiscences and Reflections
of a Medico (Nottingham, 1942). Boyhood in Cornwall; medical training at
Durham;practice in mining towns; Public Health work. Cambridge U.L.   89

ANON.Reminiscences of a Territorial
in the D.C.L.I. (Plymouth, 1919). His
military service in Egypt, Palestine,
and India in WW1; simple.   90

ANON. Reminiscences of an Old Bohemian (1882). Schools; university life
in Germany; travels; work as journalist in London; Savage Club; friend of
minor writers and artists.   91

ANON.   Reminiscences of My Boyhood
(1851).Sentimental sketches of family
life in the country in the early 19th
Century; nostalgic.   92

RENDLE, Thomas McDonald. Swings and
Roundabouts (1919). The experiences &
observations of reporter and Parliamentary correspondent;The Times; London Bohemian life, theatre, sport and
amusements from late 19 C.   93

RENIER, Gustaaf Johannes.   He Came
to England (1933). Dutch scholar and
author settled in England;the English
the Dutch and his own character; life
and loves; politics, writing, historical studies.   94

RENNIE,James. Seed Time and Harvest
(1902). Australian boyhood; return to
Scotland; shepherd,smith's apprentice
and chimney sweep; self-education and

religion; experiences as a colporter;
work in Bedfordshire.   95

RENNIE, Sir John. Autobiography (L.
1875). Professional life as civil engineer; bridges, railways, dockyards,
canals; industrial development; travels and surveys abroad; good,although
technical.   96

RENTOUL, Sir Gervais.   Sometimes I
Think (1940); This Is My Case (1944).
Oxford days;playing with OUDS; career
as a barrister, magistrate, Recorder;
career as Conservative M.P.for Lowestoft from 1922; social life, theatre,
war and public affairs, law and justice in his time.   97

RENTOUL,James A. Stray Thoughts and
Memories (1921). A boyhood in Ulster;
Queen's University; law studies; car-
eer as barrister and judge; member of
LCC and Conservative M.P. for E.Down;
Parliament,bench, bar, church, liquor
trade, Irish life.   98

RENWICK, George. War Wanderings (L.
1916). Correspondent of Daily Chronicle in WW1; Vienna,Paris, the Western
Front, Suez, Dardanelles, Balkans and
Macedonia; descriptions, travels, and
adventures.   99

REPINGTON, Lt.Col. Charles a Court.
Vestigia (1919); The First World War
(1920); After the War(1922). Military
service and travels; India,Sudan, the
Boer War;WW1; military and diplomatic
travels in Europe and America following WW1; society, social life, celebrities, gossip; rather vapid.   100

REPINGTON,Mary. Thanks for the Memory (1938). Her travels with soldier-
husband,as above; spiritualism; theosophy; social work in London; family,
troubles,consolations; her friendship
with celebrities.   101

RERESBY, Sir John. Memoirs (1734);
best edition, Memoirs (Glasgow, 1936)
Life of a Royalist in Civil War; last
Governor of York; his quarrels,brawls
and military activities;Parliamentary
affairs while M.P.; court life,gossip
and self-praise of hanger-on; terse &
good.   102

A RETIRED OFFICER.Pages from a Pri-

vate Diary(1898). Country life, books
and religion; fiction?   103

ANON.   Retrospections: A Soldier's
Story (Dublin, 1829). Service in Peninsular War; life and adventures recollected on returning home; home life
and bereavements.   104

REYNARDSON, C.T. S. Birch. Down the
Road (1875). Memories of a gentleman-
coachman;coaching revival; glories of
20's; coaches,coachmen, the road, and
its amusements.   105

REYNARDSON, Capt. H. Birch. Mesopotamia (1919). Military service in the
Bucks Light Infantry in WW1;the Mesopotamian campaign; sport; local scene
and Arab life.   106

REYNOLDS, Capt. Charles. Surveyor's
journal, 1785; journey from Surat to
Agra and Delhi; topography. MS, India
Office, Eur. B.13.   107

REYNOLDS,Clifton. Autobiography (L.
1947). Early life and experiences in
the business world by author of Glory
Hill Farm books.   108

REYNOLDS, Frederick. Life and Times
(1826). Westminster school; work as a
dramatist;London theatre and theatrical life; society, politics, law, women, clubs; his plays and their fortunes; lively and amusing.   109

REYNOLDS, Harry. Minstrel Memories
(1928). History of minstrelsy in England from 1836; his own experiences &
travels with his troupe.   110

REYNOLDS, Mrs. Herbert. At Home in
India (1903).Domestic and family life
of wife of an Indian Civil Servant in
Calcutta; Indian scene.   111

RHODES,Anthony. Sword of Bone(1942)
Engineer Stores officer with British
forces in France in WW2;light-hearted
account of blunders behind the Maginot
Line; Dunkirk; good.   112

RHODES,Benjamin. Lives of Early Methodist Preachers, ed. Thomas Jackson
(1838) III. Ministry and travels of a
Yorkshire Methodist, in North of England, later 18th Century; missionary
work; Yorkshire scene.   113

RHODES, Elizabeth. Memoir (1829). A
Methodist's account of dissolute father; triumphs over sinful men; work in
Sunday Schools in Bury; life and travel with husband in Methodist ministry
and God's mercies; lively. Methodist
Book Room.   114

RHONDDA, Margaret Haig, Viscountess
This Was My World (1933). Education &
family life; Victorian Scene; work as
a suffragette; war work; her business
life.   115

RHYS,Ernest. Everyman Remembers (L.
1931); Wales England Wed (1940). Life
in London in 80's; literary reviewing
and editing; career as publisher; the
Everyman series; memories of most of
the important writers of his time and
details of his personal life.   116

RIBBLESDALE, Thomas Lister, 4th Baron. Queen's Hounds(1897);Impressions
and Memories(1927). Staghunting, horses, nobility, royalty; Master of The
Buckhounds;boyhood in France; Harrow;
court life as Lord in Waiting; House
of Lords and politics.   117

RICE, Major-General William. Tiger
Shooting in India (1867). Hunting on
foot in Rajpootana in 50's, as young
officer.   118

RICH,Lt.Col. C. E. F. Recollections
of a Prison Governor (1932). His work
in various prisons and at Borstal;the
life,regime, problems of prison, especially at Walton Gaol.   119

RICH, Claudius James. Narrative of
a Residence in Koordistan (1836). His
work for East India Company in Bagdad
travels down the Tigris; topography &
people; vivid descriptions.   120

RICHARD, Timothy. Forty-Five Years
in China (1916). Life and work of a
Baptist medical missionary from 1869;
Chinese scene and politics.   121

RICHARDS, Coombe. Wild Goose Chase
(1948); Tight Lines (1949); Sporting
Vacations (1950). Reminiscences and
anecdotes of wild-fowling, salmon and
other fishing, shooting and yachting;
Scotland, Ireland, etc.   122

RICHARDS, Frank. Old Soldiers Never

Die (1933); Old Soldier Sahib (1936).
Service with Welch Fusiliers; Western
Front, WW1; boyhood and life as priv-
ate in India and China before the 1st
World War.   123

RICHARDS, GRANT. Memories (L. 1932)
Author Hunting (1934). City of London
School;work in Paternoster Row; journalism and publishing; literary society and business;anecdotes of society
writers, painters, etc.   124

RICHARDS, Tom L.   White Man, Brown
Woman (1932). Frank narrative of his
life and work as a trader in the Solomons;relations with natives; life with
native women; dictated.   125

RICHARDSON, Sir Benjamin Ward. Vita
Medica (1897). Study in Glasgow; medical practice and research;   work at
St. Andrew's medical school;   changes
in medical practice.   126

RICHARDSON, David. Diaries, 1829-30
and 1834-35; travel and diplomacy in
Siam; missions to chiefs of the Shan
states. MS, B.M. Add. 30354.   127

RICHARDSON, Colonel Edwin H. Forty
Years with Dogs (1930);   Fifty Years
with Dogs (1950). Career as a trainer
of army and police dogs; kennel work;
travels.   128

RICHARDSON,Ethel Mary Emily. Remembrance Wakes (1934). Wife of officer
in WW1;life in Wilts village; work in
Red Cross; service of her family, and
casualties; the war scene in England
and reflections after the war.   129

RICHARDSON, H. M. Reminiscences of
Forty Years in Bolton (Bolton, 1884).
Public and social life of an alderman
of Bolton;the local scene. Manchester
P.L.   130

RICHARDSON,Henry Handel (Mrs. Ethel
Florence Robertson).Myself When Young
(1948). Australian girlhood; solitude
life in England and Germany;evolution
as novelist; marriage; it comes up to
1895.   131

RICHARDSON, James.   Travels in the
Great Desert (L.1848); Narrative of a
Mission (L. 1853); Travels in Morocco
(1860).Travels and exploration in the

Sahara, Sudan, Morocco; Arab caravans
and German expeditions; banditti and
slaves; excitements.   132

RICHARDSON, J. W. Memoirs (Glasgow,
1911). Shipbuilder's work on Tyneside
and reminiscences of trade union activities, strikes, profit-sharing, and
politics.   133

RICHARDSON, James. Lights & Shadows
(Antananarivo, 1877). Missionary life
and work in Madagascar; teaching; his
dangers and escapes.Copy India Office
Library.   134

RICHARDSON, James C. The Living and
the Living Dead (1923). Old soldier's
service in WW1;Ypres, Flanders, Salonika; reflections on army life.   135

RICHARDSON, John. An Account of the
Life (1759). Life of a Yorkshire Quaker from 1660's to 1730's; conversion
and travels in ministry,England, Ireland, America, West Indies; his early
work as a clockmaker in Bridlington;
interesting.   136

RICHARDSON, John. Recollections (L.
1856). Clergyman's life in London and
reminiscences of London scene, first
half of the century; theatres, sport,
journalism, taverns.   137

RICHARDSON, Joseph H. From the City
to Fleet Street (1927). London scene
from 60's; work on Stock Exchange and
later work as journalist; Daily Telegraph; politics, crime, public events
and celebrities.   138

RICHARDSON,Maurice L.London's Burning (1941). His training and service
in London Fire Service in WW2; adventures in the Blitz; candid.   139

RICHARDSON,Teresa Eden. In Japanese
Hospitals (Edin. 1905). Service with
the Red Cross in Russo-Japanese War &
at Tokyo in WW1.   140

RICHARDSON, William.   A Mariner of
England (1908). Life in navy, 1780 to
1819; cabin boy to warrant officer; a
lively account of naval engagements in
Napoleonic wars, naval conditions and
the slave trade, press-gangs and life
of the lower deck; excellent story of
an old salt from South Shields.   141

RICHMOND, Sir William. The Richmond
Papers, ed. A. M. W. Stirling (1926).
His boyhood;study and work as painter
and activities at Royal Academy; the
Pre-Raphaelite painters and poets;and
his travels.   142

RICKARD, Major F. Ignacio. A Mining
Journey (1863). Engineer's travels in
the Andes, 1862-3; exploring for silver in San Juan and Mendoza on behalf
of Argentine government.   143

RICKARDS, Clifford. Prison Chaplain
(1920). Twenty-five years at Dartmoor
sympathetic account of life of prisoners; famous prisoners; escapes.   144

RICKETTS, Charles S. Self-Portrait,
(1939). Work as painter from 1874;his
interests in art, literature, and the
theatre; reading; Shannon & his other
friends; travels; his criticism & his
enthusiasms; diaries.   145

RICKMAN,Edwin. Diary of a Solitaire
(1835). Quaker's travels in Switzerland;Quaker life and reminiscences of
Quakers.   146

RICKMAN, Eric. On and Off the Race-
course (1937). Work of sporting journalist; Robin Goodfellow of the Daily
Mail; owners, jockeys, trainers, horses, bookmakers; anecdotes.   147

RICKMAN, Thomas. Notes on the Life,
by Thomas M. Rickman (1901). Selected
from diaries; architectural interests
in early 19th Century.   148

RIDDELL, Florence.   I Go Wandering
(Philadelphia, 1935). Englishwoman's
travels in four continents and activities as jack of all trades.   149

RIDDELL, Henry Scott. Autobiography
in his Poetical Works (Glasgow, 1871)
Boyhood and shepherd days in the Border country;school; Edinburgh University; early writings; ministry at Te-
viothead.   150

RIDDELL, W.G. Adventures (L. 1932);
The Thankless Years (1948). A Glasgow
marine engineer's apprenticeship;work
on merchantmen from the 80's;sea life
& adventures; marine engineers of the
past; good narrative.   151

RIDER, Dan.   Ten Years' Adventures
(1927). A librarian turned knight-er-
rant for tenants; a cavalier reformer
fighting the landlords;the Rent Acts;
lively and gay.   152

RIDGE, William Pett. A Story Teller
(1923); I Like to Remember(1925). The
novelist's memories of London from the
50's;street life and manners; theatre
and entertainments; Dickens and other
notables; songs, etc.   153

RIGBY, General Christopher Palmer.
Diary, 1858-61; travel, work and per-
sonal affairs in Zanzibar; operations
against slave-trade.   General Rigby,
Zanzibar and the Slave-Trade, edited
C. E. B. Russell (1935).   154

RIGG, James H.   Wesleyan Methodist
Reminiscences (1904). His years as an
itinerant preacher in Cornwall in the
forties; stories of the Older Wesley-
anism. Cambridge U.L.   155

RIGGE, Ambrose.   Constancy in the
Truth (1710). A Surrey man's original
wickedness & conversion to the Quaker
faith; testimony,witness, and sufferings.   156

RIJNHART,Susie C. With the Tibetans
in Tent and Temple (1901). Life of a
Canadian medical missionary on Tibet-
China border in the 90's; adventures;
Tibetan culture.   157

RILAND, John (editor). Memoirs of a
West-India Planter (1827). The life &
work of a Jamaican planter from 1778;
plantation life; negroes; the horrors
of slavery; abolition work.   158

RILEY, Patrick. Memories of a Blue-
Jacket (1927). Life in navy from 1872
and many cruises; Chinese expedition;
work as gunnery instructor;good story
of lower deck life.   159

RINGER,Frederica. Glimpses of a Varied Life(1937). Her life in the sixties; travel, nobility, social work,
painting, festivals.   160

RIPLEY, Dorothy. Extraordinary Conversion (1817). Yorkshire woman's sin
and conversion; travels in the Quaker
ministry in England and USA.   161

RITCHIE, Lady Anne Thackeray. Chapters from Some Memoirs (L.1894); From
the Porch (1913). Her girlhood in the
Thackeray household;domestic life and
literary friends of her father;charm-
ing account of her own writing; reminiscences of Victorian writers; Eliot
Dickens, Gaskell, Browning and others;
delicately done.   162

RITCHIE, James Ewing.   Christopher
Crayon's Recollections(1898). Village
life in East Anglia in 40's;religious
studies in London University;journal-
ism in London and Cardiff; London religious life; Exeter Hall; a pleasant
life of enjoyment, with his work for
social reform movements.   163

RITSON,John Holland. Abroad for the
Bible Society(1909); The World is Our
Parish(1939). Owen's and Oxford; work
and travel as colporteur in China and
Japan;work at Bible House; world tra-
vels in Methodist ministry.   164

RIVAZ,Richard C. Tail Gunner (1943)
Adventures of a Tail-End Charlie; his
bombing missions over Germany in WW2;
dangers and escapes.   165

RIVETT-CARNAC, John Henry. Many Memories of Life in India (1910). Work
in Bengal Civil Service, 1857-94; his
administrative and legal affairs; and
Indian life, culture and history; social life,sport, Queen Victoria; good
account of India in his time.   166

RIVIÈRE, Jules. My Musical Life (L.
1893). Early life in France;career in
England from 1857 as a conductor; the
English musical scene; Cremorne,Prom-
enade concerts,opera; musical society
and celebrities.   167

ROBB, Nesca A. Ulsterwoman in England (1942). Teaching in England from
1924; threat of Hitlerism; experience
in Blitz.   168

ROBERTS, A. W. Coasting Bargemaster
(1949). His life and work as a master
of a coastal barge before and during
WW2.   169

ROBERTS,Arthur. Adventures (Bristol
1895); Fifty Years of Spoof (1927). A
comedian's career in music-halls, and
in comic opera, revues and pantomime;

theatrical and Bohemian life.   170

ROBERTS,Arthur. On and Off the Beat
(1944). Commercial artist's humourous
story of his duties and experience as
war-time policeman in WW2.   171

ROBERTS, Cecil. Half Way(1931). His
first 35 years; civil servant, teacher, novelist, journalist; correspondent with British forces in WW1;editor
Nottingham Journal; literary and artistic society.   172

/ROBERTS, Charles/. Adventures of a
Poor Beggar (1820?). Carpenter's apprentice; escape to sea; residence on
Robinson Crusoe's island; return home
fiction?   173

/ROBERTS, Emyr/. Mespot Memories,by
Private 187 (Liverpool 1929).Military
service with Indian troops during WW1
in Mesopotamia;India after war; riots
in Amritsar.   174

ROBERTS,Eric S. Passing Along(Sheffield,1930); Exits & Entrances (Sheffield, 1938). Family, school, university in Sheffield;religious life; WW1
service in army; work as entertainer-
reciter;celebrations and public occasions in Sheffield. Copies, Sheffield
P.L.   175

ROBERTS, Mrs. Ernest Stewart. Sherborne, Oxford and Cambridge (1934). A
woman's life in academic circles during Victorian era; at Sherborne with
her father; Oxford and Cambridge with
her husband;pleasant reminiscences of
academic life and persons; L.Carroll,
Wilde, etc.   176

ROBERTS, Frederick Sleigh Roberts,
1st Earl. Forty-One Years in India(L.
1887). Army career from subaltern to
commander-in-chief; military and political life and events in India; the
Mutiny; Afghan Wars; good.   177

ROBERTS, George. Four Years Voyages
(1726). Trader's adventures with pirates off Cape Verde Islands;detention
and hardships;shipwreck and two years
of Crusoe-life; escape in vessel constructed by himself.   178

ROBERTS,Col. Herbert Harington. Memories of Four-Score Years (1920).His

career in the army and later career as
a painter; reminiscences of painters;
pleasant retrospection.   179

ROBERTS, Robert. Lives of Early Methodist Preachers, ed. Thomas Jackson
(1837) I. Cheshire man's ministry and
travels as a Methodist preacher;most-
ly in the Midlands.   180

ROBERTS, Robert. An Autobiography
(Birmingham, 1917). Religious life of
a Christadelphian; preaching and missionary work; work as reporter in the
Midlands and Yorkshire; working-class
life; interesting. Copy in Birmingham
P.L.   181

ROBERTS, Robert. Life and Opinions
(Cardiff, 1923). Life of Welsh scholar;early poverty and drudgery; ordination and work as a minister in North
Wales; work on Celtic language & literature; goes to 1863; good.   182

ROBERTS, Samuel. Autobiography (L.
1849). Deals with life as a young man
in late 18th Century; work for manu-
facturer-father in Sheffield; poetry;
writings in defence of common man and
the poor; factory life.   183

ROBERTSON, Mrs. The Life of (Derby,
1791?). Troubles of woman who claimed
descent from Charles I; affluence to
bankruptcy; children of her old age;
teaching and sewing to earn a living;
affected and amusing. Derby P.L.   184

ROBERTSON, George. Rural Recollections (Irvine, 1829). Farming in Ayrshire and Kincardine;Scottish country
life, work, institutions, customs and
scenes; somewhat impersonal.   185

ROBERTSON,Col.James Peter. Personal
Adventures (1906). Edinburgh Academy;
rattling account of his army career;
Crimean War;Indian Mutiny; perils and
escapes; social life, sport, pleasure
and travels; good.   186

ROBERTSON, R.Macdonald. In Scotland
With a Fishing Rod (1935); Angling in
Wildest Scotland (1936). Experiences
of sport in Highland rivers and lochs
with anecdotes and advice.   187

ROBERTSON, Walford Graham. Life Was
Worth Living (1931); Time Was (1931).

His work as a painter;family life and
social life; reminiscences of famous
actors,writers, painters of Victorian
and Edwardian days; Pre-Raphaelites,
Crane, Whistler, Wilde, Sargent, Irving, Rehan, Bernhardt, etc.   188

ROBERTSON,Sir William. From Private
to Field-Marshal (1921); Soldiers and
Statesmen (1926). His military career
and success, 1877-1920;his service in
England,India, South Africa; Boer War
and WW1;director of military training
and Quartermaster-General;work on the
General Staff in WW1; history of WW1;
strategy; political aspects.   189

ROBERTSON-GLASGOW, R. C. Forty-Six
Not Out (1948). Charterhouse, Oxford;
scholar and athlete; cricket reporter
for The Observer; cricket for Oxford,
Somerset, England; the game and players; good.   190

ROBEY, George. My Life Up Till Now
(1908); Looking Back (1933). Boyhood
in Birmingham; career as a comedian;
vaudeville, pantomime, revues, films;
Empire tours.   191

ROBINS,Elizabeth. Theatre & Friend-
ship(1934); Both Sides of the Curtain
(1940).American-born actress's career
in the English theatre;her roles; the
theatre, plays, writers, actors; Irving, Terry. Tree, Shaw, Benson; valuable and interesting.   192

ROBINSON, Benjamin Coulson.   Bench
and Bar (1889). Legal study at Temple
and Serjeants Inn; legal career of a
Serjeant-at-Law; circuit work and Old
Bailey; legal personalities; the London social scene and customs; Dickens
and the law; interesting.   193

ROBINSON, Sir Henry Augustus. Memories (1923); Further Memories (1924).
Career of an English civil servant in
Ireland; Irish politics from the 80's
and the lighter side of Irish life in
town and country.   194

ROBINSON, Capt. Herbert R. A Modern
De Quincey(1942). Army life, Burma in
inter-war period; addiction to opium;
Buddhism as an escape and its failure;
shock-treatment and cure.   195

ROBINSON,Hercules. Sea Drift (Portsea, 1858). Service in the navy, 1813 to 1856; cruises and adventures.   196

ROBINSON,Jasper. Lives of Early Methodist Preachers, ed. Thomas Jackson (1838) III. A Bucks man's work in the Methodist ministry; circuit travel in South of England.   197

ROBINSON, Sir John Richard. Recollections of, by F. M. Thomas (1904). Includes extracts from a loosely kept journal; work as journalist and social events.   198

ROBINSON, Lennox and Tom; & DORMAN, Nora. Three Homes(1938). Childhood in Ireland related by three friends;village and home life; schooling; sport; development of literary talents; work for Abbey Theatre.   199

ROBINSON, Lennox. Curtain Up (1942) Career as playwright, 1910-40; Abbey Theatre and Irish theatrical renaissance; lecturing in America; theatre in London; history of the Abbey; and reflections on himself.   200

ROBINSON, Martha. Continuity Girl (1937). Trials and tribulations; maid of all work at a small British studio producing cheap films; cheerful, artless gossip.   201

ROBINSON, Mary D. Memoirs (1802). A famous belle of the later 18th Century;mistress of George IV; roles as an actress; high society; literary society; her amours.   202

ROBINSON, Matthew. Autobiography in J. E. B.Mayor's Cambridge in the 17th Century (Cambridge,1855). Life & work of a fellow of St.John's and vicar of Burneston, Yorks; medical study, academic life, ministry; told in the 3rd person.   203

ROBINSON, Maude. Southdown Farm in the Sixties (L.1938). Sheepfarming in Sussex; country life, education, pleasures; Quaker religion.   204

ROBINSON, Sarah. Life Record (1898) Soldier's Friend (1913); My Book (L. 1914). Missionary work among soldiers and sailors at Guildford, Aldershot & Portsmouth; militant campaigns on behalf of sobriety, morality and Chris-

tianity; interesting.   205

ROBINSON,Dr. William. Sidelights on Life (Gateshead, 1939). Life and work of a Wearside surgeon from 1859; simple and thoughtful.   206

ROBINSON, William Heath. My Line of Life(1938). Boyhood; career as illustrator and cartoonist; books, advertising, journalism.   207

ROBSON,John Henry Matthews. Records and Recollections(Kuala Lumpur, 1934) Administrative work in Malaya in 90's economic development of Malaya; politics; Federal Council and his part in its work.   208

ROBSON, William. The Old Play-Goer (1846). Life in theatre;reminiscences of acting and actors; Siddons, Kemble Kean, Macready, etc.   209

ROBY, Marguerite. My Adventures (L. 1911). Her solitary expedition to the Congo; experiences with natives, biggame, white friends; troubles.   210

RODD, Sir James Rennell. Social and Diplomatic Memories (1923-25). Career in diplomatic service,1884-1919; Berlin, Athens, Rome, Paris, Cairo; social life and diplomacy.   211

RODDA, Richard. Lives of Early Methodist Preachers, ed. Thomas Jackson (1837) II. Cornish man's travels and work in the Methodist ministry; mainly in the South-West.   212

RODERICK, George. Gimcrack (1944). Life, work, reflections of a trainerowner; racehorses and hunters; riders jockeys and sportsmen.   213

ROE, William. Private Memorandums (Brighton, 1928). His life, 1775-1809 marriage and family; work as commissioner of Public Accounts to the House of Commons and as commissioner of customs; business as a landowner; garden plots for working people.   214

ROEBUCK, John Arthur. Life and Letters (1897). His life, 1802-32; education; residence in Canada and England and early legal career;his friendship with J.S.Mill, T.L. Peacock and other celebrities.   215

ROGERS,Rev. Charles. Leaves from My Autobiography (L.1876). Clerical life in Fifeshire; society, scholarly, and literary life in Edinburgh in the mid Century;founding Royal Historical Society; antiquarian studies.   216

ROGERS,Clara Kathleen (Doria). Memories (1919); Story of Two Lives (L. 1932).Cheltenham childhood in musical family;studies at Leipzig and Berlin; operatic career in Italy; musical and social life in England and America and her family life.   217

ROGERS, Edmund Dawson. Life and Experiences (1911). Norfolk man's work as chemist and journalist; mesmerism and spiritualism; spiritualist movement in London   218

ROGERS, Frederick. Labour, Life and Literature(1913). Factory work; trade unions; strikes; enthusiast for working class education and pensions; his writing in this behalf;industrial and social work; earnest.   219

ROGERS, Hester Ann. Experience and Spiritual Letters (1857).Childhood in Macclesfield; family life, illnesses, religion; Methodist activities; God's mercies; married life in Dublin; Wesley; 2nd half 18th Century.   220

ROGERS, James. A Short Account (L. 1792). Yorkshireman's sins,conversion and ministry in the Methodist faith; North of England.   221

ROGERS, James Guinness. Autobiography (1903). Cornish boyhood; study at Trinity, Dublin, and Lancashire College; congregational pastorates; country life; London ministry; his social work and political activities.   222

ROGERS, John. Some Account of the Life and Opinions (1867). Essex boyhood; Presbyterian ministry in Hunts; Fifth Monarchy Man; controversy with Cromwell; imprisonment; release, and medical practice in London and Leyden after the Restoration; good.   223

ROGERS, John. A Sketch of the Life (Southampton, 1889). Work and interests of a gardener and nurseryman;his life at Richmond,Sry; theatre, actors and social life,late 18th Century and

early 19th Century.   224

ROGERS, Joseph. Reminiscences(1889) Physician's work at the Strand Workhouse and Westminster Infirmary from 1854;practice; patients; the need for reform.   225

ROGERS, Major-General Sir Leonard. Happy Toil (1950). His career in the Indian Medical Service from 1893;medical research on leprosy and tropical diseases.   226

ROGERS, Rose Annie. Lonely Island (1926). Life and work of missionary's wife on Tristan da Cunha in twenties; domestic work; education; life of the islanders.   227

ROGERS, Samuel. Recollections, ed. W. Sharpe (L.1859); Reminiscences and Table-Talk, ed. G. H. Powell (1903). The banker-poet's anecdotes of social life,social customs and fashions, and literary and theatrical celebrities, from his youth in 1780's.   228

ROGERS, Stanley. After Forty Years (1918).Pupil at City of London School and reminiscences of Asquith;ministry at Liverpool congregational church and social life there.   229

ROGERS, William. Reminiscences (L. 1888). Eton under Keate; Oxford; his ministry at Charterhouse and St. Botolph's, Bishopsgate; work in public education; Dulwich School; Royal Commission on Education 1858.   230

ROHAN, Thomas. Confessions (1924). Work as an art dealer; glass, furniture, antiquities; the trade; notable clients.   231

ROLLS, Sam Cottingham. Steel Chariots in the Desert (1937). Adventures while driving armoured car for Duke of Westminster in Libya and for Lawrence in Arabia; hero-worship.   232

ROLT, Sir John. Memoirs (1939). His struggles as an orphan at beginning of 19th Century to obtain an education & reach the Bar; his legal career until 1871; Q.C., Attorney-General, L.C.J.; political opinions.   233

ROMILLY, Esmond, Mark, and David.

Boadilla (1937). Their activities in the Spanish International Brigade and Spanish Republican Army in 1936-7;the siege of Madrid; politics.   234

ROMILLY, Giles and Esmond. Out of Bounds (1935). Their education at prep schools and Wellington;young rebels; indictment of public schools.   235

ROMILLY, Hugh Hastings. From My Verandah in New Guinea (1889). Life and work as special commissioner; at Port Moresby; folk-lore and anthropology; personal affairs.   236

ROMILLY, Sir Samuel. Memoirs (1840) His early years, 1757-89; family life and schooling; early legal career and Parliamentary career; visits to Paris and Switzerland; diary.   237

RONALD, Sir Landon. Variations (L. 1922); Myself and Others (1931). His career as a conductor; opera, orchestras; Covent Garden; musicians, prodigies, etc.; rather dull.   238

RONALDSHAY,Lawrence John L. Dundas, Earl of. Sport and Politics (1902); A Wandering Student(1908). His official life,work and travel in India; sport; travels in Burma, China, Japan, early century; reflections on development & progress of Far East.   239

ROOK, Clarence. Hooligan Nights (L. 1899). Journalist's report of narrative of life of Alf,a young and impenitent thief;life and crime in Lambeth told in Cockney; good.   240

ROOME,William John Waterman. Tramping through Africa(1930); Through the Lands of Nyanza (1931). His extensive travels in Central Africa; missionary work for CMS in Uganda; native life; missionary rivalries.   241

ROOT,Fred. Cricket Pro's Lot (1937) Bowler with Leicester, Derby and Worc. from 1896;Test matches; his games and famous players; reflections.   242

RORIE, Col. David. Medico's Luck in the War (Aberdeen, 1929). His medical work with Highland division in France in WW1; personal experiences; activities of his division.   243

RORKE, J. D. M. A Musical Pilgrim's Progress (1921). Development of his musical tastes; musical experiences; good but specialised.   244

ROSCOE,Edward Stanley. Rambles with a Fishing-Rod (Edin. 1883). Pike and trout fishing; travels in Switzerland Germany, France for fishing.   245

ROSCOE, Sir Henry Enfield. Life and Experiences (1906). Chemist's education in Germany in 50's; teaching and professor at Manchester University and academic and scientific work; political career as M.P.for Manchester from 1885.   246

ROSCOE, John. Twenty-Five Years in East Africa (1921). Life and work as a missionary in Kenya and Uganda; the life, folk-lore and ethnology of Bantus; adventures; travels.   247

ROSE, Constance. Plain Mrs. Rose (Cheltenham, 1936). London girlhood; artistic life;marriage and removal to Gloucester; entertainment, sport, and social life at Cheltenham; production of pageants and tableaux. Gloucester City Library.   248

ROSE, Henry. Before I Forget (1942) Work of sports journalist; provincial journalism; boxing from 20's & vaudeville.   249

ROSE,Walter. Good Neighbours (1942) Memories of social life in an English village; as he remembered it, and as it was told to him by his father, and his grandfather.   250

ROSS, Sir Edward Denison. Both Ends of the Candle(1943). Education London and continental universities;linguistic studies;work as professor of Persian and Director of School of Oriental Studies; art, literature, theatre and social life.   251

ROSS, Elizabeth Ness MacBean. Lady Doctor in Bakhtiari Land (1921). Her medical work in Persia; life and customs of Bakhtiaries; religion; politics; women's life.   252

R(OSS), J. A. R. Memoirs of an Army Surgeon (Edin. 1948). Service in WW2;

North African and Italian campaigns; hospital work; vivid.   253

ROSS, Sir James Clark. A Voyage of Discovery (1847). Scientific work on an antarctic expedition, 1839-43; the scientific work, explorations, adventures and perils.   254

ROSS,Janet Ann. Early Days (1891); Fourth Generation (1912). A childhood in London society in 40's; youth with her father in Egypt; later life Italy society at home and abroad; literary acquaintances.   255

ROSS,Sir John. Years of My Pilgrimage (1924); Pilgrim Scrip (1927). His legal career in Ireland from the 80's work as barrister, judge, Lord Chancellor;public and social life, Ulster and Dublin; politicians; lawyers; and sport.   256

ROSS, John Dill. Sixty Years (1911) Trading in his own ships in Far East; Singapore;Borneo; business and adventure in Eastern seas.   257

ROSS,Margaret. Memoirs of a Private Nurse (Glasgow, 1929). Experiences in 28 years as a nurse; travels,patients and fellow-nurses.   258

ROSS,Sir Ronald. Memoirs (L. 1923). Boyhood in India;education in England and his army and medical career in India; study of malaria problem and its solution; and later study of tropical diseases in Africa.   259

ROSS-LEWIN, Major Harry. Life of a Soldier(1834). Irish soldier's career in British army;twenty-seven years in various parts of the world; with the 32nd Foot in the Peninsular War and at Waterloo;campaigns; army life & ways; good.   260

ROSSA, O'Donovan Jeremiah. Prison Life (N. Y. 1874). Political activity in Ireland from 1865; demonstrations against British Rule; his sufferings in prison.   261

ROSSETTI, William Michael. Some Reminiscences (1906). London childhood and family;work in Excise office; his relations with Dante G. Rossetti; his literary work;Pre-Raphaelite Brother-

hood; literary and artistic friends; editorial and lecturing work.   262

ROSSLYN, James F. H. St. Clair-Erskine, Earl of. My Gamble with Life (1928). Eton and Oxford; family life, travel and sport; acting and theatrical tours; sport and gambling abroad; life in Hants;society; House of Lords Boer War and WW1.   263

ROSSMORE,Derrick W.W. Westenra, 5th Baron. Things I Can Tell(1912). Irish upbringing;social life in Dublin; his army career; horseracing and sport; & anecdotes.   264

ROSTRON,Sir Arthur Henry. Home from the Sea (1931). Career at sea; commodore of Cunard Line; loss of Titanic; transport in WW1; anecdotes of celebrated passengers.   265

ROTHENSTEIN, Sir William. Men and Memories (1931-32); Since Fifty(1940) Bedford and Slade; art in Paris; work as a painter; artists, artistic movements, literary friends; anecdotes of the chief painters, writers, scholars of his time.   266

ROTHERHAM, Joseph Bryant. Reminiscences (1922). Seventy years from 1828 in Baptist religion; evangelism; work as a printer;his Emphasized Bible and his religious life.   267

ANON. Rough Notes of Journeys in... the Sandwich Islands (1875). Diaries of travels in the Near and Far East, 1868-9 and in Australia and U.S.A. in 1870-3; business; economics.   268

ROUTH, Martha. Memoirs (York, 1822) A Worcester woman's life and travels in the Quaker ministry in second half of 18th Century; visiting meetings in England and USA.   269

ROW, John. Even to Old Age (1893). His early sins; conversion; work as a minister at Tunbridge Ebenezer Chapel lively; from 1805.   270

ROWAN, Archibald Hamilton. Autobiography (Dublin, 1840). Life of United Irishman in late 18th and early 19th Century; political agitation; rebellion of 1798; his exile and return to

Ireland in 1806; useful for Irish affairs. A MS transcript in 3rd person is in Royal Irish Academy.   271

ROWAN, Arthur. I Live Again (1938). Swiss childhood; service with RAF in India and Near East; squadron-leader; interest in the occult.   272

ROWBOTHAM, Sir Thomas. Living Memories (1933). Life and work of a merchant; work for Methodism.   273

ROWE, John Tetley.   Town and Gown (Cambridge, 1891). Five years work at St. George's Mission, Camberwell; his social work and difficulties;life and attitudes of slum dwellers.   274

ROWE, Sir Thomas. Journal, 1615-18; embassy to the Great Mogul & dealings with Governor of Surat. MS, B.M. Add. 19277,6115.   275

ROWLAND, Alfred. Independent Parson (1923).   Business life; study at New College;sixty years in Congregational ministry in country and London; history of the church;celebrities he met; modest.   276

ROWLANDS,Ernest Brown Bowen. Seventy-Two Years (1924); In Court and Out (1924); In the Light of the Law(1931) Legal studies;Gray's Inn; practice of law; South Wales and Chester circuit; reminiscences of trials, judges, lawyers; good anecdotes.   277

ROWLEY,Charles. Fifty Years of Work (1896). Public career in Manchester; the Ancoats Brotherhood; art in Manchester; Pre-Raphaelites; his work in education.   278

ROWSE,Alfred Leslie. Cornish Childhood (1942). Excellent evocation of a boyhood in Cornwall; village life and family; schools;up to his going up to Oxford in 1921.   279

ROYCE, James(Jesse Godfrey Hancock) I Stand Nude(1937). London errand boy in French trenches in WW1; self-education; journalism and odd jobs after the war; humble; interesting.   280

ROYDEN, Agnes Maude. Threefold Cord (1947). Her long life in the home of Rev. Hudson Shaw and his wife; domes-

tic, religious, and social life together;marriage to Shaw on the death of his wife.   281

⟨ROYSTON,W.Stewart⟩. The Real Live Story of a Walking Stick (Warrington, 1919).Life of a bedridden invalid and his philanthropy; founding of Walking Stick Fund for wounded soldiers. 282

RUCK,Bertha. Story-Teller Tells the Truth (1935). Welsh education; study of art; journalism and novel-writing; literary practice; literary celebrities; Wales in WW1; social and family life; spiritualism.   283

RUDKIN,Mabel S. Heard at the Vicarage (1929); Inside Dover (1933). The vicar's wife;nagging reminiscences of Sussex village life & failings of the villagers; domestic and canteen work in Dover during WW1.   284

RUGGLES, Major-Gen. John. Recollections of a Lucknow Veteran (L. 1906). His military and social life in India 1845-76; service in Mutiny; the siege of Lucknow; anecdotes.   285

RULE, William Harris. Recollections (1886). Welsh Methodist; ministry and travels in England and in Malta, West Indies, Spain, Gibraltar.   286

RUMBOLD, Sir Horace. Recollections (1902); Further Recollections (1903); Final Recollections (1905). His fifty years in public service; diplomacy in Vienna, Chile, Berne, Stockholm, etc. travels, society, public affairs, anc personal life; pleasant.   287

RUMNEY, A. W. Fifty Years a Cyclist (Keswick, 1927). Athletics and travel by bicycle.   288

RUNCIMAN,Sir Walter.Before the Mast (1924). Life at sea in merchant ships to 1884; career and affairs as a ship owner; political career; good.   289

RUSHTON,Adam. My Life as a Farmer's Boy (1909). Farming in Cheshire; factory work;teaching; work as Methodist and Unitarian minister in Lancs, from 1859; self-culture; simple.   290

RUSKIN, John. Praeterita (Orpington 1885-1900). Scenes and thoughts worth

remembering, 1819-64; education, travels, family stresses; development of
his literary and artistic talents and
his literary career;psychological interest; good.   291

RUSSELL, Arthur. With the Machine
Gun Corps (1923). Simple narrative of
experiences in France and Italy, WW1;
major battles.   292

RUSSELL, Charles. Diary, 1898; work
as a riveter in Beira; lively account
of the life of a Cockney workman; in
tropical Africa. The Work, edited B.
Eastwood (1912).   293

RUSSELL, Charles Edward Mackintosh.
Bullet & Shot in Indian Forest, Plain
and Hill (1900).Life and work of lawyer and official in Forest Department
in Mysore from 70's; natural history;
big-game hunting.   294

RUSSELL, D. Stobart. Spindrift (L.
1948). Her years of travel with her
husband; cruising in Breton waters; &
Breton life and people.   295

RUSSELL,Sir Edward. That Reminds Me
(1899).Liverpool editor's memories of
politicians and other public figures,
in England and America.   296

"RUSSELL, Fox." In Scarlet and Silk
(L.1896); Cross Country Reminiscences
(1887). Foxhunting in Essex and Kent;
staghunting; steeplechasing; point to
point races; social life.   297

RUSSELL,Mrs. Frank (Phillipa A. M.)
Fragments of Auld Lang Syne (L. 1925)
Family life and London society in the
70's;with husband, military attaché ,
in Berlin;later life in Aberdeenshire
and Scottish society.   298

RUSSELL, Sir George. Reminiscences
of life at Swallowfield; meeting with
Dickens, Thackeray and other writers;
their literary opinions.In Lady Constance Russell, Swallowfield and   Its
Owners (1901).   299

RUSSELL, George. Narrative (1935).
Scottish boyhood; work for Clyde Company in Victoria and Tasmania,1830 to
1875; pioneer life in Victoria.   300

RUSSELL, George G. W. Collections &
Recollections (1898); Londoner's Log
Book(1902); One Look Back (1911). His
education at Harrow and Oxford;London
society,writers, artists, celebrities
and his Parliamentary career; Church
and social work.   301

RUSSELL, Henry. Cheer, Boys, Cheer!
(1895).Musical career from 1820; composer and singer; opera; theatrical &
musical life; much of it dealing with
his adventures in USA.   302

RUSSELL, Henry. Passing Show (1926)
Career as a voice coach;reminiscences
of opera and singers in England,Italy
and America.   303

RUSSELL,James. Three Years in Shetland (1887); Reminiscences of Yarrow
(Selkirk, 1894). Clerical and parish
life in Scotland; village life in the
border area and Far North; Wordsworth
and Coleridge interest.   304

RUSSELL, John Russell, first Earl.
Recollections and Suggestions (1875).
His Parliamentary and public career &
observations on political affairs and
public events at home and abroad 1813
to 1873; Chartism; Reform Bill; general education; statesmen.   305

RUSSELL, John F. S. Russell, second
Earl. My Life and Adventures (1923).
His education;political career; study
of law, science, religion; his marriage troubles; quizzical.   306

RUSSELL,Joshua. A Journal of a Tour
(1852). Travels of a Baptist missionary in Ceylon and India in 50's; work
of the missions.   307

RUSSELL,Norman. Village Work in India (1902).Sketches of his missionary
experience in India.   308

RUSSELL,Sir Thomas Wentworth. Egyptian Service (1949). Career as Police
Commandant in Egypt, 1902-45; crime,
riots,drug traffic; Egyptian politics
and economy; social life; sport; valuable record.   309

RUSSELL, Wing-Commander Wilfred W.
Forgotten Skies (1946). Personal nar-

rative of service with the Indian Air Force in Burma during WW2.   310

/RUSSELL,William7. Recollections of a Detective Police Officer, by Waters (1856); Experiences of a Real Detective, ed. Waters (1862). Life and work of policeman in London from 30's; his feats of apprehension; crimes, courts and the law; fiction?   311

RUSSELL, William. Invalid's Twelve Years' Experience (1893). Reminiscences of a quack; his own many diseases and his cures by purgatives; his medical theories and practice; it may be fiction.   312

RUSSELL, Sir William Howard. My Diary in India (L.1860); A Diary in the East(1869); The Prince of Wales' Tour (1877). Special correspondent for the Times during the Mutiny; on the spot observations & comments; politics and society and places in the Far East; & with the Prince in India;at courts on journey out and home.   313

RUSSELL-COTES,Merton. Home & Abroad (Bournemouth, 1921). Life in Bournemouth in second half of 19th Century; travels in many parts of world; notes on eminent writers, artists.   314

RUTHERFORD, Alison (Cockburn). Letters and Memoir (Edin. 1900). Family life in Scotland; country life in Ettrick, Selkirkshire.   315

RUTHERFORD,Nathaniel J. C. Soldiering with a Stethoscope(1937); Medical Memories (1938); Memories of an Army Surgeon(1939). Career in Army Medical Service,1898-1933; Boer War, West Africa, France and Salonika in WW1; India;Netley Hospital; Tower of London; medical work and army life;social and sport; interesting.   316

RUTTER,Edward. Cricket Memories (L. 1925). His games as an amateur;M.C.C. and Free Foresters; public school and country cricket;great players; social history of game.   317

RUTTER, Frank Vane Phipson. Since I Was Twenty-Five (1927). Merchant Taylors and Cambridge; art criticism and journalism; Today and Daily Mail; curator at Leeds; the art world,artists and art movements.   318

RUTTER, Sir Frederick Pascoe. The Twinkle (1937). Schooldays; career in insurance; London and Lancs Insurance Company; travels; telepathy.   319

RUTTER, Thomas. Some Account of the Religious Experience (1803). Boyhood in Bristol; work in shop; sins; conversion; work and travels in the Quaker ministry later 18th Century. 320

RYAN, Desmond. Remembering Sion (L. 1934). Irishman's life of trouble and quiet from 1906; scholarship, literature,theatre; politics and the rebellion; Dublin scene.   321

RYAN, Mark F. Fenian Memories (Dublin, 1945). The movement and his part in it, 1867-1908; politics, smuggling and his medical work; Sinn Fein; literary interests.   322

RYAN, Nellie. My Years at the Austrian Court (1915). Society and royal life in Vienna before WW1.   323

/RYDER, John7. Four Years' Service in India, by a Private Soldier (Leicester,1853). Boyhood; enlistment; his service in Ireland and India; brutal experiences; horrors of the Sikh campaign; dislike for India.   324

RYDER,Samuel Wills. Blue Water Ventures (1931). Life at sea from 70's; career in merchant navy; WW1 service; anti-submarine work.   325

RYE, Walter. Autobiography (Norwich 1916). Study at King's College,London in 60's; athletics, paperchasing, cycling; career as antiquarian and bibliographer; social life; good. 326

RYLAND, Frederick J. Specks on the Dusty Road (Birmingham, 1937). Forty years in London and in business, as a commercial traveller; his experiences on the road.   327

RYLAND, Thomas Henry. Reminiscences (Birmingham, 1904). Religious and business life in Birmingham in 1st half 19th Century; industrial scene; Birmingham social life and theatre;family life; useful. Birmingham P.L. 328

RYLEY,Samuel William. The Itinerant
(1808,1816, 1827). Life and adventure
of actor and playwright in later 18th
and earlier 19th Century; wild oats;
financial troubles; tours as an actor
and his plays at Drury Lane; miseries
and poverty; Dibdin and other friends
marriage troubles.   329

RYMER,James. Transplantation (1779)
Service as ship's surgeon; his quarrels about his appointment; his publications.   330

S *** ****** *****, D. C. L.Experi-
ences of a Barrister(1856). His legal
career and cases; county assizes and
Old Bailey; criminal cases.   1

S.,C.S. Reminiscences of a Midshipman's Life(1893). Voyages in 50's and
experiences in Crimean War.   2

SAFRONI-MIDLETON,Arnold. Sailor and
Beachcomber(1915); Vagabond's Odyssey
(1916); Wine-Dark Seas (1918); South
Sea Foam (1919); Tropic Shadows(1927)
In the Green Leaf (1950). Shipped to
Australia;life before mast and violin
playing; life with Maoris and natives
of South Seas islands; folk-lore; adventures; Gauguin, Stevenson, Conrad;
enchantment of heathen fairyland.   3

SAGE, Donald. Memorabilia domestica
(Wick,1889). Life and work of Presbyterian minister at Resolis; Rossshire
life, customs, people in first half of
the century.   4

ST.CLAIR, Lt. Col. Thomas Staunton.
A Residence in the West Indies (1834)
A Soldier's Recollections (1834). His
army life in West Indies, 1805-8; and
recruiting in Scotland; social, sport
and negro life.   5

ST.DENIS, Teddie. Almost a Star (L.
1940). Career of a child actress and
soubrette; on road and at the Gaiety;
theatrical social life.   6

ST. HELIER, Lady Mary. Memories of
Fifty Years (1909). Social life, Ireland and London; the Commune; travels
in Europe and America; society; poli-

tical and literary friends.   7

ST. JOHN, Charles W. G. Note-Books
(Edin. 1901). A naturalist's life at
Inverness, Nairn, Elgin, 1845-53; his
studies and sport.   8

ST. JOHN, Sir Frederick. Reminisc-
ences(1906). Career in diplomacy from
1855; Florence, Stuttgart, Pekin, Vienna,Buenos Ayres, Rio, Bogotá, Berne
etc.;public affairs and politics; and
people and places.   9

ST. JOHN, Lt.Henry Beauchamp Trefu-
sis. Journal,1843-44; army service in
Madras Infantry; religious observance
All is Well (1847).   10

ST. JOHN,Sir Spenser B. Life in the
Forests (1862); Adventures of a Naval
Officer(1905); Early Adventures(1906)
Early life in Borneo as naval cadet &
his adventures with pirates, fish and
wild beasts;later work as a consul in
Borneo.   11

ST. JOHNSTON, Sir Thomas Reginald.
South Sea Reminiscences (1922); From
a Colonial Governor's Notebook (1936)
Strange Places (1936).Thirty years as
a commissioner and governor, in Crown
colonies; Tonga, Fijis, Lau, Falkland
Islands, West Indies; administration;
law;social life and sport; and native
life and humours.   12

SAINT-MANDÉ, Wilfred. War, Wine and
Woman (1931). Personal, military, and
amorous adventures of an English soldier in WW1.   13

SALA,George Augustus. Things I Have
Seen (1894); Life & Adventures (1895)
Endless travels and acquaintances of
a Victorian journalist; his glory as
a foreign correspondent;new magazines
and the literary, theatrical, musical
and public scene; Thackeray, Dickens,
and infinite celebrities.   14

SALE, Lady Florence. Diary, 1841-2;
experiences at Kabul during rebellion
retreat and capture. A Journal of the
Disasters (1843).   15

SALISBURY, Frank. Portrait and Pageant (1944). Career of a society portrait painter in England and America;
his celebrated sitters; commentary on

contemporary art.   16

SALMON,Arthur L. A Book of Memories (1937). Childhood;country life; books religion and faith; ordinary affairs; elements of the spiritual autobiography of a poet.   17

SALMOND, David S. Reminiscences of Arbroath and St. Andrews (Arbroath, 1905).Social and public life in those places from 1850; personalities; much of it is personal.   18

SALMOND, Lady Monica. Bright Armour (1935). Society girl serving as nurse in France in WW1 and in London Hospital; Red Cross work.   19

SALT, Annie Gwendoline. My Lot (Ilfracombe, 1946). London childhood and married life in Oxford;experiences as vicar's wife in N.Z. in 20's & return to an English rectory.   20

SALT, Henry Stephens. Seventy Years (1921);Memories of Bygone Eton (1928) Company I Have Kept (1930). Eton and King's and work as assistant master at Eton under Hornby, 1866-85; friends & reading; humanitarianism; opposition to blood-sports; socialism & the free thought movement; writers, scholars & reformers.   21

SALTER, Cedric. Flight from Poland (1940). Daily Mail journalist;Spanish Civil War; Poland under its collapse; escape; experiences in the Balkans; a tough record.   22

SALTER, John Henry. Diary and Reminiscences (1933). Education; medical studies;practice in Essex village and details of social life, sport, trips to London,etc.; good picture of country life, later 19th Century.   23

SALTOUN,Alexander Fraser,17th Baron Scraps (1883). Army career in 40's in Ireland,Gibraltar, Egypt, India; travel, sport, adventure.   24

SALVESEN, Edward T. Salvesen, Lord. Memoirs,ed. Harold F. Andorsen (1949) His legal career, 1880-1922; Scottish Bar and Bench; and his later life in Norway.   25

/SALVIN, Hugh/. Diary, 1824-27; the

travels & observations of naval chaplain on the West Coast of South America; Peru; catholicism. Journal Written on Board H.M.S.Cambridge (Newcastle, 1829).   26

SAMPSON, William. Memoirs (Leesburg 1817). Ulster lawyer's political career in Ireland; agitation with United Irishmen; the rebellion of 1798; his imprisonment and exile.   27

SAMS,Sir Hubert Arthur. Pauline and Old Pauline (1933). Schooldays at St. Paul's in 90's; Walker the headmaster his contemporaries; school work, life and sport.   28

SAMSON, Charles Rumney. Fights and Flights (1930). Personal narrative of service in WW1;in charge of navy aircraft and on carrier.   29

SAMUEL,Horace B. Unholy Memories of the Holy Land (1930). Experiences of a soldier, judge, and Zionist; Palestine, 1917-29; politics.   30

SAMUEL,Herbert Louis Samuel, Visct. Memoirs (1945); Grooves of Change (L. 1946). London and Oxford education; Parliamentary career and offices;public affairs; WW1; Palestine; House of Commons and House of Lords;affairs of Liberal party.   31

SAMUELSON, James. Recollections (L. 1907). Slum life; Labour Movement and Reform; travels in Russia and Servia; Thackeray, Max Mueller, etc. Liverpool Athenaeum.   32

SAMWELL, Maj. H. P. An Infantry Officer (1945). His service with 8th Army in North Africa and Sicily; personal adventures and feelings.   33

SANDBACH, J. H. This Old Wig (1950) Life and memories of a London Police Magistrate; Marlborough Street; crime and punishment; changes in social attitudes to offenders.   34

SANDEMAN, Robert G. C. C. Mountaineer's Journal (Carmarthen, 1948). His climbs in the Cairngorms and Breconshire; dangers; naive.   35

SANDERSON, George P. Thirteen Years among the Wild Beasts of India (1899)

Life and work of the superintendent of an elephant-catching establishment in Mysore, 1864-77; work, techniques and adventures.   36

SANDERSON, Henry Sanderson Furniss, Lord. Memories(1931). Clifton and Oxford; opthalmia; study of economics; tutor and principal at Ruskin College and work in adult education; working-class movement; Liberalism; excellent record of devoted life.   37

SANDES,Maj.E. W. C. In Kut and Captivity (1919). Service with an Indian division in Mesopotamia; siege of Kut and experiences in Turkish prisons; a typical record.   38

SANDES, Elise. Enlisted (Cork 1896) Childhood in Tralee; religious life; social and evangelical work among soldiers in Ireland;founding of Soldiers Homes.   39

SANDES, Flora.Englishwoman-Sergeant (1916); Autobiography (1927). Work as nurse in Serbia in WWl; turns soldier during the retreat; warfare in trench and mountain; good.   40

SANDFORD, Daniel Augustus. Journal, 1848-49; military life in India; vigorous description of Punjab campaign. Leaves from the Journal (1849).   41

SANDWICH, Edward, 8th Earl of. The Earl of Sandwich, ed.Mrs. Steuart Erskine (1919). Assembled from diaries and letters; life of nobleman in 2nd half of 19th Century and early 20th; society,religion, estate work, public work in Hunts.   42

SANDWITH, Humphry. Humphry Sandwith by Thomas Ward (1884); compiled from autobiography. Life of army physician and adventures in Near East;the Franco Prussian War, Serbian War & Russo-Turkish war; travels.   43

SANDYS, Oliver (Marguerite Evans). Full & Frank (1941); Unbroken Thread (1948). Indian childhood; education; work as journalist and popular novelist;private life and daily activities in a Welsh country district.   44

A SANE PATIENT. My Experiences in a Lunatic Asylum (1879).Account of con-finement, escapes, brutality, alleged cures; an exposé inspired by contemporary propaganda.   45

SANGER,"Lord" George. Seventy Years (1910; 1926). Circus life from 1835; parents; fairs, gypsies, freaks, circus people, tours; triumphs with Astley's Circus; good.   46

SANSOM, Oliver. An Account of the Remarkable Passages (1710). Religious life and ministry of an early Quaker; sufferings from "priests"; troubles & imprisonment; travels and witness in the ministry.   47

SANTLEY, Sir Charles. Student and Singer (1892); Reminiscences (1909). Liverpool in 40's; musical studies in Italy;career as opera singer; travels and empire tours; musical society and musical scene.   48

SARAWAK, Gladys Milton Brooke, Dayang Muda of. Relations and Complications (1929). Social life in London; her marriage; life and society in Sarawak; travels; celebrities in literature, theatre, dancing.   49

SARAWAK,Margaret Alice Lily Brooke, Ranee of. My Life in Sarawak (1913); Good Morning and Good Night (L.1934). Her life & work at Sarawak court from 1870; settlers and natives; business; sport; social life; good.   50

SARAWAK, Sylvia Leonora, Ranee of. Reminiscences (1935); Sylvia of Sarawak (1936); A Star Fell (1940). Her childhood in Sarawak;education; court life in England and Sarawak;marriage; literary interests.   51

SARIS, Edmund. Journal, 1617-1618; travel to Cochin China and the Riu Kiu islands; business on sea and land and travel notes;interesting language and spellings. Log-Book of William Adams, ed. C. J. Purnell (1916).   52

SARJANT, John. Brief Memoirs of, by Thomas Bond (1834). Includes diary of Sarjant's life and work as a Methodist missionary in Mauritius.   53

SARL, Arthur J. Horses, Jockeys and Crooks (1935). Racing journalist; The People; experiences on the course and

Bohemian life in London.   54

SARTAIN, John. Reminiscences (N. Y. 1899). First half deals with his life in London, 1808-30; turnpike guard on Deptford Road;London theatres and social scene;work as engraver; his work for William Blake; good.   55

SASSOON,Siegfried. Memoirs of a Fox Hunting Man (1929); Memoirs of an Infantry Officer(1930); Sherston's Progress (1936); The Old Century (1938); Siegfried's Journey (1945). Country house life and sport in Kent; school, Marlborough and Cambridge; army service in France in WW1; trench life and emotional revulsion;Ireland after the war; a poet's reactions to the beauty of nature and the ugliness of war;excellent.   56

SATOW, Sir Ernest Mason. A Diplomat in Japan (1921). Work at the British legation in Tokyo, 1861-9; opening up of Japan; politics; civil war; trade. His diary, 1861-85; covering his Japanese service and also his service in Siam. MS,Public Records Office, Satow Papers, G.D. 22/14-17, 11 vols.   57

SAUNDERS, James Edwin. Reflections and Rhymes (1938). Childhood; Baptist religious life; work as miller, Stone Amersham and Slough to 1888; pleasant memories of country life.   58

SAVA, George. Healing Knife (1938); Surgeon's Destiny (1939); Ring at the Door(1940); Twice the Clock Round (L. 1940); Surgeon's Symphony (1944); The Knife Heals Again (1948). Adventures of a White Russian after the Revolution; medical studies and practice in Italy and Germany; emigration to England; success as Harley Street surgeon; his work; WW2; Blitz; excitements of his life and work.   59

SAVAGE,Henry. Receding Shore (1933) London childhood;service in Boer War; work in publisher's office; his writing career;Bohemian life, sex, travel and literature.   60

SAVAGE,John. Memoirs (Ipswich 1900) Dictated in 1810 when he was 70; life of a Suffolk miller; travels, England and abroad buying wheat. Copy, Ipswich P.L.   61

SAVAGE, Percy. Savage of Scotland Yard (1934). Career as a Metropolitan policeman and in the C.I.D.;detective stories of real life.   62

SAVAGE-LANDOR, A. Henry. Everywhere (1924). Explorer's travels and adventures in five continents; lecturing & writing;memories of Swinburne, Landor etc.   63

SAVI, Ethel Winifred. My Own Story (1947).Her upbringing in Calcutta and marriage; life on indigo plantation; career as a novelist; her later trips to India.   64

SAVORY, Arthur H. Grain and Chaff (1920). Reminiscences of village life and farming from late 19th Century in Aldington, Worc.   65

SAVORY,Isabel. Sportswoman in India (1900). Her travels in India; hunting and other sport.   66

SAVORY, William. Life of a surgeon, apothecary, midwife in Newbury; notes on medicine and popular science, folk lore, astrology, magic; much amusing and curious information. MS, Reading Public Library; see, Life, by George Peachey (1903).   67

SAWLE, Lady Rose Graves. Sketches from the Diaries (1908). Her girlhood in Bath; social life in London & Bath to 1896;travels; family life; society of whole Victorian period.   68

SAYCE, Archibald H. Reminiscences, (1923). Life of scholar; professor of Assyriology at Oxford; Biblical study and archaeology in Egypt, India, and China.   69

SAYCE, Arthur Birch. Looking Back (1924). Somerset boyhood; Oxford; his ministry in Felton,Locking, Woodlands and work as chaplain in Gibraltar and Egypt; clerical life; travel.   70

SAYE AND SELE, Geoffrey Cecil Twistleton-Wykeham-Fiennes, 18th Baron. Hearsay(1925). Education; army career 1879-1904;South Africa and India; and later career in business; politics in House of Lords; court life.   71

SAYER, T.Lewes. Gog and Magog and I

(1931).Career from 1881 in service of the City of London; city life, celebrations, officials.   72

SCARGILL,William P.   Autobiography (1834). Disillusioned narrative; the life of a Unitarian minister; studies and work; impertinences of congregations; Southwark scene.   73

SCARTH, John. Twelve Years in China (Edin. 1860). Residence in Shanghai, Canton and Foochow; politics and war; Clive; Chinese life.   74

SCHARLIEB, Dame Mary A.D. Reminiscences(1924). Career as a physician in India and later in Harley Street; her medical and social work.   75

/SCHAW,Janet/. Diary, 1774-76; her experiences in the American Revolution and social life at St. Kitts; travels in South Carolina and Portugal. Journal of a Lady of Quality (New Haven, 1921).   76

SCHIMMELPENNINCK, Mary Anne. Life, ed. C. C. Hankin (1858). Begins with childhood to 1793; Quaker life; reading, mental, spiritual training; the eminent visitors; Priestley, Darwin, etc.; excellent.   77

SCHOEN, Rev. Jacob F. and CROWTHER, Samuel A. Diaries, 1841; religion and trade in Central Africa;establishment of factories on the Niger; operations against the slave trade. Journals (L. 1842).   78

SCHOFIELD, Dr. Alfred T. Behind the Brass Plate (1928). London in fifties and medical studies;hospital work and practice; Harley Street; celebrities as patients; medical fashions.   79

SCHOFIELD, H. M. High Speed (1932). Experiences with RFC in WW1;work in high-speed planes after the war;races and Schneider Trophy; escapes.   80

SCHOFIELD, Robert Harold Ainsworth. Journals, 1873-83; studies at Owen's College, Manchester; life and work as medical missionary; with China Inland at Shansi. Memorials, ed. A. T. Schofield (1885).   81

SCHUSTER, Sir Arthur. Biographical

Fragments (1932). Boyhood in Manchester; education in Frankfurt; science; teaching and research as professor of physics at Manchester;German and English scientists; times and places in which he was interested.   82

SCOTT, Alexander. Turf Memories of Sixty Years (1925). Turf life, horses races and personalities.   83

/SCOTT, Lady Alicia E./.   A Lady's Narrative (1874). Social and domestic life with her soldier-husband; Bombay in 1834.   84

SCOTT, Charles W. A.   Scott's Book (1934). Service with RFC in WW1;later with RAF,commercial pilot, instructor and escort;record flights, celebrated passengers, etc.   85

SCOTT,Clement William. The Wheel of Life (1897); The Drama of Yesterday & Today(1898). Boyhood in Islington;law study;work as journalist and dramatic critic for Telegraph; his life in India and China in 60's and 70's;clubs; theatrical observations.   86

SCOTT, Cyril. My Years of Indiscretion (1924). Musical study; career as pianist and composer; his adventures in the theatre, philosophy, therapeutics; literary and musical friends; a rich artistic life.   87

SCOTT, Sir George G.   Personal and Professional Recollections(1879). His early life and studies; his career as an architect; Gothic Revival; work on various cathedrals & public buildings and tours abroad.   88

SCOTT, Lord George William Montagu Douglas. Fleeting Opportunity (1940). Memories of happy days; career in the cavalry from 80's;Boer War; sport and social life in Scotland.   89

SCOTT, Maj. J. Robson. My Life (L. 1921). Military career from 1890;Boer War; India; hunting, riding, fishing, India and England.   90

SCOTT, Captain James. Recollections (1834). Service in navy as young man; Napoleonic and Peninsular wars; America; battles; ships; commanders; Nelson, etc.   91

SCOTT, James. Sane in Asylum Walls
(1931). Four years of horror, lunatic
asylum;ways of doctors and attendants
and humanitarian propaganda.   92

SCOTT, John. Diary, 1837-1838; work
as magistrate in Trinidad;police; the
courts; estate life; negroes and planters; good. MS, Exeter P.L.   93

SCOTT, Adm. Sir Percy. Fifty Years
(1919). Career in the navy from 1866;
service in Egypt and Sudan, Boer War,
Boxer Rebellion, WW1.   94

SCOTT,Ralph. Soldier's Diary (1923)
Service with Royal Engineers, France
in 1918; the German offensive and the
victory; embittered.   95

SCOTT, Robert. The Life of (Dundee,
1801). Life of Scottish working-man;
the 45; apprentice; atheism & conversion; work as a wright in London, and
later return to the North and to Scotland; distress of old age.   96

SCOTT, S. Cooper. Things That Were
(1923). Boyhood in Hull in 40's;early
industrialism in Yorks; education for
ministry and parish work in Bloomsbury
and Battersea to 1875; slums & London
life.   97

SCOTT,Thomas. Force of Truth (1779)
Spiritual autobiography;surgeon's ap-
prentice; ordination; ministry, Olney
London Lock Hospital, Aston Sandford;
criticism of sects; Biblical studies;
Newton and Cowper; good.   98

SCOTT, Thomas. The Life of, by John
Scott (1822). Includes autobiography;
apprentice surgeon in 1760's; ordination; curate to Newton at Olney; memories of Cowper; work at London Lock
Hospital; biblical studies.   99

SCOTT, William Bell. Autobiographical Notes (1892). Work as painter and
poet from 30's;Newcastle; artists and
writers; Swinburne, Tennyson, Ruskin,
and Pre-Raphaelites.   100

SCRIVENOR, Lt. John Brooke. Brigade
Signals (1932). Personal experiences
of signal officer in France; service
in WW1.   101

SCUDAMORE, Frank. Sheaf of Memories

(1925). Adventures and observations;
foreign and war correspondent for the
Times and the News; Turkey, Egypt and
Sudan; from 1875 to 1890.   102

SCURRY, James. The Captivity (1824)
Devon sailor captured by French 1780;
adventures in India as prisoner; Hyder Ali and Tippoo Sahib.   103

SEAGO,Edward. Circus Company (1933)
Sons of Sawdust (1934); Tideline (L.
1948).Work and social life and observations of a painter;several years of
travel with small circuses in England
Ireland and Europe;painting of circus
life; lively narrative.   104

SEALE, Miss F. E. Memories of life
in Sevenoaks and Kent in the sixties.
MS, Sevenoaks Public Library.   105

SEATON, Sir Thomas. From Cadet to
Colonel(1866). His military career in
India, 1822-59; army life; Delhi; the
Mutiny; Indian life and politics; and
sport; good.   106

SEAVEN,Michael. Hell and High Alti-
tude (1943). Service with British Air
Force in WW1 and WW2;missions; planes
and advances in design; comparison of
service in two wars.   107

SEBRIGHT,Arthur. A Glance into the
Past (1922). Hunting, sport, country
house life in Herts and Worc.;society
in London; celebrities.   108

SECRETAN, W. Bernard. A Mixed Bag
(Reading, 1943). Youth in 90's; medical education; experiences as ship's
surgeon; medical practice at Reading;
recreations.   109

SECRETT, Sgt. T. Twenty-Five Years
(1929).Experiences as servant to Earl
Haig in South Africa, India, and during WW1.   110

SEDGWICK, Noel M. The Gun on Salt-
ings and Stubble (1949). Reminiscences of wild fowling.   111

SEEBOHM, Benjamin and Esther. Private Memoirs (1873). Early life in a
Quaker household;Germany in the early
century.   112

SEGRAVE, Henry O'Neil De Hane. Lure

of Speed (1928). Career as a motorist
and racer from 1920.   113

SEIGNE, J. W. Irish Bogs (1928). An
account of his social life and sport,
in the Irish countryside.   114

SELBORNE, Roundell Palmer, 1st Earl
Memorials (1896-98). His private and
public life; Winchester and Oxford; &
law studies; legal practice; Parliamentary career; Lord High Chancellor;
chief public movements of the time and
his part in them; Reform; Tractarian;
Disestablishment; Crimean War.   115

SELBY-LOWNDES, H.W. The Hunting and
Sporting Reminiscences (1926). Sport
and fox-hunting from 1900; MFH of the
East Kent Pack.   116

SELIGMAN, Adrian. No Stars to Guide
(1947).Military service in WW2 in the
Aegean; adventures trying to slip the
blockade; social life.   117

SELKIRK, James. Journal, 1826-1838;
life and work as missionary in Ceylon
Buddhism and native life and customs;
and Catholic rivalry.Recollections of
Ceylon (1844).   118

SELLAR, Eleanor Mary. Recollections
and Impressions (Edin. 1907). University, academic, literary, social life
in Glasgow, St.Andrews, Edinburgh and
Oxford from the fifties.   119

SELOUS, Frederick Courteney. A Hunter's Wanderings (L.1881); Travel and
Adventure (1893). Many years' travels
and big-game hunting in Africa;explo-
rations of the Zambesi, Matabele, and
Mashuni areas.   120

SEMON, Sir Felix. Autobiography (L.
1926).Early life and study in Germany
and practice as laryngologist in England from 1874; Royal Physician; his
private practice and hospital work and
his social and court life.   121

SEMPLE, Dugald. A Free Man's Philosophy (1933).Country life and farming
in Wales;spiritual life; influence of
Gandhi.   122

SEMPLE-LISLE,Maj. James George. The
Life (1799). Adventures of a soldier
of fortune; American Revolution, Rus-

sia,France, Denmark; society and love
affairs;debts and scrapes, in and out
of prison.   123

SENEX. Clerical Reminiscences(1880)
Chatty memories of parish life, Wilts;
and notes on churchmen, etc.   124

SENIOR,William. Near and Far (1888)
Angling editor of The Field; fishing;
social life; England; Australia.   125

SERGEANT-MAJOR, R.A.M.C.   With the
R.A.M.C. in Egypt(1918). Military and
medical service, WW1;with Dardanelles
and Egyptian expeditions.   126

SERRELL,Alys F. With Hound and Ter-
rier(1904). Early hunting experiences
in Dorset,Hants, Berks; the Blackmore
Vale Hunt; terriers at work.   127

SESSIONS, Harold. Two Years (1902).
Service with Remount Commissions,pur-
chasing horses in England, Spain, Argentina, USA, S. Africa.   128

SETON-KARR, Heywood W.   Ten Years'
Wild Sports (1889). World-wide travel
and exploration; climbing, shooting &
big-game hunting.   129

SEVERN, Joseph Millott. Life Story
(Hove, 1929); My Village (Brighton,
1935). Work as farmer, miner, carpenter; mainly his practice and beliefs,
as a phrenologist; village life, Derbyshire.   130

SEWELL, E. H. D. Log of a Sportsman
(1923); An Outdoor Wallah (1945). His
boyhood in India; sport and education
at Bedford School; cricket, hunting &
social life in India.   131

SEWELL, Elizabeth Missing. Autobiography (1907). Schooling, home life,
and teaching in Isle of Wight; social
life there; literary friends; writing
the Oxford Movement.   132

SEWELL, Mary. Life and Letters, by
Mrs. Bayly (1899). Begins with autobiography of childhood, country life,
marriage and domestic life, writing &
literary pursuits, Quaker religion in
earlier 19th Century.   133

SEWELL, William. Reminiscences of a
teacher; Oxford; Radley; educational

work, 1866–74; via media; interesting.
MS, Radley College.   134

SEXTON, Sir James. The Life of the
Dockers' M. P. (1936). Early life in
sailing ships; dockyard work; Labour
and Trade Union work for dockers; ILP
and career in Parliament; rise of the
Labour Party; pleasant.   135

SEYMOUR, Adm. Sir Edward. My Naval
Career (1911). His naval service from
1852; Crimean War; China command; and
troop carrying;also captain of Cunard
liner; wide friendships.   136

SEYMOUR, Richard Arthur. Pioneering
in the Pampas(1869). Sheep-farming in
Argentina in 60's;settlers & Indians;
pioneer life; return.   137

SEYMOUR, Walter. Ups and Downs (L.
1910). Sheep-farming and mining,South
America and Australia;work as a civil
servant, businessman, journalist; his
travels and adventures.   138

SHADFORD,George. Lives of Early Methodist Preachers, ed. Thomas Jackson
(1838) III.Lincs man's travels in the
Methodist ministry, 18th Cent.   139

ANON. Shadowed (1924). Experiences
of a man suffering from an incurable
disease; thoughts, emotions, moods; a
well-written record.   140

SHAFTESBURY, Anthony Ashley Cooper,
Earl of. Memoirs,Letters and Speeches
(1859). Contains fragment of autobiography, 1621-39; society of his youth
Oxford university; country life, Dorset.   141

SHAFTOE, Frances. Narrative (1707).
Her service with Catholic nobleman;is
tricked into journey into France, and
imprisoned in nunnery; conversion to
Catholicism by force.   142

SHAKESPEARE, Sir Geoffrey. Let Candles Be Brought In (1949). Political
career; secretary to Lloyd George and
minister; Macdonald and Churchill go-
vernments; National Liberal Party and
political history;   studies of Lloyd
George, Macdonald, Simon, Churchill &
other statesmen.   143

SHAND, Alexander Innes.   Old Time

Travel(1903); Days of the Past (1905)
Travels in western Europe forty years
before;scenes and conditions; work as
journalist in Edinburgh & London; the
Victorian scene; church, army, literature, scholarship, country; journalism for The Times.   144

SHANNON, Kitty. For My Children (L.
1933). Childhood in painter's family;
her parents; society life and fashion
in London;holidays abroad; effects of
WW1.   145

SHARE, Adm. Sir Hamnet. Under Great
Bear (1932). Forty years in the navy;
midshipman to admiral and paymaster &
naval engagements and voyages; Egypt;
WW1; naval development.   146

SHARLAND, John. Recollections (Tiverton, 1898). Watchmaker; Devonshire
life and ways; Palmerston and Liberal
politics from 1820's. Copy in Exeter
Public Library.   147

SHARP, Evelyn. Unfinished Adventure
(1933). London in 70's;Paris in 90's;
literary lights;Yellow Book; Beerbohm
and the Meynells;journalism; suffragism;social work and Labour Party politics after WW1; travels.   148

SHARP, Sir Henry. Goodbye India (L.
1946). Administration in India;Bengal
life and problems; famines; hunting &
social life.   149

SHARPE,Arthur Robert.Memories Grave
and Gay (Bournemouth, 1926). Mission
work in London East End; ministry in
the country; church work, social life
and anecdotes.   150

SHARPE,Fred D. ("Nutty"). Sharpe of
the Flying Squad (1938). Career as a
policeman and detective in CID; crime
murders and detection.   151

SHARPLES, Isaac. A Short Narrative
(1785). Spiritual life and travels in
the ministry of an 18th Century Quaker
from Hitchin, Herts.   152

SHAW,Alfred. Career and Reminiscences (1902). Dictated; career of Notts
cricketer;county and Test matches and
reminiscences of great players.   153

SHAW, Arthur E. Forty Years in the

Argentine Republic (1907). Memories of his business activities, travels & social life in Argentina. 154

SHAW, Charles. Personal Memoirs (L. 1837). Experiences as general in the British auxiliary service in the War of Constitutional Liberty; Portugal & Spain, 1831-37. 155

SHAW, Desmond (ed.). Love Diary of a Boy(1930). Irish boy in London; his Methodist background and poverty; his romantic yearnings; sex life; morbid, but sensitive. 156

SHAW, Frank H. Knocking Around (L. 1927); White Sails (1946); Life Owes Me Nothing (1948). Boyhood at sea and work on wool clippers, nitrate ships, tramps, liners; old sea customs; WW1 and WW2 service;Q-boats; the Murmansk route;adventures; his books; moralisings on life. 157

SHAW,James. Reminiscences of thirty years in Tynron; old Scottish customs and people.Dumfriesshire and Galloway Nat. Hist. Soc. Trans. X (1894). 158

SHAW, Kenneth E. Jottings from the Front (1918). Simple narrative of the work of Anglican chaplain in France in WW1. 159

SHAW, Mabel. God's Candlelights (L. 1932). Life and work as a missionary at Mbereshi,Northern Rhodesia; maternity and infant welfare work; interesting. 160

SHAW, Martin. Up to Now (1929). His boyhood in Hampstead; study at R.C.M. and career in music; compositions for church and theatre; personal & social life; interesting. 161

SHAW, Samuel. Guttersnipe (1946). A Birmingham man's story of slum life & delinquency;time in reformatory; work as miner;Conservative politics; journalism; anti-Socialist work; vigorous and able. 162

SHAW,William. Golden Dreams & Warning Realities(1851). Gold prospecting in California; life in San Francisco; travels in Hawaii & Philippines; very lively. 163

SHAWE, John. Memoirs (Hull, 1824; & in Yorkshire Diaries, 1875). Boyhood in Yorkshire in early 17th Century; & his religious life and ministry, Hull and Rotherham; family life & trouble; Civil War in Yorkshire; national figures; good. 164

SHAYLOR,Joseph. Sixty Years a Bookman (1923). Reminiscences of a London bookseller; the trade, auctions, collectors, etc. 165

SHEARME, John. Lively Recollections (1917). Boyhood in Cornwall; Oxford; career in Church of England; parishes in Isle of Wight and Surrey; Canon of Winchester; society. 166

SHEEPSHANKS, Rt. Rev. John. My Life in Mongolia and Siberia (1903). Work as a missionary in Mongolia; mission at Kuren; Lamas; Russian clergy; native religion. 167

SHELDON, Ann. Authentic and Interesting Memoirs (1787-8). Splendours & miseries of a fashionable courtesan & details of love and high life. 168

SHELLEY, Gerard. The Speckled Domes (1925). Experiences of interpreter at Tsar's court; WW1 events; & Bolshevik revolution; adventures. 169

SHELTON, George. It's Smee (1928). Career of a comedian;Empire tours and theatrical life;long association with J. L. Toole. 170

SHENNAN, Hay. Judicial Maid-of-All Work (Edin. 1933). Legal career, from 1891; sheriff-substitute in Scotland; legal and local social life. 171

SHEPHERD, J. W. Personal Narrative (Lucknow,1886). The experiences of an official in the Mutiny; negotiations; massacre at Cawnpore;his imprisonment Copy India Office library. 172

SHEPPARD, Lady Margaret K. Cottage in Majorca (1936).Domestic affairs in Majorca; peasant life; travels. 173

SHERARD, Robert H. Twenty Years in Paris (1905). Work as journalist; and literary life and famous writers, end of 19th Century; French & English celebrities; interesting.   174

SHERER,John Walter. Daily Life during the Indian Mutiny(1898). Personal experiences of collector in the North Western Provinces in 1857.   175

SHERER,Col. Joseph Moyle. Recollections (1823); Story of a Life (1825). His career in the army;military movements and engagements of the Peninsular war; Peninsular scenes.   176

SHERIDAN,Clare Consuelo. Nuda Veritas (1927); Redskin Interlude (1938); My Crowded Sanctuary (1945). Girlhood and literary friends (Moore, Kipling, James);marriage and family; study and work as sculptor before and after WW1 and her famous sitters;left-wing politics; famous writers and artists and her tempestuous life, including experiences on Indian Reservation.   177

SHERINGHAM, Hugh Tempest. Angler's Hours(1905); Open Creel (1910); Trout Fishing (1920). Angling journalist's fishing experiences.   178

SHERMAN,Margaret. No Time for Tears (1944).Former journalist's service in WW2;ATS; Home Front; work in Ordnance journalistic account.   179

SHERWOOD, Martyn. Coston Gun (1946) The story of his career in the navy, from his days at Osborne in WW1 to the end of WW2.   180

SHERWOOD, Mary Martha. The Life of (1854),based on her diaries and autobiographical fragments,which are also used in F.J. Harvey Darton's Life and Times (1910). Childhood in England in later 18th Century; with her soldier-husband in India; missionary work and adventures; social work in England; & association with Henry Martyn, Elizabeth Fry, Wilberforce, etc.   181

SHERWOOD, William Edward. Oxford Yesterday (1927). Oxford life in Mid-19th Century; town and university and business;social; sport; rather impersonal.   182

SHEWAN, Andrew. Great Days of Sail (1927).Experiences as sailor and master of a tea-clipper in sixties; life in London dockland; famous ships; ad-

ventures with Chinese pirates.   183

SHILLITOE, Thomas. Journal of the Life(1839). Life of influential London Quaker from mid-18th Century;ministry in British Isles; Europe and America; humanitarian and religious work.   184

SHIPLEY,Mary E. Looking Back (1879) Orphan; country childhood; visits to London;education; happy marriage; her widowhood; two lives.   185

SHIPP,John. Memoirs (1829). Suffolk man's adventures in army in India, at beginning of Century; Mahratta wars; Tippoo Sahib; his exploits; criticism of army discipline; a soldierly story well told.   186

SHIRLEY-FOX,John.Angling Adventures (1923). Sporting artist's memories of fishing, mostly S. England.   187

SHORTER, Clement King. An Autobiography (1927). Career as journalist & writer;editorial work; Sketch, Tatler Illustrated London News, Sphere; his family and social life; literary and public scene.   188

SHORTHOSE,Capt. William J. T. Sport and Adventure in Africa (1923). Army service, 1910-22; with King's African Rifles;WW1 campaigns; hunting in Central Africa.   189

SHREWSBURY, William James. Journal, 1815-35; life and work of a Methodist missionary in West Indies and Africa; negroes & slavery. Memorials, by John Shrewsbury (1867).   190

SHRUBSOLE, Edgar S. Long Casts and Sure Rises (1893). Fishing experiences and adventures.   191

SHUTE, Nerina. We Mixed Our Drinks (1945). Disturbed woman in disturbed inter-war generation;personal life on background of public events.   192

SIBBALD, Sir Robert. Memoirs (1932) Family life and education in mid-17th Century; his medical career, Scotland and Holland; physician to Charles II; experiments with medicine and herbals and his professional career; Jonson's conversations.   193

SIBBALD, Susan. Memoirs (1926). Her family, social and personal life, 1783 to 1812; Cornwall, Bath, Scotland and London; good.   194

SIBREE, James.   Madagascar and Its People(1870); Fifty Years in Madagascar (1924). Life and work of missionary from 1863; principal of missionary college; administration, education and medicine; French Colonial life; interesting.   195

SIBREE, James.   Fifty Years' Recollections (Hull, 1884). Congregational minister at Hull from 1831; his work; public life; fishermen and whalers; a general but interesting book.   196

SICHEL, Walter Sydney. Sands of Time (1923). Harrow and Oxford in sixties; legal studies; literary and biographical work; editor of Time; the literary, theatrical, artistic, and social scene and celebrities.   197

SIDDONS, Sarah Kemble. Reminisences, (Cambridge, Mass., 1942). Her parts & performances, 1773-85; theatrical life and literary and society friends; Dr. Johnson; Reynolds etc.   198

SIDGWICK, Henry. Memoir, by Arthur and Eleanor Sidgwick (1906). Contains dictated autobiographical fragment and intermittent journal; life as scholar at Cambridge; psychical work.   199

SIGMA. Personalia (N. Y. 1904). His education at Harrow in sixties; intimate memories of celebrities in legal religious, artistic, literary, noble society.   200

SILVESTER, Anson Lloyd. Royal Sussex Hero (1920). Oxford studies; service with Sussex regiment in France in WW1 and impressions of war. Copy in Colchester P.L.   201

SIME, Jessie G.   The Land of Dreams (1941). A detailed record of her dream life.   202

SIMMS, Henry. The Life (1747). Eton and riotous youth in London; crime and deportation; life of a highwayman in England; conviction.   203

SIMON, Sir John. Personal Recollec-

tions (1894). Brief account of career of a pathologist; honors.   204

SIMON, Lady Rachel. Records and Reflections(1894). Religion and Judaism Liberal politics; social life as wife of Liberal M.P.   205

ANON. Simple Annals (1936). WW1 work as civil servant; literature and journalism; widow; one of the new poor and life in Maida Vale and country.   206

SIMPSON, Alyse. Land that Never Was (1937). Experiences farming in Kenya with her husband; six years' misfortunes; nostalgia; warnings to intending colonists.   207

SIMPSON, Evelyn Mary (Spearing). From Cambridge to Camiers (1917). Newnham woman doing research in France and her involvement in WW1; Red Cross work in Flanders and France.   208

SIMPSON, Mary Charlotte Mair. Many Memories (1898). Society, political & literary, in London and Paris; mainly forties to sixties.   209

SIMPSON, P. Carnegie. Recollections (1943). Presbyterian ministry, Glasgow and Wallasey; professor of church history at Cambridge; theology & church movements; humorous and shrewd.   210

SIMPSON, William. Diary, 1841-1842; civilian on Niger expedition; trading and missionary work; native life and customs. A Private Journal Kept during the Niger Expedition (1843).   211

SIMPSON, William. Autobiography (L. 1903). Career of an illustrator; war artist for Illustrated London News in Crimea, India, Soudan, France; public events and celebrations; adventures & his work.   212

SIMPSON, William. One of Our Pilots is Safe (1942). Experiences of bomber pilot in WW2; shot down; two years in French hospitals and under the Vichy regime.   213

SIMS, George R. Glances Back (1917) My Life (1917). Life and work of London journalist and novelist; Bohemian life; literature, music, theatres and music-halls; celebrities.   214

SIMSON, James. Reminiscences (N.Y . 1882). His boyhood at Inverkeithing; Fifeshire scenes and people.   215

SINCLAIR, Alexander. Fifty Years of Newspaper Life(1895). His work on the Glasgow Herald; production, printing, advertising; rather impersonal.   216

SINCLAIR, Capt. Archibald. Reminiscences (1859). Naval life, discipline and anecdotes; rather impersonal. 217

SINCLAIR, Francis. Reminiscences of a Lawyer(1861). Boyhood at Winchester and London school; his work and cases at the bar; philosophy.   218

SINCLAIR, Col. Hugh M. Camp and Society(1926). Repton and Woolwich; and long army career; Cyprus,Syria, India and Ashanti War, Boer War, WW1; Royal Engineers; celebrities he met.   219

SINCLAIR, John, Master of. Memoirs of the Insurrection (Edin. 1858). His account of 1715 rebellion.   220

SIRCAR, Noel. Indian Boyhood (1948) Marvels of Indian life seen through a boy's eyes; Indian scene; family life and friendships; part fiction.   221

A SISTER. Life in Hospital (1884). Her work as nurse; religious endeavor and attempts to convert patients from drink and to religion.   222

SITWELL, Constance. Flowers and Elephants (1929); Bright Morning (1942) Memories of a cultured and privileged youth in Ceylon and England.   223

SITWELL, Georgiana Caroline. Autobiography to 1847, in Two Generations ed. Osbert Sitwell (1940). Excellent story of her youth at Renishaw;family life;society in the country; artistic interests.   224

SITWELL,Sir Osbert. Left Hand,Right Hand! (1944); The Scarlet Tree (1946) Great Morning (1947); Laughter in the Next Room (1948); Noble Essences (L. 1950). A richly detailed picture of himself, his family, and the society in which he grew up and lived; Renishaw, London, the Guards, Europe; society, the arts, Edwardian culture and traditions; character sketches; writers,artists, celebrities with whom he was associated; an artistic brocade & an amused self-portrait; good.   225

SITWELL, Sacheverell. All Summer in a Day(1936). An autobiographical fantasia; embroideries on a few unusual memories and experiences; a sensitive evocation of childhood.   226

SIXTY-ONE.Reminiscences of the Lews (1873). Twenty years of sport in the Hebrides.   227

SKELTON,Sara. Autobiography, edited Rachel Ferguson (1929). Her life in the theatre from childhood to old age; roles and successes; tours in England and America; theatrical life & actors may be fiction.   228

SKELTON, Thomas. Clay Under Clover (1949). His life as a navvy in County Antrim; pleasures and troubles of the work; unemployment; Irish scene, social life, people; pleasant.   229

ANON.Sketches of Naval and Military Adventure (Bath,1849). Boyhood in the navy; later military life in India; a slight affair. Cambridge U.L.   230

SKIMMING, Sylvia. Sand in My Shoes (Edin. 1948). A good account of service in WW2 as Red Cross Welfare Officer in North Africa,Italy, France and Germany.   231

SKINNER,James. Autobiography (Edin. 1893). Scottish boyhood; training in reading and scholarship; study, Edinburgh College; life and work as Free Church minister;country life in Fifeshire; mental development. Cambridge U.L.   232

SKINNER,Maj. Thomas. Fifty Years in Ceylon (1891). Military life, surveying and railway construction in Ceylon from 1818; social life.   233

SKIPPER, J. Bowline. Yarns from a Captain's Log (1912). Fifty years at sea; anecdotes of retired captain of an ocean liner.   234

SLADE, G. H. Two Sticks (1923). His naval service;crippled by disease and his spiritual life and faith; a simple record.   235

SLADEN, Douglas B. W. Twenty Years
(1913); My Long Life (1939). School &
Oxford;teaching at University of Sydney;editing Who's Who; writing poetry
and publishing; Savage Club; literary
friends.   236

SLEEMAN, Col. Sir James Lewis. From
Rifle to Camera (1947). Shooting and
photographing big game; India, Africa
and New Zealand;his conversion to the
bloodless form of hunting.   237

SLEEMAN,Lt. Col. Sir William Henry.
Rambles and Recollections (1844). His
military career in Bengal;administra-
tion, official life, society; customs
and culture of Hindus.   238

SLESSER,Sir Henry.Judgment Reserved
(1941). Legal studies and law career;
trade-union law; Fabian Society; work
in Labour Party; M.P., Solicitor-General,Lord Justice of Appeal; politics
and his philosophy.   239

SLOANE-STANLEY,Capt. Cecil. Reminiscences (1893). Midshipman in fifties
under sail; following Marryat; work &
comrades; cruises; good.   240

SLOCOMBE, George Edward. The Tumult
(1936).Career of socialist journalist
Labour Party; Daily Herald; special
correspondent in WW1, Versailles, India, Spanish revolution.   241

SLUGG, Josiah Thomas. Reminiscences
(Manchester, 1881). Experiences, Manchester in thirties; industrial scene
and social life.   242

SMALL, E.Milton (editor). Told from
the Ranks(1897). Recollections of military and war service by privates and
non-coms; Crimean War, Indian Mutiny,
Sudan, Zulu War, etc.   243

SMALLEY, George W.   Anglo-American
Memories(1911-12). Journalist's anecdotes and reminiscences of statesmen,
politicians, actors, writers, industrialists, England and USA; American-
born.   244

SMART,Sir George Thomas.Leaves from
the Journals (1907). Career as church
organist; Chapel Royal; festivals and
oratorios;friend of Beethoven & Weber
travels abroad; good; autobiography &

written up diary; first half of 19th
Century.   245

SMEATON-STUART, John Roland. Safari
for Gold(1942). Experiences prospecting for gold in Kenya in the twenties;
development of the colony.   246

SMEDLEY, Anne Constance. Crusaders
(1929). Work for Lyceum Club; modern
theatre and dance; travels in Europe,
USA, etc.; celebrities of theatrical
and literary world.   247

SMILES,Samuel. Autobiography (1905)
His life in Leeds and London; work as
biographer and friend of the Victorian
engineers and industrialists.   248

SMILLIE, Robert. My Life for Labour
(1924). Boyhood in Ireland; work in
Scottish coalmines; industrial scene
of 80's; trade union work as miners'
leader; Keir Hardie, MacDonald, other
Labour friends.   249

SMITH, A. Mervyn. Sport & Adventure
(1904).Travel and big-game hunting in
India; society experiences. India Office Library.   250

SMITH, Aaron. Atrocities of Pirates
(1824). Captivity among pirates,Cuba;
their barbarities; his sufferings and
romantic love;written up and probably
ghost-written in connection with his
own trial for piracy in 1823.   251

SMITH,Albert. Diary, 1858; notes on
Chinese scene and customs; given away
at his lectures. To China and Back(L.
1859).   252

SMITH,Alexander. Smithy (1936). His
life in Nottingham; designing of lace
curtains; service in RNAS.   253

SMITH, Annie Swan ("Annie S. Swan")
My Life (1934); We Travel Home (1935)
Scottish girlhood and her career as a
journalist and novelist;domestic life
philanthropy; spiritualism; notes on
her houses.   254

SMITH, C.Harold. The Bridge of Life
(1929). London boyhood;career of self
made businessman; travels in England,
USA, etc.; religion, social life, and
fashions.   255

SMITH, Charles. <u>Autobiography of an Old Passport</u> (1893). Wilts minister's travels in France, Belgium, Germany, Italy, Switzerland, before the coming of the railway.　256

SMITH, Charles Edward. <u>From the Deep of the Sea</u> (1922). Work and adventure of surgeon aboard a whaler in 1885-7; voyage and the work; life in the Arctic; Quaker religion; diary.　257

SMITH, Charles Manby. <u>Working Man's Way</u> (Redfield, 1854). Apprentice and journeyman printer; London; travels & unemployment; teaching and printing; good picture of working-class life in earlier 19th Century.　258

SMITH, Charles Roach. <u>Retrospections</u> (1883). Antiquarian and archaeological pursuits; scholarly and literary society and friends; London life.　259

SMITH, Prof. Chretien. Diary, 1816; botanist on Tuckey's expedition up the Congo; scientific notes. James Hingston Tuckey, <u>Narrative of an Expedition</u> (1818).　260

SMITH, Deborah. <u>My Revelation</u> (1933) Spiritual autobiography; how working-woman found God.　261

SMITH, Capt. E. A. Military journal 1889; details of a punitive expedition into Burma. MS, India Office Library, Eur. B.65.　262

SMITH, Edward. <u>Three Years in Central London</u> (1889). Religious social work at St. John's Square, Clerkenwell among London poor; aims; ideals; and methods.　263

SMITH, Edward Sharwood. <u>Faith of a Schoolmaster</u> (1935). Work at Newbury Grammar School; educational ideas and reform.　264

SMITH, Edward Tennyson. <u>From Memory's Storehouse</u> (1914). Thirty-five years as preacher and temperance lecturer & propagandist against vivisection, and cruelty to animals.　265

SMITH, Lady Eleanor Furneaux. <u>Life's a Circus</u> (1939). Girlhood romanticism influence of Borrow; travels, sport & bullfighting, gypsies, circus, ballet

and work as a novelist in these fields and her adventures.　266

SMITH, Eliza. <u>Personal Experience of Roman Catholicism</u> (1864). Conversion to Catholicism as girl; family opposition and doubts; life in a convent on the continent; disappointment; break; criticism of church.　267

SMITH, Ernest. <u>Fields of Adventure</u> (1923). Forty years as a journalist & special correspondent; Paris, Russia, Boer War, Germany, Greece, etc.　268

SMITH, Fred. <u>Scenes from the Boyhood</u> (1899). Cambridge boyhood; enthusiasm for natural history; adventures with worms, insects, fish, molluscs at Yarmouth and in country; good.　269

SMITH, Frederick. <u>Autobiographical Narrations</u> (1848). Wicked youth; his conversion; ministry and travels as a Quaker, later 18th Century.　270

SMITH, George. Trowbridge Baptist's record of his sin and redemption. Undated pamphlet in Wilts Archaeol. Soc. Devizes.　271

SMITH, George. <u>Autobiography</u> (1923) Cornish life, beginning 19th Century; school, family, apprentice; work as a carpenter and builder; work for mining safety; invention of safety fuse; simple and interesting.　272

SMITH, George Hill. <u>Rambling Reminiscences</u> (Newry, 1896). Experiences of lawyer and political speaker; travels and experiences with politicians and audiences, England, USA. Copy in Cambridge U.L.　273

SMITH, George Murray. Sidney Lee's <u>Memoir</u> (1902) includes autobiography of boyhood and early life as publisher; Leigh Hunt; discovery of Charlotte Bronte; Cornhill magazine and contributors; business affairs.　274

SMITH, George R. <u>Half-a-Century in the Dead-Letter Office</u> (Bristol 1908) Work in Post-Office; Controller of the Returned Letter Office; colleagues and techniques; public scene and effects on his work. Bodleian.　275

SMITH, Goldwin. <u>Reminiscences</u> (1910)

Boyhood at Reading; Eton and Oxford; tutor at Oxford and later professor at Oxford and Cornell; education, journalism, studies of economics; scholars and literary friends.   276

SMITH, Lt.Gen. Sir Harry G. W. The Autobiography (1902). His army career 1787-1846; soldier's life, campaigns, adventures; Peninsular War, France, USA, Netherlands, S. America, Africa, Asia;interesting and valuable account of private and public life.   277

SMITH, Lt.Col. Sir Henry. From Constable to Commissioner(1910). Boyhood in Scotland; life in Suffolk Militia; long career in London City Police and account of police life,crimes, public events, etc.   278

SMITH, Adm. Humphrey Hugh. A Yellow Admiral Remembers (1932); An Admiral Never Forgets (1936). Long career in the navy;WW1 service; his voyages and adventures; mostly anecdotes.   279

SMITH, Rev. James. Marvellous Mercy (1862). Lifetime of religious revelation and self-examination;travels and work of Methodist minister. Gloucester City Library.   280

/SMITH, James Hicks/. Reminiscences of Forty Years, by a Hereditary High Churchman (1868). Theological studies and his opposition to dissent; life & opinions of high churchman; Catholic Revival; St. Alban's, Holborn.Copy in Cambridge U.L.   281

SMITH, Capt. John. The True Travels (1630); Works (1884). His voyages and the colonisation of Virginia;colonial life, Indians,adventures, in the early 17th Century.   282

SMITH, John Benjamin. Reminiscences of a Manchester politician and Member of Parliament, 1819-32. MS, Manchester Central Library.   283

SMITH,John C. Christian Work (1883) Religious life and social work;prison and hospital visits; Sunday-schools & conversions of Scottish elder.   284

SMITH,John Thomas. Book for a Rainy Day (1845;1905). Engraver's recollections, 1766-1833; London life and art

painters, writers, engravers, customs amusing anecdotes.   285

SMITH, Joseph Manton. Stray Leaves (1885); More Stray Leaves (1889). His work in London factories; forty years of evangelism,temperance work, ragged school teaching in Stepney, missions to various parts of country; working-class life; good.   286

SMITH, Julia. Diary, 1899-1900; her travels in Ceylon, India, Burma; social work. Leaves from a Journal(1901) India Office Library.   287

SMITH, Lesley N. Four Years (1931). Young woman's service as nurse in WW1 in civilian and base hospitals; work, life of unit, flirtations.   288

SMITH, Logan Pearsall. Unforgotten Years (1938). Quaker boyhood in Pennsylvania;Harvard; travels; friendship with Whitman; business life; study at Oxford; life of a literary and scholarly expatriate in England.   289

SMITH, Malcolm Arthur. A Physician at the Court of Siam (1948). Medical work;court life; Queen Mother and her household; anecdotes.   290

SMITH, Margaret. Different Drummer (1932). Life with tea-planter husband in India early century;loneliness and problems of motherhood; training as a nurse; work at Queen Charlotte Hospital; suffragism; social life.   291

SMITH, Mary. Autobiography (1892). Life and work of nonconformist school teacher at Cropredy,Oxon. and at Carlisle; poverty, religion, social life and her poetry.   292

SMITH, Matthew. Memoirs of Secret Service (1699). Activities of spy on Jacobites in 90's; relation with the Duke of Shrewsbury; self-defence related to his ill-usage.   293

SMITH, Percy J. Con Man (1938). His experiences at Scotland Yard as C.I.D. inspector; confidence tricksters; his intelligence work in WW1.   294

SMITH, Richard Skilbeck. Subaltern in Macedonia (1930). Adventures of a chaplain in WW1;Macedonian and Palestine campaigns.   295

SMITH,Rodney ("Gipsy"). Gipsy Smith (1906). Early life as a gipsy;work as revivalist; evangelistic tours, England and America.   296

SMITH, Samuel. My Life-Work (1902). Business career in Lancs;Liberal M.P. for Lancs to 1898; public affairs and politics.   297

SMITH, Sydney T. G. Reminiscences (Mexborough,1926). Theological training and ordination; ministry in Sheffield; infirmary chaplain; civic work and social work; WW1 experience. Copy Sheffield P.L.   298

SMITH, T. Carrington. The Story of a Staffordshire Farm (Stafford, 1909) The trials and tribulations of a tenant farmer; crops, regulations, soil, etc. Salt Library, Stafford.   299

SMITH, Capt. Thomas. Narrative of a Five Years' Residence (1852). Work as a political officer in Nepal in 1840's military, political and economic matters; native life.   300

SMITH, Thomas. A Brand Plucked from the Burning(1856). Hereford youth and sins; marriage; business in Worcester and struggles with drink;his business affairs in Hereford; religion. A copy in Hereford P.L.   301

SMITH,Thomas. Extracts from the Diary of a Huntsman (1852, 1921); Life of a Fox (1897, 1926). Sporting life; foxhunting; hunting advice.   302

SMITH,Victor. Diary of a Young Civil Servant(1927). Work in Westminster during WW1; religious inclination and proletarian opinions.   303

SMITH, Wareham. Spilt Ink (1932). A career in advertising; work for Daily Mail and associated newspapers;Northcliffe, publishers, journalists.   304

SMITH,William. An Authentic Account (1750). Irish rector's son; education and various jobs; succumbs to forgery and vainly pleads for mercy; written before execution.   305

/SMITH,William John7. Autobiography

of a Rascal (1935). Respectable youth turned criminal; crimes in S. Africa, Australia; plantation overseer in Tahiti;prime minister on small island & trader; adventures.   306

SMITH, William Ramsay. In Southern Seas (1924). Wanderings of a naturalist in New Hebrides, etc.   307

SMITH-DORRIEN, Gen.Sir Horace Lockwood. Memoirs (1925). His 48 years in the army; Zulu War, Soudan, Boer War, India, Aldershot Command, WW1 service in France; campaigns and staff activities.   308

SMITHERS, Jack. Early Life (1939). Working-class life in England in early century; travels for work; publisher for Oscar Wilde; troubles.   309

SMITHSON, Annie M. P. Myself - and Others (Dublin, 1945). Her childhood in Ireland; work as nurse in London & Scotland; Ireland and the troubles; & her work as a novelist.   310

SMITHSON, George. Raffles in Real Life (1930). Work and adventures of a country-house burglar;crimes and gaol life of educated man.   311

SMYTH, Dame Ethel. Impressions that Remained (1919); Streaks of Life (L. 1922); Final Burning of Boats (1928); As Time Went On (1936); What Happened Next (1940). Musical study in Germany and her career as composer; musical & literary society and celebrities whom she knew;modern ideas on sex, women's independence; lively.   312

SMYTH,Herbert Warington. Five Years in Siam (L.1898); Chase and Chance in Indo-China (1934). Work, travels, and adventures while director of mines in Siam;service in RNVR; resources, government; social and hunting.   313

SMYTHE, Francis Sydney. Adventures of a Mountaineer (1940). His climbing experiences from 1922;Dolomites, Alps and Himalayas; Everest.   314

SMYTHE,Mrs. S. M. Ten Months in the Fiji Islands (Oxford, 1864). With her soldier-husband on a mission for cession of Fijis; travel notes; visit to New Zealand.   315

SNAPE, Joseph. Reminiscences (1881)
Training, career, cases of a dentist;
lecturer and surgeon at Liverpool Royal Infirmary; intended to remove public prejudice against dentists.   316

SNELL, Hannah.   The Female Soldier
(1750). Marriage and desertion; search
for husband disguised as sailor & soldier; adventures in India; her ruses
to conceal her sex.   317

SNELL, Henry, Baron. Men, Movements
and Myself (1936).Country boyhood and
self-education; Bradlaugh influence;
work in charity organizations, trade
unions, L.C.C. and Parliament; Labour
Peer;Fabian society and Ethical Movement; discreet record.   318

SNELL, Sidney H. Doctor at Work and
Play (1937). London medical study and
practice at Grays,Scarborough,London;
work, social life, sport.   319

SNEYD-KYNNERSLEY,Edmund M. H. M. I.
(1908); H.M.I.'s Notebook (1930). A
school inspector's career;North Wales
and Cheshire from 1870; schools, children, teachers, boards; subjects and
methods of teaching.   320

SNOW, F. H. No Names, No Pack Drill
(1932). Personal experiences of private in RAMC in WW1; sanitary work and
ways of soldiers.   321

SNOW, Lt.Col. H.W. Victorian Gothic
(1941). His army career from the Boer
War to WW2; soldiering; official life
in Canada; sporting career.   322

SNOWDEN, Nicholas. Memoirs of a Spy
(1934).Former Austro-Hungarian agent;
boyhood in Russia;espionage in Russia
during WW1; adventures.   323

SNOWDEN, Philip, Viscount. Autobiography (1934). Early work in ILP and
his political career in Labour Party;
Parliamentary life in opposition and
on Treasury bench;national and international affairs; socialism, finance,
trade unions; good.   324

SOCIETY CLAIRVOYANT. Recollections
(1911). A Frenchwoman's practice in
English society; her clients & cases;
anecdotes; superficial record.   325

SODEN, C. C. It's a Great Life (L.
1937). Life at sea from boyhood; odd
jobs and rough life in English ports,
U.S.A. and Canada.   326

SOLDENE, Emily.   My Theatrical and
Musical Recollections (1897). Musical
career of a singer from the sixties &
her operatic roles, theatrical experiences and concerts; tours.   327

ANON. A Soldier's Journal (1770). A
soldier's experiences, 1758-64; raids
on French coast; military activity in
West Indies; army life.   328

SOLLY,Henry. These Eighty Years (L.
1893).Schooling in Sussex and University of London;work in counting house
and ministerial career; social work;
trade unions, workingmen's institutes
and clubs; religion and reform.   329

ANON. Some Experiences of a Political Agent (1910). Conservative agent
in mining area in early century; work
and elections; fiction?   330

ANON. Some Personalities, by 20/1631
(1921).Light gossip and reminiscences
on writers,churchmen, politicians and
society in early century.   331

ANON.   Some Professional Recollections,by a Former Member of the Council of the Incorporated Law Society
(1883). His practice as a solicitor;
tour in India and Ceylon.   332

ANON. Some Trivial Recollections of
an Old Landscape Painter(1913). Notes
on art and painters; public events in
England and Scotland; superficial and
genial jottings.   333

SOMERVELL,Robert. Chapters of Auto-
biography(1935). Scottish family life
in mid-century;Cambridge; teaching at
Harrow 1887-1911; famous pupils, masters; education and religion.   334

SOMERVELL, Theodore Howard.   After
Everest (1936); Knife and Life in India (1940); India Calling (1948). His
experiences as a mountaineer; Everest
expedition of 1923; work as a medical
missionary in Travancore, 1923-1945 &
descriptions of hospitals and medical
conditions in India; good.   335

SOMERVILLE,Alexander. Autobiography
of a Working Man (1848); Conservative
Science of Nations (Montreal, 1860);
Somerville's Diligent Life (Montreal,
1860). Political and economic affairs
in British Isles and Europe; country
life and agriculture in Scotland; Irish affairs and European revolutionary
activities; 1832 crisis; Birmingham &
the riots; later in Canada.   336

SOMERVILLE, Edith; and ROSS, Martin
Irish Memories (1933); Happy Days (L.
1946). Irish country and social life;
family life and childhood;hunting and
country sport; Victorian scene; travels abroad; witty and pleasant.   337

SOMERVILLE, Martha. Personal Recollections (1873). Scottish social life
at Jedburgh and Edinburgh; education,
religion, theatre, life with scientific husband; two marriages; memories
of Scott; valuable.   338

SOMERVILLE, Thomas. My Own Life and
Times (Edin. 1861). Childhood at Haw-
ick;Edinburgh University; ministry at
Minto; London from 1770's; American &
French revolutions; slavery; Scottish
social history;Hume,Pitt, Wilkes, Fox
and Wesley; useful.   339

SOOTHILL, Lucy. A Passport to China
(1931). Life and work as a Methodist
missionary in Wenchow, 1884-1909; her
wide interests; Chinese life and customs; travels.   340

SOPER, Grace. Reminiscences (1839).
Plymouth woman's story of religious &
spiritual life; Methodist activities;
in letters to her children.   341

SORRELL,George. Man Before the Mast
(1928). Experiences as able seaman in
sixties and seventies; many ships and
crews; places he saw.   342

SOSKICE, Juliet M.   Chapters from
Childhood (1922).The childhood of the
granddaughter of Ford Madox Brown;the
Rossetti circle; convent school.   343

SOTHERN, Edward H. My Remembrances
(1917). Amused story of nursery days;
boyhood in theatrical family; career
in London and American theatre; anecdotes and dialogue.   344

SOUPER, William. Man from the Rocks
(1926). Life in the Highlands; Scottish social and religious life; education;quietude of glen; his spiritual
life; Rainey, Salmond etc.   345

SOUTAR,Andrew. My Sporting Life (L.
1934); With Ironside (1940). Life of
journalist and war correspondent; his
experiences in boxing and other sport
and on the expedition into N. Russia,
1919-20; personalities.   346

SOUTHEY,Robert. Life and Correspondence, ed. Charles C. Southey (1849),
Vol. I. A series of letters to J. May
recounting the poet's early life and
schooling; Bristol and Bath.   347

SOUTHWARK, Selina Mary,   Baroness.
Social and Political Reminiscences(L.
1913). Life with her M.P.husband; law
and politics in later 19th Century; &
their social life.   348

SOUTTAR, Henry Sessions. A Surgeon
in Belgium (1915). Personal narrative
of his work in field hospitals in the
early part of WW1.   349

SOUTTER, Francis William. Recollections (1923); Fights for Freedom (L.
1925). His life and work in the trade
union movement and Labour Party;work-
ing class life; Southwark; Chartism,
Socialism;industry and reform; London
social life and changes.   350

SPALDING, John. A Short Account of
John Spalding (1856). Spiritual life
and travels in the ministry of a Reading Quaker in the second half of 18th
Century.   351

SPANTON,Ernest Frederick. In German
Gaols (1917). Work as a teaching missionary; two years' imprisonment during WW1 in German East Africa.   352

SPANTON, W.S. An Art Student (1927)
Youth in sixties;art and art teaching
in Norfolk and London; Royal Academy;
Pre-Raphaelite painters and theories;
friends and teachers.   353

SPARK, Fred R. Memories of My Life
(Leeds, 1913).Life in music and jour-
nalism in Leeds, second half of 19th
Century; Leeds festivals; public life

and personalities in Leeds.   354

SPARK,William. Musical Memories (L. 1892). Church organist in Leeds;anec-dotes of celebrated musicians from the fifties.   355

SPARLING, John. Life, ed. Emma Cun-liffe (Edin.1904). Extracted from his autobiography; childhood; education; Oxford; family life, travel, personal affairs in Victoria's reign; lively & interesting. Bodleian.   356

SPARROW, Geoffrey; and ROSS, J.N.M. On Four Fronts (1918). Experiences of two naval surgeons in WW1;the Antwerp expedition; Gallipoli; Salonika, and the Western Front; personal.   357

SPARROW, Walter Shaw.   Memories of Life and Art (1925). Liverpool in the sixties;art study at the Slade and in Belgium; painting and painters; work for The Studio and career as art edi-tor; theatrical friends.   358

SPEAIGHT, Richard N.   Memoirs of a Court Photographer (1926). Work, tra-vels and acquaintances of a photogra-pher; exhibitions; sitters. Cambridge U.L.   359

SPECKMAN, Charles. Life (1763). An account of the exploits and crimes & adventures of a thief; written in New-gate before his execution.   360

SPEDDING, Charles T. Reminiscences of Transatlantic Travellers (1926). A life at sea from 1896; sailing ships; career as chief purser, Cunard Line; ship life; celebrities.   361

SPEED, Maude. Snapshots (1929). Her social life and travels; family scene and social affairs in Ireland; social changes from 19th Century.   362

SPEID, Mrs. John B. Our Last Years in India (1862). Social life, travels and personal affairs from 1858.   363

SPEISER, F. Two Years with the Nat-ives in the West Pacific (1913). His experiences in New Hebrides.   364

SPEKE, Hugh. Secret History of the Happy Revolution(1715). Somerset gen-tleman's help in bringing over William

of Orange;political agitation; finan-cial loss and imprisonment;patriotism and activity in 1688.   365

SPEKE, Capt. John Hanning. Journal, 1859-63;explorations in Abyssinia and Central Africa; topography; natives & adventures. Journal of the Discovery of the Source of the Nile (1863). 366

SPENCE,Edward F. Bar and Buskin (L. 1930). Family life in Liverpool; work as articled clerk and solicitor; bar-rister and journalist in London;sport and theatre; social; his cases.   367

SPENCER, Frederick H.   Inspector's Testament (1938). Mechanic's son; his boyhood poverty in Lancs; studies and teaching in London; work in economics the Webbs and Graham Wallas;career as inspector of schools; valuable record of a successful career.   368

SPENCER, George. Life of Father Ig-natius, by Father Pius (Dublin, 1866) Education at Eton and Cambridge; work as Anglican minister; conversion, and life as secular priest and passionist from autobiography and diary.   369

SPENCER, Rt.Rev. George John Trevor Journals, 1840-1, 1843-4; visitations of Bishop of Madras; travels in Trav-ancore and Tinnevelly; administration religious life,congregations, workers Journal of a Visitation (1842); Jour-nal of a Visitation (1845).   370

SPENCER, Herbert. An Autobiography (1904). History of his education, the genesis and evolution of his ideas and writings; personal and mental history and his work as journalist and author, an important record.   371

SPENCER,Walter.T. Forty Years in My Bookshop(1923). Life and work of Lon-don bookseller;bibliomania; books and writers; writer-friends; Dickensiana; London social life.   372

SPENCER-KNOTT,Justina (Tina). Fools Rush In (1949).Experiences of herself and her family as novice farmers;dif-ficulties; Devon life; amusing.   373

SPENDER,Harold. Fire of Life (1926) Youth in Bath;work in London journal-ism; Daily News; Liberalism; East-End social work;lecturing and writing and work in Liberal politics; travel as a foreign correspondent.　374

SPENDER, John A. Life, Journalism, and Politics (1927). London boyhood; Oxford; journalism in Hull; editor of Westminster Gazette; Liberal politics and religion;WW1; celebrities of public life and journalism.　375

SPENSER, James. Limey (1933); Limey Breaks In (1934); The Awkward Marine (1948).Slum life and criminal associations in Birmingham; Borstal; prison life; adventures as a gunman in USA; life as recalcitrant marine in WW2 and life as prisoner at Dieppe. Real name Francis Harold Guest.　376

SPERSOTT, James. Memoirs of social life at Chichester in 18th Century; a good lively record. Sussex Archaeological Collections, XXIX (1879) and XXX (1880).　377

SPEYER, Edward. My Life and Friends (1937). Boyhood in Germany; musical & social life in England from sixties; concerts, players, eminent friends to the thirties.　378

SPOONER, Lawrence. Abstract of the Gracious Dealings of God, ed. Samuel James (1774). Litchfield man; Quaker conversion;ministry and sufferings in later 17th Century. Bodleian.　379

A SPORTSMAN.Random Recollections of the Belvoir Hunt (1897). Hunting and country life of a squire; the Belvoir country and its notables.　380

SPOTTISWOODE, Col.Robert. Reminiscences (Edin.1935). Military career in the Hussars; India; the Mutiny; Egyptian campaign; Russia and Ireland; an ascetic record.　381

SPRATT, Devereux. Autobiography (L. 1886).Ministry and private and public troubles of a Protestant clergyman in Cork; rebellion; captivity in Algiers Irish life.　382

SPRING,Howard. Heaven Lies About Us (1939); In the Meantime (L.1942); And Another Thing (1946). Boyhood, school and early journalism and odd jobs;his work as provincial reporter and literary critic of Evening Standard; religious life; Plymouth Brethren; career as writer and novelist.　383

SPRINGFIELD, Lincoln. Some Piquant People (1924). Forty years as London journalist; editor of London Opinion; Bohemian life;celebrities in journalism, the arts and public life.　384

SPROT, Gen. J. Incidents and Anecdotes (Edin. 1906). Schooldays; army life in India and Ireland; the Mutiny and his recruiting work.　385

SPURGEON, Charles Haddon. Autobiography (1897-1900). Compiled from his autobiography, diary, letters; childhood;conversion; Baptist ministry and travels; public affairs.　386

SPURGIN,John. Narrative of Personal Experiences (1847). A doctor's scientific experiences and observations in confirmation of Swedenborg's theology and principles.　387

SQUIRE, J. H.　And Master of None (1937). Varied life at sea,in theatre and music; life as conductor and director; music as a trade.　388

SQUIRE, Sir John C. The Honeysuckle and the Bee (1937); Water Music(1939) Aspects of his life; school; places; books; people; personal experiences & amusements;arts and pleasures; George Moore,Kipling and other literary men; vignettes;the last organized on canoe trip up the Thames; episodic but rich and charming.　389

SQUIRE, Rose E. Thirty Years in the Public Service (1927). Inspector of factories; social and factory conditions and progress in health and sanitation; personal experiences.　390

SQUIRRELL, Mary Elizabeth. Autobiography(1853). Woman's blindness and deafness;alleged abstinence from food and drink for 25 years; mesmerism and marvels.　391

STABLES,William Gordon.Medical Life in the Navy (1868).Experiences in his joining navy; voyage to Cape Town and medical work on shipboard;slave trade good.　392

STACEY,James. James Stacey, by W.J. Townsend(1891). First half deals with his Methodist ministry in Halifax,Liverpool, London, Hanley; humble life; Joseph Barber; Yorks religious life & his literary interests.   393

STACKHOUSE, Frances Acton (Knight). Reminiscences of country life, family and childhood romance from late 18th Century; Shropshire society; Davy and 19th Century science; married life; a very interesting record. MS, Hereford City Library.   394

STACKHOUSE, Thomas. The Book-Binder Book-Printer and Book-Seller Confuted (1732). Theologian's poverty; life at Finchley; proposal for history of the Bible; quarrels; justification.   395

STACPOOLE, Henry De Vere.Men & Mice (1942); More Men and Mice(1945). Life in Ireland from sixties; work as doctor and writer; life in WW1; meetings with Wilde, Wells, Anatole France and other celebrities.   396

STACY, Col. Lewis Robert. Narrative of Services (1848). Military service on Nott's expedition to Kabul 1840-2; Baluchistan; Afghanistan; & political work at Kelat.   397

STACY,Sarah Elizabeth. Memoir (Norwich, 1849). Girlhood sins, including reading Edgeworth's novels;conversion and religious life in Norwich;friends naive;charming. Norwich P.L.   398

STALEY, Rt. Rev. Thomas Nettleship. Five Years' Church Work (1868). Diocesan administration as Bishop of Honolulu; religious affairs.   399

STAMER,William ("Mark Tapley, Jr.") Recollections (1866). Adventures and travels; Canada, USA, Australia; soldier,goldminer, pioneer; the American Civil War.   400

STAMPER,Charles William.What I Know (1913). Experiences as chauffeur and attendant to Edward VI; anecdotes of king's public life & journeys.   401

STAMPER, Joseph. Less than the Dust (1932). Wanderings and adventures of a tramp; squalid life; poor.   402

STANFORD,Sir Charles Villiers. Studies and Memories (1908); Pages from an Unwritten Diary (1914); Interludes (1922). Dublin boyhood; Irish musical life; London music and theatre; work as a composer; musical performers and movements from sixties; reminiscences of Brahms, Joachim, Tennyson.   403

STANHOPE, Aubrey. On the Track (L. 1914). Special correspondent for N.Y. Herald;England and Europe; adventures scoops; celebrities.   404

STANHOPE, Lady Hester. Memoirs (L. 1845); Travels (1846). Her adventures related to her physician; travels and excitements in the Near East by Circe of the Desert; social life.   405

STANIFORTH, Samson. Lives of Early Methodist Preachers, ed. Thomas Jackson (1837) II. A Sheffield man's life as itinerant Methodist preacher in the 18th Century; Yorkshire mainly.   406

STANLEY,Arthur G. The Smallest Drum (1936). Childhood memories; his life at Peckham and Nunhead.   407

STANLEY,Cecil Sloane. Reminiscences of a Midshipman's life (1893). Childhood; naval cadet in fifties; service in Mediterranean; Crimean war & naval engagements.   408

STANLEY, Henry Morton. How I Found Livingstone (1872); Through the Dark Continent (L.1878); In Darkest Africa 1890); My Early Travels (1895). Travels and adventures in America & Asia; explorations in Central Africa; residence with Livingstone & travels with him; jungle life; expedition to find Livingstone; native life.   409

STANLEY, Lady Maria Josepha. Early Married Life (1899). Wife of Cheshire squire in early century; country life and husband's activities; politics; & England during Napoleonic wars.   410

STANLEY, Monica M. My Diary in Serbia (1916). Personal experiences in Balkans during WW1.   411

STANLEY,William Ford. Life and Work (1911). Life of founder and head of a firm of instrument makers; his inventions; Technical schools. 412

STANMORE,Arthur Hamilton-Gordon,1st Baron. Fiji (Edin. 1879). Administrative work in Fijis in 70's; society & private life. 413

STANNARD, M. Memoirs of a Professional Lady Nurse(1873). Marriage and business failure; work as nurse; with husband in California goldrush;return to nursing after his murder; her life in England and USA. 414

STANNARD,Russell.With the Dictators of Fleet Street (1934). Work as journalist from 1912; Daily Mail; John o' London; Sunday Express; journalists & novelists. 415

STANTON, William Henry. The Journal (1929). Life and work of Deal pilot & boatman in 19th Century; life at sea; smuggling and piracy; helping vessels in distress at Deal; attractive, simple record. 416

STARK, Freya. Traveller's Prelude (1950). Her family; early life, England, France, Italy; family travels; mountaineering; service as nurse WW1; Italian campaign; Caporetto; travels in Arabia; solitude. 417

STARK, Malcolm. Pulse of the World (1915). Fleet Street journalist;Glasgow Herald; London and Scottish scene and political and social movements of preceding forty years; his work as a novelist. 418

STARKIE, Enid. Lady's Child (1941). Her girlhood in Ireland; daughter of British civil servant; education; Oxford studies and troubles; a genteel life; WW1. 419

STARKIE, Walter F. Don Gypsy (1936) Waveless Plain (1938).The holidays & travels of Irish professor; fiddling in Spain; adventures in Italy. 420

STARR, Leonora. Colonel's Lady (L. 1937).Social life in military circles in India;Staff College; clubs and society in Quetta; Indian life. 421

STATHAM,Francis Reginald. My Life's Record (1901). Liberal freethinker's fight for justice; journalism; Liver-

pool and Edinburgh; South Africa and fight for negro rights. 422

STATHAM, John. Indian Recollections (1832). Life and work as a missionary in India; education; village life and disasters; animal adventures. 423

STATHAM, Louisa Maria. Memoir, by John Statham (1842).Includes extracts from diary; religious and family life of wife of Baptist minister at Reading sickness; views on entertainments.424

STAUNTON,Sir George Thomas. Memoirs (1856). Public life and work of politician and diplomat to 1845; M.P. for South Hants and Portsmouth; Corn Laws embassy to Pekin. 425

STAYLEY, George. Life and Opinions (Dublin, 1762). Boyhood at Burton-on-Trent;school; life in Ireland; career on Dublin stage; theatrical life; his writings; quarrels; religion. 426

STEAD, James. Treasure Trek (1936). Hunting for buried treasure in Bolivia and Central America; life in Canadian wilds. 427

STEADMAN,William. Memoir, by Thomas Steadman (1838). Contains early autobiography of education and Baptist religious life; late 18th Century. 428

STEBBING, Edward Percy. Jungle By-Ways in India (1911);Diary of a Sporting Naturalist (1920). His career in the Forestry Department in India; big game hunting; natural history. 429

STEDMAN, Henry W. Battle of the Flames(1942). Bombing of London; work in Auxiliary fire Service, WW2. 430

STEED,Henry Wickham. Through Thirty Years (1924). Study in Germany; work as journalist; Times; personal history of Europe and English public life to 1922. 431

STEEL, Frank. Ditcher's Row (1939). Victorian family life among impoverished working classes; odd jobs; slum life;emigration to Canada; sociological interest. 432

STEEL,Flora Annie. Garden of Fidelity(1930). Girlhood in fifties; offi-

cial life in India with husband; social life and social work;the place of
women; work as author; later life in
Wales.   433

STEELE, Elizabeth. Memoirs of Mrs.
Sophia Baddeley (1787). Largely about
her own life as companion to the Drury
Lane actress (may be same people); an
account of love affairs,high life and
society in London.   434

STEELE, Sir Robert. Marine Officer
(1840). Service in Marines in Napoleonic and Peninsular Wars; Nile; Cape
St. Vincent; Nore; Trafalgar; Nelson;
his personal activities.   435

STEELE, Thomas. Musings of an Old
Schoolmaster (1932). Forty years as a
teacher at Bradfield and eight as student at Cranleigh;experiences of masters,boys, discipline, curricula, and
amusements.   436

STEEVENS, Col. Charles. Reminiscences of My Military Life (Winchester,
1878).Essex man's account of his army
service, 1795-1818; Egypt; Peninsular
War; personal affairs.   437

STEEVENS, George Warrington. With
Kitchener (1898). Journalist; account
of the expedition to Khartoum.   438

STEGGALL, John Henry. Real History
of a Suffolk Man (1857). Boyhood at
Needham;escape from school to gypsies
and later adventures as soldier, sailor,Cambridge student; life as curate
in Suffolk; family life.   439

STEIN,Sir Mark Aurel.On Alexander's
Track in the Indus (1929). Government
exploration on Northwest Frontier;and
history, antiquities, Buddhist life &
travel notes.   440

STENHOUSE, Mrs. Fanny. An Englishwoman in Utah (1880).Jerseywoman converted to Mormonism; her experiences
in Salt Lake City; polygamy. Published
first as "Tell It All" (Hartford,Conn.
1874).   441

STENT,George Carter. Scraps from
My Sabretasche(1882).Military life in
England and India;engagements; social
life; adventures.   442

/STEPHEN,Sir George7. Adventures of
an Attorney in Search of a Practice
(1839). Early days as a young lawyer,
London life; cases and clients; humorous and fictionalized.   443

STEPHEN, Sir Leslie. Some Early Impressions (1924). Mostly about his 14
years at Cambridge; journalism; criticism; work for DNB; literature; public affairs; Victorian life.   444

STEPHENSON, Sarah. Memoirs of the
Life (1807). Life in Cumberland; Qua-
ker ministry and travels;visit to the
USA, where she died.   445

STERN, Lt.Col. Sir Albert G. Tanks
(1919). His experiences in the development and use of the tank in WW1; an
account of experiments.   446

STERN, Gladys Bronwyn. Another Part
of the Forest (1941); Trumpet Volun-
tary (1944); Benefits Forgot (1949).
Childhood in 90's; career as a writer
European and American travels;friend-
ships; Gielgud; Waugh; gratitude for
past benefits and misfortunes;remini-
scences and meditations.   447

STEUART, Daniel Rankin. Bygone Days
(Edin. 1936). Scottish boyhood; chemistry studies at Edinburgh and Munich
and career as industrial chemist;fam-
ily life.   448

STEUART, Mary E. Everyday Life on a
Ceylon Cocoa Estate (1905). Domestic
and social life in Ceylon;estate work
and labour problems;native life; from
a woman's viewpoint.   449

STEUART, R. H. J. March, Kind Com-
rade (1931). Catholic chaplain's service in France during WW1; with Highland Light Infantry.   450

STEVENS, Alfred A. Recollections of
a Bookman (1933). His career in three
famous London bookshops; the trade; &
anecdotes of books and writers.   451

STEVENS, Gerald P. Ramblings of a
Rolling Stone (1924). Westminster and
Cambridge;law studies and practice in
Malaya and South Africa; social life;
sport.   452

STEVENS,Thomas P. Cassock & Surplus (1947). Incidents in his clerical career, mainly in London; Hon. Canon of Southwark; left-wing politics; working class life; reform.　　　453

STEVENSON,David. Fifty Years on the London & North-Western Railway (1891) Life and work of a railway man, 1837-1890.　　　454

STEVENSON,Mrs. Esmé Scott. Our Home in Cyprus (1880). Domestic and social life of wife of commissioner of Kyrenia;Turkish and Cypriot life; women's life.　　　455

STEVENSON, Frederick James. Journal 1867-69; extensive travels in Brazil, Peru, Argentina, Chile, Patagonia and Bolivia; exploration and adventures. A Traveller of the Sixties, ed. Douglas Timins (1929).　　　456

/STEVENSON,George Skelton/. Reminiscences of a Student's Life in Edinburgh, by Alisma (Edin.1918). Student life and medical and scientific study in Edinburgh in 70's;Lister and other teachers.　　　457

STEVENSON,James Arthur Radford. Din of a Smith (1932). Journalist; search for jobs; how he became a blacksmith; his smithy in Devon;wrought iron work and design; aesthetics.　　　458

STEVENSON, John. Soldier in Time of War (1841). Service in Foot Guards at Copenhagen and in Peninsular War;conversion and Methodist ministry in army simple and interesting.　　　459

STEVENSON, Robert Louis. Memoirs of Himself (Philadelphia, 1912). Account of his childhood;dreams; fears; drawing; sense of sin.　　　460

STEVENSON, William Bennet. Historical and Descriptive Narrative (1825). Twenty years in South America; travel in Peru,Chile, Colombia; Peruvian War of Independence; Cochrane.　　　461

STEWART,Alexander. The Life, edited Albert Peel (1948). Boy at sea; ten years as prisoner of France during the Napoleonic wars;later life as preacher.　　　462

STEWART, Col. Arthur Easdale. Tiger and Other Game (1927). Experiences of a big-game hunter in India.　　　463

STEWART, Charles. Haud Immemor (Edinburgh, 1901). His work as a lawyer in Edinburgh and London; social life, second half of century.　　　464

STEWART,Col.Charles Edward. Through Persia in Disguise (1910). His military service in the Mutiny; political work in Persia from 1880;intelligence work on Afghan frontier.　　　465

STEWART, Sir Donald. Military diary 1857;details of siege of Delhi; vivid picture of camp life; later experiences in Abyssinian expedition. Account of His Life, ed. George R. Elsmie (L. 1903).　　　466

STEWART, Major Herbert A. From Mons to Loos (1916).His work as supply officer in WW1; personal account of the retreat.　　　467

STEWART, Lt. J.Diary, 1898; service on an expedition against the Mendes in Sierra Leone rebellion. Sierra Leone Studies, XVII (1932).　　　468

STEWART, Maj.Gen. Sir Norman Robert My Service Days (1908). Military life in India, Afghanistan and China; service in Boxer rebellion; social life; sport.　　　469

STIBBE, Philip. Return via Rangoon (1947). WW2 experiences with Wingate in Burma; Japanese captivity; lively and picturesque.　　　470

STIBBONS, Fred. Norfolk's Caddie Poet (Holt, Norfolk, 1923). Ploughboy in Norfolk;odd jobs; work as a caddie wide reading; his verses. Copy, Norwich P.L.　　　471

STIGAND, Capt. Chauncey Hugh. Hunting the Elephant (1930). His thirteen years of travel and hunting in Africa Theodore Roosevelt; problems of African unity.　　　472

STILL, John. A Prisoner in Turkey (1920). WW1 experiences; his capture at Kut; prison experiences.　　　473

STIRLING, Anna Maria D. W.   Life's
Little Day (1934). Childhood; court &
social life in London in second half
of 19th Century; literary society and
anecdotes.   474

STIRLING,Edward. Old Drury Lane (L.
(1881). Southwark childhood; life as
actor,writer, manager; Drury Lane and
theatrical fashions; fairs; shows; reminiscences of Kean, etc.   475

STIRLING,John. Fifty Years with the
Rod (1929). Trout and salmon fishing;
Scotland; techniques.   476

STIRLING, W.Edward.Something to De-
clare (1942). Manager of English theatre abroad in 20's and 30's; tours;
repertory; theatre life.   477

STIRREDGE, Elizabeth.   Strength in
Weakness Manifest(1711). Herts Quaker
in later 17th Century; spiritual life
and observances; persecution; wickedness of "priests".   478

STIRTON, John.   Mirrors of Memory
(Aberdeen, 1923). Boyhood in Scotland
and education at St.Andrews; ministry
in Scotland; pleasant memories of his
reading, antiquarianism, country life
and Scottish society.   479

STOBART,Mabel Annie St. Clair. Mir-
acles and Adventures (1935).Sport and
travels in Europe and Africa; her Red
Cross work in Balkan War and WW1,Ser-
bia; her books and lectures.   480

STOBO, Maj. Robert. Memoirs (1800).
Adventures of soldier-of-fortune; may
be pirated fiction; cp. Benjamin Mead
Some Hidden Sources of Fiction(Philadelphia, 1909).   481

STOCK, Eugene. My Recollections (L.
1909). London boyhood in 40's; social
and religious work and travel for the
Church Missionary Society; religious
developments; Sunday Schools.   482

STOCK, John. Confessions of an Old
Smoker (1872). London apprentice; his
smoking and reform; ministry; lapses
into smoking; spiritual troubles of a
man tempted to tobacco.   483

STOCKDALE, Percival. Memoirs (1809)
Education; ministry; chaplain to Lord

Berwick;translator, poet and literary
hack; Dr.Johnson and literary society
in later 18th Century.   484

STOCKLEY, William C. Fifty Years of
Music (Birmingham, 1913). Work as an
organist and singing teacher in Birmingham from 1850;musical scene; Elgar
and Parry. Birmingham P.L.   485

STOCQUELER,Joachim Hayward. Memoirs
of a Journalist (Bombay, 1873). Education; theatrical ambitions; military
career in India; work as a journalist
in London and India; literature, theatre, celebrities; anecdotes. Copy in
India Office Library.   486

STODART, Robert. Travel diary 1626-
1629; with Cotton's mission to Persia
adventures; observations; interesting
language. The Journal, ed.Sir Denison
Ross (1935).   487

STODDART,James Henry. Recollections
of a Player (N. Y. 1902). Boyhood in
Scotland; early years on the stage in
England and Scotland; later career in
American theatre.   488

STODDART, Jane T. My Harvest of the
Years(1938). Girlhood in Kelso; study
in Germany;religious journalism; work
on British Weekly; Free Church work &
ministers.   489

STODDART,Thomas Tod.Angling Reminiscences (Edin.1837); An Angler's Rambles (Edin.1866). Fishing in Scotland
done in Walton style.   490

STOKER, George. With "The Unspeak-
ables" (1878). Experiences of surgeon
with Turkish army; the Russo-Turkish
War, 1876-8; medical work and difficulties.   491

STOKER, Com. Henry Hew Gordon Dacre
Straws in the Wind (1925). Career in
the navy; service in submarines, WW1;
lighthearted reminiscences.   492

STOKES, Adrian Durham.   Inside Out
(1947).Self-analysis of an artist and
his relation to the outer world; emotions,perceptions, and aesthetic contacts with external things; Cezanne;
interesting but often obscure.   493

STOKES, Sewell. Monologue (1934). A

journalist's adventures and work; his
meetings with celebrities in the arts
politics and crime; journalistic eth-
ics and problems.   494

STOLL, Dennis. I Give Myself Away
(1936).Work as musical journalist and
conductor; his compositions; ballet &
musical life; callow.   495

STONE, Christopher R. Christopher
Stone Speaking (1933). His career as
broadcaster with BBC;reminiscences of
a genteel disk-jockey.   496

STOPES, Marie Charlotte Carmichael.
A Journal From Japan (1910). Travels
in Japan, 1907-9; work on fossils and
notes on people and places.   497

STOREY, G. A. Sketches from Memory
(1899).His work as sculptor and painter; study in France; Victorian painters; travel; family life.   498

STOREY, Gladys. All Sorts of People
(1929). Work as painter;reminiscences
of Victorian art and artists;literary
and theatrical friends; Thackeray and
Dickens.   499

STORRS,Sir Ronald. Orientations (L.
1937). His career as diplomat; work &
travels in Egypt, Palestine, Cyprus,
1881-1932; politics, war, the Arab
revolt, WW1; Arab society and ideas;
a valuable record.   500

STORY,Christopher. Brief Account of
the Life (1726). A Quaker ministry in
England, Ireland, Scotland; troubles;
controversies.   501

STORY, George. Lives of Early Methodist Preachers, ed. Thomas Jackson,
III (1838). Ministry and travels of a
Yorkshire Methodist in second half of
18th Century.   502

STORY, Janet L. Early Reminiscences
(Glasgow, 1911); Later Reminiscences
(Glasgow,1913). Social, religious and
academic life in Glasgow from fifties;
theatre, literature, college.   503

STORY, Sommerville. Twenty Years in
Paris (1927). Life of a foreign cor-
respondent;Bohemian life; society and
WW1; celebrities.   504

STORY, Thomas. Journal of the Life
(Newcastle, 1747). Spiritual life and
ministry of a Quaker in 17th and 18th
Centuries;controversy; sufferings and
imprisonment.   505

ANON. Story of a Peninsular Veteran
(n.d.). Irish youth in army;rebellion
in Ireland; sergeant in Wellington's
campaigns; later service in England;
conversion to Methodism;work at Chelsea Royal Military Asylum.   506

STOTHARD,Anna Eliza (Bray). Memoirs
(1823); Autobiography(1884). Memories
and anecdotes of old people, heard in
her childhood;life in the country and
marriage to Stothard the painter; her
literary career and novels; anecdotes
of literary men; Southey.   507

STOTHERD, Col. Edward A. W. Sabre &
Saddle(1933). Military service in the
cavalry in Burma,India, Africa, China
and in WW1; sport.   508

STOTHERT, Capt. William. Narrative
of the Principal Events (L.1812). His
service with Foot Guards in Peninsular War; account of campaigns; rather
impersonal.   509

STOTT, Grace. Twenty-Six Years of
Missionary Work (1897). Life and work
of a missionary in China, 1866-92;and
Chinese life.   510

STOUGHTON, John. Recollections of a
Long Life(1894). London childhood and
education;work as Congregational minister in Windsor and Kensington; Dean
Stanley and other friends;church life
and personalities.   511

STOUT,William. Autobiography (1852)
Lancs boyhood in 1670's; apprentice &
successful grocer;Quaker religion and
public affairs; mostly business,trade
and family life in Lancaster. The Ms.
is in Manchester Central Library. 512

STRACHAN,Arthur W.Mauled by a Tiger
(1933). Adventures of a big-game hunter in India; perils.   513

STRACHAN,John. Explorations and Adventures (1888). A geographer's three
journeys in New Guinea;scientific observations; missionaries; natives and

native life; adventures.   514

STRACHAN, William. A Brief Autobiography (Croydon, 1860). Scottish boyhood; study at St. Andrews; classics
master in London;ordination; ministry
in Bahamas; later study in Cambridge;
West Indian affairs.   515

STRACHEY, John. Post D. (1941). His
experiences as an air-raid warden during WW2; London Blitz.   516

STRACHEY, John St.Loe. Adventure of
Living (1922); River of Life (1924).
Education; Oxford; career as journalist; Cornhill and Spectator; literary
life and politics; the great men from
late Victorian period onwards.   517

/STRAIGHT, Sir Douglas/. Harrow Recollections of an Old Harrovian, by S.
Daryl (1867). His schooldays; cricket
and football; curriculum; masters and
boys; speech days, etc.   518

STRANGE,Lt.Col. Louis Arbon. Recollections of an Airman(1933). Training
and combat service with RFC in WW1 in
France.   519

STRATHMORE, Mary E. Bowes, Countess
of. Confessions (1793). Her loves and
sins and imprudences reprinted from a
deposition; interesting.   520

STRATTON, J.   Rural Reminiscences
(Winchester, 1901). Farm life, work &
social conditions; Wilts and Hants in
the first half of 19th Century. Wilts
Archaeol. Soc., Devizes.   521

/STRAUSS, G. L. M./. Reminiscences
of an Old Bohemian (1882). Schooling;
travels in Europe; work as journalist
from 30's;Franco-Prussian war; Savage
and other clubs; theatre, literature,
law; celebrities.   522

STREATFIELD, Frank N. Reminiscences
of an Old 'Un (1911);Sporting Reminiscences (1913).Eton and Heidelberg in
50's;commerce in India and Argentine;
military service in Zulu War; work as
resident magistrate in Bechuanaland &
sporting adventures.   523

STREET,Arthur George.Farmer's Glory
(1932); Wessex Wins (1941); Landmarks
(1949). Work as a dairy-farmer, Hants

Wilts,Western Canada; farming old and
new; mechanization, economics, traditions; conflict of old and new; journalism and novels; BBC work.   524

STREET,George Slyth (ed.). Autobiography of a Boy (1894). Public school
and Oxford;love affairs; family troubles;debts; life with social outcasts
and emigration to Canada;life of Victorian eccentric and rebel.   525

STRETTON,Charles. Memoirs of a Chequered Life (1862). Schooling; sport;
poaching; amours; adventures in Ireland and Australia; goldmining, sheep
farming,frontier life; lively account
of adventures from 1810.   526

STRINGER,Mabel E. Golfing Reminiscences (1924). Long career in county &
championship golf; her games; famous
players.   527

STRONG, W. M. "Some Personal Experiences in British New Guinea." Royal
Anthrop. Soc. XLIX (1919). Life among
native races; their customs.   528

STRUDWICK,Herbert.Twenty-Five Years
Behind the Stumps (1926). Memories of
the great Surrey and England wicketkeeper; panorama of cricket.   529

STRUTHERS, John. "My Own Life" pre-
fixed to Poetical Works (Edin. 1850).
Summary account of early life, struggles as poet, life in Edinburgh, from
late 18th Century.   530

STRUTT, Col. Joseph Holden. Charles
R. Strutt, Strutt Family (1939). Contains autobiography; Winchester, Oxford from 1760's; country life, sport
and politics in Maldon;service in the
Essex militia.   531

STRUTT, William Maitland. Reminiscences of a Musical Amateur (L. 1915).
Autobiography and opinions of music &
opera by a listener.   532

STUART, Alexander Moody. Memoir, by
Kenneth M. Stuart (1899). Autobiographical passages;Paisley childhood and
religious study in Glasgow and Edinburgh; ministry and missionary travel
lives of parishioners.   533

STUART, Lt.Col. Charles. Journal of

a Residence in Northern Persia (1854)
Experiences in Persia while secretary
to British ambassador,1825-6; Persian
scene, politics, people.　　　　534

STUART, Francis. Things to Live For
(N.Y. 1935). Irish social life in the
country; politics, rebellion, sport &
Irish characters.　　　　535

STUART, James. Reminiscences (1911)
Education in Madras, St. Andrews, and
Cambridge; scholarship; professor of
Applied Mechanics at Cambridge; work
in Parliament and L.C.C.; good detail
of Cambridge life;adult education and
business in Norfolk; Dickens; Josephine Butler.　　　　536

STUART, James Montgomery. Reminiscences and Essays(1884). Literary life
and meetings with Macaulay.　　537

STUART,Col. William Keir. Reminiscences of a Soldier (1874). Service as
ranker and officer in West Indies and
India; his comrades; experiences with
dreams and superstitions.　　538

STUART-GLENNIE,John Stuart. Pilgrim
Memories (1875). Travel with Buckle,
the historian, through North Africa &
Asia Minor in 60's; philosophy, religion, the law of history, humanitarianism, holy places.　　　　539

STUBBS, Francis William. Extracts
from the Diary (Woolwich, 1894). Army
experiences of a subaltern in Mutiny;
military affairs in India. India Office Library.　　　　540

STUBBS, George. Notes for the Life;
jottings on the life and career of the
18th Century painter. MS in Liverpool
Public Library, Eq. 466.　　541

STUDLEY, J.T. Journal of a Sporting
Nomad(1912). Hunting in Canada and in
tropical Africa; whaling, sealing and
tarpon-fishing in Arctic.　　542

STURGE, Elizabeth. Reminiscences of
My Life (Bristol, 1928). Childhood in
Bristol in 50's; Quaker life; educa-
tion; social work; women's movement;
Octavia Hill and Mary Clifford. Copy,
Exeter City Library.　　　　543

STURGE, Joseph. The West Indies in

1837 (1838). Philanthropist's visit
to Antigua, Montserrat, Jamaica, with
Thomas Harvey; studies of slavery and
negro life.　　　　544

STURGE, Mary Charlotte. Some Little
Quakers (1906). Quaker childhood mid-
19th Century; Bristol; family & sur-
roundings of childhood.　　545

STURGE, William. Some Recollections
(1893). Quaker religious life;Bristol
scene;social work and working classes
and temperance movement;early days of
Victoria.　　　　546

STURT, George.　A Small Boy in the
Sixties (1927). Life in a Surrey village;scenes and sensations of boyhood
and the country life; good.　　547

ANON. A Subaltern in America (Philadelphia, 1833).Lively account of his
experiences in British Army during the
war of 1812.　　　　548

SUB-INSPECTOR.　Two Years with the
Specials (1917). Service with Special
Police during WW1.　　　　549

SUFFIELD,Charles Harbord, 5th Baron
My Memories(1913). Boyhood in Norfolk
from 1830's; military service, mostly
in India;social life and sport; anecdotes of celebrities.　　　　550

SULIVAN, George L.　Dhow Chasing in
Zanzibar Waters (1873). Experience of
a naval officer engaged in suppression
of slave trade in 50's and 60's;naval
blockades and chases.　　　551

SULLIVAN,Alexander Martin. Old Ireland (L. 1927). Childhood in Ireland;
education;career as lawyer and King's
Counsel;political life; opposition to
the IRA.　　　　552

SULLIVAN, John William Nairn.　But
for the Grace of God(1932). Intellectual and emotional conflicts of scientist and author;adventures in science
literature, love and war.　　553

SULLIVAN, Timothy Daniel. Recollections of Troubled Times (Dublin,1905)
Work as journalist; The Nation; Irish
politics in second half of 19th Century; Parnell; O'Connell: only partly
personal.　　　　554

SULLY, James. My Life and Friends (1918). Study in London and Germany in 60's; philosophy and psychology; professor at University of London; scholarship; his literary and philosopher friends.   555

SUMBEL, Leah. Memoirs (1811). Life and work of actress in provincial and London theatres from 1780's; marriage and life in high society.   556

SUMMERSBY, Kathleen. Eisenhower Was My Boss(1948). Irish girl; driving in WW2; driver and hostess for Eisenhower; celebrities she met; her success story and secondhand glory.   557

SURTEES, Robert Smith. Robert Smith Surtees, by Himself and E. D. Cuming (Edin. 1924). Autobiographical notes; schooldays in London and Brighton in early 19th Century; sport; travel and journalism; his sporting novels; literary friends; Thackeray etc.   558

SURTEES, William. Twenty-Five Years in the Rifle Brigade (1833). Military career from 1795; Quartermaster; service in Peninsular War and in America in 1812 war.   559

SUTCLIFFE, Herbert. For England and Yorkshire (1935). Career of the great batsman; county and Test cricket; his partners, captains, games.   560

SUTCLIFFE, Thomas. Sixteen Years in Chile and Peru (1841). Life and work as Governor of Juan Fernandez;Chilean war of independence;politics in South America, 1822-39.   561

SUTHERLAND, Halliday. Arches of the Years (1933); A Time to Keep (1934); In My Path (1936). Childhood and education; medical work and research and advocacy of eugenics;social criticism naval service in W.W.1; fight against consumption; vigorous and lively. 562

SUTHERLAND, James. Adventures of an Elephant Hunter (1912). His romantic life and adventures during 18 years as hunter in Africa; snakes.   563

SUTRO, Alfred. Celebrities and Simple Souls (1933). Work as playwright and novelist; critical reminiscences of famous authors;social life & clubs

in London; the theatre.   564

SUTTON,Barry. Way of a Pilot (1942) Experiences of RAF flyer;service as a squadron-leader in WW2;Battle of Britain;hospital experiences after being shot down.   565

SUTTON,Gen. Francis Arthur. One-Arm Sutton (1933). Experiences as soldier and adventurer; engineering in Mexico and prospecting in Siberia;service in WW1; Russian Revolution and civil war in China; sport.   566

SWAFFER, Hannen. Really Behind the Scenes (1929); My Greatest Story (L. 1945). Work and observations as drama critic; theatre life; psychic adventures; spiritualism and supernatural; flimsy.   567

SWAINE, Gen. Sir Leopold. Camp and Chancery (1926). Service in the Rifle Brigade and as military attaché, from 1858;Russia, Turkey, Germany, Canada; Franco-Prussian War; social life. 568

SWAN, Andrew. The Remarkable Story (1933). Dictated adventures of Scotch seaman; hairbreadth escapes from pirates, cannibals, shipwreck during his 40 odd years in South Pacific.   569

SWANN, Alfred James. Fighting the Slave-Hunters in Central Africa(1910) His 26 years in Central Africa; work and adventures around the great lakes and overturning of slave-trade.   570

SWANSTON, Sgt. Paul. Memoirs (1840) Personal adventures of a soldier during Peninsular War; battles,captivity on land and sea;picaresque and may be fictional.   571

SWANSTON, Major William Oliver. My Journal (Calcutta, 1858). Experiences of a cavalry officer in Indian Mutiny the march to Lucknow.   572

SWANWICK, Helena Maria. I Have Been Young (1935). Social life, politics, women's movement, journalism, literature from 80's; editor of Foreign Affairs.   573

SWAYNE, Capt. Harold George Charles Seventeen Trips through Somaliland(L. 1895). Exploration from 1885;big-game hunting;government and politics; native life.   574

SWAYNE,William S. Parson's Plea - sure (Edin. 1934). School and Oxford; parish work in country; Walsall, Manchester;Bishop of Lincoln; family and friends; good and happy things.   575

SWEARS,Herbert. When All's Said and Done (1937). Work in Bank of England; work in play-producing societies; reminiscences of great actors.   576

SWEENEY, John. At Scotland Yard (L. 1904). Career in police and CID; his work as bodyguard to Victoria;   jewel robberies; anarchists, etc.   577

ANON. The Sweepings of an Old Broom (1936).London girl's travels; life in Australian goldfields, Detroit, China and India; marriage; family.   578

SWETTENHAM, Sir Frank Athelstane. Malay Sketches (1913); Footprints in Malaya (1942). Administrative career in Malaya, 1871-1914; politics, law & native life;travel, social and sport; his later work for the government, in England.   579

SWINBURNE,A.J. Memories of a School Inspector (1911). Genial account of a career in Lancs and Suffolk schools & of ways of teachers, pupils, councils and their humours.   580

SWINBURNE, Algernon Charles. Autobiographical Notes (1920). The poet's war with publishers;mostly in letters to Watts-Dunton.   581

SWINNERTON,Frank Arthur. Swinnerton (1936); Tokefield Papers (1949). London boyhood; office boy; publishing; career as writer;literary friendships Bennett, Wells; Reform Club; urbane & pleasant memories of an elegant, easy life.   582

SWINTON, Alan A.C. Autobiographical and Other Writings (1930). Edinburgh boyhood; Fettes School; career as an electrical engineer and contractor in shipwork; engineering and scientific celebrities.   583

SWINTON, Gen.Sir Ernest. Eyewitness (1932). Army career in Engineers; Sth

Africa;Russo-Japanese War; originator of tanks; adoption of tank in WW1 and work as commander of Tank Corps;drama of the new weapon.   584

SWINTON,Philip Cunliffe-Lister, 1st Viscount. I Remember (1948). Politics before WW2; Conservatism; the political issues of WW2.   585

SYDENHAM OF COMBE, George Sydenham Clark, Baron. My Working Life (1927). Military career from 1870; Sudan; War Office; work on ordnance and imperial defence; journalism.   586

SYDENHAM, John. History of the Sydenham Family, by G.F.S.Sydenham (East Molesey, 1928). Whimsical and amusing autobiography, 1721-1794; boyhood and education at Tiverton;estate work and country affairs in Devon;domestic and social life; good.   587

SYKES,Capt. Clement Arthur. Service and Sport on the Tropical Nile (1903) Military life with native troops; the re-occupation of Nilotic province;and hunting in Uganda.   588

SYKES,Gen. Sir Frederick Hugh. From Many Angles (1942). Military career; Boer War, India, War Office and Staff College; with RAF and civil aviation; Governor of Bombay; political career in House of Commons.   589

SYKES, Joseph. Introduction to his Selected Works (Brighton, 1853-5), I. Boyhood in Bath; Oxford in 30's; social life and conviviality; Bath theatre;his poems and literary reputation and study of French writers; health & fast life.   590

SYKES, Major Percy Molesworth. Ten Thousand Miles in Persia (1902). Work and extensive travels as British consul in Persia; business, politics and communications; mountaineering.   591

SYMES, Sir Stewart. Tour of Duty(L. 1946). Forty years as soldier and administrator; India, Boer War, Egypt, Aden, Tanganyika, Palestine; Governor of Sudan; sage views on colonial administration.   592

SYMONDS, John Addington. John Addington Symonds, by Horatio Browne (L.

1895). Autobiography of boyhood; Harrow and Balliol; reading and literary tastes; later autobiographical notes in his diary; life as writer and critic;his health. Our Life in the Swiss Highlands(1892) contains essays written by Symonds and his daughter. 593

SYMONDSON, F. W. H. Two Years Abaft the Mast (1876). Life as apprentice-seaman;adventures and observations in the South Seas. 594

SYMONS, Arthur. Spiritual Adventure (1905); Confessions(1930). Family and country life; spiritual bewilderment; unhappy childhood; Nonconformity; his rebellion against religion; literary and language studies;insanity; escape into writing and art; good. 595

SYNNOTT,Rev.Edward Fitzgerald. Five Years' Hell (1920).His misery in Sussex parish; farming troubles & malice of parishioners;debunking of supposed beauty of country life & people. 596

SYRRETT, Netta. The Sheltering Tree (1939). Victorian Swansea and London; theatre,literature, painting, ballet, her work as novelist;friendships; and WW1 experiences. 597

TACKLINE. Holiday Sailor(1944). His life in the navy; chatty account; WW2 experiences. 1

TAFT, Mary. Memoirs of the Life (L. 1827). Religious life and conversion; Methodist labours in Lancashire,Yorkshire, Ripon. Copy in Methodist Book Room. 2

TAIT,George. Autobiography (Halifax 1884). Life and work of deaf mute,who first instructed the deaf and dumb in Halifax. 3

TALBOT,Beatrice. And That's No Lie (Cambridge, Mass., 1946). Early life, County Roscommon and County Kildare & sport and country life. 4

TALBOT, Edward Stuart. Memories of Early Life (1924). Bishop of Winchester's boyhood; religious life; Oxford in 60's; foundation of Keble College;

religion and scholarship; Pusey, Mill and Tractarian Movement. 5

TALFOURD, Sir Thomas Noon. "Gleams of Long Past Life;" "Private and Personal Memoranda."Sketchy jottings on his education and law career, 1797 to 1846; extensive jottings on law work, life and work in literary and dramatic circles, 1841-50; Dickens & other literary friends; social views; very interesting. MSS, Reading Public Library. 6

TALLENTS,Sir Stephen G. Man and Boy (1943). Boyhood; Harrow,Oxford, Grenoble; career as civil servant; Marine Dept.; Labour Exchanges; WW1 work at Ministry of Food and in munitions;administration at Riga after WW1;social work at Toynbee; politics; good. 7

TANGYE, Derek. Time Was Mine (1940) World travels of a young journalist & his evolution from gossip writing to seriousness. 8

TANGYE,Sir Richard. One and All (L. 1889). Cornish boyhood;career as Birmingham industrialist; growth of the Cornwall Works;industry, business and education and culture in Birmingham in Victorian period;career of a selfmade businessman. 9

TANNER, Henry. Life and Writings of (1807). Autobiography and some diary; life as brickmaker in Plymouth; sins; conversion by Whitefield; his spiritual wrestlings; work in the Methodist ministry. 10

TANNER, William. Memoir (1868). His early life in Bristol and later business as papermaker in Cheddar; Quaker life and ministry;work for temperance societies. 11

TASWELL, William. Autobiography and Anecdotes (Camden Soc. Misc. II, No.8 1853).Brief life of rector of Newington,Surrey, 1651-82; parish life; the Great Fire; scrappy. 12

TATE,Maurice. My Cricketing Reminiscences (1934). Career of the Sussex and England all-rounder; games, tours and triumphs; WW1 service. 13

TATLOW,Joseph. Fifty Years of Railroad Life (1920). Rise from jr. clerk to general manager;Irish railways and railway life and work from 60's.   14

TAUBMAN, Nathaniel. Memoirs of the British Fleets (1710). Naval chaplain and his experiences in naval warfare; Western Mediterranean; Portuguese and Spanish scenes.   15

TAWKE, Miss. Hunting Recollections (Rochford, 1914). Her experiences of foxhunting, largely with Essex Union; anecdotes of hunters and runs.   16

TAYLER, Charles Benjamin. Facts in a Clergyman's Life (1849). Experience and lessons of country parson;Suffolk parish life.   17

TAYLER,John Lionel. Story of a Life (1931).Victorian family and religious background; sex, romance, art, music, frustrations;study; life as Unitarian minister and as a doctor;emotions and wild opinions on everything.   18

TAYLER, William. Thirty-Eight Years in India (1881). Career in the Bengal Civil Service from 1829; commissioner of Patna; postal service; Hindu life; Anglo-Indian society; diaries.   19

TAYLOR,Algernon. Memories of a Student (1895). Music from 50's; architecture, sociology, books; Mill; Victorian celebrities.   20

TAYLOR,Allan K. From a Glasgow Slum (1949).Boyhood poverty in the Gorbals odd jobs; imprisonment; success as a free-lance journalist in Fleet Street lively and confident.   21

TAYLOR, Annie R. Diary, 1892-3; her life and work as a missionary in China; details of great hardships; good. Travel and Adventure,by William Carey (1902).   22

/TAYLOR, Frederick7. Confessions of a Horse Coper, by Ballinasloe (1860). Boyhood in the Hussars; work as horse coper;markets, taverns, sales; lively stories.   23

TAYLOR,George Cavendish. Journal of Adventures (1856). Military affairs & personal experiences in the Crimea and candid views.   24

TAYLOR, George Ledwell. Autobiography (1870).Work and study of an architect; mostly European travels in the early century; notes on cathedral and church architecture.   25

TAYLOR, Mrs. H. M. No One to Blame (1939). A psychological history since babyhood; ambition, frustration, social and political interests.   26

TAYLOR,Harold Robert. Jungle Trader (1939). Life and work as a merchant's clerk in Liberia and Grand Bassa;traders and natives; justice; adventures interesting.   27

TAYLOR, Harry Pearson. A Shetland Parish Doctor (Lerwick, 1949). Fifty years in the Shetlands; medical practice; social life; people.   28

TAYLOR,Henrietta. Scottish Nurse at Work (1920). Lively story of WW1 service in Belgium, France, Italy.   29

TAYLOR, Henry. Memoirs (N. Shields, 1811). Early life as a sailor in mid-18th Century;work for lighthouses and safety at sea; Sailors' Friend.   30

TAYLOR, Sir Henry. Autobiography of (1885). Country boyhood; work as poet and writer to 1875; London scene; society,writers, reform, politics; literary friends; useful.   31

TAYLOR,Gen. Sir Herbert. The Taylor Papers, ed. Ernest Taylor (1913). Includes reminiscences and diaries;work as secretary to George III and William IV; Foreign Office; Royal household & social and political affairs.   32

TAYLOR,Isaac. The Family Pen (1867) Essex clergyman's history of his family; includes chapter on his life and work as clergyman at Ongar.   33

TAYLOR, James Hudson. A Retrospect (1894).Medical and theological training; life and work as a medical missionary at Ningpo from 1854.   34

TAYLOR, James W. In a Country Manse (Edin. 1890). Scottish clerical life at Flisk; theology; the Disruption; & Presbyterian worship and morality;his parishioners.   35

TAYLOR, John. An Account of Some of the Labours (1710).York man's conversion by Fox in 1656;travels in Quaker ministry, England, America, W. Indies and sufferings; imprisonment in Newgate; adventures.   36

TAYLOR,John. History of the Travels and Adventures (1761). Norwich man's experiences in England and abroad, as an opthalmiater; a quack in high society; eye-quack; amusing in the Barnum manner. Cambridge U.L.   37

TAYLOR,John. Records of My Life (L. 1832). Life and anecdotes of journalist, poet, miscellaneous writer, from later 18th Century; editor of Morning Post; coffee-house gossip; actors and literary celebrities.   38

TAYLOR, John. Autobiography (Bath, 1893).Trade and religion in Bath from early century;butcher; alderman; Moravian worship and Sunday schools.Copy Bath P.L.   39

TAYLOR, John. Autobiography (Bolton 1883). Coroner and lawyer in Bolton; formerly an actor; legal, social, religious, theatrical affairs; excessively religious but useful for Lancs. affairs from 40's.   40

TAYLOR, John Henry. Golf: My Life's Work (1943). Career of famous professional golfer;caddie to champion; his games and opponents.   41

TAYLOR, Col. Meadows. Story of My Life (1877). Schooling; his business in Liverpool;service with the Nizam's army in India;work as police superintendent; romantic adventures; Dacoits and Thugs to 1860;Hindu studies; London society;the D'Orsay circle; great career; fascinating.   42

TAYLOR, Peter. Autobiography (Paisley, 1903).Village boyhood; education in Perth; work in Paisley and Kilmarnock, engineering and shipbuilding; a good story of business & workingclass life and friends.   43

TAYLOR,Samuel. Records of an Active Life (L.1886). Work in potteries from childhood; foreman and designer; political and social interests;Mechanics Institutions; penny readings; Cobden;

celebrities; interesting.   44

TAYLOR, Shephard T. Diary of a Norwich Hospital Student (Norwich 1931). Apprentice doctor 1858-60; hospitals, doctors, medical practice before Lister; ingenuous and interesting.   45

TAYLOR,Thomas. Lives of Early Methodist Preachers, ed. Thomas Jackson, III (1838). Life & work of a Yorkshire Methodist from mid 18th Century; travels in North of England; one of the best of its kind.   46

TAYLOR,Thomas E. Running the Blockade (1896). Adventures on a British ship running the blockade from Havana during American Civil War.   47

TAYLOR, Sgt. Maj. William. Scenes & Adventures (1842). Military life and experiences in India; 1838 expedition to Afghanistan.   48

TAYLOR, William. Autobiography of a Highland Minister (1897).Education in Aberdeen; ministry; spiritual wrestlings; his sin and redemption.   49

TEASDALE, Harvey. Life & Adventures (Sheffield, 1881). Clown and comedian publican; converted in Wakefield prison;lively account of circus and theatre life in Yorks and Lancs; religious life later. Sheffield P.L.   50

TEELING, Charles Hemilton. History of the Irish Rebellion (Glasgow 1828) The Irish rebellion of 1798; adventures of a United Irishman in 90's and Irish affairs.   51

TEICHMAN,Eric.Travels of a Consular Officer (Cambridge, 1922). Life, work and travels of a consul in North-West China before WW1; business, economics and politics; Chinese life.   52

TEIGNMOUTH,Charles John Shore, Lord Reminiscences (Edin.1878). School and Cambridge;Waterloo; travels in Europe literary,political, social life; local affairs in Bristol and Yorks.   53

TEIGNMOUTH-SHORE, Rev. Thomas. Some Recollections (1911). His career as a clergyman from 60's; Royal chaplain; Mayfair, royalty, churchmen; Canon of Worcester.   54

TELFORD,Thomas. Life (1838). Career of the great engineer;work on bridges harbors and roads from later 18th Century; technical; some private.   55

TELLEGEN, Lou. Women Have Been Kind (1931). Artist's model, pugilist, actor; travels; European theatre; writers and performers.   56

TEMPLE, Alfred G. Guildhall Memories (1918). Long career as curator at the Guildhall; painters and exhibitions; art in England; city life and public functions.   57

TEMPLE,Ann. Good or Bad (1944). Her experiences with human troubles as editor of Readers Problems column in the Daily Mail.   58

TEMPLE, Derek. Ivory Poacher (1938) His adventures with natives in search of big game and ivory in S.W. Central Africa.   59

TEMPLE, Sir Richard. Men and Events (1882);Journals Kept in Hyderabad (L. 1887);Life in Parliament(1893);Story of My Life (1896).His career with the East India Company and ICS from 1848; finance minister and governor; Mutiny and public events; official and society life; career in Parliament and in London municipal politics to 1895; his travels in Empire, Europe, USA.   60

TEMPLE,Sir William. Memoirs of What Passed in Christendom (1692). Work as ambassador; War of 1672; and Peace of 1679; diplomacy; public affairs.   61

TEMPLE, William. Strolling Player (1802). Picaresque adventures; travel theatre, prison, love affairs; probably fiction.   62

TEMPLEWOOD, Samuel J. G. Hoare, 1st Viscount. The Unbroken Thread (1949). Mostly reminiscences of family life, sport, gardening; humanitarianism and reform as his family tradition; work on Norfolk estate; books and natural history.   63

TENNANT, Col. John E. In the Clouds (1920).Military service in the Middle East in WWl; air-commander; fighting around Baghdad; personal.   64

TENNANT, Thomas. Lives of Early Methodist Preachers, ed. Thomas Jackson III (1838).London man's conversion by Wesley; Methodist ministry in the 2nd half of 18th Century.   65

TENNYSON, Lionel H. Tennyson, third Baron. From Verse to Worse (L. 1933); Sticky Wickets(1950). Eton; Cambridge and Coldstream Guards; WWl service on Western Front; fox hunting; career as cricketer; early escapades.   66

TERNAN, Gen. Trevor. Some Experiences (Birmingham, 1930). Bromsgrove; & army career in Afghanistan, Egypt and Uganda; pioneer life in Africa.   67

TERRISS, Ellaline. Ellaline Terriss (1928). Forty years on the stage; her career and roles;theatre life and actors; Gilbert and Sullivan.   68

TERRY, Ellen. The Story of My Life (1908); Memoirs (1932). Spirited recollections of her theatrical career, England and America; stock companies; Lyceum; roles and performances; theatrical and literary society & friendships; gay and excellent.   69

TERRY, Stephen. Diaries of Dummer, ed. A.M.W. Stirling (1934). Reminiscences of country social life,work and sport; Hampshire, 1795-1861; excellent picture and details.   70

TERTON,Alice. Lights and Shadows in a Hospital (1902). Family; life, work and friends as London nurse; merits & demerits of the career.   71

TETLEY, J.George. Old Times and New (1904); Forty Years Ago and After (L. (1910).Religious and social life from 1868;career in church; Canon of Bristol;literary and church anecdotes and account of changes.   72

TEW, E. L. H. Old Times and Friends (Winchester, 1908, 1910). Oxford and later days of Oxford Movement; education;career as country clergyman, Essex, Yorks, Hants; sketches of Newman Pusey, etc. Winchester P.L.   73

THACKERAY,Colonel Sir Edward Talbot Reminiscences (1916).Military service in India and Afghanistan; in Hodson's

Horse during the Mutiny.   74

THACKWELL, Lieut.General Sir Joseph
Military Memoirs (1908). His military
career; the Peninsular War and Indian
service; first Afghan War; Sikh and
Gwalior campaigns.   75

THADDEUS,Henry Jones. Recollections
of a Court Painter (1912). Art career
from 1870; Cork, Paris, Florence; his
work and sitters; Whistler and other
painters;social life, celebrities and
the Grande Monde of Europe.   76

THEOBALD, Sir Henry Studdy. Remembrance of Things Past (1935). Rugby &
Oxford; youth in England and Germany;
largely people and places he knew as a
youth; life as a barrister; his collections.   77

THEOBALD, R. M. Passages from the
Autobiography(1912). Schools and college in London; teachers, writers and
the theatre;work as a Baconian Shakespeare student; spiritualism.   78

THESIGER, Ernest. Practically True
(1927). Career as actor; theatre life
but mostly social and society.   79

THICKNESSE, Philip. Memoirs & Anecdotes (1793). Social life; anecdotes
of relations, friends, acquaintances;
high and low society, 1730-80.   80

THIN, James. Reminiscences of Booksellers (Edin. 1905). Impersonal account of the Edinburgh book trade and
booksellers in time of George IV.Copy
in Harvard U.L.   81

THIRKELL, Angela. Three Houses (L.
1931). Evocative reminiscences of her
childhood in London and Rottingdean;
minutiae of childhood sentiments and
experience;Burne-Jones, Kipling, Mackail, etc.; pleasant.   82

THIRKELL, Sir Herbert. A Civil Servant in Burma (1913). Administration
and personal life in India and Burma,
from 1877;Lieutenant-Governor of Burma; Burmese life and politics.   83

THODAY, Leslie R. N'Importe (1944).
Sport in Staffs and Derbyshire; service in WW1; work as insurance broker
at Lloyds; travels; friends.   84

THOMAS, Albert. Wait and See (1944)
Life as waiter and butler in hotels &
taverns of Oxford;butler at Brasenose
splendors and miseries of the waiting
profession.   85

THOMAS, Bertram. Alarms and Excursions in Arabia (1931). Life and work
as political officer in Iraq; financial adviser to the Sultan of Muscat &
Oman; Arab life and politics.   86

THOMAS, Cecil. They Also Served (L.
1939). Experiences of private in WW1;
prisoner of war;German camps and coal
mines; strikes; German revolution; an
unusual and good story.   87

THOMAS, Edward. The Childhood, ed.
Julian Thomas (1938).Autobiographical
fragment; to age 16; schools, games,
friends,books, nature study, writing;
influence of Jefferies; pleasant and
unaffected.   88

THOMAS, Edward W. Twenty-Five Years
Labour (1879). Mission work in London
slums;work among prostitutes; conversions;homes for prostitutes; sociological data; useful.   89

THOMAS, George. A Tenement in Soho
(1931); My Mind a Kingdom(1938). Con-
solations of books,music, philosophy;
life of crippled son of London dustman
and struggles of family;slum life;his
writing; good.   90

THOMAS,Gilbert Oliver.Autobiography
(1946).London boyhood in 90's;religi-
ous upbringing;Leys School; work in a
publisher's office;reviewing;writing;
spiritual and intellectual life;simple
and good.   91

THOMAS, Helen T. As It Was (1927).
Wife of Edward Thomas; story of their
romantic love.   92

THOMAS, Herbert T. Story of a West
Indian Policeman (Kingston,1927). His
47 years' service as police inspector
in Jamaica; crime, riots, native psychology; personal affairs and social
life. Royal Empire Society.   93

THOMAS,James Henry. My Story (1937)
Political career from 1909; M.P. for
Derby; his ministries; Labour Govern-
ment; Trade Unions; reminiscences of

royalty,statesmen, labour leaders and
civil servants.   94

THOMAS,Julian. Cannibals & Convicts
(1886). His travels and adventures in
New Guinea and New Hebrides; journalism; native life.   95

THOMAS, Thomas Morgan. Eleven Years
in Central South Africa (1872). Life
and work of a Welsh missionary; Dutch
settlers; gold rush; big game.   96

THOMAS,Sir William Beach. Traveller
in News(1925);The Way of a Countryman
(1944). Childhood in country rectory;
Oxford;work and travels as special and
war correspondent;Daily Mail; country
life; social changes.   97

THOMASON,Sir Edward. Memoirs during
Half a Century (1845).Career in business from boyhood in London and Birmingham;ironwork, steam-engines, toys;
Birmingham industry, arts, sciences &
inventions; friends and honors.   98

THOMPSON, Alexander Marlock. Here I
Lie (1937).Fifty years as journalist;
"Dangle" of The Clarion; radicalism &
Labour Party; theatre.   99

THOMPSON, Bonar.   Hyde Park Orator
(1934).Ulster boyhood; work as a free
lance propagandist for socialism; entertaining,reciting, lecturing in the
streets and parks of London; Bohemian
life and prison experiences; literary
friendships;Shaw; conceited, mannered
and amusing.   100

THOMPSON,Cecil Vincent R. I Lost My
English Accent (1939). Six years as a
correspondent for London newspapers in
USA; impressions; slight.   101

/THOMPSON, Maj.Gen. Charles William/
Twelve Months in the British Legion,by
an Officer of the Ninth Regiment(1836)
Service in Spain in 1835-36; personal
adventures.   102

THOMPSON, Flora. Lark Rise (1939);
Over to Candleford (1941); Candleford
Green (1943); Still Glides the Stream
(1948).Childhood and later years in a
North Oxford village;country ways and
people;old customs; her writing; very
pleasant account of life from 80's and
much sociological material.   103

THOMPSON, Rev. G. War Memories and
Sketches (Paisley, 1916). Experiences
and work of a Scottish chaplain during
WW1; Western Front.   104

THOMPSON,Herbert (1856-1945). Autobiography of the Leeds music critic;a
record of his life and career;travels
abroad,concerts, musicians, criticism
and musical history. MS,University of
Leeds, 209 fos.   105

THOMPSON, James Alan. Only the Sun
Remembers (1950). Travels and adventures in the South Pacific and other
remote areas; romantic.   106

THOMPSON, Joseph. The Singular Life
and Surprizing Adventures   (Halifax,
1810). Upbringing in Halifax; escapades; marriage, poverty, drunkenness;
life in Lancs and at sea; conversion
to Methodism and ministry.   107

THOMPSON,Marian S.Archer. Selworthy
(1907). People and day-to-day life in
the fifties;Selworthy, Minehead, Tiverton area.   108

THOMPSON, Reginald Campbell. A Pilgrim's Scrip (1915). His work as an
archaeologist in Arabia, Syria, Sudan
etc.; scholarship; diggings.   109

THOMPSON, Reginald William. Argentine Interlude (1931); Down Under (L.
1932); Glory Hole (1933): Home in Ham
(1938); Voice from the Wilderness (L.
1940). Travel and adventures of rolling stone in Australia and Argentina;
farming & family life and society in
Devonshire.   110

THOMPSON,Thomas. An Encouragement
Early to Seek the Lord (1708). Quaker
spiritual autobiography; preaching at
Quinby;George Fox; imprisonment, sufferings, etc.   111

THOMPSON, Thomas. Lancashire for Me
(1940).Life of Lancashire journalist
and writer; radio and film writer;the
Lancashire scene and people;musichall
life.   112

THOMPSON, W. H. Guard from the Yard
(1938). Work as a constable & detective
from 1913; suffragettes, anarchists &
celebrities he guarded;General Strike;
anecdotes.   113

THOMSON, Basil C. The Diversions of a Prime Minister (Edin. 1894); South Sea Yarns(1894); Savage Island (1902) Life and travels in the Pacific; his administrative work in Fijis; experiences as minister in Tonga.   114

THOMSON, Sir Basil H. Queer People (1922);The Scene Changes (1937). Eton and Oxford; his career as a detective and work at Scotland Yard during WW1; espionage; last days at Yard.   115

THOMSON, Christopher. Autobiography of an Artisan (1847). Errand-boy, apprentice,shipwright;life at sea; work as sawyer in Yorkshire;strolling player and painter;varied and interesting life with much about workingclass life in Yorks and about theatre.   116

THOMSON,Adm.George Pirie. Blue Pencil Admiral (1947). Interesting story of experiences as submarine officer in WW1 and as Chief Press Censor in WW2; handling of details about the Blitz & D-Day.   117

THOMSON,James. Charles and Allectum (Edin. 1791). Life, ministry, reflections of a Scottish clergyman; Dundee in 18th Century.   118

THOMSON, Sir Joseph John. Recollections and Reflections (1936). Work as physicist; Cambridge studies; Owen's College;Trinity College, Cambridge; & its celebrities;Sidgwick, Prior; travels to USA;work in physics; psychical interests.   119

THOMSON,William Burns.Reminiscences of Medical Missionary Work(1895). His religious study in Edinburgh and spiritual and medical work in slums there; work among street arabs.   120

THORBURN,A.Douglas. Amateur Gunners (Liverpool, 1934).Personal narrative; service with howitzers in WW1;France, Salonika, Palestine.   121

THORNDIKE, Arthur Russell. Children of the Garter (1937). Life as a choir boy at St. George's Chapel, late 19th Century; schooling, music, snobbery & bullying; life at Windsor.   122

THORNDIKE,Charles Faunce. Some Memories of Ninety Years(1912). His ear-

ly career as a gunner; emigration to Canada;ordination; rector in England; consular chaplain in Trieste.   123

THORNE, Will. My Life's Battles (L. 1925). Working-class life from 60's; London life; work in the trade union movement and Labour Party; Member of Parliament; Labour Movement.   124

THORNELY,Thomas. Cambridge Memories (1936).Sixty years at Trinity;lighter side of college life; old friends and scholars; Latham, Maine, Maitland and others.   125

THORNHILL, Christopher James. From Hobo to Cannibal King (1928); Taking Tanganyika (1937). Lively adventures; goldminer, hunter, hobo, king of the Fan tribe,ivory trader; ups and downs in Central Africa; later intelligence work; WW1 East African campaign. 126

THORNHILL, J.B. Adventures in Africa (1915).In British,Belgian, Portuguese Africa and in Rhodesia.   127

THORNHILL, Mark. Haunts and Hobbies (L. 1899); Personal Adventures(1884); Career asmagistrate and administrator in India; experiences in Mutiny; natural history;Indian life and customs; social life; anecdotes.   128

THORNTON,Alfred H.R. Diary of an Art Student (1938). Art schools, artists, painting movements from the nineties; study with Gauguin;impressionists and modernists.   129

THORNTON,Alice. Autobiography (Surtees Soc., 1875). Interesting account of life of country gentleman's wife in Yorkshire in mid-17th Century;family, children, religion, domestic.   130

THORNTON,Anne Jane.Interesting Life and Wonderful Adventures (1835). Her love for a sea-captain;search for him in America,disguised as sailor; later voyages; discovery of her sex; adventures and hardships.   131

THORNTON, Ernest and Annie. Leaves from an Afghan Scrapbook (1910). Army officer and his wife in Kabul; court and social life; Afghan ways.   132

THORNTON, James Howard. Memories of

Seven Campaigns (1895). Career of an army surgeon; 35 years in medical department in India, China, Egypt, Sudan; deputy surgeon-general.　　133

THORNTON,John. Memoirs (1843). Life of Congregational minister of Billericay, Essex; boyhood in Yorkshire village and Lancashire; apprentice; study for ministry;career; afflictions; his religious life; writings.　　134

THORNTON,Percy Melville.Some Things We Have Remembered (1912). Harrow and Cambridge;social and literary life in Bournemouth; politics; career as Conservative M.P.　　135

THORNTON,William Henry. Reminiscences and Reflections (Torquay,1897-99) two series; 3rd unpublished series in Exeter City Library.Devonshire public and social life,people and sport; reminiscences of an old West-Country parson; pleasant.　　136

THOROGOOD, Horace. East of Aldgate (1935). Journalist's experiences living in East London slums; social and sociological notes.　　137

THORP,Ellen. Quiet Skies on Salween (1945). Her childhood in Upper Burma; nostalgic and delighted account of the dream world of a child.　　138

/THORP, Joseph Peter/. Friends and Adventures (1931). Catholic education of a "spoiled Jesuit"; work in advertising,printing, and for "Punch"; his literary friendships.　　139

THORPE, James H. Happy Days (1933). Schooling;London in late 19th Century and work as artist;London Sketch Club and artistic life;pleasures of a contented Victorian.　　140

THORPE,Maj.Samuel. Narrative of Incidents(1854).His early military life including service in Peninsular War & in Canada.　　141

THORPE, William George. Still Life of the Middle Temple (1892). His life at Cambridge;travels in India; merchant in London; barrister; table-talk at the Temple; 50 years' memories of legal life and personalities.　　142

THRALE,Hester Lynch (Piozzi). Autobiography(1861). Childhood in Wales & London;married life, finances, literary activities & friends; second marriage and travels in Italy.　　143

THRUSTON, Major Arthur B. African Incidents (1900). Military service in Egypt and Unyoro; Uganda Mutiny; army social life and sport.　　144

/THURBURN, Captain/. Reminiscences of the Indian Rebellion(1889). Indian Mutiny experiences of a magistrate in Fyzabad; the flight.　　145

THURSTAN,Violetta. Field Hospital & Flying Column(1915). Experiences of a nurse in Belgium and Russia during the early days of WW1.　　146

THURTLE, Ernest. Time's Winged Chariot(1945). Experiences in WW1 and in WW2; Labour Party politics; M.P. and junior minister;working-class life in Shoreditch.　　147

THWAITES, Norman Graham. Velvet and Vinegar (1932). Work and travels of a journalist; European correspondent of New York World;Pulitzer; society, war and public affairs from 80's.　　148

TILKE, Samuel Westcott. An Autobiographical Memoir(1840). Boyhood, London and Devon; country life; study of herbs;medical theories; practice as a herbalist; London social life.　　149

TILLARD, William. Diary, 1699-1705; journey to India and work for the new East India Company of which he became president;Indian life, conditions and people;interesting language. H. M. C. 15th Report, App. X (1899).　　150

TILLETT, Benjamin. Memories and Reflections (1931).Life at sea as docker and trade union leader & M.P.; the growth of the Labour Movement;dockers and dock strikes.　　151

TILLEY,Sir John Anthony Cecil. London to Tokyo (1942). Career as a diplomat; work in Brazil & Japan; public affairs,society,travel from the 90's; political views.　　152

TILMAN, Harold William. Snow on the

Equator (1937). Mountaineering, hunting, farming and gold prospecting in Kenya after WW1.   153

TILSLEY, V. W. Other Ranks (1931). Vivid account of personal experiences with the 55th Division during WW1; on Western Front.   154

TINLING, Christine I. Memories of the Mission Field (L. 1927); India's Womanhood (1935). Missionary's career in Syria, India, China, Japan, Korea; Ludhiana; temperance; Oriental religion; justification of missions.   155

TINSLEY, William. Random Recollections of an Old Publisher (1900); Publisher's Confession (1905). Memories of literature and the chief Victorian novelists; the theatre; social life & clubs.   156

TINTON, Major Ben Thomas. War Comes to the Docks (L.1941); My Twenty-Five Years in Dockland(1946). His life and work as warden of dockland settlement and experiences in WW2; the Blitz and the refugees.   157

TOASE, William. Memorials of (1874) Work as Methodist minister in France & Channel Islands from 1802; work among French prisoners and refugees from the revolution; his spiritual life.   158

TODD,Amos. The Confessions, by John Pearce (1894).London boyhood and poverty;work as clerk;in prison for debt and adventures in New World;trading in Central America, mining in Brazil,and business ventures;views on education; adventures.   159

TODD, William Hogarth. Work, Sport, and Play (1928). The life and work of a civil engineer in India before WW1; hunting and horse-racing.   160

TOLD, Silas. An Account of the Life and Dealings with God(1786). The very lively adventures of an early Methodist converted by Wesley; perils by land & sea,from war, shipwreck, mobs; one of best of its kind.   161

TOLLEMACHE, Lionel A.   Old and Odd Memories (1908).Life in clerical family; Harrow and Oxford; recollections of celebrities;Huxley,Spencer, Milnes.

Carroll, etc.; quite interesting. 162

TOLMER, Alexander. Reminiscences(L. 1882).Education and service in British army from 40's;later career in police in Australia.   163

TOMKINS, Simon. The Adventures of a Strolling Player(n.d.). Dickensian & possibly fictitious account of theatrical life and travel; pseudonymous;a paper-back.   164

TOMKINSON,Lt.Col. William. Diary of a Cavalry Officer(1894). Service with the Light Dragoons in Peninsular War & at Waterloo.   165

TOMLIN, Jacob. Diary, 1826-29; life work and travels of a missionary; religious activities in China,Siam, Malaya, Java, Bali. Missionary Journals (1844).   166

TOMLINSON, G. A. W. Coal Miner(1937) Work in Worksop mines;conservative in politics;trade unionism;escape; country life & pleasures; literary interests.   167

TONE,Theobald Wolfe. Autobiography, edited Barry O'Brien(1893); edited S. O'Faolain (1937). Military service in French and Batavian republics;political activities in Ireland with United Irishmen; to 1796.   168

TONNA,Charlotte Elizabeth. Personal Recollections (1841).Religious issues and controversies of early 19th Century;Irvingites, Catholics and her objections to them;travels in USA; life in Ireland; social problems.   169

TOOLE, John Lawrence. Reminiscences (1889).Comedian's dictated account of his career in the theatre; plays, actors, theatrical life, tours.   170

TOOLE,Joseph. Fighting through Life (1935).Lancashire journalist and politician;Social Democracy; Salford politics; career in Parliament; Parliamentary personalities.   171

TOPHAM,Anne.Memories of the Fatherland(1916);Chronicles of the Prussian Court (1926).German life and character at the court of Wilhelm II before WW1, as seen by an English governess.   172

TORR, Cecil. Small Talk at Wreyland
(Cambridge,1926). Extracts from family
papers,including grandfather's letters
and father's diary,1833-78;family and
local affairs and history at Wreyland
and Lustleigh.   173

TORRANCE,Arthur. Junglemania (1934)
Medical work in Sudan,Abyssinia, Congo, and Borneo; adventure and romance
in the tropics; tropical diseases and
science.   174

TORRENS,William T.McCullagh. Twenty
Years in Parliament (1893). Career as
Liberal M.P. for Finsbury; politics &
politicians.   175

TOTHILL, Vincent. Doctor's Office,
(1939).Medical work in Trinidad; conditions of work; poverty,illiteracy &
need for social & medical services in
West Indies; excellent.   176

TOTTENHAM,Edith Leonora. Highnesses
of Hindostan (1934). Experiences of a
lady-in-waiting to Maharani of Baroda
1911-20; Indian courts, culture, social life and customs.   177

TOVEY, P. H. F. Action with a Click
(1940).Experiences as press photographer; WW1,Irish rebellion, Scapa Flow
Abyssinian War, Spanish war.   178

TOWNEND, John Michael. Overture to
Life (1944). Service with RAF in WW2;
training in Canada and USA;people and
ways of the New World.   179

TOWNEND,Joseph. Autobiography (1869)
Religious life and work in Rochdale and
North; working-class life; missionary
work in Australia.   180

TOWNLEY,Lady Susan M. Indiscretions
of Lady Susan (N.Y.1922). Social side
of diplomatic life from 90's; Lisbon,
Berlin,Rome, Pekin, Washington, Buch-
arest;WW1 work in censorship; gossip;
pleasant and superficial.   181

TOWNSHEND, Arthur FitzHenry. A Military Consul in Turkey (1910). Life &
work of the British representative in
Turkish Asia Minor;military and economic affairs; travels.   182

TOWNSHEND,Maj.Gen. Sir Charles Vere
Ferrers.My Campaign in Mesopotamia(L.

1920).History of the 1914-16 campaign
and his strategy; siege of Kut.   183

TOWNSHEND,Gladys E.G. E. Townshend,
Marchioness. It Was - and It Wasn't
(1937). Society, country house, and
London life;travels in USA; anecdotes
and ghost stories.   184

TOWNSHEND, Zoe. An Officer's Wife
(1932).Childhood,schooling, marriage;
life with soldier-husband,India, England and Ireland;garrison life; fresh
and simple.   185

TOYE, Francis. For What We Have Re-
ceived (1950). Winchester; his study
of music;music journalism for Morning
Post and Daily Express; opera in England; intelligence work in WW1; publishing;Director of British Institute
in Florence; friends; pleasures. 186

TOZER, Basil John. Recollections of
a Rolling Stone(1923); Life's Lighter
Side (1932); Roving Recollections (L.
1945).Travels and adventures of freelance journalist;writers and celebrities he met; theatres, amusements and
sights; Bohemian life.   187

TRANT, Thomas Abercromby. Two Years
In Ava, by An Officer (1827). Service
in Burmese War, 1824-6.   188

TRAVIS, James. Seventy-Five Years
(1914). Early religious experiences &
his posts as Primitive Methodist minster, especially in Lancs.   189

TREE, Viola. Castles in the Air (L.
1926). Experiences as a singer before
WW1 in Italy and England; in letters,
diary and reminiscences.   190

TREFUSIS,Mrs. Violet. Reminiscences
(1941);Prelude to Misadventure (1942)
European travels & opinions of a cos-
mopolitan;life in France, Austria and
Italy in thirties;Reynaud, Mussolini,
Colette, Cocteau, etc.   191

TRELAWNEY-ANSELL, Edward Clarence.
One of the Leaderless Legion (L.1937)
I Had Nine Lives (L.1938); I Followed
Gold (1939); African Odyssey (1939).
Fifty years of travels and remarkable
escapes; South Africa, Yukon, Siberia
Nevada, Mexico; goldmining, prospect-
ing, revolutions; the celebrities he

met; a lively and varied career. 192

TRELAWNY, Edward John. Adventures of a Younger Son (1831); Recollections of the Last Days of Shelley and Byron (1858). Travels and adventures at sea and on land,Mediterranean and Asia; & in Italy with the poets; an excellent story of adventure.   193

TREMAYNE,Harold. Reminiscences of a Gentleman Horse Dealer (1901). Life & anecdotes of riding-teacher at Brixton and a dealer in hunters.   194

TREMAYNE, Mrs. L. Experiences of a Psychometrist and Clairvoyant (1922). Episodes from her life as medium; society; dreams; Spiritualist Society & her beliefs.   195

TREMEARNE, Maj. Arthur John Newmann Tailed Head-Hunters of Nigeria (1912) Life and work of military & political officer in Ashanti, 1900-10; anthropology; native culture.   196

TREMLETT, Rex. Easy Going (1940). A varied life and travels;tobacco planter in Nyassaland, goldfinder in Tanganyika, journalist in Europe; WW2 & Dunkirk.   197

TRENCH,Edmund. Some Remarkable Passages (1693). Religious life of 17th Century clergyman; extracted from his diaries.   198

TRENEER, Anne. School House in the Wind(1944); Cornish Years (1949). Her childhood and schooling in St.Austell region;family life; Cornish customs & people; training as teacher; teaching in Exeter,Liverpool, etc.; a pleasant evocation of early life.   199

TREVELYAN,George Macaulay. An Autobiography and Other Essays(1949). His studies and career as historian; Cambridge; ideas of history; historical writings; WW1.   200

TREVES, Sir Frederick. The Elephant Man (1923).Reminiscences of a doctor's life,cases, & incidents, by Sergeant Surgeon to the King; travels.   201

TREVOR,John. My Quest for God (1897) Boyhood in East Anglia;studies of art literature, theology; travel,America

& Australia; Unitarian church work in London & Manchester; Labour churches; spiritual life.   202

TREWIN, John Courtney. Up from the Lizard(1948). Life and work of editor of West Country Magazine;Cornish life people and places.   203

/TRIPP,Henry/. Reminiscences of Old Times (Winchester, 1887). Boyhood in Devon; Winchester and Oxford studies; and at St. Columba's;life & interests of a classical scholar.   204

TROLLOPE, Anthony. Autobiograp h y (1883). Education; work at Post Office and his literary career and writings; commercial side of literary genius and his social life.   205

TROLLOPE, Thomas Adolphus. What I Remember (1887);Further Reminiscences (1889). His early life in London;education;Harrow and Winchester; travels in America & Europe; social life; literary reminiscences; writings.   206

TROOPER. The Four Horsemen Ride (L. 1935).Unvarnished account of personal experiences of an infantryman on Western Front during WW1.   207

TROSSE, George. The Life of (Exeter 1714). A lively account of the evils of life & his conversion,by an Exeter nonconformist.   208

TROUBRIDGE,Lady Laura. Memories and Reflections (1925). Society and sport from 70's;diplomatic life in Barbados and memories of famous writers,actors etc.; Tennyson, Browning, Watts. 209

TROUNCER, Nellie. An Old-Fashioned Miss (Surbiton, 1938). Childhood life in Sussex in 70's;travels, pleasures, social work of a spinster to WW1;life in Surbiton. Hereford City Lib.   210

TROUP, John R. With Stanley's Rear Column (1890). Travel and exploration in Central Africa 1886-88; transport officer on Emin Pasha relief expedition; self-justification.   211

TROUP, Major Walter. Sporting Memories (1924). Service in Indian Police and experiences in Rugby football and hockey; Gloucester County cricket and other sports; Rugby, hockey, etc. 212

TRUMBULL, Sir William. Autobiography of his diplomatic life to 1687; secretary of State to William III. MS, All Souls College, Oxford.   213

TRUSLER, John. Memoirs of the Life (Bath,1806); only Part I was published and the MS of the remainder is in Bath Municipal Library. Discursive, rambling jottings of an eccentric clergyman and antiquary; education at Westminster & Cambridge; ministries in Hertford and Essex; his writings; anecdotal gossip on clerical, social and literary life; often amusing.   214

TRYON, Thomas. Some Memoirs of the Life (1705). Boyhood as a shepherd and later life as London merchant; Baptist religious life; vegetarianism.   215

TUBBY, Alfred Herbert. A Consulting Surgeon in the Near East (1920). His work with RAMC in Mediterranean and in Near East during WW1.   216

TUCKER, Rt. Reverend Alfred Robert. Eighteen Years in Uganda and East Africa (1908). Life and work as missionary and bishop; organization and education; Christian rivalries; politics and revolts; important.   217

TUCKER, William Guise. Recollections of a Chaplain (1886). Travel and work as naval chaplain; missionary work in Canada; religion in the Navy.   218

/TUCKER, William Hill/. Eton of Old, by An Old Colleger (1892). Schooldays at Eton, 1811-22; mainly an impersonal account of people and customs.   219

TUCKEY, James Hingston. Diary, 1816; explorations of the Congo; scientific notes. Narrative of an Expedition (L. 1818).   220

TUCKWELL, William. Reminiscences of a Radical Parson (1905); Reminiscences of Oxford (1907). His work in country parishes; development of radical beliefs; miseries of the poor; social & intellectual life in Oxford; Pattison and other celebrities.   221

TUKER, Sir Francis Ivan Simon. While Memory Serves (1950). India in last

two years of British Rule; commander of Indian army; problems and difficulties; useful.   222

TULLOCH, Maj.Gen.Sir Alexander Bruce Recollections of Forty Years' Service (Edin.1903); A Soldier's Sailoring (L. 1912). Military life, campaigns, travels; Crimea, India, China, Egypt; and intelligence work in Australia; work & experiences while being transported on sailing ships.   223

TUPPER, Martin Farquhar. My Life as an Author (1886). Literary career and moral philosophy; visits to America & his social and domestic life; literary friendships; spiritualism.   224

TUPPER, Sir Reginald Godfrey Otway. Reminiscences (1929). Admiral's life and career, 1882 through WW1.   225

TURNER, Maj.Gen. Sir Alfred E. Sixty Years of a Soldier's Life (1912). His service in the Sudan and Ireland; Home Rule campaign; later experience at the War Office.   226

TURNER, Ben. About Myself (1930). His boyhood in Yorks; working-class life; trade unionism & textile workers; the Labour Movement in Yorkshire; work on Trades Council; politics; social life; labour leaders he knew.   227

TURNER, Charles C. My Flying Scrap-Book (1946). Experiences as balloonist and flyer from 1907; air-journalism & flying events.   228

TURNER, George. Nineteen Years in Polynesia (1861). Life and work of a missionary in New Hebrides and Samoa; London Missionary Society; paganism & native cults and cultures.   229

TURNER, Sir George R. Unorthodox Reminiscences (1931). Early days & school in London; Victorian scene; study and practice of medicine; St. George's Hospital; eminent scientists and doctors of his acquaintance.   230

TURNER, J.Arthur (ed.). The Life of a Chimney Boy (1901). Apprenticeship & work as chimney-sweep in London and in Bucks; poverty and exploitation; conversion and Methodist missionary work among sweeps; life in Hitchin.   231

TURNER,Sir James.Memoirs of His Own
Life (Edin,1829). Life of a soldier &
anti-covenanter in 17th Century;Civil
War;public affairs; service with King
and with Gustavus Adolphus.   232

TURNER, Jane. Choice Experiences of
the Kind Dealings of God (1653). Wife
of a sea-captain;spiritual experience
during husband's absence; agnosticism
and conversion.   233

TURNER, Joanna. Memoir of, by David
Bogue (1820). Religious autobiography
of a Whitefield Methodist;prayers and
ejaculations; life in Trowbridge. 234

TURNER, John Arthur. Kwang Tung (L.
1895). Life and work of a Methodist
missionary, during five years in Canton; Chinese life.   235

TURNER,Sir Llewelyn.The Memories of
(1903).His work in the Welsh slate industry in 19th Century;legal affairs,
Wales and England; work as Constable
of Carnarvon Castle.   236

TURNER, Samuel. My Climbing Adventures (1911). Climbs in the mountains
of four continents.   237

TURNER, Thomas A. Argentina and the
Argentines (1892). Five years' residence in Argentina;South American life
and politics; 1890 revolution; social
and private affairs.   238

TURNER, William Robert. Eyes of the
Press (1935). Experiences of a press
photographer;Daily Mail; journalistic
sensationalism.   239

TURNERELLI,Edward Tracy. Memoirs of
a Life of Toil(1884). Work on Russian
history and art in mid-19th Century &
Conservative politics.   240

TURQUET-MILNES, Gladys R. Apples I
Have Picked (1939). Life in the Loire
country and Sussex; farming, country
life and people.   241

TUSSER,Thomas. Last Will and Testa-
ment(Great Totham, 1846); also in the
1573 & the subsequent editions of his
Husbandry. Short metrical autobiography of his education,sins, marriages,
work as farmer in Suffolk;warnings to
the young against vice.   242

TWEEDIE,George R. Yesterday (1932).
Lecturer and political agent;Liberal-
ism and Free Trade and his changes of
opinion;eminent Victorians and Edwardians.   243

TWEEDIE, Adm. Sir Hugh J. Story of
a Naval Life(1939). His career in the
navy from 1892; experiences with destroyers.   244

TWEEDSMUIR, John Buchan, Baron. Memory Hold the Door (1940). Scottish
upbringing; impressions made on him
since childhood by outside world and
episodes and changes in his life; in
Oxford, South Africa, Parliament and
Canada; writings; public offices; an
essay in recollection.   245

TWELLS, Julia H. In the Prison City
(1919). Experiences of internment in
Brussells during WW1;the German occupation.   246

TWINING, Louisa. Recollections of
Life and Work(1893). Labour for workhouse reform;charity schools & girls'
homes; Marine Society; Education Commission of 1860.   247

TWINING, Thomas. Travels in India
(1893). Life, work, and travels 1792-
1795;work for East India Company; the
French wars; tour in USA.   248

TYACKE, Mrs. Richard Humphrey. How
I Shot My Bears(1893). Hunting in the
Central Himalayas; camp life.   249

TYERMAN, Daniel and BENNET, George.
Diary, 1821-1828; missionary work and
extensive travels in South Sea islands
China, India, New Zealand and Leeward
Islands;natives and whalers;Christian
life and hell-raising;interesting and
valuable record of impact of the West
Journal of Travels (1831).   250

TYLER, William Ferdinand. Pulling
Strings in China (1929). His work in
Chinese customs service and on revenue
cruisers from 1887; politics, war and
rebellion; Chinese life; his WW1 work
in China; lively.   251

TYNAN, Katharine (Hinkson). Twenty-
five Years' Reminiscences (1913); The
Middle Years (1916); The Years of the
Shadow(1919); The Wandering Years (L.

1922); <u>Memories</u> (1924). Childhood and family life;public, political, literary affairs in Ireland;the rebellion; her literary work and friendships;her travels in England and Europe.   252

TYNDALE, Henry Edmund Guise. <u>Mountain Paths</u> (1948). Mountain climbing before and after WW1; Alps; mountaineers and guides; emotional aspects; & natural history.   253

TYRELL, Anthony. <u>The Troubles of Our Catholic Forefathers</u>, ed. John Morris (1875), 2nd Series. Fall from faith & recantation of Catholic priest accused of plotting against the life of Queen Elizabeth.   254

TYRRELL, George. <u>Autobiography and Life</u>(1912). Irish boyhood in 60's and his conversion;training as Jesuit and religious work in Cyprus and Malta and at Stonyhurst;good example of spiritual autobiography.   255

TYRRELL, J. <u>From England to the Antipodes and India</u> (Madras,1904). Life of a private soldier in India and his long career in the government police service, 1846-1902.   256

TYRWHITT-DRAKE, Sir Garrard. <u>Beasts and Circuses</u>(1936); <u>My Life with Animals</u> (1939). Upbringing at Maidstone, Kent;cattle-ranching in the Argentine and service in Veterinary Corps during WW1;his circus work and his Maidstone zoo; Mayor of Maidstone.   257

ULLATHORNE,Rt.Rev. William Bernard. <u>From Cabin Boy to Archbishop</u>(1941).At sea as a boy;Downside; work as priest among convicts and settlers in Australia; travels; life and work as Bishop of Birmingham.   1

ULLSWATER,James W.Lowther, Viscount <u>A Speaker's Commentaries</u>(1925).School and King's College, London; career as a barrister; M.P. for Rutland; work & opinions as Speaker, House of Commons 1905-21; personal affairs.   2

ULYAT, Elizabeth Ann. <u>Memoirs of</u>,by Thomas Rogers(Boston,1823). Spiritual

life of Lincolnshire Baptist, excerpted from diary and letters.   3

UNDERHILL, Sir Arthur. <u>Change and Decay</u> (1938). Victorian life;school & Trinity College,Dublin; inns of court and work as barrister;Bencher of Lincoln's Inn; legal celebrities; social changes.   4

UNDERHILL,Edward. <u>Narratives of the Reformation</u> (Camden Soc.,1859).Lively account of the sufferings & imprisonment of a Warwickshire protestant during reign of Queen Mary.   5

UNDERWOOD,Michael.<u>Extracts from the Diary</u>(1823). Religious experience and meditations of London surgeon.   6

UNDERWOOD, Reginald. <u>Hidden Lights</u> (1937).London from late 19th Century; school,journalism, teaching, writing, Methodism, sex;Edward Carpenter, H.E. Bates.   7

/UPSON, Arthur T.7. <u>High Lights in the Near East</u>, by Abdul Fahy (1936). Life and work as missionary in Egypt; 30 years' work for Nile Mission Press Arabic scholarship; Egypt in WW1; and Egyptian scene.   8

/UPWARD,Allen7. <u>Some Personalities</u>, by 20/1631 (1921). Light veined memories of London society,literature and politics from 80's.   9

URCH, Reginald Oliver Gilling. <u>We Generally Shot Englishmen</u> (1936). An English teacher in Russia in the last years of Tsarist regime; the Revolution;Russian brutality & eccentricity and his sufferings.   10

URIE, John. <u>Reminiscences of Eighty Years</u> (Paisley, 1908). Recollections of old Paisley & Glasgow; clubs, social life,public events;work as photographer and engraver.   11

URLIN, Richard Denny. <u>Journal and Reminiscences</u> (Worthing, 1909). Legal and ecclesiastical life in Ireland and Irish society.   12

USBORNE,Adm. Cecil Vivian. <u>Smoke on the Horizon</u>(1933); <u>Blast and Counterblast</u> (1935); <u>Malta Fever</u> (1936). His naval service during WW1;mainly mine-laying and anti-submarine work in the Mediterranean.   13

UTTLEY,Alison. Ambush of Young Days (1937);Farm on the Hill (1941); Country Child(1941); Country Hoard (1943) Country Things(1946); Carts & Candlesticks (1948). Life in the country in childhood and later; family; friends; country ways,scenes, sports; memories and emotions.   14

VACHELL, Horace Annesley. Fellow-Travellers (1923); My Vagabondage (L. 1936);Distant Fields (1937); Now Came Still Evening On(1946); Twilight Grey (1948); In Sober Livery(1949); Methuselah's Diary (1950). Education; his career as novelist, playwright, etc.; travels; later days in West Country & notes on public affairs; social life & literary friendships; old age.   1

VALE,Edmund. Straw into Gold (1939) Service in WW1;fishmonger, journalist and writer;life in Anglesey & London; travels abroad; meetings with "Q" and E. V. Lucas; ideas.   2

VANBRUGH, Irene.   To Tell My Story (1948).Sixty years in the theatre;Edwardian social scene;gossip about the theatrical world.   3

VANBRUGH, Violet.   Dare to be Wise (1925).Career on the stage;theatrical life and personalities; advice to the wouldbe actor.   4

VAN DE LINDE, Gerard. Reminiscences (1917). Life as accountant & business man in later 19th Century;social life and world travels.   5

VANDENHOFF,George. Dramatic Reminiscences (1860).His career as an actor in 40's and 50's; famous plays & performers;theatre and green-room gossip in England and USA.   6

VAN DER BYL,Maj. Charles. My Fifty Years (1937). School; Cambridge; his career in cavalry from 1897;Boer War; WW1 service in remounts;sporting life and beliefs as a Buchmanite.   7

VAN DER ELST, Violet. Torture Chamber (1937); On the Gallows (L. 1938). Events in her lifetime's campaign vs. capital punishment.   8

VANDERKISTE, Robert W. Notes & Narrative (1852); Lost; But Not for Ever (1863).Methodist's five years work at London City Mission; drunkenness and crime in Clerkenwell;later adventures in Australian mountains.   9

VANDON,George. Return Ticket (1940) Nostalgic memories of Edwardian London service in WW1;Oxford and Paris after the war;country house life;literature and pleasures; pseudonymous.   10

VAN DRUTEN,John. Way to the Present (1938).Youth in suburban London; education;family life; law study; teaching law at Aberystwyth; career in the theatre; playwriting.   11

VANE, Sir Francis Patrick Fletcher. Agin the Governments(1929). Life of a soldier from 60's;schools, Oxford and Guards;Boer War, WW1, Ireland; social work at Toynbee Hall and in Boy Scouts Irish troubles.   12

VANE,Sir Henry.History of the Wrays of Glentworth,by Charles Dalton(1881) contains brief autobiography of family and financial affairs, 1649.   13

VAN HARE, G. Fifty Years of a Showman's Life (1889). Adventures,travels and devices of an English Barnum;circus performer and manager in Europe & British Isles.   14

ANON.The Vanished Pomps of Yesterday (1919).Society life in Berlin, Vienna and Russia by a British diplomat. 15

VAN WART, Reginald Bramley. Palace Days (1934). His work, adventures and misadventures while tutor in the court of Gurumpore, Southern India; Indian life, its virtues and vices.   16

VAQUERO. Adventures in Search of a Living (1911); Life and Adventure in the West Indies (1914). Six years in Mexico and Latin America; poverty and competition for jobs; travel and work in West Indies; Englishman's penniless travels.   17

VARDON,Harry. My Golfing Life(1933) Career as a sportsman; especially his life as a champion golfer and later as a golf-teacher.   18

VARLEY,Henry. Life Story (1913).His boyhood in London; ministry at Notting Hill Tabernacle;life and religious work in Australia.   19

/VASON,George7. Authentic Narrative of Four Years'Residence at Tongataboo (1810).Nottingham man's adventures as missionary among natives of Friendly Islands, end of 18th Century.   20

VASSALL—PHILLIPS, Oliver R. After Fifty Years(1928). Eton; Oxford; conversion to Catholicism;life as priest and religious reflections.   21

VAUGHAN,General Sir John Luther. My Service in the Indian Army - and After (1904). Military career in India from 1840; Afghan wars, the Mutiny, Frontier skirmishes; later service in Boer War; useful record.   22

VAUX, James Hardy. Memoirs of the First Thirty-Two Years(1819). Life of a pickpocket and swindler transported to New South Wales;descent into crime through idleness and extravagance;may be fiction; picaresque.   23

VAUX, John. Journal, 1691-1698; his administration and business activities as deputy-governor of Bombay. MS,B.M. Add. 14253.   24

VECCHI,Joseph. The Tavern is My Drum (1948). Italian-born restaurantier's experiences in London, Berlin, Kiev & St. Petersburg hotels during 1st half of century.   25

VEE, Roger. Flying Minnows (1935). American's service in RFC during WW1; training and combat in France.   26

VEITCH,Mrs. William. Religious life and sufferings of wife of Scottish covenanter in the 17th Century;family & husband;Scottish affairs. MS.36.6.22, National Library of Scotland.   27

VEITCH, William. Memoirs of William Veitch & George Bryson, ed. T.M'Crie (Edin.1825). Adventures of a Scottish covenanter;chief events of later half

of 17th Century especially in Scotland Pentland rising, Rye House Plot, Monmouth rebellion; very lively.   28

VENABLES, Bernard. Fisherman's Testament (1949). Reminiscences of fishing; pleasures and philosophy.   29

VENNAR, Richard. An Apology (1614). Life of Lincoln's Inn lawyer;troubles and imprisonment for debt;travel into Scotland, etc.   30

VERNAL, Joshua. Recollections of a Tradesman (1864). Birmingham; work in father's jewelry business;his own experiences in business; financial and legal troubles.   31

VERNE, Mathilde. Chords of Remembrance (1936).Music teacher to Duchess of York; music and musicians from the 90's; music-teaching; travels, Europe and America.   32

VERNON, B.J. Early Recollections of Jamaica (1848). Chaplain's life there in early 19th Century; Matoon war and exciting voyage to England during War of 1812.   33

VERNON, Francis V. Voyages and Travels of a Sea Officer (Dublin, 1792). Irishman's naval career and adventures from 1777; war and travel in America, West Indies, Mediterranean.   34

VERNON,William Warren.Recollections of Seventy-Two Years(1917). Study and scholarship from 30's; Oxford;Italy & Italian literature and politics; work on Dante; Lacaita.   35

VERNON-HARCOURT, Frederick C. From Stage to Cross(1902). Scottish childhood; adventures as sailor, soldier & actor; missionary work in England and France and in Boer War.   36

VETCH, Major George Anderson. The Gong (Edin.1852). Military and social life of a cadet in Bengal before Mutiny; Indian life and scene; literary interests.   37

VIATOR.Ten Years in Anglican Orders (1897).Theological study; ordination; curacy; breach with Church of England and analysis of his gradual conversion to Catholicism.   38

VIBART,Col.Edward. The Sepoy Mutiny
(1898). Military service in Delhi and
experiences in siege; relief of Lucknow; service after the Mutiny.   39

ANON. Vicissitudes in the Life of a
Scottish Soldier(1827). Glasgow man's
service in Peninsular War; details of
campaigns in Spain, Portugal, France;
life of a private soldier.   40

VIDAL, Lois. Magpie (Lon. 1934).Her
vicarage girlhood;country life, Herts
at turn of century;WW1 service, YMCA,
France and Land Army;secretary, journalist, odd jobs; travels; & academic
associations.   41

VIGERS, Edith Mary. Notebook Caval-
cade(1942). Experiences of a reporter
travels and adventures;life on liners
etc.   42

VILLIERS,Frederic. Peaceful Personalities and Warriors Bold (1907); and
Five Decades of Adventure(1921). Travels and adventures of Graphic artist
and reporter; blood, violence, pomp &
anecdotes of celebrities.   43

VILLIERS,George. Noonday & Nocturne
(1943).Poet's mystical experiences on
a background of service in WW1 and the
bitterness of daily life.   44

VILLIERS, Katharine.   Memoirs of a
Maid of Honour(1931). Her life at the
court of George V from 1911;Windsor &
Balmoral;state ceremonies; anecdotes;
reminiscences.   45

VINCENT,Henry. A Stoker's Log (1929)
Life on the lower deck during WW1;good
Smollett-like account of humours of a
blackguardly society.   46

VINCENT,John. Inside the Asylum (L.
1948). Intimate story of mental patient; troubles in childhood, youth and
marriage; asylum life.   47

VINCENT,William.Seen from the Railway Platform(1919). Fifty years' work
in railway bookstalls;country stations
Taunton,Swansea, Reading, London; the
people he met; anecdotes.   48

VINING, Maj. L. E. Held by the Bolsheviks (1924). With British Railway
Mission in Russia after WW1; service

with White Russians;capture by Reds &
experiences in Moscow prisons.   49

/VIVIAN, Herbert/. Myself Not Least
(1923). Education;Cambridge; interest
in literature and art;diplomatic life
in Europe;international affairs, WW1;
personal and public.   50

VIZETELLY, Edward.   From Cyprus to
Zanzibar (1901). Adventures and observations of a war correspondent in the
80's; Egypt; East Africa.   51

VIZETELLY,Ernest Alfred. My Days of
Adventure(1914); My Adventures in the
Commune(1914); In Seven Lands (1916).
Travels as assistant to his father and
his life as war correspondent;European
affairs & personalities; Franco-Prussian War;Illustrated London News; his
adventures.   52

VIZETELLY, Henry. Glances Back thro
Fifty Years (1893). Journalistic and
literary life in London;public events
and personalities; politics; social &
club life;good broad picture of times
and himself.   53

VOKINS,Joan.God's Mighty Power Mag-
nified (Cockermouth, 1871). The religious life and Christian witness of a
17th Century Quaker.   54

A VOLUNTEER, Military journal 1857;
service with Barrow's cavalry during
the Mutiny;Havelock; march to Lucknow
My Journal (Calcutta, 1858). Copy in
India Office Library.   55

VOSPER,Thomas Nicolls.Story of Commercial Life (Plymouth,1871).His hard
times getting started;work as a hotel
keeper and draper;Plymouth & Launce-
ston town life and people.   56

VOSS, W. J.   The Light of the Mind
(1935).Officer blinded in WW1; training for life of blindness;experiences
and reflections in blindness.   57

VULLIAMY, Colwyn Edward. Calico Pie
(1940).Boyhood in Wales; WW1 service,
Salonika; work in publishers; writing
of biography.   58

/W., Arthur7.Spiritualistic Experiences of a Lawyer (Manchester, 1937). Education;scientific study; agnosticism;psychic experience after death of his wife;spiritualism in the 20's and 30's.   1

/W., J.7. Perils,Pastimes and Pleasures of an Emigrant(1849). Pioneering and mining in Vancouver Island,California and, mostly, Australia.   2

WADDELL,Hope Masterton. Twenty-Nine Years in the West Indies and Central Africa(1863). Missionary life & work in Jamaica and Old Calabar 1829-1858; negro life and slavery.   3

WADDINGTON,George; HANBURY, Bertram Journal of a Visit (1822). Travels of two Cambridge scholars in Ethiopia and observations on local life and scene; Ismael Pasha & Mahomed Ali.   4

WADDINGTON, Samuel. Chapters of My Life(1909). Yorkshire boyhood; Oxford and civil service;travels; his poetry and literary friendships; Clough,Watson, Hall Caine, etc.   5

WADE,Maj. Alexander Gawthorp. Counterspy! (1938). Military career; Boer War and WW1;adventures as a scout and spy; moralisings.   6

WADE, Lt.Col. Sir Claude Martine. A Narrative of the Services (Ryde 1844) His career in the army and police, in Bengal, 1809-44; military, political, and social affairs.   7

/WADELTON, Maggie Jeanne7. The Book of Maggie Owen(Indianapolis, 1941). A deliberately quaint account of life of a twelve-year old child; Irish.   8

WADSWORTH,James.The Memoires of Mr. James Wadsworth(1679). With his father in Madrid; education by Jesuits; conversion to Catholicism & later recantation;intelligence work among Jesuits in France; adventures, imprisonment & hardships in public service.   9

WAGNER, Leopold. Roughing It on the Stage (1895).Stage aspirations; start in Northern Ireland;tours through the English provinces; acting in London & work in vaudeville,lecturing,theatre; growing prosperity.   10

WAITE,Arthur Edward.Shadows of Life and Thought (1938). Spiritual life; & occult,mysticism,sacramental religion and his work as poet,writer, publisher; romantic literature; his literary friendships.   11

WAKE,Charlotte Murdoch (Tait), Lady Reminiscences (1909). Her social and religious life in Scotland, Edinburgh and Midlands; public affairs.   12

WAKEFIELD, Gilbert. Memoirs of the Life (1804). His life to 1792; education;Cambridge; theological study and his ministry in Lancs and Notts; his scholarly and social writings;labours against slave-trade and for the reform of prisons.   13

WAKELAM,Capt.Henry B. T. Broadcasting Memoirs (1936); Half-Time! (1938) Marlborough and Cambridge;his service in WW1;engineering; playing Rugby for the Harlequins; journalism; work as a sports commentator for BBC;celebrities of radio.   14

WAKINSHAW,William.Gleanings from My Life(1931). Reminiscences of Wesleyan Methodist minister from 1883.   15

WALBROOK,Henry Mackinnon.Playgoer's Wanderings (1926). Work as a dramatic critic & reminiscences of the theatre & actors from 80's; partly historical essays.   16

WALDECK, Theodore J.   Treks Across the Veldt (1944); On Safari (1946). A big-game hunter in Central Africa and zoological work, collecting specimens may be American.   17

WALDEGRAVE, James, 2nd Earl. Memoir (1821).Political affairs; helping the King with new administration,1754-58; Governor to Prince of Wales.   18

WALDRON, Patrick L. Afloat & Ashore (Glasgow, 1920). School; apprentice & marine engineer; voyages & employment in Burma; Burmese life.   19

WALE,Henry John. Sword and Surplice (1880).Service in Hussars; Crimea and Balaclava; ordination and ministry in Worcester and Folksworth, Hants.   20

WALE,Thomas.My Grandfather's Pocket

Book, ed.Henry John Wale (1883). Family history & extracts from his diary 1724-95;life in Riga; family life and business in England;poultry prices; & Cambridge affairs; interesting.   21

WALES,Archbishop of. Memories(1927) boyhood at Dinas;education; work as a schoolmaster; ordination and ministry in Wales; church affairs, reform, and disestablishment. Cambridge U.L.   22

WALFORD, Lucy Bethia. Recollections of a Scottish Novelist(1910);Memories of Victorian England(1912). Childhood in Highlands;domestic life, society & sport in Edinburgh; literary life and writings;preachers, writers, painters and lecturers;Carlyle, Houghton, Jean Ingelow, etc.; anecdotes.   23

WALFORD,William. Autobiography, ed. John Stoughton (1851). His secession to Congregational Church; training at Homerton College;his ministries;tutor at Homerton; religious beliefs.   24

WALFORD, Wilmington (pseud.). Autobiography of an Indian Army Surgeon (1854). Medical studies; army service at various stations in India; mainly about social life and people.   25

WALKE, Bernard. Twenty Years at St. Hilary (1935). Life of High Churchman in a Cornish parish; village life and people;plays at St. Hilary; his radio work; chatty memories.   26

WALKER, Alexander. Hours Off and On Sentry (Montreal,1859). Military life in England, Portugal, Canada; settles in Quebec.   27

WALKER, Bettina. My Musical Experiences (1890).Piano student with Liszt Taussig, Sgambati, Bennett, etc.   28

WALKER,Sir Charles.Thirty-Six Years at the Admiralty (1933). Career as a deputy-secretary; administrations and naval personalities.   29

WALKER,David. Death at My Heels (L. 1942).Personal affairs and adventures during German invasion of Balkans;his evacuation and escape; war & politics from 1939.   30

WALKER, Fred. Destination Unkno w n

(1934). Boy stowaway;later adventures in Wild West, South & Central America among Indians,revolutionaries & headhunters.   31

WALKER, H., J.,& B.M.Recollectio n s (Leeds,1930). Their life in Yorkshire village of Levisham from 1860's; village life,schools,sport, people; and later at Leeds.   32

WALKER,Henry Francis Bell. Doctor's Diary in Damaraland(1917). Service in field ambulance unit in Southwest Africa in WW1; hardships of campaign in bush; with Botha.   33

WALKER,Kenneth. The Intruder (1936) I Talk of Dreams (1946); A Doctor Digresses (1950). Psychologist's analysis of himself and his career; dramatic form; his roles; family, personal life, medical and psychological study and travels; medicine and philosophy; the past as a guinea pig.   34

WALKER,Lieut. Robert. Private Diary (Scinde, 1885). Day-to-day events in Afghan War, 1839-42; personal and military affairs. India Office.   35

WALKER,Col.Thomas Nicholls. Through the Mutiny (1907). Military career in India, 1854-83; Mutiny; siege of Delhi; Rohilcund; campaigns against Naga Hill tribes; social life; sport.   36

WALKER, Whimsical. From Sawdust to Windsor Castle (1922). Life in circus from boyhood;clown in Sanger's circus and later in musichalls, Drury Lane & at command performances; Grimaldi and other famous clowns.   37

WALKER,William. Reminiscences(Aberdeen, 1904); Additional Reminiscences (Aberdeen, 1906). Aberdeen religious & social life from 30's as remembered by the Dean of Aberdeen;Marischal College and academic life.   38

WALL, Sir Frederick. Fifty Years of Football (1935). His experiences with Soccer;Secretary of Football Association;players, clubs, managers; mostly historical.   39

WALLACE, Alfred Russel. My Life (L. 1905). Early life in Herts; workingclass life; secularists, Owenites and

development of his scientific and social interests; work in natural science;socialism; his friends; valuable
and interesting story of Victorian affairs and intellectual movements. 40

WALLACE,Maj. Blake. Quod (1935). In
prison service from 1900;Pentonville;
Borstal;training of prison officers &
reflections on penology.   41

WALLACE, Edgar. People (1927). Life
in London slums;school;odd jobs, army
and later a war correspondent in South
Africa;his career as a novelist; told
as climb from slumdom to his succ es s
as journalist and author.   42

WALLACE,Harold Frank. Happier Years
(1944); Hunting Winds (1949). Misery
of war years; nostalgic recollections
of Eton,travels, sporting life; hunting,fishing, shooting; literature and
theatre and cinema; anecdotes.   43

WALLACE, Nisbet. The Padre Sees It
Through (1939). Record of his service
as padre during WW1; Gallipoli, Egypt
Salonika and Western Front.   44

WALLACE, Robert. Life & Last Leaves
(1903).His youth in Fifeshire in 30's
in Calvinistic family;parish schools;
family struggles.   45

WALLACE, Robert Grenville. Fifteen
Years in India (1823). Army officer's
experiences in India; social life and
Hindu life and scene.   46

WALLACE, William. Memoirs (1821). A
Hussar in Peninsular War;imprisonment
in France; mostly his adventures as a
rake; amours; gambling.   47

WALLACE, William. From Evangelical
to Catholic (Calcutta, 1922). Schools
in Ireland; clerical life & parishes;
missionary work in Bengal; studies of
Hinduism; conversion to Catholicism &
his novitiate. India Office.   48

WALLAS,Ada. Daguerrotypes (1929). A
record of her childhood in Devonshire;
family, schools, religion, pastimes &
people; pleasant.   49

WALLER,Gen. Sir William. The Poetry
of Anna Matilda(1788). Includes short
account of events in life of the Par-

liamentary general;his adventures and
escapes during the Civil War.   50

WALLETT,William Frederick. The Public Life of (1870).Forty years career
as comedian in England and America;at
circuses,pubs, cigar-stands, medicine
shows;tours of the Empire; the Queen's
Jester.   51

WALLIS,Rt.Rev. John. Autobiographical notes written 1697; education and
scientific studies;beginning of Royal
Society; writings & motives; teaching
pronunciation. MS Smith 31, Bodleian
Library.   52

WALLIS, Mary Davis. Life in Feejee
(Boston, 1851). Life and work during
five years among cannibals as a missionary; American?   53

WALLIS, Thomas Wilkinson. Autobiography (Louth, 1899). Apprentice and
journeyman carver;his career at Louth
as wood-sculptor;honours; his life at
Louth;social and political affairs of
the day; very interesting.   54

WALMSLEY, Leo. Flying and Sport in
East Africa (1920); So Many Loves (L.
1940). Service with RFC in East Africa during WW1; hunting; his Yorkshire
boyhood; county life, sport, natural
history; his writings; films and art;
varied interests; pleasant.   55

WALPOLE, Frederick. Four Years in
the Pacific(1849). Naval life and his
cruises aboard HMS Collingwood, 1844-
1848.   56

WALPOLE,Horace, 4th Earl of Orford.
Reminiscences Written in 1788 (1798);
Memoirs of the Reign of King George II
(1846); Memoirs of the Reign of King
George III(1845); Last Journals(1910)
Largely impersonal history of parliament,public affairs, court life, from
1750's;foreign news, gossip, and some
personal affairs;mostly in day-to-day
form.   57

WALSH, Langton Prendergast. Under
the Flag (n.d.). Life and work of an
official in India and on the coast of
Somaliland in 70's and 80's.   58

WALSH,Louis J. On My Keeping and In
Theirs (Dublin, 1921). Political life

of County Down lawyer;Irish nationalism; prison, internment camp, and his
experiences fleeing the British.   59

WALSH, Robert. A Residence at Constantinople (1836). Life and observations; Greek and Turkish revolutions;
Turkish life and customs.   60

WALSH,Thomas. Life and Death of, by
James Morgan (1762). Largely autobiographical notes of sinful childhood &
conversion from Catholicism to Methodism; diary notes.   61

WALSH, Capt. Thomas. Journal of the
Late Campaign in Egypt(1803). Service
in 93rd Foot; personal narrative; the
conquest of Egypt.   62

WALSHE, Maj. Blayney Townly. Sporting and Military Adventures (L.1875).
Youth in Ireland; enlistment; service
in army in Nepal and Himalayas;adven-
tures; hunting; social life.   63

WALSINGHAM, Thomas de Grey, Baron.
Hit and Miss (1927). Bird-shooting in
later 19th Century;notes on birds and
natural history.   64

WALTERS,Mrs. Arthur. My Wayside (L.
1931). Travels and changing domestic
life of wife of Methodist minister who
later settled in Cambridge; VAD work
in Birmingham hospital, WW1.   65

WALTERS, John Cuming. Knight of the
Pen (Manchester, 1933). Work as journalist in Birmingham and Manchester &
social life,theatre,personalities in
those areas.   66

WALTON,Robert. Random Recollections
of the Midland Circuit (1869). Career
as barrister and judge;circuit life &
memories of cases and lawyers.   67

A WANDERER.Reminiscences & Reveries
of a Wanderer(1935). Lifelong travels
of an Englishman born in India;Europe
Far East, the Americas.   68

WARBURTON,Ernest. Behind Boche Bars
(1920). Cheerful memories of English
officer in German prisons from 1916;a
record of German stupidity.   69

WARBURTON,John. Mercies of a Covenant God (Manchester, 1837). Spiritual

autobiography of Lancs Baptist;family
life;sins and wrestlings with his God
and preaching in Lancashire,Cheshire,
and Wiltshire.   70

WARBURTON,John. Memorials, ed. John
Hemington (1892). Spiritual life of a
Baptist minister;early idleness; work
among soldiers;ministry in Beds.; his
spiritual struggles.   71

WARBURTON,Col. Sir Robert. Eighteen
Years in the Khyber (1900). His youth
and early career in India; military &
surveying activities, 1879-98; tribes
of the frontier; sport.   72

WARD, Edward H. Give Me Air (1946).
Journalist's experiences as a prisoner
in Germany during WW2;later work as a
war correspondent in Germany.   73

WARD, Edwin A.   Recollections of a
Savage(1923). Travels in Asia, Canada
and Europe; work as a painter; sitters;
club life; anecdotes of Whistler, and
Rhodes, Harmsworth, etc.   74

WARD, Ernest. Medical Adventure (L.
1929). Reminiscences of general practitioner; by-paths of medicine; legal
adventures;experiments in spiritual -
ism, etc.   75

WARD,Francis Kingdon. Plant-Hunting
on the Edge of the World(1930); Plant
Hunter in Tibet (1934). His travel in
Burma, Assam, and Tibet in the 20's,
searching for plants and shrubs.   76

WARD, H. M. Behind the Lines (1918)
Vivid account of evangelical work during WW1; behind the Western Front; a
moving record.   77

WARD, Henrietta Mary Ada. Reminiscences (1911);Memories of Ninety Years
(1924). Her painter-father; marriage;
country life, Windsor and Slough; the
Victorian social scene; art, theatre,
writers; Dickens, Thackeray, Macready
Collins, Lytton, etc.   78

WARD, Herbert. Five Years with the
Congo Cannibals (1890); My Life with
Stanley's Rearguard (1891). Travels &
work for missionaries in Congo area;
service with Stanley and self-justification against Stanley's criticisms;
negro life and customs.   79

WARD,Mrs. Humphry. Writer's Recol-
lections(1918). Childhood and friends
at Fox How;Oxford in 60's; marriage &
life in London; her literary career &
friendships; Henry James,etc.　　80

WARD,John. Experiences of a Diplomatist (1872). Germany, 1840-70; work
as minister to Hanse towns;economics,
politics, social life.　　　　81

WARD, Col. John. With the Die Hards
in Siberia (1920). Lively account of
activities against Bolsheviks following WW1; stirring adventures.　　82

WARD, John Sebastian Marlow. Gone
West(1917);A Subaltern in Spirit Land
(1920).His psychic experiences during
WW1; death of his brother; interviews
and dialogue through mediums.　　83

WARD, Leslie. Forty Years of "Spy"
(1915). Eton;his family and their artist and theatrical friends;work as a
cartoonist; Vanity Fair; clubs; & his
friends in literature & politics.　84

WARD,Paul.Reminiscences of Cheltenham College, by an Old Cheltonian (L.
1868).Experience at the school in the
mid-century;students, masters, sports
and customs.　　　　　　85

WARD, William. Brief account of his
life in Sheffield; early years, until
conversion to Primitive Methodism 1828
MS, Sheffield City Libraries, Miscellaneous Docs. 1490.　　　　86

WARDLE,Joseph. The Story of My Life
(1924). His career in insurance, Manchester,Derby, Beeston; his travel in
America; Primitive Methodist missions;
social work.　　　　　　87

WARING, John Burley. A Record of My
Artistic Life (1873). Boyhood at Lyme
Regis;University College, Bristol and
Royal Academy; travel in Europe;notes
on painting and architecture.　　88

WARNER, Rt.Rev. John. Brief account
of the life of the 17th Century scholar and Bishop of Rochester (d. 1666).
MS, Bodleian Library, Rawlinson Mss,K
(Hearne Smith) (516) 12.　　　89

WARNER,Pelham F. My Cricketing Life
(1921). Boyhood in West Indies; Rugby

and Oxford; cricket there & with Middlesex and England;games and tours; &
his law studies.　　　　　90

WARNER, Richard. Literary Recollec-
tions(1830). Education, Lymington and
Oxford;early reading; literary career
from 1780's; eccentrics & antiquaries
he knew; Grose, Parr, Hartley; travel
in England and France; clerical life;
anecdotes; amusing.　　　　91

WARREN, Arthur. London Days (Boston
1920). A Bostonian in England,1878 to
1918;social, political, artistic, and
literary life and celebrities.　92

WARREN, C. V. Burmese Interlude (L.
1937).Life and work during five years
as a teak-forester in Burma;　Burmese
life; adventures.　　　　　93

WARREN, Clarence Henry. Boy in Kent
(1937). Pleasant memories of his youth
in Kentish village; sports, worthies,
social life, trade, hoppers, etc. 94

WARREN, George. Dangers and Doings
in a Soldier's Life,by John Young (L.
1845).Childhood misbehaviour; service
in army in Peninsular War in Spain and
at Waterloo; reported to a clergyman;
may be fiction.　　　　　95

WARRENDER,Lady Maud. My First Sixty
Years (1933). Memories and anecdotes;
society, music, theatre, literature &
celebrities.　　　　　　96

WARWICK, Frances Evelyn Greville,
Countess. Life's Ebb and Flow (1929);
Afterthoughts(1931). Girlhood at Easton and London society; the Victorian
and Edwardian scene; social work; her
activities in the socialist movement;
the Clarion; Shaw.　　　　97

WARWICK, Mary Rich, 4th Countess of
Autobiography, ed. T. C. Croker (1848)
Her early life in Ireland;marriage &
family life in England;　her troubles;
fervid devotions of a great lady of the
17th Century.　　　　　98

WARWICK AND BROOKE,Earl of.Memories
of Sixty Years (1917). His education;
country work, social life, and sport;
Society; Royal Family.　　　99

/WASHINGTON, Pat B./. Fanny Goes to

War, by Pat Beauchamp (L.1919); Fanny
Went to War (1940). Service with FANY
during WW1; nursing and hospital experience on Western Front; convoys and
first-aid; women's life in war.   100

WATERHOUSE, Francis Arthur. 'Twixt
Hell and Allah (1931);Five Sous a Day
(1934);Gun-Running in the Red Sea (L.
1935); Bloodspots in the Sand (1939);
Journey without End(1940). Service in
Foreign Legion in North Africa; Druze
rebellion;work for international gang
in Abyssinia; tough life; career as a
soldier of fortune,including his army
career in India and his work in films;
Beau Geste.   101

WATERHOUSE, T. A. With Nets & Lines
(1947).Activities of president of the
National Federation of Anglers;coarse
fishing;anti-pollution work; trials &
difficulties; fishing yarns.   102

WATERS,General Sir Wallscourt Hely-
Hutchinson.   Secret and Confidential
(1926);Private and Personal (1928). A
record of his career in the army & as
a military attaché;Versailles, Berlin
Russia and North China;personal life,
diplomacy; his opinions.   103

WATERTON,Charles. Essays on Natural
History (1838-57);Wanderings in South
America (1825).Autobiography & travel
of the eccentric and naturalist; life
and pursuits at Walton Hall; explorations and natural history observation
1812-24 in Guianas, Brazil, Demarara,
Pernambuco,etc.; scientific studies &
writings.   104

WATKINS,Miles. A Sketch of the Life
(Cheltenham, 1841). Boyhood poverty;
odd jobs; debtor's prison; shoemaker;
work for poor; teetotalism.   105

WATKINS,Owen Spencer. With Kitchener's Army(1899);With French in France
(1915).Methodist chaplain on the 1898
Nile expedition and in WW1; soldiers'
morals; hospital work.   106

WATKINS,Sir Percy Emerson. A Welch-
man Remembers (Cardiff, 1944). Career
in educational administration,Wales &
Yorks;Welsh Board of Health; Board of
Education(Wales); social service; and
Welsh public life; good.   107

WATSON,Aaron. Newspaper Man's Memo-
ries(1925).His 55 years in journalism
with Pall Mall,Echo, etc.; Parliament
politics,literature, Savage Club, and
celebrities.   108

WATSON, Alfred E. T. A Sporting and
Dramatic Career (1918). Music & drama
critic with Standard; editor Badminton
Magazine;sporting life; social life &
friends.   109

WATSON,Angus. My Life(1937). Social
work in Newcastle;Liberalism; temperance movement;business as sardine can-
ner; travels to Norway; social-minded
businessman.   110

WATSON, David. Chords of Memory (L.
1936); I Was a Parson(1948). Ministry
and social work in Glasgow; religious
and social problems of industrial society;revolt against authoritarianism
in Church; his spiritual search.   111

WATSON, Edmund Henry Lacon. Notes &
Memories (1931); I Look Back Seventy
Years (1938). Interests as a sporting
journalist; Winchester and Cambridge;
teaching, writing, journalism,and publishing; censorship in WW1; Reuter's;
colleagues and friends.   112

WATSON, Edward. History of the Hawtrey Family,by Florence Hawtrey(1903)
contains an autobiography of activity
in the Irish rebellion, 1798; service
in Peninsular War to 1811 and personal
adventures.   113

WATSON,Edward Spencer. Diary, 1857-
1858; naval service of a cadet in Indian waters; service in Mutiny; Lucknow;Cawnpore. Journal; India (Kettering, 1858). India Office.   114

WATSON,John (ed.). Confessions of a
Poacher (Edin. 1890). Activities of a
Scottish poacher; his encounters with
keepers; woodcraft.   115

WATSON,John Cameron. One Man's Fur-
row (1940). Farming and travels, from
1913;Argentina, Canada, USA, France &
Greece;tramping; writing; adventures;
odd jobs.   116

WATSON,Keith Scott. Single to Spain
(1937). A journalist's service in the

International Brigade during the Spanish Civil War; love affairs; civilian life.   117

WATSON, Lily (Mrs. Sydney). Village Maiden's Eventide(1929). Missionary's wife;religious experience; missionary work in England, WW1 and after.   118

WATSON, Rt.Rev. Richard. Anecdotes of the Life (1817). Education; career in the church;Bishop of Llandaff; and his scientific and theological studies and interests.   119

WATSON, Robert Patrick. Memoirs (L. 1899). Athlete,boxer, referee, sporting journalist;famous fights, patrons & fighters; musichalls, police courts and prisons; entertaining.   120

WATSON,Sydney. Brighter Years(1898) Life's Look-Out (1906). Hard times as a boy;life in the navy; Christian influence;work as evangelist; secretary of YMCA at Basingstoke.   121

WATSON,Thomas A. Exploring Life (L. 1926). Mechanical and telephone work; assistant to Alexander Graham Bell; & late interest in culture; with Benson theatrical company.   122

WATSON,William.Autobiography of the life and work of Sheriff-Substitute of Aberdeenshire (1796-1887),written for the young; "The Children's Sheriff." MS, Aberdeen P.L., 4 vols.   123

WATSON,William David.I Was a Parson (1948). Spiritual life and conflicts; London University; Plymouth Brethren; ordination in Church of England; work among Jews and in slums;resignation & spiritual search as layman.   124

WATSON,William Foster. Machines and Men (1935). Working-class life; work as mechanic in London factories;trade unions;unemployment; views on management; wanderings.   125

WATSON, William Henry Lowe. Adventures of a Despatch Rider (1915). His service in Royal Engineers in WW1;the Mons retreat.   126

WATT, Agnes C. P. Twenty-Five Years Mission Life (Paisley, 1896).Life and work of wife of Presbyterian mission-

ary at Tanna, New Hebrides, 1868-93; tribulations; translations.   127

WATT, Mrs. Stuart (Rachel). In the Heart of Savagedom (1913). Her life & work as a missionary in East Equatorial Africa,1885-1911; evangelism; adventures and jungle life.   128

WAUGH, Alexander Raban (Alec). Myself When Young(1923). The novelist's travels,pleasures, friends; beginning of his writing career.   129

WAUGH,Arthur. One Man's Road (1931) His life from 60's to 1918; Somerset country life;work as journalist, writer, publisher; family life; literary friendships; WW1.   130

WAWN,William T. South Sea Islanders (1893). Life at sea;operations in the Queensland labour trade; recruitment of native labour in New Guinea & West Pacific, 1875-91.   131

WAZAN, Emily (Keene), Shareefa of. My Life Story(1912). Life of Englishwoman married to a Moroccan chieftain thirty years at a Moorish court, Tangier and the desert; family life; and Moorish life and customs.   132

WEATHERLY, Frederic Edward. Piano & Gown (1926). Experiences as a teacher entertainer and lawyer; concerts; and life on circuit.   133

WEAVER, Richard (d.1896).Life Story (1913). Life of a workman-evangelist in 19th Century.   134

WEBB, Beatrice.   My Apprenticeship (1926); Our Partnership(1948). Growth of attitudes and career of the famous socialist and sociologist;childhood & Victorian scene;studies; observations of working-class life;marriage; joint work with her husband;Fabian Society ; Labour Party;Trade Unions; research & writing; London politics; celebrities in public life;valuable record of the social and intellectual history of the period.   135

WEBB, Thomas Duncan. Sailor, You've Had It(1946). Experiences in merchant navy during WW1;Atlantic and Murmansk convoys; reporter on 2nd Front;flying accident.   136

WEBLING, Archie Frederic. Something Beyond (Cambridge, 1931). A Suffolk minister's self-education, ministry & religious and personal difficulties & his spiritual quest;assistant to Hallam; Catholicism.   137

WEBLING, Peggy. Peggy (1924). Early years in later half of 19th Century in Lake District & Kensington; the Slade school;literary and theatrical interests;Ruskin; travels and pioneer life in Canada;her writing career;pleasant memories.   138

WEBSTER,Benjamin Nottingham. Acting National Drama (1837-53) Vol.VI, contains sketch of his life as strolling player, comedian, stage manager at the Haymarket and Covent Garden in the early 19th Century.   139

WEBSTER, Gerald.   I Walked at Dawn (1949). Attractive story of hardships of his youth as a cripple in Australia and of his working-class life in England; struggles for independence. 140

WEBSTER, Nesta Helen. Spacious Days (1948). Well-to-do family life in the 90's;travels; marriage; life in East; farming in England; WW1.   141

WEDDERBURN,Sir David. Life, by Mrs. E. H. Percival (1884) is based on his papers and diaries;activities of 19th Century Scottish lawyer, politician & traveller.   142

WEDGWOOD,Sir Josiah C. Essays & Adventures(1924); Memoirs of a Fighting Life (1940).Work as magistrate in the Transvaal;Boer War; radical and labor politics;socialism & taxation of land values;WW1, international socialism & movement toward WW2.   143

WEDMORE,Sir Frederick. Memories (L. 1912). Work as painter; reminiscences of French and English painters,actors and writers.   144

WEEDEN,Edward St.Clair. A Year with the Gaekwar of Baroda (1911). Clergyman's experience during his year as a guest at an Indian court; social life sport and amusements.   145

WEHL, David.   The Moon Upside Down (1948). Travels and impressions of a

soldier-artist in Burma,China, Siam & Java after WW2.   146

WELCH, Denton. Maiden Voyage (1943) Runaway from school; visits father in China; art study; sensitive record of a phase of his life.   147

WELDON,Capt. Lewen Barrington. Hard Lying(1926). His WW1 service; torpedo boats; intelligence work; in Eastern Mediterranean.   148

WELLDON,Rt.Rev. James Edward Cowell Recollections and Reflections (1915); Forty Years On(1935). Education, Eton and King's; teaching, Dulwich, Harrow etc.;career in the church in Calcutta Westminster, Manchester; work and reflections of teacher and bishop. 149

WELLER, James.   The Wonders of Free Grace (Battle, Sussex, 1845). Kentish boyhood;ploughboy;conversion; visions and evangelism of Calvinistic Baptist, in Kent and Sussex;interesting detail of life of the poor. Copy in Worthing P.L.   150

WELLESLEY,Colonel Frederick A. With the Russians in Peace and War (1905); Recollections of a Soldier-Diplomat - (1948).Eton; career in the Coldstream Guards; military attaché in Russia in the Russo-Turkish War; later work in the diplomatic service.   151

WELLS,Herbert George. Experiment in Autobiography(1934). His lower-middle class upbringing; science study, London University; struggle for a living and the development of his career as a novelist and writer; his ideas; world planning.   152

WELLS, John Carveth.   My Candle at Both Ends(1943). Travel in many lands and his ups & downs; Bohemian life in Soho.   153

WELLS, Lionel De Lautour. Letters & Recollections, by Ida C. Wells (1934) Contains diary extracts, 1915-18; his work in navy,convoys during WW1; naval vice-consul in USA.   154

WELLS,William Edwin.Nine Years with the Colours (1899). Life of a Baptist chaplain in the British army;mainly a survey of army life, with anecdotes of his work and acquaintances.   155

WELSH,Major-General James. Military Reminiscences (1830). His service in India,1790-1829; Poligar and Mahratta wars; Travancore; Ceylon; travels and inspection of defences. See also, his diary, 1845-48;scientific observation & personal affairs in Southern India. MS, India Office, Eur. D.168.   156

WENSLEY,Frederick Porter. Detective Days (1931). Forty years as policeman chief constable,detective;Whitechapel and slums; Flying Squad; adventures & amusements.   157

WESLEY,John. Wesley's Last Love, by Augustin Leger (1848). An interesting autobiographical account of courtship of Grace Murray of Newcastle;marriage views, devotion, religion; episode of 1748-49.   158

WEST,Adam. Just as They Came (1946) Soldier's letters,1942-4; army life & training as parachutist.   159

WEST,Sir Algernon Edward. Recollections (1899). Politics and society in mid-century;civil servant and private secretary; Palmerston, Gladstone,etc. and public affairs.   160

WEST,Charlotte. Ten Years Residence in France (1821). Her experiences and observations during the revolution,up to Bonaparte's advent to power;personal memories of Royal family.   161

WEST, Daniel. Travel diary, 1856-7; missionary's visits to Methodist stations on the Gold coast; negroes and their beliefs. The Life and Journals (1857).   162

WEST, Elizabeth. Memoirs (Glasgow, 1766). Edinburgh servant's religious autobiography; illness, doubts, temptations, exultations.   163

WEST, Lady Lucretia. Diary, 1823-8; a very interesting record of domestic family and social life in Bombay.Bombay in the Days of George IV, edited Frederick G. D. Drewitt (1907).   164

WEST, Thomas.   Ten Years in South-Central Polynesia (1865). Life & work of a Wesleyan Methodist missionary in

the Friendly Islands and dependencies from 1845; troubles; adventures; native conditions.   165

WEST,William.Fifty Years' Recollections (1837). Affairs of a bookseller in London;the trade; authors, artists antiquaries, actors; Grose, etc. 166

WESTELL, William Percival. My Life as a Naturalist(1918). Boyhood at St. Albans; nature lover; rambles around England; natural history study.   167

WESTERN, Colonel John Sutton Edward Reminiscences of an Indian Cavalry Officer (1922). Youth in India; school; Sandhurst; army career, India & Burma and social life and sport.   168

WESTMACOTT, George Edward. Journal, 1830; army officer's travels in India MS, India Office, Eur. C.29.   169

WESTMORELAND,Mildmay Fane, 2nd Earl Short autobiography in Latin; school and activities as royalist during the civil wars. MS, British Museum, Add. 34220.   170

WESTMORELAND, Thomas, 6th Earl. His education and public life.Extracts in Earl of Westmoreland's MSS. HMC, 10th Rep. App. Pt.IV (1885).   171

WESTON, Agnes Elizabeth. Life among the Bluejackets (1910). Her vocation & training for social work;teetotalism and work among soldiers and sailors at Portsmouth,etc.; activities at Sailors' Rest;Queen Victoria's patronage; interesting.   172

WESTON,Mary. Eliot Papers, ed.Eliot Howard(1895). Spiritual life, travels in the ministry in England and America of a Wapping Quakeress, first half of 18th Century.   173

WESTON,Fr. William. The Troubles of Our Catholic Forefathers,by John Morris (1875). Religious labours,travels adventures, imprisonment, of a Jesuit sent into England in Elizabeth's time; continued in Catholic Record Soc.Misc. I (1905).   174

WESTON-WEBB,Weston Fulford Marriott Autobiography of a British Yarn Merchant (1929). Rise from rags to riches;

business success of Nottingham merchant in Victoria's reign.   175

WETHERED, Joyce. Golfing Memories & Methods(1933). Career and experiences of a champion golfer; advice.   176

WEWEGE-SMITH,Thomas. Gran Chaco Adventure (1937). Airman's service and adventures in Foreign Legion & in the Bolivian Air Force; Gran Chaco War; & love affairs.   177

WEYLLAND,John Matthias. Valiant for the Truth (1899). London boyhood; his resistance to Catholicism; social and mission work in London slums; temperance movement, Sunday Observance, and education; Shaftesbury.   178

WEYMOUTH, Anthony (Ivo Geikie Cobb) Who'd Be a Doctor (1937). Training as doctor; work in hospitals, in general practice and in the army; excitements of medical life; novel-writing, journalism; lively.   179

WHALEY,Thomas. Memoirs (1906). His romantic travels through Europe & the Near East in 1780's;inspired by Lavater, Gibbon and Rousseau.   180

WHARTON,Hon. Goodwin. Autobiography written for his son;education; family troubles;strange afflictions, romantic adventures,visions, visitations by angels; a strange document. MS, B. M. Add. 20006-7.   181

WHATCOAT,Richard.The Lives of Early Methodist Preachers,ed.Thomas Jackson (1838) III.Gloucestershire man's life as an itinerant Methodist preacher,in West of England.   182

WHATELEY, Dame Leslie. As Thoughts Survive (1949). Her work as director of Auxiliary Territorial Service,WW2; administration.   183

WHATLEY,Charles W. Farming and Foxhunting (1940).Life of a Wilts farmer from the 70's;country life, work, and sport;service on Wilts County Council WW1 service; broadcasting.   184

WHEELER, Barbara. Life and ministry of a London Quaker,mainly in 2nd half of 18th Century. Extracts in, Journal Friends' Hist. Soc. III (1906).   185

WHEELER, Daniel. Journal, 1817-39; Quaker's travels and ministry; Russia Australia,New Zealand, Tahiti and the Sandwich Islands;native life; sociological observations;personal religion Memoirs of the Life (1842); Extracts from the Letters & Journal (1839).186

WHETSTONE,Charles. Truths No. 1, or The Memoirs of(1807). School and farm life in 1760's;work in the stocking & silk factories of Derby;child labour; working conditions. Derby P.L.   187

WHIFFEN,Mrs.Thomas (Blanche). Keeping off the Shelf (1928). Career as a singer and entertainer from the 60's; Gilbert and Sullivan; USA tours.   188

WHILE, John Henry. Fifty Years of Fire Fighting (1931);Fire!Fire!(1945) An old man's reminiscences of fires & firemen's work in London; gossipy and rather vague record.   189

WHIPPLE, Dorothy. The Other Day (L. 1936).Psychological history of childhood; emotional hurts, school compulsions, troubles, imaginings; the real stuff of childhood.   190

WHISH,Violet.Partners in Friendship (1949).Her memories combined with the memories of Lady Norah Spencer-Churchill; friendship; London social life & politics, literature, music, theatre, and society between wars. Copy, Exeter P.L.   191

WHISHAW, James. Memoirs (1935). His medical training;life and work in St. Petersburg from 70's as a shipbroker; travel and sport in Russia;the Revolution; dictated.   192

WHISTON,William.Memoirs of the Life (1749).An astronomer's account of his student days at Cambridge in 1680's & of later scientific studies;life as a clergyman; theology & his ideological troubles; reflections.   193

WHITAKER,J.P. Under the Heel of the Hun (1917). Yorkshire business man at Roubaix;experiences while interned by Germans in WW1.   194

WHITAKER,Malachi (Mary). And So Did I (1939).Sketches of her domestic life and family affairs.   195

WHITAKER, Percy. My Memoirs (1938). Hunting in Essex and Suffolk;training racehorses;Grand National experiences and his famous clients. 196

WHITALL, James. English Years (N.Y. 1935). Young American's life, England 1914-23;literary interests; translating and reviewing; literary society; Strachey, Squire, George Moore, Henry James, Symons, etc. 197

WHITE,Florence. Fire in the Kitchen (1938). Varied career as teacher,social worker,journalist, cook from 60's and work as cookery journalist. 198

WHITE, Henry. The Record of My Life (Cheltenham, 1889). Farm boyhood; his work as a servant; marriage; ventures as a grocer; itinerant waiter; social establishment at Cheltenham. 199

WHITE,Sir Herbert Thirkell. A Civil Servant in Burma(1913). Life and work as an official and judge in Burma, in 1878-1905; administration, politics & social life;Burmese life, customs and scene. 200

WHITE, James Robert. Misfit (1930). Irish soldier's adventures; Boer War; with Irish volunteers in the rebellion and his activities in trade unions and communism. 201

WHITE,John Baker. It's Gone for Good (1941). Army officer; boyhood in Kent and Hants; farming after WW1; work in circus; interest in communism & fascism; Territorial service; WW2 experiences; the Blitz. 202

WHITE, John Claude. Sikhim & Bhutan (1909). Life and work of a political officer on Northeast Frontier 1887 to 1908; travels; descriptions. 203

WHITE,Joseph Blanco. Second Travels of an Irish Gentleman in Search of a Religion (Dublin, 1833); Life, edited J. H. Thom(1845). Spiritual difficulties in the Church;his youth in Spain and life in England;Oxford; religious studies; work in the Church; unitarianism. 204

WHITE, Maude Valérie. Friends and Memories (1914); My Indian Summer (L. 1932). Career as singer & composer in 2nd half 19th Century;concerts; music and literature; travel; her friends in the arts. 205

WHITE,Rev. Newport John Davis. Some Recollections of Trinity College(Dublin, 1935). Memories of scholarship & scholars in Dublin from 1878; Dowden; academic life. 206

WHITE, Colonel Samuel Dewé. Indian Reminiscences (1880). Military career in Bengal, 1845-70; service in Mutiny Christian work; religious views. 207

WHITE,Terence Hanbury. England Have My Bones(1936). Country life; farming and sport; country people. 208

WHITE,William Hale(Mark Rutherford) The Autobiography (1881);Mark Rutherford's Deliverance(1885, 1888); Early Life of Mark Rutherford(1913). Education; religious training;Cheshunt College; work for John Chapman; his life in London;spiritual autobiography and his emancipation from Puritan dogma to a newer Puritanism;Civil Service work and graphic picture of London. 209

WHITEFIELD, George. The Experiences (1851). The life of the great Methodist until his taking orders in 1736;a vigorous picture of working-class life in Gloucester; religion. 210

WHITEHEAD, Sir Charles. Retrospections (Maidstone,1908). Public work & farming; adviser to Board of Agriculture; work for Royal Agricultural Soc. farming and sport in Kent. 211

WHITEHEAD,George.Christian Progress (1725).Ministry and hardships of 17th Century Westmoreland Quaker;trial and imprisonment;political controversies; London in plague and fire. 212

WHITEHEAD, Joseph. The Evangelist & Pastor (1879). Boyhood in Yorks; work as bookbinder;Methodist ministry; his meetings & conversions; Moody, Sankey and other evangelists. 213

WHITEHOUSE,Arthur G. J. Hell in the Heavens (1938). Personal experiences of a WW1 aerial gunner. 214

WHITEHOUSE, William Edward. Recollections of a Violincellist (L. 1930)

Anecdotes about his musical activities and friends; royal performances. 215

WHITEING, Richard. My Harvest (1915) Early life in London; work as novelist journalist and foreign correspondent; The Star; his travels; social life in Victorian London; literature. 216

WHITELAW, David. A Bonfire of Leaves (1937). Work as painter, writer, and journalist; travels in Europe and America; his eminent friends in the arts; anecdotes. 217

WHITELEY, George Cecil. Brief Life (1942). Career in the law; the Temple and criminal bar; recorder & chairman of Quarter Sessions; judge at the Old Bailey; crimes, cases, his opinions on punishment. 218

WHITELOCKE, Bulstrode. Annals of his Life; public affairs and diplomacy in 17th Century. MS, British Museum, Add. 36341-7; extracts in R.H. Whitelocke's Life (1860). 219

WHITELOCKE, Sir James. Liber Famelicus (Camden Soc., 1858). Life of judge of King's bench; legal work in the 1st quarter of 17th Century. 220

WHITFIELD, George J. Fifty Thrilling Years at Sea (1934). Life and work in sailing and steamships; merchant navy; liners; commander of RMS Arundel Castle; excitements. 221

WHITFORD, John. Trading Life (Liverpool, 1887). Life, work and travel of a trader in western and central Africa; native life. 222

WHITING, John. Persecution Expos'd (1715). His life and ministry in the Quaker faith; account of early Quakers and Quaker history. 223

WHITMAN, Sidney. German Memories (L. 1910); Turkish Memories(1914); Things I Remember (1916). Boyhood; career as journalist; special correspondent for N.Y. Herald Tribune; major events and celebrities in Europe from 90's. 224

WHITNELL, Lewis. Engines Over London (1949). Lively account of his service in WW2; training and experiences as a flyer; Battle of Britain. 225

WHITSED, Juliet De Key. Come to the Cook-House Door! (1933). Adventure and work of a nurse in VAD during WW1; the Macedonian campaign; lively. 226

WHITTAKER, James. I, James Whittaker (1934). Squalid life in slums & cotton mills; dreams of beauty and knowledge; his revolt. 227

WHITTAKER, Thomas. Life's Battles in Temperance Armour (1884). His boyhood in squalid Yorks home; factory work & sinful friends; lifelong propaganda & travel for temperance; a good picture of 19th Century industrialism. 228

WHYTE, A. P. Luscombe. Escape to Fight Again (1943). Thrilling escapes of bomber pilot in WW2. 229

WHYTE, Frederic. A Bachelor's London (1931). Work for publishers; Methuen's and Cassell's; travels; reminiscences of famous writers, before WW1. 230

WICKENDEN, William. Some Remarkable Passages in the Life (1847). Boyhood in Gloucs.; love of country; his poems teaching, study at Cambridge beginning 19th Century; friendship with Jenner; academic life. 231

WICKHAM, George. A Blue-Coat Boy's Recollections (1841). His life at the Christ's Hospital foundation in Hertford; no dates. 232

WICKHAM, Henry Alexander. Journal, 1869-70; travel from Trinidad to Pará via the Orinoco; explorations in the Orinoco and Negro basins; the Brazilian jungle. Rough Notes of a Journey (1872). 233

WICKS, Henry W. The Prisoner Speaks (1938). His trial & prison experience in 1936-37; sex, fascism, prisoners & administration. 234

WIDDICOMBE, John. Memories and Musings(1915). London in 50's; religious life; Pusey and the Puseyites; career as churchman in South Africa. 235

WIENHOLT, Arnold. Story of a Lion Hunt (1922). WW1 service with Intelligence Corps in East Africa; scouting; hunting; adventures of an intelligence officer. 236

WIGHAM, John. Memoirs of the Life of (1842). Aberdeen Quaker's account of his religious life & ministry; travel in Scotland and USA.   237

WIGHTWICK, George. Theatricals, 45 Years Ago (Portishead,1862). Theatregoer's memories of London stage;plays players and audiences.   238

WIGNACOURT, John. Odd Man in Malta (1914).Life and work of British civil servant; Maltese life and customs and his reactions.   239

WIGNALL, Trevor C. I Knew Them All (1938);Never a Dull Moment(1940). His sporting memories and work of a sports journalist in Fleet Street; Sporting Life, Mail, Standard; celebrities in sports, films, etc.   240

WILBERFORCE-BELL, Capt. Harold. War Vignettes (Bombay,1916). His personal experiences in France and England during WW1. India Office.   241

WILD, John James. At Anchor (1878). Experiences aboard HMS Challenger;exploration of depths of oceans.   242

WILD, Roland. The Rest of the Day's Your Own(1943). Gossip and humours of army life in WW2; infantry service in France.   243

WILDE, Jimmy. Fighting Was My Business (1938). Welsh boyhood; work as a miner and escape into boxing;his life as champion boxer in England and USA; behind the scenes details.   244

WILKES,John. An Unfinished Autobiography, ed. W.F. Taylor (Harrow 1888) His schooldays; exile in France and in Italy and love affair, to 1765.   245

WILKES, Paget. Missionary Joys in Japan (1913). Fifteen years' life and work of a missionary;evangelism; tent meetings; Japanese life. Copy, India Office Library.   246

WILKINS, John. The Autobiography of an English Gamekeeper(1892). An Essex man's memories of sport,gamekeeping & poachers,early 19th Century; excellent dialogue.   247

WILKINSON,Charles Allix.Reminiscen-

ces of Eton (1888). His schooldays in days of Keate;critical account of the curriculum, discipline, social life & religion.   248

WILKINSON,Dyke. A Wasted Life(1902) Rough Roads(1912). Journalist's life; the Turf, jockeys & gamblers; boyhood and schooling in Birmingham;odd jobs; work as sports journalist.   249

WILKINSON,Henry Spenser.Thirty-Five Years (1933). Life and experiences of a lawyer,journalist, military strategist from 1874; travels in Europe and the Empire; political scene.   250

WILKINSON, Kitty. Memoir (Liverpool 1927). Social work among the working classes in Liverpool in early part of 19th Century; nursing, charity work & humble service; cholera epidemic. 251

WILKINSON, Sir Nevile R. To All and Singular (1925). Harrow;career in the Coldstream Guards;Boer War; WW1 service in Egypt; Irish rebellion; Ulster King-of-Arms.   252

WILKINSON, General Osborn & General Johnson.Memoirs of the Gemini Generals (1896). Reminiscences of their military careers in India from 1848;Mutiny and Ceylon rebellion; military life, social affairs, sport.   253

WILKINSON, Rt. Rev. Thomas Edward. Twenty Years of Continental Work and Travel (1906). Work in the colonies & in factories and communities as British Bishop in North and Central Europe travel experiences.   254

WILKINSON, Tate. Memoirs of His Own Life (York, 1790); Wandering Patentee (York, 1795).Career as theatre manager in Yorkshire, from 1760's; theatre life in provinces;plays, actors, audiences,problems; anecdotes; criticism very lively and valuable.   255

WILLANS , Geoffrey. One Eye on the Clock (1943). Naval lieutenant's life on corvettes and aircraft carrier during WW2.   256

WILLCOCKS, General Sir James. From Kabul to Kumassi (1904); With the Indians in France(1920); The Romance of Soldiering and Sport (1925). His army career from 70's; India, Afghanistan, Burma, Nigeria; Ashanti War; service in France in WW1 with Indian troops;& hunting and other sports. 257

WILLCOCKS, Sir William. Sixty Years in the East (1935). Boyhood in India; work as an engineer, 1852-1914; India Persia, Egypt; canals, dams, irrigation; politics; humanitarianism. 258

WILLIAMS, Bransby. An Actor's Story (1909).Life as character-impersonator in music-halls;Dickensian roles;anecdotes of music-hall performers; travel to USA, etc. 259

WILLIAMS, Dr. Charles James Blasius Memoirs of Life and Work(1884). Study of medicine,Edinburgh and Paris; life and research work as professor of medicine,University College, London; the medical scene to 1883. 260

WILLIAMS, Clement. Journal, 1863; a journey exploring the possibility for a trade route between the Irrawaddy & the Yang-tse-Kiang; political agent's observations;native cultures. Through Burmah to Western China (1868). 261

WILLIAMS, D.R.H. Memories of Moor, Stream and Woodland (1944). Country & sporting life;mainly shooting & fishing in Yorkshire. 262

WILLIAMS, E.Harcourt. Four Years at the Old Vic (1935). Work as producer and actor; Shakespeare, Shaw, and his productions. 263

WILLIAMS, Eric Ernest. The Wooden Horse(1949). Excellent account of one of the most remarkable escapes from a German prison in WW2;making of wooden horse and tunnels; emotional aspects; novelistic in style. 264

WILLIAMS,Frederic Condé. From Journalist to Judge (Edin.1903). Practice of journalism in Birmingham and France and his later career in the law. 265

WILLIAMS,Henry Willey. Some Reminiscences (Penzance, 1918). His work on English railways & at St. Katherine's Docks;social scene and public affairs from 1830's. Harvard U.L. 266

WILLIAMS, Sir Herbert G. Politics,

Grave and Gay(1949). Rambling reminiscences and anecdotes; family affairs his candidacies and 18 years in Parliament; political scene; Baldwin, N. Chamberlain, Hitler, etc. 267

WILLIAMS,Mrs. Hwfa. It Was Such Fun (1935).Childhood in Dorset in 1870's; marriage; sport & high society in the days of Edward. 268

WILLIAMS,Isaac. Autobiography(1892) Spiritual and religious life at Oxford in first half of century,while fellow of Trinity; Pusey; Newman; Tractarian movement. 269

WILLIAMS, John. A Narrative of Missionary Enterprises(1837). Life, work and travels of a missionary in Tahiti Samoa and New Zealand in 20's; family affairs; adventures; translations and studies of native history. 270

WILLIAMS,Joseph. A Wexford Quaker's memories of the 1798 rebellion.Journal Friends Hist. Soc. II (1905). 271

WILLIAMS,Josiah. Life in the Soudan (1884). Surgeon's work and experience 1881-2; tribal life and conditions in Kunama country; hunting. 272

WILLIAMS,Leigh. Green Prison (1941) Twenty years work for teak company in Siam;forest life; teak trade; Siamese life and politics; good. 273

WILLIAMS,Montagu Stephen. Leaves of a Life(1890); Later Leaves (L. 1891); Round London (1892). Eton;army; legal career and practice;slum life & crime in East End of London;his cases;views on poverty and crime. 274

WILLIAMS,Peter.English Works of the Late Eliezer Williams (1840). Preface contains autobiography;Welsh boyhood; schools; religious life; ordination & persecution for pro-Methodism;life as itinerant preacher in Wales during the latter part of 18th Century. 275

WILLIAMS, Sir Ralph.How I Became a Governor (1913). Personal experiences and official life in Australia, Patagonia,Bechuanaland, S. Africa; Governor of Windward Isles and Newfoundland travel, politics, administration; the interests of a public servant. 276

WILLIAMS,Thomas. Diary, 1840-2; his work as a missionary in Fijis;passion for service;paganism and Christianity natural history;native culture & history; excellent. The Journal, edited G. C. Henderson (Sydney 1931).   277

WILLIAMS,Thomas Rhondda.How I Found My Faith(1938). Welsh boyhood; career as Congregational minister, Wales and England;Church Union; work in Christian socialism; Labour Party.   278

WILLIAMS,Valentine. World of Action (1938). Life of journalist, soldier & novelist; Reuter's; Daily Mail; Young Germany; WWl; war correspondent; his travels in Europe and America; novels and books. Adventures of an Ensign by Vedette(1917) records his experiences with Guards in France, WWl.   279

WILLIAMS-ELLIS, Bertram Clough. The Architect (1929). His career, aspirations and achievements; architecture in England.   280

WILLIAMSON, A. Stanley. On the Road With Bertram Mills(1938). Life & work as circus press agent;circus performers; how the show works.   281

WILLIAMSON,Alice Muriel (Mrs. C. N. Williamson). What I Found Out, by an English governess(1915); Inky Way (L. 1931). American girlhood; her work as governess in German noble family pre-WW1; marriage to English writer; social writing for Daily Mail;the motoring novel;literary friendships; Meredith, Jerome, etc.   282

WILLIAMSON, Fr.Benedict. Happy Days (1921).Catholic padre's experience in France during WWl.   283

WILLIAMSON, David. Before I Forget (1932). Journalist's career from 1890 memories of editors,journalists, writers,musicians, politicians, sportsmen, royalty, etc.   284

WILLIAMSON, George Charles. Stories of an Expert(1925); Memoirs in Miniature (1932). Art expert's anecdotes of collecting and collectors; miniatures paintings, jewels; legal and illegal acquisitions;episodes of general interest;people, antiquities, books, and places.   285

WILLIAMSON,Henry.Story of a Norfolk Farm (1941); Sun in the Sands (1945); Life in a Devon Village(1945).Experiences as farmer from novice days;life in Devon;friends and neighbours; work as writer;natural history;romanticism and Jefferies' influence.   286

W(ILLIAMSON), J(ohn).Narrative of a Commuted Pensioner (Montreal, 1838).A Scotsman's army service in India & the Far East;misfortunes in business; his emigration to Canada.   287

WILLIAMSON,John Ernest.Twenty Years under the Sea(1935). Adventures of a deep-sea diver;photography in tropical waters; big fish.   288

WILLIAMSON,William Crawford.Reminiscences of a Yorkshire Naturalist (L. 1896). Yorks boyhood; natural history studies and research;teaching in Manchester University; science in his day and academic life.   289

WILLIS, Frederick. Peace & Dripping Toast(1950). His life as a workman in late Victorian and Edwardian days;his schooling,family life, work in a publisher's and hatter's; London scene, shops, pleasures; a nostalgic, idealised but pleasant record.   290

WILLIS, George H. A. The Royal Navy as I Saw It (1924). His career in the navy from 1879;work of a paymaster; & anecdotes of naval life.   291

WILLIS,Jerome. Restless Quest(1938) It Stopped at London(1944).Journalist and traveller;mental experiences; the cynicism of inter-war period;European scene and events leading up to WW2 and his experiences as correspondent for a London evening newspaper.   292

WILLIS, R. Carrington. My Fifty-One Years at Euston(1939). London boyhood his various railway posts; registrar, LMS Railway;amateur acting, gardening and suburban pleasures.   293

WILLISON, Charles. Reminiscences of a Poor Hunting Man (1905). University education;poverty; guest in North and West Country mansions;hunting; horsedealing; love-affair; fiction?   294

/WILLMOTT-DIXON, Wilmott/. Spice of

Life, by Thormanby (1911). Boyhood in London in 50's;Cambridge & the Temple and career as journalist;anecdotes of bench, bar, theatre, clubs, taverns & Bohemian life and celebrities.   295

WILLOUGHBY DE BROKE,Richard Greville Verney, 19th Baron. The Passing Years (1924).His forebears and family;Eton, Oxford;foxhunting and country society his Parliamentary career and activity in serious House of Lords politics; a record of a contented Victorian.   296

WILLYAMS, H. V. Down West (1903). A yachtsman's experiences;his boats and cruises off South coast;departure for Boer War.   297

WILSON, Albert Edward. Playgoer's Pilgrimage (1948). His life and work as dramatic critic; The Star; plays & players.   298

WILSON,Andrew.Some Reminiscences of a Lecturer(1898). Scottish scientist; oratorical ambitions; lecture tours & Sunday Lecture movement;experience as lecturer in physiology in Scotch universities; anecdotes.   299

WILSON,Lady Anne Campbell (MacLeod) After Five Years (1895). Life of the wife of a commissioner in remote Punjab district; studies of Indian education and culture;her views on Indian needs and British rule.   300

WILSON,Sir Arnold Talbot. Loyalties (1930);Mesopotamia(1931); S.W. Persia (1941).Campaigns in Near East in WW1; work as civil commissioner and political officer;survey of military, economic and political affairs;personal & historical.   301

WILSON,Arthur.Observations of God's Providence(in Francis Peck,Desiderata Curiosa, 1735, II). Writer's memories of childhood;service with Essex & Warwick;Oxford studies; Civil War memories; views on witch-burning; 1st half 17th Century.   302

WILSON, Lady Barbara. The House of Memories (1929). Her girlhood, France before WW1; society,friends, artistic life in Paris.   303

WILSON, Caroline (Fry). An Autobio-

graphy (Philadelphia, 1849). Girlhood education, religious training; Quaker religious life;literary interests and reading.   304

WILSON, Rt. Rev. Cecil. The Wake of the Southern Cross (1932). Life and work as missionary in Melanesia, from 1893; mission on Norfolk Island & his cruises as a supervisor; administration as Bishop of Melanesia.   305

WILSON,Sir Charles Rivers. Chapters from My Official Life (1916). Family; Oxford; work in Treasury; supervisor, Egyptian finances;administrative work on Canadian railways.   306

WILSON, Colonel Sir Charles William From Korti to Khartum (Edin. 1885). A personal narrative of his services as adjutant on Nile expedition.   307

WILSON, Daniel. Life of (Woodbridge 1847-8). Childhood hardships; voyages to Greenland in 80's; conversion; his life and work as a Baptist minister in Suffolk.   308

WILSON, Right Rev. Daniel. Journal, 1832-41; missionary and diocesan work as Bishop of Calcutta; education; and religious thought; the Indian scene. Journal Letters (1863).   309

WILSON, Francesca M. In the Margins of Chaos (1944). Relief work with the Friends and others during WW1 & after; Belgium,France, Serbia, Russia, Spain etc.; victims of war.   310

WILSON, Frederick B. Sporting Pie (1922). Athletics at Elstree School & Harrow from 90's;cricket & rackets at Cambridge and Queen's Club;journalism for Daily Mail; celebrities.   311

WILSON,Sir Guy D.A. Fleetwood. Letters to a Nobody (L.1921); Letters to Somebody (1922). His youth and early life in Italy; India; work at the War Office, 1868 to end of WW1; soldiers, politicians, wars, sport, social life and his own work.   312

WILSON, Capt. Henry. Journal, 1783; shipwreck & experiences among natives of Pelew Islands; native life. George Keate, Account of the Pelew Islands (1788).   313

WILSON, Capt. Henry Allen. British Borderland (1913). Military and political work in Nairobi; the Anglo-German border; travels; hunting.   314

WILSON, Field-Marshal Henry Maitland Wilson, Baron. Eight Years Overseas (1950). Military activities from 1939; defeat of Italians in Cyrenaica; commanding Commonwealth troops in Greece Greek campaign and campaigns in Syria and Iraq; military details.   315

WILSON, Harriette. Memoirs (1825). A lively, impudent record of her life as a society whore from age 15; Esterhazy Wellington, Beau Brummell and others; excellent dialogue.   316

WILSON, Herbert Arthur. Haggerston Roundabout (1948). His experiences as parish priest in working-class parish in London, mainly in WW2; religion and sports; his people.   317

WILSON, James. Diary, 1824-25; the travels and work of Scottish merchant in Guatemala; economics; social life; good. A Brief Memoir (1829).   318

WILSON, James. Autobiography of the Blind James Wilson (1856). Boyhood in America; departure during Revolution; blind as boy; raised in Ulster; experiences there as itinerant dealer; his love of learning, poetry, philosophy & his publications; Reading Society; and marriage and family.   319

WILSON, Col. James Alban. Sport and Service in Assam (1924). Thirty-five years in the Gurkha Rifles; Manipur; garrison life; mainly sport; hunting, polo, cricket.   320

WILSON, James Hall. Life and Labour (1877). Life & work of Congregational minister in Aberdeen and London; work missions, conversions.   321

WILSON, James Maurice. Autobiography (1932). Religious life and education; Cambridge, Rugby and Clifton; teaching of science; headmaster of Clifton; the changes & reforms in education; covers 1836-1931.   322

WILSON, John. Memories of a Labour Leader (1910). Boyhood; early life at sea and in America in 60's; political

work in England; Member of Parliament; Liberalism & rise of the labour movement; Gladstone.   323

WILSON, John. Tales and Travels of a School Inspector (Glasgow, 1928). His work in Scottish schools from the 80's and experiences with teachers, schools and Boards; pleasant anecdotes; views on teaching.   324

WILSON, John Plumpton. With the Soldiers (1920). Chaplain's WW1 service in Palestine and Syria.   325

WILSON, Joseph Havelock. My Stormy Voyage (1925). Early life as a sailor; organization of Sailors and Firemen's Union; Member of Parliament; excellent details of labour movement in 2nd half of 19th Century.   326

WILSON, Margaret. Missionary diary, 1828-35; work at the Scottish mission in Bombay. A Memoir, by John Wilson (Edin. 1829).   327

WILSON, Rathmell. Pre-War (Epsom, 1937). Boyhood in Cotswolds; Sherborne and Oxford; literary activities; life as an actor; his parts and tours; London social life.   328

WILSON, Robert Francis. Short Notes of Seven Years' Work (Oxford, 1872). A Hants parson in 60's; church services; views on ritual; social work.   329

WILSON, Robert McNair. Doctor's Progress (1938). Boyhood and education in Glasgow; medical studies and practice and work as medical correspondent for The Times; London Scots; social life; his novels.   330

WILSON, Thomas. Brief Journal of the Life (Dublin, 1728). Spiritual life & travels in ministry of Cumberland Quaker; visit to America.   331

/WILSON, Maj. Thomas Fourness/. The Defence of Lucknow, by a Staff Officer (1858). Diary of military and personal affairs in the siege of Lucknow. 332

WILSON, William. Green Peas at Christmas (1924). Northants boyhood; soldier in mid-19th Century; country life; and foxhunting; MFH of Atherstone; life at Gumley.   333

WILSON-CARMICHAEL, Amy. Things as They Are (1903). Life and work of a missionary in Southern India; Tinnevelly; Indian life and customs.   334

WILTON, Horace. Wanderer's Episodes (1915).Friendly gossip on his life on the stage; minstrels, pantomimes, entertainments; later work as electioneering speaker and agent.   335

WILTON,John Henry. Scenes in a Soldier's Life (Montreal, 1848). Ups and downs; campaigns in Afghanistan, Sind and Baluchistan.   336

WINDHAM, Sir Walter. Waves, Wheels, Wings(1943). Life at sea and in army; experiences with planes;his career as King's Messenger; Empire travels; adventures.   337

WINDLASS. With the R. N. R. (1917). WW1 experience and adventures in naval patrol; life on small boats.   338

WINFRED, Daniel J. Glimpses of Police Work (Madras,1914). Life and work of a police inspector in Madras;crime and criminals. India Office.   339

WINFREY, Sir Richard. Great Men and Others I Have Met (Kettering,1943). A Liberal M.P.'s memories of politicians clergyman and journalists; his public work in Lincs; Mayor of Peterborough; Parliamentary career.   340

WINGATE,Col. Alfred Woodrow Stanley Cavalier in China(1940). His military life,travels and adventures, India to China, 1897.   341

WINGFIELD, William Edward. My Story (Stirling,1913). Irish boyhood; Woolwich; service in artillery in India & its resultant agnosticism; conversion in England;missionary work as chaplain in army; his curacies.   342

WINGFIELD-STRATFORD,Esmé.Before the Lamps Went Out (1945). English life in late Victorian period;Cambridge; Dartmoor;country life; Oscar Browning and Austen Leigh; cultural life.   343

WINN,Godfrey. Home From Sea (1944); Going My Way (1948). WW2 service;on a cruiser in Arctic patrol; life on the lower deck; adventures in America and Europe; amusing but digressive.   344

WINNINGTON-INGRAM,Rt.Rev. Arthur F. Fifty Years' Work in London (1940). A clerical career in London;Oxford House and East End social work;activitiesas Bishop of Stepney and of London;problems & controversies; temperance; his gospel.   345

WINNINGTON-INGRAM,Herbert F. Hearts of Oak (1889). Incidents in his naval career from 30's; mainly S. America & Baltic campaign; admiral.   346

WINSLOW, Lyttleton Stewart Forbes. Recollections of Forty Years (L.1910) Rugby and Cambridge; career as alienist in lunatic asylums; criminal lunacy; medical and legal experiences; & famous crimes.   347

WINTERTON, Edward Turnour, 6th Earl of. Pre-War(1932). Social life, sport travel and Tory politics in the decade before WW1.   348

WISEMAN, Cardinal Nicholas Patrick Stephen. Scraps from My Scrapbook (L. 1875).Rambling recollections of Catholic life and personages.   349

WITHERS,Percy. In a Cumberland Dale (1914); Friends in Solitude (1923). A life in a secluded cottage;nature and country life in Lake District;friends and countrymen;musings and moods in a pleasant vein.   350

WITHINGTON, T. Reminiscences of the Ministerial Life(Devonport,1895). The life and work of a Cornish Methodist; conversions,temperance work, missions Penny Readings; social life; pleasant record. Methodist Book Room.   351

WITNEY,Max Arthur. No More Hustling (Watford,1940). Early life in Germany and business life in London & Germany; conversion;spiritual life; activities in Adult Education in Watford.   352

WITT, John George. Life in the Law (1906).Cambridge boyhood; career as a barrister; Norfolk and Home circuits; judges, trials, procedure; & notes on Jefferson Davis & other American lawyers.   353

WOLFE,Humbert. Now a Stranger(1933)

Upward Anguish (1938). Experiences in boyhood & youth; his schools; life at Oxford as undergraduate;literary circle at Oxford;Flecker;military training; freely treated facts.   354

WOLFF,Sir Henry Drummond.Some Notes of the Past(1892); Rambling Recollections (1908). Family and education; & career in the Foreign Office in second half of 19th Century; his embassy at Madrid; diplomacy; society.   355

WOLFF, Joseph. Missionary Journal & Memoir(1824); Researches and Missionary Labours (1835); Journal (L.1839); Travels and Adventures (1861). Travel and missionary work in Near East, India, Persia, Afghanistan, Abyssinia & Yemen; mostly journals.   356

WOLLASTON,Alexander Frederick Richmond. Letters and Diaries (1933). His career at King's College,Cambridge; & work and travels as naturalist.   357

WOLLASTON,Francis.Secret History of a Private Man (1795).Early law study; ministry in Norfolk and Kent;his work on behalf of Dissenters; his troubles within the Church;interests in astronomy and theology.   358

WOLLASTON, William. Autobiography, written 1709; boyhood; Leicestershire interests;interests as schoolmaster & moral philosopher.MS,Leicester Museum and printed, John Nichols, History of Leicestershire (1795-1815) IV.   359

WOLLEY,Clive Phillips. Sport in the Crimea and Caucasus (1881). Pleasures of British Vice-Consul at Kertsch;his climbs, hunting, travels.   360

WOLLOCOMBE, John B. From Morn till Eve (1898). Experiences at Winchester School and Oxford,early 19th Century; travels in Europe;public affairs; and life and work as Rector of Dunterton & of Stowford.   361

WOLSELEY,Garnet Joseph Wolseley,1st Viscount.The Story of a Soldier's Life (1903).Field-marshal's account of his army career;India;Crimean War; Indian Mutiny;Ashantee War; service in China and Canada; American Civil War.   362

WONHAM,Capt.Albert R. Spun Yarns of a Naval Officer(1917). Navy career in second half of 19th Century;the manly life & adventures of a practical seaman; Sarawak; China; introduction of first ironclads.   363

WOOD, Anthony a. Early life of 17th Century antiquary;family & upbringing and Oxford career;public affairs; his historical and antiquarian studies;an amusing story. MS, Harl.5409, British Museum, 67 fos;see also, Life & Times ed. A. Clark (1891-1900).   364

WOOD,Maj.Gen. Sir Elliott. Life and Adventure (1924). Military service & campaigns,1864-1905; Egypt, S. Africa and Boer War.   365

WOOD, Ernest Egerton. Is This Theosophy(1936). Lancs boyhood; work as a shop assistant and stamp dealer;life-work as theosophist; Annie Besant and other leaders in the movement; occult phenomena; interesting.   366

WOOD, Sir Evelyn.   From Midshipman to Field Marshal (1906); Winnowed Memories (1917). Boyhood in the navy in 50's; career in the army; Crimean War and Indian Mutiny; Ashanti War; Zulu War;Sudan; Boer War; sport and social life; anecdotes; and his reflections on soldiers and soldiering.   367

WOOD,Capt. George. Subaltern Officer (1825).Service and personal adventures in Peninsular War;complaining that the narratives of privates are numerous,he writes for the subalterns.   368

WOOD,Georgie. I Had to be Wee(1948) Life and stage career of a small comedian; music-hall personalities. 369

WOOD, Harry Stotesbury. Milestones of Memory (1950). Varied life; army and medical service in India; travels and sport;retirement; various walking tours.   370

WOOD, Sir Henry J. My Life of Music (1938). Career of the conductor; RAM; Sullivan;German; opera; the Promenade concerts;musical life in London;development of public taste;reminiscences of artists and composers.   371

WOOD,Lieut. Colonel Henry S. Shikar Memories (1934). Military life, India

and Burma from 1891;social life; travels; hunting.   372

WOOD, J. A. Diary, 1857-61; details
of military and personal affairs; his
exploits and lack of reward; the Indian scene. MS, India Office Library,
Eur. B.34.   373

WOOD, John. Artist's autobiography;
boyhood at beginning of 19th Century;
family life, education, art studies &
struggles & work as artist; Victorian
social life;a very interesting record
with many drawings. MS,British Museum
Add. 37159-37167.   374

WOOD, R.Theodore. Theo Wood in Wartime and After (1931). Experiences of
crippled pacifist during WW1; No More
War and left-wing activities;troubles
with police; illnesses & unhappy love
affairs.   375

WOOD, Stuart. Shades of the Prison
House (1932); Glorious Liberty (1933)
Strange Triumph (1936). His unhappy &
maladjusted boyhood; criminal career;
prison experiences;prison ways; religious conversion by Oxford Group;work
as missionary and lecturer.   376

WOOD, Thomas. True Thomas (1936). A
musician's story of early days in the
merchant service;study at Oxford; his
career as organist; music, the occult
and other matters of interest;humane
and well-written record.   377

WOOD,Wendy. I Like Life (1938). Her
girlhood in late Victorian days; Boer
War; Boy Scout Movement; the Scottish
National Party.   378

WOOD,William. A Sussex Farmer(1938)
Country life and farming in Sussex,in
late 19th Century; Sussex people. 379

WOODARD, Capt. David. The Narrative
(1804). Shipwreck; his two years as a
captive of Malays on Island of Celebes
and his escape; native life, customs,
etc.   380

WOODBURN, M. Kathleen. Backwash of
Empire (Melbourne,1944). Her life and
adventures during a year in New Hebrides islands; native culture. Colonial
Office Library.   381

[WOODCOCK,Thomas?]. Account of Some
Remarkable Passages in the Life of a
Private Gentleman (1708). Spiritual &
contemplative life;temptations; God's
hand in his life;has been ascribed to
Defoe.   382

WOODGATE,Walter.Reminiscences of an
Old Sportsman(1909). Boyhood in Worcs.
Radley and Oxford;sports; career as a
lawyer;Thames rowing;Victorian social
scene; light-veined.   383

WOODHALL,Edwin T.Detective & Secret
Service Days (1929). Twenty years in
police and CID;secret service in WW1;
guarding VIPs;later work as a private
detective.   384

WOODHEAD, Henry George Wandesforde
A Journalist in China(1934). His work
for foreign press in Shanghai 1902-31;
Chinese politics,development, personalities; drug problem.   385

WOODLEY, Herbert George (pseudonym)
Certified (1947); That Which is Caes-
ar's(1948); Synthetic Mania (L. 1948)
Experiences as patient in lunatic asylum; sympathetic and careful account
of institution and criticism of treatment; plea for psychiatry. Real name,
H. G. Wilkins.   386

WOODROOFE, Com. Thomas. Naval Odyssey (1936); River of Golden Sand (L.
1936); In Good Company (1947); Moana-
lua (1950).Service on gunboats on the
Yangtse; convoying and anti-submarine
work in WW2; African and Sicily inva-
sions; naval life on New Zealand station and in South Seas.   387

WOODS,A.P. I Guarded the Waterfront
(1942). Experiences at Old Swan Pier;
building of new Tower Bridge;shipping
on Thames; adventures.   388

WOODS, Sir Henry Felix. Spunyarn(L.
1924). His 47 years in navy;admiral &
pasha in Turkish navy;Turkish-Russian
relations; navy and diplomacy; social
life in Constantinople.   389

WOODS, Samuel Moses James. My Reminiscences (1925).Sport at school & at
Cambridge and his experiences as Rugby
footballer and Somerset cricketer;his
other sports.   390

WOODVILLE,Richard Caton. Random Recollections (1914). Education in Germany;career as painter; travel, India
Morocco, Balkans; sport; acquaintance
with royalty.   391

WOODWARD, David. Front Page & Front
Line (1943). Travels and observations
of war correspondent; Near East,China
India, Africa; strong opinions.   392

WOODWARD, Ernest Llewellyn.   Short
Journey (1942). London boyhood in the
90's; Oxford; WW1; study and teaching
of history; travels in Far East; Lost
Generation.   393

WOODYATT, Gen. Nigel Gresley. Under
Ten Viceroys (1922); My Sporting Memories (1923). Military career in the
Gurkhas, 1880-1920; Indian wars & unrest; society and sporting adventures
in India.   394

WOOLF,Ernest P.Thirty Years of Pub-
lic Life (1913). Work in national and
London municipal politics;Conservative
Party; public speaking.   395

WOOLLEY,Frank. King of Games (1935)
Reminiscences of the Kent and England
cricketer;county and Test cricket and
players; behind the scenes.   396

WOOLMER,Joseph. Letters to a Christian Friend (Sherborne,1826). Life of
business man in Exeter;family affairs
and religious life; insurance.   397

WOOLMER, T. My Life and My Work (L.
1892). Boyhood in Yorkshire;Kingswood
School; work as teacher and itinerant
minister; Methodist affairs; governor
of Kingswood School.   398

WOOLWARD,Robert.Nigh on Sixty Years
at Sea (1894). Ramsgate man's cruises
and adventures; West Indies.   399

WOON, Basil. Eyes West (1940). Life
and adventures as hobo,prospector and
tramp-reporter,soldier, and Hollywood
writer; Canada, USA, S.America. 400

WORBY, John. The Other Half (1937);
Spiv's Progress(1939). The unpleasant
record of a man who lived by his wits;
card and coin tricks;low life & crime
adventures in Canada.   401

WORDSWORTH, Rt.Rev. Charles. Annals
of My Early Life (1891); Annals of My
Life(1893). Family; Harrow and Oxford
and teaching at Winchester;Newman and
the Oxford Movement; academic life at
Trinity; clerical career; work as the
Bishop of St. Andrew's.   402

WORDSWORTH, Elizabeth. Glimpses of
the Past (1912). Girlhood at Harrow &
Rydal; Lake poets; Oxford religious &
academic life with parents; scholarly
career; Principal, Lady Margaret Hall
Lambeth settlement work;social life &
literary friends.   403

A WORKING MAN. Scenes from My Life,
ed. R. Maguire (Islington, 1858). His
boyhood in Clerkenwell; apprentice to
weaver;unemployment; Reform Bill; the
London scene and working-classes;work
and unemployment in Exeter;conversion
and growing serenity.   404

A WORKING MAN.   Reminiscences of a
Stonemason (1908). Labourer in Kent;
bricklayer and stonemason;unemployed;
life as a tramp;travels in Canada and
USA; ups and downs of life.   405

WORKMAN, Alan. Colonial Postmaster-
General's Reminiscences (1937). Work
and travels in postal service in East
and West Africa;Uganda; Trinidad; and
anecdotes.   406

WORMELEY,Adm.Ralph Randolph. Recollections (N.Y.,1879). Life in British
Navy in early century;social life and
politics,London and Essex; the Reform
Bill; people he knew.   407

WORRALL,T.H. Reminiscences of Early
Life (Macclesfield, 1897). Childhood;
people, places, churches, shops, public affairs in Macclesfield. Copy in
Manchester P.L.   408

WRATISLAW,Albert Charles. Consul in
the East (1924). Official life & work
in Constantinople from 80's, and also
in Smyrna, Greece, Bulgaria; travels;
Balkan politics; excellent.   409

WRAXALL,Sir Nathaniel William. Memoirs of the Courts of Berlin,Dresden,
Warsaw and Vienna (1799);   Historical
Memoirs(1815); Posthumous Memoirs (L.
1836).Diplomacy and court life in the

later part of 18th Century;George III
and Pitt,Fox, Burke, Sheridan; public
affairs; politics; anecdotes.   410

WRENCH, Sir John Evelyn L.   Uphill
(1934); Struggle(1935); I Loved Germ-
any(1940); Immortal Years (1945). His
boyhood; Eton; foreign correspondent;
WWl activities;Peace Conferences; his
work in Germany between wars;Hitler &
rise of Nazis;work for Empire unity &
endless travel and speaking; Overseas
League;English-Speaking Union;friends
in politics; Daily Mail.   411

WRIGHT,Alfred. Adventures in Servia
(1884).Adventure of medical freelance
among Bashi-Bazouks;Russo-Serbian War
of 1876; lighthearted.   412

WRIGHT, Mrs. Charles Henry Hamilton
Sunbeams on My Path (1890). Christian
missionary and medical work in Sweden
Switzerland,Crimea; life with clergy-
man-husband, Yorks, Dresden, Boulogne
and Ireland. Cambridge U.L.   413

WRIGHT, Duncan. The Lives of Early
Methodist Preachers,ed.Thomas Jackson
(1837) I.Perthshire man's travels and
work in Methodist ministry, later half
of 18th Century; Scotland.   414

WRIGHT,Henry.Eighty-Six Years Young
(1938). Boyhood in North; work in tea
trade;marriage, family, travels, publications;Victorian social life, London; his life in Dublin, France, Bermudas.   415

WRIGHT,Henry Press.Recollections of
a Crimean Chaplain (1857).Ministry at
Varna Cholera Hospital;the campaign &
care of wounded; hradships.   416

WRIGHT, John Hornsby. Thoughts and
Experiences (1878); Confessions of an
Old Almsgiver (1881). His work as an
organizer of charities;pauperism; the
evils of unorganized charity; tricks
of the poor; donors; recipients. 417

WRIGHT,Joseph. Life, by E.M. Wright
(1932).First part is a dictated autobiography of his boyhood in Yorkshire;
early poverty;self-education; study &
teaching of philology.   418

WRIGHT, M. J. Three Years in Cachar
(1895). Life & work on tea-plantation

domestic and social life; Hindu life;
Moslem servants;Manipur massacre; and
hunting.   419

WRIGHT,Adm. Noel. Sun of Memory (L.
1947).His forty years in the navy and
highlights in his cruises.   420

WRIGHT, Philip A.   Ploughshare and
Pulpit(1947). Life in East Anglia and
simple details, farming, country life
church and parish; Methodism.   421

WRIGHT, Richard. Review of the Missionary Life and Labours (1824). Work
and travels of a Unitarian in England;
visit to USA.   422

WRIGHT,Thomas. Autobiography(1864).
Yorkshire clothmaker and wool manufacturer in 2nd half 18th Century;a good
picture of domestic life,religion and
Methodist disturbances.   423

WRIGHT,Thomas. Thomas Wright of Olney (1936). Schools;reading; critical
& biographical work; literary friendships; difficulties with relatives of
his subjects.   424

WROE, John. Life & Journal (Gravesend,1859) Vol. I. Yorkshire religious
fanatic;visitations from God and high
priests;their communications with him
and the import of them.   425

WYATT,James. The Life & Surprizing
Adventures (1748). Early life at sea
trumpeter on privateer; capture by the
Spanish; imprisonment; shipwreck; and
Moorish captivity and hardships. 426

WYLD,George. Notes of My Life(1903)
Scottish youth; the Carlyles; medical
study in London;many interests; smoke
abatement, investments,, theosophy and
spiritualism;Liberal Union Party; his
poems and other writings.   427

WYLDE, Augustus Blandy.   '83 to '87
in the Soudan (1888). His political &
military activities in Sudan in 80's;
account of Abyssinia.   428

WYLDE,Mary. A Housewife in Kensington (1937). Tranquil life;house, family,servants, domestic routine; books
and theatres; pleasant and wise. 429

WYLIE, Ida Alexander Ross. My Life

with George (N.Y.1940). Upbringing in
England; education; social life; WW1;
her later life in USA; her novels;her
literary life.   430

WYLLIE,Marian A. We Were One (1935)
Her childhood in France and Kent;mar-
riage to painter;his career; family &
social life;Portsmouth; share in husband's work and life.   431

WYNDHAM,Horace. The Queen's Service
(Boston, 1899). Life of a private;the
conditions and practices of army life
in the 90's.   432

/WYNDHAM,Horace/. The Nineteen Hun-
dreds,by Reginald Auberon (1922). The
London scene in 1900's;newspapers and
publishers;courts; theatres; literary
life; Bohemia.   433

WYNN,Wynn E. Ambush (1937). Service
in the East African campaign in Tanga
during WW1; adventures.   434

WYNNE,Frances. Eastward of All(Dublin, 1945); True Level (Dublin, 1948)
Girlhood in Ulster;career as a writer
influences toward Catholicism and her
conversion;travels in England, Spain,
and France to holy shrines.   435

WYNTER, Captain Philip H. M. On the
Queen's Errands (1906). Army service
in India; the Mutiny; his 35 years as
diplomatic courier to the capitals of
Europe; genial anecdotes.   436

YAPP, Sir Arthur. In the Service of
Youth(1927). Hereford boyhood; family
life;religion and temperance; work in
YMCA;secretary of movement; YMCA work
on Western Front in WW1;lecturing and
travels; celebrities he met.   1

YARDLEY,Capt. John. Papergon (1931)
Military service in Central Africa in
WW1; personal experiences.   2

YATES,Agnes. Putting the Clock Back
(1939).Childhood in Wilts Quaker home
in 60's;schools, social life, games &
pleasures; religion; pleasant.   3

YATES,Arthur. Autobiography (1924).

Work and experiences of a trainer;his
memories of riders,trainers, owners &
horses.   4

YATES,Edmund Hodgson. Recollections
and Experiences (1884).London boyhood
and work in Post Office; journalism &
literature; The World; Garrick Club &
literary friends; Dickens, Thackeray,
the theatre; visit to USA.   5

YATES, John. Travel diary, 1820-28;
life, work, and travels of a merchant
in Peru and Chile. MS, The Athenaeum,
Liverpool.   6

YEATS, John Butler. Early Memories
(Dundrum,1923). Poet's father; school
and boyhood in Ireland;early years as
a painter;conversation-piece; reflections on poetry, patriotism, anything
of interest.   7

YEATS,William Butler. Reveries over
Childhood (Dundrum, 1915); Four Years
(Dundrum,1921); Trembling of the Veil
(1922); Estrangement (Dublin, 1926);
The Death of Synge(Dublin,1928); Dra-
matis Personae (1936). Notes on life,
literature,other days, writers, Irish
life,troubles, theatre, magic, aspirations; writers of the Irish literary
revival; Abbey Theatre; reflections &
speculations; some diary notes.   8

YEATS-BROWN,Francis C. C. Caught by
the Turks(1919); Bengal Lancer (1930)
Bengal Lancer at Large (1936). Career
as a cavalry officer; prisoner of war
in Turkey during WW1; service in India before and after WW1; social life
and sport; Hindu religion, mysticism,
and philosophy; practice of Yoga; the
Indian social scene; good.   9

YEVONDE. In Camera (1940). Training
work and travels of woman photographer
celebrities she photographed.   10

YONGE,Charlotte Mary.Charlotte Mary
Yonge, by Christabel Coleridge (1903)
Contains partial autobiography;family
history and her girlhood.   11

YONGE,James. Memoirs 1684-1715; the
Plymouth Corporation & its work; life
and events in Plymouth; notes kept by
learned and curious physician. MS, at
Plymouth Institution, Plymouth, Devonshire.   12

YOUNG, A. B. R. Reminiscences of an Irish Priest (Dundalk,n.d.). Life and work in the Church of Ireland;Dublin; Ballybay;disestablishment; Irish life and people.   13

YOUNG,Capt. A. Donovan. A Subaltern in Serbia (1922). Simple narrative of experiences in Irish battalion sent to Serbia in 1915.   14

YOUNG, Alexander Bell Filson. With the Battle Cruisers(1921). Lieutenant in RNVR:North Sea battles in WW1; his meetings with Fisher, etc.; battle of Dogger Bank.   15

YOUNG, Ann. Cirencester Quaker; her religious and family life;ministry in South-West to 1768. MS in Friends Soc. Library, London, N.W.1.   16

YOUNG, Arthur. Autobiography (1898) Education and career of agriculturist 1740's to early 19th Century; farming experiments; travels and observations in England, Ireland, France; his work at Board of Agriculture;country life; London politics; excellent.   17

YOUNG, Dinsdale T. Stars of Retrospect (1920).Life and work of leading Methodist minister; travels; ministry at Westminster Central Hall;preaching; religion; reunion.   18

YOUNG, Edward Daniel. Nyassa (1877) Exploration in Central Africa; establishing an industrial mission on Lake Nyassa; Livingstonia.   19

YOUNG, Elizabeth. Christian Experience (Bristol, 1843). Religious life and Quaker observances; Minehead, and Somerset.   20

YOUNG, Ella. Flowering Dusk (1945). Irish poet and folk-lorist;a romantic picture of Ireland in early 20th Century; Gaelic revival; Dublin scene and writers;the 1916 rebellion; her later life in California.   21

YOUNG, Francis Brett. Marching on Tanga (1917).Military service in WW1; with Smuts on Tanga campaign in East Africa.   22

YOUNG, Geoffrey Winthrop. On High Hills (1926). Youth; school; literary influences;passion for mountains; his work as writer,poet, mountaineer; big climbs; excellent.   23

YOUNG, Lt. James. Journal, 1804-5; his military service with East India Company at Cawnpore;Mahratta campaign MS, B. M. Add. 38516.   24

YOUNG, James Martin. The Blue Bowl (1947).Life with his family in Angus; passion for shooting wild birds;walks in the country; Angus people.   25

YOUNG, John. Cheating Death (1937). His hairbreadth escapes; hunting big game in Kenya; farming there; & prospecting in South Seas.   26

YOUNG,Col. Keith. Military diaries, 1843-5 and 1857; military service and administration; with Napier in Scinde as advocate-general;the Mutiny; siege of Delhi. Scinde in the Forties(1912) Delhi, 1857 (Edin. 1902).   27

YOUNG,Keith Douglas. Born to Adventure (1945). Travel and adventures in New Guinea and Solomons; pearl diving and mining; native life.   28

YOUNG,Miriam. Seen and Heard (1931) Three years' work as a missionary, in a Punjab village;her attempt to assimilate to native life.   29

YOUNG, Robert. Journal, 1852-4; his life and work as Methodist missionary in Fijis and Friendly Islands; schools and religion;social scene; a visit to the Australian goldfields. The Southern World (1854).   30

YOUNG, Thomas. Narrative of a Residence on the Mosquito Shore (L.1842). Life and work as a superintendent for a British land company in Honduras 1839 to 1841; his personal and social life and hardships.   31

YOUNGE, William. Autobiography; his religious and family life at Seacroft Yorks.,to 1813; religious reflections MS, Dewsbury Public Library.   32

YOUNGER,John. Autobiography (Kelso, 1881).Homely narrative of shoemaker's work and religious life;working-class and village life at St. Boswell's;social conditions and changes; 1st half of century; interesting record.　　33

YOUNGHUSBAND,Sir Francis E.　Light of Experience(1927). Critical reminiscences and opinions; events & people of his time;Indian frontier and inner India; philosophy and literature from the 80's.　　34

YOUNGHUSBAND, Maj.Gen. Sir George J Soldier's Memories(1917); Forty Years a Soldier(1923). Military career from 1878; India, Egypt, Sth Africa, Mesopotamia;campaigns; sport; social life and anecdotes.　　35

ZIMMERMAN,Godfrey. Autobiography of (1852).Work in army commisariat dept. under Napoleon;his life in England in 1820-40.　　1

ZINCKE,Foster Barham.The Days of My Years (Ipswich, 1891). His boyhood in Jamaica; Oxford; ordination; ministry in Andover & Wherstead, Suffolk; village life; religion; literature.　　2

INDEX

Notes. 1. Each item is indexed once and most items are indexed twice or more, under headings appropriate to their main emphases. 2. The headings are chiefly professions and occupations, places & regions, reminiscences, wars, general topics: in suitable cases these headings are collected together under one general heading, and cross-references are provided. 3. When there are many entries under one single heading they are arranged in rough historical groups: items which spread over two or more of these periods are repeated only when they divide fairly evenly between the periods given. 4. Details have been merged into their appropriate broader topics: thus towns are merged into the appropriate counties, and individual political movements or events are not indexed separately from Politics and Politicians. 5. A few topics such as London, Social Life, are not indexed at all, on the ground that entries would be so numerous as to waste time rather than save it. 6. It is assumed that many owner-users will wish to make their own indices of matters in which they are specially interested and blank pages for this purpose are left at the end of the index. 7. References give the initial letters of writers' surnames followed by the numbers attached to the items in the bibliography.

[341]